THE
WIZARD OF
FOOD PRESENTS

10,001 FOOD FACTS, CHEF'S SECRETS
& HOUSEHOLD HINTS

**More usable food facts and household hints
than any single book ever published.**

By

Dr. Myles H. Bader

10,001 Food Facts, Chef's Secrets & Household Hints

Published by:
Northstar Publishing
1818 Industrial Rd Ste. 209
Las Vegas, NV 89102
(800)717-6001
www.wizardoffood.com

Printed in the United States of America
First Printing September 1998
ISBN: 0-9646741-7-3

Illustrations by:
Deborah Rose Peek

Desktop Publishing by:
Suzanne Merritt
FAX (760)931-9797

Table of Contents

Dedication

To my beautiful wife Paulette, our children and grandchildren.

Deborah, Sheryl, Nichelle, Renee, Jimmy, Dawna, Cinnimon

Veronica, Tanya, Michael, Justin, Chris, Christopher, Jessica, Mikey, Junior, Kasandra, Kaylena, Chris H., Ashleigh, Damian, Jacob, Alex, Little Paulette

and Rascal the dog

A Word About The Author

Dr. Myles H. Bader (known as the Wizard of Food) has been interviewed on over 3,000 radio and television shows in the United States and Canada and is internationally recognized as a leader in Preventive Care and Wellness. Recent television shows have included Oprah, The Discovery Channel, Crook and Chase, America's Talking, Trinity Broadcasting, QVC, etc.

Dr. Bader received his Doctoral Degree from Loma Linda University and is board certified in Preventive Care. He has practiced nutrition, weight control, exercise physiology, stress management, and lectured extensively on nutrition and anti-aging for 23 years. In recent years he has established prevention and executive health programs for numerous safety departments, city governments, and Fortune 500 companies.

Recently, Dr. Bader has formulated one of the finest nutritional supplements ever to be produced in the United States. It is one of the only complete multi-vitamin/mineral, super antioxidants called "Opti Max."

Current books that Dr. Bader has authored include 8001 Food Facts and Chef's Secrets, 2001 Food Secrets Revealed, To Supplement or Not to Supplement, and The Wellness Desk Reference.

Presently, Dr. Bader is associated with Health Quest Medical Services in a Preventive Care practice in Las Vegas, Nevada. He is always available for lectures to any organization or club and presents seminars to train weight counselors and health educators.

CHAPTER 1

It's Party Time

REMOVE THE CRUSTS FIRST

An electric knife should be used to cut small finger sandwiches that have a filling that may easily run out. Try using a miniature, long French bread for the sandwiches.

DIP HOLDERS

For an interesting dip holder, use a large green, red, or yellow pepper. Remove the top and scrape the pepper clean of ribs and seeds. If you can cut the top so that it can be replaced it makes an interesting conversation piece when you serve it. A scooped-out cucumber or small squash will also work as well.

GOBBLE, GOBBLE

If you have ever wondered how many mouthfuls a guest will eat from the appetizer tray, wonder no more. The average party-goer at a cocktail party (no meal included) will gobble-up 10-12 mouthfuls. If a meal is included you only have to figure 4-5 mouthfuls. If you are having a wine and cheese gathering, figure 4 ounces of cheese per person. If you are having a dip and crackers or chips you need to figure one cup will serve 8 people if you are serving other small goodies. One quart of dip will provide you with 150-170 cracker-sized servings. If you are having a picnic figure on 3 beers or soft drinks per person.

CHEESE IT

Unless you are very adept at preparing pizza crust it might be wise to add the cheese before the tomato sauce. This will keep the crust from becoming soggy.

FRESH IDEA

Use a hollowed-out melon, orange, or grapefruit as a holder and fill it with cut-up fruits and miniature marshmallows. You can scallop the edges, or cut it in the shape of a basket for a more attractive holder.

A CHILLING SOLUTION

If you want to place a large quantity of ice cubes out for a party and are concerned about them melting, just place a larger bowl under the ice cubes with dry ice in it. They will last through the entire party.

BEFORE IT TURNS TO VINEGAR

If you enjoy wine coolers, try freezing leftover wine in ice cube trays. Not only can they be used in wine coolers, but any dish that calls for wine.

WHOOOOOSH

If you soak sugar cubes in lemon or orange extract they will ignite to provide you with a flaming desert. The alcohol content is just high enough to do the job.

THE SANDWICH OF MANY COLORS

Cream cheese can be colored with powdered or liquid food coloring and used as a filler in dainty rolled sandwiches. Try a different color for each layer, then slice as you would a jelly roll.

CHILLY CHERRIES

For a great conversation starter, try freezing red or green cherries in ice cubes for children's drinks. For adult drinks freeze cocktail onions or olives in the ice cubes. Toothpicks can be inserted before they are frozen for easy retrieval. Also, freezing lime or lemon rinds in cubes for water glasses is a nice twist.

KEEPING REAL COOOOOL
One of the easiest way to keep a large punch bowl cold is to make large ice cubes using old milk cartons. Remember the larger the ice cube, the slower it will melt.

YOU'RE IN TROUBLE IF YOU RUN OUT
When you buy ice cubes in the bags, you will get about 10 cubes per pound. The average person at a party will go through 10-15 ice cubes depending on the type of drink. The rule of thumb is 1 pound per person. Try 2 pounds for the big boozers or better yet just don't invite them.

JOLLY GOOD FOOD
Instead of using a pastry shell around the filet when preparing Beef Wellington, try using crescent dinner rolls.

THIS WILL SURPRISE YOU
A great tasting dip can be prepared by pureeing one cup of drained white beans with a package of any herb-flavored soft cheese.

CHILDREN'S TREAT
Surprise the kids with sandwiches in the shape of animals or objects. Just use cookie cutters.

AVOIDING A CRUSTY SOLUTION
To keep your meat or cheese hors d'oeuvres moist, try placing a damp paper towel over them. Many fillings as well as the bread dry out very quickly.

DO A MAGIC ACT FOR YOUR COMPANY
Have you ever had a problem with soda pop fizzing up over the top of a glass? To prevent just place the ice cubes in the glass and rinse them for a few seconds, pour the water out, pour the soda in and you have changed the surface tension of the ice and no fizzing over.

HOT WATER FOR ICE CUBES?

If someone told you that boiling water will freeze faster than cold water, you would probably tell them that they were crazy or to prove it. Well actually boiling water does freeze faster and the reason is that even though cold water is closer to the freezing point than boiling water, the hot water evaporates faster than the cold water leaving less water to freeze. The evaporation also creates an air current over the ice cube tray which tends to actually blow on the water similar to the cooling effect of blowing on a spoon of hot soup before tasting it.

DISINTEGRATION

If you have a cork stuck inside of a wine bottle and want to keep the bottle, try pouring a small amount of ammonia into bottle and place it outside for 2-3 days. The ammonia should eat the cork away.

GO FROST A GRAPE

Choose some really nice-sized grapes, wash them and dry them thoroughly. Then dip them in a solution of ½ cup of granulated sugar and ½ cup of ice water. Freeze until ready to use. Don't freeze for more than one day for the best results.

SWEET IDEA

To save money, try purchasing solid chocolate bunnies after Easter and freeze until you need them for recipes. They are usually half price. Shave them with a potato peeler as needed.

IT'S BUNNY TIME

Natural Easter egg dyes can easily be made from grass for green, onion skins for yellow, or beets for red. Just add about 2 ounces of these foods to the water the eggs are boiling in.

A GOOD OLD SQUEEZE

If you want to serve fancy butter pats at a party, just partially melt the butter and use a pastry or cookie bag with a decorative tip. Squeeze the butter onto a cookie sheet and refrigerate until they harden.

MAKING BUTTER BALLS

If you would like little round butter balls for your party, just place a melon ball cutter in very hot water for 5 minutes and then scoop out the butter from a whole pound cake, then drop each one in a bowl of cold water with ice cubes. Store them in the refrigerator until you are ready to use them

WHOA, DISH

Dishes placed out for a buffet tend to move when people scoop food from them. Just place a damp cloth napkin under the dishes to solve this problem.

CHAPTER 2

A Baker's Secret

PLAIN OR SELF-RISING FLOUR, THE TASTE TEST

Have you ever wondered how to tell the difference in your flours after they have been placed in a flour bin. The plain flour has no taste and the self-rising has a salty taste due to the baking powder.

WHAT HAPPENS WHEN YOU TOAST BREAD?

The browning reaction of toast was first discovered by a French chemist by the name of Maillard. He discovered that when bread is heated a chemical process takes place that caramelizes the surface sugars and proteins turning the surface brown. The sugar then becomes an indigestible fiber and a percentage of the protein (amino acids) lose their nutritional value. The toast then has more fiber and less protein than a piece of bread that is not toasted. The protein is actually reduced by about 35%. If you are making your own bread you can increase the amount of protein by just reducing the amount of regular flour by 2 tablespoons and replacing it with an equal amount of a quality soy flour.

CAN POPPY SEEDS GIVE YOU A POSITIVE DRUG TEST?

Poppy seeds are commonly used in the baking industry in bagels, muffins, and cakes. However, since poppy seeds are derived from poppies from which morphine and codeine are made, it may cause a positive urine test for opiates. Even 5 hours after consuming poppy seeds your test may still be positive. In one incidence in Michigan a woman ate a lemon poppy seed muffin and gave a positive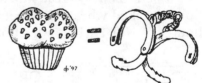

urine test. She was in trouble until the authorities and the University of Michigan solved the problem.

DEBUGGING YOUR FLOUR

It is almost impossible to purchase flour of any kind without some sort of bug infestation. In fact, the FDA allows an average of 50 insect fragments per 50 grams (about 2 ounces) of grain. It is not a danger to your health at this level and is unavoidable. Insects and their eggs may set up residence when the grain is warehoused, during transit, or even in your home. To reduce the risk of infestation, just store your grains and flours in the freezer to prevent any eggs from hatching.

DRYING OUT

Baking is a dry-heat method of cooking foods which surrounds the food with heated air. Baking for the most part dries the food and the need to control the amount of moisture lost is important.

WORK FAST

Remember on humid or very hot days most yeast doughs may rise too fast and may be very hard to knead. When this occurs there is a loss of elasticity.

VISA, VERSA

The ingredients for baking should always be warm, never cold to start. For pastry it is just the opposite, the ingredients should be cold.

READ THE LABEL

Don't be fooled by bread labeling. If the package reads whole wheat flour, cracked wheat, or wheat bread it is probably made from white flour, not 100% whole wheat or whole grain flour.

LOOKS FUNNY, TASTES GREAT

For a different type of toast, try lightly buttering a piece of bread on both sides and placing it in the waffle iron.

COOKIE CHILL
Save your used coffee cans, they make excellent containers to store cookies in. Use the original plastic lid or a piece of plastic wrap sealed with a rubber band.

BUT IT'S HEALTHIER
Whole wheat bread cannot be expected to raise as high as white breads since it has more volume due to lack of refining.

BACK, BACK
When using a dough mixer, try spraying vegetable oil on the hook or blade. This will stop the dough from climbing up the hook.

USE THE BEST BOARD FOR THE JOB
When kneading dough always do it on a wooden board. Plastic boards do not have the tacky surface needed nor the grabbing quality.

OVERSIZED BAGELS
With the increase in bagel shops and delis the sale of bagels have skyrocketed over 170% in the last 12 years. Bagels now rank as one of the most popular breakfast foods in the United States. However, the size is increasing as well, turning a normally low-fat, low-calorie food into a high-calorie food.

FRISBEE, ANYONE?
French toast, waffles, and pancakes may be made and frozen. They can then be placed into the toaster for an easy breakfast.

BUYER BEWARE
When purchasing rye bread, it would be best to read the label. Most rye bread contains white flour and very little rye flour. For the best quality the label should read "whole rye flour."

BUY RIGHT
To purchase the highest quality white bread, make sure the list of ingredients reads "unbleached flour" instead of "white flour" or just "flour."

BAKING SMART

For the best results when baking always make sure that your oven has been pre-heated for at least 10 minutes before placing the product in. In most instances it is also best to bake on the center shelf so that you will get an even circulation of the heat.

NEED MY SPACE

Airspace is important between pans, never place pans next to each other. Hot air need to circulate and not be blocked.

PUCKER UP, DOUGH

If you are in a hurry for whole wheat bread to rise, try adding one tablespoon of lemon juice to the dough as you are mixing it.

TIMING IS IMPORTANT

Make sure you turn pancakes as soon as the air pockets form on the surface for the best results.

STARCH IT

The water from boiled potatoes contains just the right amount of starch to substitute for water you might use in a bread recipe. It will also help keep the bread fresher for a longer period of time.

VITAMIN C TO THE RESCUE

As a substitute for yeast you can use one teaspoon of baking soda mixed with one teaspoon of powdered vitamin C. A similar chemical reaction will take place as with the baking soda. Ascorbic acid is just acidic enough to make the reaction work.

TRICK OF THE TRADE

The batter should always be mixed between batches of pancakes, waffles, or latkas. This will assure that settling of ingredients does not take place as well as keeping it aerated. The quality of the product will be excellent.

AN OLDIE BUT GOODIE

If you would like an old-fashioned look on top of a cake, just place a paper lace doily on top and sprinkle powdered sugar over it, then remove it. Colored powdered sugar works great too.

EASY DOES IT

Remember, when you are making 100% whole wheat bread it will come out more moist if you slowly add the flour to the water and mix gently as you do. It is the nature of whole wheat to absorb water slower than other types of flour.

YOU'VE HEARD IT BEFORE, BELIEVE IT!

Yeast must always be added to water, never place yeast in a bowl and pour water on it. The yeast is easily damaged and the weight of the water falling may harm too many of the little yeasties.

RISING TO ANY OCCASION

Yeast is a bacteria and a living organism. In a single pound you may have up to 3,000 billion cells. They prefer to live on sugar in any form and produce alcohol and carbon dioxide, which is going to do the job of rising your product. When using wheat starch the enzymes actually produce the sugar for the rising to take place.

COLD STORAGE IS BEST

Always store your dry yeast in the refrigerator. The cold slows down the metabolic processes. This works for any product containing yeast. However, make sure you allow it to warm to room temperature before using it. The yeast needs to get its act together again.

HERE YEASTIE, YEASTIE

If you have ever wondered how sour dough bread is made, wonder no longer! It is made from a live bacterial culture that is called a "starter." The starter is made from tap water and white flour which ferments and traps yeast spores from the air causing it to become sour. Starters may be kept for years. Only a small portion is removed when needed for bread making allowing more to grow.

AN EASY SOLUTION TO A CRUSTY PROBLEM

If you are worried about your bread crusts becoming too hard, just place a small container of water in the oven while the bread is baking. This will provide just enough moisture and steam to keep the bread soft.

FOILED AGAIN

An old trick is to put a small piece of aluminum foil under the cloth in your breadbasket before placing the bread or rolls in. This will help the food retain its heat for a longer period of time.

COOL IT!

The best method of cooling hot bread after it has been removed from the oven is to place the bread on an open wire rack. This will allow air to circulate around the bread and should eliminate any soggy areas.

GOING UP

If you wish to speed up the rising of bread dough which takes just a small amount of heat, try placing the pan with the dough on top of a heating pad on medium. This will easily do the trick.

FATTY LITTLE STICKS

Best to read the list of ingredients and check the fat content before you purchase bread sticks. They may contain up to 40% fat.

TOO CHEWY?

When making biscuits, never overwork the dough, be gentle, if you want to have light biscuits. Overworking the dough makes them tough and continually re-rolling may cause the biscuits to become tough.

A LITTLE DIP WILL DO YA

If you dip a biscuit cutter in flour it will keep the dough from sticking to it.

UP, UP, AND AWAY

Try substituting buttermilk for milk in a muffin recipe for the lightest muffins ever.

DON'T EXPOSE TOO MUCH OF THE SURFACES

If you want your biscuits to be soft, try brushing them with milk or melted unsalted butter, then place them in the pan so that they touch each other.

FILLER UP

The latest bread fad is called a "wrap." This is just another type of pita bread pocket filled with a variety of foods. If they are made like a pita they will contain no sugar or fat which will make them similar to a corn tortilla, and should only contain about 60 calories in a 2 ounce serving.

BREAD BUYER BEWARE

If white bread is your bread of choice, only purchase the bread if it clearly states "enriched," many do not.

ZAPPING A SANDWICH

When microwaving a sandwich, it would be best to use a firm textured bread such as French or sourdough. Toasted white bread will not remain crisp. The filling may be heated separately. If the filling is heated in the sandwich, be sure and spread it evenly over the bread and very close to the edges. Wait a few minutes before serving as the filling may remain very hot.

A NO NO

Most bread machines are timed for the use of dry yeast. Compressed fresh yeast should never be used in bread-baking machines.

GOOD OLD BREAD BOX

The dry air in the refrigerator actually draws moisture from the bread. Bread develops mold faster at room temperature, however the freshness of the bread is lost in half the time. Freezing maintains the freshness, however, liquid is released as cells burst from the freezing and the texture of the bread is never the same. Storing bread will depend on the length of time it will take for you to use the bread. For short periods of up to 5-6 days, the bread box works great. It provides a closed compartment and will keep the bread fresh, otherwise it has to go into the refrigerator or freezer to avoid mold forming.

NON-CRISPY BREAD CRUST

Do you ever wish that you could bake a loaf of bread without the crust becoming too crispy? Well the secret to a softer crust is to open the oven door and throw in a few ice cubes about midway through the baking time. This will produce a dense steam and provide just enough extra moisture to keep the crust from becoming hard and too crispy. It also will allow the bread to rise more easily giving you a nice firm, chewy inside.

THE ROLE OF SALT IN BREADMAKING

Salt is really not needed when making bread. It does, however, make the crust a little crispier as well as slowing down the growth of the yeast which will prevent the dough from increasing its volume too fast.

WHY DOES FRENCH BREAD GET STALE SO FAST

French bread is made without fat, the fat content in bread tends to slow down the loss of moisture in bread and keep it softer by reducing the percentage of gluten from forming too strong a structure. French bread may get stale after only 5-7 hours which is why the French purchase their bread supplies at least twice a day.

DOING THE TWIST

In the year 600 A.D. in a monastery in Northern Italy a monk made the first pretzel. It was during lent and he was forbidden to use any type of fat, eggs, or milk so the monk used flour, salt, and water. He formed the bread into the shape of what he thought were two arms that were crossed in prayer. He named the bread, "pretiola" which is Latin for "little gift" and gave the treat to the town children as a special reward for saying their prayers.

SWEETENERS ROLE IN BREADMAKING

Sweeteners such as honey, molasses, and cane sugar are really not required in breadmaking, however, they tend to slow down the coagulation of the protein allowing the dough to increase in volume making a fluffier loaf. They do add a few more calories to the bread, but they also extend the shelf life. If you do plan on using honey or molasses, always add a small amount of extra flour to offset the liquid sweetener.

WHAT IS AMERICA'S FAVORITE COOKIE?

It's no contest, America's favorite cookie is the Oreo which was first marketed by the National Biscuit Company of Hoboken, New Jersey in 1912. The "Oreo Biscuit" as it was originally known was described in the company literature as "a biscuit with two beautifully embossed, chocolate-flavored wafers with a rich cream filling." The company has manufactured 210 billion Oreos since they were introduced in 1912 which is an average of over 2.5 billion every year for eighty-five years. If you are a health advocate that amounts to over 8 trillion calories.

LOWER FAT, HIGHER PRICE

Reduced fat Oreo cookies contain 47 calories and 1.67 grams of fat. The original Oreo has 53 calories and 2.33 grams of fat. Not a big savings. It is still necessary to read past the reduced-fat, low-fat, and lite information to see if there is really a good fat calorie saving. Also, many of these products cost more because they are slightly lower in fat content.

THE RISE AND FALL OF A SOUFFLE

A souffle rises because of air bubbles that are trapped in the egg whites as they are beaten. When the souffle is placed in the oven the air in the bubbles expand causing the souffle to rise. If the souffle is punctured or shaken it will cause a premature release of the air and the souffle will collapse and is ruined.

WHO INVENTED TWINKIES?

Twinkies were invented by James Dewar in 1930 who attributed his long life of 88 years to the fact that he ate two twinkies every day since he invented them. I wonder how long he would have lived without them?

WHAT IS CHESS PIE?

This a regional specialty of the Southern United States. It has a rich, smooth, translucent filling made of eggs, sugar, and butter held together with flour. In the 1800's, the pie was made with molasses since sugar was relatively unavailable. It is a thin pie and may be made using a variety of flavorings, such as pineapple or even bourbon.

DISSOLVING FLOUR

Instant flour will always dissolve more readily than a regular flour. Regular flour may lump easily because the exterior of the flour molecule gelatinizes immediately when contact is made with a warm liquid, thus forming a protective shield that blocks the liquid from entering the flour's inner molecules. This forms lumps with dry insides and wet outsides. Instant flour is produced with irregular shaped molecules with jagged edges so that the liquid can enter. This irregular shape also reduces their ability to clump together to form lumps.

HOW MUCH BREAD DOES A BREAD PLANT BAKE?

Most large bread baking companies can bake 20,000 loaves an hour. The typical plant uses raw materials by the trainload since they consume 2 million pounds of flour every week delivered in steam-sterilized boxcars or specially equipped truck tankers. The flour is then stored in sealed silos until used, with each silo carefully dated. Bakeries that use this much flour have very strict rules regarding sparks or the lighting of a match since flour dust may be ignited under the right conditions.

WHAT IS A MEXICAN WEDDING CAKE?

This is really not a cake but a very rich, buttery, cookie filled with pecans or almonds. The cookies are coated with powdered sugar when they are warm and then again after they are cooled. They are sometime found in bakeries called Russian tea cakes.

HOW DOES BREAD BECOME STALE?

When the bread is baked a large percentage of the water accumulates in the starch. As the bread ages the water is released from the starch and the protein allowing the texture of the bread to become more crumbly and firm. As the bread continues to age the water content inside the bread is released and the water is absorbed by the crust, drying the crust and making it hard through evaporation of the moisture into the air. Reheating the bread allows the moisture that remains in the bread to be distributed back into the starch and partially gelatinizing. When reheating a bread it must be placed in a sealed container or wrapped in a damp non-flammable material to avoid any evaporation and the crust becoming too hard.

WHY SOUR DOUGH BREAD IS SOUR

The yeast used in bread is normally standard baker's yeast which does not work well in an acidic environment needed to produce sour dough breads. Baker's yeast works by breaking down maltose which the acids used in sour dough bread cannot do. The acids that are found in sour dough bread are 75% lactic and 25% acetic acid. The bacteria in sour dough breads also require maltose but does not break it down. The bacteria prefer a temperature of 86° F. (30°C.) and a ph of 3.8-4.5 as ideal. Standard bread prefers a ph of 5.5. Starters for sour dough have lasted for hundreds of years and are thought to be protected by bacteria that are related to penicillin mold in cheese.

HOW DOES BAKING POWDER WORK?

 Baking powder is a mixture of a number of chemicals that will leaven breads. The main chemicals are calcium acid phosphate, sodium aluminum sulfate or cream of tartar and sodium bicarbonate. This mixture of acids and bases produce a chemical reaction when water is added to it producing carbon dioxide, a gas. When this occurs the gas creates minute air pockets or will enter already existing ones in the dough or batter.

When you then place the mixture in a hot oven or hot plate, the dough rises because the heat causes additional carbon dioxide to be released from the baking powder as well as expanding the trapped carbon dioxide gas creating steam. This pressure swells the dough or batter and it expands or rises for the occasion.

Always combine the wet and dry ingredients separately. A wet measuring spoon should never be placed into a baking powder box. Use 1 teaspoon of baking powder for each 1 cup of flour. If you are mixing a batter for fried foods reduce to half the amount for each. This will give you a lighter coating.

DOES STORAGE TIME AFFECT BAKING POWDER

Baking powder does lose potency over time (about 6 months) and if you are unsure of its freshness you should test it before using it. Place ½ teaspoon of baking powder in a small bowl then pour ¼ cup of hot tap water over it. The more bubbling activity there is the fresher the baking powder. The activity must be at a good active level or the dough will not rise sufficiently. Try this test on a box of fresh baking powder so that you will be familiar with the activity level of the fresh powder. Be sure to check the date on the box when you first purchase it to be sure it's fresh.

WHAT THICKENERS WORK BEST IN FRUIT PIES?

For apple pies you should not need a thickener, for all other fruit pies the best thickening agent is a combination of 2 tablespoons each of cornstarch and tapioca. Just mix them with the sugar before adding to the fruit. When baking remember that cornstarch has twice the thickening power of flour.

BAKING WITH BUTTERMILK AS A SUBSTITUTE FOR MILK

When you substitute buttermilk in place of milk you are adding additional acid to the dough and upsetting the ratio of acid to base needed for the leavening agent to release the maximum amount of carbon dioxide. This will reduce the amount of carbon dioxide that is generated.

To offset the additional acid you need to add a small amount of baking soda in place of an equal amount of baking powder. The basic rule of thumb is to reduce the amount of baking powder by 2 teaspoons and replace it with ½ teaspoon of baking soda for every cup of buttermilk you use in place of the milk.

HOW MANY EGGS CAN A BAKER BREAK, IF A BAKER BREAKS EGGS?

Large baking companies will rarely have their bakers take the time to break open every egg. In some cases either the yolk or the white will be used and the baker would have to separate the egg yolk or whites before he could go to work. Eggs are usually purchased frozen which eliminates the problem especially if the bakery uses more egg yolks than whites (or visa versa). The financial saving could be substantial over the course of a year. Frozen eggs are delivered under refrigeration at -15°F.(-26.1°C.) and must be thawed before they can be used. Defrosting takes 6-8 hours in a special thawing tank of cool, running water.

WHAT CAN YOU USE TO REPLACE FAT IN BAKED GOODS?

First, we need to realize that fat has a number of important purposes in baked goods. They extend shelf life, tenderize the product, add flavor, and contribute to the texture. When fat is replaced the baked product may be altered to such a degree that the finished product will not be acceptable. Replacements include; skim milk, egg whites, and certain starches and gums. These will all lower the fat content and reduce the total calories. The gums and starches cannot replace the fat completely, however, they do help to retain moisture.

HOME FORMULA FOR BAKING POWDER

The following formula for making one teaspoon of baking powder is to use ½ teaspoon of cream of tartar and ¼ teaspoon of baking soda. If you plan on storing a quantity of the powder for a few days then add ¼ teaspoon of corn starch to absorb moisture from the air preventing a chemical reaction to take place before you are ready to use it. This formula tends to cause the release of carbon dioxide faster and the mixture should be used as fast as possible when you use it. Commercially produced powders work at a higher temperature giving them a longer period of time before they react.

SOLVING THE MYSTERY OF CAKE PROBLEMS

» LAYER CAKES

If your cake has a coarse texture or is heavy and solid you probably didn't beat the sugar and Crisco, margarine, or butter long enough. These ingredients need to be mixed together very thoroughly for the best results.

If your cake is dry this may indicate overcooking and failure to check the doneness after the minimum cooking time. Another reason this occurs is that you may have overbeaten the egg whites.

If your cake has elongated holes this is a sign of overmixing the batter when the flour was added. Ingredients should be mixed only enough to combine them totally.

» ANGEL FOOD, CHIFFON, AND SPONGE CAKES

If your cake has poor volume you may not have beaten the egg whites long enough, only beat them, however, until they stand in straight peaks. They should look moist and glossy when the beaters are removed. Another problem occurs if you overmix the batter when you add the flour. The ingredients should be gently folded in and combined until the batter is just smooth.

If your cake shrinks or falls the egg whites have probably been beaten too long. Another problem may be that you forgot to cool the cake upside down allowing the steam to dissipate throughout the cake, thus creating a lighter, more fluffy cake.

If your cake is tough you probably overmixed the batter at the time when the dry ingredients were added. Ingredients should be blended only until they are mixed.

If your sponge cake has layers you didn't beat the egg yolks long enough. They should be beaten until they are thick and lemon-colored.

If your chiffon cake has yellow streaks you have added the yolks directly into the dry ingredients instead of making a "well" in the center of the dry ingredients then adding the oil and then the egg yolks.

If your chiffon cake has a layer you probably have either overbeaten or underbeaten the egg whites. Only beat the egg whites until they are stiff and look moist and glossy.

I WONDER WHERE THE YELLOW WENT?

When flour is processed it still tends to retain a yellowish tint which is not very appealing. This yellow tint is caused by a chemical group called "xanthophylls" which remains in the flour. Bleaching is needed to remove the yellow tint, however, when this is done it destroys the vitamin E in the flour. The yellow color is left in pasta which is why seminola is never white. The bleaching is done by using chlorine dioxide gas. Higher quality flours are naturally aged thus allowing the air to bleach them.

HOW DO THEY MAKE COMMERCIAL CAKES SO LIGHT

Commercial cakes are difficult to duplicate from scratch and are always light and tender. The reason for this is that they use chlorinated flour and special fat emulsifiers. These items are available, however, not always easy to find in the supermarket unless you know what to look for. To produce the chlorinated flour, bleaching agents are mixed with chlorine gas. The chlorinated flour changes the surface properties of both the starch and flour fats, then inhibits the gluten proteins from coming together. This special flour can tolerate more structural damage by the sugar and shortening than normal flour, resulting in a sweeter, more tender product.

HARD WATER MAY AFFECT YOUR BAKED PRODUCT

The high mineral content of hard water may retard fermentation by causing the gluten to become tough. The minerals will prevent the protein from absorbing water the way it normally would. To counteract this problem there are a number of methods you may wish to try, such as using bottled water, adding a small amount of vinegar to reduce the ph, or adding more yeast. Water that is too soft can cause the dough to be sticky. If you are having a problem you may want to consider using a dough improver.

WORLD'S GREATEST PANCAKES! HERE'S THE SECRET

There are a number of tricks that chefs use to prepare the best pancake batter. The first is to use club soda in place of whatever liquid the recipe calls for to increase the amount of air in the pancake and make it fluffier. The second is not to overmix the batter otherwise it will cause the gluten to overdevelop resulting in a 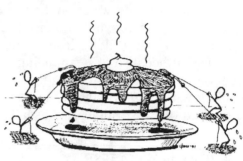 tougher pancake. Overmixing can also force out more of the trapped carbon dioxide that assists in the leavening. Most people tend to mix the batter until all the small lumps of flour are dissolved, this is overkill.

Instead stop mixing before this occurs and place the batter in the refrigerator slowing the development of the gluten and the activity level of baking powder or yeast. Third, adding sugar to your recipe causes carmelization and produces a golden brown outside, the more sugar, the more carmelization that will take place, and the browner the pancake will be.

WHAT IS A SHOOFLY PIE?

Shoofly pie is an old Pennsylvania Dutch specialty which is a very sweet spicy pie that has a standard bottom pastry shell and a custard filling made from molasses and boiling water. It is usually covered with a crumb topping made with brown sugar and a variety of spices. Sometimes the custard is on top and the crumbs are inside. The name originated because of the flies that would hang around the pie trying to get at the molasses.

A FOOL MAKES A GREAT DESSERT

This is actually a classic British dessert made from fruit and whipped cream. The "fool" is usually made with a cooked fruit puree which is chilled, sweetened, and then folded into the whipped cream and served like a parfait, then layered in a tall glass. The fruit of choice is the gooseberry and the "fool" probably originated in the 15th century.

THE HOT GRIDDLE BOUNCING-WATER TEST

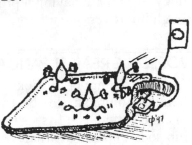

Pancakes should be cooked on a griddle that is approximately 325°F. (162.8°C.) for the best results. To be sure of having the proper temperature just dribble a drop or two of cold water on the hot griddle. The water should bounce around on the top of the griddle close to the spot you drop it because of steam being generated and gravity forcing the water back down to the griddle. If the griddle is too hot the water drops will be propelled off the griddle, this usually occurs at about 425° F.(218.3°C.).

THE BLIND OREO TEST

Tufts University conducted a "blind" test on 36 consumers who agreed to taste Oreo cookies to see if they were able to tell the difference in the regular Oreo and the new reduced-fat version. The reduced-fat version barely won the test with 18 tasters favoring the reduced-fat and 17 preferring the regular Oreo. The reduced-fat Oreo has 47 calories and 1.67 grams of fat per cookie, compared to 53 calories and 2.33 grams of fat in the regular Oreo cookie. The difference is so minor that people will not easily be able to tell the difference.

YEAST AND ITS BAKING USES

A block of yeast is composed of millions of one-celled fungi that will multiply at a fast rate given their favorite carbohydrate food either sugar or starch in a moist environment. Yeast reproduces ideally at 110°-115°F. (43.3°-46.1°C.) except when used for bread dough, does best at 80°-90°F. (26.7°-32.2°C.). Yeast causes the carbohydrate to convert into a simple sugar, glucose, which then ferments into alcohol and carbon dioxide. It is the carbon dioxide that will leaven the baked goods similar to the reaction of baking powder expanding the air and creating steam. There is no risk from the production of alcohol, since the heat from the baking evaporates the alcohol as well as killing the live yeast cells.

A SLUMP YOU CAN REALLY GET INTO

A "slump" is a New England dessert that dates back to the 1700's and is a deep-dish fruit dessert that is topped with a biscuit-like crust. It is similar to the "grunt" except that it is baked instead of steamed. The dough used for the "slump" is a dumpling dough which will stay moist on the inside while becoming crisp on the surface. The name "slump" was derived from the fact that the dessert does not hold its shape well and usually slumped over when served.

IS KNEADING REALLY KNEADED?

Kneading is required to evenly distribute the yeast and other ingredients throughout the dough. If this is not done efficiently the dough will not rise evenly resulting in a product with a shorter shelf life. Dough kneading machines make this chore easy and if you knead dough frequently a machine is a worthwhile necessity.

WILL BREAD RISE IN A MICROWAVE?

It is possible for bread to rise in a microwave oven in approximately $1/3$ of the time it would take through normal methods. The only problem is that it may affect the flavor somewhat because the slower it rises, the more time there is to develop the flavor and have it permeate the dough. If you do decide to use this method your microwave needs to have a 10% power setting. If you try to use any higher temperature the dough will turn into a half-baked glob. To rise dough for one standard loaf, place $1/2$ cup of hot water in the back corner of the oven. Place the dough in a microwave bowl that is well-greased and cover it with plastic wrap, then cover the plastic wrap with a damp towel. With the power level set at 10% cook the dough for 6 minutes, then allow it to rest for 4-5 minutes. Repeat the procedure if the dough has not doubled its size.

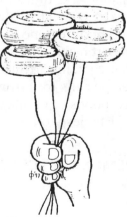

WHY AREN'T THE BISCUITS LIGHT AND FLUFFY?

Check your baking powder for freshness and make sure that you sift all the dry ingredients together. This will provide you with the texture you desire. If you don't have a sifter, then just place all the ingredients into a large sieve and shake them all out, it's the even blending of the ingredients that is the key. Shortening is also the preferred fat over butter since shortening is a more refined product and adds lightness. Butter will make a biscuit more solid.

WHAT IS FONDANT ICING?

Fondant icing is produced from glucose, sucrose, and water that is cooked to 240°F. (115.6°C.) *then quickly cooled off to* 110°F. (43.3°C.) and rapidly worked until it is a white, creamy, smooth texture. To ice with the mixture, cool it down to 100°F. (37.8°C.) and it will flow smoothly. Normally, it is used as a base for buttercream icing.

WHAT IS A SNICKERDOODLE?

The "Snickerdoodle" is a true American cookie that originated in the 1800's in the Northeastern United States. It is a buttery cookie filled with dried fruit, nuts, and spices, usually nutmeg or cinnamon. The top of the Snickerdoodle is sprinkled with powdered sugar before it is baked producing a crinkly top and may be found either hard or soft.

THE CURE FOR DOME-TOP CAKES

This problem is usually the result of adding too much flour to your batter. Thick batter does not circulate in the pan well and the batter around the edges tends to set before the batter in the center. This causes a reduction in the amount of heat that is transferred to the center and the center will take too long to harden, thus allowing the center more time to rise into a dome.

WHAT IS ARROWROOT?

Arrowroot is derived from the rootstalks of a South American tuber which is finely powdered and used as a thickener. Its thickening power is about 1-2 times that of all-purpose flour and like cornstarch should be mixed with adequate cold water to produce a paste before adding it to a hot mixture. One of the best features about arrowroot is that it will not impart a chalky taste if it is overcooked. Best not to overstir a mixture that contains arrowroot or it will revert and become thin again. If your recipe calls for arrowroot and you don't have any just use 2 ¼ teaspoons of cornstarch or 1 ½ tablespoons of all-purpose flour in place of 1 tablespoon of arrowroot.

REMOVING BREADS AND CAKES FROM PANS

When breads and cakes are baked they build up steam inside which needs to be released after they are removed from the oven. If the steam is not allowed to escape it will convert to water as it comes in contact with the cooler air and be absorbed back into the product, thus making the product soggy. To avoid this problem, remove the pan from the oven and allow the product to remain in the pan and to just rest for a few minutes. The product should then be removed and placed on a cooling rack which will allow more of the area to release additional steam and stop any moisture from going to the bottom of the product, causing the bottom to become soggy

DRY AND COMPRESSED YEAST

Compressed yeast has a higher level of moisture, about 70% compared to the standard dry yeast at 8%. Compressed yeast should be stored in the refrigerator and only lasts for about 2 weeks before losing its effectiveness. Dry yeast should always be stored in an airtight container since it absorbs water rather easily. The yeasts are interchangeable with 1 packet of the active dry yeast equaling the leavening power of 1 cake of the compressed yeast.

WHY CHOCOLATE CAKES NEED TO BE LEAVENED WITH BAKING SODA, NEVER BAKING POWDER

Chocolate has a high acid level, so high that it would upset the balance between the acid (cream of tartar) and the base of baking powder. When baking soda (sodium bicarbonate) is used it may make the chocolate cake too basic and most recipes also call for the addition of a sour-milk product such as yogurt or sour cream to assure that the batter will not be too alkaline (basic). If the batter did become too alkaline the color of the cake would turn red instead of brown and taste bitter.

THE SECRET TO MAKING FLUFFY BISCUITS

Whatever recipe you are using it probably calls for you to use yeast. Instead of the yeast substitute 1 teaspoon of baking soda and 1 teaspoon of powdered ascorbic acid (vitamin C) for the yeast. By doing this you will not have to wait for the dough to rise. The addition of these products will react with the other ingredients and the dough will rise naturally during the baking process.

WHAT IS CREAM OF TARTAR?

Tartar is derived from grapes during and after the process of fermentation. Two pinkish crystalline sediments remain in wine casks after the wine has fermented, they are "argol" which collects on the sides of the cask and "lees" which collects on the bottom. These substances are actually crude tartar. The crude tartar is then decrystallized by cooking in boiling water and then allowing the remains to crystallize again. This substance is then bleached pure white and further crystallized. As this process concludes a thin layer of very thin white crystals are formed on the surface. The name cream of tartar is derived from this thin top layer that looks like cream. It is used to produce baking powder when mixed with baking soda.

WHAT IS BAKING SODA?

Baking soda is actually bicarbonate of soda which is derived from the manufacture of common washing soda, also known as "sal soda." Baking soda is composed carbon and oxygen molecules which combine to form carbon dioxide gas. If a batter has a sufficient acidic nature then only baking soda is needed to produce carbon dioxide. If the batter does not have sufficient acid then baking powder which carries both acid and alkali is needed. All baking soda in North America is mined from the mineral, trona, which is found in Green River, Wyoming.

The large deposit was discovered in the 1930's. Trona is actually composed of sodium bicarbonate and sodium carbonate, a very close relative. The ore is mined from deep mines, crushed, rinsed, and heated to produce sodium carbonate. The sodium carbonate is then dissolved in water and carbon dioxide is forced through the solution releasing the sodium bicarbonate crystals which are then washed, dried and packaged as baking soda.

When baking soda is added to a recipe, it has an immediate rising action with the release of the gas which means that your oven must be preheated and your pans greased before you even combine the ingredients. Baking soda should be added to dry ingredients first and the wet ingredients just before placing the food into the oven.

Baking soda will last for approximately 6 months if stored in an airtight container and in a cool, dry location. If you are not sure of the activity level of baking soda, try placing ¼ teaspoon in about 2 teaspoons of white vinegar, if carbon dioxide bubbles appear it still has good activity.

Sodium bicarbonate is also produced in the human body to assist in maintaining the acidity (ph) level of the blood. It is also found in saliva and will neutralize plaque acids which might otherwise dissolve our teeth. Another action in the body is to neutralize stomach acid so that we don't get ulcers as well as assisting in the breathing process by transporting carbon dioxide from the tissues to the lungs for disposal.

MAKING A TURKISH DELIGHT

This is a chewy, rubbery textured dessert made from fruit juice, honey, and a number of different sugars, cornstarch, or gelatin. It is colored pink or green and usually contains a variety of nuts for added texture. It is usually found in squares and covered with powdered sugar.

WHAT IS AMMONIUM CARBONATE?

This product is similar to sodium bicarbonate, however, it does not need either acid or alkali mediums to produce carbon dioxide. The addition of moist heat causes the reaction to occur. Since it decomposes rapidly it is usually only used in cream puffs and soft cookies when a fast release and expansion of carbon dioxide gas is needed.

POOR RISING DOUGH YOUR PROBLEM?

One of the most frequent encountered problems is that yeast dough doesn't rise adequately. There are a number of reasons for this. First, the dough may be too cool and reduce the level of yeast activity. The temperature needs to be between 80°-90°F. (26.7° - 32.2°C.) for the best results. Second, the yeast may have been prepared with water that was too hot, which is a frequent problem. The water must be below 140°F. (60°C.) for optimum results. Third, you forgot to test the yeast and it was ready for retirement.

JUMBLE, JUMBLE, IT'S NOT A DANCE CRAZE

It's a great-tasting cookie that was first introduced in the United States 200 years ago and is still being sold today. It is a sugar cookie baked in a circular shape, flavored with sour cream, and then scented with rose water. Sometimes nuts are added to the top.

YEAST, DEAD OR ALIVE?

Yeast should be tested before you use it in all instances. Just mix a small amount in ¼ cup of warm water that has ¼ teaspoon of sugar mixed in. The mixture should begin bubbling (happy yeasties) within about 5-7 minutes. If this does not occur they are either dead or too inactive to provide the leavening function.

THE COMPOSITION OF PASTA

Pasta is composed of two main ingredients, water and either standard flour or the coarsest part of the wheat called seminola. Pasta dough needs to be very stiff and is therefore only 25% water compared to bread dough which is about 40% water. Durum wheat seminola is the choice for most of the better quality pastas and contains a very low percentage of starch and a high percentage of protein. The gluten matrix is very strong since the protein does not have to compete with the starch for the moisture. Because the protein is strong it can be extruded by machine without falling apart. Standard flour pasta is easily broken and is the poorer quality product.

THE NAPKIN TEST

There is an easy method of determining whether a baked goods product has a high fat level which is simply called the "napkin test." Place the baked goods in question on a paper napkin or a piece of paper towel. If the product leaves a grease stain, it contains more than three grams of fat. If you would like to reduce the fat content of pizza, dab a napkin on the surface of the pizza to absorb some of the fat.

HERMITS ARE CHEWY

This type of hermit is a chewy, spicy cookie that is usually flavored with brown sugar, cinnamon, nutmeg, and cloves. Occasionally, raisins and nuts are added and they are either drop or bar cookies.

UNBLEACHED VS. BLEACHED FLOUR

Unbleached flour would be the best choice for most baking projects that call for one or the other. The unbleached will have a more natural taste since it lacks the chemical additives and bleaching agents used in bleached flour. Bleached flour is also less expensive to produce since it doesn't require aging. Aging, however, strengthens the gluten content of the unbleached flour. Best not to skimp when buying the unbleached flour, not all companies may allow the flour to age adequately.

WHY DOESN'T BREAD COLLAPSE ONCE THE STEAM IS RELEASED?

The structure of the bread is supported by the coagulation of the proteins and the gelatinization of the complex carbohydrates. If this did not occur all baked goods would collapse once they started to cool and the steam and carbon dioxide dissipate.

WHAT IS A BATH BUN?

It is a yeast-risen type of roll that is filled with candied citrus peels and raisins or currents. They are usually topped with powdered sugar and occasionally caraway seeds. They are commonly found in England and originated in the town of Bath. The creator of the popular roll was Dr. W. Oliver Bath in the mid-1800's when the town was a popular vacation spa.

MAKING IT WITH A TWIST

Pretzels are made from a stiff thin, yeast-raised dough which is baked so that the pretzel will have a hard surface. Once the pretzel dough is shaped it is sprayed with a 1% solution of lye (sodium hydroxide) or sodium carbonate that is heated to 200°F. (93.3°C.). It is this process of spraying and heat that causes the surface starch to become gelatinized. The surface is then lightly salted or left plain and baked in a high heat oven for 4-5 minutes. The gelatinized starch will harden and leave a shiny surface. Lye then creates an alkaline condition on the surface which causes the intense brown color. The lye reacts with carbon dioxide while it is cooking to form a harmless carbonate substance. The final cooking stage takes about 25 minutes and dries the pretzel out or with less cooking time will produce a soft pretzel.

COOKIE FACTS

Cookies are made from doughs that are high in sugar and fats and lower in water content than other types of doughs. Because of this there is a shortage of available water to starch granules and gluten protein. The sugar will draw moisture from the mixture more than other ingredients and between this and the fact that a cookie dough mixture is not mixed the same as other doughs, the gluten development is minimized. If you desire a cookie with a cake-texture this can be achieved by mixing the shortening, eggs, sugar, and liquid together, then gently folding in the flour and leavening agent. To prepare a more dense cookie, just mix all the ingredients together very slowly. Because of the way cookies are mixed and the limited use of liquid, the starch is only able to gelatinize slightly.

WHAT HAPPENS WHEN YOU USE MARGARINE IN COOKIES?

When margarine is used to make cookies, the firmness of the dough will depend on the type of margarine you use. One of the most important things to remember when choosing margarine for cookies is that the package says "margarine" not "spread." If the margarine is made from 100% corn oil it will make the dough softer. When using margarine you will need to adjust the "chilling time" and may have to place the dough in the freezer instead of the refrigerator. If your making "cutout" cookies the chilling time should be at least 5 hours in the refrigerator. Bar and drop cookie doughs do not have to be chilled.

YOU'VE GOT TO LOVE A GRUNT

This "grunt" was first introduced in the late 1700's in America and is a type of cobbler. It was made with berries or other fruit and topped with a biscuit pastry dough, then steamed in a kettle with a lid while hanging over an open fire. Water was added to the fruit and as it steamed sugar is added to the grunt forming a syrup on top of the fruit. The name originated in Massachusetts and the "grunt" comes from the sound that the fruit makes as it releases the steam. Grunts are still served in the New England States with ice cream on the side.

SOURCES FOR BAKING EQUIPMENT

Albert Uster Imports, Inc. 9211 Gaither Rd. Gaithersburg, MD 20877 (800) 231-8154	Dean & DeLuca 560 Broadway New York, NY 10010 800) 221-7714
The Kitchen Witch 127 N. El Camino Real Ste. D Encinitas, CA 92024 (619) 942-3228	Gourmet Shop Williams-Sonoma P.O. Box 7456 San Francisco, CA 94120 800) 541-2233
C.A. Paradis, Inc 1314 Bank St. Ottawa, Ontario, K1S 3Y4 Canada (613) 731-2866	

WHY DIFFERENT BAKING TIMES FOR DIFFERENT BAKED GOODS?

Baked goods should always be baked at high temperatures such as 425°-450°F. (218.3° - 232.2°C.). This will allow the expanding gasses to sufficiently increase the dough's volume before the protein has a chance to coagulate which will set the structure for the food. Small biscuits, because of their size can easily be baked at the above temperatures without a problem. However, a lower temperature is preferred for breads of about 400°F. (204.4°C.)since the higher temperature would probably burn the crust before the insides were baked. If you are baking a bread with a high sugar content you need a lower temperature of about 325°-375°F. (162.8°-190.6°C.)since sugar will caramelize at a very high temperature and cause the crust to turn black.

WHAT IS THE FASTEST GROWING BAKED GOODS PRODUCT?
The baking industry today is gearing up for tortillas and tortilla chips. Americans are consuming more tortillas than they are bagels, English muffins, and pitas combined. In 1997 we consumed over 64 billion tortillas (not including tortilla chip sales) totalling over $2 billion in sales. According to the Tortilla Industry Association this equates to 225 tortillas per person annually.

HOW OLD IS THE BAGEL?
The name bagel comes from the German word "beugel" meaning "a round loaf of bread." The first mention of the bagel was in 1610 in Kracow, Poland when it was mentioned in a piece of literature that it would be given to women in childbirth. The earliest picture of a bagel was in 1683 in an advertisement by a Jewish baker in Vienna, Austria.

WHO MAKES THE BEST SOURDOUGH BREAD IN AMERICA?
Baldwin Hills Bakery in Phillipston, Massachusetts owned by Hy Lerner makes the finest 100% all natural sourdough bread. After studying in Europe he learned the method of fermenting wheat to form a special sourdough starter. He uses a wood-fired oven that holds 2,000 loaves and the water comes from a 500 foot deep artesian well. All the ingredients used are organically grown, even the sesame seeds and raisins and he even imports his sea salt from France. The finest spring wheat is purchased from the Little Bear Trading Company in Winona, Minnesota. He does not use sweeteners, however, the bread has a light, sweet flavor. To order the bread call (508)249-4691.

WHAT IS A ONE BOWL CAKE?
It is a layer cake which is made by mixing the batter in one-bowl. When this is done you omit the step of creaming the shortening or butter and the sugar. Using the one-bowl method you add the shortening, liquid,

and the flavorings to the dry ingredients and beat. The eggs are then added and the batter beaten again.

WHERE CAN YOU FIND THE WORLD'S BEST MACAROONS?

The best macaroons are made by White Oak Farms and are called the St. Julien Macaroons. They are named after a fourteenth-century mystic, St. Julien. The macaroons are fat-free, low in calories and are made French-style with crushed almonds, egg whites, sugar, and flavorings. They need to be kept cold due to the lack of preservatives. To order the macaroons call (508)653-5953.

WHAT IS A MOON PIE?

A Moon Pie is simply marshmallow between two vanilla cookies or graham crackers and because of its round shape people thought it resembled the moon. It was originally called the "Lookout Marshmallow" and was know as the largest five-cent snack cake on the market. Later the name was changed to the "Lookout Moon Pie." It was a regional bakery novelty that had its origins in Chattanooga, Tennessee at the Chattanooga Bakery. It was only sold in the Southern United States. The snack cake caught on nationally and has sold over 2 billion since its creation in 1917. The Moon Pie is still manufactured by the Chattanooga Bakery on King Street. The bakery produces 300,000 Moon Pies every day. The company does no advertising due to its loyal followers over the years. Call (800)251-3404 for their catalog.

DOES YOUR PASTRY HAVE PUFFY ENDS?

Puff pastry dough is made from flour, butter, and water. A small amount of butter is placed between the layers of dough before it is folded several times which may produce as many as 700 layers. When the dough is cut, be sure and only slice the dough with a very sharp knife and cut straight down, never pull the knife through the dough or cut the dough at an angle. If you do it will cause the ends to puff up unevenly as the pastry bakes.

AMERICA'S GREATEST FRUITCAKE

The best fruitcake in the United States is made by the Gethsemani Monks at their farm in central Kentucky. The fruitcake is a dark cake, made with cherries, raisins, dates, pineapple, and high quality nuts. Almost all ingredients are grown in their own gardens and if you expect to purchase the fruitcake for Christmas you need to order early at (502)549-3117.

WHAT DIFFERENT LIQUIDS CREATE DIFFERENT TEXTURED BREADS?

Liquids tend to impart their own significant characteristics to breads. Water, for instance, will cause the top of the bread to be more crisp and significantly intensifies the flavor of the wheat. Water that remains after potatoes are boiled (potato water) will add a unique flavor and make the crust smooth as well as causing the bread to rise faster due to the higher starch content. Any liquid dairy product will change the color of the bread to a richer creamy color and leave the bread with a finer texture and a soft, brown crust. Eggs are capable of changing the crust so that it will be more moist.

If any liquid sweetener such as molasses, maple syrup, or honey is used it will cause the crust to be dark brown and will keep the crust moist. A vegetable or meat broth will give the bread a special flavor and provide you with a lighter, crisper crust. Alcohol of any type will give the bread a smooth crust with a flavor that may be similar to the alcohol used, especially beer. Coffee and tea are commonly used to provide a darker, richer color and a crisper crust.

WHAT IS THE BAKER'S SECRET TO GREASE & FLOUR?

 When baking a variety of foods the recipe may call for you to "grease and flour" the pan before adding any ingredients. The standard method is to grease the pan with an oil and then sprinkle flour in and tap the pan or move it around to allow the flour to distribute as evenly as possible. However, sticking still may occur unless you place a piece of waxed paper on top of the grease, then grease the waxed paper and then flour. One of the professional chef's secrets is to use what is known as the "baker's magic" method, which is to prepare a mixture of ½ cup of room temperature vegetable shortening, ½ cup of vegetable oil, and ½ cup of all-purpose flour. Blend the mixture well and use the mixture to grease the pans. The mixture can be stored in an airtight container for up to 6 months under refrigeration.

THE FOUR MOST POPULAR TYPES OF BREAD

» Batter Breads
These are yeast-leavened breads that are always beaten instead of kneaded.

» Quick Breads
Going Up! If you ever wondered what quick bread is, it is bread that is leavened with baking powder or baking soda instead of the standard yeast. It does not require any rising time since there is an

instant reaction with water and between the oven temperature and the acidic nature of the dough carbon dioxide is formed to expedite the rising process.

» Unleavened Breads
This would include matzo, which is flat due to the lack of a leavening agent.

» Yeast Breads
These are leavened with yeast and are always kneaded to stretch the gluten in the flour. If you use room-temperature ingredients in the yeast and quick-bread types it will accelerate the rising and baking times.

CHEWY! PHOOEY!

Check the label of commercial baked goods to see if the word "hydrogenated oil" is on the list of ingredients, if so these products will be higher in saturated fat. Hydrogenation changes the texture of the product giving it added body. It provides more of a "feel" to the food in your mouth.

HOT, HOT, MILK

If you are using raw or unpasteurized milk in your recipe, make sure you scald the milk before using it. Raw milk contains an organism that tends to break down the protein structure of the gluten.

PEEK-A-BOO

Always check baking bread at least 10-15 minutes before the baking time is completed to be sure your oven temperature is accurate.

OVEN SPYING

The best method of reheating biscuits or rolls is to put them into a slightly dampened paper bag sealed with a tie. Place the bag into the oven at a very low temperature. It should only take about 5 minutes and it is best if you keep your eye on the bag just to be safe.

BREAD BIOCHEMISTRY

If your bread is a "low-riser" it may mean that you used old yeast, too little water, or water that was too cold or hot. Remember too high a heat kills yeast activity. Try again with fresh yeast and warm water.

TIMMMMBER

If your bread is a "high-riser" or has collapsed you may have added too much yeast or water. Use less next time. Remember a small amount of sugar is "yeastie food" and will feed the yeast and make the dough rise faster. If too much sugar is used then it will actually act to inhibit the rising.

I'M FALLING, HELP ME!

Occasionally a dough rises too much before the bread starts to bake, thus causing the gluten strands to become weak and too thin leading to the escape of carbon dioxide gas. When this occurs the bread may rise, then collapse and have a sunken top.

BREAD MAKING 101

For the best results never use a shiny bread pan. It is best to use a dull finish aluminum pan to bake your bread in. A dark pan may cool too quickly and a shiny pan reflects heat to such a degree that you may not get even cooking.

A GAS LEAK

Occasionally a dough rises too much before the bread starts to bake, thus causing the gluten strands to become weak and too thin leading to the escape of carbon dioxide gas. When this occurs the bread may rise, then collapse and have a sunken top.

EVENING THINGS OUT

If your bread has a crumbly texture you might try adding a small amount of salt, which will give the bread a more even texture.

TUCKING IN THE BREAD

If you are going to freeze a loaf of bread, make sure you include a piece of paper towel in the package to absorb moisture. This will keep the bread from becoming mushy when it is thawed out.

ARTIFICIAL COLOR?

If you ever wondered how pumpernickel bread gets its dark color, it comes from adding a dark caramel to the white or rye flour. The better pumpernickel breads are made from rye flour only.

CUT UP

One of easiest methods of cutting a pizza is to use a scissors with long blades. Make sure it is sharp and only use it for that purpose. Pizza cutters do work fairly well providing they are always kept very sharp. However, they tend to dull quickly since most are made of poor quality metal.

THE OCTOPUS MOLD

If you see the slightest sign of mold on baked goods throw the item out. Mold tends to send out feelers that cannot be seen in most instances.

SCRUB-A-DUB

If you burn bread, try removing the burned area with a grater.

JOLLY POOR SHOW

If you eat an English muffin in the morning and think that it is healthier than white bread you are wrong. English muffins have about the same or possibly less nutritional value unless they are enriched, then they may be equal.

JUST A TEASPOON OF SUGAR

If you like your biscuits and rolls to be a rich golden color, just add one teaspoon of sugar to the dry ingredients. It only adds 16 calories to the whole batch.

SLOWING DOWN THE RISING

If you would like to slow down the rising time, just add one extra cube of yeast to the batter. It should slow things down about 45 minutes to one hour without changing the taste of the product.

CRANK UP THE MACHINE

If you use a bread machine and want the finest all-natural flour money can buy, try calling (800)827-6836. King Arthur Flour is located in Norwich, VT and offers a unique strain of white whole wheat flour.

OR USE A BELLOWS

If you want the lightest dumplings every time, just puncture them when they are through cooking with a fork and allow air to circulate within them.

IT'S A WRAP

To replace lost moisture in a loaf of bread that has hardened, try wrapping it tightly in a damp towel for about 2-3 minutes then place the bread in the oven at 350°F. (176.7°C.) for 15-20 minutes. Moisture can easily be replaced in French or Italian bread by just sprinkling the crust with cold water and placing them in a 350°F. (176.7°C.) oven for 8-10 minutes.

VOILA

To remove muffins, rolls, or biscuits from a sectioned pan, try placing the pan on a damp towel for about 30 seconds. Use an old towel, it might stick.

EASY, NOT DIFFICULT

For a thick dough that is difficult to knead, just place a small amount of vegetable oil on your hands. Placing the dough in a plastic bag also may help.

SEALING IT UP

One of the best methods of keeping the insides of a cake from drying out is to place a piece of fresh white bread next to the exposed surface. The bread can be affixed with a short piece of spaghetti.

KEEPING IT ALL TOGETHER

If you have problems keeping a cake together when you are icing it, try holding it together with a few pieces of thick spaghetti.

THINNING IT OUT

Icing tends to become thick and difficult to work with after a short period of time. If this happens just add 2-3 drops of lemon juice and re-mix the icing.

UNSALTED IF YOU PLEASE

Next time you make an icing, try adding 1 teaspoon of butter to the chocolate while it is melting to improve the consistency.

NO HANGERS ON HERE

To eliminate the problem of icing sticking to your knife, just dip your knife in cold water frequently.

WHIPPING IT UP

When you are whipping cream, try adding a small amount of lemon juice or salt to the cream to make the job easier. For a unique flavor also add just a small amount of honey.

GETTING ARTISTIC

Before baking rolls, try glazing the tops. Just beat one egg white lightly with one tablespoon of milk and brush on. When glazing a cake, try using 1 tablespoon of milk with a small amount of brown sugar dissolved in it.

HELP, I NEED AIR

When cream cheese is used in any recipe, make sure you blend it well so that it's light and fluffy before adding any other ingredients to it, especially eggs.

TOSS IT!

If a cake gets hard and stale, throw it out, don't try to repair it.

THROW IN THE COLD TOWEL

When your baked food gets stuck to the bottom of the pan, try wrapping the cake pan in a towel when it is still hot or place the pan on a cold, wet towel for a few minutes.

POOR BUBBLES

If you are having problems with bubbles in the batter, try holding the pan about 5 inches off the floor and drop it. It may take 2-3 times but the bubbles will be all gone, the cake might be too if you are not careful.

CHEESECAKE TO DIE FOR

When preparing a cheesecake, never make any substitutions, go exactly by the recipe. Cheesecakes will come out excellent if the recipe is followed to the letter. Also, when making cheesecake, be sure that the cheese is at room temperature before using it and remember the slower you bake a cheesecake, the less chance there will be of shrinkage.

The oven should never be opened for the first 25-30 minutes when baking cheesecake, or you may cause the cheesecake to develop cracks or partially collapse. To avoid cheesecake cracking from the evaporation of moisture, it will be necessary to increase the humidity in the oven by placing a pan of hot water on the lower shelf before you preheat the oven. Cheesecake cracks can be repaired with creamed cream cheese or sweetened sour cream.

Never substitute a different size pan for a cheesecake recipe, use the exact size recommended.

STAYING SOFT

To keep boiled icing from hardening, just add a small amount of white vinegar to the water while it is cooking.

I PREFER THE REAL THING

If you are in a hurry to make a frosting, try mashing a small boiled potato, then beat in 1/3 cup of confectioners sugar and a small amount of vanilla.

DOTH YOUR CAKE RUNNETH OVER

If you sprinkle a thin layer of corn starch on top of a cake before you ice it the icing won't run down the sides.

THE BEST FLOUR FOR CAKES

Remember cake flour will make a lighter cake due to its lower gluten content. If you don't have any cake flour, try using all-purpose flour, but reduce the amount 2 tablespoons for each cup of cake flour called for. One of the best recipes for making a light textured cake is to use 50% unbleached cake flour and 50% whole wheat flour.

BEAT ME, BEAT ME
Butter or shortening when mixed with sugar needs to be beaten for the complete time the recipe calls for. If you shorten the time you may end up with a coarse-textured or heavy cake.

WORKS, BUT NOT A HEALTHY TIP
A richer cake will be produced by substituting 2 egg yolks for 1 whole egg as long as you don't have to worry about your cholesterol.

GIVE ME ROOM, LOTS OF ROOM
Remember never to fill the baking pan more than ¼ full. The cake needs room to expand.

CAKEQUAKE
During the first 15-20 minutes of baking, never open the oven or the cake may fall from the sudden change in temperature.

HEAVENLY FOOD
An angel food cake may be left in the pan and covered tightly with tin foil for a maximum of 24 hours, or until you are ready to frost it.

THE BLOB?
The juices from pies will not spread when you dish it out if you blend 1 egg white which has been beaten until stiff with 2 tablespoons of sugar and add it to the filling before baking.

BE THE FLAKIEST!
There are a number of ways to make a flakier pie crust, the following are just a few;
(1) adding a teaspoon of vinegar to the pie dough,
(2) substituting sour cream or whipping cream for any water,
(3) replacing your shortening or butter with lard, lard has larger fat crystals and 3 times the polyunsaturates as butter.

DOWN WE GO, USED THE WRONG FAT AGAIN
Low-fat margarine or whipped butter should not be used for baking purposes. They both have too high a water and air content and this may

cause your cakes or cookies to collapse or flatten out. For the best result, always try and use the type of fat recommended in the recipe.

MAKE THE RIGHT GRADE

Most cook books never mention the fact that when eggs are called for in a recipe and the size not mentioned, you should always use large eggs. The volume difference in a small egg compared to a large egg may be enough to change the consistency and the quality of the final product.

JUST WHAT THE RECIPE NEEDED

A pastry chef's trick to add flavor to a lemon tart or pie is to rub a few sugar cubes over the surface of an orange or lemon then include the cubes in the recipe as part of the total sugar. The sugar tends to extract just enough of the natural oils from these fruits to add some excellent flavor.

ROOM TEMPERATURE WORKS BEST

If you have ever baked a butter cake and it was too heavy chefs have a trick that works great. Incorporating air into the batter to make the butter cake light and airy. All you have to do is to cream the sugar with the fat at room temperature. Shortening of any type does not blend well when it is too cold.

CAKE TENDERIZER?????

The texture of a cake will change depending on the type of sweetener used. Sweeteners may determine how tender the cake will be so make sure you use the right one. Never substitute a standard granulated sugar for a powdered sugar, powdered should only be used for icings and glazes. Granulated is recommended for baking. If you are baking any cake that has a crumb texture, make sure that you use oil in place of a solid fat.

FOLLOW INSTRUCTIONS TO THE LETTER

Many people do not read all the instructions carefully in a recipe. If a recipe says for a pan to be greased it may not mean to grease the entire pan including the sides. A number of cakes need to go up the sides and only the bottom of the pan should be greased.

UP, UP, AND AWAY

When mixing batter, spray the beaters with a vegetable oil spray before using them and the batter won't climb up the beaters.

BUTTER BEWARE

Butter is frequently called for in recipes. Be aware that when it is, make sure that you do not automatically melt the butter. Most recipes, especially cake recipes, will have a better texture if the butter is just softened.

GUARANTEEING A DRY BOTTOM

If you have a problem with fruit or fruit juices soaking the bottom of your pie crust and making them soggy, try brushing the bottom with egg whites. This will seal the pie crust and solve the problem. Other methods include: spreading a thin layer of butter on the pie plate bottom before placing the dough in; warming the pan before placing in the undercrust, and making sure that the crust is fully thawed out if it was frozen.

MAKE A COOOOL CRUST

When making a pie crust, be sure and have the kitchen cool. A hot kitchen will affect the results. All pie ingredients should be cold when preparing a crust.

KEEPING IT FIRM

When using a cream filling in a pie, coat the crust with granulated sugar before adding the cream. This usually eliminates a soggy crust.

MUST BE JUST RIGHT

All-purpose flour is best for pie crusts, cake flour is too soft and won't give the crust the body it needs, while bread flour contains too high a gluten content to make a tender crust.

NO SMOOTHIES WANTED HERE

If you use some sugar in the pastry recipe it will tenderize the dough. Pastry dough should look like coarse crumbs.

CHILLING OUT

Never add water to pie dough unless it is ice water. However, ice cold sour cream added to your recipe instead of ice water will result in a more flaky pie crust.

KEEPING IN SHAPE

Never stretch pie dough when you are placing it in the pan. Stretched dough will usually shrink away from the sides.

GLASS COOKWARE

Glass baking dishes will conduct heat more efficiently than metal pans. When you use a glass baking dish, remember to lower the temperature by 25°F. (-3.9°C.).This will reduce the risk of burning the bottom of your cake.

OUCH THAT HURT

If you have a problem with burning the bottoms of cookies when making a number of batches, all you have to do is to run the bottom of the pan only under cool water before placing the next batch on the pan. When you start with too hot a surface the cookies may burn their bottoms. The desired shape of the cookies may also change if placed on the hot pan.

TYPES OF COOKIES

» Bar Cookies
Soft dough is used and the batter is then placed into a shallow pan and cut into small bars after baking.

» Drop Cookies
Made by dropping small amounts of dough onto a cookie sheet.

» Hand-Formed Cookies
Made by shaping cookie dough into balls or other shapes by hand.

» Pressed Cookies
Made by pressing the cookie dough through a cookie press or bag with a decorative top to make fancy designs or shapes.

» Refrigerator Cookies
Made by shaping cookie dough into logs, then refrigerated until firm. They are then sliced and baked.

» Rolled Cookies
The cookie dough is rolled out and made into thin layers. Cookie cutters are then used to make different shapes.

HELP, LET ME OUT

Cookies tend to burn easily. One method of eliminating this problem is to remove them from the oven before they are completely done and allow the hot pan to finish the job.

DEEP POCKETS

Whipped butter, margarine, or any other soft spread that is high in air and water content should never be used in a cookie recipe.

EXTRA WORK

When making cookies, sifting the flour is usually unnecessary.

DOUBLE DECKER

If you don't have a thick cookie pan, try baking the cookies on two pans, one on top of the other. It will eliminate burned bottoms.

RACK 'EM UP

Cookies should be cooled on an open rack not left in the pan. They should be fully cooled before you store them or they may become soggy.

SAME ADVICE GIVEN FOR BISCUITS

When mixing the cookie dough, remember that if you over-stir the cookies may be tough.

IT NEVER TASTES THE SAME

Unbaked cookie dough may be frozen for 10-12 months. Wrap as airtight as you can in freezer bags.

STAYING A SOFTEEE

Soft cookies will always stay soft if you add half an apple or a slice of fresh white bread to the jar. This will provide just enough moisture to keep the cookies from becoming hard.

PERK UP YOUR PEAKS

There are a number of methods for making world-class meringue and high peaks. (1) Make sure that your egg whites are at room temperature before adding a small amount of baking powder, then as you beat them add 2-3 tablespoons of a quality granulated sugar for each egg used. Keep beating until the peaks stand up without  drooping. (2) To keep the peaks firmer for a longer period of time, try adding ¼ teaspoon of white vinegar for each 3 eggs (whites), while beating. Also, add 4-5 drops of lemon juice for each cup of cream. Remember, if the weather is bad, rainy, or even damp out, the meringue peaks will not remain upright.

WON'T MAKE THEM SOGGY

Fruitcakes will retain their moisture if wrapped in a damp towel.

VALENTINE'S DAY SPECIAL

A heart-shaped cake is easier to make than you might think. All you have to do is to bake a normal round cake and a square cake. Cut the round cake in half, then place the square cake so that one of the corners faces you and add the halves of the round cake on either side.

HEAVENLY CAKES

Never bake an angel food cake on the top or middle rack of the oven. They will retain their moisture better if you bake them on the bottom shelf and always at 325°F. (162.8°C.). The best method of cutting the cake would be to use an electric knife or unwaxed dental floss.

CRUNCHY, CRUNCHY

When making oatmeal cookies, try lightly toasting the oatmeal on a cookie sheet before adding it to the batter. The best way to do this is to heat the oatmeal at 185°F. (85°C.) for about 10 minutes. The flakes should turn a golden brown.

SWEET TRICK

If you want your sugar cookies to remain a little soft, try rolling the dough out in granulated sugar instead of flour.

WATER RETENTION?

If you are having a problem with icing getting crumbly, just add a pinch of baking soda to the powdered sugar. The icing won't get crumbly and this will also help to retain some moisture so that the icing will not dry out as fast.

ELIMINATING MERINGUE TEARS

The nature of meringue is to develop small droplets of water on the surface shortly after it is removed from the oven. This is a common problem with tarts and pies and can easily be eliminated by just allowing the tart or pie to remain in the oven until it cools off somewhat. Turn the oven off a few minutes before the dish has completed cooking to avoid over-cooking it. This will also eliminate the problem of cracking.

FRUIT PIE TIP

The acidic (ascorbic acid) nature of fruit pies and tarts may cause a reaction with a metal pan and discolor the food. Always use a glass dish when baking a fruit pie or tart for the best results. Remember to reduce your baking time or lower the temperature of the oven.

THE INCREDIBLE SHRINKING PIE

Most recipes tell you to make sure that pastry and pie dough is chilled before placing it into the tin or dish. The reason for this is that the cold will help to firm up the fat or shortening and relax the gluten in the flour. This will cause it to retain its shape and reduce shrinkage.

SLIPPING AND SLIDING

A chef's secret when using measuring cups and you have to measure both eggs and an oil is to measure the eggs before the oil. The egg will coat the cup and allow the oil to flow out more easily.

A MUST TO REMEMBER

When the recipe calls for a greased pan, make sure you always use unsalted butter. Salted butter has a tendency to cause food to stick to the pan.

ACCURACY COUNTS
A bakery chef will always sift the flour first before measuring it for a more accurate measurement.

GOOD RULE TO FOLLOW
A souffle must be served as soon as it is removed from the oven. When an item is steam-baked it has a tendency to collapse as soon as it starts to cool down. Best to serve it in its baking dish or on a very warm plate.

A CLEAN GRIDDLE IS A HEALTHY GRIDDLE
Pancakes will never stick to the cooking surface if you clean the surface after every batch with coarse salt wrapped up in a piece of cheesecloth. The salt will provide a light abrasive cleaning and won't harm the surface if you are gentle.

TO CRUNCH OR NOT TO CRUNCH
If you are using a 100% whole wheat flour and want the crunchiest cookies ever, try using butter instead of any other shortening. Never use oil, it will make the cookies soft.

RUNNY IS NOT FUNNY
If you have a problem with juices bubbling out or oozing out when baking a pie, try adding a tablespoon of tapioca to the filling. This will thicken the filling just enough. Another method is to insert a tube-wide macaroni in the center of the top allowing air to escape.

OLD NEW ENGLAND TRICK
A tablespoon of REAL maple syrup added to your pancake batter will really improve the taste.

CLOSE THE DOORS AND WINDOWS
When chefs make pancakes they never use milk or water, they substitute club soda to make the pancakes so light they will float around the house and you will have a problem finding them.

KEEPING A MOIST TOP

If you place a few slices of fresh white bread on top of your pie while it is baking this will eliminate blistering. Remove the bread about 5 minutes before the pie is finished to allow the top crust to brown.

POP GOES THE MARSHMALLOW

For a unique pumpkin pie, try placing small marshmallows on the bottom of the pie. The marshmallows will rise to the top as the pie bakes and look great. This feat is accomplished by the air expanding in the marshmallows.

TRY BLENDING IN

When baking it is important for all the ingredients to be blended well. If the recipe calls for flour to be sifted, try adding other dry ingredients such as the leavening and salt to the flour before you sift.

GOING UP

When cookies do not brown properly, try placing them on a higher shelf in the oven.

ONE FOR THE COUNTY FAIR

If you want to try something different, make your own cake flour by mixing 2 tablespoons of cornstarch in 1 cup of cake flour. It will produce a light, moist cake.

TASTES GREAT

Vanilla extract can be used to replace sugar. Use 5 drops to replace 1/4 cup of granulated sugar.

GRAPE WORKS BEST

If you are having difficulty keeping your soft cookies moist and keeping the moisture in cakes and pancakes, just add a teaspoon of jelly to the batter.

THIN IS IN

To stop your dough from crumbling when worked and to make a thinner dough for pie shells, try coating the surface you are rolling on with olive oil.

SLICK MOVE

Spray a small amount of vegetable oil on your knife before cutting a pie with a soft filling. This will stop the filling from sticking to the knife.

WORLD'S GREATEST DOUGHNUT

Doughnut dough should be allowed to rest for about 20 minutes before frying. The air in the dough will have time to escape giving the doughnut a better texture. This will also allow the doughnut to absorb less fat. One of the best methods of reducing the total fat in a doughnut is to place it into boiling water the second it is removed from the frying vat. Any fat that is clinging to the doughnut drops off in the hot water, then just remove the doughnut after 3-5 seconds and allow to drain on a metal rack. Frying temperature should be 365°F. (185°C.) for about 50 seconds on each side. Never turn them more than once and allow room for expansion in the frying vat.

RETAINS MOISTURE

Cookie jars should always have a loose-fitting lid to allow air to circulate around the cookies if you want them to stay crisp.

DIP IT, DIP IT

If you would like a sharp edge on your cookies when using a cutter, try dipping the cutter in warm oil occasionally during the cutting.

A CENTER CUT

Next time you cut a cake, try cutting it from the center so that you can move the pieces together keeping the edges moist.

CHILLY DOUGH

If your cookie dough is cold it will not stick to the rolling pin. Chill the dough for no more than 20 minutes in the refrigerator for the best results.

WELL SLIVER MY CANDY

Why purchase chocolate slivers, when all you have to do is use your potato peeler on a Hershey bar.

WORKS LIKE A CHARM

Pies with graham cracker crusts are difficult to remove from the pan. However, if you just place the pan in warm water for 5-10 seconds it will come right out without any damage.

BE GENTLE

The best way to cool an angel food cake is to turn it upside down on an ice cube tray or place it upside down in the freezer for just a few minutes.

FOWL FACT

Never allow anyone in your family to sample batter if it contains raw eggs. Over 3,200 people became ill in 1997 from tasting batter, homemade eggnog, and Caesar salad made the old fashioned way. Chicken ovaries may be contaminated with salmonella and even though eggs look OK and are not cracked they may still be contaminated.

SUGARTIME

Never place a freshly baked cake on a plate without shaking a thin layer of sugar on the plate first, This will prevent the cake from sticking.

A REVIVAL

It really isn't worth the trouble but if you want to revive a cake that has gone stale, just very quickly dip it in low-fat milk and place it in a 350°F. (176.7°C.) oven for 10-15 minutes.

FLOUR

Flour is ground from grains, fruits, vegetables, beans, nuts, herbs, and seeds. Primarily, it is used in muffins, pies, cakes, cookies, and all other types of baked goods. It is also used as a thickener in soups, gravies, and stews. Many products are "floured" before they are breaded to help the breading adhere better.

The production of flour is mainly the "roller process" in which the grain is sent through high speed rollers and sifters which crack the grain, separate it from the bran and germ, then grind it into the consistency we are used to.

Wheat flours are more popular than all other types of flour because of its ability to produce "gluten." This protein gives wheat its strength and elasticity, which is important in the production of breads.

TYPES OF FLOURS

» All-Purpose Flour (General-Purpose Flour)
This flour is a blend of hard and soft wheat flour. It has a balanced protein/starch content which makes it an excellent choice for breads, rolls, and pastries. It may be used for cakes when cake flour is unavailable. Pre-sifted, all-purpose flour has been milled to a fine texture, is aerated, and is best for biscuits, waffles, and pancakes.

» Bleached Flour
A white flour with a higher gluten-producing potential than other flours. Used mainly to make bread.

» Bran Flour
A whole wheat flour that is mixed with all-purpose white flour and tends to produce a dry effect on baked products.

» Bread Flour
A hard-wheat, white flour with a high gluten content used to make breads.

» Bromated Flour
White flour in which bromate is added to the flour to increase the usefulness of the gluten. This will make the dough knead more easily and may be used in commercial bread making plants.

» Browned Flour
This is really just a heated white flour that turns brown adding color to your recipe.

» Brown Rice
Flour contains rice bran as well as the germ and has a nutty flavor. Commonly substituted for wheat flour.

» Cake Flour
A very fine white flour, made entirely of soft wheat flour and is best for baking cakes. Tends to produce a soft-textured, moist cake. Also excellent for soft cookies.

» Corn Flour
Usually a very starchy flour used in sauces as a thickener with a slightly sweet flavor.

» Cottonseed Flour
A high protein flour used in baked goods to increase the protein content.

» Durham Flour
A white flour that has the highest protein content of all purpose white flour. Best for light pastries and biscuits.

» Potato Flour
Provides a thickening texture and used mainly for stews, soups, and sauces.

» Rice Flour
Excellent for making delicately textured cakes.

» Self-Rising Flour
A soft-wheat, white flour that should not be used in yeast-leavened baked goods. Contains a leavening agent that tends to cause deterioration. The flour should be used within 1-2 months of purchase.

» Seminola
A white flour with a yellow tint made from Durham. Used mainly in commercial pasta and bread. Has a high protein content.

» Soy Flour
Produced from raw soy beans which are lightly toasted. It has a somewhat sweet flavor and tends to retain its freshness longer than most baked goods.

» White Rice Flour
This type of flour will absorb more liquid and may need additional liquid as well as increasing the mixing time.

» Whole Wheat Flour
This a reconstituted flour made from white flour with the addition of the bran and endosperm. It is sometimes sold as graham flour and has small specks of brown. Whole wheat flour is more difficult to digest than white flour. It tends to cause flatulence and intestinal upsets in susceptible individuals.

YOU'LL NEVER TASTE THE WINE
An old trick to stop waffles from sticking to the waffle iron is to add a teaspoon of white wine to the batter.

SHAME ON YOU
The reason a custard pie shrinks away from the crust is that you have cooked it too long in an oven that was too hot.

INCREASING THE HUMIDITY
If you are having a problem with bread browning too fast, try placing a dish of water on the shelf just above the bread. The added humidity in

the oven will slow down the browning. This will work with cakes as well.

STAY FRUIT, STAY

Dried fruits tend to go to the bottom of the baked goods when cooked because they lose some moisture and become more solid. If you coat them with the same flour that you are using in the recipe they will stay put.

A BIG ONE WORKS BEST

Use a salt shaker filled with powdered or colored sugar for sprinkling candy or cookies. Make the holes larger if needed.

FAT REDUCTION

Substituting light cream or "lite" sour cream for the liquid in a recipe in a packaged mix will not make a difference in most instances.

DON'T GET YOUR BOTTOMS WET

The bottoms of dumplings always seem to get soggy. To avoid this problem all you have to do is wait until the dish is bubbling hot before you place them on top. They will cook faster, be lighter, and absorb less moisture. For a great fruit cobbler place the top on after it starts bubbling.

SQUIRT, SQUIRT

To resolve the problem of removing gelatin from a mold, try spraying the mold with a light coating of vegetable oil.

IT'S PARTY TIME

If you are going to cut an unfrosted cake and make decorative designs, try freezing the cake first. This will make it much easier to slice and make the designs. Fresh cakes are hard to work with without making a big mess.

DOUBLE DUTY

It's very handy to keep a shaker of ¾ salt and ¼ pepper next to the range or food preparation area.

ADD AN APPLE TO A CAKE
If you need to store a cake more than 1-2 days you should add ½ an apple to the cake saver. This will provide just enough moisture to stop the cake from drying out too soon.

NOT VERY PROFESSIONAL
Warped pans should be discarded. They will spoil the quality of the product especially if you place batter directly on the pan.

LET THE ARTIST OUT
A baker's trick when placing a design on top of a cake is to take a toothpick and trace the design before sprinkling on the topping.

THE TOP SELLING COOKIES IN THE UNITED STATES IN 1997
1. Oreo . . . . 128 Million Pounds
2. Generic Brand Icing Sandwich . . . 119 Million Pounds
3. Chocolate Chip Cookies . . . . . . 114 Million Pounds
4. Fig And Apple Newtons . . . . . . 86 Million Pounds

GETTING HIGH
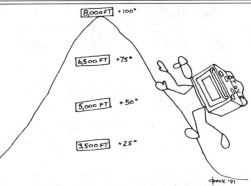

When baking at an altitude of over 3,500 feet it is necessary to increase the temperature 25° and add 1 tablespoon of flour to the recipe. Then continue adding 1 tablespoon for every 1,500 feet increase in elevation. If you are using leavening and 1 teaspoon is needed at sea level, then use ⅔ teaspoon at 3,500 feet, and ½ teaspoon at 5,000 feet. Use ¼ teaspoon at 6,500 or above.

ATTACK OF THE SPORES
Fresh bread will not get moldy as fast if you wrap it in waxed paper and place it in the refrigerator.

SOUFFLES

When preparing a souffle, be sure and use a souffle dish with straight sides which will force the expanding souffle upwards. Also, always use the exact size dish called for in the recipe.

» GREASE ME, GREASE ME
A souffle dish should always be buttered unless the recipe says not to use any type of fat on the sides of the dish.

» CLOSE THE WINDOWS
If more egg whites than yolks are used, the souffle will be lighter.

» CALL THE PARAMEDICS
The egg whites should be beaten in such a way as to insure the highest amount of air be trapped. Never over-beat or they will become too dry and cause a collapse.

» CURIOSITY KILLED THE SOUFFLE
The oven door should never be opened when the souffle is cooking for at least ¾ of the cooking time.

» WELL HAUTE DA
European souffles are usually served a little underdone with a custard textured center. This is the preferred method in the finer restaurants.

» A ROYAL MISHAP
A souffle must be served as soon as it is taken from the oven or the crown may collapse as it cools.

GREAT ALL-NATURAL BREAD

If you want to order the best raisin pumpernickel bread you have ever tasted, just call Bread Alone, Inc. in Boiceville, NY at (914)657-3328. They also have a free catalog.

FLAVORED WHIPPED CREAM

» Whipped cream can be flavored by adding the following:

» Chocolate - Add 3 tablespoons of granulated sugar, 1 tablespoon of cocoa, ¾ teaspoon of natural vanilla extract.

» Coffee - Add 1 ½ tablespoons of granualted sugar, 1 teaspoon of instant coffee.

» Lemon/Lime- Add 2 tablespoons of granulated sugar, 1 teaspoon concentrated lemon or lime juice.

CHAPTER 3

The Secrets of Cooking and Preparation

VEGETABLE COOKING

» BAKING

Leave the skins on to preserve most of their nutrients. Make sure that the vegetable has a high enough water content or it will dry out in a very short period of time. The harder root vegetables are more suited to baking, these include; potatoes, winter squash, jicama, and beets.

» ARE YOU STEAMING?

Steaming cooks vegetables in a short period of time and retains most of the nutrients. Start with the more solid vegetables such as carrots then add the softer ones later.

Artichokes	6-10 minutes
Green beans	45 minutes
Beets	45 minutes
Broccoli with stalk	25 minutes
Brussels Sprouts	20 minutes
Cabbage	15 minutes
Carrots	25 minutes
Cauliflower	12 minutes
Celery	20 minutes
Corn on Cob	15 minutes
Green Peas	20-40 minutes
Green Peppers	5 minutes
Onions	20-30 minutes
Potatoes (all)	35 minutes
Tomatoes	15 minutes

» PRESSURE COOKERS
Needs to be controlled more. Can be too difficult for vegetables and overcooking is a common occurrence.

» WOK
This is a fast method providing the pan is well heated with a very small amount of vegetable oil first. The only problem that may occur is that if you cook the vegetables too long in oil some of the fat soluble vitamins may be lost.

» WATERLESS COOKWARE
Best for green leafy vegetables, using only the water that adheres to their leaves after washing, and usually takes only 3-5 minutes.

» BOILING
When boiling vegetables there are a few good rules to follow:

1. Vegetables should always be placed in the water after it has started to boil. The shorter the time in the water the more nutrients that will be retained. Vitamin C is lost very quickly.

2. The water should be allowed to boil for 2 minutes to release a percentage of the oxygen which will also cause a reduction in nutrients.

3. Leave the skins on and the vegetables in as large a piece as possible. The more surface you expose the more nutrients will be lost.

» CROCK POT
Vegetables should never be placed in a crock pot for prolonged cooking. Most of the nutrients will be lost to the heat and the liquid.

» MICROWAVE
Usually results in short cooking times which retains the nutrients. The water content of the vegetables will determine just how well they will cook. Microwave ovens should have a movable turntable so that the food will not have "cold spots." This can result in the food being undercooked.

If you wish to brown foods in the microwave, be sure and use a special dish for that purpose. The dish should always be preheated first for the best results. If you don't have a browning dish, try brushing the meat with soy or teriyaki sauce.

A steak will continue cooking after it is removed from the microwave and it is best to slightly undercook it.

THERMOMETERS

» DEEP-FAT/CANDY
The bulb should be fully immersed in the candy or food and should

never be allowed to touch the bottom of the cooking container. To check the accuracy of the thermometer, place it in boiling water for 3-4 minutes. The temperature should read 212°F. or 100°C.

» FREEZER/REFRIGERATOR
These thermometers read from -20° to 80°F. (-28.9° to 26.7°C.). Frozen foods should always be stored at 0°F. (17.8°C.) or below to slow nutrient loss and maintain the quality of the food.

» MEAT
Insert the thermometer into the center or thickest part of the meat, making sure that it is not resting on a bone.

» OVEN
It is wise to check your oven temperature accuracy at least once a month. If the temperature is not accurate it can affect the results of the food being prepared, especially baked goods. The thermometer should be placed in the middle of the center rack.

MEASUREMENT FACTS

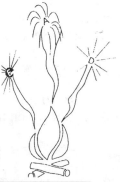

60 drops =	5 ml. =	1 tsp
3 tsp =	1 tbl	
2 tbl =	30 ml. =	1 fl. oz.
8 tbl =	½ cup	
Juice of 1 orange =	5-6 tsp.	
5 large eggs =	1 cup	
2 tbl butter =	1 oz.	
1 oz. = 30 g.		

Cooking Temperatures Degrees		
	Fahrenheit	Centigrade
Ground Beef, pork, lamb	160°	71.1°
Beef, Lamb, Veal		
Rare	140°	60°
Medium rare	145°	62.8°
Medium	160°	71.1°
Medium well	165°	73.9°
Well done	170°	76.7°
Pork		
Medium	160°	71.1°
Well-Done	170°	76.7°

Cooking Temperatures Degrees		
	Fahrenheit	**Centigrade**
Precooked	140°	60°
Poultry		
Ground Meat	165°	73.9°
Whole Birds	185°	85°
Parts	175°	79.4°
Stuffing (alone or in bird)	170°	76.7°
Egg Dishes	165°	73.9°
Leftovers	170°	76.7°

KEEP YOUR SUNNY SIDE UP

If you want to keep food wrapped in aluminum foil from overbrowning, keep the shiny side of the foil out.

OIL CHANGE

If you need to place a thin layer of oil on food, try using a spray bottle with oil in it. Beats using a brush and reduces the amount of oil used.

PIC'ER UPPER

If you are having problems keeping a pot from boiling over, try placing a toothpick between the lid and the pot.

LE PEW

If odors are a problem with a particular dish, try placing a cloth that has been dampened with ½ water and ½ vinegar over the pot. Make sure that the edges are not near the flame or intense heat.

PUNCTUATION

When cooking potatoes, try piercing the skin with a fork to allow the steam to escape.

CRISP IT

If you would like a crisp topping on your casserole, try leaving the lid off while it is cooking.

SAFETY FIRST

If a child accidentally turns on the microwave damage may occur. To avoid a problem just keep a cup of water in the microwave when it is not in use.

KEEP THE ENERGY FOCUSED

If the meat has a bone, microwaving will send more energy to the bone than the meat and the meat may not cook evenly. If possible remove the bone and give it to the dog or cat (only if it's a really big one).

WHEN USED PROPERLY

A microwave oven is just as safe as a regular oven. However, make sure you never place a sealed container in a microwave.

WHAT IS THE FORMULA FOR AN ALL-AROUND BREADING FOR ANY FOOD?

The following blend should make any food taste better and enhance the flavor. Mix all ingredients together well and store in the refrigerator until needed. Allow to stand at room temperature for 20 minutes before using.

2 cups of whole wheat pastry flour
½ tablespoon paprika
1 tablespoon of dry mustard
¾ teaspoon of finely ground celery seed
1 teaspoon ground black pepper
1 teaspoon dried basil
1 teaspoon dried marjoram
¾ teaspoon dried thyme

DON'T BE AN EGG POPPER

When cooking eggs in the microwave, remember that whole eggs may explode and when cooking an egg with a whole yolk intact, make a small hole in the yolk with a pin to allow for expansion.

OUCH!

The best oil for deep fat frying is Canola. It has the highest smoke point and will not break down easily. Oils can only be cooked to 400°F.(204.4°C.) before serious deterioration starts to occur.

RAPESEED TO THE RESCUE

To use butter, margarine, or lard for frying or sauteing add a small amount of Canola oil to them to raise the smoke point. This will allow you to cook with them without their breaking down for a longer period of time.

NOT AN OLD WIVES TALE

 If you are having problems keeping a pot from boiling over, try placing a toothpick between the lid and the pot. Other tricks include placing a wooden spoon across the top and rubbing butter around the inside lip of the pot. Also, if you add 1 ½ teaspoons of butter to a cooking pasta or soup it will not boil over. This doesn't work with vegetable oil and of course, adds calories and cholesterol.

FAT REDUCTION

Cooking meat in oil will not lower the fat content to any great degree. However, all other methods of cooking will lower the fat content.

WOK IT, WIPE IT

Depending on the type of metal your wok is made of, it may rust. Always wipe off the inner surface with vegetable oil after each use.

HOW DRY I AM

To avoid foods splattering when fried, be sure and dry them thoroughly before placing them into the hot oil. Also, place all fried foods on a piece of paper towel for a few minutes before serving to allow the excess oil to drain off.

GIVE ME AIR

Always use a shallow pot for cooking roasts, this will allow air to circulate more efficiently. Placing fresh celery stalks under the roast also helps.

AN UPLIFTING EXPERIENCE

A frequent problem that occurs when frying is trying to fry too much food at once. The fat may overflow (bubble over) from the temperature difference of the cold food and the hot fat. Also, to avoid food from sticking together, the basket should be lifted out of the fat several times before allowing it to remain in the fat.

PUNCTUATION

When baking potatoes, try piercing the skin with a fork to allow the steam to escape. This will stop the skin from cracking. Also, rubbing a small amount of oil on the skin helps.

JUST POP YOUR TOP

To develop a crisp topping on your casserole, try leaving the lid off while it is cooking.

NO SKINHEAD HERE

If you want to eliminate the skin forming on your custard, just cover the dish with a piece of waxed paper while it is still very hot.

CHOP, CHOP

If you want to save money when purchasing canned tomatoes, just buy a can of whole tomatoes and when you need chopped tomatoes, place a sharp scissors in the can and slice away.

HELP, I'M DROWNING

Most foods should be refrigerated as soon as possible to help retain the potency of the nutrients. An example of nutrient loss is boiled carrots, which if allowed to remain whole will retain 90% of their vitamin C and most of their minerals, however, if they are sliced before cooking, they will lose almost all of the vitamin C and niacin content.

NUTRIENT DAMAGE CONTROL

Baking soda should not be added to foods while they are cooking, it may destroy certain B vitamins.

LOW HEAT IS BEST

To avoid curdling when cooking with dairy products always cook at a lower temperature setting.

POSITION IS EVERYTHING

The thicker, tougher areas of the food should always be placed toward the outer edges of the cooking pan to obtain the best results in a microwave oven.

PREPARATION OF FOODS

» WASHING/SOAKING
The water soluble vitamins are very delicate and can be lost if the vegetable or fruit is allowed to remain soaking in water for too long. Carrots or celery stored in a bowl of water in the refrigerator may cause the loss of all the natural sugars, most of the B vitamins, vitamin C, and vitamin D as well as all minerals except calcium.

» PEELING/SLICING/SHREDDING
When you shred vegetables for salads you will lose 20% of the vitamin C content. Then if you allow the salad to stand for 1 hour before serving it you will lose another 20%.

» SKIN 'EM
There should be no concern about removing the skin from fruits and vegetables just before eating them. Less than 10% of the total nutrients are found in the skin. Removing the skin may be a good thing to do with many foods since pesticide and fertilizer residues are usually found in the skin.

COOKWARE, CURRENT 1998 FACTS

» ALUMINUM
The majority of cookware sold in the United States is aluminum which is an excellent heat conductor. Recent studies report that there is no risk from using this type of cookware unless you are deep-scraping the sides and bottoms of the pots continually, allowing aluminum to be released. Rarely does anyone do this.

» IRON
May supply a small amount of iron in elemental form to your diet, but not enough to be of that much use. Certain acidic foods such as tomato sauce or citrus fruit may absorb some iron but not enough to supply you with adequate daily supplemental levels. Conducts heat fairly well.

» STAINLESS STEEL
To be a good heat conductor they need to have a copper or aluminum bottom. Acidic foods cooked in stainless steel may acquire a number of metals into the food which may include chlorine, iron, and nickel.

» NON-STICK

These include Teflon and Silverstone and are made of a type of fluorocarbon resin that may be capable of reacting with acidic foods. If you do chip off a small piece and it gets into the food, don't be concerned, it will just pass harmlessly through the body.

Never allow any brand of "non-stick" surface pan to boil dry. The pan may release toxic fumes if heated above 400°F. (204.4°C.) for more than 20 minutes. This could be serious for any small pet.

» GLASS, COPPER, ENAMELLED

These will not react with any food and are safe to cook in. Copper is one of the best heat conductors and is preferred by many chefs. Copper pans, however, should only be purchased if they have a liner of tin or stainless steel to be safe, otherwise they may leach metals into the food. When you cook in glass, remember to reduce the oven temperature by 25° F. (-3.9°C.).

» CLAY POTS

Remember to always immerse both the top and the bottom in lukewarm water for at least 15 minutes prior to using. Always start to cook in a cold oven and adjust the heat after the cookware is placed into the oven. If sudden changes occur, the cookware may be cracked. Never place a clay cooker on top of the range.

» CONVECTION OVEN

This method provides a fan that continuously circulates the hot air and cooks the food more evenly and up to three times faster than conventional oven methods. It is great for baked goods and roasts. Make sure you follow the manufacturer's recommendations as to temperature since you will be cooking at 20° to 75° less than you would normally. Baked goods, however, are easily overbrowned and need to be watched closely.

» BARBECUING FOOD FACTS

A number of different herbs can be placed on the coals to flavor the food. The best are savory, rosemary, or dried basil seed pods. Lettuce leaves can be placed on the coals if they become too hot or flare up.

Charcoal briquettes should always be stored in airtight plastic bags since they will absorb moisture very easily.

» BYE, BYE, EYEBROWS

Coat your grill with a spray vegetable oil before starting the fire, then clean it shortly after you are through. Never spray the oil on the grill after the fire has started, it may cause a flare-up.

Window cleaner sprayed on a warm grill will make it easier to clean.

HEALTH HINT
If you are using real charcoal briquettes be aware that if the fat from meat drips on a briquette a chemical reaction will take place sending a carcinogen called a "pyrobenzine" onto the surface of the meat from the smoke. This dark-colored coating should be scraped off before you eat the meat, otherwise consuming a 12 oz. steak can provide you the same cancer risk as smoking 15 non-filtered cigarettes. There is no risk if you use artificial charcoal or a gas grill. Americans spend over $400 million dollars each year on charcoal briquettes.

SAUTEING

When sauteing make sure that you only use a small amount of oil. If you wish to have the food turn out crisp you need to heat the oil to a high temperature before adding the food. To test the temperature of the oil, try dropping a small piece of food into the pan, if it sizzles it is ready for you to saute.

Remember to always have the food at room temperature if you wish the food to brown faster and more evenly. Cold foods tend to stick to the pan. During the sauteing process the pan should be moved gently back and forth a number of times to assure that the browning will be even.

Before sauteing carrots, potatoes or any dense food, try parboiling them first. This will assure that all the food will be done at the same time.

Foods that are to be sauteed should be dry. Never salt any food that is to be sauteed, salt tends to retard the browning of foods.

Before sauteing meats, try sprinkling a small amount of sugar on the surface of the meat. The sugar will react with the juices, caramelize, and cause a deeper browning as well as improving the flavor.

Never overcrowd a pan that you are sauteing in. Overcrowding causes poor heat distribution resulting in food that is not evenly browned.

If the fat builds up from the foods that are being sauteed, remove the excess with a bulb baster.

Never cover a pan when sauteing. Steam tends to build up and the food may become mushy.

DIGITAL COOKING?

We are all aware that if you place your hand into a pot of boiling water at 212°F. (100°C.) you will definitely get burned. However, when you place your hand into a 325°F. (162.8°C.) oven all you feel is the intense heat and do not get burned. The reason for this is that air does not transfer nor retain heat as well as water.

THE CHEMISTRY OF COOKING

When you use heat to cook food, basically you are increasing the speed of the molecules of that food. The faster they move, the more they collide, the more heat is generated, and the hotter the food gets. This changes the texture, flavor, and even the color of the food. For every 20°F. (-6.7°C.) you raise the temperature over the normal cooking temperature you will actually increase the molecular activity by 100 percent, not 20 percent.

CAKE PANS MUST RISE TO THE OCCASION

Cake pans are a very important part of making a cake. Some factors will influence the outcome more than others, such as the thickness of the pan which is not very important, however, the finish of the pan and its relative volume to the size of the cake is very important. If a cake is heated faster, the gas cells will expand faster and the better the batter will set. The perfect pan for the job should be the actual size of the finished product. If the sides of the pan are too high, the unused area can shield the batter from needed radiant energy and slow the rate at which the batter is heated making the cake drier. This is also the cause of humps in the cake. Never use a baking pan with a bright surface since they will reflect radiant heat and transmit the heat too slowly, thereby slowing the baking process.

MOIST HEAT OR DRY HEAT?

Foods that contain a large percentage of connective tissue, such as meat, or have a tough fibrous structure such as those found in certain vegetables, should be cooked using moist heat. These foods are not naturally tender, therefore they must be tenderized by the moist heat. There are, of course, exceptions to the rule, one of which is if the meat is heavily marbled or frequently basted.

WHO BARBECUES, MOM OR DAD?

When it comes to slaving over the hot barbecue in the backyard it's dad who gets the chore 60% of the time. However, it's mom who chooses what is to be barbecued almost 100% of the time. The most common items to barbecue are burgers, chicken, hot dogs, and corn on the cob.

PUT A LID ON IT

When you are boiling water, place a lid on the pot and the water will come to a boil in shorter period of time. However, this is only true after the water reaches 150° F. (65.6°C.). Before this point it doesn't matter if the pot has the lid on it or not. The water will not produce enough steam until it hits the 150°F. (65.6°C.) level and at that level it is best to trap the steam in the pot. To raise 1 gallon of water from 60°F. to 212°F. (15.6°-100°C.) (boiling) on a gas range top takes 23 minutes with the lid on, without the lid it takes about 35 minutes.

COOKING IN A RECREATIONAL VEHICLE, IT MAY BE A HAZARD

Over 262 Americans were killed and thousands have become ill from carbon monoxide (CO) poisoning while cooking and using heaters in motor homes in 1997. The gas is odorless, is produced from faulty heating and cooking units. Every motor home should be equipped with a CO detector which sounds an alarm like a smoke detector and costs $40-$80.

THE SECRET OF WORLD-CLASS GRAVY

One of the most frequent problems with gravy is the temptation of the cook to use too much flour to thicken the gravy. When this is done it tends to detract from the gravy's flavor which is dependent on the small amount of drippings used. Chefs rarely use flour and usually deglaze the roasting pan with water to trap the drippings that have adhered to the bottom of the pan, Try adding a small amount of butter and reduce the mixture over heat, stirring frequently, until it is thick. Try not to prepare gravy too thick since it will thicken as it cools, and may be relatively solid by the time it is poured.

QUICK, SHUT THE DOOR

If anyone has ever driven you crazy because you opened the oven door when something was cooking, this is your chance to tell them that when the door is opened or left ajar for a few minutes it only takes 40-50 seconds for the temperature to return to the preset temperature. It is not really a big deal and will not affect the food.

ARE THERE DIFFERENT TEMPERATURES OF BOILING?

When we see water bubbling either lightly or more rapidly, the temperature will always be the same 212°F. (100° C.) There is the possibility of 1°F. difference at times but for the most part it remains constant. The only difference in the rapidly boiling water is that the food may cook somewhat faster due to the increased activity of the heat-carrying molecules. The food will cook more evenly and the food will retain more nutrients if the water is not rapidly boiling. Hard water, due to its high mineral content will boil 1-2°F. above soft water.

NEVER SALT FOODS TO BE FRIED

Salt tends to draw moisture from foods. If a food is salted before placing it in the fryer, it will draw moisture to the surface and cause spattering when the food is placed into the heated oil.

NEVER REUSE FRYING OIL

When oil is used for frying the temperature is raised to such a high level that a percentage of the oil is broken down (begins smoking) and decomposes into trans-fatty acid oil as well as turning a percentage of the polyunsaturated oil into a saturated oil. Trans-fatty acids even though edible, tend to cause an increase in free-radicals (abnormal cells) in the body and may also raise the bad cholesterol levels (LDL) and lower the good cholesterol levels (HDL). Best to use fresh Canola oil everytime you fry.

SMOKE, FLASH, & FIRE POINTS OF OILS

The smoke point of an oil is the point at which the oil starts deteriorating. All oils have different smoke points, Canola oil having one of the highest makes it the best oil for frying. Flavor would be another determining factor in using an oil with a lower smoke point. The smoke point is the point at which the oil is starting to convert a percentage of the oil into trans-fatty acids. The flash point is the point that the oil starts to show a small amount of flame emanating from the surface of the oil, this usually occurs at about 600°F. (315.6°C.) and should tell you that the oil has reached a dangerous level. The fire point is about 700°F. (371.1°C.) and this is the point that you had better have a fire extinguisher ready and remember never to use water on a grease fire. The fire needs to be smothered to extinguish it.

SMOKE POINTS OF FATS

Fat	Smoke Point
Canola Oil	525° F. (273.9°C.)
Safflower Oil	510° F. (265.6°C.)
Soybean Oil	495° F. (257.2°C.)
Corn Oil	475° F. (246.1°C.)
Peanut Oil	440° F. (226.7°C.)
Sesame Oil	420° F. (215.6°C.)
Animal Lard	400° F. (204.4°C.)
Vegetable Shortening	375° F. (190.6°C.)
Unclarified Butter	250° F. (121.1°C.)

JUST HOW HOT IS HOT!

Your gas range at home will burn at 3000°F. (1648.9°C.).It is an easily controllable heat and therefore the heat of choice for almost all chefs. Electric ranges will only heat up to 2000°F.(1093.3°C.) and it is more difficult to control small temperature changes. Depending on the dish this can become a problem, especially with boil-overs.

COOKING STUFFED TURKEY

The best temperature for cooking turkey is 325°F. (162.8°C.) since a lower temperature will allow bacteria in the stuffing to multiply for too long a period. Higher temperatures may shorten the cooking time, causing undercooked stuffing. Slow overnight cooking with the dressing in the bird has been the cause of numerous cases of food poisoning.

NEVER CROWD WHEN DEEP FRYING

When food is added to hot oil it tends to lower the temperature. Foods will absorb too much oil when this occurs unless the oil is returned to the normal frying temperature in a very short period of time. To reduce the effects of a lower frying temperature one of two methods are recommended. First, never add too much food to the oil at once, it not only lowers the temperature, but causes overcrowding and will not allow all the food to be fried evenly. Second, start the temperature about 15°F.(-9.4°C.) above the recommended frying temperature so that when you do add the cold food it will still be approximately the desired temperature. Whenever possible food should be left out for a short period before placing it into the fryer, the closer to room temperature the higher the frying temperature after the food is added. If the food is too cold the oil may drop down to the greasy range of about 300°-325°F. (148.9° - 162.8°C.) and the oil may never get to the proper temperature.

CANDY-MAKING SECRET

Sugar crystallization is one of the more frequent problems when making candy. This usually occurs when the slightest grain of sugar that may be trapped on the side of the pan falls down into the syrup mixture. This can easily be prevented by heating the sugar over low heat and do not stir, until the sugar is completely dissolved. Then to dissolve any sugar crystals that are still clinging to the sides of the pan, tightly place the lid on the pan and continue cooking the syrup for 3-4 minutes. The steam that is generated will melt the clinging sugar grains.

HOT SPOT, COLD SPOT

Your cooking pans should be made of a material that will dissipate the heat evenly throughout the bottom of the pan so that the food will cook evenly. Unfortunately many pans do not have this ability and develop cold spots. To check your pan, place a thin layer of about 4-5 tablespoons of sugar that has been mixed with 2 tablespoons of water on the bottom of your pan and spread it out as evenly as you can. The sugar over the hot spots will caramelize and turn brown forming a pattern of the hot spots. Hopefully, you will not have a pattern and the sugar will caramelize all at about the same time. If you do have a problem, use a heat diffuser under the pan or try the same test using a lower heat setting.

TESTING YOUR METAL

There are a number of materials that are used to manufacture pots and pans, many of which do not really do the job adequately. Remember, the thicker the gauge of the metal the more uniformly it tends to distribute the heat. The finish on the metal will also affect the efficiency of the cookware.

> » Copper
> One of the worst types of cookware is the thin stamped stainless steel pots with a thin copper-coated bottom. The copper coating is approximately $\frac{1}{50}$ of an inch in thickness and too thin to distribute the heat efficiently and uniformly.
>
> The "real" copper cookware provides excellent, even heat distribution on the bottom as well as the sides of the pan. The copper, however, needs to be kept clean and if black carbon deposits form to any degree it will affect the heat distribution significantly. These pots are usually lined with tin which must be replaced if it wears out

otherwise excess copper may leach into the food causing a health risk. Foods that are high in acid will increase the release of copper. The metal ions in copper will also react with vitamin C and reduce the amount available.

» Aluminum

Aluminum cookware stains very easily, especially if you are using hard water to cook with. Certain foods will also cause the pans to stain easily such as potatoes. If you cook a high-acid content food such as tomatoes, onions, wine, or if lemon juice is used in aluminum it will probably remove some of the stain. However, if the pan is stained when the acidic foods are cooked it may transfer the stain to the food possibly turning your foods a brownish color.

Aluminum pans also tend to warp if they are subjected to rapid temperature changes, especially if they are made of a thin gauge aluminum. If they are made of a thick gauge, they will have excellent heat-flow efficiency and will not rust, thus making the thick the best for use as cookware.

» Cast Iron/Carbon Steel

These are both non-stainless steel, iron-based metals that have a somewhat porous, jagged surface. These pots need to be "seasoned." To accomplish this you need to rub the cooking surfaces with Canola oil and heat it at 300°F. (148.9°C.) for about 40-50 minutes in the oven, then allow it to cool to room temperature before using. The oil has the ability to cool and seal the pores and even provide a somewhat non-stick surface. Another factor is that when the oil is in the pores, water cannot enter and possibly cause the formation of rust.

These pots should be washed daily using a mild soap and dried immediately. Never use salt to clean the pot, since this may cause rusting. If a cleaner is needed, be sure it is a mild one. Iron pots tend to release metal ions that react with vitamin C and reduce its potency.

» Teflon/Silverstone

These non-stick surfaces are the result of a chemically inert fluorocarbon plastic material being baked on the surface of the cookware or other type of cooking utensil. Silverstone is the highest quality of these non-stick items. The food is actually cooked on jagged peaks that protrude from the bottom, which will not allow food a chance to stick to a smooth surface. The surface is commercially "seasoned" producing the final slick surface.

The major contribution of a non-stick surface is that of allowing you to cook without the use of fats, thus reducing the calories of foods that would ordinarily be cooked with fats. The less expensive non-stick cookware usually has a very thin coating and will not last very long with everyday use. With heavy usage and continual cleaning, the coating will eventually wear thin.

» Multi-ply Pans
The bottoms of these pans usually have three layers. They are constructed with a layer of aluminum between two layers of stainless steel. Stainless steel does not have the hot spot problem and the heat will be more evenly diffused by the aluminum.

» Enamel Cookware
While the enamel does resist corrosion, it is still a metal coated with a thin layer of enamel. The coating is produced by fusing powdered glass into the metal surface, which is in most instances cast iron. The cookware can chip easily if hit against another object and can even shatter if placed from a very hot range into cold water.

» Glass Cookware
Rapid temperature changes may cause the glass to crack or break in many brands. Glass has a very low "heat-flow" efficiency rating and when boiling water is poured into the glass cookware, the actual heat that is transferred from the boiling water to the bottom of the cookware will travel slowly back to the top of the pot. Because of this, the bottom of the pot will swell and the top of the pot does not expand creating a structural type of stress and a crack is very possible. Corningware and Pyrex in that order would be the only choices for glass cookware, since both will resist most stresses.

CRUCIFEROUS COOKING

When you cook a cruciferous vegetable such as cauliflower, never use an aluminum or iron pot. The sulfur compounds will react with the aluminum turning the cauliflower yellow. If cooked in an iron pot it will turn the cauliflower brown or a bluish-green.

THE PRESSURE OF PRESSURE COOKING

Pressure cooking is more desirable for people that live at higher altitudes since water boils at 203°F.(95°C.) at 5,000 feet elevations instead of the standard 212°F. (100°C.) at or near sea level. Normally, a food would take longer to cook at the higher elevations. With a pressure cooker it allows the water to reach a temperature of 250°F. (121.1°C.) by increasing the atmospheric pressure in the pot and using the steam to cook the food faster. Steam conducts heat better than air and forces the heat into the food.

COOKING IN A BROWN BAG? DON'T EVEN THINK OF IT

When grandma cooked her turkey in a brown bag years ago the quality of the brown bag was totally different than the ones we get today from the supermarket. The majority of the brown bags of today are produced from recycled paper using a number of harmful chemicals. When heated these chemicals may be released into the foods and may produce free radicals.

MAKING THE BREADING STAY PUT

Preventing the breading from falling off foods can sometimes create a real headache unless you follow a few simple rules. First, make sure that the food that is to be breaded is very dry and use room temperature eggs, overbeating the eggs will also cause a problem. Second, after you apply the breading place the food into the refrigerator for 1 hour before allowing the food to remain  out for 20 minutes before frying. Homemade breadcrumbs are the best because of their uneven texture they tend to hold better.

COOKING WITH ALCOHOL

The boiling point of alcohol is 175°F. (79.4°C.), much lower than the boiling point for water of 212°F. (100°C.).When alcohol is added to a recipe it will lower the boiling point until it evaporates. For example, if you decide to change your recipe by adding some wine to replace some of the water, you will need to increase your cooking time by about 10 percent.

SALTING YOUR COOKING WATER

If you add 1 teaspoon of salt to your cooking water it will raise the temperature 1-2°F. (17.2-16.7°C.). Sugar and many other ingredients will also raise the temperature of the water. Unless the recipe calls for this raise, it is best not to add salt because salt has the tendency to cause toughness

BOILING POINT VS. ALTITUDE

As the altitude increases, the atmospheric pressure decreases placing less pressure on water that is trying to boil. When this occurs it makes it easier for the water to boil and the water molecules are able to be released more easily. Water will boil at a lower temperature at the 5,000 elevation. For every 1,000 feet water will boil at approximately 2°F. (16.7°C.) less than at sea level.

Altitude (feet)	Fahrenheit	Centigrade
0	212°	100°
1,000	210°	99°
2,000	208°	98°
3,000	207°	97°
4,000	205°	96°
5,000	203°	95°
10,000	194°	90°

HOW A CONVECTION OVEN WORKS

The standard oven and the convection oven work very similar to each other. The notable difference in the convection oven is that it has a fan that increases the distribution of the heat molecules providing heat to all areas more evenly and faster. Because of the fan and the efficiency of the heat circulation, a lower temperature is usually required, thereby conserving energy. Roasts especially do well in a convection oven, because of the lower heat, the meat tends to be juicier.

WHY PANS WARP

Metal pans have a higher heat-flow efficiency rating than other materials as well as having a tougher internal structure. Metal pans warp due to structural stress that is caused by sudden changes in temperature. The thinner the metal pan, the more easily it will warp, the thicker the pan the less likely it is to warp.

HOW DOES HEAT COOK FOOD?

There are three main methods of transferring heat to food; radiation, convection, and conduction. Basically, you are transferring heat from a hot object to a cold one. Radiant heat is in the form of electromagnetic waves, such as those from a toaster to the toast. It does not require any assistance from air and water. The energy travels at 186,000 miles per second, the speed of light. Convection cooking employs circulating molecules which are propelled by either gas or liquid. The heat is placed at the bottom of the food or liquid and as the heat rises it allows the colder food or liquid to fall toward the heat. The air or water currents provide the convection cooking as a vehicle for the heat. Conduction cooking utilizes an oven where the hotter molecules pass along the heat from the surface to the interior of the food. When an aluminum spike is inserted in a potato the heat is allowed to pass more easily to the inside and heat the food from both the inside and the outside at the same time.

NEVER USE PLASTIC WRAP IN A MICROWAVE

When foods become hot, chemicals from plastic wrap may be released and migrate into the food. The wrap may also stick to the food, especially fatty or sugary foods. Waxed paper, paper towels, or a plate work well.

SOLVING PROBLEMS THAT MAY OCCUR IN SAUCE BEARNAISE

Sauce bearnaise is one of the most popular sauces in the United States restaurants. It is an emulsion sauce that combines oil and water. It was developed in France in the 1830's and goes well with meats and fish dishes. When preparing the sauce the most frequent problem is that of overheating. One of two problems may occur; the first is that if the egg proteins are overheated they tend to coagulate forming small curds in a liquid that is supposed to be creamy. The second problem is that overheating may cause a breakdown of the emulsion causing it to separate. To prevent the protein from coagulating, try placing a small amount of vinegar in the sauce to lower the ph.

WHY CHEFS LEAVE THE BROILER DOOR AJAR

When the door is left ajar it will actually improve the broiling aspects and reduce the roasting aspects. When the door is left ajar the pan and the air inside the broiler doesn't become as hot as it normally would and reduces the effects of conduction heat cooking. It still allows the same heat intensity to occur and improves the flavor and imparts a more crusty texture to meats.

IS GAS OR ELECTRIC COOKING BEST?

There is no contest here, it is definitely gas that wins on the range top, since you are able to change the temperature quickly, as well as have instant heat control which is preferred by all chefs. Boilovers are more easily controlled than electric in all instances. The oven, however, is a different story, electric ovens will reach the desired temperature more rapidly and hold it more evenly with excellent accuracy.

MICROWAVE MAGIC?

A microwave oven actually works by emitting high-frequency electromagnetic waves from a tube called a "magnetron." This type of radiation is scattered throughout the inside of the oven by a "stirrer." The "stirrer" is a fanlike reflector which causes the waves to penetrate the food, reversing the polarity of the water molecules billions of times per second, causing them to bombard each other and creating friction that heats the food.

DO I, OR DON'T I MICROWAVE IT?

Microwave cooking is less expensive than most other methods of cooking, however, it is only desirable for certain types of foods. If you are baking a dish it will rise higher in a microwave oven, however, meats do not seem to have the desired texture and seem a bit mushy. When it comes to placing something frozen in the microwave, it will take longer to cook since it is difficult to agitate the water molecules when they are frozen.

WHY YOUR POT LID MAY STICK

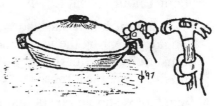

When you are cooking a food the air space that is inside the pot increases in pressure and raises the lid very slightly allowing the heated air (gas) to escape. When the heat is turned off, however, the pressure and temperature is decreased and with the help of water molecules sealing around the rim of the lid, the lid is pulled tightly shut. The longer the lid is left on, the tighter the seal. If this occurs never place the pot in cold water, just place the pot on moderate heat for a minute or so to return the pressure to a more equal level with the outside.

CAN'T TOP A RESTAURANT WOK

The big difference is in the more intense heat that is developed in a professional wok. Your home gas range is only capable of producing less than 10,000 BTU's. The BTU's produced in a professional wok is almost twice that high due to a larger gas feeder line and larger burner opening diameters. Also, the specially built wok has a series of burners, not just one. The higher heat tends to seal the juices and flavors in and the amount of juice that remains in the wok is less, allowing the juices that are there to stick to the vegetables more readily. Beware of special woks built with flat bottoms for electric ranges. The flat bottoms make it very difficult to stir and cook the vegetables properly.

SELF-CLEANING OVENS, IT'S HOTTER THAN HADES

Electric ovens are capable of much higher temperatures than gas ovens. Since the electric ovens go as high as 1000°F during the self-cleaning phase, it literally disintegrates any food or grease particles and turns them into dust that only needs to be wiped away.

AS IGOR WOULD SAY, WOK THIS WAY

Cooking in a wok originated in China over 2,000 years ago during the Han Dynasty. It was prompted by the lack of cooking oil. It cooked the food fast and was an energy saver. There are a few things that every cook should be aware of when stir frying foods:

» Before cooking beef, pork, or chicken, partially freeze the meat for about 1 hour so that it will be easy to slice thin, even-sized pieces.

» Place the meat in a marinade for great flavor for a few minutes while you are preparing the vegetables. Adding a small amount of cornstarch to the marinade will protect the meat from the high heat and make the meat more tender and juicy.

» Vegetables should be cut into uniform bite-size pieces to insure that they will cook evenly. If vegetables are preferred in different sizes then they will have to be added at different times which makes the cooking more difficult.

» Oil should be used very sparingly, approximately one tablespoon is all that is needed for four servings which is just enough to place a thin coating on the bottom of the wok.

» Never stir-fry more than ½ pound at a time for the best results.

WOKS, A GOOD SOURCE OF IRON?

Most woks are made from steel which is 98% iron. A study performed at Texas Tech University found that if you stir-fry in a steel wok it will increase the iron content in foods by as much as 200-500%. The amount of iron in a 3 ½ ounce portion of vegetables may rise from 0.4 mg. to 3.5 mg. when cooked in a wok. If the wok is made of stainless steel it will only release an insignificant amount of iron.

QUICK, QUICHE ME

Quiches should be served right from the oven to the table and never allowed to cool. Quiches are usually made with onions and mushrooms which have a high water content. Because of this fact the quiche will lose a large amount of moisture as it cools causing the crust to become soggy and weepy.

WHEN WAS THE MICROWAVE OVEN INVENTED?

In 1946 Dr. Percy Spencer, an engineer at Raytheon Laboratories was working with a magnetron tube which produces microwaves. He had a candy bar in his pocket which he went to eat and found that it had melted and there was no heat source for that to occur. The only thing he could think of that would cause this to occur was the magnetron tube he was working with. He then tried placing a small amount of popcorn near the tube and the popcorn popped in a few seconds. He then tried focusing the beam through a box at an egg, which exploded on one of his associates much to both of their surprise. The result was the first microwave oven called the Amana Radar Range introduced in 1977. The use of the word "radar" was used since the actual beam was invented in England and used as microwave radar to detect Hitler's planes in 1940.

WHO INVENTED THE TOASTER?

The first people to toast bread was the Egyptians in 2500 B.C. using long-handled forks. The inventor of the toaster as we know it today was Charles Strite who received a patent for the toaster in 1919. However, the toaster didn't really work as well as he would have liked and it took him a few more years after a number of poor field tests to produce the first pop-up toaster in 1926 with the brand name of Toastmaster. The toaster had a darkness timer and sales went wild. Congress was so impressed they declared March 1927 as National Toaster Month.

CROCK POT AKA SLOW-COOKER

The Crock Pot was invented in 1971 by Rival. Many consumers still question whether the pot is safe or a breeding ground for bacteria since it advocates all day cooking at a low temperature. The fact is that most slow cookers have settings that range from 170° to 280°F. (76.6° to 137.8°C.).Bacteria die at 140°F. (60°C.) which is below the lowest possible temperature that can be used. However, if the lid is left off it may cause a problem with food not being fully cooked and harboring bacteria that is still alive. To minimize the risk of food poisoning the following should be followed:

» All foods should be at refrigerator temperature.
  No frozen or partially thawed foods.

» Only cook cut up pieces of meat, not whole roasts or fowl to allow the heat to penetrate fully.

» Make sure that the cooker is at least ½ to ⅔ full or the food will not absorb enough heat to kill any bacteria.

» The food must be covered with liquid to generate sufficient steam.

» The original lid should always be used and should be tight-fitting.

» When possible allow the cooker to cook on the high setting for the first hour then it can be reduced.

» Never use the cooker to reheat leftovers. A number of bacteria are usually found on leftovers and it takes a high heat to kill them.

» Always follow the manufacturer's directions for temperature settings.

THE CUTTING EDGE

One of the most important utensils in a kitchen is your knife. There are a number of different materials used in knife blades, many of which are relatively new and need to be evaluated as to which will suit you best. Make sure the handle is secured with at least three rivets. It should feel comfortable and always avoid plastic grips. When cutting foods the best surface would be a soft wooden cutting board. Hardwoods and plastic boards tend to dull the blade faster and also reduce the life of the knife.

» Carbon Steel
  This is by far the best for taking the sharpest edge and is the preferred knife for the serious chef. However, if the blade is not constantly kept dry it will rust. Acids in foods may also take their toll and turn the blade black which can be imparted back to foods.

» Superstainless Steel
  This not one of the better quality blades. Once it dulls and loses its original well-honed sharpness it is almost impossible to restore to a decent level of sharpness. However, it does resist rust and staining.

» Stainless Steel
  Has the ability to resist rust and the acid effects from foods. Will take

a sharper edge than the superstainless steel, but will dull and does not really take a very sharp edge.

» High Carbon Stainless Steel
This is the most expensive of the four types mentioned here and will not rust or stain. It does not have to be washed and dried continually when in use. Can be sharpened to a sharper edge than either of the other stainless steel knives.

HOW DO YOU SHARPEN A KNIFE?

The one method that should never be used on a good kitchen knife is that of allowing a coarse grinding wheel to be used. The blade will only last a few years if you do and will become thinner and thinner. Rotating steel disks are not recommended either. The preferred method is the "butcher's steel." This is just a rough-surfaced, hard metal rod with a protective handle. If the butcher's steel is used frequently it will keep the edge on the knife.

If you have a problem keeping the edge it may mean that you are not using the sharpener as frequently as you should and you may have to use a "whetstone" to return the edge. The whetstone is made of silicon carbide (carborundum).

WHAT IS THE PROPER WAY TO STORE A KNIFE?

One of the best ways to store a quality knife is to keep it in a wooden countertop knife holder that was made for the knife. However, not all wooden holders are quality ones and the holder should not have a hard surface for the blade to lie on. The higher quality holders will have a protective liner that allows the edge of the blade to rest free. When a knife is stored in a drawer with other utensils it will end up with small nicks on the blade and that will eventually ruin a high quality knife.

WHAT SHOULD I LOOK FOR WHEN BUYING A KNIFE?

Purchasing a knife is an investment that you need to make. It is a kitchen tool that is indispensable and unless you buy a quality knife you will not have it very long and not be very satisfied with the results. Purchase either carbon-steel or high-carbon steel knives. The manufacturer should be a recognized name such as Trident, Wusthof, or Heckles and be sure that the blade and the handle are one piece and that the handle is not attached to the blade. If the knife has a plastic hilt it is not recommended.

BOILED FOODS TAKE LONGER TO COOK ON BAD WEATHER DAYS

When the weather is bad and stormy, the atmospheric pressure goes down. The lower the pressure gets, the lower the boiling temperature of water gets. The decreased temperature is usually about 1-2 degrees and it will take a little longer to cook boiled foods.

CHECK YOUR OVEN TEMPERATURE WITHOUT A THERMOMETER

Place about 1 tablespoon of flour on the bottom of a cookie sheet and place it into a preheated oven for about 5 minutes. When the flour turns a light tan the temperature is between 250° to 325°F. (121.1° to 162.8°C.). If the flour turns a golden brown the oven is at 325° to 400°F. (162.8° to 204.4°C.). When it turns a dark brown the temperature is 400° to 450°F. and almost a black color the oven will be 450° to 525°F. (232.2° to 273.9°C.).

CHAPTER 4

Fruits and Garden Bounties

When choosing fruits it is always best to choose the healthiest looking and if possible check the original box it came in to see if the fruit was graded "U.S. Grade No.1" or at least has a USDA stamp on the box or crate.

To preserve the nutritional quality of fruits, leave them in their original packaging material if frozen. This will reduce the risk of exposure to air which may result in a loss of flavor and cause discolorization.

Brown areas on fruits mean that oxidation has taken place from exposure to the air of the more sensitive inner flesh and that the vitamin C content has been lost. Brown discolorization can be reduced if you slice bananas, apples, plums, and peaches with a stainless steel knife, then either combine them with any citrus fruit or sprinkle them with lemon or pineapple juice. The citric acid from the lemon or pineapple neutralizes the effects of the oxidation.

FRUITS & VEGETABLES VS. REFRIGERATION

The majority of fruits and vegetables are able to handle cold fairly well with the exception of tropical fruits whose cells are just not used to the cold. bananas will suffer cell damage and release a skin browning chemical and avocados will refuse to ripen in the cold when stored below 45°F. (7.2°C.) and oranges will develop a brown spotted skin. The best temperature for squash, tomatoes, cucumbers, melons, green peppers, pineapple, and most other fruits and vegetables is actually at about 50°F. (10°C.). A few exceptions are lettuce, carrots, and cabbage who prefer 32°F. (0°C.). The humidity is also a big factor and most fruits and vegetables need to be stored in the storage drawers which will protect them from drying out.

PECTIN

The nutrition "buzzword" these days is pectin. Studies are reporting that pectin has the ability to lower LDL (bad cholesterol) levels and is being used to treat bowel diseases. There may be good validity to these studies and pectin supplement sales are on the rise. There are, however, many natural sources for pectin. The following are a few of the better ones.

FOOD	GRAMS OF PECTIN
Soybeans - 1 cup cooked	2.6
Figs - 5 fruit, dried	2.3
Orange - 1 medium	2.2
Chestnuts - 1 ounce, dried	2.1
Pear - 1 medium	1.8
Potato - 1 medium	1.8
Sweet Potato - ½ cup mashed	1.3
Brussels Sprouts - ½ cup, frozen	1.1
Apple - 1 medium	1.1
Papaya - ½ fruit	1.1
Broccoli - ½ cup	1.0
Banana - 1 medium	1.0
Strawberries - 1 cup	9
Tomato - 1 medium	9
Lima beans - ½ cup boiled	9
Hazelnuts - 1 ounce, raw	9
Carrot - 1 medium	8
Pistachio Nuts - 1 ounce, dried	8
Peach - 1 medium	7
Peas - ½ cup, boiled	6
Almonds - 1 ounce, dried	6
Walnuts - 1 ounce, dried	6
Green Beans - ½ cup, boiled	5
Lemon - 1 medium	5
Summer Squash - ½ cup, boiled	5
Grapefruit - ½ medium	3
Spinach - ½ cup, raw	2

GETTING RESULTS

Baking soda will not help vegetables to retain their color when added to the cooking water, milk or a small amount of white vinegar will.

FRUITS AND VEGETABLES

Fruits and vegetables are the easiest targets for loss of nutrients due to their soft skins. They are easily bruised and their meat is easily damaged by the air, light, and heat. When cooking or preparing produce for a meal it is best to leave the produce in as large a pieces as possible until you are ready to serve it. Exposing the surface of any fruit or vegetable will cause nutrients to be lost immediately and the longer the surfaces are exposed, the higher the losses. In some fruits the vitamin C can be totally lost in less than 1 hour of exposure.

SHOULD YOU BUY A FROSTED PACKAGE OF VEGETABLES?

No! This usually means that the food has thawed either partially or completely and a percentage of moisture has already been lost. The fact that one package of that product is damaged means that the chances are very good that the balance of the shipment may also have deteriorated.

DOUBLING UP

Any salad bar item that uses a dairy product as a dressing should be kept cold. The easiest method is to place a larger bowl with ice or dry ice under the food dish. This will keep the temperature cold enough so that bacteria should not be a problem before it is refrigerated.

WAX COATINGS ON FRUITS AND VEGETABLES

A thin coating of wax helps seal the moisture in and extends the storage time and by keeping more moisture in reduces the weight loss, providing a higher profit. A secondary benefit to the industry is that it gives the produce a sheen which is eye catching. The wax coating is safe to eat, but may give the produce an off-flavor. One of the drawbacks is that it does make it more difficult to clean the produce, especially if there were pesticide residues left on under the wax coating.

HELP! I CAN'T SEE MY "C" ANYMORE, IT'S GETTING DARK

Fruits contain a "phenolic" compound which is responsible for turning the exposed meat brown when they are cut up or bitten into. This happens fairly rapidly, especially to apples, bananas, pears, potatoes, and avocado. The browning is caused by the enzyme "polyphenoloxidase," which causes the oxidation (breakdown by oxygen) of the phenolic compound in the cells with the conversion to a brown color. This is a similar action that occurs when you tan from the sun. Citrus fruits, melons, and tomatoes lack the enzyme and therefore can't turn brown through this chemical reaction, however, if they are allowed to sit out with their flesh exposed to oxygen for any length of time they will turn brown through normal oxidation of their flesh.

The browning can be slowed down, even if the flesh is exposed by refrigerating the fruit at 40°F. (4.4°C.), however, boiling will actually destroy the enzyme. Salt will also slow down the enzyme but will negatively affect the flavor. Placing the fruit in cold water will slow the process by keeping the surface from the air. Brushing lemon juice on the surface or spraying the surface with an ascorbic acid spray (vitamin C mixed with water) also works well.

HOW DOES FRUIT RIPEN IN A BROWN PAPER BAG?

Fruit normally gives off ethylene gas which hastens the ripening. Some fruits give off more gas than other and ripen faster while other fruits are picked too soon and need a bit of help. By placing a piece of unripe fruit in a closed container, such as a brown paper bag the ethylene gas that is given off does not dissipate into the air but is trapped and builds to a higher concentration thus causing the fruit to ripen faster.

ARE CHIPS MADE FROM VEGETABLES HEALTHIER THAN OTHER CHIPS?

The calories in a vegetable chip such as the new carrot chip is about the same as any potato chip since it is fried in oil. Any chip that is fried will be high in calories and fat and almost void of any nutritional value. If the chip is baked it will have fewer calories, however, because of the high-heat processing that is used, the nutritional value is reduced significantly.

TENDERIZING VEGETABLES

The major component in the cell wall of fruits and vegetables is a complex carbohydrate called "cellulose." The higher the cellulose content, the firmer the fruit or vegetable. To tenderize the cellulose, heat and moisture are used, however, certain vegetables have different levels of cellulose in their various parts. Stems have more than tips, which is why it is necessary to remove the outer covering with a vegetable peeler before cooking broccoli or asparagus, otherwise the tips will be mushy and the stalks tender. When heat or moisture is applied to the vegetable it tends to destroy the cell's capability to retain and release moisture which causes a structural breakdown resulting in tenderness. It also dissolves some of the pectin which is active in holding the cell's walls together.

LOSING COLOR IN VEGETABLES

When vegetables lose their color it is the result of the loss of pigment by a chemical reaction of the pigment with the acid that is being released by the cooking process. A variety of colors may actually appear in the same vegetable depending on the length of time it is cooked. After a period of cooking the liquid medium may deplete the acid and turn alkaline changing the color of the vegetable again. In green vegetables the acid that is released reacts with the chlorophyll lightening the color. In cabbage the pigment chemical "anthocyanin" may be changed from red to purple depending on the acid or alkaline nature of the liquid. baking soda placed in the water will help reduce and neutralize the effects of the acid and keep some vegetables close to their natural color but will destroy a number of vitamins especially C and thiamin. The best method of retaining color is to steam your vegetables.

CAN VITAMIN C SURVIVE IN COMMERCIALLY PREPARED PRODUCTS?

The methods of preparation and packaging will determine the level of vitamin C that will remain in a commercial product or juice that has been placed in a container by a market. Frozen orange juice only loses about 2% of its vitamin C content over a 3 month period of home freezer storage. If the juice is sold in glass bottles it will retain almost 100% of the vitamin C, however, if it is stored in plastic or waxed cardboard containers oxygen will be able to pass through and reduce the potency depending on the storage time. The best juice to buy is the juice that is squeezed and sold fresh in the market. All commercially prepared bottled juices are pasteurized and the natural enzymes are destroyed by the heat.

STORING COOKED VEGETABLES

The best method of storing vegetables that have been cooked is to store them in a well-sealed plastic container in the refrigerator. They will last about 3-5 days. If you wish to freeze them, then seal them in an airtight bag or a container in which most of the air can be removed. Since cells will burst releasing some of their liquid they will be somewhat soggy but can be used in soups and stews. They will last from 8-12 months and still be edible.

CAN PRUNES REALLY RELIEVE CONSTIPATION?

Prunes contain the organic chemical "diphenylisatin" which is a relative of another compound "biscodyl" that is the active ingredient in some of the over-the-counter laxatives. Biscodyl tends to increase the secretion of fluids in the bowel and will stimulate contractions of the intestines, thereby pushing the waste material on its way. Prunes are also a good source of minerals and a "natural" laxative is always better than a laboratory prepared chemical concoction.

DOES COOKING CHANGE GARLIC?

When garlic is heated the chemical that gives garlic its unique flavor is partially destroyed. The chemical is "diallyl disulfide" which is a sulfur compound. If garlic is allowed to sprout most of the chemical will enter the new sprouts and the garlic will become milder.

WHAT IS THE CHINESE LANTERN FRUIT?

The fruit is the "physalis" which is a round berry that is encased in a pod that exactly resembles a Chinese lantern. It is also known as the "cape gooseberry" and used as an ornamental garden plant. The berry is cultivated in South Africa and Peru and is an extremely rich source of vitamin A as well as an excellent source of vitamin C.

HAIRY FRUIT?

The "rambutan" is one of the most unusual looking pieces of fruit you will ever see. The fruit resembles a small lime and is covered with what looks like "hair." The name of the fruit is from the Malayan word for "hairy." The skin, however, is harmless and peels off easily and the fruit is usually sold in cans.

IS IT SAFE TO EAT FIDDLEHEAD FERN?

The fiddlehead fern is a member of the ostrich fern family and is shaped like a musical note with a long stem and a circular bottom. It is are about 2-5 inches long and about 2 inches in diameter. The texture of the fern is similar to that of green beans, with a flavor between asparagus and green beans. It is occasionally used in salads, stir-fried, or steamed. Fiddlehead fern should never be eaten raw or lightly sauteed, a number of people have become ill due to a toxin that is only destroyed if the fern is boiled for 10 minutes before it is consumed or used in dishes. All illnesses were in upstate New York and Banff, Alberta, Canada and in all cases the fiddlehead was eaten raw or only partially cooked.

PUCKER UP!

If you have ever bitten into a piece of fruit that was not ripe or tried eating a lemon, or even took a sip of strong tea, then you have experienced a reaction, resulting in dryness of the mouth, puckering, and constricting of the lips that is known as "astringency." It is how your mouth feels as it comes in contact with a class of phenolic compounds called "tannins." The tannins affect the protein in the saliva and mucous membranes of the mouth resulting in puckering.

DEGASSING THE SUNROOT

The Jerusalem artichoke or sunroot contains a number of indigestible carbohydrates that cause flatulence in susceptible individuals. These annoying carbohydrates can be almost entirely eliminated naturally from the vegetable by a month of cold storage in the refrigerator before being used. About half of the remaining carbohydrates can be eliminated through cooking providing the sunroot is sliced and boiled for 15 minutes.

The only way to eliminate all the problem carbohydrate is to cook the whole root for about 24 hours which will break the carbohydrates down to fructose. Sunroot is very high in iron which may cause them to turn gray with cooking. If you add ¼ of a teaspoon of cream of tartar to the boiling water 5 minutes before they are done it will prevent the discoloration. If you add 1 tablespoon of lemon juice to the boiling water when you first start cooking it will keep the root crisp and eliminate the color change.

WHAT IS THE OLDEST KNOWN CITRUS FRUIT?

To date the oldest records of a citrus fruit dates back to 500 B.C. The "citron" originated in Hadramaut which is located in a mountainous region of the Arabian peninsula. The "citron" is frequently confused with other fruits, especially the "citron-melon." The fruit resembles a knobby lemon and may be sold in a variety of sizes depending on the country where it is grown. There are a number of varieties, one of which is the "etog" which is used in the Jewish festival of Sukkot. They may be found in most supermarkets from September to March.

SOME VEGETABLES MAY FORM CARCINOGENS FROM NITRITES

Certain vegetables contain nitrites, these include; beets, celery, eggplant, radishes, spinach, and collard and turnip greens. When they enter the stomach they may convert to "nitrosamines" which are known carcinogens. The problem can become even worse when these vegetables are left at room temperature for any length of time allowing the microorganisms to multiply and convert more of the nitrites into "nitrosamines." A normal healthy adult with a healthy immune system does not have a problem with these foods, however, some may not be recommended for infants. In moderation these vegetables are not a problem.

WHAT IS A FEIJOA?

It is a small green-skinned fruit with a similar taste to a guava. The "feijoa" is popular in the Southwestern United States as well as South America and New Zealand. It has black seeds and red pulp and is available during the summer months.

SOME RUSSIAN RECIPES CALL FOR CORNELS, WHAT IS IT?

Cornels are members of the dogwood family and resemble an olive. The trees are mainly found in Southern Europe. They are frequently used in Russian cooking and have a taste similar to a sour cherry. They tend to give dishes a sweet and sour taste, especially when used in meat and dessert recipes. The French pickle cornels like olives and also make them into a unique preserve.

WHAT IS AN ACEROLA?

The acerola is a fruit that resembles a cherry. It grows on a thick bush that is used as hedge in some tropical and sub-tropical areas. It is a native to the Caribbean and has become very popular in Florida. Recently, it has become an important fruit to nutritionists in that it is the richest fruit source of vitamin C. Approximately 4,000 mg. of vitamin C can be found in 3 ½ ounces of the fruit. The acerola is sometimes called the Surinam cherry but is too sour to be eaten raw.

WHAT IS A MOG INSPECTOR?

Grapes that are shipped from the orchard to wineries are routinely inspected for MOG (material other than grapes). These people are called MOG inspectors and look for leaves, rocks, and snakes. When these items are found the orchards are fined.

CANCER CAUSING FERN THAT LOOKS LIKE ASPARAGUS

An asparagus look-a-like called bracken fern is sometimes difficult to distinguish from real asparagus and contains a powerful cancer-causing agent. Occasionally cows will eat the fern and develop bone marrow damage as well as inflammation of the bladder membranes.

WHAT IS A JACKFRUIT?

This is the largest fruit known to exist and can measure up to 3 feet long, 20 inches across, and weigh up to 90 pounds (40 kg). The jackfruit is actually a combination of many different fruits which have fused together. It has a hard green-colored skin with pointed warts and large seeds that can be roasted and are similar to chestnuts. The seeds have a high calcium content and contain 12 percent protein. The fruit originated in India and East Africa.

WHAT IS CHOWCHOW?

Chowchow is a relish made from chopped vegetables, usually cabbage, peppers, cucumbers, and onions. It is then packed in a sugar-vinegar solution and seasoned with special mustard and pickling spices. Normally, served with meats and sausages.

BABACO AS A MEAT TENDERIZER?

One of the latest arrivals in supermarket produce departments is the fruit "babaco." It is an exotic tropical fruit and is presently grown for export by New Zealand. It is a relative of papaya and has a yellow-green skin when ripe with pale yellow flesh. The fruit, however, has no pips (small black seeds) and the skin is edible. Babaco is high in vitamin C, has a low sugar content, and contains the same enzyme papain that is used as a meat tenderizer.

FRESH PRODUCE VS. HARMFUL BACTERIA

As more and more produce is being imported from foreign countries, more outbreaks of foodborne illness are being reported, especially related to the same bacteria that caused major concerns related to undercooked hamburger, E. coli 0157:57. This deadly strain of bacteria is usually the result of fecal contamination of meats during slaughtering and processing. However, the strain is now showing up on vegetables and fruits. In 1996 four outbreaks were reported related to lettuce by the Center for Disease Control and Prevention. Salmonella has been found on melons and tomatoes and other dangerous bacteria have been found on cabbage and mushrooms. In one instance more than 245 people became ill from cantaloupe in 30 states. Seventy percent of all produce is now imported from third world countries.

When it comes to buying fresh produce, make sure that you only purchase what you need for a short period of time. If bacteria is present, the longer you store it, the more it will multiply. Wash your hands before handling produce and wash the produce thoroughly before cutting it with a knife. Wash the produce in cold water using a special organic produce cleaner from a health food store and a brush.

SWEET AND SOUR FRUIT

The main source of energy for a fruit is its sugar content, which is also utilized for the manufacture of the fruit's organic materials. The sugar content of most fruits averages 10-15% by weight. The lime, however, has only 1% compared to the date which is over 60%. The sugar is produced by starch which is stored in the plant's leaves, and as the fruit ripens, the starch is converted into sugar. Also, as the fruit ripens the acid content of the fruit declines and the sourness in reduced. Most fruit is sour before it ripens. A number of organic acids are responsible for the plant's acidic nature, these include citric, malic, tartaric, and oxalic acids. Almost all fruits and vegetables are usually slightly acidic.

DANGEROUS CITRUS PEELS

Unless the citrus is organically grown it would be wise not to eat any product that uses citrus peels including orange and lime zests which are often grated into desserts. Citrus crops in the United States are routinely sprayed with a number of carcinogenic pesticides according to the EPA. These pesticides tend to remain in the skin. They include; acephate, benomyl, chlorobenzilate, dicofol, methomyl, 0-phenylphenol, and even Parathion. A thorough cleaning and scrubbing will not remove most of these chemicals.

JUJUBE, CHEWY CANDY OR DATE?

A "jujube" is also known as a Chinese date which has no relationship to the date we are used to seeing in the market. It is not even a member of the same botanical family even though it does look similar in both color and texture. The nutrient content is high in vitamin C, calcium, iron, and potassium and they are usually sold as a dried fruit.

WHAT IS A JOHNNYCAKE?

Johnnycake is a homemade cornmeal bread that may be made in a bread form or as a pancake. It is made from cornmeal, salt, and cold milk or boiling water. It originated with the American Indians and the word "johnnycake" was derived from the Indian word "joniken." Purists believe that "johnnycake" can only be made with a special type of low-yield Indian corn from Rhode Island.

COOKING FRUITS

The last thing a cook wants is mushy fruit. This frequently encountered problem can be resolved by just adding some sugar to the cooking syrup. This will strengthen the cell walls with an artificial sugar "cell" wall. The sugar will also have the effect of drawing some of the fluid back into the cell to slow down the drying out of the fruit and retaining the desired appealing consistency.

REDUCE THE RISK OF STROKE

A study of 800 middle-aged men who participated in the Framingham Heart Study reduced their risk of stroke by 22% by eating three servings of vegetables daily.

AROMATIC VEGETABLES?

A number of relatives of the carrot family have strong-scented oils and have over 3,000 species. These include coriander, anise, cumin, dill, caraway, fennel, and parsley. Garlic has no aroma until the tissues are disturbed and the sulfur-containing amino acid cysteine is released.

ODORIFEROUS CRUCIFEROUS?

We have all smelled broccoli, cabbage, Brussels sprouts, and cauliflower cooking and it is not a pleasant aroma. When these vegetables are heated it causes a chemical to break down and release a strong-smelling sulfur compound composed of ammonia and hydrogen sulfide (rotten egg smell). The more you cook them, the more intense the smell, and the more compounds that are released. If you cook broccoli too long the compounds will react with the chlorophyll (the green color) and turn the broccoli brown. If you cook broccoli in a small amount of water it will slow down the reaction.

PAUL BUNYAN'S FRUITS AND VEGETABLES

The largest watermelon that has ever been grown weighed in at 262 pounds. The world's longest zucchini grew to almost 70 inches. The world's largest squash was 654 pounds. The largest cabbage was 123 pounds. The world's largest lemon was 5 pounds 13 ounces and the world's largest tomato was 4 pounds 4 ounces.

DON'T BE FOILED

Aluminum foil wrap should never come in contact with acidic fruits or vegetables such as; lemons, oranges, tomatoes, grapefruits, etc. A chemical reaction may take place and it is possible that it will corrode through the aluminum foil. A common method of preparing meat loaf is to place the tomato sauce on top while it is cooking and then cover it with aluminum foil. Tomato sauce or paste will eat right through aluminum foil.

PRESERVES AND PECTIN

Many a cook still believes that preserves acquire their smooth, semi-solid consistency from the amount of sugar that is added. Actually, the consistency is controlled by the level of pectin which is extracted from the cell wall of the fruit. Pectin is similar to cement in that it holds the cell wall together then forms a stringlike network that traps liquids and converts them into a solid. A number of fruits such as grapes, and a few varieties of berries contain enough of their own pectin to gel without the addition of more pectin, while other fruits such as apricots, peaches, and cherries need additional pectin to gel.

The most popular sources of pectin is from either apples or the white layer, just under the skin of citrus fruits. The balance between sugar and pectin is a very delicate one and the optimum ph (acid/base balance) is between 2.8 and 3.4. The pectin concentration needs to be no more than 0.5-1.0% with a sugar concentration of no more than 60-65%. Due to the obvious complexity of these exacting percentages it would be best to stick to your recipe to the letter and not make any changes. Low-cal preserves are made with a special pectin that gels using very little sugar and contains calcium ions.

HOW DO FRUITS AND VEGETABLES MAKE VITAMIN C?

All plants manufacture vitamin C from sugars which are derived from the leaves and produced by photosynthesis. The more light a plant gets, the more sugars are produced and the more vitamin C the plant can produce. Another factor is that the more light a plant receives, the more chlorophyll and carotenoids the plant needs to handle its energy input which causes the leaves to be darker. The darker the leaves of a vegetable the more precursor it contains to produce vitamins A and C.

WHAT ARE THE BEST GREENS?

The following vegetables are by nutritional value, in descending order.

Beta Carotene, Carotenoids	Vitamin C
Dandelion Greens	Kale
Kale	Arugula
Turnip Greens	Mustard greens
Arugula	Turnip Greens
Spinach	
Beet Greens	
Mustard Greens	
Calcium	**Iron**
Arugula	Beet Greens
Turnip Greens	Spinach
Dandelion Greens	Dandelion Greens
	Swiss Chard
	Chard
	Kale
Fiber	
Kale	
Spinach	
Turnip Greens	
Mustard Greens	

CAN A SWEET LEMON BE GROWN?

There is a fruit that is called a "limetta" or sweet lemon that is grown in Italy and California. They resemble a cross between a lemon and a lime and are so sweet that you will never pucker. The California variety is called the "millsweet" but they have not really been that popular at the markets. They have a taste similar to lemonade and are excellent for lemonade, pie filling, and lemon sauces.

NO CURDLING HERE

When pouring cream over fruits, try adding a small amount of baking soda to the cream to stop the possibility of curdling. Baking soda will reduce the acidity which may cause curdling.

VEGGIE STATS

The following are the latest 1997 statistics on a few of the vegetables we consume in sufficient quantity to be worth even talking about:

Vegetable	Pounds Per Year
Potatoes	87
Lettuce	29
Onions	17
Tomato	18
Carrots	8
Sweet Potatoes/Yams	7
Broccoli	4

WHAT IS A KIWANO?

The "kiwano" is a member of the cucumber family and is actually an African horned melon. It is exported from New Zealand and was given a name similar to the Kiwi for easier recognition and association with New Zealand. The Kiwi was actually re-named and was originally a Chinese gooseberry. The shape of the "kiwano" is similar to a large gherkin, however, it is bright orange with a number of small horns protruding from the skin. The flavor is similar to that of a mango and a pineapple combined. It is very tasty and should become more popular and less expensive as the demand increases.

WHAT IS THE MOST POPULAR CHINESE FRUIT?

There is really no contest, even though China does grow many great fruits, the "lychee" is definitely the most popular. In one report an ancient Chinese poet bragged about his lychee habit claiming to eat 300 every day and as much as one thousand in a day. The first fruit culture book ever written was in 1056 and was solely devoted to growing lychee. The skin is tough, brown, and scaly with a slight red tinge, however, it peels easily. They may be found either fresh or dried, especially in Chinese markets.

WHAT IS THE EGGPLANT OF THE MUSHROOM WORLD?
Puffballs can be found dried or picked from the forest during the hot humid summer months. They are called the "eggplant of the mushroom world" because they are very large, oval shaped and white.

WHAT PIE IS SERVED NEAR THE KILAUEA VOLCANO?
On the Big Island of Hawaii a special fruit is grown called the "ohelo." The berry is a relative of the cranberry, however, it is much sweeter and is used to prepare jams and pies and served at the Volcano House on the rim of the Kilauea crater. Be sure and try this unique pie if you are ever visiting the island of Hawaii.

THE TOP 20 NUTRITIOUS VEGETABLES
The following list of vegetables start with the most nutritious calculated from their nutrient levels of 10 of the most important nutrients. They must contain all 10 which included: protein, iron, calcium, niacin, vitamins A & C, potassium, phosphorus, thiamin, and riboflavin.

1. Collard Greens
2. Lima beans
3. Peas
4. Spinach
5. Sweet Potatoes
6. Turnip Greens
7. Winter Squash
8. Broccoli
9. Kale
10. Brussels Sprouts
11. Mustard Greens
12. Swiss Chard
13. Parsley
14. Tomatoes
15. Corn
16. Beet Greens
17. Pumpkin
18. Okra
19. Potatoes
20. Carrots

WHAT'S A ZESTER?
The sweet flavor in a citrus fruit is contained in the outer rind or "zest." The tool used to remove the rind is called a "zester." It only removes the rind not the bitter white pith. The thin blade is able to only remove the extreme outer layer.

EXPOSURE

Peeling thin-skinned fruits and vegetables can be an easy task if you just place them in a bowl and cover them with boiling water, then allow them to stand for 1-2 minutes. The skin can easily be removed with a sharp paring knife. You can also spear the food with a fork and hold it about 6 inches over a gas flame until the skin cracks.

Peeling thick-skinned fruits or vegetables is much easier. Cut a small portion of the peel from the top and bottom then set the food on an acrylic cutting board and remove the balance of the peel in strips from top to bottom.

UNIQUE FLAVOR

A tasty dressing for fruits can be prepared by grating an orange rind and adding it to orange juice and low-fat sour cream.

NUTRIENT RICH

Three of the most nutritious fruits are papaya, tomatoes, and cantaloupe.

THE GOOD GUYS

When any fruit or vegetable is cooked, the natural enzymes will be destroyed. These enzymes are needed by the body to initiate biochemical reactions.

CLERK ALERT

When your foods are being bagged in the supermarket, be sure and ask the clerk not to place your fruits and vegetables in the same bag with any type of meat product. The slightest amount of leakage may ruin the food.

A POSITIVE NOTE

Fruit consumption in the United States has risen from 101 pounds per person in 1970 to 134 pounds in 1997.

BEWARE, PIT ALERT

There are a number of fruits that contain pits which contain the chemical "amygdalin." If a pit containing this chemical is crushed and heated it may release the poison, cyanide in very small amounts. Fruits, such as apricots, apples, pears, cherries, and peaches may contain this chemical.

DRIED FRUITS

» Vitamin C is lost when fruits are dried or dehydrated. However, most of the other vitamins and minerals are retained.

» Sulfites are commonly used to preserve dried fruits. This chemical may cause an allergic reaction in susceptible individuals. Best to shy away from any product that contains sulfites.

» Most fruits and dried fruits are graded; extra fancy, fancy, extra choice, choice and standard is the lowest grade. The grading is based on size, color, condition after being dried, and water content.

» Dried fruits, if frozen in a liquid, should be thawed in the same liquid to retain the flavor.

» If you store dried fruits in airtight containers they will keep for up to 6 months. If placed in a cool, dry location or refrigerated they will last for about one year. Refrigeration tends to place the fruit cells in a state of suspended animation and helps retain their flavor. After refrigeration storage it would be best to allow the fruit to remain at room temperature before eating for about 30 minutes to acquire the best taste.

ORDER OF THE NUTRITIONAL QUALITY OF FRUITS

1. Fresh, if brought to market in a short period of time.
2. Dehydrated, if Grade A or No. 1.
3. Freeze Dried, if packaged at the site where grown.
4. Frozen, if packaged within 12 hours of harvest.
5. Canned.

JELLY PRESERVATION

When cooking fruits for preserves and jellies, add a small pat of butter and there will be no foam to skim off the top. The fat tends to act as a sealant which does not allow the air to rise and accumulate on top as foam. The air just dissipates harmlessly in the product.

SIT UP, JELLY

If you have problems with fruit jelly setting-up, try placing the jars in a shallow pan half-filled with cold water, then bake in a moderate oven for 30 minutes. This will reduce the moisture content of the jelly enough to set them up.

In Australia you can purchase a "green plum." The green plum contains 3,000 mg. of vitamin C in a 4 ounce serving. The average orange contains only 70 mg.

In Tanzania enjoy the "kongoroko fruit" which contains 526 mg. of calcium. An 8 ounce glass of milk has only 290 mg. of calcium.

The African Cape Buffalo contains 1.5% omega-3 fatty acids which are usually only found at this level in fish. American beef has only a small trace. Cod liver oil which is considered one of the best sources contains 5%.

INDIVIDUAL FRUITS

AKEE
Grown in Jamaica and very popular throughout the Caribbean. When mature the fruit splits open exposing the edible white aril, the outer covering of the seed.

APPLES
Certain varieties of apples may have a different taste depending on the time of year it was purchased. If you are buying large quantities, it would be best to purchase a few and taste them. They should be firm, have no holes, should not be bruised, and have a good even color. If the apple is not ripe, leave it at room temperature for a day or two, but not in direct sunlight.

» STORING APPLES
Apples will ripen very quickly at room temperature. If you are not sure of their level of ripeness, just leave them out for 2-3 days before refrigerating them. Apples should be stored in the refrigerator to stop the ripening process. They may be washed, dried and placed into a plastic bag. When refrigerated apples will stay fresh for 2-4 weeks. Apples may also be stored in a cool, dry location in a barrel that has sawdust in it. The apples should never touch each other and will last 4-6 months. To freeze apples they need to be cored, peeled, washed, and sliced. Spray them with a solution of 2 teaspoons of ascorbic acid (vitamin C) in 12 tablespoons of cold water then place them in a container leaving ½ inch at the top.

APPLE VARIETIES
» Akane
Should be used shortly after purchasing and will have a sweet-tart flavor. The skin is thin and usually tender enough so that it doesn't

need peeling. They retain their shape well when baked and will maintain their tartness.

» Braeburn
These store exceptionally well. The skin is tender, the flavor is moderately tart and they keep their shape well when baked.

» Cortland
These are very fragile and need to be stored separated to avoid bruising. They are high in vitamin C and because of this resist browning better than most other apples. Normally very thin-skinned and have a slight tart-sweet taste. Keep their shape well when baked.

» Criterion
These should be a nice yellow color, very fragile, and difficult to handle without bruising. Their high vitamin C content resists browning. The skin is tender, but the flavor is somewhat bland and not recommended for baking.

» Elstar
Stores well in a sawdust barrel with their tart flavor mellowing with storage. They have tender skin and retain their flavor and shape well when baked.

» Fiji
Stores well when firm and has a tangy-sweet flavor. Will retain its shape when baked, but takes longer to bake than most apples. Appearance is similar to an Asian pear.

» Gala
These apples have a pale-yellow background and light reddish stripes. They are sweet with a slight bit of tartness and have tender skin. They hold their shape well when baked, however, they tend to lose flavor when heated.

» Golden Delicious
These will store for 3-4 months fairly well in a very cool location but spoil fast at room temperature. Should be light-yellow, not greenish. Skin is tender and the flavor is sweet. Since they are high in vitamin C they resist browning. Retain their shape well when baked. There are over 150 varieties of Red and Golden Delicious apples and are grown worldwide, more than any other apple.

» Granny Smith
These should be a light green color, but not intensely green and could even have a slight yellow tint. They are high in vitamin C and resist browning. Nicely balanced sweet-tart flavor makes them one of the best apples for making applesauce, however, they are too tart for baking.

» Idared

They store exceptionally well and become sweeter during storage. They resemble Jonathans and have tender skin. They bake well and will retain their full flavor.

» Jonagold

Tends to have a good sweet-tart balance and is a very juicy apple with tender skin.

» Jonathan

Grown mostly in California and harvested around mid-August. They tend to become soft and mealy very quickly. Thin skinned, they cook tender and make a good applesauce. They retain their shape well when baked.

» McIntosh

The majority are grown in British Columbia. They tend to get mushy and mealy very easily and the skin is tough and will not separate from the flesh easily. They are not recommended for baking or for pies since they fall apart.

» Melrose

The majority are grown in the Pacific Northwest. They tend to store very well and their flavor actually improves after 1-2 months of storage. Well-balanced sweet but somewhat tart flavor and they retain their shape well when cooked in pies.

» Mutsu

These may be sold as Crispin and look like Golden Delicious but are greener and more irregular in shape. They store well and have a sweet but spicy taste with a fairly coarse texture. A good apple for applesauce, just cook, peel, and strain.

» Newton Pippin

The color should not be too green, wait until you find them a light green for the sweetest flavor. They keep their shape well when baked or used in pies and make a thick applesauce.

» Northern Spy

They are tart, green apples that are excellent for pies but not for baking.

» Red Delicious

May range in color from red to red-striped. Will store for up to 12 months but will not last long at room temperature, best to refrigerate. Avoid any bruised ones and never place a bruised one next to an unbruised one. They are normally sweet and mellow with just a hint of tartness. When cooked they will hold their flavor well.

» Rhode Island Greening
This is one of the best choices for pies, but rarely available. They can only be found in October and November on the East Coast.

» Rome Beauty
Will not store for long periods and they tend to get bland and mealy. Very mild and have a low acid level which means that they will brown easily. The skin is fairly thick, but tender and is excellent for baking since it will hold its shape well.

» Spartan
Cannot be stored for long periods without getting mushy and mealy. Is sweet-flavored and very aromatic, but flavor becomes very weak when cooked, therefore it is not recommended for baking.

» Stayman Winesap
Tends to stores well. Has a spicy-tart flavor and is a good crisp apple. It has a thick skin which will separate easily. A good cooking apple that will retain its flavor well, making it excellent for baking and pies.

APPLE FACTS

» ETHYLENE GAS VS. APPLES AND BANANAS
Never store an apple near a banana unless you wish to ripen the banana in a very short period of time. Apples tend to give off more ethylene gas than most other fruits (except green tomatoes) and will hasten the ripening of many fruits and vegetables. Ethylene gas is a natural gas that is released by all fruits and vegetables as they ripen. Ethylene has been used for centuries to ripen fruits and

vegetables. Fruits and vegetables may be gassed to ripen them as they are trucked to market. Ethylene increases the permeability of the cell membrane allowing the cell to respire more and use oxygen to produce carbon dioxide up to five times faster than it ordinarily would. This increased activity of the cell causes the fruit or vegetable to ripen faster.

» SECRET TO MAKING A SMOOTH OR CHUNKY APPLESAUCE?
The difference to preparing a smooth or chunky applesauce all depends on when the sugar is added. If you prefer a chunky applesauce then add the sugar before cooking the apples. If you

prefer a smooth applesauce then add the sugar after the apples are cooked and mashed.

» THE DIFFERENCE BETWEEN APPLE JUICE AND CIDER
In both products the apples are pressed and the juice extracted. However, apple juice is sterilized by pasteurization, whereas apple cider is not. Apple cider is sold at roadside stands and in markets without the protection of pasteurization. Occasionally when apples fall to the ground they come in contact with fecal material from farm animals and may be contaminated with the bacteria E. coli. Pasteurized cider may be available in some markets and should be the cider of choice. Cider needs to labeled "cider." If it does not have the name then it is just apple juice in a gallon jug.

In 1991, 23 people drank apple cider produced by a small cider mill in Massachusetts and were infected with E. coli. If you do decide to purchase cider from a stand, be sure and inquire whether the apples were washed and inspected before being used for cider.

» WHY DOES AN APPLE COLLAPSE WHEN COOKED?
If you place a whole apple in the oven and bake it, the peel will withstand the heat and manage to retain its shape as long as it can. The peel contains an insoluble cellulose and ligan which reinforce the peel and keep it intact. The flesh of the apple, however, will partially disintegrate as the pectin in its cell walls is dissolved by the water being released from the cells. The cells rupture and the apple turns to applesauce. The reason apples stay relatively firm in apple pies is that bakers add calcium to the apples.

» DO APPLES HAVE ANY MEDICINAL USE?
Apples have been used for hundreds of years as a folk remedy for diarrhea. Thinly sliced raw apple contains an excellent level of pectin which is one of the main ingredients in over-the-counter antidiarrheals such as Kaopectate. The pectin also tends to interfere with the body's absorption of dietary fats. Pectins tend to produce a type of fat-absorbing gel in the stomach when it comes into contact with the stomach acid.

» IT'S DUNKING TIME
Apples are capable of floating since 25% of their volume is made up of air pockets between the cells. The soft texture of cooked apples is caused by the heat collapsing the air pockets between the cells.

» NO BUTTER ADDED?
Apple butter contains no fat if prepared properly with cinnamon and allspice.

» OUCH, MY SKIN
Pare apples by pouring scalding water on them just before peeling them. This will make the skin loosen and they will be easier to peel.

» OLD AGE?
To avoid wrinkled skin on apples when baking them, just cut a few slits in the skin to allow for expansion.

» REVIVAL TIME AGAIN
If the apples are losing their moisture and taste, try slicing them up, placing them in a dish and pouring cold apple juice over them and refrigerating for 30 minutes.

» WILL HAVE A BREAKDOWN EARLY
Frozen apple concentrate will only last for a few weeks after it is thawed.

» PUCKER UP
The tartness of an apple is derived from the balance of malic acid and the fruit's natural sugars.

» NATURAL IS BEST
Commercially prepared sweetened applesauce can contain as much as 77% more calories than unsweetened varieties.

» WE'RE EVEN
Nutritionally, there is no difference between "natural" and "regular" apple juice, even the fiber content is the same. However, apple juice is not high on the nutritional scale. Most varieties only contain a small amount of natural vitamin C.

» AN APPLE A DAY
Americans consume approximately 22 pounds of apples per person annually. Pesticides were identified as being present in 33% of all apples tested by the USDA. Forty-three different pesticides were detected and identified.

» APPLES AS A STRESS RELIEVER?
Researchers at Yale University recently discovered that the fragrance of apples will relax a person. A calming effect was noted in a number of instances when the person sniffed apple spice fragrance. When they smelled mulled cider or baked apple it actually reduced anxiety attacks. Try it, you'll like it!

» CAN AN APPLE SEED POISON YOU?
Apple seeds do contain the poison cyanide, which is a deadly poison. However, the poison is encased in a seed that cannot be broken down by the body and is harmlessly excreted. If the seed was to split open

risk. Other fruit seeds containing cyanide are apricots and peaches. These seeds are more easily split, however, they do not pose any risk to a healthy person.

» AN APPLE FOR THE TEACHER
A survey performed by USA Today asked teachers what apple they would prefer if a student brought one to them. The results were as follows:

Red Delicious	39 percent
Golden Delicious	24 percent
Granny Smith	20 percent
McIntosh	10 percent

REPORTED HEALTH BENEFITS
Studies have shown that apples will stimulate all body secretions. Apples contain malic and tartaric acids, which may aid in relieving disturbances of the liver and general digestion. In populations that drink unsweetened apple juice on a regular basis, kidney stones are unknown. The low acidity level of apples tends to stimulate salivary flow and stimulates gum tissue. Studies also indicate that consuming apples daily will reduce the severity of arthritis and asthma. The skin of the apple contains an excellent level of pectin which is active in raising HDL levels (good cholesterol).

APRICOTS

Apricots are usually the first fruit of the summer season. It is a relative of the peach and in one ounce may contain enough beta-carotene to supply 20% of your daily vitamin A requirement. Apricots were a favorite food for astronauts on the Apollo moon mission.

They were originally grown in China over 4,000 years ago and were brought to California by the Spanish in the late 18th century. California is still the largest producer of apricots with over half the apricots grown being canned due to their short growing season. Apricots that are not ripe will ripen quickly at room temperature, then should be refrigerated.

» WORD TO THE WISE
Dried apricots contain over 40% sugar. When purchasing dried apricots, it is best to purchase the unsulfured variety.

» WHY IS IT SO HARD TO FIND A FRESH APRICOT?
Apricots are mainly grown on 17,000 acres in the Santa Clara Valley in California. They were introduced by Spanish missionaries in the 1700's when they were establishing their missions along the California coast. Because they are so fragile and bruise very easily

they do not transport well or last very long once they ripen. Barely 5% of the United States population has ever tasted a ripe apricot since they are unable to travel the thousands of miles to Midwest and Eastern markets.

REPORTED HEALTH BENEFITS
Apricots contain a high level of iron making it a beneficial fruit for cases of anemia, TB, asthma and blood impurities. may be effective in destroying intestinal worms, relieving diarrhea, and pimples.

ATEMOYA

This fruit is grown in Florida and is available from August through October. They are a pale-green fruit that should not be purchased if it is cracked open. Looks like an artichoke and has a cream-colored flesh that is sweet and almost fat and sodium-free. It is an excellent source of potassium.

AVOCADOS

Originally grown in Central America and were first grown in the United States in the 1800's in Florida and California. California produces 90% of all avocados sold. The most popular varieties are the Fuerte and Hass. The Florida avocado has half the fat of the California varieties and only ⅔ of the calories.

Approximately 71-80% of the calories in avocados come from fat. However, most of the fat is of the monounsaturated type, the same type found in olive oil and Canola oil.

They are available year round and should be fresh in appearance with colors ranging from green to purple-black. They should feel heavy for their size and be slightly firm. Avoid ones with soft spots and discolorizations. Refrigerate, if ripe, and use within 5 days after purchase.

  » SNUGGLE-UP
    Avocados will ripen in a short period of time if placed in a brown paper bag and set in a warm location. They will ripen even faster if you place them in a woolen sock.

» AVOCADOS LOVE WOOLEN SOCKS
To ripen an avocado, just place it in a woolen sock in the back of a dark closet for 2 days. Avocados should never be stored in the refrigerator when they are not fully ripe. When they are ripe they should be stored in the vegetable drawer in the refrigerator and should stay fresh for 10-14 days. Avocados may only be frozen for three to six months if pureed.

» HOW GREEN I AM
Have you ever heard someone say that if you leave the pit in the guacamole it will not turn black. I'm sure you have, and you have probably tried it to no avail unless you covered the entire dish tightly with plastic wrap. The plastic wrap, not the pit, did the trick because it would not allow oxygen to oxidize the guacamole turning it black. Guacamole will oxidize on the surface in about 60-90 minutes if left out uncovered. The area under the pit was not exposed to the air which is why it never turned black. Oxygen is not our friend when it comes to exposed foods. Another method that works is to spread a thin layer of mayonnaise on the top of the guacamole dip. Spraying the surface with a solution of powdered vitamin C and water also will work.

» CAN YOU COOK AN AVOCADO?
No! Never cook an avocado because a reaction will take place that releases a bitter chemical compound. It would be rare to ever see a recipe that calls for cooked avocado. When restaurants do serve avocado on a hot dish they will always place the avocado on the dish just before serving it. If you just slice an avocado, the enzyme "phenoloxidase" is released from the damaged cells and converts "phenols" into a brownish compound. Ascorbic acid will neutralize this reaction for a period of time, slowing the reaction.

» EN GARDE
To remove an avocado pit, just thrust the blade of a sharp knife into the pit, twist slightly and the pit comes right out.

» FAUX RIPE
If an avocado is too hard and needs to be used, try placing it in the microwave using high power for 40-70 seconds. Make sure and rotate it half way through. This procedure won't ripen it but will soften it.

REPORTED HEALTH BENEFITS
Used for inflammations of mucous membranes, especially in the intestines.

BANANAS

They are available all year round since they grow in a climate with no winter. They should be plump and the skin should be free of bruises as well as brown or black spots. Bananas should be purchased green or at least with some green tint and allowed to ripen at home.

» MONKEY'S FAVORITE FOOD

As soon as a banana ripens at room temperature it should be stored in the refrigerator to slow down the ripening process. The skin will turn black, however, this does not affect the flesh for a number of days. Bananas will freeze well for a short period of time, however, they will be a bit mushy when thawed and are better used in dishes. Frozen banana treats are eaten while the banana is still frozen solid which does not give them the thawing time to make them mushy.

The new miniature bananas have more taste than many of the larger ones and can be consumed in the same manner. Excellent spices to use on bananas are cinnamon and nutmeg.

Bananas are often sold as chips and should not be considered a healthy snack food since they are usually fried in a saturated fat oil. It would be best to choose an air-dried chip if you can find one. Only one ounce of fried banana chips can contain 150 calories and up to 10 grams of fat, most of which is saturated.

» BERRY INTERESTING

Bananas contain less water than most other fruits. They are a type of berry from a tree classified as an herb tree which can grow up to 30 feet high, and are the largest plant in the world with a woody stem.

» OUCH!

If you are not sure if a banana is ripe, just insert a toothpick in the stem end. If it comes out clean and with ease, the banana is ripe.

Ouch!

» RIPENING TID-BITS

If you wish to ripen bananas more quickly, wrap them in a wet paper towel and place them into a brown paper sack or place a green banana next to a ripe banana. More ethylene gas is released from the green banana. If you place an apple next to a banana it will also ripen very quickly, since apples give off more ethylene gas than other fruits. Another fast method is to place the banana in the oven at 350°F. (176.6°C.) for about 8-10 minutes.

» BROWN SPOTS ON BANANAS TELL THE SUGAR CONTENT

 Bananas are always picked when they are green. If they are allowed to ripen on the tree they tend to lose their taste and become mealy. The sugar content increases from 2% to 20% as soon as the banana is picked. The more yellow the skin becomes, the sweeter the banana. Brown spots are the result of the sugar level increasing over the 25% level. The browner, the higher the sugar content. In 1997 we consumed 27 pounds of bananas per person. Banana imports top 15 billion bananas a day amounting to a $5 billion business in the United States. Bananas are mainly grown in tropical climates, however, they are also grown in Iceland in soil heated by volcanic steam vents.

» CAN YOU GET HIGH FROM SMOKING BANANA PEELS?
Banana peels became popular during the 1960's when scientists announced that they contained minute amounts of psychoactive compounds such as serotonin, norepinephrine, and dopamine. Banana peels were dried, ground up into a fine powder and rolled in paper cigarette wrappers. The fad didn't last too long since the effects were weak and few people were actually getting high. The majority of the bananas being exported to the United States today are from Ecuador.

» Bananas will freeze for about 6-7 months if left in their skins.

BANANA VARIETIES

» CAVANDISH
The standard curved banana that we normally purchase, these are mainly imported from South American countries.

» MANZANO
Known as the "finger banana" and tends to turn black when it is ripe.

» PLANTAINS
A very large green banana which has a high starch content and is more palatable when prepared like a vegetable. They are often substituted for potatoes in South American dishes.

» RED BANANA
Usually straight instead of the curved standard banana, they tend to turn a purplish color when ripe and have a sweet flavor.

REPORTED HEALTH BENEFITS
Historically, bananas have been reported used to improve conditions such as stomach ulcers, colitis, diarrhea, hemorrhoids, and even to increase energy levels. The inner surface of banana skins were used on burns and boils.

BERRIES

All berries should be firm and their color bright. Berries should be refrigerated and never allowed to dry-out. They should be used within 2-3 days after they are purchased for the best flavor and nutritional value. Berries do not ripen after being picked.

Choose only bright red strawberries and plump firm blueberries that are light to dark blue.

Checking the bottom of berry containers is a must to be sure they are not stained from rotting or moldy berries. Mold on berries tends to spread quickly and you never want to leave a moldy one next to a good one. This actually goes for all fruits.

Never hull strawberries until after they are washed or they will absorb too much water and become mushy and waterlogged.

Berries can be defrosted by placing them in a plastic bag and immersing them in cold water for about 10-12 minutes.

> » BOTTOMS UP
> If you are making a dish with berries, make sure the batter or consistency is thick enough to hold the berries in suspension. Berries placed into thin batters just go to the bottom.
>
> Blueberries and strawberries are higher in vitamin A than most berries. Fresh cranberries may contain up to 86% more vitamin C than canned cranberries, due to the heat processing and storage times. Strawberries are one of more nutritious berries with just one containing only 55 calories and considerably more calcium, phosphorus, vitamin C, and potassium than blueberries and raspberries.
>
> Blueberries and blackberries contain an enzyme that may reduce the absorption of vitamin B_1. These berries are best if cooked, since cooking will neutralize the enzyme.
>
> Berry juice stains can usually be removed from your hands with lemon juice.

> » WHAT HAPPENS WHEN YOU SPRINKLE SUGAR ON A STRAWBERRY?
> Strawberries can easily be sweetened by sprinkling powdered sugar on them and allowing them to stand for a short while. When the sugar is placed on the surface of the berry it mixes with the moisture that is naturally being released producing a solution that is somewhat denser than the liquid inside the berry. Through osmosis the liquid with the less density flows toward the liquid which is more dense placing the sugar inside the strawberry cells and sweetening the berry.

» A LOTTA BERRIES
In 1997 California grew enough strawberries to circle the earth fifteen times. The largest strawberry ever grown was 8.17 ounces.

» BERRY, BERRY, INTERESTING
The largest producer of blueberries in the United States is New Jersey followed by Michigan. Blueberries are second only to strawberries in berry consumption.

» IS THERE A BLACK RASPBERRY?
Raspberries are actually grown in three colors. The traditional red which we see in the markets during the summer and the black and golden or yellow which are sold in different areas of the country and are relatively common.

REPORTED HEALTH BENEFITS
Blackberries have been used for relieving symptoms of arthritis, weak kidneys, anemia, gout and minor skin irritations. Blueberries have been used as a blood cleanser, anti-diarrheal, reduce inflammations and menstrual disorders. Strawberries have been used effectively as a skin cleanser and blood cleanser as well as relieving the symptoms of asthma, gout, arthritis, and lowering blood pressure.

BREADFRUIT

Has the appearance of a large melon and may weigh up to 5 pounds. It is high in starch and vitamins and is a staple food for the Pacific Islanders. The outside is a greenish color with a scaly covering and pale-yellow flesh. When ripe it is very sweet. Make sure you choose a relatively hard breadfruit then allow it to ripen at room temperature until it has a degree of give.

CANTALOUPE

They are best if purchased between June and September. They should be round, smooth, and have a depressed scar at the stem end. Be aware, that if the scar appears rough or the stem is still attached, the melon will not ripen well. Cantaloupes are best if the netting is an even yellow color with little or no green. Melons can be left at room temperature to ripen, they do not ripen under refrigeration. The aroma will usually indicate if it is ripe and sweet, then refrigerate as soon as possible.

» Whole melons will last for a week if kept refrigerated.

» Cut melons, wrapped in plastic with seeds, and refrigerated, are best eaten in 2-3 days.

» If you shake a ripe cantaloupe the seeds should rattle. The "belly button" should be somewhat soft, but make sure that the melon is not soft all over.

» One average size cantaloupe will produce about 45-50 melon balls or about 4 cups of diced fruit.

REPORTED HEALTH BENEFITS
Has been used to lower high fevers, to reduce blood pressure, relieve the symptoms of arthritis, alleviate bladder problems, and stop constipation.

CARAMBOLA

The color, when ripe, should be golden-yellow and when sliced will yield perfect star-shaped sections. It has a sweet but somewhat tart flavor and may be purchased green and allowed to ripen at room temperature. Excellent natural source of vitamin C.

CHERRIES

Cherries are grown in 20 countries worldwide. The United States grows 150,000 tons of cherries annually, 50% of which are sweet cherries and 90% sour cherries. Most cherries are canned or frozen.

Cherries were a favorite fruit of the Romans, Greeks and Chinese thousands of years ago. Cherries originated in Asia Minor and were named for the Turkish town Cerasus, which is presently called Giresun, and is located on the Black Sea. It is believed that birds brought the cherry pits to Europe. Europeans enjoy a chilled cherry soup as a summertime treat.

French colonists from Normandy brought pits that they planted along the Saint Lawrence River and throughout the Great Lakes areas. Sweet cherries are primarily grown on the West Coast, while tart cherries are grown in the Grand Traverse Region of Michigan.

» CHERRY-PICKING TIME
Cherries should be stored in the refrigerator with as high a humidity as possible. They should be placed unwashed in a plastic bag and allowed to stand at room temperature for 30 minutes before eating for the best flavor. Cherries will last about 4 days in the refrigerator. If you freeze cherries they must be pitted first and sealed airtight in a plastic bag, otherwise they will taste like almonds.

CHERRY VARIETIES

» MONTMORENCY
Usually round but slightly compressed. Very juicy and a clear medium-red color. Excellent for pies, tarts, and jams. This is the most widely grown tart cherry in the United States.

» EARLY RICHMOND
Round, medium-red colored, with tender flesh and a tough, thin skin. Not generally grown in the United States.

» ENGLISH MORELLO
A round-shaped cherry, very deep red in color becoming almost black. The flesh is red, tender, and somewhat tart. It is not grown commercially in large quantities in the United States.

» SWEET REPUBLICAN (Lewellan)
It is small to medium-sized, heart-shaped with crisp flesh ranging from very red to purplish-black. The juice is very dark and sweet.

» ROYAL ANN (Napoleon or Emperor Francis)
These are heart-shaped and a light golden color. The flesh may be pink to light red, usually firm and juicy, with an excellent flavor. The light flesh variety is used commercially in canning.

» BING
These are usually very large, heart-shaped with flesh that ranges in color from deep red to almost black. The skin is usually smooth and glossy.

» SCHMIDT
Similar to a Bing cherry.

» TARTARIAN
Very large, heart-shaped, with purplish to black flesh. Very tender and sweet, is thin skinned and one of the most popular cherries of the mid-season.

» CHAPMAN
Large round, purplish-black flesh. Produced from a seedling of the Black Tartarian variety. The fruit usually matures early in the season.

» LAMBERT
A very large, usually round cherry with dark to very dark red flesh. Very firm and meaty.

REPORTED HEALTH BENEFITS
Very high in magnesium, iron, and silicon making them valuable in arthritis, as a blood cleanser, worms, asthma and high blood pressure. They tend to stimulate the secretion of digestive enzymes. Numerous people have reported that consuming 8-10 Bing cherries per day relieved symptoms of arthritis. This claim has not been substantiated.

COCONUT

Coconuts are always available. When choosing one be sure that it's heavy for its size and you can hear the sound of liquid when you shake it. If the eyes are damp it would be best not to buy it. Coconuts can be stored at room temperature for 6-8 months depending on how fresh it was when it was purchased. If you are going to grate coconut for a recipe, make sure that you place the meat in the freezer for at least 30 minutes. This will harden the meat and make it easier to grate.

» A COCONUT SEPARATION
To easily separate the outer shell of a coconut from the inner meat, just bake the coconut for 20-25 minutes at 325°F. (162.8°C.) then tap the shell lightly with a hammer. The moisture from the meat will try and escape in the form of steam and establish a thin space between the meat and the shell separating the two. The coconut milk (which unlike the coconut and the meat is low in saturated fat) should be removed first by piercing 2 of the 3 eyes with an ice pick. One hole will allow the air to enter as the milk comes out the other one.

CRANBERRIES

Cranberries are usually too tart to eat raw and are therefore made into sauces, relishes, and preserves. Only 10% of the commercial crop in the United States is sold in supermarkets, the balance is made into cranberry sauce or juice.

Canned cranberries have only 14% of the vitamin C content than that of fresh and 3 times the calories. Cranberries contain "ellagic acid," a phytochemical.

When choosing a fresh cranberry in the supermarket, make sure it bounces. Another name for cranberries is "bounce berries." Buy berries that are hard, bright, light to dark-red, and sealed in plastic bags. When frozen they will keep for up to one year.

Cranberries should only be cooked until they "pop." Additional cooking will only make them sour and bitter. When cooking cranberries, it is best to add one teaspoon of unsalted butter to each pound, this will eliminate overboiling and reduce the foam that develops.

» IS CRANBERRY JUICE HELPFUL FOR BLADDER PROBLEMS?
Recently, researchers at Youngstown University found the "cranberry factor" which may interfere with the ability of bacteria to adhere to the surface of bladder cells as well as the urinary tract. The factor tends to show up in the urine of humans and animals within 2-3 hours after drinking cranberry juice and stays active for about 12 hours. Research is continuing and may show promise that there is actual scientific data that proves cranberries may help to relieve a urinary infection.

» POP GOES THE CRANBERRY
Cranberries will not handle a great amount of heat before the water inside produces enough steam to burst the berry. When a cranberry pops and bursts it is best to stop the cooking process otherwise the cranberry will become bitter and very tart. The addition of lemon juice and a small amount of sugar added to the water will help to preserve the color, since the heat will cause the pigment (anthocyanin) to be dissolved and turn the cooking water red.

IT'S THE BERRIES
If you want to taste the greatest cranberry candy ever made, call Cranberry Sweets Company in Bandon, Oregon at (503)347-9475. This chewy cranberry and walnut treat can't be beat.

> REPORTED HEALTH BENEFITS
> Cranberries have been used for numerous skin disorders, reducing high blood pressure, and for liver and kidney disorders. It has been extensively used as a urinary tract cleanser for hundreds of years.

DATES
Dates contain a higher sugar content than any other fruit and some varieties may contain up to 70% sugar. California and Arizona are the major suppliers for the United States, however, Africa and the Middle East have been cultivating them for 4,000 years. The Medjool date, considered the best date grown was first brought to the United States from French Morocco in 1927. Date palms require a lot of tender care if

they are to produce the maximum of about 200 pounds of dates every year.

The palms must be climbed eighteen times each year to perform a number of hand operations so that they will produce. Dates are classified as either soft, semi-soft, or dry. Semi-soft dates are the most common sold in the United States and Deglet Noor is the most common variety. Two of the other popular varieties are Zahidi and Medjool.

A date cluster may weigh up to 25 pounds. Ounce for ounce they supply 250% more potassium than an orange and 64% more than a banana. Dates are a concentrated source of calories and not a diet food. Medjool dates will last for about 45-60 days at room temperature because of their high moisture level. If only refrigerated, they will last for about 5 months.

» THE GREATEST MEDJOOLS
If you would like to purchase your dates direct from the grower, just call the Sphinx Date Ranch in Scottsdale, Arizona at (602)941-2261 and ask for a free catalog.

> REPORTED HEALTH BENEFITS
> Used in cases of anemia, raising low blood pressure, colitis, and improving sexual potency. Crushed dates have been made into syrup for coughs and sore throats.

FIGS

Figs can be traced back to ancient Egypt and are one of the oldest known fruits. The majority of the figs grown are sold dried, less than 10% reach markets in their original form. They were brought to California by the Spaniards and most are still grown in California. The most common fig found in supermarkets is the Calimyrna. Figs are pollinated by a small fig wasp which if killed off by pesticides ends the crop. Dried figs have 17% more calcium than milk but are very high in calories for their size.

» IS IT TRUE THAT FIGS CAN TENDERIZE A STEAK?
It is a fact that figs have the ability to tenderize meats. Fresh figs contain the chemical "ficin" which is called a proteolytic enzyme, one that is capable of breaking down proteins with a similar action to that of "papain" from papayas or "bromelain" from pineapples. Ficin is effective in the heat ranges of 140° - 160° F. (60° -71.1°C.), which is the most common temperature to simmer stews. If fresh figs are added to the stew it will help to tenderize the meat and impart an excellent flavor. However, if

the temperature rises above 160°F. (71.1°C.) "ficin" is inactivated. Canned figs will not work since they have been heated to very high temperatures during their sterilization process.

Varieties include; Black Mission, Kadota, Calimyrna, Brown Turkey, and Smyrna.

REPORTED HEALTH BENEFITS
Beneficial for constipation, anemia, asthma, gout, and a number of skin irritations. Fig juice makes an excellent natural laxative as well as used in a poultice for boils.

GRAPEFRUIT

The heavier the grapefruit, the juicier it will be. Florida grapefruit are usually juicier than those from the Southwestern States. However, fruit grown in the Western United States has a thicker skin which makes it easier to peel. When refrigerated, grapefruit should last for 2-3 weeks. Grapefruit should be firm, the skin unblemished, with no discolorization. Fruit that is pointed at the end tend to be thick-skinned and have less meat and juice. White fruit has a stronger flavor than the pink variety. They are available year round, but are best January through May.

Grapefruits were cross-bred from oranges and shaddocks. Shaddocks are not a common fruit since they have almost no juice, are thick skinned, have a sour taste, and too many seeds.

» FOR GRAPEFRUIT LOVERS EVERYWHERE
If you want to taste the world's greatest and sweetest orange-grapefruit call Red Cooper at (800)876-4733 in Alamo, Texas and ask for his catalog. He grows a hybrid grapefruit that is a one and only.

Always rinse citrus fruit in case there are still traces of pesticides on them, especially before cutting.

» IT'S MAGIC
A small amount of salt will make a grapefruit taste sweeter.

» GRAPEFRUIT AND DRUGS, DO THEY MIX?
Recent studies have shown that grapefruit will increase the absorption rate of a number of drugs. A researcher at the University of Western Ontario found that grapefruit juice caused a three-fold absorption rate for a blood pressure medication. The enzyme in the gastrointestinal tract "3YP3A4" tends to neutralize a controlling

mechanism. Some of the drugs that are affected are calcium-channel blockers Procardia and Adalat, the antihistamine Seldane, immunosuppressant Cyclosporine, short-acting sedative Halcion, and the estrogens Estinyl. The race is now on worldwide to isolate the actual ingredient that is causing the reaction.

» GRAPEFRUIT WHITE OUT
The white material just under the skin of a grapefruit (pectin) may be easily removed by either immersing the grapefruit in very hot water for 5-6 minutes or by placing it in boiling water for 3 minutes. However, this material is also very high in an antioxidant known as carotene and is worth eating even though it may be a bit bitter. Recent studies have associated grapefruit pectin as being effective in lowering the bad cholesterol LDL.

> REPORTED HEALTH BENEFITS
> Used in the dissolution of inorganic calcium found in the cartilage of the joints of arthritics. Fresh grapefruit contains organic "salicylic acid" which is the active agent.

GRAPES

All varieties of grapes are really berries and are native to Asia Minor where they were cultivated for 6,000 years. Grapes are presently grown on six continents. The growing of grapes is known as "viticulture." California produces 97% and Arizona produces 3% of all European varieties grown in the United States.

Grapes should be plump and firm, and attached to a green stem. They should have good color and never faded. Grapes do not ripen off the vine, so be sure that they are sweet and ripe when purchased. It is always best to try and taste a grape from the bunch you are buying before you buy them, however, this caused a problem for supermarkets so they now place bunches in mesh bags. If it is not possible to taste them only purchase a small quantity, then taste. Grapes will only stay fresh for 5-7 days even if refrigerated.

Raisins will not stick to food choppers if they are soaked in cold water for 10 minutes.

GRAPES, BIGGEST INDUSTRY IN THE WORLD

The grape industry is reported to be the largest single food industry in the world. This includes table grapes, raisin grapes, wine grapes, and juice grapes. Grapes need to be stored in a plastic bag and in the coldest part of the refrigerator. They should not be washed before being stored, but need to washed very well before eating. Grapes do not freeze well since they are high in water content and become mushy when thawed. They are OK to eat frozen or used in dishes and will freeze well for about 1 year.

» THE POPULAR DRIED GRAPE
Raisins are just dried grapes and may be dried either artificially or naturally. They are sold in a number of varieties such as:

» GOLDEN SEEDLESS
Produced from Thompson seedless grapes but are somewhat tart. In order to retain their golden color, sulphur dioxide is used to prevent them from becoming dark.

» MUSCAT
These raisins are made from Muscat grapes and are always sun dried. They are larger than Thompson seedless and darker in color. They are naturally very sweet.

» NATURAL SEEDLESS
These are very sweet and produced from Thompson seedless grapes. They are the most common grape sold and are always a dark brown color and sun dried.

» SULTANAS
These are always sun dried and have a somewhat tart taste.

» ZANTE CURRANTS
These are produced from the Black Corinth grape and are always sun dried and smaller than most other grapes. They have a dark brown color and are somewhat tart. These grapes are normally used more in baking because of their size.

» CHUBBY RAISIN
If you would like nice plump raisins, just place them in a small bowl with a few drops of water, cover them and bake in a pre-heated 325° oven for 6-8 minutes.

COMMON GRAPE VARIETIES

» BLACK BEAUTY
A seedless black grape.

» CALMERIA
These are a dark red grape with a light gray finish and only a few seeds.

» CHAMPAGNE
These are usually used to make currents or sold through gourmet markets.

» CONCORD
A common variety of American grape. The color is usually blue-black with a sweet but somewhat tart flavor.

» DELAWARE
These are a smaller grape that is pink-colored with a tender skin.

» EMPEROR
These are a very popular small grape. They are a reddish-purple color and seedless.

» EXOTIC
A blue-black grape with seeds.

» FLAME SEEDLESS
These are deep red and usually found seedless and about the same size as the Emperor, but somewhat more tart.

» ITALIA
Also called Muscat and used mainly for winemaking. Green-gold grape with seeds.

» NIAGARA
These large amber-colored grapes may be somewhat egg-shaped and not as sweet as most other varieties.

» PERLETTE SEEDLESS
A green grape usually imported from Mexico or South America.

» QUEEN
A large red grape that has a mild sweet flavor.

» RED GLOBE
A very large grape with seeds and a delicate flavor.

» RED MALAGA
A thick-skinned reddish grape that is usually fairly sweet.

» RIBIER
One of the larger grapes. It is blue-black with tender skin.

» RUBY SEEDLESS
A very sweet deep red grape.

» STEUBEN
A blue-black grape that resembles the Concord grape.

» THOMPSON SEEDLESS
The most common grape sold in the United States. They are a small green grape with a sweet flavor. The most common raisin grape.

» TOKAY
A much sweeter version of the Flame Seedless grape.

HONEYDEW MELONS

The most desirable will be creamy white or pale yellow with a slight silky finish. Best if purchased between June and October. A faint smell usually indicates ripeness. Blossom end (opposite from the stem) should be slightly soft. Like most melons, honeydews taste better if left unrefrigerated for a few days. Whole ones keep fresh for up to one week when refrigerated. Store cut half-melons with seeds in plastic bags and eat within 2 days. If the seeds have been removed it would be best not to purchase them unless they are eaten the same day.

> REPORTED HEALTH BENEFITS
> Used for kidney problems, a diuretic and to improve a person's complexion.

KIWI

Originated in China and was brought to New Zealand in 1906. The original name was "Chinese gooseberry." It was renamed for the New Zealand bird and has been known as "Kiwi." It is a commercial crop in California and with the reverse growing seasons between California and New Zealand they are available year round. They store for up to 10 months in cold storage.

» Firm Kiwis, left at room temperature, soften and sweeten in 3-5 days. Ripe Kiwis feel like ripe peaches. Refrigerated, they stay fresh for weeks with their average size approximately 2-3 inches long. They have a furry brown skin which is peeled off before eating. The inside should be lime green.

» Two Kiwis = the fiber in 1 cup of bran flakes and is an excellent source of vitamin C. Best to peel with a sharp vegetable peeler for less waste.

» Kiwi will ripen faster if placed next to an apple or a banana in a brown paper bag.

» KIWI, A GREAT MEAT TENDERIZER?
While we are familiar with the tenderizing properties of the enzymes in papaya and pineapple, we rarely hear about Kiwi. Kiwi contains the enzyme "actinidin" which is an excellent meat tenderizer. Fresh Kiwi needs to be pureed and can be used as a marinade for any type of meat, poultry, or pork. If you prefer, the pureed Kiwi may be rubbed on the meat before cooking, just allow the meat to sit in the refrigerator for about 30 minutes before cooking it. The meat will retain its own flavor and not pick up the Kiwi

flavor. Actinidin will also prevent gelatin from setting up, so you will have to add Kiwi to a gelatin dish just before serving, preferably on the top. Cooking the fruit, however, will inactivate the enzyme.

LEMONS AND LIMES

Lemons and limes were probably brought to this country by one of the early explorers and were grown in Florida around the sixteenth century. The commercial industry was started around 1880 for lemons and around 1912 for limes. California is now the largest producer of lemons.

» There are two types of lemons, the very tart and the sweet. We are more used to the tart, however, the sweet are grown mostly by home gardeners. Limes originated on Tahiti. Key limes are a smaller variety with a higher acid content. The California variety of limes are known as the "Bears" and is a seedless lime.

» If sprinkled with water and refrigerated in plastic bags, lemons and limes will last for 1-2 months. If frozen, both their juices and grated peels will last about 4 months. Look for lemons and limes with the smoothest skin and the smallest points on each end. They have more juice and a better flavor. Also, submerging a lemon or lime in hot water for 15 minutes before squeezing will produce almost twice the amount of juice. Also, warming the lemon in the oven for a few minutes will work.

» If you only need a few drops of juice, slightly puncture one end with a skewer before squeezing out the desired amount. Return the lemon to the refrigerator and the hole will seal up and the balance of the fruit will still be usable.

» Lemons and limes will keep longer in the refrigerator if you place them in a clean jar, cover them with cold water and seal the jar well. After using ½ of the fruit, store the other half in the freezer in a plastic bag. This reduces the loss of moisture and retards bacterial growth.

» When lemon is used as a flavoring, it tends to mask the craving for the addition of salt. Lemon and lime peelings may cause skin irritation on susceptible people. They contain the oil "limonene."

THE MYTH REGARDING LIME JUICE

A recent article in the New York Times referred to cooking raw meats and fish in lime juice without heat. This concept is also used in Latin America where people think that the acid in lime juice is "strong enough to kill bacteria." A Latin American dish called "ceviche" is made from fish or shellfish and only marinated in lime juice before being consumed. Lime juice will not kill E. Coli nor will it kill any parasites that are in the fish flesh. If the raw fish is commercially frozen well below zero for 3 days then it may be safe to eat.

> **REPORTED HEALTH BENEFITS**
> Used as a natural antiseptic to destroy harmful bacteria that may cause infections and as a topical agent for relief of acne and other skin irritations (peelings are not used).

MAMEY

Resembles a small coconut and is the national fruit of Cuba. It has a brown, suede-like skin and the inside is salmon-colored or bright red. The pulp is scooped out and eaten or added to milk and made into a shake.

MANGOES

Mangoes originated in India and that country is still the primary producer. Mangoes come in hundreds of varieties and a number of shapes and sizes. The majority of the mangoes sold in the United States are imported from Mexico, Central America and Hawaii. Only about 10% of the commercially sold fruit is grown in Florida. The most popular variety is the Tommy Atkins, which is an oval-shaped fruit with a bland taste.

They are available in late December through August. Mangoes are an excellent source of vitamins A and C and should be eaten when soft. They ripen easily at room temperature. Recently, they have been found to contain traces of a carcinogenic fumigant, ethylene dibromide (EDB). Purchase only mangoes and papayas grown in Hawaii or Florida.

Mangoes are one of the best sources of beta-carotene, they contain 20% more than cantaloupe and 50% more than apricots. Mangoes will last for about 5 days if refrigerated in a plastic bag. Green, hard mangoes may never ripen, try to purchase them ripe and ready to eat.

> **REPORTED HEALTH BENEFITS**
> May be beneficial for kidney diseases and to reduce acidity and aid digestion. Also, used for reducing fevers and asthmatic symptoms. When crushed and used as a paste it helps to cleanse the skin pores.

NECTARINES

Nectarines have been around for hundreds of years and are not a new fruit as many people think. The Greeks gave them the name of "nektar" which is where the present name was derived from. California grows 98% of all nectarines sold in the United States. Basically, they are just a peach without fuzz with over 150 varieties worldwide.

Their peak season is July and August. They are a combination of a peach and a plum. Their color should be rich and bright. If they are too hard, allow them to ripen at room temperature for a few days, they will not ripen in the refrigerator. Avoid the very hard dull-looking nectarines.

> REPORTED HEALTH BENEFITS
> Used as a digestive aid and to relieve flatulence. It has also been used to lower high blood pressure and relieve arthritis.

ORANGES

Commercially oranges were first grown in St. Augustine, Florida in 1820. Florida grows more citrus than any other state. When frozen orange juice was invented in the 1940's oranges became the chief crop of the United States. Florida still produces 70% of the United States crop.

The color of an orange does not necessarily indicate its quality, since oranges are usually dyed to improve their appearance. Brown spots on the skin indicates a good quality orange. Pick a sweet orange by examining the navel, ones with the largest navel will usually be the best. If you place an orange into a hot oven for 2-3 minutes before peeling it, no white fibers will be visible and the pectin will melt into the flesh.

Oranges that look green have undergone a natural process called "regreening." This is due to a ripe orange absorbing chlorophyll pigment from the leaves. They are excellent eating and usually very sweet. Mandarins are a very close relative to the orange, are more easily peeled, and the sections are more pronounced. They come in a number of varieties.

The rinds of oranges and grapefruits should be stored in a tightly sealed jar and refrigerated. They may be grated and used for flavoring cakes, frostings and cookies.

» THE NO WASTE ORANGE
  The orange juice industry uses every bit of every orange it processes. The residues from the production of orange juice is a multi-million dollar

industry. Everything, including the pulp, seeds, and peel are used in food products such as candy, cake mixes, soft drinks, paints, and even perfumes. Over 100 million pounds of "peel oil" is sold for cooking uses and is also made into a synthetic spearmint base for the Coca Cola company to be used as a flavoring agent.

» ORANGE JUICE AND ANTACIDS DO NOT MIX
If you take an antacid that contains aluminum, avoid drinking any kind of citrus juice. A four ounce glass of orange juice can increase the absorption of aluminum found in antacids tenfold. Aluminum can collect in the tissues and high levels may affect your health. Allow at least 3 hours after taking an antacid before drinking citrus juice.

» HOW DO YOU MAKE AN ORANGE JUICE FIZZ?
A real fun drink for children is when you add ¼ teaspoon of baking soda to 8-10 ounces of orange juice, lemonade, or other acidic fruit drink. Stir the drink well and it will do a great deal of fizzing much to the kid's delight. It will also reduce the acidity level of the drink.

» GREEN ORANGES?
Florida oranges normally have more of green tint than oranges from California or Arizona. This occurs due to the warm days and nights allowing the orange to retain more of the chlorophyll. A number of companies that sell Florida oranges may dye the oranges since we are not used to purchasing green oranges and think that they are not ripe. When oranges are dyed they must be labeled "Color Added" on the shipping container. The cooler nights in California and Arizona remove the green, however, both states have laws prohibiting adding any color to citrus fruits.

ORANGE VARIETIES

» BLOOD
The flesh is a blood-red color, and they are sweet and juicy. They are imported from the Mediterranean countries. The reddish color of the flesh comes from anthocyanin pigments.

» HAMLIN
Grown primarily in Florida and best for juicing. Averages 46 mg. of vitamin C per 3 ½ oz serving.

» JAFFA
Imported from Israel and similar to Valencia, but are sweeter.

» NAVEL
A large thick-skinned orange that is easily identified by its "belly-button" located at the blossom end. It is seedless and sweet, easily peeled, and one of the favorites in the United States.

» PARSON BROWN
Good juice orange from Florida. Averages 50mg. of vitamin C per
3 ½ oz. serving.

» PINEAPPLE
They have been named for their aroma which is similar to a
pineapple. Very flavorful and juicy. Averages 55mg. of vitamin C
per 3 ½ oz. serving.

» TEMPLE
Sweet-tasting juice orange. Averages 50mg. of vitamin C per 3½ oz.
serving.

» VALENCIA
Most widely grown of any orange used mostly for juice. Averages
50mg. of vitamin C per 3 ½ oz. serving.

> REPORTED HEALTH BENEFITS
> Recommended for asthma, bronchitis, arthritis, and to reduce
> high blood pressure. The desire for alcohol is reduced by
> drinking orange juice.

PAPAYAS

The papaya is also known as the "pawpaw," however, this is a different
fruit. They originated in South America and are now extensively grown in
Hawaii, the United States and Mexico. The fruit can weigh from ½ to 20
pounds and can be in any number of shapes, from pear to oblong.

The papaya seeds are edible and can be used as a garnish similar to capers.
They may also be dried and ground, then used like pepper. The Hawaiian
papayas are the sweetest and the most common in the markets. The
Mexican papayas are much larger and not as sweet.

It is an excellent meat tenderizer utilizing an enzyme called "papain." Only
papayas that are not fully ripe have sufficient papain to be useful as a meat
tenderizer. The more ripe a papaya the less papain content. The papaya
leaves also contain the tenderizer and meat is commonly wrapped in these
leaves while it is cooked in Hawaii.

When ripe they will be completely yellow. They will take 3-5 days to ripen
at room temperature.

> REPORTED HEALTH BENEFITS
> Used as a digestive aid, because of the papain content also, as
> an intestinal cleanser. The juice has been used to relieve
> infections in the colon and has a tendency to break down
> mucous.

PEACHES

Peaches are natives of China and were brought to the United States in the 1600's and planted along the eastern seaboard. It has been a commercial crop since the 1800's with Georgia actually being known as the Peach State.

Peaches can be ripened by placing them in a box covered with newspaper. Gasses given off are sealed in and it should only take 2-3 days to complete the ripening process. The skins are easily removed with a vegetable peeler. Peaches rarely get sweeter after being picked, they will just become softer and more edible.

There are two main varieties of peaches, clingstones and freestones. The clingstones are best for canning, making preserves, and general cooking. The freestone is the best for eating since the meat separates easily from the pit. Remember, never cook peaches with the pit in, since it may impart a bitter taste to the product. The reddish area around the pit may also contain a bitter flavor and should be removed as well.

» WHERE DID THE FUZZY PEACHES GO?

Peach fuzz was a term given to young boy's facial hair when they were nearing the age when they start shaving. The term came from the fuzz on the outside of peaches which was a nuisance to many people who loved peaches but hated the fuzz. The peach industry was unable to develop a fuzzless peach so they have developed a machine that mechanically gently brushes the surface of the peach removing most of the fuzz. Sales of peaches rose almost 50% after this was done. They are an excellent source of vitamin C and are available in many varieties, the favorite being the Alberta.

> REPORTED HEALTH BENEFITS
> Valuable for anemia due to its high vitamin and mineral content. Has also been used for reducing high blood pressure, bronchitis, asthma, bladder and kidney stones and de-worming.

PEARS

Pear trees will live and produce for approximately 90 years and were brought to the Americas by early European settlers. The skins of pears are an excellent source of fiber and a member of the rose family. The majority of the vitamin C in a pear is concentrated in the skin which is why canned pears are not a good source.

PEAR VARIETIES

» ANJOU

A winter pear with a smooth yellow-green skin that has a taste which is not as sweet as most pears.

» BARTLETT

A summer pear and one of the most popular in the United States, accounting for 65% of all commercial production. It is a large, juicy pear and is best when purchased golden yellow or allowed to ripen to that stage.

» BOSC

Has a long tapering neck and is excellent for baking.

» COMICE

This is the sweetest pear and a favorite among chefs when preparing pears for dessert recipes. it is usually found in gift baskets.

Other pear varieties include; Red Bartlett, Seckel, Asian Pear, and Clapp.

Ripen pears at room temperature for 2-3 days by placing them in a brown paper bag along with a ripe apple. Punch a few holes in the bag and store in a cool, dry location. Apples give off ethylene gas which will help speed the ripening of most fruits. As pears ripen their starch content turns to sugar and they may become somewhat mealy.

> REPORTED HEALTH BENEFITS
> Excellent for constipation and as a digestive aid. Has also been used for skin irritations.

PERSIMMONS

The persimmon is a native of Japan, and is widely grown there. Persimmons are high in vitamins and minerals but have never really caught on as a popular fruit in the United States. The Japanese persimmons sold in the United States are the Hachiya and Fuyu. The Fuyu is the smaller of the two and shaped like a tomato.

They are available October through January. Persimmons have a smooth, shiny, bright-orange skin, which should be removed before eating or they will taste very sour.

» REMOVING THE PUCKER FROM PERSIMMONS?

Persimmons are a very astringent fruit due to their natural level of tannins. When the fruit becomes ripe the tannins are somewhat bound up and the fruit is edible. If carbon dioxide is present, however, in larger quantities, the astringency can be reduced before the fruit is soft. Just wrap the persimmon as tight as you can in 3 layers of plastic wrap and allow it to remain in a very warm location for at least 12 hours. Return the persimmon to room temperature for another 12 hours. If you don't have a very warm location allow the wrapped persimmon to be placed in a gas oven with only the pilot light overnight or if an electric oven is used leave the light on overnight or place a pot of boiling water in the oven with it to provide heat. Freezing a persimmon will also remove most of the astringency. Leave the fruit in the freezer for about 2 months before eating it.

> REPORTED HEALTH BENEFITS
> Used to increase energy levels, and treat stomach ulcers and colitis. Have also been used for pleurisy and sore throats.

PINEAPPLE

Pineapples originated in South America and were brought to the Hawaiian Islands in the 1700's for cultivation. It became the main crop of Hawaii and was canned there for the first time. Pineapples are similar to melons in that the starch which converts to sugar as a fruit ripens is found only in the stem until just before the fruit reaches maturity. The starch then converts to sugar and enters the fruit. The fruit will not become any sweeter after it is picked. To check for ripeness, gently pull at a leaf anywhere on the stem, if the leaf comes off easily, the pineapple is ripe. It should also smell sweet.

It is available year round, but is best March through June. Buy as large and heavy as possible and be sure the leaves are deep green. Do not purchase if soft spots are present and refrigerate as soon as possible.

Fresh pineapple contains the enzyme "bromelain" that will prevent gelatin from setting up. This enzyme may also be used as a meat tenderizer. Studies in the future may also show that bromelain may be effective in reducing the plaque in arterial walls.

The easiest method of ripening a pineapple is to cut off the top, remove the skin, and slice. Place the pineapple in a pot and cover with water, add sugar and sweeten to taste then boil for 5 minutes, cool and refrigerate.

» DRIED PINEAPPLE FROM TAIWAN
Most of the dried pineapple that is sold in the United States is being imported from Taiwan and is saturated with refined sugar instead of pineapple juice. The sugar-sweetened pineapple will be very plump and will have a coating of sugar crystals, while the naturally sweetened pineapple will look somewhat mottled, fibrous and will lack the surface crystals.

REPORTED HEALTH BENEFITS
Found to assist in gland regulation, as an aid to digestion, and to relieve arthritic symptoms.

PLUMS

There are over 140 varieties of plums and they are found growing worldwide. The majority of the United States crop is the Santa Rosa variety which was developed by Luther Burbank in 1907. Plums are used for making prunes and their flavor varies from sweet to tart. The California French plum is the most common variety for prunes.

They are available June through September. Buy only firm to slightly soft plums, hard plums will not ripen well. To ripen, allow to stand at room temperature until fairly soft. Do not place in a window where they will be in direct sunlight, as this will eliminate their vitamin C content. They should be refrigerated after ripening and only last for 2-3 days.

» YOU'LL NEVER FORGET THE TASTE OF WILD PLUM
A rare wild plum found in Southern Oregon is made into the finest plum products you will ever taste. Three products produced by Stringer's Orchard in New Pine, Oregon is wild plum wine, pancake syrup, and preserves. All have a unique taste of their own. Call for their catalog (916)946-4112.

» WE'VE BEEN HOODWINKED
The traditional "English Plum Pudding" never contained plums, only currents and raisins.

REPORTED HEALTH BENEFITS
Used for liver disorders, constipation, to relieve flatulence, and bronchitis.

POMEGRANATES

This has always been a difficult fruit to eat and has never gained popularity. The seeds and pulp are edible, however, it is best to just juice the fruit to obtain its vitamins and minerals. The pulp-like membrane is bitter and not usually eaten. Pomegranate juice is used to make grenadine syrup. They are an excellent source of potassium and are available September through December.

REPORTED HEALTH BENEFITS
Used as a blood purifier and for worm problems, especially tapeworm. Possible benefit in cases of arthritis.

PRICKLY PEARS

A type of cactus fruit that has a yellowish skin, is covered with spines, and has a purple-red inside. It has a sweet taste similar to watermelon. Other names it may go by are Indian fig, and Barberry fig.

SAPOTES

Also, called "custard apples." They have green skins and creamy white pulp. They are a good source of vitamin A and potassium.

STAR APPLES

The skin is usually dull purple or light green. A cross section reveals a star-like shape. Used in jellies and eaten like an apple.

UGLI FRUIT

Produced by cross-breeding a grapefruit with an orange or tangerine. It has pinkish-orange flesh, nearly seedless and sweeter than a grapefruit. The fruit originated in Jamaica and is grown in Florida. Choose the heaviest fruit. It has a yellow, pebbly skin with green blotches that will turn orange when the fruit is ripe. It makes excellent eating and is high in vitamin C. Looks Ugli!

WATERMELON

The exterior color of a ripe watermelon should be a smooth, waxy-green color with or without stripes. If cut, choose one with a bright, crisp even-colored flesh. Whole melons will stay fresh if refrigerated for 2-3 days. Once cut, they should be kept refrigerated and covered with plastic wrap.

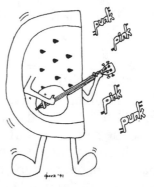

A good test for ripeness is to snap your thumb and third finger against the melon, if you hear a sound that says "pink" in a high shrill tone, the melon is not ripe. If you hear "punk" in a deep low tone, the melon is more likely to be ready to eat and should be sweet.

> » WATERMELON POPCORN?
> In China watermelon seeds are a treat and are roasted, salted, and eaten like popcorn. It is, however, a high-fat treat with 65% of its 535 calories in a 100 gram serving coming from fat.

» INSULATOR
Watermelon can be placed in a double brown paper bag for 1 hour after it has been cooled if you need the refrigerator space.

VEGETABLES

NEW NAMES TO LEARN
A new category of fruits and vegetables has recently arrived on the scene called "fruit-vegetables." These include; new varieties of eggplant, squash, peppers and tomatoes and are the seed-bearing bodies of these plants. Cross-breeding has also produced new vegetables such as the cross between broccoli and cauliflower. Other new arrivals are the sea vegetables called "wakame" and "kombu." These are derived from seaweed and have a very high mineral content.

MAKING THE GRADE
Fruits and vegetables are sold in three grades; U.S. Grade A Fancy, U.S.Grade B Choice or Extra Standard, and U.S. Grade C Standard. Grades B and C are just as nutritious but have more blemishes. The grades refer to all canned, frozen, or dried products.

FRESH PRODUCE GRADING
Fresh fruits and vegetables can also be found in three grades; U.S. Fancy, U.S. Fancy #1, and U.S. Fancy #2. These grades are determined by the product's size, color, shape, maturity and the number of visible defects.

NO MORE SOGGY SALADS
You will never have another soggy salad if you just place an inverted saucer in the bottom of a salad bowl. The excess water left after washing the vegetables and greens will drain off under the saucer and leave the salad greens high and dry.

HELP, I'M DRYING OUT
Salting the water when cooking any fruit or vegetable will draw a percentage of the liquid out. This may change the desired consistency and they may not cook evenly.

PAIN IN THE JOINT

Solanine has been associated with arthritis pain in a study by Rutgers University. Foods high in solanine are: green potatoes, tomatoes, red and green bell peppers, eggplant, and paprika. Best to avoid them.

HARMFUL LITTLE CRITTERS

Home-canned vegetables should always be cooked before eating since bacterial contamination is very common in these products.

USE THE REAL THING

Try placing a few sponges in your vegetable drawer to absorb moisture.

THYROID ALERT

The thyroid gland is very sensitive to certain chemicals, cabbage, turnips, kale, watercress, and rapeseed (Canola oil) contain a harmful chemical called a "thioglucoside," which may adversely affect the gland. However, this chemical is destroyed by cooking.

SNIP, SNIP

A chemical group found in parsnips is called "psoralens." This chemical causes cancer readily in laboratory animals. Parsnips should be peeled and cooked to eliminate these toxins.

KEEP YOUR BONES STRONG

Some plants high in oxalic acid should be avoided as you approach middle-age and beyond, especially women who have gone through menopause. These include; spinach, rhubarb, and cocoa bean (chocolate). Oxalic acid may interfere with calcium absorption and cause excess calcium to be excreted in the urine.

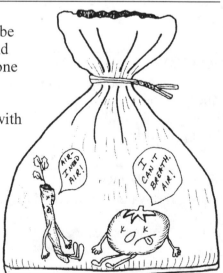

GIMME AIR

Wrap all produce loosely, air must be allowed to circulate around them to reduce spoilage.

EATING PARSLEY, BEST TO STAY INDOORS

Parsley contains a chemical that may make your skin sensitive to sunlight.

CLEAN 'EM UP REAL GOOD

During a routine sampling of domestic and imported produce by the FDA, they found pesticide residues in 33% of the 3,750 vegetables tested in 1996. The FDA, however, is only able to test about 1% of all vegetables sold in the United States. Laws regarding the use of pesticides are not very well regulated in foreign countries.

MAD SCIENTIST

Avoid using baking soda around fruits and vegetables. Baking soda is a base and many fruits and vegetables are somewhat acidic. When you mix a base and an acid you may end up with a salt and significant loss of taste.

NOT A HEALTHY MOVE

Since the 1950's, we have reduced our purchase of fresh vegetables by 12%, and increased our purchase of frozen and canned by 50%. This may cause an enzyme deficiency and more fresh produce is recommended.

Choosing The Healthiest And Most Nutritious Greens	
Dandelion	Young leaves are the best
Arugula	Has a slight mustard green flavor.
Kale	Young leaves are the best.
Romain	One of the best lettuces.
Spinach	High in nutrients, but contains oxalates. Use in moderation.
Beet	Small young leaves are best.
Endive	Contains oxalates, use in moderation.
Iceberg	Most popular green and the least nutritious due to water content.

SNAP, CRACKLE

If cut-up greens need to be crisped, dry them and place them in the freezer in a metal bowl for 5-10 minutes.

HOW CAESAR SALAD ORIGINATED

It wasn't invented in France by a renowned chef. Caesar Salad was actually named after a restaurateur who lived in Tijuana, Mexico named Caesar Cardini. One day Caesar ran out of food, took a large bowl, and placed everything he had left over in the restaurant in the bowl then served it as "Caesar Salad." Egg substitutes may be used to replace raw eggs in a Caesar salad, this will eliminate the risk of possible salmonella poisoning.

PECANS TO THE RESCUE

Unless you really like the smell, try placing a few unshelled pecans in your saucepan when cooking kale, cabbage, or collard greens to reduce the odor. When cooking onions or cabbage, boil a small amount of vinegar in a pan to remove the odor.

GETTING THE LITTLE CRITTERS OUT

When washing your vegetables place a small amount of salt in a sink full of cold water to draw out any sand and insects.

SWEETENS THEM UP TOO

Caramelizing vegetables will make the flavors and colors more intense. If you toss them in extra virgin olive oil then roast them in a 500°F. (260°C.) oven for about 30-40 minutes they should turn a nice golden brown. Great flavor but a big loss of nutrients.

JUST A WEE BIT

Adding a small amount of sugar to vegetables when they are cooking will bring out the flavor, this is especially true with corn.

STOP BOILING OVER

Next time you are cooking greens, either stir constantly or rub a small film of butter on the sides of the pan to prevent boiling over. The butter tends to stop the buildup of air bubbles.

COLOR SET

Try adding a small amount of milk or vinegar to your cooking water, it will help retain the color of vegetables.

ATTENSHUN

If your celery, carrots, or potatoes get soft and limp, try placing them into a bowl of water with ice cubes in the refrigerator for 45 minutes. Sometimes adding a small amount of lemon juice may help.

LOOK FOR THE PAPER LINING

It is always a good idea to line your refrigerator produce drawers with a piece of paper towel to absorb excess moisture. Mold spores love moisture.

POPULARITY CONTEST

The most popular salad items are tomatoes, cucumbers, and carrots in that order. The ones that are the least popular are Lima beans and peas.

SHAPE UP!

Use a well-greased muffin tin to bake tomatoes, apples, or bell peppers, this will keep them in shape.

LET'S HAVE A COMING OUT PARTY

By the end of 1998, a new plastic wrap may be released for sale that was developed by the USDA to extend the life of wrapped vegetables.

THE TOP 10 FRUITS AND VEGETABLES

Broccoli
Papaya
Cantaloupe
Sweet Potato
Carrots
Kale
Spinach

Red Bell Pepper
Pumpkin
Mango

ARTICHOKE

Originated in Italy and was brought to the Unites States by the Europeans in the 1800's. Almost all artichokes sold in the Unites States are grown in California. The artichoke is an unopened flower bud from a thistlelike plant. The most tender and edible part is the "heart" or center of the plant. They tend to vary in size and produce a sweet aftertaste caused by the chemical "cynarin."

There are 50 varieties and it is best to purchase them March through May. Choose from compact, tightly closed heads with green, clean-looking leaves. Their size is not related to quality. Avoid ones that have brown leaves or show signs of mold. Leaves that are separated, show that it is too old and will be tough and bitter.

Best to wear rubber gloves when working with artichokes. Artichokes should never be cooked in aluminum pots as they tend to turn the pots a gray color. They are easily burned and should be kept covered by water while they are cooking, however, they are also easy to overcook. Stainless steel knives should be used to cut artichokes. Carbon blades tend to react with the chemicals and darken the flesh.

A better flavor may be obtained when cooking artichokes if you add a small amount of sugar and salt to the water. They will have a sweeter taste and will retain their color better. If they are still too bland, try adding a small amount of fennel to the cooking water, about ⅛ - ¼ teaspoon.

Artichokes can be stored in a plastic bag in the refrigerator, unwashed, for 5-6 days.

» THE PROPER WAY TO EAT AN ARTICHOKE
This large globelike vegetable tends to scare people away and many people never get to taste one. If you do eat an artichoke remember that the best part to eat is at the base of the leaves, since the rest of the leaf is bitter and tough. Place the leaf into your mouth and draw the leaf through your teeth removing the tender meat. After eating all meat on the leaves you will be left with the "choke" or the heart of the artichoke which can be eaten with a fork and is the most succulent portion of the vegetable.

» ARTICHOKES, A REAL SWEET TREAT
Artichokes contain the chemical "cyanarin." Any food that is consumed immediately after eating artichokes will taste sweet. The chemical "cyanarin" stimulates the taste buds that are involved in the sweet taste and keeps them stimulated for 3-4 minutes. After eating artichokes, best to rinse your mouth with a glass of water.

» THE COLOR OF ARTICHOKES
When an artichoke is cooked, the chlorophyll in the green leaves reacts with the acids in the artichoke or cooking water and forms the compound "pheophytin" which turns the leaves brown. This is why many cooked artichokes have a bronze tint. If the artichoke is cooked fairly rapidly, this reaction will not take place and it will remain

green. Also, if you rub lemon on the leaves that have been cut, they will not discolor. Another method is to soak the artichoke for 20-30 minutes in a quart of water with 1 ½ tablespoons of white vinegar. The vinegar will stabilize the chemical that produces the color and the taste is also improved.

» WORLD'S GREATEST ARTICHOKES
If you want the greatest tasting artichoke direct from the grower, just call Giant Artichoke in Castroville, California at (408)633-2778.

REPORTED HEALTH BENEFITS
The juice of the leaves have been used as a powerful diuretic and in liver disorders and to relieve bad breathe. Other uses include arthritis, neuritis, and glandular disorders.

ASPARAGUS

Asparagus can be traced back to ancient Greece and has been referred to as the "aristocrat of vegetables." It is a member of the lily family and related to onions and garlic. It is an excellent source of vitamins and minerals. There are two types of asparagus, white and green. Canned asparagus contains less vitamin C due to losses by heat and water in the can. It is recommended to use the water in other dishes.

White asparagus is the result of planting under a layer of soil which does not allow the sun to reach the asparagus. Fresh asparagus stalks are more fibrous and need to be tenderized by removing a single layer with a potato peeler. Asparagus loses approximately 50% of its vitamin C content within 2 days after picking as well as some of its sugars. Fresh asparagus should be eaten within a day of purchase.

When choosing asparagus the stalks should be green with compact, closed tips and tender. Avoid flat stalks or stalks that contain white streaks. Never purchase them if they are being stored in water. The best time of year to purchase asparagus is March through June.

Refrigeration will help to retain the nutrients providing you cut a small piece off the ends, wrap the ends in moist paper towel and seal them in a plastic bag.

» ASPARAGUS LOSES SUGAR?

 Fresh asparagus loses sugar very rapidly and each day it is stored in a plastic bag in the refrigerator it will lose about 10-15% of its natural sugar. As the natural sugars are lost the asparagus will also become tougher. The tips should be kept as dry as possible or they will become mushy and fall apart when they are cooked. To tenderize the stalks, just use your potato peeler and remove the first layer of the stalk. To freeze asparagus remove the last 2 inches of the stalk then blanch in boiling water for 2-4 minutes depending on the thickness of the stalks. If you steam, blanch then add 1 minute. Tray freeze before placing into a plastic bag to retain the tips in good condition.

» ASPARAGUS, A FOUL ODOR, BEETS ARE COLORFUL
Asparagus contains a sulfur compound that is converted during the digestive process into a foul smelling sulfur compound. When some people urinate after eating asparagus their urine may have a foul smell. Almost 40% of all people that eat asparagus have this problem caused by a specific gene that causes the harmless reaction. Beets contain a pigment called "betacyanin" which will harmlessly turn the urine and feces red. Only 15% of the population have the problem of not being able to metabolize this substance.

» MALE & FEMALE ASPARAGUS STALKS?
The male asparagus flower has a stamen that will produce a spore. The female asparagus flower has a pistil, or ovary. The male asparagus stalks are thinner, while the female stalks are fatter. The darker the color of asparagus, the more tender, the greener or the whiter the better.

» TOPSY TURVY
Asparagus is usually canned upside down, it would be wise to read the top of the can before opening.

» CHOP, CHOP
If the asparagus is overcooked, try cutting the asparagus into small pieces and adding the asparagus to a can of creamed soup.

» THIS WILL STRAIGHTEN THEM OUT
Asparagus that has become limp can be revived by placing them in ice cold water with ice cubes for 30-45 minutes.

To improve the taste of asparagus, try adding a bouillon cube or a small amount of soy sauce to the cooking water.

REPORTED HEALTH BENEFITS
The juice has been used to break up oxalic acid crystals in the kidneys. It has also been used for arthritis.

BEANS (Edible Pods)

This type of bean is picked before they are fully ripe and as the inner seed (bean) is just starting to form. These immature seeds contain a higher level of beta-carotene and vitamin C. The dried seeds are high in protein and carbohydrate.

Beans may be green, purple or yellow and should have no scars or discolorizations. When broken they should have a crisp snap. They are available all year round, but are best May through August. Refrigerate whole and unprocessed beans to retain their nutrient content. Never leave beans soaking in water.

» LEGUMES, A PAIN IN THE ABDOMEN?

Almost all legumes, including beans, peas, and lentils (fresh or dried) contain a toxin called a "lectin" which is capable of causing abdominal pain, nausea, diarrhea, and severe indigestion. To destroy this toxin, legumes must be cooked at a rolling boil for 10 minutes before lowering the heat to a simmer. Peas and lentils only need to boil for 2-3 minutes to kill the toxin.

» CHILI-MAKING, ITS BEAN A SECRET

The first aim is to soften the bean and turn it into mush, without it falling apart. The cell wall needs to be weakened and the starch granules need to be gelatinized. Initially, beans are soaked in water containing 1-2 teaspoons of fennel seed and ½ teaspoon of baking soda for 3-4 hours. This will soften the bean and allow the fennel seed to neutralize the complex sugars that causes flatulence. The beans are then cooked in boiling water with another ½ teaspoon of baking soda added until they are tender but not overly mushy. The texture of the bean will remain more stable if the cooking is performed in a somewhat alkaline solution instead of an acidic one. This is why you add the baking soda to the cooking water. Chili sauce is too acidic a solution for the bean until it is fully cooked since it will not soften any further in an acidic environment. Many cooks try to save time by relying on the acidic chili sauce to complete the cooking of the bean and end up with hard beans.

» ROASTED BEANS

Only two legumes are commonly roasted, soybeans and peanuts. This is because of their high oil content which compensates for their dryness. When roasted both legumes tend to change flavor and texture. The low water content and the high temperature used for roasting is responsible for the browning of the outer coating. Unless you desire a very hard bean after it is roasted it is best to partially cook the bean first. This will partially gelatinize the starch making it more crisp than hard as a rock. Beans are similar to nuts when it comes to roasting and they should be roasted slowly at 250° F. (121°C.) to avoid burning the surface before the insides are done.

» COMMON BEANS

The following list provides information that was released by the USDA's Western Laboratory in Berkeley, California. The list of beans is in the order of those that produce the most gas, or are higher in the sugar that causes the problem, to the beans that are lower, rated on a scale of 1-10.

Soybeans	10 (mask required)
Pea Beans	9
Black Beans	8.5
Pinto Beans	8.5
California Small White Beans	8
Great Northern Beans	7
Lima Beans	6.5
Garbanzos (chick-peas)	6
Black-Eyed Peas	5 (livable)

» GOODBYE TO FLATULENCE

When it comes to eating beans many of us have a problem with flatulence (gas). The gas is produced by the fermentation of the complex sugar oligosacchaide found in beans and some other vegetables, such as cabbage and broccoli. The small intestine does not have the proper enzyme to break this sugar down and it passes into the large intestine where bacteria break it down and unfortunately ferment the sugar producing hydrogen, methane, and carbon dioxide gases.

However, when you are in a Mexican restaurant eating refried or black beans you don't stand a chance unless you consume an equal amount of rice. Rice has the ability to neutralize the gas in the beans. We found this out in Mexico when we asked a restaurant owner why no one ever seems to have a gas problem in Mexico when they consume large quantities of beans daily, we were told about the rice and have tried it with perfect success everytime.

The problem of flatulence was studied when it became a problem for pilots since the gas expands, the higher the altitude, and can cause pain and discomfort. At 35,000 feet the gas will expand to 5.4 times more than at sea level. Almost 50% of the gas is nitrogen with about 40% being carbon dioxide produced by aerobic bacteria in the intestinal tract. The remains are a combination of methane, hydrogen sulfide, hydrogen, ammonia, and the really bad odor makers, the indoles and skatoles. In the late 1960's astronauts had to be selected who would not produce large amounts of gas. The two beans that cause the most problems were found to be Navy and Lima beans with Pinto beans coming in a close third.

BEAN VARIETIES (Edible Pod)

» CHINESE LONG BEANS
Mild-tasting, long, thin beans. These can be as long as 18" and have been called the "yard-long" bean. Best when young and tender.

» HARICOTS VERTS
A slender variety of a snap bean developed originally in France.

» ITALIAN GREEN BEANS
Also known as Romano beans. Have a broad, flat, bright green pod and are a popular frozen bean.

» PURPLE WAX BEAN
Has a dark purple pod that changes color to green when cooked. Looks similar to a small yellow wax bean.

» SCARLET RUNNER BEAN
Pods are broad and flat, the pod is green and the seeds are a reddish color. The blossom is also edible.

» SNAP BEANS
Have tender, crisp pods that will easily snap in half. The ends are usually just "snapped off" instead of cutting them. These are the familiar green beans or yellow wax beans. Formerly known as "string beans." The string has been bred out from the inside and their name has been changed.

» Cooked beans have a refrigerator life of approximately 5 days. If you boil the beans whole without even removing the ends you will retain 50% more of the nutrients. If you place a very small amount of sugar in the cooking water of beans it will bring out the flavor. baking soda should never be added to green beans while they are being cooked as it will reduce the nutrient content of the beans.

» Acidic foods such as tomatoes will cause the color of green beans to be lightened.

» BEANS (Shell)
These are actually mature fresh seeds that are between the fresh seeds and dried seeds. Shell beans have a higher level of vitamins and dried beans are higher in protein, potassium and iron.

REPORTED HEALTH BENEFITS
Have been used for hemorrhoids and anemia.

BEAN VARIETIES (Shell)

» CRANBERRY BEAN
Identified by their red markings on the white pods as well as the actual bean.

» FAVA BEAN
Similar to Lima beans in taste and texture. Has been called "broad bean" but the pods are longer than Lima beans. A popular favorite in salads.

» LIMA BEAN
The most common shell bean in the United States. Originated in Peru. Almost all of the domestic crop goes for canning or freezing. They are very perishable and should be used as soon as purchased. If you add a small amount of sugar to the cooking water it will help bring out the flavor.

» POISONOUS LIMA BEANS?
Lima beans tend to produce an enzyme called "cyanogen" which is a form of cyanide. Some countries have laws that restrict certain varieties of Lima beans from being grown. European and American farmers have developed new breeds of Lima beans that do not produce as much of the toxin and are safer to eat. These potentially harmful toxins may be removed by boiling the beans in a pot without a lid allowing the hydrogen cyanide gas to escape with the steam. Neither raw Lima beans or their sprouts should be eaten raw.

» SOYBEANS
Usually sold as a dried bean, however, they are more popular in the orient as a fresh bean. They have a high protein content and a mild flavor. Soybeans contain a complete protein which makes it equivalent to animal products in relation to the quality of the protein.

» SOYBEANS, GETTING POPULAR
Soybeans are now the single largest cash crop in the United States producing more protein products and oil than any other source. The soybean originated in China and was popularized by the Buddhists who were vegetarians. They became popular in the United States after Commodore Matthew Perry's expeditions brought back two varieties in 1854 from the Far East. The bean has a high protein content of 40% and an oil content of 20% and was originally used in paints, soaps, and varnishes. It was not used in foods due to an off-flavor until the process of hydrogenation was invented which

placed water into the soybean making it more acceptable as a food product. The first use in the food industry was in margarine to replace butter during World War II.

A FEW OF THE MORE COMMON SOY PRODUCTS

» TOFU HOW IS BEAN CURD, AKA TOFU MADE?
Tofu is prepared by boiling soybeans in water then grinding the beans into a paste and adding calcium sulfate to coagulate the curd, making it a better source of calcium than raw soybeans. However, most Japanese and Chinese tofu is made without the addition of the calcium sulfate, instead they use an acid such as lemon juice or vinegar. The proteins in bean curd is 90% digestible which is close to milk. The curds are compressed into blocks then stored in water under refrigeration or vacuum-packed. If you purchase unpackaged tofu be sure and change the water it is stored in daily. Low-fat tofu is now being sold. If this is done tofu will last for 3-5 days from the "sell date" and possibly 2 weeks if it is very fresh when purchased. If you are going to freeze tofu then it should be frozen as soon as it purchased in its original water and container. It can be frozen for about 2 months at 0°F. (-17.8°C.). After it is thawed it will, however, be a little bit more fragile and will disintegrate unless added to disheS just before serving.

» TEMPEH
Made from whole cooked soybeans that are infused with a starter bacteria then allowed to ferment. This produces a product that is very dense and chewy with a nutty flavor. Can be fried, grilled, or used for veggie burgers. Because of the fermentation process, it contains one of the only vegetable sources of vitamin B_{12}.

» MISO
This is a fermented soybean paste. It is high in protein, isoflavones, and antioxidants. Has a high sodium content. Used more as a condiment and flavoring agent.

» SOY MILK
Extracted from soybeans and consumed by people who have an allergy to cow's milk. Usually, found supplemented with vitamin D and B_{12}. Commonly found flavored with chocolate.

» TEXTURED SOY PROTEIN (TSP)
Made from compressing soy flour. Excellent source of calcium and because of its consistency is used as a replacement for hamburger meat in many recipes. Try replacing 30-50% of your ground beef with TSP next time you make a meatloaf.

» Shell beans should have a bulge and a tightly closed pod. If the pods are sealed, they should last for 2-3 days. When they are cooked, add a small amount of baking soda to the cooking water to help stabilize their color.

» Gas-free Lima beans are now being grown, They will contain less of the hard-to-digest complex sugar that causes the problem.

REPORTED HEALTH BENEFITS
Lima beans are very rich in iron and have been used to treat anemia. Soybeans have been given to athletes because of their high quality protein.

» BEANS
Pinto beans are a dried bean that is an excellent source of protein. They should have a bright uniform color, fading is a sign of aging or long storage periods. When preparing pinto beans, try and purchase ones of uniform size, the smaller ones may become mushy before the larger ones are cooked. If you feel that this may be a problem, try adding a small amount of baking soda to the water while they are cooking.

» STORING DRIED LEGUMES
If legumes are kept in a dry, cool location below 70°F. (21.1°C.) they will last for up to 1 year and retain most of their nutrient content. They may be stored in their original bag or container or transferred to a sealed glass jar. Never mix old beans with new beans as they will not cook evenly. It is not necessary to freeze dried beans, it will not help to retain their nutrient content any longer. Beans in cooked dishes may be frozen, however, they may be somewhat mushy when thawed but can last for up to 6 months. Pinto beans contain about 22% protein while beef has only 18%, and eggs 13%.

» BEAN OVERBOARD
When you are cooking dried beans, make sure you add 3 teaspoons of a pure vegetable oil to the water, this will help prevent boilovers.

» COOKING TIPS
To tell whether a bean is fully cooked squeeze the bean, you should never feel a hard core. If you are cooking the beans in an acid medium, such as with tomatoes, this will slow down the cooking time and testing the tenderness of the beans is a must. The taste of beans can be improved by adding a small amount of brown sugar or molasses.

» BEAN COOKING TIME VS. LOSS OF NUTRIENTS
Many people worry about the loss of nutrients due to the long

cooking and soaking times for beans and other legumes. Studies performed by the USDA, however, have proved that legumes, even if they require 1-1 ½ hours of cooking time will still retain from 70-90 percent of their vitamin content and almost 95 percent of their mineral content. The most affected were the B vitamins of which about 45-50 percent were lost.

» LINING THEM UP

Beans rank as one of the best vegetable sources of protein, first is kidney beans, followed by navy beans, Lima beans, lentils, chickpeas, and split peas.

Bean Cooking Chart		
Bean	**Pre-Soak**	**Cooking Time**
Adzuka Beans	yes	1 hour
Black Beans	yes	1 - 2 hours
Black-eyed Peas	no	1 - 1½ hours
Chick Peas(garbanzos)	yes	2½ - 3 hours
Great White Beans	yes	1½ - 2 hours
Kidney Beans	yes	1½ - 2 hours
Lentils	no	30 - 40 min.
Lima Beans	yes	1 hour
Mung Beans	no	45 min. - 1 hour
Navy Beans	yes	1 - 1½ hours
Split Peas	no	1 - 1½ hours
Pinto Beans	yes	1½ - 2 hours
Soy Beans	yes	3+ hours

BEETS

Beets have the highest sugar content of any vegetable, however, they are low in calories and are an excellent source of vitamins and minerals. Both the roots and the leaves are edible. Beets are a relative of spinach. It is best to buy only small or medium-sized beets, the larger beets are not very tender and may have a stronger flavor. Never purchase beets if they look shriveled or flabby, they should be firm.

Beet greens should be used as soon as purchased and the roots within 5-7 days. Beets should be cooked whole and unpeeled to retain their nutrients. Beets contain the chemical pigment "betacyanin" which gives the beets their red color. Some people cannot metabolize this pigment and it turns their feces and urine red for a few days, however, it is harmless. When preparing any dish that contains beets, be sure and add the beets last. Beets will lose some of their color and color the other foods red.

» BETTER BEETWARE
Betacyanin "beet red" is difficult to remove from your hands and disposable rubber gloves are recommended when working with beets.

» SWEET BEET
Sugar beets are 20% sucrose by weight and have twice the sugar content of standard beets. It takes 100 pounds of sugar beets to produce 5 pounds of sugar.

» OFF WITH THEIR TOPS
As with any vegetable with a leaf top, the leaf top should be removed when they are purchased and stored. The leaf top will leach moisture from the root or bulb and shorten their shelf life.

> REPORTED HEALTH BENEFITS
> Used to relieve headaches and toothaches. Two pounds of raw mashed beets consumed daily have been used for tumors and leukemia. Beet greens have a higher iron content than spinach and have been used to treat anemia.

BROCCOLI

A member of the "cruciferous" family of vegetables which also include cabbage and Brussels sprouts. It was first grown in United States in the 1920's and is one of the more nutritious vegetables. They will have a higher nutrient content if eaten fresh.

Broccoli is available year round and is best from October through May. The stem should not be too thick and the leaves should not be wilted. If the buds are open or yellow the broccoli is old and will have a significant loss of nutrients. The florets should be closed and should be a good solid green color, they contain 8 times the beta-carotene as the stalks.

One cup of broccoli contains 90% of the USRDA of vitamin A, 200% of vitamin C, 6% of niacin, 10% of calcium, 10% of thiamin, 10% of phosphorus, and 8% of iron. It also provide 25% of your daily fiber needs and even has 5 grams of protein.

Broccoli should be washed in a good organic cleaner since the EPA has registered more than 50 pesticides that can be used on broccoli. Seventy percent of these cannot be detected by the FDA after harvesting. In a recent study it was reported that 13% of broccoli still retained pesticide residues even after initial processing. Organic broccoli would be an excellent choice or consume in moderation.

Broccoli consumption has risen over 50% since 1983 to 23 servings per person in 1997. Cooked broccoli still contains 15% more vitamin C than an orange.

Broccoli should be cooked as quickly as possible to retain its green color. Broccoli's color is also very sensitive to acidic foods.

» STORING BROCCOLI

Broccoli should be stored in a plastic bag in the refrigerator. It will keep for only 3-5 days before the florets start opening and a loss of nutrients occur. To freeze broccoli, the leaves need to be removed and the stalks peeled. The broccoli should be cut into small lengthwise strips and blanched for 5 minutes, chilled and drained well then placed in a sealed plastic bag. May be frozen for 10-12 months at 0° F. (-17.8°C.)

A recent study at the University of Kentucky compared the vitamin C content of whole broccoli and plastic wrapped broccoli. Broccoli that was left out in the air lost 30% of its vitamin C content in four days while the broccoli that was wrapped in plastic only lost 17% and retained its color better. The respiration rate of the broccoli was slowed down conserving the nutrients.

» WHY IS IT THE LONGER I COOK BROCCOLI, THE WORSE IT SMELLS?

Broccoli as well as Brussels sprouts contains the natural chemical called mustard oil "isocyanates." This chemical, when heated breaks down into a foul smelling sulfur compound, hydrogen sulfide and ammonia. In fact, you should never cook these vegetables in an aluminum pot or the reaction will cause an even more intense smell. The longer you cook the vegetables, the more chemicals are released and the smellier the kitchen. Cook them for as short a time as possible. If you keep a lid on the pot and place a piece of fresh bread on the top of the broccoli or Brussels sprouts while they are cooking, the bread will absorb some of the odor, then discard the bread.

> REPORTED HEALTH BENEFITS
> Used for constipation, to reduce high blood pressure and as a digestive aid.

BROCCOFLOWER

A cross between broccoli and cauliflower and looks more like a cauliflower with a light green color. It has a milder flavor than either of its relatives. Make sure that the florets are tightly closed for maximum nutritional content.

BRUSSELS SPROUTS

This vegetable was named after the capital of Belgium, where it originated. A relative of the cabbage family, it even resembles small heads of cabbage. They were brought to America in the 1800's from England and were first grown in Louisiana. They are an excellent source of protein, but not a complete protein unless you eat them with a grain.

They are easily overcooked and will become mushy. Best to store them in the refrigerator to keep the leaves a green color instead of yellow.

> » X MARKS THE SPOT
> If you cut an "X" on the stalk end of each Brussels sprout with a sharp knife before cooking them, the sprout will retain its shape and not fall apart. The small opening will allow the steam to be released through the bottom instead of being forced through the leaves.

REPORTED HEALTH BENEFITS
Used as a general tonic for blood cleansing, constipation and to reduce hardening of the arteries.

CABBAGE

Originated in the eastern Mediterranean region and was popular among the ancient Greeks. It is available year round in three main varieties; red, green, and savoy which has crinkly leaves. Avoid cabbage with worm holes and be sure to smell the core for sweetness. Green and red cabbage should have firm tight leaves with good color, Cabbage should be refrigerated in plastic bags and used within 7-14 days.

Cabbage along with its other cruciferous family members are being studied in cancer prevention due to its "indole" content. Initial studies indicate that if you consume ½ of a standard cabbage daily you may prevent a number of cancers.

When you need cabbage leaves for stuffed cabbage, try freezing the whole cabbage first, then let it thaw, and the leaves will come apart without tearing.

Cabbage will last longer if stored in the refrigerator sealed tightly in a plastic bag. It should stay for about 2 weeks.

Flatulence problems from cabbage can be eliminated by boiling the cabbage for about 5-6 minutes then draining the water and continuing to boil it in fresh water. The chemical that causes the problem is released during the first few minutes of cooking.

If you are preparing a recipe that calls for cabbage wedges, try steaming them instead of boiling them, they will retain their shape better.

» SAUERKRAUT TO THE RESCUE
Sauerkraut was popularized by Genghis Khan when his marauding hordes brought the recipe back from China. The recipe found its way throughout Europe and to Germany where the cabbage was fermented with salt instead of wine and given the name of "sauerkraut." However, sauerkraut became a real hero in 1772 when Captain James Cook who had heard of the possible health properties of sauerkraut decided to bring 25,000 pounds of it on his second journey to explore the Pacific Ocean. Since sauerkraut has vitamin C he only lost one sailor to scurvy in over 1,000 days at sea. The sauerkraut supply lasted one year without going bad.

CABBAGE VARIETIES

» BOK CHOY
Looks like a cross between celery and Swiss chard. When cooked bok choy will have a slightly sharp flavor, but the stalks are rarely bitter. They contain an excellent amount of calcium and vitamin A.

» GREEN
Has smooth, dark to pale outer leaves, while the inner leaves are pale green or white.

» NAPA
Has a more delicate flavor than most cabbages. Is high in vitamins and minerals.

» RED
Has a solid red to purple outer leaf, usually with white veins or streaks on the inside leaves.

» SAVOY
Has a crinkled, ruffled yellow-green leaf and is less compact than most cabbage.

REPORTED HEALTH BENEFITS
Used for asthma, blood cleansing, healthier hair and nails, bladder disorders and skin irritations.

CARROTS

Carrots are the best source of beta-carotene of any vegetable. Studies show that carrots may lower blood cholesterol levels, however, drinking an excessive amount of carrot juice may turn your skin orange due to high level of carotenoid pigment. Reducing the intake will alleviate this color problem.

They are available year round and should have smooth skin, a solid orange color and be well-formed. Should be stored in the refrigerator and never placed in water for any period of time, especially if peeled.

If carrots are to used in a stir-fry, try boiling them first, then place them in cold water until needed. It takes longer to cook the carrots since they are so solid. To slip the skin off carrots, drop them in boiling water, let stand for 5 minutes, then place them into cold water for a few seconds.

To curl carrots, peel slices with a potato peeler and drop them into a bowl of ice water. When grating carrots, leave a portion of the green top on to use as a handle. This will keep your fingers from becoming shorter.

» WHY SOAK CELERY AND CARROTS?
A number of vegetables tend to lose their moisture before you are able to use them up and become limp. There is no need to discard them when all you have to do is immerse them in a bowl of ice cubes and water for 1 hour in the refrigerator. The cells will absorb the water, return to their normal size, thus making the vegetable hard and crisp again. Soaking fresh vegetables for long periods of time, however, may have the opposite effect because of excess water buildup in the spaces between the cells.

» WHY IS THE BETA CAROTENE INCREASING IN CARROTS?
According to the USDA scientists have been improving carrots to such a degree that they presently have twice the beta carotene level as they did in 1950. By the year 2000 the beta carotene level is expected to double again thanks to genetic research.

» OFF WITH THEIR TOPS
Carrots and beets need to have their tops removed before they are stored. The tops will draw moisture from the vegetable, cause them to become bitter, and reduce their storage life, however, leave about two inches of the root if it is still there to keep the bottom sealed. Carrots and beets need to be stored in a sealed plastic bag in the refrigerator. Both are very susceptible to a number of microbes that will cause them to decay. Carrots will freeze well with only minimal blanching, beets should be boiled until they are fork tender before freezing.

» PURPLE CARROTS?
Originally, carrots were purple until the early 17th century when the orange color variety was developed in England. The beta-carotene levels were not always as high as they are today. Carrots were originally grown to have a higher level of beta-carotene to help the World War II British aviators acquire better night vision. The iron

supply in carrots is also absorbed more efficiently than most other vegetable sources.

» CARROTS, EASIER TO DIGEST WHEN COOKED
Carrots are not affected to any great extent by heat and cooking, therefore there is almost no loss of the vitamin A content. Carrots will retain their color, which is the result of the chemical carotene. When carrots are cooked a percentage of the hemicellulose (fiber) will become softer making the carrot more easily digestible and allowing the digestive juices to reach inside the cells and release the nutrients for easier utilization by the body.

» GOING FOR A PHYSICAL? DON'T EAT CARROTS
Your physician needs to be advised if you consume a large amount of carrots. Your skin may have a yellow tinge due to the excess amount of carotenoids you are consuming and the physician may think you have jaundice. Another concern is if you are asked to take a guiac test for occult blood in your feces. The active ingredient in the guiac slide is alphaguaiaconic acid which turns blue in the presence of blood. Carrots contain the enzyme peroxidase which also turns blue when combined with alphaguaiaconic acid, and gives you a false-positive test showing that you have blood in your feces.

» FRESH YOUNG ONES ARE BEST
A good rule to remember when purchasing vegetables for freezing is to purchase "young ones." The nutrient content will be higher and they will contain less starch. Freeze as soon as purchased. Remember, fresh produce has stronger cell walls and will handle freezing better.

» VERY NUTRITIOUS
Carrot greens are high in vitamin K and E which are lacking in the carrot.

» COOKING SLIGHTLY HELPS EVEN MORE
The USDA has completed studies showing that 7 ounces of carrots consumed every day for 3 weeks lowered cholesterol levels by 11%. This was probably due to calcium pectate, a type of fiber found in carrots and usually lost during the juicing process.

REPORTED HEALTH BENEFITS
Carrot juice has been used for the treatment of asthma, insomnia, colitis, improving eyesight, and healthy hair and nails. It is also an excellent antioxidant.

CAULIFLOWER

Another member of the cruciferous family, it has a very compact head and grows on a single stalk. It is surrounded by green leaves which protect it from the sun and cause the cauliflower to remain white instead of producing chlorophyll.

It is best purchased September through January, but is available year round. Do not purchase if the clusters are open or if there is a speckled surface, this is a sign of insect injury, mold, or rot. Should be stored in the refrigerator, unwrapped.

Cauliflower can be kept white during cooking by just adding a small amount of lemon or lemon peel to the water. Overcooking tends to darken cauliflower and make it tough. To reduce the odor when cooking cauliflower, replace the water after it has cooked for 5-7 minutes. Due to certain minerals found in cauliflower it is best not to cook it in an aluminum or iron pot, Contact with these metals will turn cauliflower yellow, brown or blue-green.

» STORING CAULIFLOWER

One of the most important things to remember is never bump or injure the florets. This will cause the head to loosen and spread too fast and cause discoloration. Store the head in a plastic bag that is not wrapped too tight around the head and store it in the vegetable crisper. Never wash the cauliflower before it is stored and it should keep for 4-6 days. Wash the head thoroughly before eating since a number of chemicals are often used to preserve their freshness. To freeze, just cut the cauliflower into small pieces, wash in lightly cold salted water, then blanch in salt water for 5 minutes. Drain and chill them before placing them into a plastic bag.

> REPORTED HEALTH BENEFITS
> Used as a blood cleanser and for kidney and bladder disorders.
> Also, in some cases of asthma, gout, and high blood pressure.

CELERY

Arrived in United States from Europe in the 1800's. Celery has a very high water content and is low in calories. It is available year round, Stalks should be solid, with no hint of softness along any of the stalks which will denote a pithiness. If even one stalk is wilted, do not purchase. Celery will only store in the refrigerator for 7-10 days and should not be placed in water.

Don't discard the celery leaves; dry them, then rub the leaves through a sieve turning them into a powder that can be used to flavor soups, stews, and salad dressings. This can also be made into celery salt.

Celery, carrots and lettuce will crisp up quickly if placed into a pan of cold water with a few slices of raw potatoe. To prevent celery from turning brown, soak in lemon juice and cold water before refrigerating for only a few minutes.

» CELERY STRINGS
Celery is easy to cook, the pectin in the cells will easily break down in water. However, the "strings" which are made of cellulose and lignin are virtually indestructible and will not break down under normal cooking conditions. The body even has a difficult time breaking them down and many people cannot digest them at all. Best to use a potato peeler and remove the strings before using the celery. When preparing stuffed celery stalks for a party, always be sure and remove the strings.

» HOW DID CELERY TURN INTO A SWIZZLE STICK?
Placing a stalk of celery into a Bloody Mary and using it as a swizzle stick came about in the 1960's when a celebrity (who wishes to remain anonymous) needed something to stir his drink with and grabbed a stalk of celery from a nearby relish tray in a restaurant at the Ambassador East Hotel in Chicago. Celery was first grown in the United States in Kalamazoo, Michigan in 1874 and to popularize celery it was given to train passengers free. Presently, 2 billion pounds are grown annually.

» MEDICAL CONCERNS WITH CELERY?
Celery contains the chemical "limonene" which is an essential oil and known to cause contact dermatitis in susceptible individuals. This chemical is also found in other foods such as; dill, caraway seeds, and the peelings of lemons and limes. Photosensitivity has also been a problem with workers who handle celery on a daily basis unless they wear gloves. The chemical that is responsible for this problem is "furocoumarin psoralens" and increase contact may make your skin sensitive to light.

REPORTED HEALTH BENEFITS
The juice has been used as a tonic to reduce stress. Other uses include; asthma, diabetes, as a diuretic, and to reduce the incidence of gall stones.

CELERIAC
An edible root vegetable that resembles a turnip and may be prepared like any other root vegetable. It has an ivory interior and has a strong celery taste with a dash of parsley. Celeriac should be firm and have a

minimum of rootlets and knobs. Excellent in salads and can be shredded like carrots.

CELTUCE

A hybrid of celery and lettuce, it does not have a high nutritional content and is prepared similar to cabbage.

CORN

Corn was first grown in Mexico or Central America and was an early staple of the American Indian. Corn is a good source of protein and can be part of a complete protein by serving it with rice. When ground for tortillas, an excellent amount of niacin is released. Corn contains 5-6% sugar making it a taste favorite. Americans consume about 25 pounds of corn per person annually.

It is available May through September and the kernels should be a good yellow color. Do not purchase if the husks are a straw color, they should be green. The straw color indicates decay or worm infestation. Yellow corn usually has a more appealing flavor than white and is higher in vitamin A content.

The easiest method of removing kernels from an ear of corn is to slide a shoehorn or spoon down the ear. The best tasting corn is grown in Florida and is known as "Florida Sweet."

» WHY DOES CORN OCCASIONALLY TURN RUBBERY?
When corn is cooked the protein goes through a chemical change called "denaturization" which simply means that the chains of amino acids (proteins) are broken apart and reformed into a network of protein molecules that squeeze the moisture out of the kernel turning the corn rubbery. The heat also causes the starch granules to absorb water and swell up and rupture the kernel, thereby releasing the nutrients. Corn should be cooked just long enough to cause the kernels to barely rupture which allows the protein to remain tender and not tough. When corn is boiled in water 50% of the vitamin C is destroyed, however, if you cook it in a microwave without water almost all of the vitamin C is retained. Worldwide there are 200 varieties of corn. However, corn ranks as a vegetable low on the overall nutritional scale.

» DON'T STORE CORN
Corn is one vegetable that is always better if eaten when it is fresh, preferably the same day you purchase it. As soon as corn is picked it immediately starts to convert the sugars to starch. The milky liquid in the kernel that makes corn sweet will turn pulpy and bland in only

2-3 days. This is the reason that many people add sugar to the water when cooking corn. This guarantees the taste which was probably lost during just a few days storage. Leftover fresh corn should be cooked for a few minutes just to inactivate the enzymes and store the ears in a sealed plastic bag for 1-2 days before using.

If you plan on freezing corn it needs to be cleaned and blanched for 4 minutes in boiling water. First allow the water to drain, tray freeze, keeping room between the ears so that the kernels will retain their shape and not be crushed, then seal in plastic bags. Frozen corn will freeze for 1 year.

» WELL FANCY THAT
When wrapping corn in tin foil for barbecuing, try placing a sprig of marjoram next to each ear of corn.

» CORN SMARTS
If you plan on storing corn, always keep it in a cool, dry location and try not to place the ears touching each other to avoid mold. Remember as corn warms up the sugar tends to convert into starch very quickly. In fact, when corn is piled high in bins in the market and is allowed to stand for days, the bottom ones will be less sweet due to the heat generated by the weight of the ones on top.

» COOKING CORN?
Steaming corn for 6-10 minutes is one of the preferred cooking methods. To store corn longer, cut a small piece off the stalk end, leave the leaves on, then store the ears in a pot with about an inch of water, stems down.

» ALMOST NO NUTRITIONAL VALUE
The color of a corn or potato chip will not affect the calories or fat content. However, if the label reads baked it will probably be a lower fat product.

» CORN FACT
Cornmeal may be purchased in two varieties; steel-ground which has the husk and germ almost all removed, and stone or water-ground which retains a portion of the hull and germ and is usually only available in health food stores.

» CORNSTARCH, THE IDEAL THICKENER
Cornstarch is a thick, powdery flour that is made from the corn's endosperm. It is an excellent thickener for sauces but tends to form lumps easily unless it is mixed slowly into a cold liquid and then added to a hot liquid. Stir the cornstarch until it mixes thoroughly then boil it for a few minutes to thicken the sauce or

stew. When you are thickening a stew or soup, be sure and remove as much fat as possible before adding the cornstarch.

» FRESH CORN, THE BEST CORN
If you want to taste the sweetest corn ever, then it needs to be as fresh as possible, no more than 1-2 days at the most from the farm to you. The sugar in corn will start converting to starch as soon as the corn is picked reducing its sweetness. When you heat the corn it also speeds up the sugar conversion. Refrigeration will slow the process down. Salt should never be placed in the water when cooking corn since it will toughen the kernels, since table salt contains traces of calcium. Salt in the water will also toughen almost all types of legumes.

» KERNEL CORN
Choosing fresh corn can be a difficult task unless you have some "corn knowledge." If the corn still has its husk it will be necessary to peel back a small area and examine the kernels. The kernels should be packed tightly together with no gaps between the rows. Gaps between rows mean that the ear is overmature. If the tip has no kernels the corn was picked too soon and not allowed to mature. The kernels should always be plump and juicy and should spurt a milky, starchy, liquid. If the center of the kernel is sinking inward it is drying out and will not be as sweet. Always purchase corn with the smaller kernels at the tip of an ear of corn, larger kernels are usually a sign of over maturity.

POPCORN FACTS

» WHAT MAKES POPCORN POP?
When the popcorn kernel is heated, the moisture inside turns to steam and as the pressure builds it has to vent and bursts the kernel. The explosion forms a fluffy white starch. Normal corn will not explode because it does not have as high a moisture content as special popcorn. As soon as the popcorn is popped it is best to open the bag or remove the lid as soon as possible to avoid the popcorn absorbing the steam and becoming soggy. Popcorn should always be stored in a well sealed container so that it will retain as much of its moisture as possible.

» CALLING ROTO-ROOTER, HELP!
Popcorn is composed of a complex carbohydrate (starch), and includes insoluble fiber (cellulose), which may help prevent constipation. It is always best, however, to drink plenty of fluids when consuming any large amount of insoluble fiber. Insoluble fiber tends to absorb water from the intestinal tract and will add bulk. The

only risk that might exist would be if you ate a large tub of popcorn without drinking any liquids, then you may have a major traffic jam.

» WISING UP
The 1997 annual popcorn consumption in the United States was about 50 quarts of popcorn per person. In 1994 this figure dropped to about 40 quarts after the information that the high saturated fat coconut oil was being used to pop the corn. One quart of popcorn (a small bag) equals the calories in just 7 large potato chips.

» ON WITH THE SHOW
Movies switched to Canola oil and by 1995 popcorn consumption was back to its original level. Using Canola oil did not change the fat content, just gave us a healthier oil.

» PROBABLY NEEDED SALT AND BUTTER
The first recorded popcorn event in history was by the Aztecs. However, they used it for decoration instead of eating it.

» PASS THE POPCORN TENDERIZER?
It may be healthier to air pop your popcorn, however, all this does is make larger blossoms that are tougher and not as crispy.

» SAVING AN OLD MAID
Old maids are kernels of corn that are too pooped to pop. These kernels usually have lost sufficient moisture and can be revived by just placing a handful of them into a sealed container with 1-2 tablespoons of water, then shake for at least 3-4 minutes. The container should then be placed in a cool (not cold) location for about 3 days. This should revive them and you should have no problem popping them.

» TOO BAD, YUPPIES
Nutritionally regular popcorn and gourmet popcorn are equals. The only difference is that gourmet popcorn pops into larger blossoms.

REPORTED HEALTH BENEFITS
Used for anemia and constipation.

CUCUMBERS

Originated in Asia, cucumbers were brought to the Americas by Columbus. They are grown in all sizes from the smallest 1" gherkins to as large as 20" long. They have a very high water content and are an excellent source of fiber. The Greenhouse or English cucumber is becoming more and more popular, however, the price of this thin-skinned, skinny "cuke" is considerably higher than the standard market cucumber.

Cucumbers should be firm and a good green color, either dark or light, but not yellow. Purchase only firm cucumbers and refrigerate. Large thick ones tend to be pithy and will give when squeezed. Cucumbers only have 13 calories per 3 ½ ounce serving due to their high water content.

» CUCUMBER, BITTERNESS REMOVER
This fact really surprised me, and I thought it was just another old wives tale again, one that had been passed down through the years and really didn't work. To my surprise it actually worked. Next time you purchase a standard cucumber, not the long, skinny English variety, cut about one inch off the end and then rub the two exposed areas together in a circular motion while occasionally pulling them apart. This will cause enough suction to release a substance that causes some cucumbers to have a bitter taste. Then discard the small end you used to release the bitterness.

» WHY ARE CUCUMBERS WAXED?
Cucumbers tend to shrink during shipping and storage. The wax coating is to prevent the shrinkage and is edible. The skin should never be removed until you are ready to eat the cucumber or it will lose most of its vitamin C content. The cucumber is capable of holding 30 times its weight in water and is a member of the "gourd family." If you can remember back to the 1930's "cucumber" was a slang word for a one dollar bill.

» DO CUCUMBERS SWEETEN AFTER THEY ARE PICKED?
Cucumbers do not contain any starch therefore they are unable to produce sugar to sweeten them. They will, however, get softer as they age and absorb more moisture into the pectin. If the cucumber gets too soft, just soak the slices in lightly salted cold water to crisp them up. The reaction that occurs removes the unsalted, lower-density water from the cells and replaces it with the higher-density salted water.

» HOW DOES A PICKLE GET PICKLED?
It all starts with a fresh cucumber arriving at the pickle factory. There are three processes to control their fermentation. The first is a type of processing that begins with the "curing stage", where the cucumbers are stored for up to 3 years in large tanks filled with a salt-brine mixture. Next they are washed and placed in a vat of fresh water,

then heated to remove any excess salt residues. After being cleaned and heated they are packed in a final "liquor" solution which turns them into the dark green color we are used to purchasing.

The second type of processing is for "fresh pack" pickles which eliminates the holding tanks and speeds the cucumbers into a flavored "brine" or "syrup" then immediately into pasteurization. The pickles emerge less salty than the cured pickles and are a lighter green in color.

The third method of processing is done totally under refrigeration. These special pickles are known as "deli dills." They are cleaned and graded and proceed right to the flavored brine without any further stages. They are never cooked or pasteurized and remain very cucumberlike in flavor and texture. These pickles are always found in the refrigerated section of the market and must be stored under refrigeration.

Sour pickles are completed in a solution of vinegar and special spices. Sweet pickles are just sour pickles that have been drained of all traces of brine and bathed in a mixture of vinegar, sugar, and spices. The most popular being the small gherkins.

» PICKLED CALORIES
Pickled dill cucumbers have 3 calories per ounce compared to sweet pickles at 30 calories per ounce.

» GETTING PICKLED
When making pickles, remove 1/4 inch from each end. The ends contain an enzyme that may cause the pickles to soften prematurely.

» ARE YOUR CUCUMBERS GASPING FOR AIR
Cucumbers should be stored unwashed in a plastic bag with holes to allow air to circulate around the cucumber or should be placed in the vegetable drawer if your refrigerator has one. Cucumbers will only keep for 3-5 days and do best in the warmest part of the refrigerator around 40°F. (4.4°C.). Cucumbers do not freeze well because of their high water content, too many cells tend to burst making the cucumber mushy.

» Pickle juice should be saved and used for making coleslaw, potato salad, etc.

» GRANDMOTHER'S TRICK
If you add a small piece of horseradish to the pickle jar, it will keep the vinegar active while keeping the pickles from becoming soft.

> REPORTED HEALTH BENEFITS
> Used as a natural diuretic and to help lower high blood
> pressure. Cucumbers contain the enzyme "erepsin" which aids
> in the digestion of proteins.

EGGPLANT

Eggplant is a member of the "nightshade" family of vegetables which
also include potatoes, tomatoes, and peppers. It is not very high on the
nutrient scale and varieties include: Chinese purple eggplant, globular
eggplant, Japanese eggplant and Italian eggplant. Eggplant contains the
chemical "solanine" which is destroyed when it is cooked. It is best
never to eat raw eggplant.

» EGGPLANT BITTER? SALT IT
Since eggplants will only last a few days even under refrigeration it is
best to use them the same day or no later than the next day after they
are purchased. Eggplants tend to be a bit bitter and the easiest method
of eliminating this problem is to slice the eggplant in ½ inch slices,
then lightly salt the slices and allow them to drain on a wire rack for
30 minutes. This will also reduce the amount of oil that is absorbed
when frying.

Eggplant is available year round but are best during August and
September. Their outer purple-black skin should be smooth and
glossy, free of scars and they should be firm. Soft eggplants are
usually bitter. Keep them cool after purchase and use in 2-3 days.

» WHY IS EGGPLANT ALWAYS SERVED IN A PUDDLE OF OIL?
The cells in a fresh eggplant have a very high air content that will
escape when the eggplant is heated. When you cook an eggplant in
oil the air escapes and the cells absorb a large quantity of oil. As the
cells fill up with oil and as the eggplant is moved about they
eventually collapse and release the oil. Eggplants in a recent study
absorbed more fat when fried than any other vegetable, 83 grams in
70 seconds - four times more than an equal portion of French fries,
thus adding 700 calories to the low-calorie eggplant. Eggplant
parmigiana is always served in a pool of olive oil for this reason.
Eggplant should never be cooked in an aluminum pot, this will cause
the eggplant to become discolored.

> REPORTED HEALTH BENEFITS
> Used for constipation, colitis, and various nervous disorders.

FENNEL

Fennel is a member of the parsley family and looks like a very plump bunch of celery. Fennel tastes like "anise" and has a sweet flavor. It is very low in calories, can easily be substituted for celery, and is high in vitamin A, calcium and potassium.

The bulbs should be firm and clean with fresh-looking leaves. If any brown spots are seen, avoid the fennel. It tends to dry out quickly and should be wrapped and used within 3-4 days.

HORSERADISH

Horseradish is usually available year round and stores very well. Make sure that you purchase only firm roots with no signs of soft spots or withering. If tightly wrapped in a plastic bag it should last up to 3 weeks in the refrigerator. If not used in 3-4 weeks it may turn bitter and lose its hot bite.

Try mixing a small amount of horseradish with applesauce as a unique condiment when serving pork.

JERUSALEM ARTICHOKES

These are members of the sunflower family and also known as the "sunchoke." Do not buy them if they are tinged with green or have any soft spots. They should be firm and look fresh. They will stay fresh under refrigeration for about a week and are easily peeled with a vegetable peeler, however, they do contain a fair amount of nutrition in the skin.

It has a somewhat nutty, sweet flavor, and should be crunchy. It can be boiled, sauteed, or even breaded and fried.

JICAMA

Originated in Mexico and is becoming very popular in the United States. It is a root vegetable that can weigh up to 5 pounds or more. The skin is brown and the flesh is white. It can be used in salads either diced or in small sticks. Choose only unblemished jicama with no soft spots. Excellent for stir-fries. Excellent source of vitamin C.

It has a slightly sweet flavor and can be substituted for potatoes. One pound equals about 3 cups. The texture is similar to a water chestnut.

LEEKS

Leeks are a close relative of the onion family, but are milder and sweeter. They are more nutritious, having a wide variety of vitamins and minerals. They are best purchased between September and November. The tops should be green with white necks 2-3 inches from the roots. Do not purchase if tops are wilted or if there appears to be signs of aging. Refrigerate and use within 5-7 days after purchase.

LETTUCE

Lettuce can be traced back to Roman days and was originally named for the Romans (Romaine). Lettuce is second only to potatoes in popularity in the United States. It is mainly used in salads and as garnish.

It is available year round and should be heavy and solid, depending on the variety. The greener the leaves the higher the nutrient content. Never add salt to lettuce prior to serving as this may cause the lettuce to wilt.

» THE GOOD AND THE BAD
Americans consume approximately 11 pounds of lettuce per person, per year. Romaine lettuce has 6 times as much vitamin C and 8 times as much vitamin A as iceberg lettuce.

» LETTUCE SCRUB
Over 60 chemical agents can be applied to lettuce. Most can be removed by washing with a good organic cleaner or by placing the head stem side up in a sink with 6-8 inches of cold, lightly salted water for a minute while shaking and swirling it around.

» OUCH, OUCH
Before you store your lettuce you should remove the core by hitting the core once against a hard surface, then twist the core out.

» SALAD DRESSING SOAKS INTO LETTUCE, WHY WON'T WATER?
Lettuce leaves as well as many plants have a waxy cuticle, which is a water-repelling mixture of various chemicals that are all related to repelling water and assisting the leaves from becoming waterlogged. This cuticle also protects the leaves from losing too much of their internal moisture. The oils in salad dressing are related to the chemicals that keep the water out and to at least allow the oils to stick to the surface. Water molecules also tend to bead up and fall off the leaf, while the oil spreads out and coats the surface.

» TO TEAR IT OR TO CUT IT
Recently, I watched two different cooking shows on television and watched one chefs tear the lettuce and the other cut the lettuce with a knife. The chef who tore the lettuce mentioned that tearing it would

extend the life of the lettuce before it would turn brown. After trying this, I found out that it makes no difference at all whether you tear or cut lettuce. It will brown and oxidize in the same amount of time.

» STORING LETTUCE
All types of lettuce love the cold and the closer the temperature gets to 32°F. (0°C.) without going below that, the longer it will last and the crispier the lettuce will be. Most refrigerators range between 35°-40°F. (1.7°-4.4°C.) which is good, but not the ideal temperature for lettuce. The lettuce should be stored without washing in a sealed plastic bag with a small hole or two for ventilation. Lettuce will turn brown easily if allowed to remain near most other fruits or vegetables due to the level of ethylene gas given off by most fruits and vegetables. Iceberg lettuce will remain fresher than any other type of lettuce due to its higher water content and will store for 7-14 days, romaine lasts for 6-10 days, and butterhead for only 3-4 days. If you need to crisp lettuce leaves, place them in the freezer for no more than 2-3 minutes, any more and you may have to discard them.

LETTUCE VARIETIES

» BUTTERHEAD
Has a soft "buttery" texture and a is a "loose" head lettuce. Also, known as Boston or bibb lettuce. The leaves are a dark green to grass-colored green.

» ICEBERG
This is the most popular and extensively sold in the United States. It is the least nutritious lettuce of all the green vegetables except Belgium endive which has an even higher high water content. Best to choose any other lettuce.

» LOOSELEAF
The leaves are loosely packed and joined at the stem. The leaves are usually green with a tinge of red near the edges. It is a crisp lettuce with a mild and delicate flavor.

» ROMAINE
Has long green leaves and is usually very crisp. It is mainly used in Caesar salads. Romaine lettuce has 6 times as much vitamin C and 8 times as much vitamin A as iceberg lettuce.

» STEM
Has a thick edible stem, approximately 6-8 inches long. Widely grown in China. The United States grown variety has been called Celtuce. It has a mild flavor.

» ARUGULA
A solid green lettuce with a high beta-carotene and vitamin C content. Has small flat leaves on long stems and resembles dandelion greens with a somewhat peppery flavor. A cruciferous vegetable which may be studied regarding cancer prevention.

» BELGIUM ENDIVE
Related to chicory and escarole. Has a bullet-like head with tightly closed creamy white or somewhat yellow leaves. Low in vitamins and minerals, even lower than iceberg lettuce.

» CHICORY
Has loosely bunched ragged leaves on a long stem. The outer leaves are dark green and it has a somewhat bitter taste. The center leaves, however, are yellow and have a mild taste.

» ESCAROLE
Has broad wavy leaves with smooth edges and a bitter flavor.

» MACHE
Has a delicate green colored leaf, is very perishable, and more expensive than most lettuce. The leaves have a fingerlike shape with a mild taste and mache is only sold in small bunches.

» RADICCHIO
A chicory-family member that looks like a small head of red cabbage with leaves in a variety of colors.

» WATERCRESS
Another member of the cruciferous family with dark green leaves and a mustardlike flavor. More popular as a garnish than for use in salads.

» THROW THE LETTUCE IN THE WASHING MACHINE
Greens need to be thoroughly washed before using them in a salad and they are not always as dry as they should be if you are in a hurry to prepare the salad. When this happens, just put the greens in a clean pillowcase and place them in the washing machine on the fast spin cycle for no more than 2 minutes.

REPORTED HEALTH BENEFITS
The cruciferous lettuce varieties are being studied in cancer prevention. Endive has been used in cases of asthma, gout, high blood pressure, arthritis and liver ailments.

MUSHROOMS

Mushrooms can be traced back to the Egyptian pharaohs. They are an excellent source of nutrients and are a fungus without any roots or leaves. There are approximately 38,000 varieties of mushrooms, many toxic, and a few varieties that are edible. It is best never to pick and eat a wild mushroom.

Mushrooms contain the chemical substance "hydrazine," which is found mainly in the stems. Cooking tends to neutralize this chemical, therefore mushrooms should be cooked. However, most of the "hydrazine" is found in the stems. Studies from the University of Nebraska showed that mice developed malignant tumors from ingesting large quantities of mushrooms. Never eat the stems of raw mushrooms.

They are available year round but are best November through March. Be sure that the caps are closed around the stem and refrigerate soon after purchasing. Mushrooms can be kept white and firm when sauteing if you just add a teaspoon of lemon juice to each quarter pound of butter or ½ cup of olive oil.

» MUSHROOMS NEED ROOM TO BREATHE
Fresh mushrooms have a very short shelf life of only 2-3 days and need to be stored in an open container in the refrigerator. Plastic containers should never be used since they tend to retain moisture. Best to use the original container or a paper product to store them in. Never clean them before storing them, they will retain moisture and become soggy. If you need to keep them stored for a few days place a piece of single-layer cheesecloth on top of the container. If they do become shriveled, they can be sliced and used in dishes. When freezing mushrooms, just wipe them off with a piece of damp paper towel, slice them, saute them in a small amount of butter until they are almost done, allow them to cool, then place them in an airtight plastic bag and freeze. They should keep for 1 year.

» THE FLAVOR OF MUSHROOMS, MSG?
The unique flavor of fresh mushrooms are caused by glutamic acid, the natural version of the same flavor enhancer used in the flavor enhancer, Monosodium Glutamate (MSG). Mushrooms, however, do not have any sodium.

MUSHROOM VARIETIES

» BUTTON
The standard mushroom that is widely cultivated throughout the world. A large majority of the production goes into jars and is canned and dried. They are a short, stubby mushroom with a round cap and gills on the underneath side. Sizes can vary from 1-10 inches.

» CEPE
Has a stout stem and a spongy surface, instead of gills on the underneath side it has a solid brown cap. It is also known as the

Bolete, Cep and Porcino mushroom. They range in size from 1-10 inches and are one of the best tasting mushrooms.

» CHANTERELLE

These are shaped like trumpets. They are large with frilly caps and range in color from gold to yellow-orange.

» ENOKI

These are sproutlike and have very small caps on a long thin stem. Their color is a creamy white and they have a mild flavor. Best served raw in salads or soups and are sometimes called "enokitake" mushrooms.

» ITALIAN BROWN

These are less expensive mushrooms and are similar in appearance to the standard button mushroom. They have a good flavor and are not as tender as button mushrooms.

» KOMBUCHA

Also known as Japanese tea fungus. Claims have been made recently that it is a cure-all for numerous diseases and recommended for the prevention of hair-loss, arthritis, psoriasis, and cancer. According to recent information from the FDA, scientific evidence is lacking. Cornell University is studying the mushroom and has found it to have properties that may have an anti-tumor effect.

A West African study showed that the tea caused organ damage in rats. A report from the Iowa Department of Public Health stated that two women who drank the tea for several weeks suffered from acidosis.

Never use ceramic or lead crystal for storing this tea, its high acidic nature may leach the lead out.

» MOREL

These are one of the more high-priced mushrooms, They are a dark brown mushroom with conical shaped, spongy caps. They also have a honey-combed surface.

» OYSTER

A wild variety, ranging in color from off-white to a gray-brown, they grow in clusters and have a very dense chewy texture. More flavorful when cooked.

» PORTOBELLO

Also known as Roma mushrooms, they have a hearty flavor, circular caps and long, thick stems. Cut off the woody part.

» SHIITAKE

At one time these were only grown in Japan, but are now grown and are available in the United States. They are grown on artificial logs and are umbrella-shaped, and brown-black in color. They have a rich flavor and are excellent in salads. They may also be called: golden oak, forest, oriental black, or Chinese black mushrooms. Remove stems.

» WOOD EAR
May have anti-coagulant properties and health claims are presently showing up in the literature. There are no conclusive studies at present in relation to the avoidance of heart attacks. They are mostly sold dried and have flattened caps that tend to vary in size with a crunchy texture. They have also been known as tree ear, and black tree fungus.

» TRUFFLES
These are fungi that grow underground, and are only found by pigs and trained truffle-seeking dogs. They have excellent flavor, and are a very expensive delicacy. There are two types, the black truffles from France and Italy and the white truffles from Northern Italy.

REPORTED HEALTH BENEFITS
In Japan a chemical compound extracted from shiitake mushrooms has been approved as an anticancer drug. Studies showed that it repressed cancer cell growth.

OKRA

Originated in Ethiopia or North Africa and brought to the United States in the 1700's. has been a Southern favorite and used in many Creole dishes. The taste is a cross between eggplant and asparagus and because of its sticky juice has been mainly used in soups and stews. It is a good source of vitamins and minerals.

Okra pods should always be green and tender and should not be purchased if the pods look dry or shriveled, since they will lack flavor and be tough. Okra tends to spoil rapidly and should be refrigerated soon after purchasing. It is usually best between May and October. Never wash okra until you are ready to use it or the protective coating will be removed that keeps the pods from becoming slimy.

Try grilling okra with a small amount of olive oil brushed on.

» OKRA IS AN EXCELLENT THICKENER
Okra is actually a vegetable that consists of numerous unripe seed capsules. It is a very high carbohydrate food that is high in fiber and starch and contains a good amount of pectin and gums. The combination of these food elements provide an excellent thickener for soups and stews. As okra is heated the starch granules absorb water and increase in size. They soon rupture and release "amylose"

and "amylopectin" molecules as well as some of its gums and pectin. These then attract additional water molecules and increase the volume, thus thickening the food.

> REPORTED HEALTH BENEFITS
> Due to its mucilaginous nature it has been used as a treatment for stomach ulcers.

ONIONS

Probably originated in prehistoric times and was a popular favorite in ancient Egypt and Rome. They are members of a family that has over 500 varieties. They are low in calories and some are an excellent source of vitamin A.

» SOLID AS AN ONION
Onions should only be purchased hard and dry, avoid onions with wet necks, this indicates decay. Also, avoid onions that have sprouted. They can easily be stored at room temperature or refrigerated.

» TOP OF THE ONION TO YOU
If you are only going to need half an onion use the top half, since the root half will store longer in the refrigerator.

» STORING ONIONS
Onions should be stored ideally in hanging bags which will allow the air to circulate around them. Never purchase an onion if it has the slightest hint of decay since it will spread rapidly to healthy onions. The location should be cool and dry. If the weather is hot and humid it will cut the storage time in half otherwise they should last about 2-3 weeks. If you refrigerate onions they will last for about 2 months but may pass their aroma on to other foods in the refrigerator, even eggs. Sprouted onions are still good to use as well as the sprouts. To freeze onions just slice them (do not blanch them) and place them into a sealed plastic bag. They will freeze well for about 1 year.

The smell of onions can be removed with a strong solution of salt water or a small amount of white vinegar.

Chives need to be refrigerated and used within 3-4 days after purchase for the best flavor. If frozen, they can be added to any dish while still frozen. Chives can be stored in the refrigerator wrapped in paper towels in a plastic bag. They should last for about 1 week.

» HOW SWEET IT IS
Vidalia onions are a variety of sweet onion, grown in Georgia and one of the best tasting onions. Sweet onions brown better in the

microwave and most are over 12% sugar. Place 1 cup of sliced onions in an uncovered dish with 2 tablespoons of butter for approximately 15 minutes on high. No need to cover as there should be no splattering and they will not brown if covered. To order Vidalia onions from Bland Farms in Glennville, Georgia, just call (800)843-2542.

» RING MY ONION
When preparing onion rings, make sure you place the onions in the dish as evenly as you can to assure even cooking.

» PITHY TO THROW IT OUT
An onion that has become pithy and has started to sprout should be placed in a pot on a window sill and as it continues to sprout, just snip off pieces of the sprout for salad seasoning.

» COOKING ONIONS AND GARLIC TOGETHER
When sauteing onions and garlic together, be sure and saute the onions first for at least ½ their cooking time. If the garlic is placed in at the same time it will over cook and possibly burn and release a chemical that will make the dish bitter.

» POP GOES THE ONION, INSIDES ONLY
Have you ever cooked a whole onion only to have the insides pop out and ruin the appearance of the dish you are preparing. This is a very common occurrence and happens almost everytime unless you pierce the onion with a thin skewer once or twice allowing the steam to escape. Another method, similar to one that is done to chestnuts so they won't explode, is to cut an "X" on the root end which will allow the steam to be released without damaging the onion.

» SHEDDING A TEAR FOR ONIONS
When you slice into an onion a gas is released that affects the lachrymal glands in the eyes and causes a defensive reaction by the body against the chemical "propanethiol S-oxide" which reacts with the fluid in your eyes forming sulfuric acid. The body protects itself from the acid by tearing action which washes out the eyes ridding itself of the irritant. One of the best methods to avoid tearing is to wear solid plastic goggles.

» Other methods if you prefer not to shed tears is to cut the root off last, freeze the onion for 10 minutes, or refrigerate for 1 hour before slicing. Other tricks that have worked is to ball up a piece of white bread and place it on the tip of the knife to absorb the fumes. Chewing gum may also help.

» COOKING AN ONION
Cooking an onion will actually turn the sulfurs in the onion into

sugars which is why onions tend to have a sweeter flavor after cooking. As onions are browned the sugars and protein change and become a deep brown color and caramelize which also intensify the flavor. The reaction is called the "Maillard Reaction." Onions will also change color when cooked and turn a creamy white color from the chemical "anthocyanin." This chemical should not come into contact with metal ions from aluminum or iron pots or it will turn brown. When onions are sliced with a carbon-steel knife the same reaction takes place and may change the color of the onion.

ONION VARIETIES

» BERMUDA
These are the most common large, white onions. The flavor is somewhat mild and they are commonly used in salads.

» PURPLE ONION
These are usually one of the sweetest and have the strongest flavor. They are commonly found on hamburgers and in salads.

» SPANISH
These are a light brown color, are larger than most onions and is the standard onion for cooking. When cooked it caramelizes easily and is very sweet.

» WHITE
Smaller than most onions, they are usually used in soups, stews, or dishes that are creamed.

REPORTED HEALTH BENEFITS
Used as a diuretic to increase the flow of urine, has laxative effects, and has been used as an antiseptic.

PARSNIPS

Looks like a top heavy ivory-colored carrot. It has a celerylike, nutty flavor. Waterhemlock is occasionally confused with parsnips but is a poisonous root. Parsnips are more easily digested when cooked since they are very fibrous and have strong cell walls.

REPORTED HEALTH BENEFITS
Used for gout and as a diuretic.

PEAS

Peas are actually legumes, plants that are pod-bearing with inner seeds. Green peas are one of the best vegetable sources of protein and have been used as a food source since ancient times. Only 5% of all green peas arrive at the market fresh, almost all are frozen or canned.

Always select pods that are well-filled without bulging. Never purchase flabby, spotted, or yellow pods and refrigerate and use within 1 week. When cooking fresh peas, always add a few washed pods to the water, this will improve the flavor and give the peas a richer green color. If peas are cooked in their pods, the pods will open allowing the peas to rise to the surface, either method is acceptable. When dried peas are placed in water, the good ones will sink to the bottom and the bad ones will float to the top for removal. Snow peas, however, can be served fresh in salads or cooked without removing the pea.

» PEAS ARE BEST WHEN USED IN SOUPS OR STEWS
The difference between fresh green peas and dried split peas is that the dried peas are actually mature seeds and usually have twice as much starch as the fresh peas. Dried peas contain an excellent source of protein. It is best not to soak split peas before using since the water you will discard will contain a good percentage of the B vitamins. When you use the split peas for soups or stews you will normally consume the liquid which will have some of the B vitamins still available.

» THE GREATEST PEAS
If you want the greatest peas and especially black-eyed peas, just call (800)767-PEAS. This will put you in touch with Peas On Earth in Athens, Texas.

REPORTED HEALTH BENEFITS
Peas contain nicotinic acid and may lower cholesterol levels.

PEPPERS

When purchasing peppers, be sure the sides of the pepper are firm. Do not purchase if the colors are dull. Refrigerate and use within 3 days. They are a good source of vitamin A and C, in fact studies have shown that eating hot peppers does not cause stomach ulcers and may even speed the healing process by increasing circulation.

Sweet red peppers contain more vitamin C than an orange. When making stuffed bell peppers, coat the outside of the pepper with vegetable oil and it will retain its color.

» WHY WON'T THE COLOR IN YELLOW
OR RED PEPPERS FADE?
Green peppers contain chlorophyll as the coloring agent which is sensitive to the acids in the pepper and when the pepper is cooked they are released and cause discoloration. Red and yellow peppers

rely on carotenoid pigments for their color. These pigments are not affected by the acids or the heat from cooking.

» RED PEPPERS VS. GREEN PEPPERS
Nutritionally speaking sweet red peppers are superior by quite a bit. They are 11 times higher in beta carotene and have one and a half times more vitamin C than a sweet green pepper. Hot red peppers contain about 14 times more beta carotene and than a hot green pepper, however, the vitamin C content is the same.

» PEPPER PROTECTION
Some of the hotter peppers will cause eye irritation and it is recommended that you wear rubber gloves so that your hands will not touch the pepper and accidentally touch your eyes. Once you get hot pepper juice in your eyes you will remember the experience for some time to come.

Recent studies have shown that New Mexico has one of the lowest incidences of cardiovascular disease. The study stated that chemicals in hot chili peppers may actually lower cholesterol levels and increase blood coagulation time. In New Mexico over 55,000 tons are eaten annually.

Chilies are probably the oldest known spice, having been found in archaeological digs in Mexico that have been dated to 7,000 B.C.

» A MOLE THAT TASTES GOOD
A "mole" is actually a Mexican sauce made from chili peppers and tomatoes. The combination of ingredients, especially the variety of chili pepper, will determine whether the "mole" is spicy or mild. The most popular "mole" is "mole poblano," which is a spicy red sauce that even includes unsweetened chocolate and is served over turkey. Green "mole" is made from green chilies and cilantro.

» INDIAN TEAR GAS
The American Indians burned chili peppers when they were fighting off the invading English. The fumes were so potent the English stayed away.

» THE COLOR AND HOTNESS OF CHILI PEPPERS
The color of chilies is only an indication of the level of ripeness of the vegetable. If the chili is picked before full maturity it will be green and contain more chlorophyll than a red chili that has matured and lost its chlorophyll. The highest concentration of capsaicin (hot-stuff) is located in the white ribs that the seeds are attached to. If you remove the ribs and seeds and wash the insides a few times in cold water, you will eliminate 70-80% of the hotness. When the chili

is then fried or boiled it will lose even more. People that consume chilies frequently are less susceptible to the hot effects and tend to become immune to the bite.

Remember there are two liquids that will neutralize the hot bite, they are whole milk (most dairy products will work) and beer.

» THE HOTTEST OF THE HOT

The hotness of chili peppers is attributed to the chemical "capsaicinoid" which acts directly on the pain receptors in the mucosal lining of the mouth and the throat. A single drop of this pure chemical diluted in 100,000 drops of water will still cause a blister to form on a person's tongue. This chemical is measured in parts per million which are converted into heat units called Scoville units. This is how the degree of hotness of a chili pepper is measured. One part per million of "capsaicinoid" is equal to 15 Scoville units. The hottest known pepper the Habaneros has a 200,000-300,000 Scoville unit rating, next is the Thai piquin at 100,000, the Jalapeno at about 85,000, the Tecpin cayenne at 50,000, the De Arbol at 25,000, the Serrano at 12,000, and the Morita cascabel at 5,000.

» THIS WILL MAKE A CHIHUAHUA STAND ON ITS EAR

Texas Gunpowder, Inc. sells one of the hottest pepper seasonings in the world. If you would like their catalog, just call (800)637-9780.

SWEET PEPPER VARIETIES

» BELL

Sweet bell peppers are available in four colors, green, red, orange or yellow. They are all relatively sweet but each has its own distinctive flavor difference. When the four are mixed in a salad it is a real taste treat. Bell peppers contain a recessive gene which neutralizes capsaicin, which is why they are not spicy.

Bell peppers should be stored in the refrigerator in a plastic bag, they will stay fresh about a week. They can be frozen for 6 months and retain a good amount of their nutrients.

To seed a bell pepper is to hold on to it tight and hit the stem end on the counter hard. This will loosen the seed core and it should pull out easily.

Sweet peppers contain more vitamin C than an orange.

» WELL EXCUSE ME

If you find that you "burp" too much after eating bell peppers, try peeling the skin off before you use them.

» BANANA Mild yellow peppers resembling bananas and available fresh or pickled.

» CUBANELLE
Long tapered pepper about 4 inches long. Sold in either green or yellow.

» PIMENTO
Heart-shaped peppers which are generally sold in jars are usually found in gourmet markets.

HOT PEPPER VARIETIES

» ANAHEIM
One of the most common chilies with a mild to moderately hot bite. Consumed in either the green or red stages of growth. Often found in long string of red peppers. Used for chili rellanos.

» ANCHO
Dried peppers that are flat, wrinkled and usually heart-shaped. Mild to moderately hot and usually ground and used in sauces and salsa.

» CASCABEL
Moderately hot red chili with seeds that tend to rattle. When dried their skin turns a brownish-red.

» CAYENNE
These are one of the hottest chilies, They are long with sharply pointed, curled tips and usually dried and made into a spice for chili and salsa.

» CHERRY
Shaped like a cherry and range from mild to moderately hot; either sold fresh or commonly found in jars.

» HABANERO
Lantern-shaped peppers which grow to about 2-3 inches. Their color is yellow-orange and it is the hottest pepper grown. They are known for extending their bite for some time, best to have milk handy for this one.

» HUNGARIAN WAX
Moderately hot yellow-orange pepper. May be purchased fresh or pickled.

» JALAPENO
One of the most common peppers. They are usually moderately hot to very hot and are sold at their green stage. The red stage which is full maturity is super hot. Canned jalapenos are usually milder because the seeds are removed and they are packed in liquid.

» SERRANO
A popular chili in Mexico. They look like a small torpedo and are very hot.

RADISHES

Originated in China thousands of years ago. They are a cruciferous vegetable and contain phytochemicals that are under investigation relating to cancer prevention. Their green tops are edible and tend to have a peppery flavor. Radishes are a good source of vitamin C.

They are available year round. Larger radishes tend to be somewhat pithy while smaller ones are usually more solid. Squeeze to be sure they are not mushy and don't buy if the tops are yellow or if there is any sign of decay.

A number of varieties are sold, these include California Mammoth Whites, Daikons, Red Globe, and White Icicles.

REPORTED HEALTH BENEFITS
Used as an appetite stimulant, to relieve nervousness, constipation, and to dissolve gallstones.

SALISIFY

This odd-shaped plant has also been called the "oyster plant" since their appearance is similar to an oyster. The plant's blossoms always close at high noon and it is also known as the "Johnny go to bed at noon" plant.

SPINACH

Was first grown in the United States in the 1700's. It is high in vitamins and minerals as well as being one of the best vegetable sources of protein. Spinach, however, does contain the chemical "oxalate" which tends to bind with certain minerals such as calcium and limits their usefulness by the body.

» THE EYE IN POPEYE
Spinach contains two special antioxidants that belong to the carotenoid family; lutein and zeaxanthin. These antioxidants in recent studies have proving to be important in an age-related disease of the eye known as "macular degeneration." This form of

blindness is prevalent in people over 65 and is the leading cause of blindness. Experts believe that overexposure to sunlight, pollution, and smog over a period of years may contribute to this problem. Consuming foods that are high in these carotenoids such as kale, collard greens, spinach, sweet red peppers, mustard greens, and hot chili peppers may significantly lower the risk by as much as 75%.

» COLOR ME GREEN
A trick to keeping the nice green color in spinach used by chefs is to cook spinach with the pot uncovered. The buildup of too much steam will cause the chemicals that create the color to lose their ability to maintain the dark green.

» SHOULD SPINACH BE EATEN RAW?
While most vegetables should be eaten raw, especially to retain their enzymes, spinach has a tough cellular wall that will only release the maximum amount of nutrients if it is cooked. Carrots are actually better cooked as well for the same reason. Our digestive system cannot break these two vegetables down sufficiently to gain the most from them. Cook in as little water as possible and for the shortest period of time. In fact, boiling in one cup of water instead of two cups will help the spinach retain twice as much of its nutrients.

» STORING POPEYE'S FAVORITE
Spinach will only store for 2-3 days providing it is stored in a sealed plastic bag. Do not wash it or cut it before you are ready to serve it. When purchasing spinach that has been prepackaged, be sure and open the bag and remove any brown or darkened leaves since they may cause the balance of the leaves to deteriorate at a faster rate. When freezing spinach, do not freeze the stems, only the whole leaves. This will allow the leaf to retain more of its moisture. To store spinach for a longer period it should be washed in cold water, dried carefully and thoroughly with paper towel and stored in the freezer in an airtight bag. It should keep for 10-12 months if the freezer is kept at 0° F. (-17.8°C.).

REPORTED HEALTH BENEFITS
Used for anemia, tumors, arthritis, high blood pressure, and bronchitis.

SPROUTS

When seeds are moistened they change into edible sprouts or shoots. When this occurs the seed utilizes its carbohydrates and fat and leaves a good percentage of its vitamins intact, making sprouts a healthy food. Their nutrient content, while preserved is not appreciably high compared to most mature vegetables, however, they are healthy and a pleasant departure from the standard vegetables.

» LITTLE SPROUTS
When purchasing fresh sprouts, remember that they can only be stored in the refrigerator for 7-10 days providing they are left in their original container, refrigerated, and placed in a plastic bag and should be lightly moistened before putting them into the bag and sealed. Too much water in the bag will cause decay. Remember the shorter the tendril the more tender and younger the sprout. Sprouts cannot be frozen successfully, they become mushy and bland.

COMMON SPROUT VARIETIES

» ADZUKI BEAN
Very sweet, small-bean shaped with grasslike sprouts. has a nutty taste.

» ALFALFA
Threadlike white sprouts that have small green tops and a mild nutty flavor.

» CLOVER
Looks similar to the alfalfa sprout, with tiny seeds that look like poppy seeds.

» DAIKON RADISH
Have a silky stem and leafy top. The taste is somewhat peppery and spicy hot.

» MUNG BEAN
These are larger than the alfalfa sprouts and have a blander taste. They are thick white sprouts and used in many oriental dishes.

» SOYBEAN
Sprouts have a somewhat strong flavor but a good source of protein. They contain a small amount of a toxin and large amounts should be avoided. Cooking for at least 5 minutes tends to neutralize the toxin.

» SUNFLOWER
Crunchier than alfalfa and has a milder flavor.

SQUASH

Squash is a fleshy vegetable with a solid protective rind. It has been a staple vegetable for thousands of years. They are a low calorie food and contain an excellent level of vitamins and minerals which vary depending on the variety. It is available year round. The soft-skinned types should be smooth and glossy. The hard-shelled type should have a firm rind. Refrigerate all soft-skinned varieties and use within a few days.

Summer squash varieties include: chayote, patty pan, yellow crookneck, yellow straightneck and zucchini. Winter squash varieties include: acorn, banana, buttercup, butternut, calabaza, delicata, golden nugget, hubbard, spaghetti, sweet dumpling, turan and pumpkin. The winter squash varieties tend to develop a higher beta-carotene (precursor for vitamin A) content after being stored than it has immediately after being picked. Also, the smaller the squash, the more flavor it tends to develop.

Squash blossoms are edible and have an excellent flavor. They make a great garnish for many dishes and can even be battered and fried. Try stuffing them with cream cheese for a real treat.

When pureeing squash the strings should be easy to remove when you are using the blender. The strings will entwine around the blades and can easily be removed.

» WHAT IS THE NEW Freedom II SQUASH?
The Asgrow Company of Michigan has developed a new strain of squash called the "Freedom II" squash that is resistant to viruses transmitted by aphids. This is expected to make squash more available and lower the prices due to less pesticide use. The company is also developing virus-resistant cantaloupe, watermelon, and cucumbers.

» "A" WINNER
One of the best sources of vitamin A and beta carotene is the pumpkin. An 8 ounce, 40 calorie serving contains about 27,000IU.

» JACK-O-LANTERN MIRACLE
One of the biggest problems every Halloween is that the pumpkin will get soft and mushy a few hours after it has been carved. The problem is the result of the air coming in contact with inside flesh, thus allowing bacteria to grow at a rapid pace. Spraying the inside of the pumpkin with an antiseptic spray will retard the bacterial growth and reduce the time of deterioration. Make sure you do not eat the pumpkin or the seeds after it has been sprayed.

> REPORTED HEALTH BENEFITS
> Zucchini has been used in cases of high blood pressure.

TOMATILLOS

These look like small green tomatoes but with a thin parchment-like skin. They are also called Mexican green tomatoes and they have a somewhat lemon-apple flavor. They are popular in salads and salsas. Purchase only firm tomatillos. They are usually available year round.

TOMATOES

The question of whether the tomato is a fruit or a vegetable was settled by the Supreme Court in 1893 when it was officially declared a vegetable. Botanically, it is still a fruit, actually a berry. It is a member of the nightshade family making it a relative of potatoes, bell peppers, and eggplant. It is available year round and should be well formed and free of blemishes. Green tomatoes will eventually turn red, but will not have a good flavor. A vine-ripened tomato is best. Refrigerate, but do not allow to freeze.

To peel tomatoes easily, place them in boiling water and remove from heat, allow to stand for 1 minute then plunge them into cold water. Tomatoes will store longer if you store them stem down. Never allow tomatoes to ripen in direct sunlight, they will lose most of their vitamin C.

Americans consume approximately 24 pounds of tomatoes per person, per year. If you are expecting a frost and have tomatoes on the vine, pull them up by the roots and hang them upside down in a cool basement until the fruit ripens. Green tomatoes will ripen faster if you store them with apples.

» TOMATO AROMA ONLY LASTS FOR THREE MINUTES?
If you like the aroma of fresh tomatoes in your salad don't refrigerate them. Tomatoes should be left at room temperature if they are going to be used within 2-3 days after purchase. They should never be sliced or peeled until just before you are going to serve them. The aroma is produced by the chemical z-3-hexenal which is released when the tomato is sliced open. The aroma chemical only lasts at the "maximum aroma" level for three minutes before it starts to lose its scent. If you do refrigerate a tomato the chemical becomes dormant, but if you allow it to return to room temperature before you slice it the aroma will still be active.

If the storage temperature is below 50°F. (10°C.) it will interfere with the ripening process and stop it cold. Even if the tomato does turn from green to red it will still not be ripe.

» HOW DO YOU REDUCE ACIDITY IN TOMATO PRODUCTS?
Some people are unable to eat spaghetti sauces and other tomato based foods due to their higher acidic content. When chopped carrots are added to any of these dishes it will reduce the acidity without affecting the taste. The high fiber content of the carrot seems to do the job.

» THE BEST DRIED FRUIT AND TOMATOES, ANYWHERE
The finest, all natural fruits and tomatoes can be found at Timber Crest Farms in Healdsburg, California. All products are unsulfured and packaged without any preservatives or additives. The farm is owned by Ron and Ruthie Waltenspiel who have ben producing the finest quality products for 32 years. Almost all the products are grown on their ranch with most being grown under strict organic regulations of the California Health and Safety Code. This one of the cleanest operations of its kind I have ever had the privilege of visiting. To order or receive a catalog call (707)433-8251 or write to Timber Crest Farms 4791 Dry Creek Road, Healdsburg, California 95448.

» WHAT IS A DESIGNER LABEL TOMATO?
A new tomato is making an appearance in supermarkets everywhere called the "FlavrSavr." This is a genetically engineered tomato that can be shipped vine-ripened without rotting and is the first whole food to be born of biotechnology. Most tomatoes are shipped green and gassed with ethylene gas to turn them red before they get to the market. The only downside is that the new tomato will cost about $2.00 per pound.

» AYE CHIHUAHUA
Salsa has replaced ketchup as the top selling condiment in the United States. A new product due out in 1998 will be a salsa/ketchup combination.

» PUREE CONCENTRATE
One ounce of tomato puree has twice the vitamin C and 20% more beta-carotene than one ounce of fresh tomato.

» KA BOOM, KA BOOM
Never place a whole tomato in the microwave, it will explode.

REPORTED HEALTH BENEFITS
Tomatoes have been used as a natural antiseptic and may protect against infection. It has been used to improve skin tone and as a blood cleanser.

TURNIPS
Turnips are related to cabbage, grow easily, even in poor soil conditions and are a good source of complex carbohydrates. It is a cruciferous vegetable and can weigh up to 50 pounds. Turnips are a better source of fiber than an apple. I'd rather eat an apple.

WATER CHESTNUTS

Chestnuts are actually grown underground and are the tip of a tuber. They are the carbohydrate storage depot for the plant's growth. They must be kept cool or they will sprout and are an excellent source of trace minerals, especially potassium. Also, they contain vitamin C.

X MARKS THE SPOT

Always remember to cut an "X" before you place chestnuts in the oven for roasting. If you don't, you may hear a small explosion. This also makes them easier to peel.

THE 900 CALORIE SALAD

Amount	Food	Calories
1 cup	Lettuce	9
½	Medium Tomato	16
½ cup	Cottage Cheese	120
4	Cucumber Slices	5
½ cup	Mixed Beans	60
¼ cup	Macaroni Salad	90
2 small ladles	Salad Dressing	230
¼ cup	Cheddar Cheese	116
2	Black Olives	40
2	Hot Peppers	5
$\frac{1}{10}$ cup	Sunflower Seeds	75
$\frac{1}{10}$ cup	Croutons	50

FRUITS AND VEGETABLES

Carbohydrate Content Analysis		
Very Low	Low	Medium
Asparagus	Beets	Artichokes
Bean Sprouts	Brussels Sprouts	Kidney
Beet Greens	Carrots	Parsnips
Broccoli	Chives	Peas (green)
Cabbage	Collards	Apples
Cauliflower	Dandelion Greens	Cherries
Celery	Eggplant	Grapes
Chard, Swiss	Kale	Olives
Chicory	Kohlrabi	Pears
Cucumber	Leeks	Pineapple

Carbohydrate Content Analysis		
Very Low	**Low**	**Medium**
Endive	Okra	Mango
Escarole	Onions	Blueberries
Lettuce	Parsley	Mushrooms
Peppers (green)	Mustard Greens	Pumpkin
Radishes	String Beans	Spinach
Rutabagas	Tomatoes	Turnips
Cantaloupe	Apricots	Strawberries
Cranberries	Watermelon	Oranges
High		**Very High**
Corn	Lima Beans	Rice
Dried Beans	Pickles (sweet)	Potato (sweet)
Avocado	Bananas	Yams
Figs	Prunes	
Raisins		

COMPLIMENTING COMBINATIONS

Certain vegetables go better with each other and will compliment the taste of the others when mixed together. Some of the tasty combinationas are: Brussels sprouts + peas + onions, green beans + carrots + mini-onions, peas + corn + zucchini, parsnips + peas + corn, celery + corn + peas.

THE BEST IN ORGANICS

One of the best quality organic farms in the United States is the Diamond Organics in Freedom, CA. Most of the fruits and vegetables are picked when ordered and shipped immediately. To get your catalog call (800)922-2396.

GETTING LOW ON WATER?

When cooking vegetables in a pot of hot water, always add as hot a water as you can if the water level gets too low. Adding cold water may affect the cell wall and cause the vegetable to become tough.

CHAPTER 5

All About Potatoes

POTATOES (SWEET)

They are usually only available around Thanksgiving, however, yams are available year round. Sweet potato skins are normally a light copper color while yams are more reddish. They should not be purchased if they have any soft spots, visible mold, or white areas. Sweet potatoes and yams tend to decay faster than white potatoes due to their high sugar content.

Yams originated in Asia and are a close relative to the sweet potato but are less sweet and contain 10-20% less nutrients. Sweet potatoes have 10 calories per ounce less than yams.

» THE SWEET NATURE OF SWEET POTATOES
Sweet potatoes cook somewhat different than regular white potatoes in that they tend to become sweeter the more you cook them. A percentage of the starch in a sweet potato converts to sugar when the potato is heated. The cells in a sweet potato are not as strong as those in a white potato and when it is boiled it will easily absorb water and swell up.

» YAM-A-DABA-DO
The best way to tell the difference between sweet potatoes and yams is to look at the flesh which should be orange in a sweet potato and reddish in a yam. Supermarkets commonly label yams as sweet potatoes.

» Sweet potatoes contain the same number of calories as white potatoes, however, they contain more vitamin C and 3 times the beta-carotene.

» The best sweet potato is called a "boniato" or "Cuban" sweet potato and has a very light yellow flesh.

» DROP THEM SKINS
To peel a sweet potato easily, take them from the boiling water and immediately immerse them in a bowl of ice cold water for about 20-30 seconds. The skins should almost fall off by themselves.

» SPUD STORAGE
Sweet potatoes, yams, and white potatoes are actually an enlarged stem called a "tuber" that extends from the plant underground and is the storage depot for the plants excess carbohydrates. The potato plant bears a vegetable similar to a small mini tomato and is not that good to eat. If potatoes are stored below 40° F.(4.4°C.), they tend to release more sugar and turn sweet. Potatoes will last longer and remain solid longer if they are stored in a cool, dry location, preferably at 45°-50°F. (7.2°-10°C.). Air must be allowed to circulate around potatoes, moisture will cause them to decay. Potatoes do not freeze well, since a large majority of the cells tend to burst causing the potato to become mushy and watery when thawed. Commercially processed potatoes will freeze.

» HOW SWEET IT IS
Sweet potatoes unlike white potatoes will freeze without becoming mushy if fully cooked, either boiled or baked. They need to be placed in a well sealed plastic container and as much air as possible bled out. The container then needs to be placed into a large sealed plastic bag. They will keep for 10-12 months.

POTATOES (WHITE)

White potatoes originated in South America and were introduced to Europe in the 16th century. They are one of the most nutritious vegetables and a member of the "nightshade" family.

Americans consume approximately 125 pounds of potatoes per person annually with the United States producing 35 billion pounds per year. In the last 30 years Americans have reduced their consumption of fresh potatoes by 40%.

» BAKED POTATO, MAY NOT BE A GOOD CHOICE
Carl's Jr. has outdone itself by serving the worst baked potato in the United States. Carl's Jr. Bacon and Cheese baked potato has 730 calories and 43 grams of fat, 15 of which is saturated. A Burger King Whopper would be better with 630 calories and 39 grams of fat, 11 of which is saturated. Not that either is a very healthy meal. If you want a good baked potato have a Rax Cheese-Broccoli at only 280 calories and zero fat.

» WHO INVENTED POTATO CHIPS?
In the summer of 1853 a Native American by the name of George Crum was the chief chef at the Moon Lake Lodge in Saratoga Springs, New York. A guest who had ordered French fries complained that they were too thick. Chef Crum sliced up another batch of potatoes, somewhat thinner and served them, only to have them rejected again. The chef who was very upset decided to slice the potatoes paper thin to get even. The guest was delighted with the thin potatoes, they became a hit, and the trademark of the restaurant and were called "Saratoga Chips." In 1997 the Frito-Lay Company used 7 million pounds of potatoes a day, in 35 plants to keep us supplied with potato chips.

» HOT POTATO, BAKED POTATO
When baking a potato, many people tend to wrap the potato in aluminum foil thinking that it will speed up the cooking time. After trying to bake potatoes a number of different ways to see which method was the fastest, I was surprised to find that by oiling the skin with vegetable oil, the skin reached a higher temperature faster and baked the potato in a shorted period of time than when it was wrapped in aluminum foil. The only method that did speed up the cooking time was inserting an aluminum nail or scewer into the center of the potato, thereby transferring heat inside.

» I KNOW WHERE THE YELLOW WENT....
If you would like a richer color to your potato salad, try adding a small amount of yellow food coloring when you are mixing it. Mustard will also work.

» HIDE AND SEEK
Potatoes should be stored at room temperature in a dark area and not refrigerated. Refrigeration tends to turn potato starch to sugar. However, if the potato is removed from the refrigerator and left at room temperature the sugar will convert back to starch.

POTATO VARIETIES

There are many varieties of potatoes such as the Russets, White Rose, Red Pontiac, Katahdin, and Finnish Yellow. The most popular is the Russet which is mainly grown in Idaho and may weigh up to a pound or more.

STAYING FRESH LONGER

» It is best to purchase potatoes in bulk bins and not in bags. It is too difficult to determine which ones are bruised. If ginger root is stored with potatoes it will help them stay fresh longer. If half an apple is stored with potatoes it will stop the sprouting by absorbing any moisture before the potato does.

POTATO FACTS

To boil potatoes in less time, remove a small strip of skin from one side. After they are cooked the balance of the skin will be more easily removed. To keep peeled potatoes white, place them in a bowl of cold water, add a few drops of white vinegar then refrigerate. White potatoes should have a small amount of sugar added to the cooking water which will revive a percentage of the lost flavor. Potatoes prefer to be stored in pantyhose. Just cut a leg off and drop the potatoes in, then hang it up in a cool, dry location.

OLD POTATO, NEW POTATO, BEST POTATO?

A new potato will have more moisture than an old potato, however, both can be used for different dishes. A new potato should be used for dishes such as potato salad since they will absorb less water when boiled and less mayonnaise when prepared, thus adding less fat to the dish. They are stronger and won't break as easily when the salad is stirred. Idaho, and other varieties of older potatoes are best for baking and french fries. They are drier, meatier, and starchier. Because of this they will bake fluffier and have a lighter texture. When French fries are made with an older potato the frying fat will splatter less because of the potato's lower water content. When baking a potato make sure you pierce the potato to allow steam to escape otherwise it may become soggy.

ARE GREEN POTATOES SAFE TO EAT?

When you see a potato with green spots or with a greenish tint, it would be best not to purchase it. Overexposure to light causes a chemical reaction that increases a chlorophyll buildup and the production of the chemical "solanine." Solanine will impart a bitter taste to the potato and high levels can actually cause serious medical problems such as interfering with nerve impulse transmission, abdominal discomfort, nausea, and diarrhea. When potatoes are stored it is best to store them in a dark location to avoid solanine buildup. This may also be a risk factor for people with arthritis.

REMOVING INDIGESTION FROM POTATO PANCAKES

For some reason a number of people have a problem tolerating fried potato pancakes and always get indigestion. This problem is easily solved by just adding 1 teaspoon of baking soda to the potato pancake batter.

WHY SOAK FRIES IN WATER?

The surface of a cut potato deteriorates very quickly when exposed to air. When this occurs a layer of sticky starch is formed as soon as the potatoes are placed into the frying vat. The potatoes may stick to each other as well as the pan and it will be almost impossible to serve them. If you soak the potatoes in ice water for 5-7 minutes before frying them it will wash off a large percentage of the surface starch and the problem will not occur. They should also be drained on paper towel and be good and dry when you fry them otherwise you will have hot oil splatter.

MASHED POTATO EDUCATION

There are number of hints to follow when preparing mashed potatoes. First, never pour cold milk into the potatoes, it has a tendency to mix with the starch that has been released through the mashing process and may make the potatoes heavy, soggy, and even create lumps. The milk should be warmed in a pan with a small amount of chives for flavor before being added. Buttermilk will give the potatoes a great flavor. A pinch or two of baking powder will give them extra fluff. Second, never overmix or overcook the potatoes. Both of these will cause the cell walls to rupture releasing an excess of starch and produce a soggy, sticky product. Potatoes should be stirred with a vertical motion and never circular stirred. This will lessen the damage which occurs by crushing the cells on the wall of the bowl. Never put baking soda in potatoes it will turn them black. Instead of adding liquid milk to the potatoes when making mashed, try adding powdered milk or instant potato flakes for extra fluffy mashed potatoes.

SKINNY FRENCH FRIES, IS THERE A REASON?

A number of the fast food chains like McDonald's serve their french fries thinner than most other restaurants. When raw potatoes are thin pre-cut exposing the surface, a percentage of the complex carbohydrates have time to convert to sugar. The extra sugar causes the french fries to brown faster and the thinner fry will cook faster. If they tried to serve normal size fries they would be too brown or undercooked.

WHAT IS A NewLeaf POTATO?

The Monsanto Company has genetically engineered a potato that provides the potato with natural resistance to the Colorado potato beetle which will reduce the need for additional pesticides. They are also working on a new potato that will absorb less fat when they are made into French fries.

CAN A POTATO EXPLODE IN THE OVEN?

It is not unusual for a white potato to explode in the oven if the skin is not pierced. It doesn't really explode, however, it may crack open and make a mess since potatoes are very high in water content and will build up a good head of steam as they bake. It is best to pierce the skin with a fork before baking.

POTATOES AND ONIONS, NOT GOOD FRIENDS

Onions should never be stored with potatoes in the same bag. Onions tend to release gases that will alter the flavor of a potato. Cooking the two together is not a problem unless you overdo the quantity of onions and it takes over the flavor and aroma of the potato.

WHAT IS DUCHESS POTATOES?

It is a light, fluffy combination of mashed potatoes, egg yolk, sweet cream butter, and seasonings to taste. The mixture is then placed into a pastry tube and piped around meats, poultry, casseroles, or fish dishes as a decorative touch.

WHY DO COOKED POTATOES HAVE MORE NUTRIENTS AVAILABLE?

Nutrients from raw potatoes are more difficult for the body to utilize. The potato cells tend to hold the nutrients until the potato is softened and cooked and our digestive systems are unable to break the cell walls down adequately to release the nutrients. Potatoes should never be cooked in aluminum or iron pots or they will turn yellowish, nor can they be sliced with a carbon-steel knife. Best to cook potatoes in a glass or enamel pot if you wish them to be a nice pale color.

THAT'S ALL FOLKS

If you store a boiled or baked potato in the refrigerator for 3-4 days it will lose approximately 90% of its nutrient value. Potatoes should only be stored for 1-2 days. When boiling potatoes, place them into a mesh frying basket to make them easier to remove and drain since they may get somewhat mushy.

GETTING HARD

To reharden potatoes, try placing soft raw potatoes in ice water for ½ hour or until they become hard. Brown areas on potatoes are the result of oxidation and vitamin C losses.

LONG DIGESTIVE TIME

The digestive time for a medium potato is approximately 2 hours. Cooking a potato with its skin will result in the retention of most of its nutrients. Recommendation is not to eat potato skins. They are one of the only vegetable skins that tends to hold pesticide and fertilizer residues even after washing and cooking. The EPA has registered 90 different pesticides for use on potatoes. The FDA laboratories can only detect 55% of these. Some of the problem pesticides are Chlordane, Aldicarb, and Dieldrin.

A FRENCH FRY FIT FOR A KING

For the greatest gourmet french fries, try allowing crinkle-cut potatoes to stand in ice cold water and refrigerated for 1 hour before frying. This will harden the potato so that they will not absorb as much fat. Dry them thoroughly before frying and then fry them twice. The first time for only a few minutes, dry them well, sprinkle a small amount of flour on them and fry them until they are a golden brown.

TAKING A BIG LOSS

Mashed potatoes that sit out on a buffet will lose up to 100% of all their nutrients after 1 hour. The loss is due to the constant heat, lights, mashing, exposing more of the surface to oxidation, and cooking in boiling water.

TWO GOOD TIPS

If you have problems peeling the potato, drop it into a bowl of ice water for a few seconds to loosen the skin. To keep peeled potatoes white during cooking add a small amount of white vinegar to the water.

HOT POTATO, COLD POTATO

Cold potato soup is called Vichyssoise and was invented when King Louis XV of France was worried about being poisoned. He insisted that his servants taste all his food before he ate it. When the hot soup was passed around, however, it got cold by the time it reached him. He enjoyed the cold soup and from that day on had it served that way.

IS IT TRUE OR FALSE?

With two people in the family working, potato products have been processed to make them easier to use. These products which include flaked, frozen, and powdered potatoes have risen in sales by over 500% in the last 30 years. Remember, the more you process a potato, the more nutrients are lost.

WATCH OUT FOR THE RADICALS

 Potato chips are produced by cooking the potatoes in long vats of oil (75 feet long) with the oil being filtered and rarely changed. Present day production is about 200 pounds an hour. This method of high temperature cooking (375° F.)(190.6°C.) causes the oil to contain mostly trans-fatty acid oil, a potentially harmful oil which may increase free-radicals production. Potato, corn, or tortilla chips contain 10 times more fat than pretzels or air-popped popcorn. Most potato chips are 61% fat. Presently, there are 30 flavors of potato chips sold in supermarkets nationally.

THE REAL THING

To make a quality potato chip, cut potatoes in half crosswise, exposing two flat surfaces. A potato peeler is then used to cut paper thin slices which are sprayed with vegetable oil and placed on a cookie sheet. Brush the tops of the potatoes with a very small amount of fresh pure vegetable oil, preferably corn or safflower oil, then bake at 450°F. (232.1°C.) for about 10-12 minutes or until they are a light golden brown. Finally, place the chips in a brown paper bag with a small amount of sea salt (¼ teaspoon per whole potato) and shake. This will allow them to become somewhat salty and remove some of the fat.

CHAPTER 6

The Cold Facts and Food Storage

SHOULD I FREEZE IT?

There is always an uncertainty in the public's mind regarding whether or not to freeze or refreeze a food and if it is frozen, how long it will retain its nutrient value, as well as its flavor and consistency. Many foods do not do well when frozen, some get tough, some develop ice crystals shortly after being placed in the freezer, while others get mushy when defrosted.

BRRRRRRRRRRRRRR

If you are going to try and freeze any dish that has alcohol in it, remember alcohol will not freeze like water and may need to be frozen at a lower temperature.

CLOSE IT UP, SEAL IT UP

The longer a food is frozen the higher the nutrient loss. Seal all freezer stored foods as well as possible to avoid freezer burn and the formation of ice crystals. While ice crystals are not a serious problem they can affect the food as it is being thawed and make the food mushy.

VACATION TRICK

A good trick when you go away on vacation is to place a baggie with a few ice cubes in the freezer. If a power failure occurs while you are gone and the food thaws and refreezes, you will be aware of this fact and discard the food.

COLD DAMAGE

There are a number of foods that should never be refrigerated since the cold causes either loss of flavor, sprouting, or the starch turning to sugar. These include, garlic, onions, shallots, potatoes, and tomatoes.

GOOD TRICK

Frozen sandwiches will thaw by lunchtime. If the bread is buttered prior to freezing, the bread will not become soggy and absorb any filling.

FREEZER TEMPERATURE AND FOODS

Freezer Temperature	Quality Changes After
30°F. (-1.1°C.)	5 days
25°F. (-3.9°C.)	10 days
20°F. (-6.7°C.)	3 weeks
15°F. (-9.4°C.)	6 weeks
10°F. (-12.2°C.)	4 months
5°F. (-15°C.)	6 months
0°F. (-17.8°C.)	1 year

FOOD PRESERVATION

The preservation of food is possible only if some method is used to destroy or control the growth of microorganisms that cause spoilage. There are a number of methods which include: drying, dehydrating, salting, smoking, radiation, heating, freezing, and the use of chemical agents (preservatives, etc.).

The microorganisms that cause food spoilage can be found everywhere. They are in the water, air, counter surfaces, brought home on foods, and even in the product itself. In many cases the food is contaminated as a natural occurrence, such as salmonella being present in the chicken's ovary. Microorganisms can exist in two forms, either visible to the naked eye, such as in colonies or in small spores which are for the most part invisible to the naked eye and carried by the air.

There are three divisions of microorganisms, molds, yeast, and bacteria.

MOLDS, YEAST, AND BACTERIA

Molds are usually airborne "spores" or "seeds" that may light on a food product and start to multiply. They tend to send out "feelers" or "filaments" and grow in colonies which may be seen in many colors depending on their food source. Mold spores will move from one food to another, especially fruits, so it would be wise to check your foods when you bring them home to be sure that none has any mold on them.

Yeasts are small one-celled fungus cells that produce enzymes which convert sugars to alcohol and carbon dioxide in a process called fermentation. It is also an excellent dietary source of folic acid.

Bacteria need only a small amount of organic material and some moisture to grow and multiply. They grow by splitting their cells and may develop either acid or alkaline properties.

When there is no moisture or the available moisture is used up, growth in all of these microorganisms cease and they dry up and become dormant until moisture is again introduced.

WAS NAPOLEON RESPONSIBLE FOR FOOD PRESERVATION?

Napoleon's army was becoming sick and many of his men were dying from scurvy and other diseases related to lack of essential nutrients. Because of their long marches far from the food sources all they could bring with them was salted meats. Napoleon talked the rulers at the time in offering a reward equal to $250,000 in today's money if anyone could develop a method of preserving foods. Nicholas Appert, a Paris confectioner, after 14 years of trial and error finally invented a method of preservation. His method was to place food in a glass jar, allowing for expansion, and place a hand-hewn cork in the jar attached firmly with a piece of wire. Each jar was then wrapped in a burlap sack and lowered into a pot of boiling water. The length of time the jar was left in seemed to vary with the type of food. He was successful in preserving eggs, milk products, fruits, vegetables, and meats. He was awarded the prize money in 1810 by Napoleon and was labeled as "the man who discovered the art of making the seasons stand still."

WHO MADE THE FIRST TIN CAN?

Canning was invented in 1810 by Peter Durand, an Englishman, who called it a "tin canister." This would be an improvement over the glass jar, especially for transportation to outlying areas without breakage. The first "tin cans" had to be made by hand with workers cutting the can from sheets of tin-plate then soldering them together leaving a small hole in the top to place the food in. The hole was then covered with a small tin disc and soldered closed. A tin worker was able to produce about 60 cans a day. The United States started a canning operation in the 1820's and within 20 years the canning of foods was being done all over the country. In 1860 Isaac Solomon in Baltimore found that if he added calcium chloride to the water when it was boiling he could raise the temperature from 212° F to 240°F. (100° to 148.9°C.) and thus reduce the processing time from about 6 hours to 45 minutes. A processing plant could now produce 20,000 cans a day instead of 2,500. The longest food to date that has been eaten safely was canned meat that was 114 years old.

WHO CAME UP WITH THE NAME BIRDSEYE?

The Birdseye food company was founded by Clarence Birdseye, an American businessman who invented the process of freezing food in small packages. He discovered the process by accident while hunting in Labrador in 1915. Some portions of caribou and fish were frozen by the dry Arctic air and when thawed were tender and still tasty. He developed a process that duplicated the Arctic conditions and started a company. Birdseye Seafoods was founded in 1923 and by 1929 had expanded its product line to other foods. In 1929 Birdseye sold the company to General Foods.

NEGATIVE EFFECTS OF FREEZING FOODS

When food is frozen a percentage of the cells tend to burst releasing their liquids. This will occur in all foods regardless of the method of freezing or the type of wrap. Ice crystals are formed from the lost liquid and the food never has the same texture or exactly the same flavor as it originally had when it was freshly prepared. Biologically, the process that occurs is referred to as "osmosis." Osmosis is the process by which a liquid passes through a semi-permeable membrane (cell wall) in order to equalize the pressure. When the food is frozen the solids inside of the cell cause the water to become more concentrated allowing the liquid from outside the cell to enter, form crystals, and eventually cause a number of the cells to burst. Since some of the flavor of the food is contained in each cell a percentage of the flavor is also lost. Meats, fruits, and most seafood are more negatively affected than vegetables.

BE SMART WHEN FREEZING FOODS

There are a number of important facts that should be adhered to if you wish to freeze foods successfully:

» When preparing any vegetable for freezing, be sure and undercook it. Reheating will complete the cooking.

» Freezing tends to intensify the flavor in spices such as garlic, pepper, oregano, and cloves so you should use less then add more before serving. Additional onions can be used since freezing tends to cause the flavor to be lost. Salt should be used in moderation or not at all. Salt tends to slow down the freezing process.

» Never use quick-cooking rice in a dish that will be frozen as it tends to become mushy. Use regular or converted rice.

» Artificial flavorings and sweeteners do not do well when frozen.

» Toppings should always be added before serving. Cheeses and bread crumbs on foods do not do well.

» Freezing causes old potatoes to fall apart, always use new potatoes in dishes that are to be frozen.

» Gravies and sauces need to be made somewhat thicker than normal since they will usually separate.

» Cool foods first in the refrigerator before freezing.

WHY IS A FULL FREEZER MORE ENERGY EFFICIENT?

A freezer that is full will use less energy than a half-full freezer because frozen foods retain cold air for a long period. The freezer will run less hours a day and save considerable money in electricity.

BLANCHING BEFORE FREEZING, A MUST

When vegetables are frozen, enzymes may still remain active and cause changes in the color, texture, and taste in the vegetable even if they have been previously stored under refrigeration. Freezing will slow the changes down, however, it will not totally inactivate the enzymes. If vegetables are blanched by either boiling them in water that has boiled for 2 minutes first (to release oxygen) or steaming them for 3-4 minutes it will not cook them but will inactivate the enzymes and the vegetables will retain their color, texture, and taste. Of course, the enzymes are important to good nutrition and it would be more desirable to only purchase enough for a few days at a time.

CHEST FREEZER VS. UPRIGHT FREEZERS

This debate has been around for a long time, however, the answer has always been a fairly simple one. The chest freezer, even though the door may be larger will retain its cold setting longer when the door is opened since cold air is heavier than hot air and tends to stay put. The upright freezer tends to release most

of its cold air the minute the door is opened. Chest freezers will maintain and hold the preferred 0°F. (-17.8°C.) freezer level to maximize food storage times before spoilage.

SMOKE CURING FOODS

The use of smoke to cure foods is one of the oldest methods of food preservation and one that provides a number of risks to the body from the toxins that may be placed into the food from the smoke. Smoke may contain as many as 200 different chemical components which include alcohols, acids, phenolic compounds, pyrobenzine, and other carcinogenic chemicals. Many of these toxic substances do, however, retard microbial growth. Salt curing methods and smoking are frequently combined to minimize the oxidation of the fats that cause rancidity.

NEW STORAGE BAGS, A MUST FOR EVERY KITCHEN

A new plastic storage bag for fruits and vegetables is now on the market. The bag contains hundreds of microscopic holes that allow air to circulate around the produce. The bag is also impregnated with "oya" which is a natural substance that will absorb ethylene gas, which is released by the produce as it ripens and helps the produce ripen. Unfortunately, the more ethylene gas the produce expels and remains around the food, the faster the food ripens and spoils. The bags are tinted green to lessen the effects of light reducing the potency of the vitamins. The bag is marketed under the name "Evert-Fresh."

Produce stored in these bags will last 10 times longer than standard plastic storage bags and in tests over a 12 day period 50% more of the vitamin C was retained. If you are unable to locate them call (800)822-8141 to order your supply.

STORING MARGARINE

Margarine will absorb odors from foods that are stored nearby very readily. It should be sealed as tightly as possible and should store for 4-6 months in the refrigerator. Margarine freezes well and will keep for 1 year if the temperature is kept at 0°F. (-17.8°C.).

FREEZER STORAGE TIMES AT ZERO DEGREES FAHRENHEIT

Storage Times For Refrigerated Dairy Products		
Product	Days Under Refrigeration	Months In Freezer 0°F.
Butter	45-90	7-8
Butter, Clarified	60-90	7-8
Buttermilk	7-14	3
Cream	3-5	3
Cream, Whipped		
Commercial	30	Do Not Freeze
Homemade	1	2
Eggnog	3-5	6
Half & Half	3-4	4
Ice Cream, Commercial		2-3
Frozen Desserts		1-2
Margarine		
Regular & Soft	120	12
Diet	90	
Milk	3-7	3
Non-dairy Creamer	21	12
Non-Dairy Toppings		
Container	7	12
Aerosol can	90	Do Not Freeze
Sour Cream	14	
Yogurt	14	2

Storage Times For Cheeses	
Cheese	Weeks Under Refrigeration
Appenzellar	4
Bel Paese	4
Bleu Cheese	2-4
Brick	4-8
Brie	3-5 Days
Camembert	3-5 Days
Cheddar	5-8
Cheshire	5-8
Colby	4-8
Cold Pack Cheese	2-3
Cottage Cheese, all curds	1
Cream Cheese	1-2
Derby	4-8

Storage Times For Cheeses	
Cheese	**Weeks Under Refrigeration**
Edam	4-8
Farmer's	1-2
Firm-type Cheeses	4-8
Feta	8-12
Fontina	4
Goat	2-4
Gorgonzola	2-4
Gouda	4-8
Gruyere	2-4
Havarti	3-4
Herkimer	4-8
Jarlsberg	4
Liederkranz	3-5 Days
Limburger	1-2
Mascarpone	1
Monastery Type	2-4
Monterey Jack	2-4
Muenster	1-3
Mozzarella, fresh	2-3 Days
Mozzarella, dry	2-4
Neufchatel	1-2
Parmesan	10-12
Port Du Salut	2-4
Pot Cheese	1
Processed Cheese, opened	3-4
Provolone	8-12
Ricotta	1
Roquefort	2-4
Semi-soft Type	2-4
Stilton	2-4
Swiss	4-5
Tillamook	4-8
Tilsiter	2-4

NOTE: The unprocessed natural cheeses will freeze for 4-6 months and retain most of their flavor.

Storage Times For Meats		
Meat	**Days Under Refrigeration**	**Months In Freezer**
Beef		
Roasts, Steaks	3-5	9
Ground, Stew	1-2	2-4
Organs	1-2	2-4
Veal		
Roasts, Chops, Ribs	3-5	6-9
Ground, Cutlet, Stew	1-2	3-4
Organs	1-2	1-2
Pork		
Roasts, Chops, Ribs	2-4	3-6
Ground, Sausage	1-2	1-2
Organs	1-2	1-2
Lamb		
Roasts, Chops, Ribs	2-4	6-9
Ground, Stew	1-2	3-4
Organs	1-2	1-2

Storage Times For Baking Staples	
Product	**Shelf Life**
Arrowroot	1 Year
Baking Powder	3-6 Months
Baking Soda	18 Months
Cornstarch	1 Year
Cream Of Tartar	1 Year
Extracts	1 Year
Gelatin, Boxed	1 Year
Salt	Forever If Kept Dry
Tapioca	1 Year
Vinegar	1 Year
Yeast	Date On Package

Refrigerator Storage Times For Vegetables	
Vegetable	**Days In Refrigerator**
Artichoke	6-7
Arugula	3
Asparagus	4-6
Bamboo Shoots	7
Beans, Lima	2-3
Beans, Green	3-5

Refrigerator Storage Times For Vegetables	
Vegetable	Days In Refrigerator
Beets	7-10
Bitter Melon	5
Black-eyed Peas	2-3
Bok Choy	3-4
Broccoli	4-5
Brussels Sprouts	3-5
Cabbage	8-14
Carrots	7-14
Cauliflower	4-7
Celery	7-14
Celery Root	2-3
Chickpeas	2-3
Chicory	3-5
Chinese Cabbage	4-5
Cooked Fresh Vegetables	3-5
Corn	1
Cucumbers	4-5
Eggplant	3-4
Escarole	3-5
Fennel	7-14
Ginger	7-14
Green Onions	7-14
Greens, Dandelion, Mustard	1-2
Horseradish	10-20
Jicama	7-14
Kale	2-3
Kohlrabi	4-5
Leeks	7-14
Lettuce, Iceberg	7-14
Lettuce, All Others	6-10
Mushrooms	4-5
Okra	2-3
Onions	7-14
Peas	7-10
Peppers, Green & Chili	4-6
Peppers, Sweet Red & Yellow	2-3
Radishes	2-3
Rutabagas	7-14
Salisify	7-14
Sauerkraut, Fresh	6-7

| Refrigerator Storage Times For Vegetables ||
Vegetable	Days In Refrigerator
Soy	2-3
Spinach	2-3
Sprouts	2-3
Squash, Summer	4-5
Swiss Chard	2-3
Tomatoes	3-5
Tofu	3-10
Turnips	5-7
Water Chestnuts	6-7
Watercress	2-3

NOTE: Unless otherwise noted in this chapter, all vegetables should be in perforated plastic bags.

| Storage Times For Fresh Fruit |||
Fruit	Ripen After Harvesting	Refrigerator Storage Time
Apples	Yes	2-4 Weeks
Apricots	Yes	2-3 Days
Avocados	Yes	10-14 Days
Bananas	Yes	1 Week
Berries	No	3-7 Days
Melons	Yes	7-10 Days
Cherries	No	2-4 Days
Cranberries	No	1 Month
Currents	No	1-2 Days
Dates	No	1-2 Months
Figs, Fresh	No	1-2 Days
Grapefruit	No	10-14 Days
Grapes	No	3-5 Days
Guava	Yes	2 Weeks
Kiwifruit	Yes	1 Week
Kumquats	No	3 Weeks
Lemons	No	2-3 Weeks
Limes	No	3-4 Weeks
Litchis	No	1 Week
Mangoes	Yes	2-3 Days
Nectarines	Yes	3-5 Days
Oranges	No	10-14 Days
Papayas	Yes	2 Weeks

Storage Times For Fresh Fruit		
Fruit	Ripen After Harvesting	Refrigerator Storage Time
Peaches	Yes	3-5 Days
Pears	Yes	3-5 Days
Persimmons	Yes	1-2 Days
Pineapple	Yes	3-5 Days
Plums	Yes	3-5 Days
Pomegranates	No	2-3 Weeks
Prunes	Yes	3-5 Days
Rhubarb	No	4-6 Days
Star Fruit	Yes	5-7 Days
Uglifruit	No	10-14 Days
Watermelons	No	1 Week

Storage Times For Nuts In The Shell			
Nut	Cupboard	Refrigerator	Freezer
Almonds	1 Year	1 Year	1 Year
Brazil Nut		9 Months	9 Months
Canned Nuts	1 Year	1 Year	1 Year
Cashews		6 Months	9 Months
Chestnuts		6 Months	9 Months
Coconuts		1 Month	
Filberts	3 Months	9 Months	1 Year
Macadamia Nuts		6 Months	1 Year
Mixed Nuts	9 Months	1 Year	
Peanuts, Raw	2 Months	6 Months	1 Year
Peanuts, Roasted	1 Month	3 Months	9 Months
Pecans	2-3 Months	6 Months	1 Year
Pinenuts		1 Month	6 Months
Pistachios		3 Months	1 Year
Pumpkin Seeds	2-3 Months	1 Year	1 Year
Sunflower Seeds	2-3 Months	1 Year	1 Year
Walnuts	2-3 Months	1 Year	1 Year

PROBLEMS WITH ALUMINUM FOIL

Foods wrapped in aluminum foil may be subjected to two problems. The first is that since aluminum foil is such a great insulator it tends to slow down the heat transfer and the food will not freeze as fast as you may want it to. Bacteria may grow and not be killed when the food is re-heated. Secondly is that when you crinkle the aluminum foil to place it around the food, microcracks develop which may allow air and moisture to penetrate the food. If you plan on storing food for more than 2-3 days in the refrigerator in aluminum foil you should probably wrap the food in plastic wrap first. Aluminum foil will also react with foods that are acidic or salty and may impart a strange taste to the food.

WHICH IS BETTER, A THERMAL BOTTLE, OR A VACUUM BOTTLE?

When a hot beverage is placed in a container for storage, the heat is lost to the colder air through conduction, and a cold beverage will lose the cold and gain heat from its surroundings. Both a thermal or a vacuum bottle slow the transfer of heat and cold between the beverage and its surroundings by placing a barrier between the food or beverage and the environment. A vacuum bottle places the food in a space within a vacuum surrounding the food. The unit is hermetically sealed between the bottle's inner and outer glass lining. In the thermal bottle, the exterior is solid and a poor conductor of heat, but not as poor as a vacuum bottle. Thermal bottles will not break as easily since they do not have the glass interior.

THE DANGERS IN RAW FOODS

The bacteria salmonella comes from the intestines of humans and animals and is often found in raw meats and eggs. Salmonella can be present after foods are dried, processed, or frozen for long periods. The bacteria can also be transferred to food by insects or human hands, especially infants and people with poor cleanliness habits. Salmonella is easily killed with high heat which is why raw meats need to be cooked thoroughly. Food preparation surfaces that are not cleaned adequately after preparing raw meats and egg dishes are usually the cause of most cases of salmonella related illnesses.

COLD FACTS

If ice cream thaws it should not be re-frozen. Jelly, salad dressing, and mayonnaise do not freeze well on bread products. The freezer in your refrigerator is not the same as a supermarket food freezer. It is best used for storing foods for short periods only. Foods should be frozen as quickly as possible and temperatures should be 0°F. (-17.8°C.) or below. Potatoes become mushy when frozen in stews or casseroles. Their cells have a high water content and break easily when frozen. However, mashed potatoes freeze well. Any bakery item with a cream filling should not be frozen. They will become soggy. Custard and meringue pies do not freeze well. The custard tends to separate and the meringue becomes tough. Waffles and pancakes may be frozen, thawed and placed in the toaster.

CHAPTER 7

Condiments, Sauces, & Such

HOW FOODS BECOME EMULSIFIED

Emulsification is the process of combining two liquids that do not normally wish to come together. A good example of this is oil and water. Oil and vinegar is another example and if they are used to make salad dressing you know that it takes a bit of shaking to bring them together before you can pour the dressing out of the bottle. When the oil and vinegar solution is shaken the oil is broken into small droplets for a short period of time. There are a number of emulsifying agents that will help keep the liquids in suspension. One of the best emulsifiers for oil and vinegar is lecithin. Lecithin, a natural fat emulsifier, can be obtained at any health food store in ampoules and only one or two of the ampoules emptied into the mixture will place the ingredients into suspension. Lecithin is found naturally in egg white which is why egg whites are used in many sauces to keep the ingredients in suspension.

GELATIN, THE GREAT THICKENER

Gelatin can be acquired from a number of different sources, however, the most common source is animal hoofs, muscle, bones, and connective tissue. Other sources include seaweed from which agar-agar is produced and Irish moss from which carregeenan is made. Both of these are these are popular commercial thickeners, carregeenan is especially useful for thickening ice cream products.

Gelatin granules have the capability of trapping water molecules and then expanding to ten times their original size. The firmness of a product will depend on the gelatin/water ratio. If the product becomes too firm, a small amount of heat is all that is needed to change the firmness closer to a liquid, if you chill the product it will become firm again. Since gelatin is high in protein you can never use fresh figs, Kiwi, papaya, or pineapple in the product since these contain an enzyme that breaks down protein thus ruining the product. The enzyme in pineapple, bromelain, can be neutralized by simmering the pineapple for a few minutes.

When using gelatin for a dish, be sure and moisten the gelatin first with a small amount of cold water, then use the hot water to completely dissolve the gelatin. When hot water is poured into the dry gelatin a number of the granules will lump and some will not totally dissolve which may cause your dish to be somewhat grainy. The hot water should never be over 180°F. (82.2°C.) for the best results. If your recipe calls for an equal amount of sugar to gelatin, the cold water step is not required since the sugar will stop the clumping. However, you still never pour the hot water into the gelatin, place the gelatin in the water.

WHO REALLY INVENTED KETCHUP OR IS IT CATSUP?

The original name for what we know as "ketchup" was "ketsiap." The sauce was invented in China in the seventeenth century and mainly used on fish dishes. It was made from fish entrails, vinegar, and hot spices. The Chinese imported the sauce to Malaya and it was renamed "kechap." The Malayan's sold the kechap to the English sailors during the eighteenth century, the sailors brought it back to England and mushrooms were substituted for the fish entrails. In 1792 a cookbook by Richard Briggs "The New Art Of Cookery" named the sauce "catsup" and included tomatoes as one of the main ingredients. Ketchup became popular in the United States in 1830 when Colonel Robert Gibbon Johnson ate a tomato on the courthouse steps in Salem, New Jersey and didn't die. Tomatoes at that time were thought to be poisonous.
H.J. Heinz started producing ketchup in the early 1870's, the company today is a $6.6 billion dollar company.

HANDY CONTAINERS

Empty plastic ketchup and mustard containers are great for holding icings and oils. Allow a mixture of warm water and baking soda to sit overnight in the containers then rinse thoroughly with hot water.

HOW DID HEINZ BECOME THE NUMBER ONE KETCHUP?

In the 1940's Hunt's was the number one selling ketchup in the United States, mainly because it poured more easily and this was viewed as a real asset since you didn't have to fight with the bottle to get the ketchup out. Heinz was also selling ketchup but sales were lagging far behind the Hunt's product. An effort was made to change the public awareness that just because the Hunt's ketchup poured more easily that doesn't necessarily mean that it is the best product. In the 1950's Heinz placed simple TV ads stating that "Heinz, Slowest ketchup in the West—East—North—South." The public then started viewing the quality of ketchup as a measure of the viscosity and Heinz with the thickest product took the market away from Hunt's and Hunt's has never regained it back even though all ketchups are now slow. Quality ketchups now flow at 4-6.5 centimeters in 30 seconds. Government standards (USDA) for ketchup flow is 3-7 centimeters in 30 seconds. Ketchup is a $600 million dollar industry with sales of seven 14 ounce bottles sold per person in the United States annually.

ALL ABOUT VINEGAR

Vinegar can be found in a number of varieties depending on the food that is used to produce it. It is a mild acid called "acetic acid." The actual amount of acid that is in the vinegar varies from 4-7 percent with the average being 5 percent. Common types include apple cider vinegar, plain white distilled, red and white wine, barley, malt, rice, and balsamic. The acetic acid content of vinegar is referred to by "grains". A 5 percent acetic acid content is known as a 50 grain vinegar. the 50 grain means that the product is 50% water and 50% vinegar. A 6-7 percent vinegar will keep foods fresher longer because of the higher acid content. Vinegar will have a shelf life and retain its effectiveness for about 18 months.

THE JELLY THICKENER

Pectin, a carbohydrate, is the most common thickener for jellies. If your jelly doesn't set it will probably be the result of too little pectin or the wrong proportions of other ingredients. For certain types of fruit jellies only a small amount of pectin may be needed since most fruits are relatively high in pectin. Some of the higher pectin fruits include: all citrus fruits, apples, and cranberries. The ones with less pectin include: peaches, cherries, raspberries, apricots, and strawberries. To get the most out of the pectin that is found in the fruit, the fruit should be very fresh. The fresher the fruit, the more active pectin will be available for processing the jelly. Jelly requires a number of ingredients to set properly, pectin is only one of the most important. The acid and sugar content will both affect the properties of the product in regard to setting up. Cooking the jelly at too high a temperature will destroy the pectin.

HOW WAS WORCESTERSHIRE SAUCE INVENTED?

Actually, Worcestershire Sauce was produced by accident by John Lea and William Perrins. In 1835 Lea and Perrins were running a small drug store in Worcester, England when Lord Marcus Sandys came in and asked if they could produce his favorite Indian sauce he had liked while in Bengal. They mixed up a batch of sauce prepared from vegetables and fish, didn't like the smell or flavor and placed the mixture in their cellar for storage. While cleaning the cellar two years later they accidentally found the sauce, tried it and were surprised at the taste. Lea & Perrin's Worcestershire Sauce is now one of the most popular steak sauces in the world.

The recipe has hardly changed from the original 1835 one using anchovies layered in brine, tamarinds in molasses, garlic in vinegar, chilies, cloves, shallots, and as a sweetener sugar. The mixture must still age for 2 years before being sold, the solids are filtered out, and preservatives and citric acid are added.

CHAPTER 8

The Fats in the Foods

FATS (Lipids)

Fats are substances such as oils, waxes, lard, butter and other compounds that are insoluble (unable to mix with) in water. Some fats are readily visible, such as fat on meats, butter, cream cheese, bacon, and salad dressing. Other fats are less visible, such as fat in egg yoke, nuts, avocado and milk.

Fats are a combination of "fatty acids" which are their "building blocks" or basic "sub-units." The type of fat depends on the specific mixture of these fatty acids. The body uses fat as its energy storage reserves, padding to protect organs, as a constituent in hormones, an important building block of a healthy cell wall, and insulation.

Fats fall into three main categories

1. Simple Fats
   These are basic fats called a triglyceride and are composed of a glycerol base with three fatty acids.

2. Compound Fats
   These are a combination of fats and other components. One of the more important being the lipoproteins, which are fats that combine with proteins. Lipoproteins are the main transport system for fats. They may contain cholesterol, triglycerides, neutral fats, and fatty acids. Since fat is insoluble it needs a vehicle to carry it around the body.

3. Derived Fats
   Produced from fatty substances through digestive breakdown.

The fats you eat are composed of three chemical elements:
Carbon C, Hydrogen H and Oxygen O.

The carbon atoms are like a skeleton and can be compared to the framework on a house. In a saturated fat, all the carbons are completely surrounded by hydrogen and oxygen atoms. Since the carbons are totally saturated this type of fat is solid at room temperature.

In a polyunsaturated fat some of the carbons have a free space where an atom of hydrogen could be attached. It is because of these openings that a polyunsaturated fat is liquid at room temperature. If all the carbons have hydrogens attached then the fat is saturated and solid at room temperature. There is also a middle of the road fat called a monounsaturated fat which the body likes better than any other.

THE THREE MAJOR TYPES OF FATS

» POLYUNSATURATED FATS (PUFA)
Always remains a liquid at room temperature. Examples are: safflower, corn, and peanut. Studies have shown that some PUFA and MUFA fats may have a tendency to lower blood cholesterol levels.

» MONOUNSATURATED FATS (MUFA)
These tend to thicken when refrigerated but are still liquid at room temperature. Examples are; olive and Canola oil. Recent studies show that MUFA oils may be more effective in lowering blood cholesterol levels than PUFA oils.

» SATURATED FATS (SFA)
Normally, these are either solid or semi-solid at room temperature. Examples are butter, lard, shortening, and hard margarine. The exceptions to the rule are coconut oil and palm oil which are liquid at room temperature and may be listed on the list of ingredients as "tropical oils." SFA's have the tendency to raise cholesterol levels even though they may not actually contain cholesterol.

» HYDROGENATION
Many products will say that they are hydrogenated on the label. This simply means that the manufacturer has added hydrogen atoms from water to saturate the carbons, harden the fat in the product, making it more "saturated," thus adding a different texture to the food to make it more palatable and possibly last longer.

A liquid fat can be turned into a solid in this manner, however, you can turn a good fat into a bad saturated fat. Remember, the more hydrogenated a product, the higher the saturated fat level in the product.

THE BAD PARTS OF A GOOD FAT

We have now covered a number of important points regarding fats and their relationship to the foods we eat, however, we now need to discuss the fact that those "good guys", the polyunsaturated fats and the monounsaturated fats may have a bad side to them.

An example of this is eating at a fast food restaurant and ordering a potatoe patty for breakfast. Since it is early morning and the frying vat has just been filled with a good fresh vegetable oil (we hope), the majority of the fat will probably be a good polyunsaturated fat.

However, when you go back to that same restaurant for lunch, they have now fried in that oil for four hours and the majority of the oil has converted to a bad oil called a trans-fatty acid. Studies have implicated this oil in the acceleration of the aging process, raising the bad cholesterol, and lowering the good cholesterol.

When you purchase oil from the supermarket for the most part your buying good oil or the "cis" form. The "trans " form should be avoided as much as possible.

» Cis-Form Fatty Acids

A horseshoe shaped molecule of polyunsaturated fat that occurs naturally in nature and is normally incorporated into a healthy cell wall. The health of the cell wall depends on a supply of "cis" form fatty acids. When these acids are not available the cell wall is constructed with abnormal openings (ports of entry) that may allow foreign substances to enter and cause a disease process to start.

» Trans-Form Fatty Acid

Instead of the normal horseshoe form, the trans-fatty acids are found in a straight line shape. This form of the fat is difficult for the cell to utilize in the construction of a healthy wall. The blueprint calls for a horseshoe shape, not a straight line. Margarines may contain up to 54% trans-fatty acids and shortenings as much as 58%. Heating and storage of these fats increases these percentages.

INCREASING THE FAT

Fast food restaurants may deep-fat or par-fry French fries before they arrive at the restaurant to save time. This may cause a higher level of trans-fatty acids in the fries. As much as 10 grams of fat may come from the par-frying.

GOOD TO THE LAST DROP

If you really want to get all the shortening out of a can, try pouring 2 cups of boiling water into the container and swish it around until all the fat melts. Place the container into the refrigerator until it sets up and the fat is on the top. Then just skim off the fat.

LOG JAM AHEAD

Used oil should never be poured down the drain. It may solidify and clog the drain. Save the oil in a metal can and dispose of it in the garbage.

KEEPING BUTTER, BETTER

If you would like to have your butter ready and spreadable at all times, go to a kitchen store and purchase a "British" butter dish. It is a butter dish made from terra cotta, the top of which needs to be soaked in cold water every day.

ADDITIVE HELPS

Cooking wine will stay fresher longer if you add a tablespoon of very fresh vegetable oil to the bottle.

CHEF'S SECRET

If your recipe requires that you cream shortening with a sugary substance, try adding a few drops of water to the mixture. This will make it easier to stir. When creaming butter in the blender, cut the butter in small pieces.

BUTTER FACT

The highest quality butter is U.S. Grade AA which is produced from fresh sweet cream. U.S. Grade A is almost as good but has a lower flavor rating. U.S. Grade B is usually produced from sour cream. The milk-fat content of butter must be at least 80%.

SUCKING UP TO FAT

A few pieces of dried bread placed in the bottom of the broiler pan should absorb fat drippings. This will eliminate smoking fat and should reduce any fire hazard.

BUYER BEWARE

The best quality oil is "cold-pressed" extra virgin olive oil. It is made from the plumpest, "Grade A" olives, has the best flavor, and is processed by pressing the oil from the olives with as little heat and friction as possible. The next best is virgin olive oil then pure olive oil which is a  blend of both. Many companies are using "cold-processed" instead of "cold-pressed." Cold-processed may mean the olive oil is produced by using a chemical solvent to extract the oil. Chemical residues are not uncommon. Read the labels and watch for this intentional use of a similar phrase which does not denote a quality processing.

DON'T LET OLIVE OIL HAVE A BREAKDOWN

Olive oil is one of the healthiest oils to use in salads or for low temperature cooking. It has a low smoke point which means that it will break down easily and start smoking. You can extend the usable life of olive oil and slow its breakdown by adding a small amount of Canola oil to the olive oil. Canola has a very high smoke point. This will also work well with butter when you are sauteing.

WHOOOOSH

A good test to tell whether a hot oil is still usable and not high in trans-fatty acids is to drop a piece of white bread into the pan. If the bread develops dark specs, the oil has reached an unsafe level of deterioration. Never allow oil to heat to the smoke point, as it may ignite. It will also make the food taste bitter and may even irritate your eyes. The oils with the highest smoke points are Canola, safflower, and corn oil.

GRANDMOTHER'S FRYING OIL TRICK, NOT A GOOD ONE

When my grandmother fried foods she always cleaned the oil out with a few slices of raw potato, then threw them away and stored the oil in the ice box to reuse it. When oil is reused the level of trans-fatty acid rises until it is 100%, which doesn't take too long. Oil should never be reused.

LIGHTEN-UP

When you deep-fat fry, try adding ½ teaspoon of baking powder per ½ cup of flour in your batter to produce a lighter coating and fewer calories.

FAT'S IN THE FIRE

If the frying fat is not hot enough, food will absorb more fat. However, if you get it too hot it will smoke, burn, and produce trans-fatty acids. Use a thermometer, the temperature should be 360° to 375°F. (182.2° to 190.6°C.).

PIG ABS

Lard is derived from the abdomen of pigs and is used in chewing gum bases, shaving creams, soaps, and cosmetics. Future studies may implicate lard in shortened life-spans as well as a factor in osteoporosis. Leaf lard is derived from the kidney area of the pig and is a higher quality than all other types of lard (best for pie crust).

FATTY PATE

Pates are bordered with pork fat from the flank of the pig.

PUTTING ON THE RITZ

Some of the highest fat content crackers are Ritz, Town House, and Goldfish, which contain about 6 grams of fat per ounce.

LARD HAS LARGER FAT CRYSTALS

Lard can be stored at room temperature for 6-8 months. If you substitute lard for butter or shortening, reduce the amount you use by 25%.

MAYONNAISE OR SALAD DRESSING?

Mayonnaise must contain at least 65% oil by weight, any less and it must be called salad dressing. Most fat-free mayonnaise contains more sodium than "real" mayonnaise. A tablespoon of mayonnaise contains only 5-10 mg. of cholesterol since very little egg yolk is really used.

CRISPY CRITTER

When you are greasing a pan, make sure you don't use too much grease or you may cause the food to overbrown.

KEEPING PIGS WARM

The age-old favorite of small pancakes wrapped around sausages was 60% fat and almost all saturated fat.

A REAL WHOPPER
Every ounce of fat contains 250% more calories than an ounce of carbohydrate or protein.

NOT THE BOTTOM OF THE CHURN
Buttermilk can be substituted for 2% or whole milk in most recipes. Buttermilk is less than 1% fat, almost equal to skim milk, however, it has a thicker consistency.

AND AWAY IT GOES
A high fat intake has been related to calcium losses through the urine.

BEAT ME, BEAT ME
Butter will go farther and have fewer calories per serving if you beat it well, increasing the volume with air.

YOLKS AWAY
When preparing any recipe or omelet, try replacing the egg yolks with an equal amount of egg substitute or just reduce the number of yolks.

LONGEVITY
The most popular oil is olive oil with soy oil coming in second. Olive oil will stay fresh longer than most oils while soy oil tends to lose its flavor the longer it is stored due to the linolenic acid it contains.

YUMMY, YUMMY
Eight ounces of potato chips are the equivalent of eating 16-20 teaspoons of fat.

NEEDS SHADES
Only purchase oils in containers if you cannot see the oil. Oil is very sensitive to light and will become rancid. All oils with the exception of cold-pressed olive oil starts oxidizing as soon as it is heat processed and continues to breaks down until it becomes rancid.

WHY CAROB?
When carob is made into candy products, fat is usually added to improve the texture. This usually brings the fat content close to real

chocolate. In fact, cocoa butter used in real chocolate is 60% saturated fat while the fat used in a carob candy is 85% saturated fat.

MARGARINE FACT
Most margarines contain over 90% fat. Diet margarines usually contain 80% fat, 16% water, 2% salt, and 2% non-fat milk solids. Margarines are naturally white, colorings and additives are added to all margarines. A liquid diet margarine, however, may contain as low as 40% fat.

A FATTY SEPARATION
If you are going to make your own mayonnaise, be sure that the weather report is clear. If the temperature or humidity is too high it will cause the mayonnaise to come out heavier and greasier than normal.

THE DEBATE
The margarine, butter controversy is still going on with neither side really winning. Margarines have the bad fat, trans-fatty acids due to the method of heat processing they must go through and butter contains cholesterol. My preferred choice would be whipped, unsalted butter in moderation.

WHERE, OH WHERE, HAVE MY VITAMINS GONE
Refined corn oil is a chemical extraction, a triglyceride, with no relationship to the nutrients in a "real" ear of corn. The vitamins that would normally assist with the digestion of corn oil are absent, even the vitamin E is lost.

DIETARY FIASCO
A burrito topped with sour cream and guacamole may contain up to 1,000 calories and 59% fat. Add cheese sauce for another 300 calories.

THE BIG "C"
Diets high in total fat and especially trans-fatty acids (from heated fats) have been related to cancers of the colon, prostate, and breast. Studies are also showing that the efficiency of the immune system may be depressed by a high fat diet. Recommended dietary fat levels are 20-25% of your total daily calories, however, a person can actually survive on only 5% dietary fat if the fat is of the essential fatty acid type. Dietary fats are being implicated as a key factor in over 300,000 cases of skin cancer reported annually.

GOOD FAT, BAD FAT?

Recent studies have shown that stearic acid, one of the saturated fats has little effect on raising cholesterol levels. As our laboratory tests become more sophisticated more information about which fats will actually raise your cholesterol will be forthcoming. Then we can avoid only those foods that may be harmful.

SALAD AND COOKING OIL USE

1909	1.5 pounds per person
1972	18 pounds per person
1990	29 pounds per person
1995	33 pounds per person
1997	34 pounds per person

MARGARINE USE

1950	6 pounds per person
1972	11 pounds per person
1990	16 pounds per person
1995	18 pounds per person
1997	19 pounds per person

HOW MUCH FAT CAN YOUR STOMACH CLEAR?

Approximately 10 grams of fat is cleared from the stomach per hour. Two scrambled eggs, bread and butter, coffee, and milk = 50 grams of fat. Assimilation time is 5-6 hours. An example of high fat foods are bacon and cheddar cheese. The percent of fat to calories in each is 75% fat. Americans spend $3 billion per year on bacon.

ASK FOR IT

Most non-dairy creamers are made from coconut oil, which is high in saturated fat. Mocha Mix is your best bet.

FATS ARE MORE SATISFYING

Studies now show that dieters miss fats more than sweets.

EDUCATION A MUST

Americans consumed 53 pounds of hard fats (meats, etc.), shortenings (baked goods, etc.) and cooking fats (oils, etc.) per person in 1972. In

1997 the consumption has risen to 68 pounds, not a good direction. Poor nutrition education and the increased eating out at fast food restaurants is to blame. There are 312 fats that are available for use in frying alone.

TOP FRYING OIL

Rapeseed (Canola oil) for years has been grown as a forage crop for animals in the United States and Canada. Originally, it was banned in the U.S. when imports from Canada showed high levels of "erucic acid." However, new varieties have shown to contain lower levels and is now being produced and sold in large quantities. It is high in monounsaturated fat and has a high smoke point, making it the preferred oil for frying.

THE COLOR OF FAT

Current studies show that if your body is higher in "brown fat" rather than "white fat" your have a higher percentage of the more active type, which may relate to why some people are able to control their weight easier than others. Studies are being conducted at Harvard University regarding these fats and their effect on human metabolism.

INSOMNIA?

Most fat should be consumed either at breakfast or lunch, few, if any for dinner. High fat meals late in the day may cause the digestive system to overwork while you are sleeping, causing restless sleep patterns.

SUGAR IN, FAT OUT, CALORIES THE SAME

The new reduced-fat peanut butter has the same number of calories per serving as the regular peanut butter, about 190 per serving, sweeteners were added in place of the fat.

CREAM-IT

To make a creamy salad dressing, try pouring cold-pressed olive oil very slowly into a running blender containing the other ingredients and spices.

WORK LIKE A PRO

Purchase empty plastic ketchup bottles to use for your oils. The narrow spout makes it easy to pour oils when cooking. Label them with a permanent felt-tip marker.

FAT SCIENCE

When oils are refrigerated and become cloudy, it is due to the buildup of harmless crystals. Manufacturers will sometimes pre-chill the oils and remove the crystals in a process known as "winterization." These oils will remain clear when refrigerated. Lard has larger fat crystals than butter, this has a lot to do with the texture of these fats and is controlled during processing. The large fat crystals in lard will make it the choice for a number of baked goods where a flakier crust is preferred, especially pies. Moderation in eating these lard products, however, is the key word.

TYPICAL AMERICAN DIET

The average American diet is about 44% fat. Dietary guidelines suggest no more than 30% of total calories. My recommendation is no more than 20% or less with the type of fats leaning toward the PUFA and MUFA types. The 30% figure is workable if the fat calories are all of the best type of fat which may be difficult for most people.

GOOD FAT?

Medium-chain triglycerides (MCT) are sold in health food stores for people who have trouble absorbing fats. They are for the most part produced from coconut oil, have a very low smoke point, and can be used for cooking without producing trans-fatty acids. Body builders tend to use this fat to increase caloric intake, but studies to date are not conclusive.

OVERWORKING YOUR DIGESTIVE SYSTEM

One 8 ounce bag of potato chips contains 6 tablespoons of oil amounting to 80 grams of fat.

FAT SUBSTITUTES

It's 1998 and the new "fat substitutes" are appearing in our foods. These synthetically produced products should be viewed with caution and used in *moderation* only.

OLESTRA

Olestra is a large synthetic fat molecule, so large that it passes through the intestinal tract undigested. This increase of undigested material may cause diarrhea. Olestra as it goes through the system, however, tends to attract the fat-soluble vitamins A, D, E, and K and may bind with them.

Proctor and Gamble, the inventor of the product, is familiar with the problem and may have to fortify the products with vitamins, however, this may not solve the problem.

A more significant problem may be that the carotenoid family are also fat soluble and the over 500 carotenoids may also be in trouble. A percentage of carotenoids may be washed out of the body. These include beta-carotene, alpha-carotene, lutein, lycopene, and the rest of the family. Since these are not considered to be essential nutrients P & G does not feel that they have to include them through fortification. The carotenoids are a nutrient that is under investigation as a possible cancer preventive nutrient.

The official name that will appear on products with olestra is Olean. Olean has only been approved for snack foods. It is being added to snack chips, crackers, tortilla chips, cheese puffs, and potato chips initially. The FDA is requiring that a warning label be added which reads:

> This product contains Olestra. Olestra may cause abdominal cramping and loose stools. Olestra inhibits the absorption of some vitamins and other nutrients. Vitamins A, D, E, and K have been added.

The "fake-fat chip" will have a caloric reduction of about 34%. The downside to all of this is that people may consume more junk foods and still end up with the same number of total calories. P & G is presently marketing the product under the brand name "WOW."

HYDROLYZED OAT FLOUR

This fat substitute may even be good for you. It is oat flour that has been treated with water to break down the starches into individual sugars. This causes a change in the texture and provides the fat texture that people like in their foods. The flour is high in "beta-glucan" which may have a cholesterol-absorbing ability. The product was developed by the USDA. It contains only 1 calorie per gram instead of the 9 calories per gram in fat.

Studies have shown a definite cholesterol lowering correlation in the 24 volunteers that took part in the study. Over 40 new products are being developed and it will be necessary to read the label to find it. It may also be called "hydrated oat flour" or use the brand name "Oatrim." Currently, it may be found in cookies, cheeses, low-fat hot dogs, and low-fat lunch meats. It is a safer alternative than the Olean products.

FAT CALORIES IN COMMON FOODS

The following is information regarding fat in relation to total calories in a person's diet:

Foods	Percent Of Fats
Bacon, butter, margarine, lard, mayonnaise, solid shortenings, cooking oils, olives, baking chocolate, cream cheese.	90-100
Macadamias, salad dressings, pecans, walnuts, avocados, sausages, corned beef, coconut.	80-90
Hot dogs, peanuts, most chips, bleu cheese, cashews, lunch meats, peanut butter, prime rib, tuna in oil, Swiss cheese, sunflower seeds.	65-80
Hamburger, rib steak, chicken with skin, canned ham, salmon, trout, bass, veal cutlet, eggs, ice cream.	50-65
Most baked goods, lean hamburger, ground turkey, Canadian bacon, ham, steak, whole milk, round steak.	35-50
Low-fat yogurt, 2% milk, veal chop, loin and rump cuts of beef, sweet breads.	20-35
Crab, baked chicken without skin, most shellfish, tuna in water, low-fat cottage cheese, low-fat broiled fish.	10-20
Buttermilk, skim milk, rice, cereals, potatoes, pasta, fruits, vegetables, egg whites.	Very small amount.

SOURCE: Nutritive Values of Foods, USDA 1994.

Percent Saturation Of Commonly Used Fats			
	PUFA	MUFA	SFA
Vegetable Oils & Shortenings			
Safflower Oil	75	12	9
Sunflower Oil	66	20	10
Corn Oil	59	14	13
Soybean Oil	58	23	14
Cottonseed Oil	52	18	26
Canola Oil	33	55	7

Percent Saturation Of Commonly Used Fats			
	PUFA	MUFA	SFA
Olive Oil	8	74	13
Peanut Oil	32	46	17
Soft Tub Margarine	31	47	18
Stick Margarine	18	59	19
Vegetable Shortening	14	51	31
Palm Oil	9	37	49
Coconut Oil	2	6	86
Palm Kernel Oil	2	11	81
Animal Fats			
Tuna Fat	37	26	27
Chicken Fat	21	45	30
Lard	11	45	40
Mutton Fat	8	41	47
Beef Fat	4	42	50
Butter Fat	4	29	62

PUFA - Polyunsaturated Fatty Acids
MUFA - Monounsaturated Fatty Acids
SFA - Saturated Fatty Acids
Source: National Heart, Lung, and Blood Institute

High Fat Vs. Low Fat Luncheon Foods		
High Fat		
Food	Calories	Fat (g.)
Cheddar cheese (1oz.)	110	9
Swiss Cheese (1oz.)	110	8
American Cheese (1oz.)	110	9
Provolone (1oz.)	100	7
Bologna (4oz.)	360	32
Sausage (2oz.)	140	11
Hot Dog (1 med.)	160	12
Cream Cheese (1oz.)	100	10
Potato Chips (1oz.)	150	10
Cream of Mushroom Soup (1 cup)	100	7
Cola Drink (12oz.)	145	0
Double Burger w/ Cheese	695	45
Vanilla Shake (12oz.)	290	11
Onion Rings (reg. order)	270	16
Butter/Margarine (1 Tbl.)	85	9
Mayonnaise (1 Tbl.)	100	11
Tartar Sauce (1 Tbl.)	70	8

High Fat Vs. Low Fat Luncheon Foods		
High Fat		
Food	**Calories**	**Fat (g.)**
Avocado (½ Haas)	150	14
Croissant Roll (1 small)	170	9
Low Fat		
Danish Ham (4oz.)	100	4
Turkey (3oz.)	110	3
Turkey Pastrami (3oz.)	100	4
Mustard (1 Tbl.)	12	0
Mayo Lite (1 Tbl.)	45	5
Ketchup (1 Tbl.)	16	0
Pickle Relish (1 Tbl.)	30	0
Pretzels (1oz.)	110	1
Diet Soda (12oz.)	1	0
Vegetable Soup (1 cup)	60	2
Lettuce (1 cup)	12	2
Tomato (1 small)	15	1
Mozzarella Cheese (1oz. skim)	80	5
Lite-Line American Cheese (1oz.)	50	2
Lite-Line Swiss Cheese (1oz.)	50	2
Hamburger (reg.)	275	12
Chicken Hot Dog (1 reg.)	125	8
Pita Bread (1 pocket)	75	7

SHORTENING VS. OIL

Shortening is just a solid form of fat and is always a solid at room temperature. It can be made from either an animal or vegetable source or a combination of the two. Shortenings that are made from vegetable sources are hydrogenated, which is the addition of water to a liquid fat until it becomes the consistency that is desired by the manufacturer. The term "pure shortening" means that the product can contain either vegetable or animal sources or a combination of both. If the product is labeled "pure vegetable shortening" it has to be made from only vegetables sources. If the product does not have the word "pure" on the label then a number of additives were added to increase the shelf life, however, when this is done it does lower the smoke point and is not as good a product. One of the best shortenings is Crisco which has a balanced saturated fat to unsaturated fat of one to one.

WHY FRYING OIL LANDS ON THE INSIDE OF LENSES

If you wear eyeglasses and fry foods, you may have
noticed that the oil droplets collect on the inner surface of
the lens rather than the outer surface. The reason for this
is because when you are frying the minute droplets
become airborne and then fall back toward the floor.
When you are bending over working at your cooking task the oil
droplets fall on the inside of the lens.

WHY OIL CAN'T BE USED FOR BAKING

Because of its liquid nature, oils tend to collect instead of evenly
distributing through the dough. This may cause the baked goods to
become grainy. When a solid fat is used, baked items tend to be more
fluffy and retain their moisture better. Especially bad are the
"all-purpose" oils which even though they say that they can be used for
baking and frying are not up to the standards that most cooks desire. To
produce these oils a number of additives are used which may affect the
flavor and taste of the food.

FRYING TEMPERATURES ARE CRITICAL

It is never wise to fry at too low a temperature, especially if the food is
breaded. The oil will not be hot enough to seal the breading or outer surface
of the food and too much of the oil is allowed to enter the food before the
sealing takes place. When the oil is too hot then the food may end up being
burned on the outside and not allow the insides to be cooked through. Most
breaded foods that are fried are normally fired at 375°F. (190.6°C.) best to
check the recipe for the particular food you are frying for the correct frying
temperature. Chicken should be fried at 365°F. (185°C.) for 10-20 minutes
for the best results and meats at 360°F. (182.2°C.).

WHO INVENTED MARGARINE?

Margarine was invented by a French chemist in the late 1800's upon
request by Napoleon III who wanted a low-cost fat. Originally, it was
produced from animal fat, however, today it is made from vegetables oil
(mainly soy), milk solids, salt, air, and water.

SOME CANOLA OIL IS NOW BEING RUINED BY BIOTECHNOLOGY

Canola oil is now being altered through genetic engineering and contains
high levels of the saturated fat "laurate." Laurate is not normally found in
Canola oil. By producing a high saturated fat product it may now be used in

the baking industry replacing palm and coconut (tropical oils) which are more expensive to import. The public has become aware that Canola oil is high in monounsaturated oil which is good for the body in moderation. The public may view the product containing Canola oil to be a product that contains a "good oil." The new Canola oil will be used initially in non-dairy products such as coffee creamers and whipped toppings.

CHAPTER 9

Soups and Gravies

The varieties of soup are endless, however, there are a few common types that most of us are familiar with, these include:

» BISQUE

A relatively thick, creamy soup, prepared from a variety of shellfish, fish, tomatoes, and seasonings. Can be served as a main meal dish.

» BOUILLON

This is clarified, concentrated soup stock that is made from any type of meat, meat bone, or poultry meat.

» BROTH

This usually a clear liquid that is made from simmering meats or vegetables in water.

» CHOWDER

A relatively thick soup that is made with a fish or clam base with vegetables, especially potatoes. Cream is usually used in the base and all the contents stewed.

» CONSOMME

A very strong, clarified soup made from a heavy brown stock which has been produced from meat or poultry.

» CREAM TYPE SOUPS

Usually made with the addition of milk, cream, or butter. Sometimes all three are used. They can be thickened with tapioca or flour. Make sure you never boil a cream soup or it will develop a film on the surface.

THE FLOATING FAT

When fat floats to the top of gravy, soups, or stews it is easily removed by placing a slice of fresh white bread on top of the fat for a few seconds. The fat will be quickly absorbed and the bread should be disposed of. Be sure to not leave the bread on too long or it will deteriorate and fall apart in your food.

ELIMINATING FATS FROM SOUPS AND STEWS

Fats can be eliminated through the use of lettuce and ice without refrigerating the food and taking the time for the fat to rise to the top. A good percentage of fat can be eliminated by either placing 4-5 ice cubes in a piece of ordinary cheesecloth and swirling it around in the soup or stew or by placing a few lettuce leaves in the food and stirring them for a few minutes then removing them and throwing them away. Fat is attracted to the cold and tends to have an affinity for lettuce leaves. Another method is to gently place a piece of paper towel on the top and absorb the excess fat (works great on pizzas too).

STOP GRAVY FROM SEPARATING

One of the more frequent problems when cooking gravy is when the gravy decides to separate into fat globules. To solve the problem all you have to do is add a pinch or two of baking soda to emulsify the fat globules in a matter of seconds.

GO FOR PAUL'S

Spaghetti sauce are really best if they are homemade. Commercial sauces are for the most part higher in fat content and calories. Prego Extra Chunky with sausage and green peppers is 47% fat. Ragu Marinara is 40% fat. The only sauce I recommend is Newman's Own. The mushroom sauce is only 22% fat.

WHAT CAN YOU DO TO STOP CURDLING?

There is always the risk of curdling especially if you are preparing cream soups and sauces. To avoid the problem you should always wait until you have thickened the mixture with flour or cornstarch before adding any ingredients that are acidic, such as wine, any type of citrus, or tomatoes. Remember heavy whipping cream won't curdle when you boil it.

A CHEMICAL BUFFET

When at all possible make your own sauces and gravies. Packaged products are lower quality convenience items that contain numerous additives, preservatives, and coloring agents.

A LITTLE BONE, A LITTLE ?

Spaghetti sauces that contain meat may not really have much of the actual muscle protein. By law, companies only need to include 6% actual meat. It would be best to add your own meat and you will know what you are eating.

THE SECRET TO SAVING A CURDLED HOLLANDAISE SAUCE

The secret to saving the hollandaise sauce is to catch the problem and nip it in the bud. As soon as the sauce starts to curdle, add 1-2 tablespoons of hot water to about ¾ of a cup of the sauce and beat it vigorously until it is smooth. Repeat this for the balance of the sauce. If the sauce has already curdled, just beat a tablespoon of cold water into the sauce and it will bring back the smooth texture.

CHEWY GRAVY?

Use your blender to smooth lumpy gravy or add a pinch of salt to the flour before adding any liquid. Also, you can add a teaspoon of peanut butter to cover up the burnt flavor of gravy if it burns without altering the taste.

A SAUTEING SECRET

Never use salted butter for sauteing, always use unsalted butter since the salt separates from the butter when heated and may impart a bitter taste to the dish.

PERK UP YOUR GRAVY

If you would like your gravy to have a rich dark brown color, just spread the flour on a cookie pan and cook over a low heat, stirring occasionally until brown, then add a small amount of coffee to the gravy during the last few minutes before serving.

IN OLDEN TIMES

A method used in the 19th century was to add onion skins to the gravy while it is cooking to give it a brown color, just make sure you remove them after a few minutes and discard.

SHAKE IT!

To help a semi-solid soup slide right out of the can, try shaking the can first and then open it from the bottom.

TESTING, TESTING

A high-fat gravy (which should only be eaten in moderation) will have a better consistency if you add ¼ teaspoon of baking soda to it. If it has a high starch content, don't add baking soda or it will turn it black. Try a small amount first before going the distance.

AMAZING, BUT TRUE

If your stew meat gets tough it may be because when you add water to the cooking stew you add boiling water, always use cold water, boiling water may toughen the meat.

EASY DOES IT

For the best results and to keep the flavors intact, soups and stews should only be allowed to simmer, never boil.

DO-IT-YOURSELF

Make your own TV dinner by just placing leftover stews into individual baking dishes or small casserole dishes, cover with pie crust or dumpling mix and bake.

UP, UP, AND AWAY

Basil is a common spice for use in soups and stews, however, basil tends to lose much of its flavor after about 15 minutes of cooking and should be added about 10 minutes before the food is done for the best results.

KEEP 'EM HANDY

To make dips and sauces, try using dry soup mixes which are usually additive-free and only contain a few dried vegetables and seasonings, however, they are usually high in salt.

REMOVING LUMPS

Wire whisks work better than any other kitchen tool for removing lumps in soups and sauces.

STRETCHING IT OUT

To make soup go farther, just add pasta, rice or barley to it.

STIR GENTLY TILL THE LUMPS ARE GONE

If you need to thicken a stew or sauce, try mixing 2 tablespoons of cornstarch, potato flour, or arrowroot in 3 tablespoons of water, then adding the mixture to the food. Do this for every cup of liquid in the product. If you just wish a medium amount of thickening reduce it to 1 tablespoon of cornstarch mixed with 2 tablespoons of water for every cup.

RECOMMENDED BY A CHIHUAHUA

To change your stew just a little, try taking a stack of tortillas and cut them into long thin pieces. Add them to the stew during the last 15 minutes of cooking. If you don't want the extra fat use corn tortillas instead of flour.

TEA AS A TENDERIZER?

The tannic acid in strong tea can tenderize meat and reduce your cooking time. Just add ½ cup of strong tea to the stew.

OLD TIME TRICK

Grandmother used to freeze leftover soup in a cube tray and then use the cubes in soups and stews at another time.

MAKING QUICKSAND

An easy method of thickening stews is to add a small amount of quick-cooking oats, a grated potato, or some instant potatoes or onions.

DON'T DROWN THEM

When preparing a vegetable soup only pour enough water into the pot to cover the vegetables by two inches. Too much water makes the soup too watery.

SALT REDUCTION

If you have a problem with oversalting your soup or stew, just add a can of peeled tomatoes. Other methods include, adding a small amount of brown sugar or placing a slice or two of apple or raw potato in, mixing it up, and then discarding them.

CARROTS PROVIDE SWEETNESS

Instead of sugar to give your soup or stew a sweeter taste, try adding a small amount of pureed carrots.

BAD BONES

Dark-colored bones should never be used for cooking. They are probably too old and have deteriorated.

A MILK CURDLING EXPERIENCE

To avoid curdling when you are making tomato soup with milk, try adding the tomato base/soup to the milk instead of the milk to the tomato base. If you add a small amount of flour to the milk and beat it, it would also help.

A REAL WINNER

Next time you make soup or stew, try using a metal pasta cooker basket. Just place the basket into your pot and cook all your ingredients. When you remove the basket it will contain all the veggies or bones you may not want.

THE PARSLEY MAGNET

When you overdo the garlic, just place a few parsley flakes in a tea ball to soak up the excess garlic. Garlic tends to be attracted to parsley.

ON A CLEAR SOUP, YOU CAN SEE FOREVER

To make a clear noodle soup, cook the noodles, then drain before adding them to the soup. When noodles are cooked in the soup, the excess starch will turn the soup cloudy.

REAL SMOOTH

Next time you make a cream soup, try adding a little flour to the milk. it will make it smoother and it will work even with 1% milk.

SOUP SECRETS

Always make soup at least a day ahead of time, so that the seasonings will have time to improve the flavor. Never use salt or pepper to season soups until you are almost finished with the cooking process. Both of these seasonings will intensify and may give the soup too strong a flavor. When cooking soup, always cook with the lid on to help the flavors become better absorbed. When you make a cold soup, remember that a cold soup needs more seasoning than a hot soup. The heat tends to drive the flavors into the product more efficiently.

CHAPTER 10

Meat Matters

GENERAL INFORMATION

Americans have always been a society that consumed large amounts of meats and poultry as far back as colonial days. The cattle industry during the 1800's thrived, and methods were improved as to transportation and preservation of meats so that the entire country could have their beef. Meat and poultry were the most important main dishes and this has stayed with 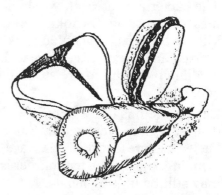 us until recent years when we discovered that excessive meat intake may increase the blood fat levels of fat and cholesterol to such a degree as to cause serious health problems.

Recently, other factors have placed meat and poultry in the media in a negative light. The fact that the inspection procedures may be lacking the tools and manpower to do an efficient job. Mad cow disease, E. coli contaminated meats, salmonella in chickens and eggs, and hormone residues in meats are just a few of the problems that may exist.

Education is the key factor if you are to continue to consume meat and poultry. The public must learn what types of meats are the healthiest and the safest, how to prepare the meats, what signs to be aware of, and even how to clean up after you work with meat and poultry.

Americans consume 34% of all meat products in the world even though we are only 7% of the world population. We presently eat 180 pounds of meat and poultry per person, per year. Red meat consumption, however, has declined since the 1970's and poultry has increased significantly to a 50/50 level in the mid-1990's. Numerous medical studies have surfaced in recent years that leave no doubt that a high red meat diet, high in saturated fat, is one of the key factors in causing colon cancer. Meat does provide a number of significant nutrients and in moderation should still be considered a healthy food.

Meats should be treated as more of a side dish and not the main course. Meat and poultry are composed mainly of muscle, which is approximately 73% water, 21% protein and 6% fat in beef and 3% fat in poultry.

In the last few years the bacteria E. coli has been associated with the risks of eating beef. However, more of an explanation is needed regarding the actual risk and how it can be eliminated if it is present at all. The bacteria E. coli is an intestinal bacteria that may not be washed off after processing. It is capable of causing severe illness or even death.

The bacteria, if present, would normally be found on the surface of the meat and searing or cooking a piece of meat on both sides would easily kill the bacteria. When you cook a steak or roast all sides are normally cooked and the risk is eliminated. This means that if you wish to eat a medium or medium-rare steak there is no risk if the meat is properly cooked.

The problem is more significant in regard to hamburger or raw meat dishes, such as steak tartar. Since hamburgers are ground beef, if the bacteria is present on the surface, it will move to the inside during grinding, then if the hamburger is not cooked thoroughly, the bacteria may still be lurking inside.

The following facts are meant to be usable in the choosing and preparation of meat and poultry as well as providing some general information that might be of interest.

MEATS FACTS—USDA MEAT GRADING

» PRIME - Very tender due to higher fat content. Well marbled. Most expensive. Calories from fat = 50%.

» CHOICE - Relatively tender, still fairly expensive and becoming harder to find in supermarkets. Calories from fat = 39%.

» GOOD - Due to its present pricing has become the most common grade in supermarkets. Has less fat and may need some tenderizing. Calories from fat = 30%.

» COMMERCIAL - Tougher beef from older animals used mainly in TV dinners and canned meat products.

» UTILITY, CUTTER AND CANNER - These are usually leftover bits and pieces used in processed meat products. May be very tough.

TRY IT ONCE FOR A REAL SURPRISE

The finest USDA Prime beef can be purchased from Omaha Steaks International in Omaha, Nebraska. Call for their catalog at (800)288-9055.

> **BUYER BEWARE**
> Supermarkets are using their own wording on meat packages to make you think that you are buying a better grade than it really is. Most of the major chains are buying more "Good Grade" beef and may call it by a number of fancy names such as "Top Premium Beef," "Prime Quality Cut," "Select Choice," "Markets Choice," or "Premium Cut." Since the public does not want to pay the higher price for USDA Choice they have found a way to make the "Good Grade" sound better.

THE INSIDE STORY OF A COW

There are eight major cuts of beef butchered in the United States; they are: shank, flank, brisket, chuck, round, rib, plate and loin. The eight cuts are given a number of additional names which will be more recognizable to the consumer. These include  names such as; sirloin, porterhouse, top round, eye of the round, New York, T-bone, etc. These explain the way the eight major cuts are actually cut up. The tenderness of beef will depend on the location of the cut and the method of cutting.

Some cuts are tougher than others. These include pot roasts (chuck roasts), which are cut from the neck area of the cow and will be the least expensive.

» CHUCK CUTS (ROASTS)
These are the toughest cuts and should be cooked in a small amount of liquid and they may need to be tenderized.

» RIB CUTS (RIBS)
Markets may label these as baby back ribs, rib steaks, rib roasts, or just back ribs. For the best results they should be prepared by grilling

or placed in the oven and cooked slowly. The taste can be improved by adding a sauce or using a marinade.

» LOIN CUTS (TENDERLOIN)
Cut from behind the ribs they are the most tender. They include filet, spencer, porterhouse, and New York steaks.

» ROUND CUTS (ROASTS)
Most of these will be tender and can be cooked a number of different ways. They include; top round, eye of the round, and bottom round. They can be pot roasted or spit barbecued.

» FLANK AND PLATE CUTS
Most of the time if USDA Good grade is purchased they will need tenderizing. Prime and Choice are much better choices for these cuts. They are usually cut in strips and used for stir frying.

» BRISKET CUTS
The brisket is cut from behind a cow's front leg or may be cut from the leg itself. Normally a tough cut of beef it needs to be cooked in liquid for about 2-3 hours. If you wish to get the best results when preparing a brisket rotate the roast ½ turn every 25 minutes. The brisket is fully cooked when you see the fat just starting to roll off. However, if the fat can easily be removed with your fingers the brisket is over-done.

CONSUME IT OR FREEZE IT

Small cuts of meat will spoil more rapidly and should not be kept in the refrigerator without freezing for more than 2-3 days. Liver, sweetbreads, cubed meats, and marinated meats should be used within 1 day or frozen.

STEAK SHAKE?

To tenderize meat when barbecueing, add green papaya (papain) to the barbecue sauce. Don't leave the meat in too long or it will start to break down and liquefy. Bromelein from pineapple will also have the same effect.

THE CASE FOR WELL DONE BEEF

When meat is cooked it becomes more easily digested and utilized by the body. Cooking meats to medium-well (170°F.) (76.7°C.) will increase the availability of vitamin B_1 by 15% over well-done beef (185°F.) (82°C.). Amino acids, the building blocks of protein will be absorbed more efficiently and more fully utilized when they come from beef. The absorption rate of beef is about 90%, grains are 80% and legumes (beans) are 60-75%.

RUB-A-DUB-DUB

A common method of seasoning the exterior of meats and poultry is called a "rub." This is simply a blend of various herbs and spices that do not penetrate the meat. It never blends with the flavor of the meat, however, it does provide a tasty coating which usually forms a brown crust of these concentrated flavors. Rub the seasoning on before you begin to cook and allow it time to take hold.

DUNKEN LAMB?

Lamb stew will have a great flavor if you cook it in black coffee. The meat will come out dark and more flavorful.

BISON BURGERS?

Beware of the wording on meat packages. If the steak packaging reads "lean" the steak cannot have more than 10% fat, "extra lean" cannot have more than 5% fat. The only time I have seen this low a fat content in a steak was a Buffalo steak. Ground beef when labeled "lean" is allowed to have as much as 22% fat.

HONOR AMONGST BEEFS?

The USDA normally monitors only 1-2% of all beef carcasses for illegal drug residues, or about 1.5 pounds out of the 89 pounds each person consumes each year. There are almost 2 million beef producers which for the most part control themselves regarding the use of hormones. If a problem with hormones is found it is usually too late and the beef has been sold. The problem rarely surfaces since it exists more in older cattle which are processed for canned meat products, soups, beef stews, pot pies, and packaged frozen dinners.

COLOR MATTERS

All meat should be thawed as quickly as possible, preferably under refrigeration, then cooked immediately. The color of fresh beef should be a bright red color which is from the muscle pigment. The darker the red color, the older the cow. Beef fat, if fresh, is always white not yellow.

A TALL TAIL AND A TRUE ONE

In Adelaide, Australia they serve an excellent kangaroo tail soup. However, the soup is not really made from a kangaroo's tail, it is made from the "kakuda plum," a native fruit of Australia. However, oxtail soup is made from the tail of a cow. This soup needs to be cooked for a long period, very slowly.

HARPOON THAT SANDWICH

In 1997 Japanese fishermen had 2,000 tons of surplus whale meat. Instead of discarding the meat it was used for school lunch sandwiches.

GLANDULAR FAT

If you have ever wondered what sweetbreads are, they are the thymus gland of a calf. The gland assists the young animal in fighting disease. It then atrophies and disappears six months after they are born. They are a high fat food with only 3 ounces containing about 21 grams of fat or 189 fat calories.

CHOLESTEROL VS. FATHER'S DAY

On Father's Day we tend to really outdo ourselves and consume over 80 million pounds of beef in one day. This the biggest barbecuing day of the year next to the Fourth of July.

LOVE MEAT TENDER

Sealing in the juices by lightly flouring the surface of meats works very well. When storing a roast, always place the roast back into its own juices whenever possible. When reheating meats, try placing the slices in a casserole dish with lettuce leaves between the slices. This will provide just the right amount of moisture to keep the slices from drying out.

MEAT FACT

Tomatoes or tomato sauce will act as a natural tenderizer for all types of beef. Meat should always be cut across the grain whenever possible, the meat will be more tender and have a better appearance.

CODDLED CATTLE

In Japan they can brag about having the most expensive per pound priced cattle in the world. Their Kobe beef are fed a specially prepared diet of soybeans, rice, and beer and then given a massage daily. The meat has almost 3 times the fat content of USDA Prime Beef.

PREMATURE AGING

Meats may turn a grayish color if they are cooked in a pot where there is insufficient room for them. Overcrowding tends to generate excess steam, give them some room to breathe for better results.

FAT RATING OF NON-VEGETABLE PROTEINS

1. Fish
2. Turkey
3. Chicken
4. Veal
5. Buffalo
6. Venison
7. Lamb
8. Pork
9. Goat
10. Beef

YUM, YUM, POWDERED BONE

One of the worst sources of protein is the hot dog. They have less protein in a 3 ½ ounce serving than any other type of meat. Legally, they can contain up to 56% water, edible offal, and 3% powdered bone which may even be listed on the list of ingredients. Sugar is a very popular ingredient in hot dogs and may show up on the label as corn syrup.

MEAT MARKET TREASURE HUNT

When purchasing a chuck roast look for the white cartilage near the top of the roast. If you can spot a roast with this showing you have found the first cut which will be the most tender. When purchasing an eye of the round roast, look for one that is the same size on either end and you will have located the most tender one. However, with round steaks purchase ones that have uneven cuts and you have found the one closest to the sirloin.

BEST NOT TO EAT READY-TO-EAT HOT DOGS

The bacteria Listeria monocytogenes may be lurking in a
number of foods, such as hot dogs, sausage, raw milk,
chicken, and deli-prepared salads and sandwiches.
Listeria first became noticed when 48 people died from
eating a Mexican-style cheese in 1985. The number one
food related risk in the United States is from bacterial food
contamination not pesticides or fertilizers. The Listeria organism can
survive refrigeration or freezing and over 1,700 cases of food poisoning
are reported annually. People with weak immune systems are more at
risk. To avoid the problem the following should be adhered to:

> » Be sure to cook all ready-to-eat hot dogs, sausage, and leftovers until
>   good and hot.
>
> » Chicken should be cooked until the juices run clear.
>
> » Never drink raw milk, only pasteurized milk.
>
> » Foods should always be kept hot (above 140°F.) (60°C.) until they
>   are ready to eat.
>
> » Be aware of "Sell by" and "Use by" dates on all processed food
>   products.

CELERY TO THE RESCUE

Roasts will never stick to the bottom of the pan again if
you just place a few stalks of fresh celery under the roast.
This works great with other meats and meatloaf as well.

BIG DOGGIE

The United States consumes more hot dogs than the rest of the world put
together. This amounts to almost 2 billion hot dogs per year, almost
enough to circle the globe.

MOIST BUNS

When boiling hot dogs, try using the top of the double boiler to keep
your buns warm.

JUST THE FACTS

16.4 billion pounds of raw beef were sold in the United States in 1997
compared to 19 billion pounds in 1976. During the same period, raw
chicken sales increased from 43 pounds per person to 69 pounds per
person.

EASY MATH

When purchasing meats you should figure the cost per pound and realize that boneless cuts usually cost less per serving. The bone weight contributes considerable cost to the meat making the cost per serving higher in most instances.

SPRUCING IT UP

When preparing a fatty-looking roast, refrigerate the roast after it is partially cooked. The fat will then solidify and can easily be removed. Then return the roast to the oven and complete the cooking time.

EN GARDE

If you need to cook hamburgers really fast, try puncturing the burgers with a fork a few times to allow the heat to enter more easily.

SECRET TO THIN SLICES

If you would like to have thin meat slices for sandwiches, just place the roast in the freezer for 30 minutes before slicing.

L'IL DOGGIE

The source of veal is from young milk-fed calves. Veal is very low-fat, tender, and more costly, but contains less hormones than most beef. It contains $\frac{1}{10}$ the fat of lean beef and the cholesterol content is lower.

GINGER ALE TO THE RESCUE

Game meats dry out quickly and should not be overcooked. They usually have less fat content than pen-bred cattle. Use a small can of ginger ale to cook in if you want to eliminate the gamy flavor.

BURGERS AROUND THE WORLD

» BRAZIL, ARGENTINA and CHILE
  Hamburgers are always broiled instead of fried and are usually served on a piece of pumpernickel (dark brown bread) with a slice of cheese and a poached or fried egg on top.

» GERMANY AND AUSTRIA
  Ground beef is mixed with small bits of wet bread or crackers then onions, mustard, and sometimes an egg is added to glue it all together.

» SWITZERLAND
Hamburgers can be found with the typical toppings of cheese, etc., however, they are never held in your hand but are eaten with a knife and fork.

» KOREA, VIETNAM and CHINA
These countries eat a unique hamburger, if you can call it that after they get through adding special hot mustards, kimchee, pickled beet sauce, and a brown cream sauce with fried onions and even a bit of ligonberry preserves.

KEEPS IT MOIST

When you are preparing meatloaf, try rubbing a small amount of water on top and on the sides instead of tomato sauce. This will stop the meatloaf from cracking as it cooks and dries out. The tomato sauce can be added 15 minutes before it is fully cooked.

SHAPING UP

When you are going to make hamburger patties or meatballs, place the meat in the refrigerator for 30 minutes before forming the patties or meatballs and they will form better and stay in shape when cooking. If you place a small piece of ice inside your meatballs before browning, they will be more moist.

OUCH!

When you burn or scorch a roast, remove it from the pan and cover it with a hot water dampened towel for about 5 minutes to stop the cooking. Remove or scrape off any burnt areas with a sharp instrument and finish cooking.

SMOKE A STEAK

When you barbecue a one pound steak remember that you may be ingesting the equivalent cancer-forming agents (carcinogens) that would be found in 15 cigarettes. The problem only exists if there is sufficient fat dripping on the "real" charcoal briquettes which cause a chemical reaction to take place that coats the meats with "pyrobenzines." Wrapping the meat in foil or scraping the black material off will alleviate the problem.

HERBS THAT IMPROVE THE TASTE OF MEATS

Beef . . . . Garlic, onion powder, basil, thyme, summer savory, and rosemary.

Buffalo . . . . . . Rosemary, basil, garlic, and sage.

Veal . . . . Rosemary, garlic, thyme, tarragon, mint, and basil

Lamb . . . . Mint, ginger, and basil.

Pork . . . . Sweet marjoram, sage, chives, garlic, and basil.

Poultry . . . . . . Sage, basil, sweet marjoram, chervil, and summer savory.

Fish . . . . Sage, fennel, parsley, dill, basil, and chives.

WASTE OF RESOURCES

Pigs require about 8 pounds of grain to produce 1 pound of meat. It requires 16 pounds of grain to produce 1 pound of beef while chickens only require 3 pounds to bring them to market size. The latest statistics are that there are 1.6 billion cattle worldwide. These cattle consume 1/3 of all the world's grain which is not a very efficient use of a natural resource.

MUST BE CLEAN LIVING

The USDA has now published information stating that only 1 in 1,000 pigs are now found to contain the trichinosis parasite. My recommendation, however, is to still cook pork until the internal temperature is 160°F. (71°C.). The trichinosis parasite is killed at 137°F. (58°C.).

BASIC BACON CHEMISTRY

Bacon is one meat that is highly nitrated. The higher nitrite content is found in the fat which means you need to choose the leanest bacon you can find. Bacon can be prepared in the microwave on a piece of paper towel or under the broiler so that the fat drips down. When your shopping for a bacon substitute remember that almost all of these products still contain nitrites. Check the label and try to find a "nitrite-free" product.

MINERAL BATH

Cured hams are immersed in a solution of brine salts, sugar, and nitrites which are injected into the ham. The ham will increase in weight due to these added solutions and if the total weight goes up by 8%, the label must read "ham, with natural juices." If the weight of the ham increases more than 8%, the label must now read "water added."

HIGH FAT & FREEZING DON'T MIX WELL

Most sausage products may contain up to 60% fat. If you purchase a pork ground product they only have a freezer life of 1-2 months.

DAMAGE CONTROL

To stop sausages from splitting open when they are fried, try making a few small punctures in the skins while they are cooking. If you roll them in flour before cooking it will also reduce shrinkage.

HAM BONE CONNECTED TO THE

Removing a ham rind (bone) can be easy if you slit the ham above the rind lengthwise, down to the rind, before placing it into the pan. While it is baking the meat will pull away and the rind can easily be removed.

DESALTING YOUR BUTT

Since ham is naturally salty, try pouring a can of ginger ale over the ham and then rubbing the meaty side with salt at least 1 hour before placing the ham into the oven. This will cause the salt water in the pork to come to the surface and reduce the saltiness of the ham.

POOR RUDOLPH, GOT ZAPPED

Unfortunately Finland was in the path of radiation fallout from the 1986 Chernobyl disaster. Reindeer meat from Finland should not be consumed, even into the late 1990's.

HOT DOGGIE, WE'RE GETTING FATTER

1937 Frankfurter	1998 Frankfurter
Fat — 19%	Fat — 29%
Protein — 20%	Protein — 11%

MOST ARE POOR SOURCE OF PROTEIN

If hot dogs are labeled "All Meat" or "All Beef" they must contain at least 85% meat or beef. The "All Meat" variety can contain a blend of beef, pork, chicken or turkey meat. It can also contain bone, water, etc. Kosher hot dogs are only pure beef muscle meat and are the better source of protein. However, they all still contain nitrites.

TENDER LIVER

The acidic nature of tomato juice will tenderize liver. Just soak it for 1-2 hours in the refrigerator before cooking. Milk will also work on young calf's liver.

LAMB FACTS

If you are buying lamb be sure it comes from New Zealand, since they do not allow the lamb to be hormonized. When buying leg of lamb, always buy a small one (two if need be) since the larger legs are from older animals and have a stronger flavor.

SITTING AROUND

Stews are usually best if prepared the day before allowing the flavors to be incorporated throughout the stew.

STEWING

Bones from poultry and beef should always be frozen and saved for soups and stews. Allow them to remain in the soup or stew from the start of the cooking to just before serving.

ADAM'S RIB FACT

Ribs should always be marinated in the refrigerator before cooking. A ready-made barbecue sauce is fine and the ribs may be placed in the broiler for a few minutes if desired.

TIMING

Roasts will take about 12-14 minutes per pound for rare and 13-15 minutes for medium at 325°F. (162.8°C.).

IT'S A MATTER OF TASTE

Beef and veal kidneys have more than one lobe while lamb and pigs have only one lobe. They should be firm, not mushy, and should have a pale color. Before you cook them, be sure to remove the excess skin and fat.

NAUGHTY, NAUGHTY

Products that are ready-to-eat meat usually contain more fat than fresh meat. When these products are manufactured more of the meat by-products can be added which also increases the fat content.

LOVE ME TENDER

Some of the best tenderizers for meats have an alcohol base such as beer and hard cider. The fermentation chemical process gives the products the tenderizing quality. Other meat tenderizers are made from papaya (papain), pineapple (bromelein), and Kiwi.

TO FREEZE OR NOT TO FREEZE

When any type of meat or lunch meat that contains fat is re-frozen the salt content may cause the fat to become rancid. This is one reason why meats should not be re-frozen. However, leftover cooked meats can be kept refrigerated safely for 4-5 days.

OVEREXPOSURE

Any meat that has been ground up has had a large percentage of its surface exposed to the air and light. Oxygen and light cause a breakdown in the meat and tend to change the color as well as making the meat go bad in a very short period of time. Exposure to oxygen especially leads to a deteriorization known as "self-oxidation." Grinding meats also speeds up the loss of vital nutrients.

BAA-WARE

When purchasing a lamb shank, be sure that it weighs at least 4 pounds, any smaller and it will contain too high a percentage of bone and less meat.

IMPROVING YOUR RECIPE

When preparing hamburger or meatloaf and you have purchased a very low-fat meat, try mixing in one well beaten egg white for every pound of meat. Also, adding a package of instant onion soup mix will really make a difference. A small amount of small curd cottage cheese or instant potatoes placed in the center of a meatloaf makes for a different taste treat while keeping the meat moist.

HIGH FAT FOOD

The most commonly purchased meat in the United States is hamburger, it also provides us with most of our meat fat intake and most of the fat is of the saturated type.

BEEFALO IS GREAT

Game meats are lower in fat than most of the beef we normally purchase, however, it is more difficult to find in the stores. Many game meats also contain appreciable amounts of an omega-3 fatty acid. The following are two mail order sources for game meat:

Broken Arrow Ranch
P.O. Box 530
Ingram, TX 78025
(800) 962-4263

Whitefeather Bison Co.
3360 Greenwich St.
Wadsworth, OH 44281
(800) 328-2476

» A LOW-FAT MEAT TREAT
Buffalo (bison) meat is gaining in popularity throughout the United States. The meat is low in fat, cholesterol, and even calories compared to beef. Today's herds total about 135,000 head and growing steadily. The National Bison Association has 2,300 members.

SCIENTIFIC FACT

A study performed by Dr. Martin Marchello, of North Dakota State University, Department of Animal and Range Sciences found that in 26 species of domestic game meat, bison meat was lower in fat than beef, pork or lamb. 3.0 ounces of bison contained only 93 calories, only 43 mg. of cholesterol, was low in sodium, and high in iron. Bison does not have the gamy flavor of many of the game meat animals.

RABBIT FACTS

The American rabbit that is domesticated and sold in markets is mainly white meat. It does not get very much time to exercise. The European rabbit is more moist and tender since they do get their regular exercise period.

HOW TO COOK A SAFE BURGER

While undercooked burgers may pose a risk of E. coli, a well done burger may pose a risk of a potentially harmful carcinogen called a heterocyclic aromatic amine (HAA). This compound is formed when meat is cooked to high temperatures. If you microwave the meat for a few minutes before cooking, this will make the meat safer and remove a large percentage of the HAA's.

1. Choose a lean cut of beef. Have the butcher remove all the visible fat from around the edges, and grind it through the meat grinder twice. That will break up the remaining fat.

2. Place the hamburger in a microwave oven just before you are preparing to use it for 1-3 minutes on high power. Pour off the excess liquid which will contain additional fat and the creatine and creatinine that form the HAA's.

3. Reduce the meat content of the burgers by adding mashed black beans or cooked rice and you will have a safer and great tasting medium-well burger.

SKELETAL PROBLEM ALERT

Any type of beef consumed in large quantities may inhibit the absorption of the mineral manganese as well as cause an increased loss of calcium in the urine.

SETTING A SPEED RECORD

When you need to barbecue for a large crowd and your grill isn't big enough, you can save time by using a cookie sheet and placing a few layers of hamburgers between layers of tin foil and baking the burgers at 350°F. (176.7°C.) for 25 minutes, then finish them on the grill in only 5-10 minutes. Hot dogs may be done the same way but only cook for 10 minutes.

LIKE A JUICY STEAK, DON'T SEAR IT

There's an old wives tale that has been handed down from generation to generation regarding searing a steak to keep the juices in. This really didn't seem to have a good ring to it so it was put to the test. The results are in, and it turns out that searing a piece of steak does not help in any way to retain the juices (many chefs won't agree), in fact the steak dried out faster because of the more rapid higher temperature cooking. The investigation found out that if the steak is cooked at a lower heat and more slowly it will be more tender and retain more of its juices.

SUPER GLUED

If you're going to buy a canned ham, purchase the largest you can afford. Smaller canned hams are usually made from bits and pieces and glued together with gelatin.

ARE WE LOSING OUR FORESTS FOR A HAMBURGER?

Presently, in the continental United States we are cutting down our forests at the rate of 12 acres every minute. The land is needed to produce feed for livestock, or for grazing. The deforestation is seriously reducing land that is the habitat for thousands of species of

wildlife. Animals are actually being slaughtered during the reforestation process. The same problem, but on a much larger scale, is occurring in Central and South America to produce more feed and livestock.

HOW IS VEAL PRODUCED?

Veal is from a calf that has been fed a special diet from the day they complete their weaning to the time of slaughtering which is usually at about 3 months old. Their diet lacks iron which would turn the meat a reddish undesirable color for veal. The animal is placed into a stall and not allowed to even lick a pail or anything else which might contain the slightest amount of iron. They are not allowed to exercise and fed a formula of either special milk (milk-fed veal) or a formula consisting of water, milk solids, fats, and special nutrients for growth. When the calf is about 3-4 months old the texture of the meat is perfect for tender veal. The most desirable is the milk-fed at 3 months old. However, the second formula is being used more since the calf will be larger at 4 months resulting in more salable meat.

THE COLOR OF COOKED HAM

After ham is cured it contains nitrite salt. This chemical reacts with the myoglobin in the meat and changes it into nitrosomyoglobin. This biochemical alteration forces the meat to remain reddish even if cooked to a high temperature.

HAM SLICES SALTY? GIVE THEM A DRINK OF MILK

If your ham slices are too salty, try placing them in a dish of low-fat milk for 20 minutes then rinse them off in cold water and dry with paper towels before you cook them. The ham will not pick up the taste of the milk.

IS THERE A BLACK MARKET IN DRUGS TO LIVESTOCK PRODUCERS?

The FDA cracked down in the 1980's on illegal drug traffic to livestock producers, however, the problem may still exist. The FDA is still trying to control the problem with only minimal success. FDA testing of beef has shown that a number of drugs are still being used. One common unapproved drug is the antibiotic "chloramphenicol," which if it shows up in your beef in sufficient amounts can cause aplastic anemia and a number of nervous disorders. A number of other illegal livestock drugs that are still showing up include: Carbadox, Nitrofuazone, Dimetridazole, and Ipronidazole, all known to be carcinogens.

IS A RARE STEAK REALLY BLOODY?

No! The blood in meats is drained at the slaughterhouses and hardly any ever remains in the meat. There is a pigment called myoglobin in all meat that contributes to the reddish color of the meat. Myoglobin is found in the muscles not the arteries. Blood obtains its color from hemoglobin. Those red juices are for the most part colored by myoglobin (and water) not hemoglobin. Beef will have a more reddish color than pork since it contains more myoglobin in the meat.

TESTING FOR DONENESS

The experienced chef rarely uses a thermometer when cooking a steak. Meat has a certain resiliency that after testing thousands of steaks the chef will just place their finger on the steak and exert a small amount of pressure, telling them if the meat is rare, medium-rare, medium, medium-well, or well done. When meat cooks it tends to lose water and loses some of the flabbiness, the more it cooks the firmer it becomes.

WHY IS THE FELL LEFT ON LARGER CUTS OF LAMB?

The "fell" is a thin parchmentlike membrane or thin piece of tissue that covers the fat on a lamb. It is usually removed from certain cuts such as lamb chops before they are marketed, however, it is usually left on the larger cuts to help retain the shape of a roast and to retain the juices, producing a more moist roast.

IS A FATTY, MARBLED STEAK THE BEST?

Those white streaks running through the meat is fat. It is a storage depot for energy and for the meat to be well- marbled the animal must be fed a diet high in rich grains such as corn, which is where the old saying that corn-fed beef was the best. The fat imparts a flavor to the meat and provides a level of moisture which helps tenderize the meat. The presence of fat means that the animal did not exercise a lot and the meat will be more tender.

BEST WAY TO THAW MEAT

When thawing meat there are two considerations to be aware of. First, you want to reduce any damage from the freezing process and second you need to be cautious of bacterial contamination. Rapid thawing may cause excessive juices to be lost since some of the flavor is in the juices which is now combined with water and ice crystals. To thaw the meat and avoid excessive loss of flavor and reduce the risk of bacterial contamination it is best to thaw the meat in the refrigerator once it is removed from the freezer. This means that you will have to plan ahead. Placing the meat in the microwave to quick defrost will cause a loss of flavor and possibly a dried out piece of meat after it is cooked.

WHICH CAME FIRST? THE HOT DOG OR THE SAUSAGE

Actually the sausage was first on the scene in 900 B.C. Hot dogs were first called a number of names such as frankfurters and weiners in Germany and Austria and even "dachshund sausages" in the United States. Hot dogs as we know them were first sold at Coney Island in Brooklyn, New York in 1880 by a German immigrant by the name of Charles Feltman who called them frankfurters. The actual name "hot dog" was coined at a New York Giants baseball game in 1901 by concessionaire Harry Stevens. The weather was too cold to sell his normal ice cream treats, so he started selling "dachshund sausages" and instructed his sales team to yell out "Get 'em while they're hot."

A newspaper cartoonist seeing this drew a cartoon showing the sales people selling the sausages, but since he didn't know how to spell "dachshund" called the food a "hot dog." Hot dogs were sold at Coney Island from carts owned by Nathan Handwerker (Nathan's Hot Dogs). His employees sold the dogs dressed in white coats and wearing stethoscopes to denote cleanliness. In 1913 it was a dark year for hot dogs since they were banned at Coney Island when a rumor was started that they were made from ground dog meat. It was cleared up and they were allowed to be sold again a few months later.

HOW MANY NAMES ARE THERE FOR SAUSAGE?

The following are a few of the names for sausage: blood sausage, bologna, bratwurst, cervelat, chorizo, cotto salami, weiners, Genoa, kielbasa, knackwurst, liver sausage, pepperoni, bockwurst, mettwurst, braunschweiger, kiszka, liver loaf, yachtwurst, mortadella, Krakow, prasky, smoked thuringer, teawurst, Vienna, frizzes, Kosher sausage, Lebanon bologna, Lyons, medwurst, metz, Milano, and thuringer.

THE WAHOO WIENER, ONE OF THE LAST HANDMADE HOT DOGS

The finest homemade hot dogs are made by the O.K. Market in Wahoo, Nebraska. The hot dogs have no preservatives or fillers and the ground hamburger and pork are placed in Australian sheep casings. The casings are expensive and imported but make the finest hot dog with just the right texture and flexibility. The market has been in business since 1926 and if you want to taste a hot dog without nitrites call Harold Horak at (402)443-3015.

SPAM, HAWAIIANS' FAVORITE CANNED MEAT

In 1937 Spam, a spiced ham canned product was introduced by the Geo. A. Hormel & Company. Spam was extremely popular with the troops during World War II as a military ration. It is actually scraps of shredded pork, with added fat, salt, water, sugar, and a dose of sodium nitrite as a preservative and bacterial retardant. The consumption of Spam in the United States is about 114 million cans annually. Hawaii outdoes itself with an annual consumption of 12 cans per person. Alaska comes in second with 6 cans per person with Texas, Alabama, and Arkansas all tying for third place with an average of 3 cans per person.

BUYING THE BEST HAMBURGER MEAT

Hamburger meat really depends on your taste. The news is full of information telling you to purchase only the leanest hamburger meat you can find, and over the years I have been telling my patients the same thing. However, after reading of experiments that were conducted on hamburger meat relating to fat content and flavor, I have decided to change my mind and start purchasing the ground chuck instead of ground round. For the most part the extra fat content tends to be released from the meat during cooking if the meat is cooked on a small platform or grate allowing the fat to drip below the cooking surface. The flavor of the hamburger is far superior to the ground round since the chuck cut is from an area of the animal that is more exercised. However, make sure that the ground meat is very fresh to avoid bacterial contamination.

HOW MANY HAMBURGERS DO AMERICANS ORDER IN ONE SECOND?

In 1997 estimates are that 252 hamburgers are ordered every second 24 hours a day in the United States at the over 150,450 fast-food outlets. These hamburgers are ordered by about 47 million people.

WHAT IS WOOL ON A STICK

If you are a Texan you will know this phrase. It refers to lamb, and in Texas that's a nasty word. However, there are 100,000 sheep farms in the United States producing 340 million pounds of lamb. New Zealand and Australia, which is always thought of as a big producer, exports only 40 million pounds per year. In Colorado sheep ranchers are using llamas to protect the sheep, which are more effective than dogs.

FRIED RATTLESNAKE

Rattlesnake is actually a good eating meat. To prepare it just cut off the head and make sure you bury it in a hole at least 12-18 inches deep. Slit the skin near the head and peel it back an inch or so, then tie a cord around the peeled back area and hang the snake on a tree limb. This will allow you to have both hands free to peel the skin off using a sharp knife. Just loosen the skin from the flesh on the balance of the snake, then slit the belly open to remove the intestines. Rinse the snake in cold, salted water several times then cut into bite sized pieces, flour, and fry as you would chicken or add to soups or stews.

THE ROOM TEMPERATURE ROAST

When a roast is brought to room temperature or at least near room temperature it will cook more quickly than one that is placed into the oven directly from the refrigerator. Also, it will protect the roast from the exterior becoming overcooked and dried out before the inside is cooked. The only caution is that if the roast is very thick (over 6 inches in diameter) there may be a problem with bacterial contamination from spores in the air. Leaving a refrigerated roast out for about 1 hour should be sufficient to warm it without risking contamination. However, this should not be done in a warm, humid climate.

WHY IS LIVER ONLY RECOMMENDED ONCE A WEEK OR LESS?

The liver acts as a filtration plant for the body and may concentrate toxins in its cells. These may include pesticides and heavy metals depending what the animal's diet consists of. The liver is also extremely high in cholesterol, more than any beef product. A 3.5 ounce serving of beef liver contains 390 mg. of cholesterol compared to 3.5 ounces of grilled hamburger at 95 mg.

WHEN SHOULD SOUP BONES BE ADDED TO SOUP

A frequent mistake made by people when they are preparing soup is to place the animal bone into the boiling water. In most instances this tends to seal the bone to some degree and not allow all the flavor and nutrients to be released. The soup bone should be added to the pot when the pot is first placed on the range in cold water. This will allow the maximum release of the flavors, nutrients, and especially the gelatinous thickening agents to be released. Store soup bones in the freezer.

RESTING YOUR ROAST

A roast should never be carved until it has had a chance to rest and allow the juices to dissipate evenly throughout the roast. When you cook a roast the juices tend to be forced to the center as the juices near the surface evaporate from the heat. A roast should be left to stand for about 15 minutes before carving. This will also allow the meat to firm up a bit making it easier to carve thinner slices.

SHOULD YOU EAT MORE WILD GAME?

Restaurants, mail-order food catalogues, and gourmet stores nationwide are now selling more wild game than ever before. The most popular are buffalo, venison, wild boar, and pheasant. The majority of the wild game sold is farm-raised, not hunted, since the supply would be too limited. Venison hamburger is selling for $4.00 per pound while a steak sells for $14.00 a pound. Most game has a high price tag, however, it seems to be selling and gaining in popularity. Most wild animals don't get fat, therefore their meat is lower in fat, calories, and cholesterol than our conventional meat fare. The lower fat content of wild game may require marinating to produce the tenderness we are used to. To remove the ''gamy flavor'' just add some ginger ale to the marinade or soak the meat in the ginger ale for 1 hour before cooking. Beware of overcooking because this will cause many of the cuts to become tougher.

ROOM TEMPERATURE HAM

Many times you will see hams placed on the shelves in the market and not under refrigeration. These hams are actually sterilized to retard bacterial growth for longer periods of time. This sterilization, however, tends to detract from the flavor, texture, and nutritional values of the ham. Best to purchase one that is under refrigeration.

PORKERS LIKE TO PLAY WITH PIGSKINS

In England pigs are now given footballs to play with which is keeping them from chewing on each other's ears and tails. Pigs do like being penned up and pester each other all day. The pigs are more contented and are gaining weight at a faster rate.

WHY IS HAM SO POPULAR AT EASTER?

Serving ham for a special festival predates Christianity. When fresh meats were not available in the early spring months, Pagans buried fresh pork butts in the sand close to the ocean during the early winter months. The pork was cured by the "marinating" action of the salt water which killed the harmful microbes. When spring arrived, the salt-preserved meat was dug up and cooked over wood fires.

THE IRIDESCENT HAM

 I'm sure at one time or another you have purchased a ham that has shown some signs of a multicolored sheen that glistens and is somewhat greenish. This occasionally occurs from a ham when it is sliced and the surface is exposed to the effects of oxidation. It is not a sign of spoilage, but is caused by the nitrite-modification of the iron content of the meat which tends to undergo a biochemical change in pigmentation.

THE COLORS OF FAT

The color of fat that surrounds a steak can give you some insight as to what the cow ate and the quality of the beef. If the fat has a yellowish tint it indicates that the cow was grass-fed, and if the fat is white the cow was fed a corn and cereal grain diet. The meat with the white fat will be more tender and probably more expensive.

RE-WRAP ME

Always remove meat from store packaging materials and re-wrap using special freezer paper if you are planning to freeze the meat for more than 2 weeks. Chops, cutlets, and hamburger should be freezer-wrapped individually. This will assure maximum freshness and convenience.

FROZEN PREHISTORIC BURGERS?

Russians have claimed to have recovered a Mammoth with its meat still edible in the ice of Siberia. The Mammoth is estimated to be 20,000 years old. If they decide to clone it we may be eating Mammoth burgers. In the Yukon frozen prehistoric horse bones, estimated to be 50,000 years old were discovered in the ice. The marrow was determined to be safe to eat and was served at an exclusive New York dinner party.

WHY IS THE BEEF INDUSTRY FORCED TO HORMONIZE COWS?

If the beef industry did not use growth hormones the price of beef would increase about 27 cents per pound. With the use of hormones cows increase in size at a faster rate and have more body mass that is converted to usable meat. This will reduce the cost of raising cattle by about $70 per steer. Over 90% of all cattle raised for beef in the United States are given hormones. The hormone capsule is implanted in the skin on the back of the animal's ear.

COOKING VS. MEAT COLOR

As we cook beef we can see that the color of the meat changes depending on how long we cook it. The red pigment of the myoglobin changes from a bright red in a rare steak to brown in a well done one. The internal temperature in a rare steak is 135°F. (57°C.), medium-rare is 145°F. (62.8°C.), medium is 155°F. (68.3°C.), and well done is 160°F. (60°C.).

IS THE SURFACE OF MEAT BEING TREATED?

In many instances when we purchase meats the outside is a nice red color and the insides are darker almost with a brownish tint. Butchers have been accused of dying or spraying the meats, however, it is really not their fault. Actually, when the animal is slaughtered and the oxygen-rich blood is not pumped to the muscles, the myoglobin tends to lose some of its reddish color and may turn a brownish color. Then when the meat is further exposed to the air through the plastic wrap, oxidation tends to turn the myoglobin a red color. Butchers call this process the "bloom" of the meat. If you would like to see the insides a bright red color, just slice the insides open and leave the meat in the refrigerator for a short period of time. The air will turn the meat a reddish color. Remember, however, that if the meat is exposed for too long a period the oxygen will eventually turn the meat brown.

THE SPLATTERING BACON

If bacon was still produced the old fashioned way by curing it slowly and using a dry salt it would not be splattering all over the place. Today's bacon is cured using a brine which speeds up the process. The brine tends to saturate the bacon more causing the grease to be released and splatter more. To reduce splattering, use a lower heat setting, this will also reduce the number of nitrites you will convert into a carcinogen since the higher heat tends to convert the nitrites faster. Another method that might work is to soak the bacon in ice cold water for 2-4 minutes, then dry the bacon well with paper towels before frying. Also, try sprinkling the bacon with a small amount of flour, if that doesn't work, as a last resort poke some holes in them with your golf shoes.

POUND PER POUND BETTER THAN BEEF

The Chinese farmers knew that pork was one of the most efficient forms of livestock in providing meat over 2,000 years ago. Pigs are efficient at converting fodder into edible meat and far surpasses the cow. For every 100 pounds of food a pig consumes they produce 20 pounds of edible meat. For every 300 pounds of food a cow consumes they produce 20 pounds of edible meat. More of the pig is also edible than any other animal. Fish farmers can produce a pound of fish for every pound of feed and chickens only need 2 pounds of feed to produce a pound of meat.

HOW TO RUIN WILD GAME

How many times have you seen a deer strapped to a bumper of a car and being transported home with the proud hunter grinning all the way. Well he may have enjoyed the macho feeling but what he has done to the kill is to destroy it before he got it home. The heat from the car engine can increase the level of bacterial growth 10 fold and render the meat worthless by the time he gets it home. The animal should be bled in the field, cleanly gutted, cooled if possible, and placed on top of the car, covered on a rack.

WHY BAD MEAT SMELLS BAD

Bacteria, spores, mold may all be either airborne or already on the surface of the meat because of poor sanitary condition when the animal was slaughtered and processed. These contaminants break down the surface of the meat, liquefying the carbohydrates and proteins and producing a putrid film on the meat. This film produces carbon dioxide and ammonia gases which result in a noxious offensive odor. The meat may also be discolored by this action on the myoglobin (red coloring pigment) in the meat converting the myoglobin into yellow and green bile pigments. The more the reaction is allowed to take place the farther the breakdown occurs and converts the protein into "mercaptans" a chemical that contains a substance related to "skunk spray" as well as hydrogen sulfide which has the "rotten egg" smell. Meats must be kept refrigerated and not allowed to remain at room temperature for more than a short period of time.

WHAT IS MEAT COMPOSED OF?

Meat	% Water	% Protein	% Fat
Beef	60	18	22
Pork	42	14	45
Lamb	56	16	28
Turkey	58	20	20
Chicken	65	30	6
Fish	70	20	9

MARINADE FACTS

If you ever wondered why meats turn brown too quickly when they are cooked on a shish kebab or similar method of cooking, it's the marinade. Marinade has a high acid content that tends to react with the myoglobin (a muscle pigment) and turns it brown very quickly.

The lower the temperature, the slower the marinade will react, turn brown, and tenderize the meat. If you marinade at room temperature it will take less time than if you do it in the refrigerator. However, it's safer under refrigeration.

The acid in most marinades may reduce the moisture retaining properties of the meat and the meat may not be as moist as you would expect. This problem is usually countered by the fact that the meat will have a better flavor and may contain some of the marinade.

Marinade may be a product that contains papain, bromelein, tomato juice, lemon juice, white vinegar, etc.

Large pieces of meat should be placed into a large tightly sealed plastic bag to conserve the amount of marinade needed. Smaller foods can be marinated in a glass container with excellent results. The acidic nature of the marinades may react with metals and give the food a poor flavor.

Never baste the food with marinade that the food was in. Bacteria from the food may contaminate the cooking food and the food may not cook long enough to kill the new bacteria.

Always cover the food that is marinating, and keep it refrigerated. Also, make sure the food that is in the marinade is fully covered with the marinade.

MARINADE TIMES UNDER REFRIGERATION

Fish . . . . 20-40 minutes
Poultry . . . . 3-4 hours
Meat . . . . 1-2 days

If the pieces of meat are cut into small pieces the marinade time should be shortened.

THE COOLER THE MEAT, THE TOUGHER

When meat cools on your plate it will get tougher because the collagen which has turned to a tender gelatin thickens and becomes tougher. The best way to counter this problem is to be sure you are served a steak on a warmed or metal plate. After carving a roast it would be best to keep it in a warmer or back in the oven with the door ajar.

BACTERIA RISKS, HAM COMPARED TO CHICKEN

Recent studies have shown that a typical piece of pork found in a supermarket may only have a few hundred bacteria per square centimeter, compared to over 100,000 bacteria in the same area of a piece of chicken. This is one of the reasons it is so important to clean up well after handling poultry.

I WONDER WHERE THE FLAVOR WENT

When cooked beef is refrigerated the flavor changes noticeably. After only a few hours fat which is the main source of the flavor, tends to produce an "off-flavor" within the meat. This "off-flavor" is caused by the heating process which tends to release reactive substances from the muscle tissue and produces oxidation of the fats, especially the phospholipids and the polyunsaturated fats in the muscle itself. One of the reasons this occurs is that the iron in the muscles is broken down and released from the hemoglobin and myoglobin and encourages the oxidation reaction. To slow the process down and fight the "off-flavor" problem, try to avoid using iron or aluminum pots and pans, and try not to salt meats until you are ready to eat them. Pepper and onions, however, seem to slow the process down and even inhibit them.

CAN A COW BE TENDERIZED BEFORE SLAUGHTERING?

A number of slaughterhouses in the United States are injecting animals with a papain solution shortly before they are slaughtered. The solution is carried to the muscles via the bloodstream and then remains in the meat, since it does not have time to be broken down before the animal is killed. When the meat is cooked, the enzyme is activated at 150°F. (65.6°C.). This method does have it drawbacks, however, since the flesh occasionally becomes mushy and lacks the firmness we are used to.

SHOULD A STEAK BE SALTED OR PEPPERED BEFORE COOKING?

The rule is never to use a seasoning that contains salt before cooking. The salt tends to draw liquid from the meat, the liquid then boils in the pan and the surface of the meat may not have the desired texture or brown color you desire. The salt does not work its way into the meat to flavor it unless you puncture the meat which is not recommended. If you wish the flavor of a seasoned salt, the best method is to season both sides of the meat just before serving. Ground pepper should never be placed on any meat that is cooked in a pan using dry heat. Pepper tends to become bitter when scorched.

WHEN WERE ANIMALS DOMESTICATED?

Animal	Approximate Date B.C.	Country
Sheep	9000	Middle East
Dog	8400	North America
Goat	7500	Middle East
Pig	7000	Middle East
Cattle	6500	Middle East
Horse	3000	Russia
Chicken	2000	India

THE DIFFERENCE IN FREEZER LIFE BETWEEN CHICKEN AND BEEF

Chicken has a shorter freezer life due to its higher polyunsaturated fat to saturated fat content. Polyunsaturates are more prone to destruction by oxidation and subsequently rancidity. There are more hydrogen sites in a polyunsaturated fat for oxygen to attach to. Beef is higher in saturated fat and has hardly any open sites.

WHY ARE CERTAIN CUTS OF BEEF MORE TENDER?

There are a number of factors that relate to the tenderness of a piece of meat, they are: the actual location the meat is cut from, the activity level of the animal, and the age of the animal. The areas of the animal that are the least exercised are the areas that will be the most tender. However, even if a steak is labeled sirloin and expected to be tender, it will still depend on which end it is cut from. If it is cut from the short loin end it will be more tender than if cut from the area near where the round steaks are cut. Activity levels in most beef is kept to a minimum so that they will develop only minimum levels of connective tissue. Kobe beef from Japan actually are massaged by "beef masseurs" to relax them since stress and tension may cause muscles to flex thus resulting in exercise that would increase the level of connective tissue.

TO AGE OR NOT TO AGE?

Aging meat causes the enzymes in the meat to soften the connective tissue and the meat to become more tender. When aging beef, the temperature is very important, and must be kept between 34° and 38°F. (1.1C. and 3.3°C.).The meat should not be frozen since the enzymes are inactivated, also too high a temperature will cause bacterial growth.

HOW MUCH BEEF TO BUY FOR EACH PERSON?

Type Of Beef	Per Serving
Chuck Roast/Rib Roast	½ lb.
Hamburger	¼ lb.
Pot Roast with bone	¼ lb.
Ribs	1 lb.
Round Beef Roast with bone	¼ lb.
Round Steak	½ lb.
Sliced Lunch Meats	¼ lb.
Steaks without bones	7 oz.
Steaks with bone	12 oz.
Stew Meat	¼ lb.
Tenderloin of Beef	½ lb.

RELAX THE ANIMAL BEFORE SLAUGHTERING

The mental state of the animal hours before they are slaughtered is important to the storage life of the meat. When you slaughter an animal that is stressed out, tense, or afraid its body gears up for the flight or fight reflex and starts to convert glycogen (carbohydrate) into glucose for quick energy needs. This will provide the animal with greater strength but when it is slaughtered the excess glucose shortens the storage life of the meat. The glycogen is needed to remain in the muscles to convert to lactic acid and help retard bacterial growth. When you are hunting the meat will be better if the animal is killed instantly instead of wounding it and allowing it to live and convert the glycogen. Most slaughterhouses are aware of this problem and see to it that the animal is well relaxed, most of the time by playing soothing music, before they kill it.

RIGOR MORTIS AND TENDERNESS

The process of rigor mortis occurs in all animals and is characterized by the stiffening of the meat and occurs a few hours after slaughtering. If meat is not consumed immediately after it is slaughtered then you should wait at least 15-36 hours which gives the enzymes a chance to soften the connective tissue.

WILL FREEZING RAW MEAT MAKE IT SAFE TO EAT RARE?

Unfortunately freezing will not kill all the bacteria in meat or chicken and you will still have a risk if the meat is consumed without fully cooking it. Some microbes will survive the freezing and will multiply very quickly as the meat is thawed. If you desire a rare hamburger, just purchase a steak, sear it well on both sides, grind it in your meat grinder and cook it immediately.

WHY SHOULD MEATS BE WRAPPED TIGHTLY WHEN FREEZING?

When you freeze foods evaporation continues and fluids are lost. The entire surface area of the meat needs to be protected from the loss of moisture with a moisture-resistant wrap. The best wrap for freezing meats is plastic wrap with a protective freezer paper over the wrap. This does not 100% protect the meat from a percentage of evaporation taking place in which water vapor causes freezer burn. A good tight wrap will, however, reduce the risk of oxidation and rancidity.

TENDERIZING MEATS

Since the main problem with tough cuts of beef is the level of collagen (protein substance) in the connective tissue it is necessary to use a moist heat to break down the collagen and soften the connective tissue. A slow moist heat will solve the problem, however, if you cook the meat too long it will actually cause the meat to get tough again due to another constituent in the connective tissue called elastin which does not soften and become tender. The best method of slow cooking meat is to cook it at 180° F. (82.2°C.) for about 2-3 hours using a moist heat. Boiling is not effective nor is slow cooking at 140°F. (60°C.) for an extended period. Meat tenderizers that actually break down the protein are papain, and bromelein. Baking soda is the easiest product to use when tenderizing beef since all you have to do is rub it on the meat and allow it to stand for 3-5 hours before you rinse and cook it.

WHAT IS A CHITLIN?

Chitlins, chitlings, or chitterlings are all the same southern delicacy made from pigs' intestines. One 3 ounce serving of simmered chitlings contains 260 calories, 222 of which come from fat.

SHOULD A ROAST BE COOKED IN A COVERED PAN?

When cooking a roast there are two methods that are normally used, either using dry heat (without liquid) or moist heat (with liquid). When the meat is covered it is cooked with steam that is trapped in the pan. Many cooks use this method to prevent the roast from drying out. Dry heat with the lid off will keep the outside of the roast crisp instead of mushy and if you wish the roast can be basted every 15 minutes to provide the desired moisture. This is the preferred method by most chefs. However, if you do roast with a lid on and in liquid, you must lower the temperature by 25°F. (-3.9°C.). Roasts should always be cooked on a rack or stalks of celery and never allowed to sit in the liquid on the bottom of the pan giving you a mushy bottom.

WHAT IS THE FAVORITE PIZZA TOPPING?

Pepperoni is at the top of the list. Americans consume 300 million pounds on pizza every year. If you placed all the pepperoni pizzas eaten in the United States next to each other they would take up an area the size of 13,000 football fields.

HAM IT UP

The Italian name for ham is "prosciutto." Prosciutto is never smoked and is prepared by a salt-curing process, seasoned and then air dried. Prosciutto cotta means that the ham has been cooked and is common terminology in a deli.

RELEASE ME

The flavor of a fully cooked ham can be improved by cooking. Cooking releases the juices.

HAMBRRRRRR

If you want thin ham slices, place the ham in the freezer for 20 minutes before you begin slicing.

BASTE ME, BASTE ME

When cooking a pork loin roast, place the fat side down for the first 20 minutes. This will cause the fat to release juices, then turn the roast over for the balance of the cooking time to allow the fat to baste the roast.

COLA HITS THE SPOT

If you want a moist ham, place the contents of a 12 ounce can of cola in your pan and wrap the ham in tin foil. About 30 minutes before the ham is done, remove the tin foil and allow the ham juices to mix with the cola.

BACON FACTS

Sliced bacon will only stay fresh for 1 week under refrigeration once the package is opened and the bacon is exposed to air. If you allow bacon to sit at room temperature for 20-30 minutes before cooking it will separate more easily. Never buy bacon if it looks slimy, chances are that it's not fresh.

GIMME AN "A"

Lamb is graded Prime, Choice, Good, Utility, or Cull. Prime is only sold to better restaurants. Most supermarket lamb is Good."

Fat And Calories In Meat			
Fat(gm.)	% Fat	Calories	Total Calories
Beef			
Round Bone	4	19	152
Sirloin Roast	4	19	156
Round Steak	5	22	161
Sirloin (dbl bone)	5	22	162
Chuck Arm	6	25	164
Flank Steak	6	25	167

Fat And Calories In Meat			
Fat(gm.)	% Fat	Calories	Total Calories
Beef			
Porterhouse	6	24	168
T-Bone	6	25	170
Sirloin Steak	8	30	184
Rump Roast	8	30	184
Club Steak	11	36	208
Chuck Rib	12	37	212
Ground Beef (lean)	15	44	230
Ground Beef (reg.)	17	46	245
Lamb			
Foreshank	5	23	152
Sirloin of Leg	6	26	154
Loin Chop	8	32	176
Blade Chop	10	37	178
Arm Chop	12	35	230
Pork			
Loin, Tenderloin	5	20	142
Ham Leg (rump)	9	32	188
Ham Leg (shank)	9	33	183
Shoulder	11	38	194
Loin	12	38	209
Veal			
Veal Cutlet	4	17	155
Sirloin Chop	5	20	167
Blade Steak	5	19	156
Rib Roast	5	24	136
Loin Chop	7	25	179

CHAPTER 11

Poultry Plus

Most chickens in the United States are processed in long metal vats with a controlled water temperature of 125°F. (51.7°C.) to 132°F. (55.7°C.). This is the temperature that bacterial growth is at a high level. Hot water also opens the pores in chickens and may allow the entry of undesirable matter that is floating in the hot bloody water of this communal bath.

Commercial chickens must be cooked to an internal temperature of 185°F. (85°C.) to kill any bacteria that may be present. If the chicken is fully cooked and you see traces of pink near the bone, it is not a sign of undercooking. It is probably only the bone pigment that has leached out during the cooking process. This is more common in smaller birds or ones that have been frozen and defrosted. The meat is perfectly safe to eat. This effect can be avoided by purchasing older birds.

Any kitchen item, whether it is a washcloth, sponge or the counter must be thoroughly cleaned after working with chicken to eliminate the possibility of contamination of other foods and utensils if any harmful bacteria is present.

Recent television expose shows have uncovered the fact that there is a potential health risk with chicken due to present processing techniques. Most of the pathogens related to poultry are rarely detected using the present poultry inspection procedures. Studies conducted by the National Academy of Science reported that 48% of food poisonings in the United States are caused by contaminated poultry. One person in every fifty who eat chicken regularly are at risk of some form of food poisoning.

In 1997 the USDA ordered food inspectors to increase inspections of all U.S. chicken slaughtering plants. However, due to budget restraints the overall number of inspectors has decreased.

HOW ARE CHICKENS SLAUGHTERED AND INSPECTED?

When the chicken is approximately six weeks old they are ready for harvesting. The live chickens are packed into cases of 22 birds per case and sent to the slaughterhouse, the cages are dumped onto a conveyer belt, workers grab the bird and hang them upside down with their feet hooked into a type of locking device. Workers can grab a bird and lock them up in about one second. They are then dampened with a spray and sent past an electrically charged grid that they cannot avoid, the charge is only 18 volts and just enough to stun them so that they won't put up a fight. As the limp chicken moves on the conveyer, it passes a mechanical knife that slits its throat and allows it to bleed freely. After a minute the blood has drained and the conveyer reaches a scalding water bath in which they are literally dragged through. The 135°F. (57°C.) water temperature loosens their feathers.

Next they pass the defeathering machine which consists of six-inch spinning rubber projections which literally flogs all the feathers off the bird. The bird now arrives at the point where a machine or a worker cuts off the chicken's head, cuts open the cavity and removes the entrails. The USDA inspector will inspect the bird at this point for diseases, tumors, or infections. The inspector is given a whole 2 seconds to accomplish this task that should take at least 20 seconds or more. If the bird has one tumor it is removed and the bird is passed. If it has two or more it is rejected. Cleaning is then done with 5,000 chickens to a bath of chilled water. One billion pounds of chicken are shipped in the United States every week.

THE PROCESSING OF KOSHER POULTRY

Kosher poultry is defeathered in cold water not warm or hot water. It is then soaked, totally submerged for 30-40 minutes in ice cold water, hand salted inside and out to clean it out, then allowed to hang for about 1 hour to remove any remaining blood residue. The birds are then salted and rinsed 3 more times to remove any remaining salt. Kosher chickens have a fresher, cleaner taste than the standard market chicken. Many Kosher processed chickens never make it to the marketplace even when passed by government inspectors. The quality control differs from most other processors and the standards are higher.

FOOD FACT

When purchasing chicken, be aware that a 3 pound chicken will yield about 1 ½ pounds of edible meat.

BUGS WILL HAVE A FIELD DAY

Stuffing or cooked poultry should never be allowed to remain at room temperature for more than 40 minutes before refrigerating. Salmonella thrives at temperatures of 60° F. (15.6°C.) to 125°F. (51.7°C.). All stuffing should be removed when the bird is ready for carving, never leave even a small amount of stuffing in the bird. Hot stuffing will keep the temperature just right for bacteria to grow for a long time.

DON'T BE TOO SPEEDY

When you make a chicken or turkey salad be sure that the meat has been cooked to 180°F. (82.2°C.), then allow the meat to cool in the refrigerator before adding the salad dressing or mayonnaise.

CHICKEN TENDERS

Lemon is a natural tenderizer for chicken and gives it a unique flavor; also you might try basting it with a small amount of Zinfandel. Remember, a low to moderate cooking temperature will produce a juicier chicken, since more fat and moisture are retained.

FOWL CUBES

Do-it-yourself bouillon cubes can be made by freezing leftover chicken broth in ice cube trays. They can be stored in baggies and kept frozen until needed for a recipe or soup. They are easily thawed in the microwave.

SHORT TIMERS

Raw poultry and hamburger meat should not be kept in the refrigerator for more than 2 days without being frozen.

CLIP, CLIP

If you want to save money when buying chicken, buy the whole chickens then cut them with a poultry scissors and freeze the sections you want together. When you purchase whole birds, try not to buy the larger ones, these are older birds and not as tender. Young chickens and turkeys also have less fat.

TRY IT, YOU WILL NOTICE THE DIFFERENCE
Chefs tenderize and improve the taste of chicken by submerging the chicken parts in buttermilk for 2-3 hours in the refrigerator before cooking.

ONLY BUY 4.0 CHICKENS
Chickens are Grade A, Grade B, or Grade C. Grades B and C are usually blemished and only used in canning, frozen foods, and TV dinners. Grade A chickens are sold in supermarket meat departments.

NO CREATURE COMFORT HERE
Production chickens are raised in large "coop farms" that house 10,000+ chickens each. The chickens are placed in holding boxes and fed around the clock to fatten them up. The boxes are well lighted 24 hours a day so that the chickens do not get much sleep.

CALL THE MASSEUR
Poultry in foreign countries are never subjected to the conditions we allow in the United States. You will also notice a difference in taste. If you do notice an odor from the market production chickens, try rubbing a small amount of lemon juice into the skin. The bird will enjoy this and it will totally remove the odor.

ASK THE BUTCHER
When you see a chicken labeled fresh, you should ask the butcher whether it was previously frozen. If it has been frozen once it would be best not to re-freeze it.

REAL SICK BIRDS?
Chicken farmers purchased $393 million dollars worth of antibiotics in 1997.

MASS CHICKENDUCTION
One chicken farm is capable of shipping 26 million chickens per week and over 43 million chickens are processed in the U.S. every day according to the National Broiler Council.

SKIP THE INJECTION

Try cooking your next turkey upside down on a "V" rack for the first hour. The juices will flow to the breast and make the meat moist and tender. Remove the "V" rack after the first hour. You will never buy another fat-basted bird.

LET'S TALK TURKEY

In 1997 Americans consumed approximately 28 pounds of turkey. In 1991 they consumed 20 pounds but in 1930 ate only 2 pounds.

SMART STUFF

Supermarkets are now selling stuffing bags to be placed in the cavity of the bird before you place the stuffing in. This is an excellent idea since all the stuffing can be removed at once. However, it is less expensive to just use any piece of cheesecloth.

RELAX!

Once the turkey has finished cooking it should be allowed to rest for about 20 minutes before carving it. This will allow the steam to dissipate and the meat will not fall apart.

BACTERIA HAVEN

Never stuff a turkey or other fowl and leave it overnight in the refrigerator thinking it's safe. The inside of the bird acts like an incubator allowing rapid bacterial growth to occur. When the bird is cooked all the bacteria may not be killed. This results in hundreds of cases of food poisoning annually.

FAUX BUFFALO

Chicken wings alias "buffalo wings" usually supply up to 25 grams of fat in a serving of 3 wings.

STAYING POWER

If you want to store chicken for 3-4 days in the refrigerator, change the wrapping to plastic wrap or waxed paper. The supermarket wrapping often contains blood residue.

HOME, HOME ON THE RANGE

A free range chicken has an average of 14% fat compared to a standard cooped-up production chicken at 18-20% fat.

RUBDOWN

Brush or apply a thin layer of white vermouth to the skin of a turkey about 15 minutes before you are ready to remove it from the oven. The skin will develop a nice rich brown tone and the turkey should really enjoy it.

BAD BUGS A GO GO

Any kitchen item, whether it is a washcloth, sponge or the counter must be thoroughly cleaned after working with chicken to eliminate the possibility of contamination of other foods and utensils if any harmful bacteria is present.

BROWN PARTS

If you wish your chicken or parts to be browned, try brushing them with a low-salt soy sauce.

THAWING OUT

Poultry thaws at approximately 1 pound every 5 hours.

HERE A DUCK, THERE A DUCK

A farm raised duck will have more meat than a wild duck. Ducks are not good candidates for stuffing. Their fat content is so high that the fat is absorbed into the stuffing when you are cooking them.

WHERE'S CHICKEY?

Miniature chickens are called Cornish game hens. These are chickens that are only 4-6 weeks old and only weigh about 2 pounds each.

GREAT CHICKEN RANCH

One of the finest chicken ranches in the United States is Shelton's in Pomona, California (909) 623-4361. They raise only free range chickens, use no antibiotics, and hand process every chicken.

BUYER BEWARE
It would be best to compare nutrition labels when purchasing ground turkey, chicken, or pork. You may be surprised that in most instances they will have as high a fat content as lean hamburger.

SCRUB A DUB DUB
The safest method of thawing poultry is to place it in a bowl of cold water. If you add salt to the water it will improve the flavor of the poultry as well as provide a measure of additional cleaning.

OUR TAX DOLLARS AT WORK?
In 1995 the U.S. Government conducted a study, (that I hope didn't cost us anything), that determined that 80% of the public referred to the "stuff" inside a turkey as "stuffing," while 20% called it "dressing." The most important fact was that of the 20% group most were all over 65.

SPUD IT
When stuffing a bird the opening may be sealed with a piece of raw potato.

SOME FOWL FACTS
Americans averaged 74 pounds of chicken in 1997, about 24 birds per person. Approximately 35% of all meat sold in the U.S. is chicken, with 5.4 billion pounds of the total 7 billion pounds produced being sold by fast food restaurants. Chicken farming is a $15 billion dollar industry.

LIKE DARK MEAT? EAT WILD FOWL!
The dark meat on fowl is the result of using the breast muscles more providing them with a greater blood supply. The breast muscles are rarely used in a production bird since they are cooped up all of their lives. The breast meat on wild fowl is always dark since these fowl must fly for long journeys and use the muscles extensively.

FOWL ANTIBIOTICS
Because of the way chickens are cooped up and the questionable sanitary conditions they must endure, diseases are common occurrences. Almost all poultry, approximately 85% of all pigs, and 60% of all beef in the United States are fed either penicillin or tetracycline. Almost 50% of all antibiotics manufactured are used on animals. The fear is now that the animals will develop antibiotic-resistant bacteria. In Europe many

countries will not allow the indiscriminate use of antibiotics for this reason.

CHUBBY CHICKEN

According to the latest USDA reports chickens are being marketed at higher weights than ever before. Using forced feeding and hormones may be the answer why they arrive at markets at top weight in only 7 weeks. Five years ago it took 12-14 weeks. Turkeys reach maturity in 14-22 weeks and are usually more tender than chickens as well as having less fat.

FOWL PLUCKING

If you need to pluck a duck, make sure the water you dip the duck in is at least 155°F. (83.3°C.). It is easier to pluck out the feathers if they are hot and wet. If you are plucking a goose, pheasant, or quail, the water should be at least 135°F. (57°C.).

A CHICKEN BY ANY OTHER NAME

Free-range chickens - These chickens are allowed to forage for food and consume a well-balanced diet. The cage doors must be kept open according to USDA rules and the chickens are usually sold whole. The exercise a free-range chicken gets increases its flavor. The meat is of a better quality and they have a higher meat to bone ratio.

» Organic chickens — May only be raised on land that has never had any chemical fertilizer or pesticide used on it for at least 3 years. They must also be fed chemical-free grains and are for the most part free-range chickens.

» Mass-produced chickens — Commercially raised in crowded coops and never allowed to run free. They are marketed in exact sizes in the same number of months.

» Kosher chickens — Chickens which have been slaughtered and cleaned in compliance with Jewish dietary laws.

» Broilers/Fryers — These are 7 week old birds that weigh from 3-4 pounds.

» Roasting chickens — These are usually hens that weigh in at 5-8 pounds with more fat than broilers.

» Stewing hens — Usually weigh 4-8 pounds and are a year old. Basically, these are retired laying hens. They are tough old birds and need to be slow-cooked but are flavorful.

» Capons — These are castrated roosters which average 10 weeks old and weigh 8-10 pounds. They usually have large white meat breasts from making a lot of noise.

» Poussins — These are baby chicks only 1 month old and weighing about one pound. They lack flavor and are only used for grilling.

» Cornish hens — These are baby chicks that are 5-6 weeks old and weigh about 2 pounds. They are best grilled or roasted.

YOUR IN A MUDDLE IF THERE'S A PUDDLE

When choosing meat or poultry in the supermarket, make sure that there is no liquid residue either wet or frozen on the bottom of the package. If there is, it means that the food has been frozen and the cells have released a percentage of their fluids. When cooked the bones will be noticeably darker than a fresher product.

WHICH CAME FIRST, THE CHICKEN OR THE TURKEY?

According to the history books, the chicken was forced to come to the Western Hemisphere by Spanish explorers who weren't sure what kind of meat they would find when they arrived and wanted a meat they were familiar with. The turkey, however, is a native American and was introduced to Europe by the same explorers. The Europeans didn't know what to call the turkey and the Spanish were not sure where they landed. Thinking that it was India they called the turkey "Bird of India" or "Calcutta Hen."

STICKY CHICKEN SKIN

When cooking chicken on a barbecue rack always grease the rack well first. The collagen in the skin will turn into a sticky gelatin which causes it to stick to the rack. To really solve the problem, try baking the chicken for 15-20 minutes in a preheated oven breast side up allowing the gelatin time to infuse into the fat and meat or to be released into the pan.

HOW FAST DO BACTERIA ON CHICKEN MULTIPLY?

If a piece of chicken has 10,000 bacteria on a 1 square centimeter area when it is processed and reaches the supermarket it will increase 10,000 times that figure if left in the refrigerator at about 40°F. (4.4°C.) for 6 days. The Center for Disease Control in Atlanta estimates that 9,000 people die each year from foodborne illness with thousands of other becoming ill from bacterial, chemical, fertilizer, and pesticide residues left on foods and poultry. According to the USDA 40% of all chickens are contaminated with salmonella and even if contaminated they can still pass the USDA inspection. Almost 50% of all animal feed may contain salmonella.

MINI-PIGEON?

If you ever wondered what a squab is, it is just a "mini-pigeon" that is no more than 1 month old. They are specially bred to be plump and are raised to be marketed. They are usually sold frozen and will not weigh over 1 pound. Look for birds with pale skin and the plumper the better. Squab will store frozen for about 6 months at 0°F. (-17.8°C.).

BEST METHOD OF CLEANING A CHICKEN

Chickens need to be cleaned thoroughly inside and out before cooking them to remove any residues that are left from the slaughtering process. While it is impossible to completely clean the bird you should at least do the best you can. The preferred method is to place 1 tablespoon of baking soda in the water that you will use to clean the chicken and rinse the bird several times, then rinse with clean water several times. The mild acidic action and abrasiveness of the baking soda will do the job.

HOW MUCH CHICKEN TO BUY FOR EACH PERSON?

5 pounds of chicken will provide about 3 cups of meat.

Type of Chicken	Amount Per Person
Broiler/Fryer	½ lb.
Capon	¾ lb.
Cornish Game Hen	1 bird
Whole Chicken with bones	1 lb.
Breast	½ breast
Drumstick	2 drumsticks
Thighs	2 thighs

IS BARBECUED BITTER CHICKEN A PROBLEM?

If you are going to use a barbecue sauce you need to know when to apply it otherwise the chicken will have an acid taste. Barbecue sauces contain sugar and high heat tends to burn sugar very easily as well as some of the spices. The barbecue sauce should never be placed on the bird until about 15 minutes before the bird is fully cooked. Another secret to the perfect barbecued bird is to use lower heat and leave the bird on for a longer period of time. Never place the bird too close to the coals.

NEVER COOK STEW AT A FULL BOIL

Stew should be cooked at a medium heat and not allowed to boil. The turbulence causes all the ingredients to be blended with each other and flavors intermingle instead of picking up the flavor of the base. Stew meat should not be too lean or the taste will suffer since the taste for the most part comes from the fat. Fish stew on the other hand is made with some olive oil and needs to be boiled somewhat vigorously to blend the oil in with the ingredients, bouillabaisse is a good example.

SKIN COLOR VS. QUALITY

Since the public would prefer to see a nice yellowish-colored chicken skin instead of a bluish-white sickly looking skin, farmers are now placing marigold petals into the chicken feed to make their skin yellow. Production chickens are never allowed to run free and soak up the sunlight to make their skins yellow and their skins are actually a sickly bluish color. Since the marigold petals are "all-natural" they do not have to be listed anywhere on the packaging. Free-range chickens always have yellowish skins as well as being more flavorful.

SKINNY TIP

The easiest way to skin a chicken is to slightly freeze it first. The skin will come right off with hardly any effort.

QUAIL, A DANGEROUS BIRD?

Over the years a number of people have become ill with symptoms of nausea, vomiting, shivers, and even a type of slow-spreading paralysis from eating quail. The problem may be the result of their diet in certain parts of the country. Occasionally a quail may consume hemlock, which may be toxic to humans, as part of their feeding pattern. The green quail of Algeria has caused a number of illnesses. If you do experience illness after eating quail it would be best to contact the local health authorities.

COOKING WHITE MEAT VS. DARK MEAT

When you cook white and dark meat chicken parts together, remember that the white meat cooks faster than the dark, so start the dark meat a little sooner. The higher fat content in the dark meat is why this occurs. The white meat may be too dry if you cook them together.

GIBLET COOKING

When you cook giblets, make sure that you place the liver in during the last 20 minutes. The liver tends to flavor all the giblets when cooked with them from the beginning.

MEAT AND POULTRY HOTLINE 1-(800)535-4555

CHAPTER 12

Real Fishy

The popularity of fish has risen since the 1980's and more varieties of fish have become available. Consumption of fish in 1997 averaged 19 pounds per person. More fish than ever are now raised in aquaculture fish farms. The fats in fish are high in polyunsaturates and contain the omega-3 fatty acids that may protect us from heart attacks by keeping the blood from coagulating too easily.

Studies show that even canned or frozen fish retain most of their omega-3 fatty acids. However, many fish and shellfish may still harbor certain bacteria and parasites. Cooking is a must, fish and shellfish should never be eaten raw. Also, never consume the skin or visible fat on fish as most of the contaminants, if present, will be located there.

CHOOSING FRESH FISH IN THE SUPERMARKET

» Skin
The skin should always have a shiny look to it and when finger pressure is applied it should easily spring back to its original shape. The meat should be firm to the touch with no visible blemishes. Never buy fish if the skin has any dark discolorizations.

» Eyes
When you look into the fishes' eyes they should be bulging and not sunken into the head which is a sign of a dried out fish. The eyes should also be clear and not cloudy. If the fish winks at you this is a very good sign.

» Scales
The scales should not be falling off. If you notice loose scales don't buy the fish. The scales should also have a healthy bright and shiny appearance.

» Gills

The gills must look clean with no sign of any slime. Their healthy color is a reddish-pink. Gray gills are a sign of an old fish that has seen better days.

» Odor

A fresh fish never smells "fishy." If the fish does have a strong odor about it, it is probably from the flesh decomposing and releasing the chemical compound "trimethylamine."

Seafood should be as fresh as possible, usually no more than 2-3 days out of the water.

CHOOSING FROZEN FISH IN THE SUPERMARKET

» Odor

If frozen fish has an odor it has probably thawed and been re-frozen. When it is thawed it should still have hardly any odor.

» Skin

Be sure that the skin and flesh are frozen solid and that there are no discolorization or soft spots. The skin should be totally intact with no areas missing.

» Wrappings

The wrapping should be intact with no tears or ice crystals and be sure that the fish is frozen solid.

SMELLS FISHY

Before handling fish, try washing your hands in plain cold water. Chances are you won't have a fish smell on them afterwards. A small amount of white vinegar placed into the pan you have fried fish in will eliminate the odor.

COLD FISH?

When fish is frozen it tends to lose some of its flavor. If you place the frozen fish in low-fat milk when it is thawing some of the original flavor will return. It is recommended by chefs not to completely thaw a frozen fish before cooking since the fish might become mushy. Frozen fish is easier to skin than a fresh one.

TASTE BUD TREAT

If you are going to bake fish, try wrapping it in aluminum foil with a sprig of dill and a small amount of chopped onion.

MILD ACID TO THE RESCUE

If you need to scale a fish, try rubbing white vinegar on the scales and then allow it to sit for about 10 minutes.

BIG DIFFERENCE

Saturated fat only accounts for 10-25% of the total fat in seafood compared to an average of 42% in beef and pork.

GIFT WRAP?

Baking fish is an excellent method of cooking. One of the better methods is to place the fish in a piece of parchment paper or wrap it in aluminum foil. This will help to retain the moisture.

COOKING CONTAMINANTS

Fish that feed on the bottom of lakes, such as Carp and Bass have a higher risk of becoming contaminated. However, cooking will neutralize most of the contaminants which tend to be located in the skin and fat.

HAVE YOUR ROD AND REEL READY

If you are not sure if a fish is really fresh, place it in cold water, if it floats, it's fresh.

SAFETY FIRST

When marinating fish it should always be done under refrigeration. Fish decomposes rapidly at temperatures above 60°F. (15.6°C.).

THE STEAMY SIDE OF FISH

When steaming fish, it should be wrapped in a piece of plain (no design) moistened paper towel. Place the fish in the microwave for 2-3 minutes on each side.

Fat Content In 3 ½ Ounces	
Lean Seafood	**Grams**
Shrimp	1.2
Crab	1.3
Shark	2.0
Swordfish	2.2
Oyster	2.4
Bass	2.4

| Fat Content In 3 ½ Ounces ||
Lean Seafood	Grams
Grouper	2.8
Ocean Perch	2.9
Mullet	3.0
Sole	3.3
Flounder	3.9
Pollack	4.3
Halibut	4.3
Red Snapper	4.5
Cod	4.6
Haddock	5.0
Hake	5.2
Tuna (Bluefish)	6.5
Fatty Seafood	**Grams**
Striped Bass	8.4
Butterfish	8.6
Salmon	8.6
Herring	9.0
Pompano	9.5
Porgie	10.5
Mackerel	13.8

DIAL THE FISH HOTLINE — (305)361-4619
The majority of fish caught in the oceans are safe. However, in the warmer waters it would be best to call the fish hotline to be sure that the type of fish you are going to catch does not have a problem with "ciguatera." This is a cause of a number of cases of fish food poisoning.

NEED A BIG FREEZER

Fish can be frozen in clean milk cartons full of water. When thawing, use the water as a fertilizer for your house plants.

COMMON FORMS OF SUPERMARKET FISH

» WHOLE FISH
Complete with entrails, needs to be sold shortly after it is caught.

» DRAWN FISH
A whole fish with only the entrails removed.

» DRESSED FISH
Totally cleaned up with entrails removed and ready to party or cook.

» FISH FILLETS/STEAKS Large pieces of fish with the bones removed. When both sides are removed they are sometimes called butterfly fillets.

» CURED FISH
These are usually sold as smoked, pickled, or salted fish. If the fish is sold as "cold smoked" it was only partially dried and will have a very short shelve life. If the label reads "hot smoked" the fish was not fully cooked and should be kept frozen until used.

» DRIED FISH
Fish that has been processed using dry heat, then salted to preserve it.

» SALTED FISH
These fish are used mainly for pickling in a brine solution.

A WORD TO THE WISE
If you see a seafood product with "USG INSPECTED" on the label, report it to authorities, this is not a legal designation. The label should read "Packed Under Federal Inspection" or (PUFI). This means that it was packed in the presence of, or at least inspected by, a Federal Inspector.

SHELLFISH — POLLUTION AND SHELLFISH STILL A PROBLEM
Presently, about 34% of all shellfish beds in the United States have been officially closed because of pollution. All coastal waters worldwide are in jeopardy of also being closed to fishing. One of the world's best known seaports, Boston Harbor is so polluted that fisherman are advised not to fish there anymore. Mutant fish are being caught in Boston Harbor with tumors and bacterial infections. The sewage problem is so bad in the Gulf States of Louisiana and Florida that 67% of the oyster beds have been closed to fishing. In Europe about 90% of the sewage is still dumped into coastal waters.

I'M JUST A SWEETIE
For the most part shellfish are sweeter tasting than fish. The reason for this, is that they have a higher percentage of glycogen, a carbohydrate, which converts to glucose. The amino acid glycine is also capable of providing some degree of sweetness from their protein. Lobsters are the sweetest shellfish, while crab and shrimp come in second and third. However, if they are stored for more than 1-2 days the sweetness will be reduced.

ABALONE

Abalone is becoming one of the rarest shellfish to find off the coast of California. The "foot" is the tough edible portion which must be literally pounded into tenderness. The price is high and they must be cooked 12-24 hours after they are captured otherwise they will become bitter.

EXPENSIVE CHEWING GUM

The method of tenderizing abalone, is to cut the abalone into the thinnest slices possible and then pound those slices even thinner using a special meat-tenderizing hammer. If this is not done properly the abalone will be tough.

TIMES UP

When abalone is cooked it should never be cooked for more than 30 seconds on each side. Overcooking makes it tough. Before cooking place small slashes about an inch apart across the whole piece to avoid curling.

SOUTHERN EXPOSURE

When purchasing abalone, make sure that the exposed foot muscle moves when you touch it. Never buy shellfish if it is dead.

CLAMS

The most popular clam is the hard-shell clam. The geoduck clam, a soft-shell clam is unable to close its shell because its neck sticks out too far and is too big. It can weigh up to 3 pounds and is not as tasty as the hard-shell clams. Packaged soups and canned clam products are produced from large sea clams.

KNOW WHERE THEY ARE RAISED

 All shellfish are called "filter feeders." They rely on food entering their systems in the water that goes by them which may contain almost any type of toxic material and even sewage. Over time any toxic material that is ingested may increase to a harmful level to humans if adequate amounts of toxic shellfish are consumed. Diseases such as hepatitis can be transmitted if the shellfish were feeding in areas that were contaminated with sewage. Shellfish are capable of filtering up to 20 gallons of water a day looking for food.

Shellfish are rarely, if ever, inspected. Some of the contaminants are rendered harmless if the shellfish is cooked. Raw shellfish should only be eaten in moderation unless they are aquacultured.

OPEN WIDE, SAY AHHHH

To open shellfish, rinse them in cold tap water for 5 minutes then place them into a baggie and place it into the freezer for about 30 minutes. They should be cooked in heavily salted water to draw out the sea salt. Remember, shellfish are naturally high in sodium and not recommended for a low-sodium diet.

FRESH WATER'S A KILLER

Once clams are dug up they must be cleansed of sand and debris or they will not be edible. To accomplish this, the clams should be allowed to soak in clean sea water (never fresh water) for about 20 minutes. Change the water every 4-5 minutes to clear the debris from the water.

DEAD OR ALIVE?

A healthy clam should have its shell closed when being cooked, however, they should relax and open after they are boiled. If you keep the clams on ice they will probably relax and open their shell, to test their condition just tap their shell and they should close. If they don't close then they are sick or dying and should not be used. After they are cooked if the shells do not open they should be discarded and the shell never forced open.

CLAW RENEWAL

Crabs and lobsters have the capability to regenerate a new claw when one is broken off. The crab industry in many areas now catch crabs and break off one of the claws then release the crab to grow another one. The crab is able to protect itself and forage for food as long as it has one claw.

THIS CLAM WILL REALLY FILL YOU UP

In 1956 the largest clam on record was caught off the coast of Manila and weighed in at 750 pounds. Clams are all males unless they decide to change to female later in life, luckily many do.

THE CHOWDER TRICK

Chefs will always add the sliced clams during the last 15-20 minutes of cooking time. When clams are added early in the cooking of chowder they tend to become tough or too soft.

CRAB

Different species of crabs are found in different oceans or seas. Crabs caught in the Gulf of Mexico or Atlantic Ocean are called Blue Crabs. Crabs caught in the Pacific Ocean are known as the Dungeness. The most prized crabs and the largest are the King Crabs, these are caught off the coast of Alaska and Northern Canada. The smaller Stone Crab is found in the waters off the coast of Florida.

Crabs should only be purchased if they are active and heavy for their size. Refrigerate them as soon as possible and cover them with a damp towel. Live crabs should be cooked the day they are purchased.

The soft-sell crabs can be found in a variety of sizes. The smallest are called "spiders" which are almost too small to keep. They only measure about 3 ½ inches across which is the bare legal size. The "hotel prime" measure in at about 4 ½ inches across and the "prime" at 5 ½ inches. The largest are called "jumbo" and measure in at a whopping 6-7 inches across.

» If canned crabmeat has a metallic taste, soak it in ice water for 5-8 minutes, then drain and blot dry with paper towels.

» WHAT IS IMITATION CRAB?
Hundreds of years ago the Japanese invented a process to make imitation shellfish called "surimi." In recent years it has become a booming industry in the United States. Presently, we are producing imitation crab meat, lobster, shrimp, and scallops, most of which is made from a deep ocean whitefish, pollack. Surimi contains less cholesterol than the average shellfish and contains high quality proteins, and very little fat. Unfortunately, most surimi does contain high levels of salt (sometimes 10 times that of the real shellfish) and in some products MSG is used to bring out the flavor. The processing also lowers the level of other nutrients that would ordinarily be found in the fresh pollack.

» COOL IT!
If crab shells are orange after they are cooked the crabs were old and may not have the best flavor. Their shells should be a bright red after cooking which means that the chemical in the shell was still very active.

CRAYFISH

These look like miniature shrimp and are a relative. The largest producer in the world is the state of Louisiana. They produce over 22 million pounds of these little "crawdads" a year.

» THE SECRET TO REMOVING THE MEAT FROM CRAYFISH
To begin with crayfish are always cooked live similar to lobsters and crabs. They have a much sweeter flavor and are affectionately known as "crawdads." All the meat is found in the tail of the crayfish. To easily remove the meat, gently twist the tail away from the body, then unwrap the first three sections of the shell to expose the meat. Next you need to pinch the end of the meat while holding the tail in the other hand and pulling the meat out in one piece. If you wish you can also suck out the flavorful juices from the head.

LANGOSTINOS

Another relative of the shrimp these small crustaceans are also called "rock shrimp." They can usually be found in the market frozen and are mainly used for salads, soups, or stews.

LOBSTER

The two most common species of lobster consumed in the United States are Maine and Spiny. Maine lobsters are the most prized and are mainly harvested off the northeastern seaboard. It is an excellent flavored lobster and the meat when cooked is a snow-white color. A smaller lobster but still a popular one is the Spiny lobster which can be identified by the smaller claws. Never purchase a lobster unless you see movement in the claws or if their tail turns under them when carefully touched.

» CUDDLE 'EM
Before you start to tear a lobster apart, make sure you cover it with a towel so that the juices don't squirt out.

» USE THE MICROWAVE
Lobster should be added to dishes just before serving in order to retain their flavor. Overcooking is the biggest problem in retaining the taste of lobster.

» WHAT DOES NEWBURG MEAN IN LOBSTER NEWBURG?
The "Newburg" is any seafood dish means that the recipe contains a special cream sauce that includes sherry. The name "Newburg" refers to a Scottish fishing village called "Newburg." The dish was first introduced in the early 1900's in the United States and has

remained a popular way of serving lobster. Most restaurants tend to purchase the Spiny lobster for these type of dishes since they are the least expensive.

» A LEFT-HANDED LOBSTER?
Believe it or not Maine lobsters may be either right or left-handed. They are not symmetrical with identical sides. The two claws are different and are used differently, one is larger with very coarse teeth for crushing, and the other has fine teeth for ripping or tearing. Depending on which side the larger, coarse-teethed claw is on will determine whether the lobster is right or left-handed. However, the flesh found in the smaller fine-toothed claw is sweeter and more tender.

» CAN A LOBSTER BE MICROWAVED?
Microwaving a lobster is actually the preferred method in many of the better restaurants. The taste and texture are far superior to boiled or steamed lobster. Microwaving allows all the natural juices to be retained. The color of the lobster is better as well. The problem some restaurants have is that it takes too many microwave ovens to handle a large volume of business. To microwave a lobster you need to place the lobster in a large microwave plastic bag and knot it loosely. A 1½ pound lobster should take about 5-6 minutes on high power providing you have a 600 to 700 watt oven.

If you have a lower wattage oven allow about 8 minutes. To be sure that the lobster is fully cooked, just separate the tail from the body and if the tomalley (mushy stuff in cavity) has turned green the lobster is fully cooked. The lobster must still be cooked live due to the enzymatic breakdown action problem which occurs immediately upon their death. If you are bothered by the lobster's movements when cooking, which is just reflex, then place the lobster in the freezer for 10 minutes to dull its senses and it will only have a reflex reaction for about 20 seconds.

» WHY LOBSTERS TURN RED WHEN BOILED
The red coloring was always there, however, it is not visible until the lobster is boiled. The lobster along with other shellfish and some insects have an external skeleton which is made up of "chitin." Chitin contains a bright red pigment called "astaxanthin" which is bonded to several proteins. While the "chitin" is bonded it remains a brownish-red color, however, when the protein is heated by the boiling water the bonds are broken releasing the "astaxanthin" and the exo-skeleton turns a bright red color.

» LOBSTER LIVER, A DELICACY?
Shellfish lovers seem to think that a special treat is to consume the

green "tomalley" or liver found in lobsters or the "mustard" found in crabs. These organs are similar to our livers and are involved in detoxifying and filtering toxins out of the shellfish. Many of these organs do retain a percentage of the toxins and possibly even some PCB's or heavy metal contaminants. Since in most instances you are not aware of the areas these crustaceans are found, you should never eat these organs. However, the roe (coral) found in female lobsters is safe to eat. Lobster roe (eggs) are a delicacy in many countries.

» STAYING ALIVE, STAYING ALIVE

Lobsters and crabs have very potent digestive enzymes which will immediately start to decompose their flesh when they die. Both should be kept alive until they are to be cooked. The complexity and location of their digestive organs make it too difficult to remove them. If you are uncertain as to whether a lobster is alive or dead, just pick it up and if the tail curls under the lobster its alive. Lobsters should never be placed into boiling water as a method of killing them. The best way is to sever the spinal cord at the base of the neck with the end of a knife, then place them into the water. In some restaurants the lobster will be placed into a pot filled with beer for a few minutes to get them drunk before placing them into the boiling water.

MUSSELS

» ROPE ME A MUSSEL

Aquaculture mussel farming has become big business in the United States. Mussels are raised on rope ladders which keep them away from any debris on the bottom. This produces a cleaner, healthier mussel, and reduces the likelihood of disease. When grown in this manner, they are also much larger. Be sure that the mussels are alive when purchased. Try tapping their shell, if they are open, the shell should snap closed, if not, they are probably a goner. When mussels are shucked, the liquid that comes out should be clear.

» OPEN WIDE

When you are cooking mussels, they will be done when their shell opens. If the shells remain closed they should not be forced open and eaten.

» DOUBLE DECKER

Live mussels, covered with a damp towel may be stored for about 2-3 days on a tray in the refrigerator. Never place one on top of the other.

» CUT OFF THEIR BEARD AND THEY DIE

Mussels are a common shellfish that is enclosed in a bluish shell and are for the most part aquafarm raised. They should always be purchased live and should be cleaned with a stiff brush under cold water. The visible "beard" needs to be removed, however, once they are debearded they will die.

OYSTER

Oysters are considered a delicacy worldwide. Consumption is over 95 million pounds annually with almost 50% produced by aquaculture farming methods. Oysters will have a distinct flavor and texture that will vary depending on what part of the world they were harvested from.

» ARE OYSTERS SAFE TO EAT IN THE MONTHS WITHOUT AN "R"?
This may have been true decades ago before refrigeration, however, there is really no medical evidence that shows it to be dangerous to eat oysters in any month of the year. However, oysters tend to be less flavorful and less meaty during the summer months which do not have an "R" because it is the time of the year that they spawn.

» NOT ALL IT,S CRACKED UP TO BE
If you purchase an oyster and the shell is broken or cracked, discard it, it may be contaminated.

» OYSTERS, A SHELLFISH GAME?
Be cautious of oysters that are harvested from the Gulf of Mexico during June, July, and August. These summer months are months when the oysters may be contaminated with a bacteria called "Vibro vulnificus." Cooking the oysters will kill the bacteria, however, raw oysters can be deadly to people who suffer from diabetes, liver disease, cancer, and some gastrointestinal disorders. The bacteria kills about 20 people a year. The FDA may require that all Gulf Coast oysters caught in the summer months be shucked and bottled with a warning not to consume them raw.

» KEEP 'EM COOL
Store live oysters in the refrigerator in a single layer with the larger shell down and covered with a damp towel. They should be consumed within 3 days.

» AGING
Shucked oysters will stay fresh frozen for up to 3 months if they are stored in their liquid and only 1-2 days under refrigeration. Oysters should be scrubbed with a hard plastic bristle brush under cold water before shucking them.

» TOUGH GUY
If you are poaching oysters, only poach them until their edges start to curl. Oysters are easy to overcook and get tough.

» POP GOES THE OYSTER
Oysters are easy to remove from their shell if you just soak them in unflavored club soda for 5-10 minutes or until they open their shell to see what kind of weird solution you placed them in.

» CLEANEST OYSTERS IN AMERICA
If you want to be sure of the breeding and cleanliness of the oysters you eat, better call (206)875-5494, The Ekone Oyster Company. These oysters are aquacultured on an 80 acre farm and can be shipped either fresh or try the world's greatest smoked oysters.

SCALLOPS

A member of the shellfish family that has a very short lifespan after it has been removed from the water. They tend to become tough very easily if they are overcooked. The varieties seem almost endless with over 400 varieties presently identified. Two types of scallops are available, the sea scallop which are about 2 inches wide, and the bay scallop which are about ½ inch wide. Bay scallops are the more tender of the two. They should be sold moist, not dried out and should never have a strong odor.

» YOU'LL NEVER SEE SCALLOPS ON THE HALF SHELL
There is a major difference in this bivalve from clams, lobsters, and mussels in that it cannot close its shell to protect itself in a closed liquid environment. The scallop does have two shells, however, these shells never close tightly, because of this when they are caught they are unable to protect their juices allowing the juices to be released. When this occurs the process of deterioration and enzymatic breakdown begins very quickly and therefore once they are caught they must be shucked on the boat, the viscera thrown away and the muscle preserved on ice.

SHRIMP

Shrimp are sold in a variety of sizes and will be classified on the package. Their size determines the number of shrimp per pound. The largest is the "jumbo" shrimp which averages 18-26 shrimp per pound. The "large" shrimp usually average 22-30 per pound, while the "medium" shrimp averages 26-40 per pound. The smallest variety sold is the "bay" shrimp which can average 60-70 per pound. Shrimp has a high water content and therefore will reduce down from one pound to about ¾ of a pound or less after cooking. Worldwide there are over 250 species of shrimp of which the largest called "prawns" are a member of the family.

Depending on where the shrimp feed and are caught they may be found in a variety of colors from white, the more desirable color, to brown which mainly feed on algae and have a stronger flavor.

» WHAT IS THE BLACK TUBE ON A SHRIMP'S BACK?
The intestinal tract of the shrimp can be found running the length of its back. It would be best to remove it since it does harbor bacteria but is safe to eat if the shrimp is cooked, which will kill any bacteria. If you do eat it and you notice that the shrimp is somewhat gritty, it is because the intestinal tube remained intact containing sand granules. Deveining the shrimp is relatively simple, all you have to do is run a small ice pick down the back and the tube will fall out.

» DECAPITATION A MUST
Shrimp with heads are more perishable than those without heads. The head contains almost all its vital organs and the majority of the digestive system.

» IS A PRAWN A SHRIMP OR IS A SHRIMP A PRAWN?
Biologically a prawn is different from a shrimp in that it has pincer claws similar to a lobster. A relative of the prawn is the scampi, both of which are considerably larger than the average shrimp. Restaurants in the United States rarely serve real prawns, they are just jumbo shrimp. Jumbo shrimp cost less than the giant prawns but are not as tasty. If you do eat a "real" prawn you will know the difference.

» GOOD ADVICE
If shrimp develops a strong odor, it is probably ammonia, which means that the shrimp has started to deteriorate and if not cooked immediately should be discarded. Shrimp cannot be re-frozen and remember almost all shrimp you buy has been frozen. This means that if you don't eat the shrimp that same day or possibly the next day it should be thrown out.

» NAUGHTY, NAUGHTY
A common problem with purchasing shrimp that has already been breaded is that a number of firms have been overbreading to increase the weight of the packages. The FDA has taken action against some companies for this practice.

» MODERATION IS THE KEY
The cholesterol content of shrimp may be higher than most other fish, however, it is lower than any other type of meat product and does not contain a high level of saturated fat.

» THE PROBLEM WITH CANNING
If you purchase canned shrimp, always place the can into a pan of ice cold water for about 1-2 hours before opening. This will usually

eliminate the "off flavor" from the can. If a canned taste still exists, try soaking the shrimp for 15 minutes in a mixture of lemon juice and cold water.

» TENDER LITTLE ONES
Shrimp will always cook up nice and tender if you cool them down before cooking them. Either place them into the freezer for 10-15 minutes or in a bowl of ice cubes and water for about 5 minutes. They should then be prepared by placing them into a warm pot (not over a hot burner), sprinkle with a small amount of sea salt, then pour boiling water over them and cover the pot. The larger shrimp cook in about 6 minutes, the average size ones are cooked in about 4 minutes, and the small shrimp in about 2 minutes. The size of the shrimp should not affect their quality.

SQUID
Squid is a member of the shellfish family and may be sold as "calamari." It tends to become tough very easily when cooked and should only be cooked for 3 minutes for the best results. When adding squid to a cooked dish it should be added toward the end of the cooking cycle when there is no more than 15 minutes left. Squid is the only shellfish that has more cholesterol than shrimp. The entire squid is edible.

"YUK"
The most unpopular foods among Americans are shark, squid and snails. Shark, however, is making a comeback since people are finding out that it is a healthy, low-fat, good tasting fish.

DON'T OVERCOOK SHELLFISH
When you cook shellfish, try not to overdo it or they may become very tough. Clams, crab, and lobster only need to be steamed for 5-10 minutes. Crayfish and mussels only need 4-8 minutes. Always remember to turn all shellfish except lobsters. Grilling an 8 ounce lobster tail only takes 10-12 minutes.

SALTWATER FISH

ANCHOVY
Anchovies are a popular poultry feed. Most of the over 200 million pounds caught annually are ground up and used for feed. Anchovies

used for canning range in size from 4-6 inches, they are also used as a pizza topping and in "real" Caesar salad.

THE SALT OF THE SEA

Anchovies can be desalted to some degree by soaking them in ice water for about 15 minutes. They should then be placed into the refrigerator for another 45 minutes before adding them to a recipe.

Anchovies will last about 2 months under refrigeration after the can is opened and up to 1 year without refrigeration in a sealed can due to their high salt content. Opened ones should be kept covered with olive oil.

If you use anchovies in any dish, taste the dish before adding any further seasoning.

ANGLERFISH (Lotte)

The angler species of fish may include several other unusual varieties such as; bellyfish, goosefish, sea devil, and monkfish. They have a relatively firm texture and are all low-fat. Monkfish are appearing on menus and are mainly used as a substitute for lobster since the only part that is worth eating is the tail. Anglerfish can weigh from as little as 3 pounds to as high as 25 pounds. They are more popular in France than in the United States.

BARRACUDA

Weighs in at an average of 6.5 pounds and is a moderately-fat fish, usually caught in the Pacific Ocean. Most barracuda have very toxic flesh due to their type of diet. The only edible variety is the Pacific barracuda.

BLUE-FISH

This fish tends to deteriorate very rapidly and does not even freeze well. They usually weigh around 5 pounds and have a thin strip of flesh running down its middle that should be removed before cooking or it may affect the flavor.

COD

Cod is one of the lower-fat fishes with a very firm texture. Three varieties may be found in the fishmarket. They are; Atlantic cod, Pacific cod, and scrod. The scrod are the smallest of the cod family. As a substitute for cod you might try the cuskfish which is excellent for soups or chowders and has a taste similar to cod.

CROAKER

All varieties are low-fat except for the corvina. They are a small fish usually weighing in at around ¼ to ½ pounds and up to over 30 pounds if you are lucky enough to catch a redfish. These are a popular fish for making chowder.

EEL

Popular in Japan and in some European countries more than the United States. It is a firm-textured tasty fish that resembles a snake and can grow to 3-4 feet long. The skin must be removed before cooking since it is very tough.

FLOUNDER

This the most popular fish sold in the markets and may appear as "sole." There are over 100 varieties and has a mild flavor and nice light texture. It is one of the low-fat fishes and weighs in anywhere from 1-10 pounds. Dover sole may be found on a menu and is imported from England. These are safer if they are aquacultured since they are a scavenger fish.

GROUPER

These are also known as "sea bass" and can weigh up to 25 pounds. Before cooking be sure and remove the skin. The skin is similar to the eel skin and is very tough. Grouper has a firm texture and is an easy fish to cook either baked or fried.

HADDOCK

Related to the cod and usually caught in the North Atlantic. A common smoked form of the fish is sold in markets and called "Finnan Haddie." The flesh of haddock will be somewhat softer than cod, which is a close relative.

HAKE

An Atlantic Ocean fish that has a firm texture and is relatively low-fat. It has a mild flavor and usually weighs in at about 3-7 pounds.

HALIBUT

Similar to a flounder with a low-fat, firm texture. Normally weighs in at a healthy 15-20 pounds and marketed as steaks or fillets. Can replace the more expensive salmon in most recipes.

HERRING

Normally sold pickled or smoked it is a high-fat fish with a very fine texture. When caught they only weigh-in at around ¾ pound. Sardines are a member of the herring family. The best quality sardine is the Norwegian bristling. Norwegian sardines are the best source of omega-3 fatty acids, next to Chinook salmon. Their scales are pulverized and used in the cosmetic industry and they usually end up as an appetizer.

MACKEREL

This a high-fat, relatively oily fish similar to tuna. You may find it under a variety of names such as; Atlantic mackerel, wahoo, Pacific jack, kingfish or Spanish mackerel. It may be sold canned in a red meat variety and has an excellent level of omega-3 fatty acids. Best cooked in an acid marinade using white vinegar.

MAHI MAHI

Even though it has been called the "dolphin fish" it is not related to the dolphin. There is a slight resemblance but the greenish color gives it its own unique look. These may weigh up to 40 pounds and are one of the better eating fishes caught in Hawaiian waters. Usually sold as steaks or fillets.

MULLET

The majority of mullet is caught off the coast of Florida. It has an unusually firm texture and a relatively mild flavor. The flesh can be found in a variety of light and dark meats. It is somewhat oily and good for barbecueing.

ORANGE ROUGHY

Almost all orange roughy is imported from New Zealand and is a low-fat fish. The taste is slightly sweet and it has a texture similar to sole. May be cooked by any method and when imported normally comes in frozen fillets.

PERCH

A true perch is only caught in freshwater, however, the ocean perch that is sold is really a rockfish. Perch is relatively low-fat with a fairly firm texture. The majority of perch sold in the United States comes from the Great Lakes. They weigh-in at about 1-2 pounds and are available fresh or frozen.

POLLACK

Pollack is mainly used for fish sticks and surimi. It has a firm texture and a rich flavor. The darker layer of the flesh is not as mild as the lighter flesh. A very common fish used in chowders.

POMPANO

Found mainly off the coast of Florida and has recently been affected by overfishing making it one of the more expensive fishes. It is an oily, firm textured fish, sometimes called a Boston bluefish which it is not related to.

SABLEFISH

The sablefish is commonly called the "black cod." It has a high-fat content but a very light texture. Commonly found smoked but can also be prepared by baking, poaching, or frying.

SALMON

This is by far one of the tastiest fish you will ever eat. The fattest salmon is the Chinook (king salmon). The Coho salmon have less fat and are a smaller variety. The lower quality are the sockeye and pink salmon. Coho salmon deposit about 2,500 eggs during their 5 days of spawning.

WHITE LOX?

More and more salmon are being farm-raised which may mean that the color of salmon may someday be white instead of salmon-colored. The farm-raised salmon are not exposed to the same food supply in a pen that they are in the wild. Fish farmers are now adding synthetic pigments to the farm-raised salmon's food supply to make the color salmon.

» SINCE RAW FISH MAY CONTAIN PARASITES, WHAT
ABOUT LOX?

 Good news for bagel and lox lovers! Smoked salmon,
lox, or Nova that are commercially processed should
pose no health threat. When processed lox is heavily
salted. Nova is salmon that originally came from Nova
Scotia and is not as heavily salted. According to
researchers at the Center for Disease Control and the
FDA, no cases of parasitic contamination has ever been reported in
lox or Nova. Occasionally parasites are found in wild salmon but
almost all the lox sold in the United States is aquacultured.
Cold-smoked salmon is always kept frozen which will kill any
parasites.

SALMON (RUSSIAN) ROULETTE

If you are a sushi lover and eat salmon, be aware that raw salmon has a
10% chance of being contaminated with the parasite roundworm
"anisakis." This information comes from an FDA report regarding
samples taken from over 30 sushi bars.

SARDINES

Sardines are an excellent source of calcium. In only 3 ½ ounces they
contain more than an 8 ounce glass of milk. Milk has vitamin D added
to help metabolize the calcium while the sardines also supply vitamin D
and phosphorus. Ounce for ounce sardines can also supply you with
more protein than a steak.

SEA TROUT

These trout are usually caught off the shores of Georgia and the
Carolinas. They are somewhat fatty but have a good solid texture and
are good for baking or broiling.

SHAD

This is one of the fattiest fishes and excellent for barbecueing. It is
usually cooked whole with just the entrails removed since it is very hard
to fillet. The roe (fish eggs) is one of the more highly prized caviars.

SHARK

Shark flesh is becoming more and more popular everyday since it is a tasty, low-fat fish with an excellent level of nutrients. Over 300 species of shark have been identified to date.

» MMMM, MMMMMM, GOOD
If you go to China you will find shark fin soup a popular menu item at around $55 per bowl. In Hong Kong, herb shops sell dried shark fins for up to $60 per pound. At the rate sharks are being fished they may become an endangered species within the next 20 years. In 1997 over 122 million sharks were caught.

» BETTER GET A BIGGER NET
The largest shark in the world is the whale shark at about 60 feet long.

SKATE

A relative of the shark family it has rays or wings which are the most edible part of the fish. The taste is similar to scallops and the meat looks like crab meat because of the striations. Try to buy skate that does not have an odor of ammonia.

SWORDFISH

Has been found to contain high levels of mercury in its flesh and is not recommended as one of the safer fish to eat unless you know that they have been caught well off shore. Usually sold in boneless loins and is excellent for barbecuing. It has a good flavor and fairly firm texture.

» THREE CHEERS FOR THE CHEFS
Since swordfish are close to becoming extinct, chefs all over America are now refusing to prepare swordfish until it is more readily available and the overfishing stops.

TUNA

When purchasing tuna, make sure you purchase the best grade which is the "albacore white." The other classes of tuna are darker in color and have a stronger flavor and aroma. They may be labeled: light, dark, or blended. These tuna are also very oily and usually higher in calories even if water-packed. Some brands use other types of fish in a related family and sell them as just "tuna." These fish include bonita, bluefin tuna, and skipjack. Bluefin tuna may weigh up to 1,000 pounds. When tuna is packed in oil it is sometimes called "tonno tuna."

» THERE'S A CATCH TO THIS FISH STORY
You probably think that if you purchase tuna in water it will have
fewer calories than the type that is packed in oil. Well the truth is that
albacore tuna may have a fat content that will vary by as much as
500%. Tuna manufacturers always try to use low-fat tuna in their
product with about 1 gram of fat per serving. However, when the
demand for the product gets extremely high, they have to resort to
packaging the higher fat albacore which contains 4-5 grams of fat per
serving. Best to check the label.

» PACK IT IN
Solid-pack is tuna composed of the loins with the addition of a few
flakes. Chunk tuna may have parts of the tougher muscle structure,
while flake tuna has mostly muscle structure and smaller bits all
under ½ inch. Grated tuna is as close to a paste product as you can
buy. If the chemical "pyrophosphate" (a preservative) appears on the
label it would be best not to buy the tuna.

» SAVING FLIPPER
Choosing tuna for tuna salad is more a matter of taste than the type of
tuna. If you have noticed that tuna in cans is darker than it used to be,
you are right, the reason being is that smaller nets are being used so
that the porpoises won't be netted. This means that the larger tuna
won't be netted either. The smaller tuna has the darker meat.

» NUMERO UNO
In 1997 tuna was ranked as the most popular fish sold in the United
States. Shrimp came in an easy second, while cod was third, and
Alaskan pollack next due to its use in imitation shrimp and crabmeat.
Americans consume about 4 pounds of tuna per person annually.

» IS CANNED TUNA SAFE TO EAT?
A study performed in 1992 and reported in Consumer Reports stated
that tuna for the most part is safe to eat. Only a few insect parts were
found and the level of mercury was too low to be a health threat.

» NO CANNED TUNA ODOR HERE
If you are a tuna lover you have probably never tasted "real" high
quality canned tuna. If you want a gourmet treat, call Lazio Family
Products in Eureka, California at (800)737-6688 for their catalog.
They only use the finest superior quality white albacore tuna.

FRESHWATER FISH

BUFFALO FISH

A common fish caught in the Mississippi River and the Great Lakes region of the United States. It has a fairly firm texture and has enough fat that it can be barbecued. The average weight is around 4-6 pounds.

CARP

Used to make "gefilte fish." It is a scavenger fish that may carry a degree of contamination. They should only be purchased if the label says that they are raised on a fish farm. Extremely difficult to skin and should be purchased as a fillet.

CATFISH

One of the more popular and tasty fish. Since they are scavengers 85% are presently aquacultured in the United States. They are a low-fat fish with a relatively firm texture and not that good for barbecueing.

PIKE

If you can find a walleyed pike it is an excellent eating fish. They have literally been fished out of existence and should be on the endangered list until they make a comeback.

SMELT

One of the smallest fish, it is usually eaten whole with just the entrails removed. Best prepared pan-fried, they are a high-fat fish with a firm texture.

STURGEON

Sturgeon caviar (roe) is one of the finest. These fish can weigh up to 1,500 pounds and are the largest of all freshwater fish. They are high-fat and excellent for barbecuing. About 65% of the calories in sturgeon caviar are from fat.

TROUT

Trout is one of the most common fish caught in the United States next to catfish. The most popular variety of trout is the rainbow trout, which is one of the tastiest fish. Almost all trout sold has been raised on fish farms.

WHITEFISH

A relative of the trout it is also one of the best eating fish. It is high-fat and best barbecued, broiled, or baked. Commonly found in abundance in the Great Lakes.

All fish purchased in supermarkets should be labeled Grade A.

CAVIAR

» BELUGA
Comes from the Beluga sturgeon from the Caspian Sea. The roe (eggs) range in size, but are usually pea size and silver-gray to black. This is the most popular in the United States.

» OESTRA
Somewhat smaller than the Beluga. The color is a gray to brownish-gray.

» SEVRUGA
Even smaller than the oestra and gray in color.

» WHITEFISH, LUMPFISH, AND SALMON
These are the least expensive caviars, sometimes called "red caviar."

» CAVIAR FACTS
If you see the Russian word "malossol" on the caviar container, it means that only a small amount of salt was used to process it. This caviar will not have a long shelf life. Caviar loses much of its flavor and texture when cooked. Best to eat it cold. Caviar should be stored in the refrigerator and will last for 1 month if the temperature is about 28°F. (-2.2°C.).

» VERY EXPENSIVE CURE
In many European countries, caviar has been used to treat hangovers due to its acetylcholine content.

PRESERVATION

Fish should always be cooked at a relatively low temperature to retain its moisture and provide a more tender product. Fish dries out very quickly and should never be cooked at temperatures exceeding 350°F. (176.7°C.)

» PRESSURE TEST
To test a cooked fish to see if it is finished cooking, try pressing your finger on the side of the fish. No dent should remain, however, the fish may flake under the pressure.

» NEVER OVERCOOK
When cooking fish in a microwave, many manufacturers suggest that the fish is cooked at 50% power for more even cooking. Check your instruction manual for your particular microwave oven.

» MODERATION, IF YOU ARE PREGNANT
The latest studies are showing that a number of fish with high possible contamination problems should not be consumed by pregnant women. A number of tuna canneries tend to use bonita in place of tuna in the less expensive brands. Bonita caught in the Pacific Ocean may contain PCB's. Another popular fish, white croakers have also been found to contain PCB's as well as DDT. Eating fish twice a week is probably safe. However if the fish are aquacultured there should be no problem. The healthiest and safest fish to eat are salmon, halibut, sole, skipjack tuna, and aquacultured catfish, trout, and turbot.

» TO SUSHI OR NOT TO SUSHI
There is a risk of sushi containing the larva of a parasite called "anisakis," a roundworm. Violent pains set in about 12 hours after ingestion, however, some symptoms may not show up for at least a week. For safety sake, all fish prepared for use in sushi should be either cooked to an internal temperature of 140°F. (60°C.) or at least frozen for 3 days at -5°F. (-15°C.) to kill any larva that might be present. Also, consuming raw fish too frequently may cause you to be deficient in a number of B vitamins. Raw fish contains an enzyme that tends to affect the absorption of these vitamins.

» CONTAMINATION POSSIBLE?
The majority of all fish consumed in the United States is imported from over 100 foreign countries, most of these countries have no inspection and poor sanitary conditions in the processing plants. When the fish enter the U.S. only 5-10% are ever inspected. In the U.S. we only have about 300 fish inspectors to inspect over 2,100 processing facilities and over 70,000 fishing vessels.

HOW DRY I AM

If you are going to broil, barbecue, or grill fish, be sure and purchase fish steaks that are at least 1 inch thick. Fish will dry out very quickly and the thicker the better, especially for barbecueing. The skin should be left on fillets when grilling, then remove it after cooking. When frying fish, make sure that the surface of the fish is dry.

LOVE ME TENDER

Fish only needs to be cooked for a very short time. Fish is naturally tender. However, if you overcook it you will lose some of the flavor.

MORE BOUNCE TO THE OUNCE

Saltwater fish have thicker, more dense bones than freshwater fish, which have thin, minuscule bones. The reason for this is that saltwater has more buoyancy. If you hate fighting the bones, purchase saltwater fish, such as cod and flounder.

WHAT ARE ANGELS ON HORSEBACK?

Angels on Horseback are appetizers made by wrapping bacon around a shucked oyster then cooking it. It is then served on toast and accompanied by a lemon wedge or hollandaise sauce.

FISHERCISE

River fishes have more flavor since they must swim against the currents thus exercising more than lake fish. For this reason trout are one of the best eating fishes. Cooler water fishes also have a higher fat content which imparts more flavor.

RED SPOTS ARE NOT MEASLES

If you see red spots on fish filets it means that the fish has been bruised and has been handled roughly. This may occur from roughly throwing the fish around when it is caught or if it is poorly filleted. Too many bruises may affect the flavor of the fillet by causing deterioration of the surrounding flesh.

CAN 45,000 MEN BE WRONG?

Researchers at Harvard University tracked 45,000 men and their dietary habits in relation to eating fish. They found that the heart attack rates for men who ate fish six times per week was the same as those who ate fish approximately twice per month.

TENDER FISH

Fish and shellfish do not have the extensive connective tissue that is found in land animals. Since the amount is small it doesn't take a lot of cooking to gelatinize the connective tissue with moist heat. If you overcook fish it will toughen the muscle fibers. A fish will be more tender when cooked if you leave the head and tail on, this will cause more of the liquid to be retained during the cooking process.

ROBOT SUSHI CHEF

The Japanese have developed a robotic sushi chef that is capable of producing 1,200 pieces of sushi in one hour. The record of 200 pieces in one hour is held by a Japanese sushi chef under ideal conditions. The sushi chef robot costs about $65,000.

WHAT FISH ARE AQUACULTURED IN THE UNITED STATES?

Aquaculture or fish farming originated in 2,000 B.C. in China. The first fish to be farmed was carp. China and Japan presently lead the world in aquacultured fish farms with the United States coming in fifth. At present almost 90% of all trout sold in supermarkets and fish markets are aquacultured. In 1997 farmed fish will total over 1.3 billion pounds, about 17% of the nation's seafood. There are 3,600 fish farms in 25 states raising catfish, salmon, striped bass, sturgeon, tilapia, and trout. Over 462 million pounds of catfish are marketed annually and 12 million pounds of salmon.

PORCUPINE FISH, A JAPANESE DELICACY, OR A POTENT POISON?

This fish may go by a number of names including; fugu fish or balloon fish. However, it may contain a very potent poison "tetradotoxin" which is concentrated in the liver, ovaries, and testes. If the poison is eaten the person may experience numbness of the lips, tongue, and fingertips with death following in a few hours. In Japan, chefs who prepare the fish must be licensed by the government and are trained to discard the poisonous organs.

SHOULD FRESH FISH BE DE-GILLED?

If the fish is caught fresh and prepared shortly afterwards, then it not necessary to remove the gills. However, if the fish is more than 24 hours old the gills should be removed. The gills tend to spoil faster than the rest of the fish and the overall flavor affected.

SEAFOOD POISONING

Seafood is becoming more and more of a problem. The consumer hardly ever knows where the seafood is coming from and whether it is contaminated or not. Two types of poisoning are the most prevalent; "mytilotoxism," which is found in mollusks, clams, and oysters since these filter feeders may feed on microorganism that are toxic; and "ciguatera," which may be found in any type of seafood. Both types are serious enough to either make you very ill or kill you. Commercial fisherman have a better idea where the safe fishing beds are. A person who is just out fishing in a river or lake and not aware of any contamination that may be present is at high risk in many areas of the United States.

FISH SPOILAGE AND STORAGE

The sooner a fish is gutted the better. The enzymes in a fish's gut tend to breakdown fish very quickly if allowed to remain for too long a period. They are very aggressive and very powerful which is one reason why fish is easier to digest than any other form of meat. When storing fish you need to remember that the muscle tissue in fish is high in glycogen which is their energy source. When the fish is killed this carbohydrate is converted into lactic acid, which is usually an excellent preservative, however, the fish tends to use up too much of its energy source thrashing around when it is caught trying to escape. Another problem with lengthy storage is that certain bacteria tend to be located outside of the digestive tract unlike that of beef and will remain active even below the freezing point.

NEVER FLIP YOUR FILLET

Fillets are so thin that they cook through in a very short period of time. The meat of the fillet is also so delicate that it has the tendency to flake apart when over-cooked or if it is even turned. To avoid the fillet sticking to the pan, just use a liquid oil spray.

ADDING AN ACID, A MUST, WHEN POACHING FISH

When poaching fish the contents of the pot are usually somewhat on the alkali side and may react with a pigment in the flesh of the fish known as "flavone." If this is allowed to occur the flesh may become yellow instead of the desired white color. If you add a small amount of wine, lemon juice, or other acid to the pot it will neutralize the alkalinity and render the "flavone" harmless. If the mixture turns slightly acidic it will actually whiten the meat more than it would normally be. Also, when poaching fish, keep the fish in single layers and be sure that the poaching liquid reaches the top of the fish.

HOW CAN YOU TELL IF A FISH IS FULLY COOKED?

The flesh of a fish is normally translucent. When it turns opaque and a solid white color it means that the protein has coagulated and the fish is fully cooked. If you wish to be really sure then you will have to cut into the center at the thickest part with a fork and if the flesh flakes it means that there was sufficient heat to gelatinize the collagen in the myocommata (fish connective tissue). Fish flesh contains very thin, parallel rows of muscle fibers that are held together by the connective tissue. It is these separate sheets of muscle fibers that flake.

WHY YOU SHOULD NEVER FISH FROM A BRIDGE

One of the more popular locations for people to fish is from a bridge near the highway. Fishermen in the know, will never fish from a highway bridge because of the auto exhaust pollution as well as the garbage that is thrown off the bridge by the passersby. Waters near bridges are polluted to such a degree that many are already posted with "No Fishing" signs. Fishermen think that the signs are posted to protect the fishermen from the passing cars, when it is actually to save them from becoming ill.

HOT PLATE SPECIAL

Fish tends to cool very quickly and should be served on warm plates or on a warmed server.

SNAILS

Snails are considered a fair source of protein and are cultivated in the United States and Europe on snail farms. Fresh snails have been a gourmet treat for hundreds of years in Europe. If you have a recipe calling for snails, fresh snails must be trimmed and cooked before they can be used in a recipe to replace canned snails.

» YUM, YUM?
  Fresh snails should always be cooked the day they are purchased and should be kept in the refrigerator until you prepare them.

» SNAIL STUFFING
  When purchasing snails in a gourmet shop, the shells will be separated from the snails. The shell should be cleaned before using

them by boiling them for 30 minutes in a solution of 1 quart of water, 3 tablespoons of baking soda, and 1 tablespoon of sea salt. Make sure that you dry the insides of the shell before using them with a hair dryer if necessary. Commercially purchased snail shells may be reused as long as they are boiled (as instructed) after each use and again before adding the new snails.

CHAPTER 13

It's Sugartime, Real vs. Artificial

American sugar intake per person in 1822 was 8.9 pounds a year, presently it is 16 times that amount. The average daily refined sugar consumption per person in the United States is over 40 teaspoons or 147 pounds per year.

It is hard to believe that we could eat so much sugar in a day, but sugar is hidden in many foods besides the suhagar bowl. It can be found in thousands of foods including: soft drinks, candy, baked goods, toothpastes, cereals, lipstick, etc. If you read the labels on foods you will be surprised at the foods that contain one form of sugar or another.

Consuming excessive amounts of sugar can be a health hazard since sugar requires B vitamins and minerals to enable the body to metabolize it into glucose, yet it contains none of these. Therefore, it must steal nutrients away from other sites where the nutrients may be needed more. Sugar may also increase the rate at which we excrete the mineral calcium, making bones more fragile as well as weakening the heart action. Sugar also requires chromium which is crucial for the regulation of blood sugar levels.

COMMON SWEETENERS

CORN SYRUP

» One of the most common sweeteners due to its low cost to produce. It is actually made from a mixture of starch granules derived from corn which are then processed with acids or enzymes to convert it into a heavy sweet syrup. The corn syrup is then artificially flavored and used for literally thousands of products including: pancake syrups, candy making, ice creams, etc. The fact that corn syrup tends to retard crystallization makes it a good choice for candies, preserves, and frostings.

HONEY

» The highest quality honey will be labeled "100% pure unfiltered," "raw," or "uncooked." This honey will not be nutrient-depleted by the heat processing. Honey is sold in three varieties: liquid honey, which is extracted directly from the "honeycomb," chunk-style honey, which contains pieces of the honeycomb, and comb honey, which contains a larger section of the honeycomb. One pound of honey = 1⅓cups.

Honey is a unique sugar in that it will not grow bacteria. It is the only food that has this unique quality, however, when using it, it is twice as sweet as granulated sugar. Crystallized honey can be liquefied by just placing it into the microwave for about 1 minute depending on the size of the jar and the wattage of the microwave. Never allow honey to boil or get too hot since it will break down and must be discarded.

» CERTAIN HONEY CAN BE DANGEROUS
Honey that is produced from certain geological areas may contain substances that are harmful to the human body. Farmers call this honey "mad honey." Bees that obtain nectar from flowers such as the rhododendron, azalea, and laurel family may cause symptoms of numbness in the extremities, vomiting, and muscle weakness. These are rarely fatal but will cause a bit of discomfort for a few days. Honey should never be given to babies since their digestive system is too immature to handle the botulism bacillus if it is present and they tend to develop a form of infant botulism.

» THE REMARKABLE HONEY STORY
Bees gather honey by drawing the flower nectar into their proboscis (tube extending from their head). The nectar then passes through their esophagus into a honey sac (storage pod) located just before the intestine. The nectar is stored until the bee arrives back at the hive. While the nectar is in the sac, enzymes are secreted that begin to breakdown the starch into simple sugars and fructose. The hive contains one mature queen, about 100 male drones, and 20,000 female workers. The bees utilize 8 pounds of honey for daily activities for every one pound that reaches the market. Bees must forage an equivalent of 3 times around the earth to provide sufficient nectar to make one pound of honey utilizing only one ounce for the

trip. For every gallon of honey the bees consume they travel 7 million miles, or 7 million miles to the gallon if you prefer. When the workers reach the hive they pump and mix the nectar in and out of their proboscis until the carbohydrate concentration is about 50-60%, then it is deposited into the honeycomb.

Honey storage is very important and honey should be stored in as airtight a container as possible since the sugars are "moisture attracting" and will absorb water from the air very easily especially if the humidity is over 60%. If the water content of honey goes above 17% the honey and yeast will activate, the honey will ferment, and the sugars will change to alcohol and carbon dioxide. Honey tends to crystallize easily causing the glucose to be released from the sugars. Heating the honey slightly will force the glucose back into the sugar molecule and return the honey to a liquid.

MAPLE SUGAR
» THE REAL SAP, MAPLE SYRUP

The "sap run" is one of the more interesting mysteries that nature has recently shared with us. Pure maple syrup is the product of the rock maple tree, which is the only tree that produces a high quality syrup. The sap is only collected in the spring providing ideal conditions exist. The amount of syrup available is dependent on the leaves converting the right proportions of sunlight, water, and carbon dioxide into sugar. Sap is only collected from the first major spring thaw until the leaf buds begin to burst. If the sap collection is not discontinued at this point the syrup will have a bitter flavor.

Conditions must be near perfect to have a good "sap run." The winter must be severe enough to freeze the tree's roots, the snow cover must extend to the spring to keep the roots very cold, the temperature must be extreme from day to night, and the tree must have excellent exposure to adequate sunlight. To produce sap the tree needs to have stored sugar from the previous season in the trunk, especially in specialized cells known as "xylem" cells. Transport tubes are formed in the tree from both live and dead cells in which the xylem normally carries water and nutrients from the tree's root system to the leaves and trunk.

In early spring when the rock maple tree thaws, the xylem cells tend to pump sugar into specialized xylem vessels, the transport tubes are now activated and the increase in sugar content in the xylem vessels creates a pressure that draws water into the vessels, increasing the water pressure. As the pressure increases, the xylem cells become more active and start to release waste products and carbon dioxide.

The carbon dioxide gas level in the water tends to decrease with the rise in spring temperature, the trunk of the tree warms causing the gas pressure and water to build up in the xylem tissues forcing the sap to run and be collected.

Maple tree sap is about 3% sucrose with one tree averaging about 10-12 gallons of sap per spring season. To produce one gallon of "pure maple syrup" it requires 35 gallons of sap. The final syrup is composed of 62% sucrose, 35% water, 1% glucose and fructose, and 1% malic acid. The more the syrup is boiled during processing, the darker the syrup becomes due to a reaction between the sugars and proteins.

» THE REAL THING

When a product is labeled "maple sugar" it must contain a minimum of 35% "real" maple syrup. Try to find a product where the color is very light, the lighter the color, the higher the quality. Maple syrup is best stored in the refrigerator after it is opened to retain its flavor and retard the growth of mold. If it granulates, just warm it up slightly. It should last about 1 year and is best used at room temperature or slightly heated.

Read the label well! Make sure it doesn't say "maple flavored," "maple-blended," or use the word "imitation." The real thing is rare and does contain an excellent blend of natural nutrients, especially iron and calcium. The typical pancake syrup is almost pure corn syrup and artificial maple flavoring.

» VERY LIMITED SUPPLY

The finest maple syrup in the United States is made by Everett and Kathryn Palmer of Waisfield, VT. The supply is always limited and you have to order ahead to buy this purest of the pure product. Just call (802)496-3696.

MOLASSES

Made from sugar cane going through a complex processing and removing all nutrients, resulting in a white sugar. The residue that remains after processing, is the actual blackstrap molasses. Unsulfured molasses is actually produced to make molasses and not the results of the processing to make sugar. Unsulfured molasses has a lighter, cleaner flavor than sulfured. Blackstrap molasses is collected from the top layer and is higher in nutrients than any other type of molasses. It is an excellent source of iron, calcium, and potassium.

If a recipe calls for dark molasses, you can use light molasses without a problem. When you bake with molasses, be sure and reduce the heat about 25°F. (-3.9°C.) or the food may overbrown.

If you need to measure molasses for a recipe, try coating the measuring utensil with a spray vegetable oil and it will flow better with a more accurate measurement.

Molasses has a degree of acidity that can be neutralized by adding 1 teaspoon of baking soda to the dry ingredients for every cup of molasses the recipe calls for. Molasses is best used in gingerbread and baked beans because of its robust flavor.

RAW SUGAR (TURBINADO)
Still a refined sugar and almost exactly like refined white sugar, except with the addition of molasses for color. Has no advantage over normal refined sugar except the price is higher. As with all sugar it can be labeled "natural" to make you think that it is better for you.

ARTIFICIAL SWEETENERS

» ACESULFAME K
A non-caloric sweetener, which is sold under two brand names, "Sunette" or "Sweet-One." It will provide sweetening and cannot be metabolized by the body, but passes through and is excreted. It has an advantage over Equal in that it can be used for high temperature baking and cooking. It is about 200 times sweeter than sugar and commonly used commercially in chewing gums, beverage mixes, candies, puddings, and custards. Received FDA approval in 1989 and it is in use worldwide.

» ALLTAME
A sweetener that is produced from two amino acids (proteins) and has 2,000 times the sweetness of sugar. It is metabolized by the body with almost no caloric value. It is a good all around sweetener that may be used in most recipes and baked goods.

» ASPARTAME (NUTRASWEET, EQUAL)
This approved sweetener is produced from phenylalanine, aspartic acid (two amino acids) and methanol. It has been implicated in animal laboratory testing related to nerve disease, however, testing is not conclusive and the studies were being conducted using high dosages which may skew the outcome. Aspartame may also lower the acidity level of the urine causing a reduction in the susceptibility to disease.

> Caution must be taken when Aspartame is heated since a percentage may turn into methyl alcohol. It is not recommended for use in baked goods and any drink that requires a liquid being brought to the boiling point. Recent negative study results by leading universities and the Arizona Department of Health Sciences were regarded by the FDA as "unfounded fears."

Symptoms are becoming more frequently reported relating to Equal consumption and include: sleep disorders, headaches, vision problems, dizziness, and neural disorders. A double blind study of diabetics using the products reported more adverse symptoms in the group consuming Equal. The study was conducted using a measured quantity of Equal, equivalent to 14 diet drinks per day. However, even if you don't consume that many diet drinks, Equal is now found in hundreds of other products.

When Equal was approved in 1980, the FDA set a maximum recommended amount of 34 mg. per Kg. of body weight per day. This equates to a 140 pound person drinking 12 diet drinks per day or the equivalent in foods containing Equal, Nutrasweet, or Aspartame. The World Health Organization recommended a maximum of 40 mg. per Kg. of body weight for adults. A child in an average day consuming an assortment of cereals, gum, candy, puddings, ades, soft drinks, etc. could easily exceed the adult maximum amounts. Future testing may prove very interesting.

» CYCLAMATES
May be found again in baked goods and other products. The FDA reversed a decision and is now allowing the use of this artificial sweetener. However, it would still be best to read the label and try and avoid most artificial sweeteners.

» L-SUGARS
Artificial sweetener that contains no calories or aftertaste and is available to replace a number of other sweeteners. Can be substituted cup for cup for granulated sugar in recipes and may be available shortly.

» SACCHARIN
This sweetener has been around since 1879 and is 300 times sweeter than sugar. It is used in many common products such as mouthwashes and lipsticks. Presently, it is under additional testing by the FDA. Products that do contain saccharin must have a warning label stating that saccharin may be hazardous to your health.

» STEVIA, IS THIS NEW SWEETENER SAFE TO USE?
This sweetener is new to the United States but has been used in South America and Japan for a number of years as a calorie-free sweetener. Stevia is an herbal extract from a member of the chrysanthemum family that is being sold in health food stores as a "dietary supplement." Since it is a natural herbal product the Dietary Supplement Act of 1994 applies and the product was allowed into the country. However, the FDA is still not sure of any potential problems that might arise since testing is not conclusive at present. However, research from Japan says it is safe and may even prevent yeast infections, act to boost energy levels, and doesn't promote tooth decay. The extract is concentrated and is 200-300 times sweeter than table sugar. It is being used for cooking and may leave a licorice flavored aftertaste.

» SUCRALOSE
Refined from common table sugar but has been concentrated to where it is 600 times sweeter with no calories. A very stable product in foods and carbonated beverages. Sold in Canada under the brand name "Splenda."

SWEET FACTS

A GOOD SWEETENER?
Fruit is high in the sugar "fructose." However, all studies show that there is no risk factor involved with this sugar and consumption does not have to be limited. Fructose breaks down slower than most sugars giving the body more time to utilize it before it is completely broken down to glucose.

WE'RE SUPPOSED TO BE SMARTER
Over 50% of all chocolate sold in the United States is purchased by adults. The most popular chocolate is dark (semi-sweet) chocolate. The chocolate bar was invented by Fry & Sons in 1847 in England. To be able to use the term "milk chocolate" the chocolate must contain at least 10% chocolate liqueur and a minimum of 12% milk solids. To be called "dark chocolate" (semi-sweet) it must contain at least 15% chocolate liqueur and no more than 12% milk solids.

DENTIST'S RETIREMENT FOOD
Sucking on hard candy or lollypops causes a greater risk of tooth decay than consuming large quantities of cake, ice cream, or doughnuts. Hard

candy dissolves slower and may surround each tooth with a coating of sugar for a longer period of time. A study reported that fluid movement around teeth is slowed to a crawl by a high intake of sugar and sweetened foods.

OFF TO THE GYM
Americans are consuming about 250,000 calories of sweeteners annually. This is enough calories to put 70 pounds on the average person.

BOY, IS HERSHEY'S SMILING
Americans consumed about $3.9 billion worth of candy products in 1997 and over 1.6 billion pounds of chocolate candy bars. Over $642 million was spent on advertising junk foods in 1997.

CHOCOHOLICS BEWARE
The chemical theobromine found in chocolate may reduce the amount of available protein that is absorbed through the intestinal wall. Sugar also reduces the body's ability to destroy bacteria. Oxalates, another chemical found in chocolate may unite with available calcium carrying it through the intestine as an insoluble compound, rendering it unusable.

SHAKING SUGAR
In Europe confectioners' sugar is called "icing sugar." Most recipes call for confectioners' sugar to be sifted. It is also used frequently for "dusting" and some should always be kept handy in a shaker.

OVERWORKING YOUR LIVER
Most candies, especially if they are multicolored, contain a number of additives that may be a hazard to your health. These include; Red Dye #3 and #40, Green Dye #3, Blue Dye #2 and #12, Yellow Dye #5, and glycerides. Check out your favorite candy for any of these additives. Remember your liver is the organ that must cleanse these potentially toxic chemicals from the body.

PRECISION COUNTS
If you are making candy, be sure and follow directions to the letter. Candy recipes are very exacting and variances can cause a poor quality product. Candy must be cooked at the temperature that is recommended, never try and speed up the process by increasing the heat. The lower the

final temperature of the candy after it is cooked will determine the softness of the final product. In fact, if the humidity in the kitchen is over 60% it will adversely affect the final product.

BEAT ME, BEAT ME

Fudge should be stirred or beaten with a wooden spoon. Beating the fudge is one of the most important techniques. Beat the fudge from its glossy, thin consistency to a slightly thick consistency. This is when you will need to add raisins or nuts and place into a pan to cool. Also, next time you prepare fudge, try adding a teaspoon of corn starch when you first begin mixing the ingredients, this will make the fudge set up better.

CRYSTAL CLEAR

When adding water to a candy recipe, always add very hot water for the best results and a clearer candy. Most freshly made candy will remain fresh for 2-3 weeks.

DON'T TAKE A BEETING

Cane sugar should always be used for candies, beet sugar tends to cause more foam.

Foods that may contain sugar that may surprise you:

Cough Drops	Lipstick	Canned Beans	Breads
Rolls	Relish	Licorice	Crackers
Ketchup	Canned Fish	Breathe Mints	Soy Sauce
Salt	Laxatives	Soup Mixes	Stamp Adhesives
Vitamins	Pickles	Egg Nog	Gravies
Bacon	Peanut Butter	Baby Foods	Tenderizer
Waffle Mixes	Lip Gloss	Tooth Paste	Snails

PUFF, PUFF, DRINK, DRINK

Smokers frequently consume more sugar than non-smokers, probably due to the fact that smokers drink more sweetened coffee.

SUGAR DISASTER

Freezing has a negative effect on a number of candies and they never taste the same and may even loose their consistency. Hard candies may crumble, jellies become granular, cereal products and popcorn candy become mushy, and the rest lose their original consistencies due to the expansion of the liquid in their cells.

TONS AND TONS OF SUGAR

During Easter 1997, 60 million chocolate bunnies and 600 million marshmallow bunnies and chicks were sold in the United States.

MAKING CANDY, COOL IT!

If you are making candy and the weather is hot and humid, don't try and make chocolates unless the room is well air conditioned. The best temperature to make chocolates, divinity, hard candy, and fudge is between 62°and 68°F. (62° and 20°C.) with low humidity. These candies absorb moisture from the air very easily.

FRESH 'N FRUITY

Jams and jellies are now being produced from a number of artificial ingredients. Best to read the label and make sure that the product you purchase is made from the "real fruit." If they are, and are labeled "lite" that would be even better since the sugar content has been reduced.

SNIP, SNIP

Marshmallows will store for a longer period of time if they are stored in the freezer. Just cut them with a scissors that has been dipped in very hot water to get them apart.

MOISTURIZE ME

Adding a slice of very fresh white bread or half an apple to a bag of marshmallows to soften them up works great. Just leave them alone for 1-2 days until they absorb the moisture.

DE-LUMPING YOUR SUGAR

Brown sugar has a tendency to lose moisture rather quickly and develop lumps. To soften brown sugar, try placing the sugar in the microwave with a slice of fresh white bread or half an apple, cover the dish tightly and heat for about 15 seconds. The moisture from the bread or apple will produce just enough steam to soften the sugar without melting it. If you store brown sugar in the freezer it won't develop lumps.

ZAP IT!

To remove hardened brown sugar from a box, wrap it tightly in a towel and hit it on the counter a few good whacks. If that doesn't do it just add a few drops of water to the box and microwave on full power for a few seconds. If neither one works, run over it with you car or throw it out and buy some more. Other than a touch of molasses brown sugar is chemically identical to white sugar.

DON'T RAIN ON MY PRESERVES

Remember, never make preserves or jelly if the humidity is over 50% or if it is a rainy day.

THAT'S A FEW EXTRA CALORIES

Ice cream sales in the United States in 1997 were approximately $2.6 billion dollars. We averaged almost 15.6 quarts of ice cream per person.

CANDY CHEF'S SECRET

To successfully defrost candy, the temperature should be raised gradually. Place the candy to be thawed, still in the original wrapper, in a brown paper bag lined with a paper towel. This will absorb any moisture that may collect during defrosting.

WELL EXCUUUUSE ME

Bloatiness and flatulence may be caused by frequent swallowing when people chew gum and suck on hard candy. The salivary glands produce saliva at a higher rate than normal, thus causing the frequent swallowing.

YOU WON'T BELIEVE IT UNTIL YOU TRY IT

Try using a small amount of vegetable oil on the threads of a syrup bottle; it will stop the syrup from running down the sides of the bottle.

IT'S NOT THE REAL THING

To be called chocolate you must use chocolate liqueur in the product. White chocolate doesn't use the liqueur and is not really chocolate. It is produced from sugar, milk powder, and cocoa butter. Cocoa butter is produced from chocolate liqueur and loses its chocolate flavor during the processing.

THE PERCENT OF SUGAR IN SOME COMMON FOODS:

Jello	82.0%
Breakfast cereals	up to 68.0%
Candy Corn	59.5%
3 Musketeers	41.0%
Milky Way	40.3%
Oreo Cookie	40.1%
Ketchup	29.0%
Hamburger Helper	24.0%

HEAT KILLS

If you think that a fruit jam or jelly will have vitamin C, think again!
The processing kills almost all the vitamin C.

THE NOSE KNOWS

Candies stored in the refrigerator can pick up foreign odors and should
be stored properly in a closed container.

FREE FLOWING

Sugar will never cake-up if you just place a few salt-free crackers in the
canister to absorb the moisture. Crackers should be replaced every week.

BUBBLE, BUBBLE, TOIL AND TROUBLE

If you have a problem with candy boilovers, just place a wooden spoon
over the pan to break the bubbles.

NO CANDY FOR DADDY

Adults are just as prone to hyperactivity as children from high sugar
intakes. However, new studies are showing that there may not be much
validity to this assumption.

JUST A SPOONFUL OF SUGAR MAKES THE MEDICINE GO DOWN

The chemicals used to produce cough drops are so bitter the sugar
content can be as high as 50%. In fact, approximately 30% of all cough
syrups and drops are at least 25% sugar.

A REAL SURPRISE

America's favorite desserts are pie, cheesecake, and ice cream, in that order.

POP A CUBE, BUT NOT TOO OFTEN

If you must satisfy a sugar craving and don't want the calories, try eating a sugar cube. They only contain 12 calories each and contain no fat or preservatives.

A VACATION AT YOUR EXPENSE

When you consume too much sugar it reduces the effectiveness of the body's healing mechanism, causing a prolongation in the healing time. Normally, white blood cells which aid in the healing process go to the site of the injury and assist the body by removing debris and starting the healing process, however, when there is an overabundance of sugar circulating in the bloodstream, they tend to get lazy and don't want to go to work. This increases the healing time.

FOOD ADDITIVES

Almost 98% (by actual weight) of food additives are corn syrup, pepper, mustard, baking soda, baking powder, citric acid, salt, or a natural or artificial coloring agent.

Sugar has many names, the following are a few of the more common ones:

Glucose	Molasses	Hexatol	Lactose
Fructose	Dextrose	Mannitol	Honey
Maltose	Corn Syrup	Turbinado	Beet Sugar
Sucrose	Sorghum	Xylatol	Levulose

HOW SWEET IT IS

In a recent study by Dr. Andrew Waterhouse at the University of California at Davis, chocolate was found to contain an antioxidant called "phenols." This is the same compound found in red wine that was thought to lower the risk of heart disease in France. The study found that cocoa powder prevented the oxidation or breakdown of LDL's (bad cholesterol). When LDL's are broken down they tend to convert into fatty plaque forming particles that may contribute to the clogging of healthy arteries, thus becoming a risk factor for heart disease. A 1 ½ ounce chocolate bar has the same amount of "phenols" as a 5 ounce glass of red wine.

THE BIRTH OF THE LOLLYPOP
In 1909 an employee named George Smith made a new confection on a stick while employed by a Connecticut candy maker. He was an avid race fan and named the confection after one of the most popular race horses of that time "Lolly Pop."

CAN BABIES DETECT SWEET TASTES?
Babies that are only 1 day old can detect the taste of sweet, however, it will take them 6 weeks to respond to the taste of salt. Taste buds are able to detect sweetness in a food if the food has only 1 part sweetness in 200. Saltiness can be detected if the food only has 1 part in 400.

WHAT IS A GOO-GOO CLUSTER?
This has been one of the favorite candies of the South since 1912 when Howell H. Campbell went into the candy business. He prepared the candy from chocolate, marshmallow, caramel, and peanuts. The candy is occasionally found in some of the better stores in major cities around the country. The candy was named by a Nashville woman who suggested that Campbell name the bar after the only two words his infant son could utter, "goo-goo." The Goo-Goo Cluster was the first combination candy bar produced in the United States. To order some of the bars call (615)889-6360.

ELIMINATE A SWEET CRAVING
There are two ways to eliminate the craving for sweets. First, place a small amount of salt on your tongue. Second, dissolve about 1 teaspoon of baking soda in a glass of warm tap water, then rinse your mouth out and don't swallow the water. The salt or baking soda tend to stimulate the hypothalamus gland causing the papillae to become active and secrete saliva which will eliminate the craving for sweets.

GOURMET CHOCOLATE
For years wine has been labeled from a particular vineyard or region and many connoisseurs will only drink wines from that particular vintage or region. Wine tasters can tell you by sipping a wine the complete history of that wine and its level of quality. Well, chocolate has finally come of

age and the latest craze is to purchase chocolates from a particular epicurean grower and from a particular variety of the cocoa bean.

WHAT IS CHOCOLATE PLASTIC?

This actually is a pliable decorating paste prepared from a mixture of chocolate and corn syrup and has a texture similar to marzipan. It is used to wrap around the outside of cakes to make a ribbon, ruffles, decorative flowers, or any other complex design. It can be rolled out to make a thin layer with a rolling pin.

WAS THE BABY RUTH CANDY BAR NAMED AFTER BABE RUTH?

Many people think that the Baby Ruth candy bar was named after the famous baseball player, especially since he did wish to produce a candy bar with his name on it. The candy bar was actually named after the daughter of then President Grover Cleveland after she was born in the White House to honor her. Ruth did take the matter to court and lost.

DOES YOUR CHOCOLATE STIFFEN TOO SOON?

When you are melting chocolate, water droplets, excess condensation, and high temperatures may cause the chocolate to stiffen prematurely. To alleviate this problem, add a teaspoon of corn oil to the pan and stir. More oil can be added if needed to assure the proper consistency.

IT'S JUST DIVINITY

Divinity fudge cannot be made on humid days. The air must be relatively dry, since the ingredients used and the type of preparation tends to attract moisture and will ruin the fudge.

THE CANDY MAN CAN

Hershey's Candy Company produces 2,200,000 Kisses everyday, however, the Dutch outdo us when it comes to candy consumption. They consume 64 pounds of candy per person annually, while Americans only consume 21 pounds.

ORIGIN OF CHEWING GUM

A variety of gums, resins, and plant latexes have been chewed for thousands of years. The first recorded history of mixing a gum with sugar can be traced to the Arab sugar traders who mixed the sugar with acacia, known as "Gum Arabic." A number of gums were even used in early days as carriers for a variety of medications which allowed the medicine to be released gradually. Commercially, chewing gums as we know it today were first produced in Bangor, Maine in 1850 by the Curtis family with only mediocre results. However, in 1859 a New Yorker by the name of Thomas Adams used "chicle" the dried latex material of the sapodilla tree of Central America. In 1871 a patent was issued to Adams for "chicle gum."

Then in 1885 William J. White of Cleveland further refined and improved the gum by adding corn syrup and flavoring the gum with peppermint which was very successful. In 1893 William Wrigley invented Juicy Fruit and Spearmint gums and in 1900 Frank Fleer of Philadelphia placed a hard shell on the gum and called it Chiclets. Bubble gum was invented in 1928 by Fleer.

The gums of today are produced from synthetic polymers, mostly styrene-butadiene rubbers and polyvinyl acetate. The final product is composed of 60% sugar, 20% corn syrup, and only 20% actual gum material.

A TRICK TO STOP SYRUP FROM CRYSTALLIZING

When boiling syrup one of the more frequent and annoying problems is that of the syrup crystallizing when you are cooking it. The easiest method of avoiding this problem is to put a pinch of baking soda in the syrup while it is cooking. This will prevent the syrup from crystallizing by adding just a small amount of acidity.

THE JELLY BEAN RULE

Jelly beans have zero fat, no cholesterol, and no nutritive value at all. The FDA has a new rule for advertisers of worthless foods to follow so that they will not be able to label a food such as jelly beans as a "healthy" food. This rule is actually called the "jelly bean rule." For a food to be called "healthy," a food must contain a minimum of 10% of the Daily Values for any one of several key nutrients. The food must also be low-fat, low-saturated fat, and be low in sodium and cholesterol.

THE DIFFERENCE IN CANE, BEET, WHITE, AND BROWN SUGAR

Basically, all table sugar is sucrose, a simple carbohydrate, that breaks down in the body to glucose in a short period of time. Both cane and beet sugars are not noticeably different in appearance or taste. Brown sugar still contains traces of molasses which is a by-product of the sugar refining process. The nutritional difference between white and brown sugar is so insignificant it is not worth purchasing brown over white unless it is called for in a recipe.

WHAT IS SORGHUM?

Sorghum is usually thought of as just another type of molasses, however, there is a difference and it is really a unique product. While molasses is produced from the juice of the sugarcane stalk, sorghum is made from the juice of a different breed of sugar cane stalk called the sweet-sorghum cane which is normally grown for animal feed. Molasses is usually darker and may be a slight bit bitter since much of the sugar is refined out. Sorghum retains its sugar and is sweeter as well as containing more nutritional value. Sorghum has more calcium, iron, and potassium than honey, molasses, or any other commercial syrup. The finest sorghum in the United States is made by Golden Mill Sorghum (316)226-3368.

WHAT IS CHOCOLATE LIQUEUR?

Real chocolate is made from chocolate liqueur, which is produced from cocoa pods. It is not really liquor in the sense most of us think of liquor, but the name given to the processed product obtained from the fruit of the cocoa tree. The cocoa tree is a member of the evergreen family and can only be found in equatorial climates. The tree grows to about 20 feet and the pods that contain the cocoa bean are about 8-10 inches long with each pod averaging 30 each. In 1997 the cocoa bean crop was about 1.7 million tons most of which came from West Africa. The first step in the processing is actually in the field with the pods being opened and the beans allowed to sit in the sun.

This exposure causes a number of microbes to multiply killing the seeds' embryo as well as producing changes in the structure of the cells. The cell walls deteriorate releasing substances that mix together resulting in the bitter phenolic compounds binding to each other and reducing the degree of bitter taste. The beans are then cleaned and dried and shipped to other countries.

The bean now must be processed into the chocolate liqueur. They are roasted for about 1 hour at 250°F. (121.1°C.) which finally gives them the chocolate flavor. This involves approximately 300 different chemicals and results in the "browning reaction" and the color of chocolate. After they are browned, they are cracked open and the "nibs" (kernels) separated from the shells. The nibs are then ground up to release the cocoa butter, carbohydrates, and proteins which are all in the thick liquid oil called "chocolate liqueur." The refining process continues until the mixture ends up as a coarse chocolate or a powder.

WHY DOES CAROB POWDER BURN INSTEAD OF MELTING?

When you heat cocoa powder used in "real" chocolate it contains fat which allows it to melt. Carob does not contain any fat therefore it will not melt, it will only burn. When carob flour is heated with water the starch granules absorb moisture and rupture. This releases a gum that is used as a stabilizer and thickener in processed foods. If you use carob flour in a cake recipe it will act like any other flour.

WHAT IS BLOWN-SUGAR

This is sugar that has been cooked to a point just below the hard crack stage, is then poured onto an oiled marble slab and worked with a metal spatula until it has cooled enough to be worked by hand. The sugar is "satinized" by pulling it back and forth until it has a glossy, smooth sheen. It is then formed into a ball and an air hose attached to a pump inserted into the ball of sugar and air is gently blown in. As it expands the sugar is gently formed into sugar animals or other shapes, similar to glass blowing. The finished objects are then painted with a food coloring and used for display or consumed. They will last for months at room temperature if stored in an airtight container.

WHY ALL THE XXXXXXX'S ON SUGAR BAGS

The "X" symbol on sugar bags pertains to the fineness of the sugar. The more X's, the finer the grade of sugar you are purchasing. It actually indicates the number of holes per inch in the screening material used to form the size of the sugar crystals. If the package has four X's, then there were four holes per inch in the screen. A ten "X" sugar is usually a confectioners' sugar.

CAROB, NO BETTER THAN CHOCOLATE

Carob in its pure form does contain less fat than chocolate. Carob powder that is used to make carob confections is less than 1% fat, but has up to 48% sugar. Cocoa powder used in the manufacture of chocolate bars is 23% fat and only 5% sugar. However, when either one is processed into candy or chocolate bars the differences are for the most part erased. In fact, some carob bars contain a higher level of saturated fat than a Hershey bar and more sugar than a scoop of regular ice cream. Carob does not, however, contain caffeine which is found in chocolate.

SUGARLESS GUM, FRIEND OR FOE?

Sugarless products that contain sorbitol or mannitol as the artificial sweetening agent may now be suspect of causing tooth decay just as much as regular gum. Neither one of these sweeteners actually cause tooth decay, however, they tend to provide nourishment for a bacteria that is influential in causing tooth decay. The bacteria in question is Streptococcus mutans which has the tendency to stick to your teeth and is relatively harmless until it obtains sweets. The bacteria seems to thrive on sorbitol and mannitol, just as they do with real sugars. This was reported by Dr. Paul Keyes, founder of the International Dental Health Foundation.

COKE BUYS MORE SUGAR THAN ANY COMPANY WORLDWIDE

Coca Cola is consumed over 190 million times every 24 hours in more than 35 countries speaking 80 languages. Colas have a higher physiological dependency than smoking and alcohol and is harder to give up. The Coca Cola Company is the world's largest purchaser of sugar and vanilla. The vanilla is mainly supplied by Madagascar which was placed into a panic situation when Coke switched to the "New Coke" which had no vanilla. Lucky for Madagascar, the New Coke was rejected and Coke had to place the vanilla back in the product. Americans consume about 500 bottles/cans or 48 gallons of soft drinks annually per person.

A SERIOUS INVESTIGATION?

The Mars company actually does continuing research to determine the colors and the number of each color that will be found in their packages of M & M's. The following is the current breakdown, which changes as their research is updated at regular intervals:

Color	Plain	Peanut
Brown	30	30
Yellow	20	20
Red	20	20
Green	10	20
Orange	10	10
Tan	10	0
The different colors have nothing to do with a flavor, all M & M's contain the same chocolate inside.		

HOW MANY POUNDS OF CANDY ARE YOU EATING?

In 1980 Americans were consuming 16.1 pounds of candy per person annually and by 1993 the figure was up to 20 pounds. The candy industry had set their sights on a goal of "25 by '95." They were hoping that they could reach that goal but failed. The current estimates are that they will reach their goal by 1999. For the companies to reach their goal you will have to eat the equivalent of 195 candy bars per year. The candy companies are trying to have the government set one day in May aside to be known as "Candy Carnival Day" as a National holiday.

AGING VS. TASTE BUDS

The tongue contains a number of clusters of specialized cells that form "taste buds." Each taste bud contains about 50 of these cells attached to a small projection which adheres to the upper surface of the tongue. Most adults have a few thousand of these taste buds, however, some adults have only a few hundred. Most of our taste buds are concentrated on the back of the tongue, however, the taste of sweet and salt are located in the front of the tongue and sour on either side. Children have considerably more taste buds than adults with locations on the back of the throat, the tongue, even the inner surfaces of the cheeks. Taste buds gradually decrease with age especially after the age of 50. The cells that compose the taste bud only have a life of about 10 days which is just as well if we burn our tongue regularly.

CHAPTER 14

Savoring the Flavors?

PROTECTING YOUR HERBS

The best location to store spices is in a cool, dry spot where they will not be around heat. Storing spices near a microwave exhaust fan or over the range are two of the worst locations. If you decide to store them in the refrigerator, make sure you remove them at least 30 minutes before you plan to use them. This will allow the herb to warm up enough to release its

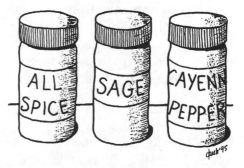

flavor and aroma. Herbs that contain oil readily oxidize and should always be stored in the refrigerator. The flavor of fresh herbs are milder than those from the supermarket that have been dried.

GARLIC FLOAT?

When cooking with whole garlic cloves and you don't want them in the dish when you serve it, just place a toothpick firmly into the garlic and it will be easy to retrieve. Another trick is to use a tea infuser for a number of herbs that fall apart easily.

TO SEASON OR NOT TO SEASON, THAT IS THE QUESTION

When you need to increase the amount of food in a recipe and are not sure if you should increase the seasonings in the same proportion as the original recipe called for, the answer is never increase the seasonings to the full degree. If you double the recipe, increase the seasonings only by 1 ½, if you increase by three times, only increase two times the original.

If the recipe is a complicated one it would be best to make two batches. Never increase sugar in tomato sauce dishes. Never increase salt more than a pinch or two at the most.

THAT'S A BLAST

If you crush dried herbs before using them it will intensify their flavor. You can also intensify their flavor by soaking them for a few seconds in hot water, especially before adding them to a salad. This also works well if they have lost their flavor. When doubling a recipe, never double the seasoning until you taste the dish.

SPICES

ALLSPICE

The flavor is similar to that of cinnamon, cloves, and nutmeg. The majority is imported from Jamaica, Central America, and South America and it is sold in both whole and ground forms. The spice is used in pickling, meats, fish, baked goods, relishes, puddings, and fruit preserves. Allspice is a common herb and can be found in a number of ready-to-serve foods such as, hot dogs, soups, and baked beans.

ANISE

Gives licorice its unique flavor and is mainly imported from Mexico and Spain. Usually sold as anise seed, it can be found in licorice candy, cookies, pickling, and in soft drinks. Also, used to make Anisette and can replace ginger in some recipes.

BASIL

There are more than 60 varieties of basil found worldwide. Common seasoning for fish, meat, tomato dishes, soups, stews, pizza sauce, dressings, and used on salads. A relative of the mint family, it is usually imported from India. Basil is also grown in the United States and known as "sweet basil." Best to store fresh basil in the refrigerator in a slightly moistened plastic bag. It should retain its flavor and aroma for about 4 days.

Basil tends to lose much of its flavor after about 15 minutes of cooking and should be added about 10 minutes before the food is done for the best results. There are a number of varieties of basil which include: lemon and cinnamon basil which have green leaves and opal basil which has purple leaves.

BAY LEAF

Usually sold as whole leaves and commonly used in stews, sauces, soups, French dressing, dill pickles, meat dishes, veal, and poultry. Also, used in numerous ready-to-serve foods.

Remember to remove bay leaves from foods before you serve them. If someone eats a piece it will be like eating a mouthful of straw. Never crumble up a bay leaf when using it in a recipe and stir gently so as not to break the bay leaf up. The Turkish variety of bay leaf has a milder flavor than the California variety and is wider and shorter.

CAPERS

Normally sold either whole or pickled in brine. Commonly used on smoked fish, chicken dishes, eggs, or veal.

CARAWAY SEEDS

Somewhat similar flavor to licorice (anise) and are harvested at night before the dew evaporates. The majority sold in the United States are imported from the Netherlands and commonly used in rye bread, cookies, organ meats, dips, cabbage, sauerkraut, soft cheese spreads, sweet pickles, Sauerbraten, and French dressing.

CARDAMOM SEED

A member of the ginger family with a slight lemon flavor. Best used in pickling, pastries, grape jellies, hot dogs, pumpkin dishes, sweet potatoes, and Asian dishes. Usually imported from India and sold whole or ground. The seeds have a tendency to cover up bad breathe very effectively.

CAYENNE PEPPER

A common spice also called capsaicin or red pepper. Sold in crushed, ground, or whole forms. Commonly used in curries, relishes, salsas, chili products, most Mexican dishes, Italian and Indian foods, sausages, and dressings.

CELERY SEED

Sold in the seed form and as celery salt and used in soups, stews, salad dressings, fish dishes, salads, pickling, and many vegetable dishes. Celery flakes are made from dehydrated leaves and the stalks and used in the same dishes.

CHERVIL
Imported from France and used in salad dressings and anything that you would use parsley for.

CHILI PEPPERS
The best method of preparing chili peppers for use in recipes is to first roast them. Just use a long handled fork on top of the stove and singe them until the skin blisters. Place the hot peppers on a cloth and cover them. Allowing them to steam makes the skin relax and easily pull away allowing the seeds and veins to be removed. The pulp will be very spicy but the seeds and veins will be even hotter. Try not to use too many of the seeds unless you desire a hot fiery dish.

CHILI POWDER—BETTER GLUE YOUR HAT DOWN
Prepared from a combination of cumin seed, hot chili peppers, oregano, salt, cayenne pepper, garlic, and allspice. This will give you a jolt if you are not used to it. Have a glass of milk ready.

CHIVES
Chives have a light onion flavor and are commonly used to flavor dips, sauces, soups, baked potatoes, or to replace onion flavor in a recipe.

CILANTRO
Sold as fresh coriander as a fresh herb and looks a lot like parsley. Commonly used in Mexican dishes and in salad dressings and salsa.

CINNAMON
Imported from China and Indonesia and is harvested from the bark of the Laurel tree. The variety commonly sold in the United States is usually imported from Vietnam and called the "cassia" variety and is used in its whole form for preserving spiced beverages, chicken, meat, flavoring puddings, pickling, cider, and hot wine drinks. The ground form is used for baked goods, ketchup, vegetables, apple butter, mustards, and spiced peaches. However, the "real" cinnamon is from the laurel tree. The color is the giveaway, true cinnamon is actually a light tan color, while "cassia" is a dark reddish-brown.

CLOVE
Imported from Indonesia and usually sold as whole cloves. A strong spice used in moderation in baked beans, pickling, ham roasts, sweet potatoes, baked goods, puddings, mustards, soups, hot dogs, sausages, and barbecue sauces.

CORIANDER SEED
A relative of the carrot family, it has a sweet musky flavor. The seed or ground form is used in gingerbread, cookies, cakes, biscuits, poultry stuffing, pork, spiced dishes, pea soup, and cheese dishes.

CUMIN SEED
Used mainly in its ground form in curry, chili powder, soups, stuffed eggs, fruit pies, stews, soft cheeses, and chili con carne.

CURRY POWDER
Curry powder is a blend of at least 20 spices, herbs, and seeds. Ingredients may include; chili peppers, cloves, coriander, fennel seed, nutmeg, mace, cayenne, black pepper, sesame seed, saffron, and turmeric. The yellow color comes from the turmeric. Usually used in Indian cooking, poultry, stews, soups, sauces, and meat dishes.

DILL
Sold in whole or ground seed form or as a fresh herb. Usually used in cottage cheese, chowders, pickling, soups, sauerkraut, salads, fish, meat sauces, potato salad, green apple pie, and spiced vinegar. Great for livening up egg salad.

FENNEL
The flavor is similar to anise but is somewhat sweeter. Usually used in pork dishes, squash, Italian sausage, sweet pickles, fish dishes, candies, cabbage, pastries, oxtail soup, and pizza sauce. When you choose fresh fennel, make sure you choose clean, crisp bulbs that are not browning. The stalks and greenery should be removed before using. Fennel bulbs and the base may be used raw in salads.

FENUGREEK
The aroma is similar to curry powder and is mainly used to make imitation maple syrup, and a digestive aid as a tea.

GARLIC

Grown worldwide and sold in fresh clove form or as garlic salt or powder. It is commonly used in hundreds of dishes especially, Italian cooking, sauces, chicken dishes, etc. Has been used as a medication for a number of illnesses throughout history. Americans consume 250 million pounds of garlic annually with a large percentage grown in Gilroy, California.

Garlic can be peeled easily by placing it in very hot water for 2-3 minutes. When actually peeling garlic, try rinsing the garlic under hot water first to loosen the skin. For a special flavor rub a clove of crushed garlic on the sides of your salad bowl before mixing your salad.

There are hundreds of varieties of garlic grown worldwide. Elephant garlic is not really a member of the garlic family, but is a form of leek with a milder flavor than most garlic.

If you wish to store garlic for an extended period do not peel it, just leave the cloves intact, and it will store for 3 months in a cool, dark, dry location. When garlic sprouts, some of the garlic flavor will go into the sprouts, however, the sprouts can then be used for salads. Garlic should not be frozen. If garlic is damaged or nicked with a knife it must be used or it will develop mold very quickly.

Garlic vinegar can be made by placing 2-3 fresh cloves in each pint of white vinegar, then allow to stand for at least 2 weeks before using.

» HEAVY-HANDED WITH THE GARLIC
If you have used too much garlic in your soup or stew, just simmer a sprig or small quantity of parsley in it for about 10 minutes. To remove the garlic odor from your hands, try rubbing your hands with salt or a slice of lemon.

Read the label before you buy a garlic product. Garlic products should contain an antibacterial or acidifying agent such as phosphoric acid or citric acid. If this is not on the label the product must be sold and stored under refrigeration at all times. Garlic butter does not have a long shelf life and should be stored in the refrigerator for no more than 14 days. Most butters are not made with a preservative. Garlic, once processed, is more perishable than most other herbs.

GARLIC, MORE THAN A REMEDY FOR VAMPIRES
Garlic has been under investigation for a number of years in relation to heart disease with studies published in The American Journal of Clinical Nutrition. Most studies were done using garlic oil in which the active ingredients were retained. Studies showed that garlic inhibited the coagulation of blood, reduced the level of LDL (bad cholesterol), and raised the level of HDL (good cholesterol). The

subjects consumed the equivalent of 10 cloves of garlic daily, blood levels of cholesterol dropped 14% and the HDL levels were raised by 41%. Most garlic products in health food stores, it was stated, had most of their active ingredients removed by processing.

» GARLIC, THE PUNGENT COUSIN OF THE ONION
Storing garlic is relatively simple, all you have to do is place the garlic in a cool, dry location as close to 50°F. (10°C.) as possible or even at room temperature and it will easily last for about 1-2 months. Garlic will retain its flavor better if it not stored in the refrigerator, however, there is no harm in storing it there. Storing garlic in a small jar of olive oil is the chef's way of keeping the flavor in the garlic for 2-3 months. Garlic should never be frozen, it will lose its flavor.

GINGER
Has a pungent spicy flavor and is grown in India and West Africa. Sold in whole or ground form and is used in pickling, conserves, dried fruits, gingerbread, and pumpkin pie.

MACE
Mace is the dried out husk of the nutmeg shell. It is sold in ground form and used in pound cake and chocolate dishes. In its whole form it is used in jellies, beverages, pickling, ketchup, baked , soups, deviled chicken, ham spreads, and French dressing.

MARJORAM
Related to the oregano family with a sweet nutty flavor. It can be purchased in leaves and is imported from France, Chile, and Peru. Usually, combined with other herbs and used in soups, Greek salad, potato dishes, stews, poultry seasoning, sauces, and fish dishes.

MINT FLAKES
These are dehydrated flakes of the peppermint and spearmint plants and have a strong sweet flavor. Grown in the United States and Europe and used to flavor lamb dishes, fish, stews, soups, peas, sauces, desserts, and jellies. For an instant breath freshener, try chewing a few mint leaves.

MUSTARD
Yellow or white seeds will produce a mild mustard, while the brown seeds produce the more spicy variety. Powdered mustard has almost no aroma until mixed with a liquid. Mustard has hundreds of uses and is

one of the popular spices worldwide. Most mustards will last about 2 years if kept under refrigeration.

If a recipe calls for a particular type of mustard, it would be best to use that one. Using the wrong mustard will make a difference in the taste desired. Mustard oil, which is pressed from brown mustard seeds is extremely hot and sometimes used in Chinese or other oriental dishes.

MUSTARD TYPES

» American Mustard
The typical hot dog mustard is produced from a mild yellow mustard seed, sweetener, vinegar, and usually colored with the herb turmeric. It has a fairly smooth texture.

» Chinese Mustard
Found in small ceramic dishes in all Chinese restaurants. It is produced from powdered mustard, water, and a strong vinegar. The sweetener is left out and the mustard will only retain its bite for 1-2 hours.

» Dijon Mustard
Originated in Dijon, France. Produced from brown mustard seeds, white wine, unfermented grape juice and a variety of seasonings. It has a smooth texture and is usually a grayish-yellow color.

» English Mustard
This mustard is produced from both white and black mustard seeds, a small amount of flour, and turmeric for coloring. This is one of the hottest mustards sold.

» German Mustard
Produced from a variety of mustard seeds. The color varies and the flavor is somewhat mild due to a small amount of sugar used in the production.

NUTMEG

A relatively sweet spice that is available in ground form and imported from the East and West Indies. Commonly used in sauces, puddings, as a topping for custards, creamed foods, eggnogs, whipped cream, sausages, frankfurters, and ravioli. The most pungent is the freshly ground nutmeg. Special nutmeg graters are sold in kitchen specialty shops.

OREGANO

A relative of the mint family, and may be found by the names origanum and Mexican sage. Commonly sold in leaf or ground forms. A common herb on Italian specialties such as pizza and spaghetti sauces. Try oregano on a grilled cheese sandwich and you will never eat another one without it.

PAPRIKA

The best paprika is imported from Hungary in the form of ground pods. The milder variety, red sweet, is grown in the United States. It is commonly used in a wide variety of dishes such as cream sauces, vegetables, mustards, salad dressings, ketchup, sausages, and fish dishes. Makes an excellent powdered garnish.

PARSLEY

The best variety with an excellent flavor is the Italian flat-leaf. This variety is also grown in the United States and Southern Europe and used in cheese sauces, marinades, salads, soups, vegetable dishes, chicken pot pies, herb dressings, and even peppermint soup. It is high in nutrients, especially vitamins E and K and will alleviate bad breath. Store it in a plastic bag in the freezer. Parsley can be dried in the microwave then crumbled.

PEPPER

This one of the most popular spices in the world and is commonly sold in both black and white varieties. It is imported from India, Indonesia, and Borneo, is sold in whole or ground forms and used in almost any dish.

After pepper has been ground, it tends to lose its flavor rather quickly. Best to use a pepper grinder so that your pepper will be fresh and flavorful. Grind white pepper and you won't change the color of your dish.

Szechuan pepper berries are harvested from the prickly ash tree and have a very tiny seed and a somewhat hot taste. Cayenne pepper is produced from chili peppers. Pink peppercorns are harvested from the Baies rose plant and have a very pungent odor and a somewhat sweet flavor.

» PEPPERCORNS—GREEN, BLACK, AND WHITE
   Basically, these are all the same with the only differences being that they are harvested at different times of maturity and the method

processing. The green peppercorns are picked before they are fully ripe and are preserved and used mainly in the pickling industry and in dishes that do not require a strong pepper flavor. Black peppercorns are picked when they are only just slightly immature and are the wrinkled peppercorns we use in our household pepper shakers or in the fresh pepper grinders. The white peppercorns are harvested when the peppercorn is fully ripe and have a smooth surface. These are used in dishes where the color of the black peppercorns would detract from the color of the dish, such as a white cream sauce.

PEPPERMINT, AN HERB AND MORE

Peppermint is related to the spearmint family and contains the active oil, menthol. Menthol is used in cigarettes, candies, liquors, toothpaste, mouthwash, etc. Menthol in low concentrations can also be used to raise the threshold temperature of our skin making a warm area feel cool. It has also been used as an anesthetic or as an irritant. Menthol is the active ingredient that will also chase the rodent population from your house or property. A small amount of oil of peppermint on a cotton ball placed anywhere you have a problem will solve it instantly. Works great on underground rodents too.

POPPY SEED

Has a rich, nut-like flavor and is used in salads, cookies, pastry fillings, Indian dishes, and baked goods.

POULTRY SEASONING

Commonly used in poultry dressings, and soups. The major ingredients are: sage, thyme, marjoram, and savoy.

ROSEMARY

A sweet, fragrant, spicy herb, with a very pungent aroma. Imported from Spain and Portugal and used in stews, meat dishes, dressings, and Italian foods.

SAFFRON

This is one of the more difficult herbs to acquire as well as one of the most expensive. It is extracted from the stigma of a flowering crocus and is only imported from Spain. It is used in moderation in poultry, baked goods and rice dishes.

SAGE

A very strong herb that is a member of the mint family and available in leaf or ground form. Commonly used in veal dishes, pork products, stuffings, salads, fish dishes, and pizza sauces.

SALT

(Sodium Chloride) While salt contains important minerals that are beneficial to the body, in excess it may be detrimental. Body fluids and their distribution in the body depend on the location and concentrations of sodium and potassium ions.

Our kidneys regulate the blood sodium levels and provide the bloodstream with the exact amount as needed. When blood levels rise due to excess sodium ingestion, the body's thirst receptors are stimulated and fluid intake increases to balance the sodium to water ratio. The excess sodium and water is then excreted by the kidneys. When this balance cannot be maintained the result may be higher blood pressure and an increased deposition of atherosclerotic plaque material.

When salt is processed the native minerals are stripped away and it is then enriched with iodine and dextrose to stabilize it, sodium bicarbonate to keep it white, and anti-caking agents to keep it "free-flowing." Morton's Special Salt is one of the only salts that has no additives. Salt is used in almost every food that is processed and is one of the best preservatives.

It is estimated by the National Institute of Health that over 10 million people over the age of 65 have some degree of high blood pressure problems. Since sodium is found in thousands of food items, it is recommended that "added salt" be avoided to help control your total sodium intake.

» When preparing food and seasoning with salt the recommended amounts for certain dishes is:
1 teaspoon for soups and sauces
1 teaspoon for raw meat dishes
1 teaspoon for every 4 cups of flour (dough)
1 teaspoon for every 2 cups of liquid used in cooked cereals

» 40% of regular table salt is sodium. Lite salt has only 20% sodium content.

» SALT INTAKE HIGH, BEWARE
If you eat a piece of bacon and it doesn't taste salty you are consuming too much salt. Excess sodium intake builds up in the bloodstream, kidneys are unable to clear the excess water it retains,

an increase in blood volume occurs and the heart has to work harder causing higher blood pressure.

SALT, THE MICROBE INHIBITOR

For thousands of years salt has been used to preserve foods by inhibiting microbial growth. Salt has the ability to draw liquids from tissues and freeing water that is bound by breaking down proteins. The mechanism involves salt's ability to create a concentration of "ions" (electrically charged particles) outside of the bacteria and mold cells encompassing the microbe drawing out its water and either drying it up and killing it or slowing down its replication. It is the drying out feature of salt that makes it such a good preservative. To preserve meats in England the meat was covered with very large grains of salt that resembled "corn" hence the name "corned beef" was coined.

Fast food restaurants may use high levels of salt to hide the offensive flavors of low quality foods.

Kelp can be ground up and used in a shaker to replace salt. It only contains 4% sodium and the taste is very close.

» SALT OF THE EARTH

The average person consumes about 4,500 mg. of salt daily, which amounts to about 2 teaspoons. The body only requires 200 mg. daily unless we are perspiring heavily. Mother's milk contains 16 mg. of sodium per 3 1/2oz. Canned baby food may contain 300 mg. per 3 1/2oz. Canned peas have 100 times the sodium of raw peas.

It is necessary to read labels and be aware that many foods contain ingredients that contain sodium, such as MSG. Many spices also contain sodium as a normal part of their makeup.

The following list are some spices and flavorings that are sodium-free:	
Allspice	Paprika
Almond Extract	Parsley
Bay Leaves	Pepper
Caraway Seeds	Pimiento
Cinnamon	Rosemary
Curry Powder	Peppermint Extract
Garlic	Sage
Ginger	Sesame Seed
Lemon Extract	Thyme
Mace	Turmeric
Maple Extract	Vanilla Extract
Marjoram	Walnut Extract

The following list are some spices and flavorings that are sodium-free:	
Mustard Powder	Vinegar
Nutmeg	

Sodium Dietary Restrictions

The following foods should be avoided, due to their high sodium content:

Avoid

Meats and Luncheon Meats	Snack foods
All pickled products	Salted crackers
All smoked products	Salted nuts
Salted popcorn	Dried beef (jerky)
Pretzels	Pastrami
Potato chips	Sausages
Corn chips	Frankfurters
Tortilla chips	Salt sticks
Luncheon meats	Canned meat/fish
Ham/pork	Candy bars/nuts
Pickles	Sauerkraut

Soups

Vegetables in Brine	Regular broth
Canned soups	Bouillion/cubes

Miscellaneous

Soy sauce	All salts including "Lite"
Fast food sandwiches	Tomato juice
Ready-to-eat meals	Prepared mustard
French fries	Steak sauce
Processed foods	Commercial sauces
Worcestershire sauce	Chili sauce
Meat tenderizer	Commercial gravies
Softened water	MSG/Accent
Mineral water	Commercial salad dressing
Seasoned salts	Dried packaged seasonings
Packaged pasta mixes	Olives
Dehydrated soups	Pickle relish
Seasonings	Condiments

Sodium Content Of Common Foods
High Sodium Foods

Food Item	Serving Size	Sodium Mg.
Dill Pickle	1 large	1935
Turkey Dinner (frozen)	1 large	1830
Macaroni & cheese (frozen)	1 cup	1090
Pretzels	1 oz.	890

Sodium Content Of Common Foods		
High Sodium Foods		
Food Item	**Serving Size**	**Sodium Mg.**
Tuna (oil packed)	3 ½ oz.	800
Peanuts (roasted in oil)	1 cup	662
Creamed Corn	1 cup	671
Beef Frankfurters	1 reg.	495
Tomato Soup	5 oz.	475
Bologna	2 slices	450
Medium Sodium Foods		
American cheese (processed)	1 oz.	447
Pancakes (mix)	3-4" cakes	435
Mashed Potatoes (instant)	½ cup	375
Cheese Pizza (frozen)	1 med.slice	370
Carrots (canned)	1 cup	366
Cottage Cheese (creamed)	½ cup	320
Tomato Juice	½ cup	320
Corn Flakes	¾ cup	305
Buttermilk	1 cup	225
Doughnut (packaged)	1 med.	210
Oatmeal (cooked)	3 oz.	175
Green Olive	1 large	155
Angel Food Cake (mix) ,$\frac{1}{12}$cake	130	
Whole Milk	1 cup	120
Low Sodium Foods		
Graham Cracker	1 large	95
Mayonnaise	1 Tbl.	80
Egg	1 med.	70
Turkey (roasted)	3 oz.	70
Margarine (salted)	1 Tbl.	40
Cottage Cheese (unsalted)	½ cup	30
Fruit Cocktail	½ cup	7
Orange Juice (canned, fresh)	½ cup	2
Fruit (canned, most)	½ cup	1
Macaroni (cooked)	1 cup	1

» SEA SALT, TABLE SALT, KOSHER SALT
The majority of the salt used in the United States is mined from salt deposits that were laid down thousands of years ago and are readily accessible.

TYPES OF SALT

» Iodized Salt
Standard table salt with iodine added.

» Kosher Salt
Has an excellent flavor and texture as well as being additive-free. Kosher salt has larger salt crystals and a more jagged shape which means that they will cling to food better. Because of its characteristics, kosher salt has the ability to draw more blood from meats, since kosher meats must be as free from blood as possible to meet the strict Jewish dietary laws.

» Pickling Salt
A fine-grained salt that is additive-free and used in the preparation of pickles and sauerkraut.

» Rock Salt
A poorly refined salt that has a grayish appearance with large crystals. Combines with ice to make ice cream.

» Sea Salt
Has a fresh flavor and is available in fine or coarse-grained varieties. It is usually imported and preferred by chefs. Sea salt as its name implies is acquired by allowing salt water to accumulate in pools and having the sun evaporate off the water leaving a stronger flavored salt with a few more trace minerals than table salt. Actually, there is not that big of a difference to pay the extra price for sea salt.

» Table Salt
A highly refined salt that contains additives. Very fine-grained making it free-flowing.

SAVOY

Has a slight peppery flavor and is a member of the mint family. Commonly sold in leaf and ground forms and is primarily used to flavor eggs, meats, poultry, and fish.

SESAME

Has a rich, nut-like flavor and a high oil content. Commonly used as a topping for baked goods and in halavah.

TARRAGON

Has a strong flavor similar to licorice. It is native to Siberia with the majority imported from Spain and France. Commonly used in bearnaise sauce, meat dishes, salads, herb dressings, and tomato casseroles.

THYME
Has a strong, very spicy flavor and is available in leaf and ground forms. Commonly used in tomato-based soups, stews, sauces, chipped beef (an old army favorite), mushrooms, sausages, clam chowder, herb dressings, and mock turtle soup.

TURMERIC
Imported from India and Peru and used in chicken, pickles, meat dishes, dressings, curry powder, Spanish rice, relishes, and mustards.

VANILLA
» VANILLA BEAN RUSTLERS?
The vanilla pod is the only food produced by a plant member of the orchid family. The reason "real" vanilla is so expensive is that it is hand pollinated when grown commercially. In the wild it is pollinated by only one species of hummingbird. Since they are so expensive to grow and over 75% of the beans are grown in Madagascar where the pods are actually branded with the grower's brand because of "vanilla bean rustlers" stealing the crop. Pure vanilla extract can only be made by percolating the bean similar to making coffee. Imitation vanilla is produced from the chemical vanillin which is a by-product of the wood pulp industry.

» BEANS
They are grown on trees and look like long, thin dark brown beans. They are expensive and not as easy to use as the extract. In order to use the bean you need to split it, then scrape out the powder-fine seeds. Seeds from a single vanilla bean is equal to about 2-3 teaspoons of extract. The beans need to be stored in a sealed plastic baggie, then refrigerated.

» PURE EXTRACT
If it says "pure" then it must come from the vanilla bean, however, the taste will be less intense. It still has an excellent flavor similar to the real bean.

» IMITATION EXTRACT
Imitation means just that! Imitation. It is produced from artificial flavorings and has a stronger, harsher, taste than pure vanilla. It should only be used in recipes when the vanilla flavor will not predominate the dish.

» MEXICAN EXTRACT
This may be a dangerous product and not recommended for use. The

product has been found to contain the blood thinner coumarin which is a banned drug in the United States. Other possible toxins have been found in the product as well.

VINEGAR
This is produced from ethyl alcohol utilizing a bacteria, acetobacter, which feeds on the alcohol, converting it into acetic acid (vinegar). Vinegar, however, can also be made from a number of other foods which is the preferred variety to use such as, apples or grains. The distilled vinegar is best used for cleaning purposes and not for a food additive. Vinegar tends to stimulate the taste buds and make them more receptive to other flavors.

TYPES OF VINEGAR

» Apple Cider Vinegar
Produced from apple juice and is mainly used in salads. It has a mild, somewhat sweet, fruity flavor.

» Balsamic Vinegar
Most is produced in Italy and aged 3-12 years before being sold. The aging produces a mellow, brown vinegar that is relatively sweet. It is one of the best cooking vinegars and made from sugars that are converted to alcohol with the addition of boiled down grape juice. It is best used in salad dressing and will bring out the flavor of many vegetables.

» Distilled White Vinegar
This is produced from grain alcohol and is too coarse for salad dressings, but is excellent for pickling.

» Herb Flavored Wine Vinegar
Produced from white wine with the addition of any herb that is compatible. Tarragon wine vinegar is commonly used by chefs for shellfish dishes, and poultry. Rosemary wine vinegar is excellent with lamb dishes.

» Malt Vinegar
Produced from beer and used in chutneys, fish, french fries, sauces, and pickles.

» Raspberry Vinegar
Produced by soaking raspberries in white wine providing the vinegar with a pleasant fruity flavor. Commonly used with pork dishes, poultry, as a salad dressing, and on fruits.

» Rice Vinegar
Produced from liquefied rice. It has a slightly sweet flavor and is used in fish marinades, oriental sauces, sushi, and pickles.

» Sherry Vinegar
A product of Spanish sherry fermentation. The flavor is somewhat nutty and it is used mainly in vegetable dishes.

» Wine Vinegar
Produced from red or white wine, it is the most frequently used wine vinegar. The red is used for meat dishes and the white for poultry and fish dishes. A common wine for marinades and as a salad dressing.

SUBSTITUTING HERBS

HERB	SUBSTITUTE
Allspice	Cinnamon+dash cloves
Anise Seed	Fennel Seed
Basil	Oregano
Caraway Seed	Anise Seed
Chives	Green Onion
Cinnamon	Nutmeg
Cloves	Allspice
Cuimin	Chili Powder
Fennel Seed	Anise Seed
Ginger	Cardamom
Mace	Allspice
Mint	Rosemary
Parsley	Cilantro

HOW SHOULD HERBS BE ADDED TO A DISH?

Herbs are noted for their aroma more than for their taste in most instances. Chefs know how to appeal to your sense of smell when preparing a dish and will add either some or all of the herbs just before the dish is served, since many herbs lose some of their flavor during the cooking process.

CAN THE OIL OF THE SAME HERB BE SUBSTITUTED FOR THAT HERB?

This is never a good idea, however, it is tried all the time. Oils are so concentrated that it is almost impossible to calculate the amount that you will need to replace the herb to acquire the same taste. A good example is cinnamon of which the oil is 50 times stronger than the ground cinnamon. If you did want to substitute the oil to replace the cinnamon extract, you would only need to use 1-2 drops of the oil to replace ½ teaspoon of the extract in candy or frostings.

THE COLOR OF PESTO

Pesto sauce tends to turns brown in a very short period of time instead of remaining the pleasant medium green we are used to seeing. The browning, which is almost black at times is caused by enzymes in one of the herbal ingredients, basil. Both the stems and the leaves of basil will cause the pasta to quickly be discolored with brown spots as well as turning the sauce brown. When nuts are added such as walnuts, sunflower seeds, or pine nuts the sauce will turn almost black. There is little to be done unless the pesto and pasta are prepared and served as soon as possible. One method of keeping the pasta yellow is to add ¼cup of lemon juice or 1⅓tablespoons of cream of tartar to each quart of cooking water. You may have to stir your noodles more frequently and keep the water boiling rapidly to keep the noodles from sticking together since the acid tends to cause excess attraction between the noodles.

LICORICE, SWEETER THAN SUGAR

The word licorice actually means ''sweet root.'' The plant is a member of the legume family and was used by the Egyptians over 4,000 years ago as a medicinal. The most common form found today is in candy and tobacco. The licorice extract is produced by boiling the yellow roots of the plant in water and then extracting the solid through evaporation. The black solid mass has two components, the oil ''anethole'' which contributes the flavor and ''glycerrhetic acid'' which is the sweet component. Glycerrhetic acid is derived from glycerrhizin found in the raw root which is 50 times sweeter than table sugar (sucrose). The Egyptians used to chew the raw root for its sugary flavor.

IT'S TURKEY TIME

Poultry seasoning is the one ingredient that really makes stuffing, stuffing. All poultry seasonings are not alike, there is a big difference in the freshness of the herbs and the methods of blending and storage before shipping. The finest poultry seasoning is produced by Brady Enterprises of East Weymouth, Massachusetts. The poultry seasoning was created around 1864 by William Bell. Bell's Poultry seasoning is more potent than what you may be used to so if you do use it remember that a little goes a long way. If you can't find it in a specialty market call (617)337-5000.

GARLIC OR HERBS STORED IN OIL MAY BE HARMFUL

Many chefs and cooks have been known for years to store garlic or other herbs in oil for longer shelf life and to flavor their olive oil. The latest studies are showing some possible health hazards that may become serious from this practice. The mixture may contain the rare and deadly Clostridium botulinum bacteria which is present in the environment and may be present on herbs. The bacteria does not like an oxygen environment but loves a closed environment such as in the oil.

When the herb is placed in oil it gives the bacteria a perfect oxygen-free place to multiply. A microbiologist at the FDA has warned that a number of people have become ill from placing store-bought chopped garlic in an oil medium. This type of mixture should be refrigerated and used within ten days to be on the safe side. When purchasing an herb and olive oil mixture from the market they will be labeled to be refrigerated and will contain a preservative, probably phosphoric acid or citric acid.

THE TOP TEN SELLING HERBS/BOTANICALS

1. Chamomile	2. Echinacea
3. Ephedra	4. Feverfew
5. Garlic	6. Ginger
7. Gingko	8. Ginseng
9. Peppermint	10. Valerian

WHAT IS CHINESE FIVE-SPICE POWDER?

This a common, fragrant spice mixture used in a number of Chinese dishes. It is a combination of cinnamon, aniseed, fennel, black pepper, and cloves. The formula is 3 tablespoons of ground cinnamon; 2 teaspoons of anise seed; 1 ½ teaspoons of fennel seed; 1 ½ teaspoons of black pepper; and¾teaspoons of ground cloves. Combine all the ingredients in a blender until they are powdered.

THE ROYAL BREATH CLEANSER

In the year 300 B.C. the Chinese Emperor had a breath problem and was given cloves to sweeten his breath. Cloves contain the chemical "eugenol" which is the same chemical that is used in a number of mouthwashes. Eugenol (oil of cloves) is also used to stop the pain of a toothache.

SOME HERBS NEED TO BE ROASTED BEFORE BEING USED

Allspice berries and peppercorns should be roasted before being used to intensify their flavor. Roast them in a 325°F.(162.8°C.) oven on a small cookie sheet for 10-15 minutes before using them and you will be surprised at the difference in their flavor and aroma. They can also be pan-roasted if you prefer over a medium-high heat for about 5 minutes with the same result.

UNSAFE HERBS

The following herbs are classified as unsafe for human consumption and should not be used in any food or beverage. This is only a partial listing of the hundreds of unsafe herbs.

Name	Scientific Name	Danger
Bittersweet, Woody Nightshade, Climbing Nightshade	Solanum dulcamara	Contains the toxin glycoalkaloid solanine as well as solanidine and dulcamarin.
Bloodroot, Red Puccoon	Saguinaris canadensis	Contains the poisonous alkaloid sanguinarine as well as other alkaloids.
Buckeyes, Horse Chestnut	Aesculus hippocasteranum	Contains alkaloids that may cause liver damage.
Hemlock, Spotted Hemlock, California Or Nebraska Fern	Conium maculatum	Contains a poisonous alkaloid (coniine). Slows the heartbeat and eventually causes coma and death.
Henbane, Hog's Bean, Devil's Eye	Hyoscyamus niger	Contains the alkaloid hyoscyamine
Indian Tobacco, Asthma Weed, Emetic Weed	Lobelia inflata	Contains the alkaloid lobeline.
Jalap Root, High John Root, St. John The Conqueror Root	Ipomoea jalapa	Usually found in Mexico, its resin contains a powerful poison.
Jimson Weed, Thornapple, Tolguacha	Datura stramonium	Contains the alkaloid atropine

Name	Scientific Name	Danger
Lily Of The Valley, May Lily	Convalleria majalis	Contains the toxic cardic glycoside convallatoxin.
American Mandrake, May Apple, Wild Lemon	Podophyllum pelatum	A poisonous plant containing a polycyclic substance.
Mistletoe	Phoradendron flavescens, Viscum album	Contains the toxic pressor amines B-phenylethylamine and tyramine.
Morning Glory	Ipomoea purpurea	Contains a purgative resin. Seeds contain lysergeic acid.
Periwinkle	Vinca major, Vinca minor	Contains toxic alkaloids. Can injure the liver and kidneys.
Pokeweed, Skoke, Pigeonberry	Phytolacca americana	Contains unidentified poisons.
Scotch Broom, Broom	Cytisus scoparius	Contains the toxin sparteine and other alkaloids.
Spindle-tree	Euonymus europaeus	Produces violent purges.
Sweet Flag, Sweet Root, Sweet Cane, Sweet Cinnamon	Acorus calamus	Jamma variety is a carcinogen. Prohibited by the FDA.
Tonka Bean	Dipteryx odorata	Seeds contain coumarin. Can cause serious liver damage.
Water Hemlock, Cowbane, Poison Parsnip, Wild Carrot	Cicuta maculata	Contains an unsaturated higher alcohol called cicutoxin.
White Snakeroot, Snakeroot, Richweed	Eupatorium rugosum	Contains a toxic alcohol substance.
Wolf's Bane, Leopard's Bane, Mountain Tobacco	Arnica montana	Unidentified substances. Produces violent toxic effects.

Name	Scientific Name	Danger
Wormwood, Madderwort, Mugwort	Artemisia absinthium	Contains oil of wormwood, an active narcotic poison. Never purchase the liquor Absinthe unless it is produced in the United States.
Yohimbe, Yohimbi	Corynanthe yohimbi	Contains toxic alkaloids.

CHAPTER 15

Hidden Dangers in Additives

GENERAL INFORMATION

The following additives and chemicals are some of the more common ones that may be recognized by the general public or ones that will easily be found on labels. The information contained in this chapter pertains only to the more pertinent facts regarding these substances and will not be overly technical. In 1997 over 820 million pounds of additives  were used in the manufacture of foods. The USDA and FDA has classified food additives into 32 different categories.

Keep in mind that you are rarely aware of the quantity of additives you consume. Almost all these additives require vitamins and minerals to assist with their breakdown, so that they can be properly disposed of, usually by the liver. These additional nutrients must be obtained from somewhere in the body that could use them more effectively.

1. **Anticaking and free-flowing agents** are usually added to foods that are finely powdered or in a crystalline form to prevent them from caking or becoming lumpy.

2. **Antimicrobial agents** are substances used in food preservation to prevent the growth of bacteria which might cause spoilage.

3. **Antioxidants** are used to preserve foods by limiting their deterioration, rancidity, or discolorization caused by oxidation. Oxygen is one of food's, worst enemies.

4. **Coloring agents** are mainly used to enhance the color of foods and are classified as color stabilizers, color fixatives, or color retention agents.

5. **Curing and pickling agents** are used to provide flavor and retard bacterial growth as well as increasing shelf life.

6. **Dough strengtheners** are used to modify starch and gluten to produce a stable dough.

7. **Drying agents** are substances that have a moisture-absorbing ability which keeps the humidity in the product at a standard moisture level.

8. **Emulsifiers** keep oil and water in suspension so that they do not separate after being mixed.

9. **Enzymes** are used to assist in food processing by helping the chemical reactions take place in an orderly fashion.

10. **Firming agents** are added to assist in the precipitation of residual pectins stengthening the tissue that supports the food. This prevents the food from collapsing during processing and storage.

11. **Flavor enhancers** are added to either enhance or change the original taste or aroma of the food. The substance must not change the normal taste or aroma, just improve it.

12. **Flavoring agents** add a specific flavor to food.

13. **Flour-treating agents** are added to flour that has been milled to improve its color or baking qualities.

14. **Formulation aids** are used to bring about a desired physical characteristic or special texture in the food. These include carriers, binders, fillers, plasticizers, film-formers, and tableting aids.

15. **Fumigants** are more volatile substances that are used for pest and insect control.

16. **Humectants** are substances added to foods to assist the food in retaining moisture.

17. **Leavening agents** are used to either produce or stimulate the production of carbon dioxide gas in baked goods. This helps give the food a light texture. A number of yeasts or salts are used.

18. **Lubricants** and release agents are added to surfaces that come into contact with foods to stop the foods from sticking to them.

19. **Non-nutritive sweeteners** are sweeteners that contain less than 2% of the caloric value of sucrose (table sugar) per equivalent of sweetening capacity.

20. **Nutrient supplementation** are substances that are necessary for a person's metabolic and nutritional needs.

21. **Nutritive sweeteners** must have more than 2% of the caloric value of sucrose per equivalent unit of sweetening capacity.

22. **Oxidizing and reducing agents** chemically oxidize or reduce specific food ingredients to produce a more stable food.

23. **Ph control agents** are added to assist in the maintenance of acid/base balance in the food. These include buffers, acids, alkalis, and neutralizing agents.

24. **Processing aids** are used to enhance the appeal or the utility of a food or ingredient of a food and include clarifying agents, clouding agents, catalysts, flocculents, filter aids, and crystalline inhibitors.

25. **Propellants, aerating agents, and gases** are used to add force in expelling a product or used to limit the amount of oxygen that will come into contact with the food during packaging.

26. **Sequestrants** are substances that combine with certain metal ions which change them into a metal complex that will blend into water or other liquid to improve the stability of that product.

27. **Solvents** are used to extract or dissolve substances placing them into solution.

28. **Stabilizers and thickeners** are used to produce a blended solution or disperse substances to give foods more body, to improve the consistency, stabilize an emulsion, and assist in the setting of jellies.

29. **Surface-active agents** are used to change the surface of liquid foods, other than emulsifiers. These include stabilizing agents, dispersants, detergents, wetting agents, rehydration enhancers, whipping agents, foaming agents, and defoaming agents.

30. **Surface-finishing agents** are used to increase the palatability of foods, preserve their natural glean, inhibit discolorization, and also included are glazes, polishes, waxes, and protective coatings.

31. **Synergists** are substances that will react with other food ingredients causing them to be more effective when incorporated into a food product.

32. **Texturizers** affect the appearance or "mouth feel" of the food.

YOUR OVERWORKED LIVER

The foods we consume today contain over $500 million dollars worth of additives. Americans eat approximately 6-9 pounds of these chemicals annually which amounts to over 1 billion pounds of additives consumed every year. Your liver is in charge of detoxifying this garbage. It is the major organ that must breakdown and dispose of these chemicals. In many cases it requires a number of nutrients to assist in their breakdown, nutrients that would prefer to be useful in other roles.

HIDE AND SEEK

Many preservatives may be hidden in the wrappers of foods. White bread may have as many as 16 chemical preservatives and additives just to keep it fresh.

IT'S THE OTHER 2% THAT MAY GET YOU

Almost 98% (by actual weight) of food additives that are used in food are corn syrup, pepper, mustard, baking soda, baking powder, citric acid, salt, or a vegetable coloring agent.

ACETIC ACID

Known as the acid which makes vinegar acidic. Vinegar is about 4-6% acetic acid. It is used as a solvent for resins, gums, and volatile oils, can stop bleeding and has been used to stimulate scalp circulation. Commercially, it has been used in freckle-bleaching products, hand lotions, and hair dyes. In nature, it occurs in apples, cheeses, cocoa, coffee, oranges, pineapples, skim milk, and a number of other fruits and plants. A solution of about 14% is used in the pickling industry and as a flavor enhancer for cheese.

ACID-MODIFIED STARCHES

These starches are produced by mixing an acid, usually hydrochloric or sulfuric with water and starch at temperatures that are too low for the starch to gelatinize. After the starch has been reduced to the desired consistency, the acid is neutralized, the starch is filtered, and then dried. The modification produces a starch that can be cooked and used at higher concentrations than the standard unmodified starches. The acid-modified starch is mainly used to thicken salad dressings and puddings.

ALUM

Alum may go under a number of different names such as potash alum, aluminum ammonium, aluminum sulfate, or potassium sulfate. Aluminum sulfate (cake alum) is used in the food industry to produce sweet and dill pickles and as a modifier for starch. The other chemicals are used in astringent lotions such as after-shave lotions to remove phosphates from waste water, harden gelatin, and waterproof fabrics.

AMMONIUM BICARBONATE

An alkali leavening agent, used in the production of baked goods, candies, and chocolate products. Prepared by forcing carbon dioxide gas through concentrated ammonia water. Also, used commercially in products that will break up intestinal gas.

AMMONIUM CHLORIDE

Has a mild salt taste and does not blend well with alkalis. It is mainly used in yeast foods, rolls, buns, and as a dough conditioner. Commercially, it is used in permanent wave solution, eye lotions, batteries, safety explosives, and medically as a diuretic.

AMYLASE

An enzyme that breaks down starch into sugar, commercially derived from the pancreas of hogs. It is used in flour and as a texturizer in cosmetics. Sometimes used medically to fight inflammations and is completely non-toxic.

BETA-CAROTENE

A natural substance found in plants and animals. Has the ability to produce vitamin A. Found in many fruits and vegetables and has a yellowish-orange color. Used as a food coloring agent in numerous food products and cosmetics. Recent studies have shown beta-carotene to be a potent antioxidant. Since there is no toxicity involved with it, it is usually recommended over vitamin A.

BHA AND BHT, FRIEND OR FOE?

Both of these chemical substances are frequently found in foods and are potent antioxidants. They are used in beverages, ice creams, chewing gum, potato flakes, baked goods, dry breakfast cereals, gelatin desserts, and soup bases. It is used as a preservative, antioxidant to retard rancidity, and as a stabilizer. Some animal studies have shown that abnormal behavior patterns and brain abnormalities appeared in offsprings after ingestion of these substances by the adults. The percentages of BHA that are allowed in foods are 1,000 ppm in dry yeast, 200 ppm in shortenings, 50 ppm in potato flakes, and 50 ppm when BHA is combined with BHT. The percentages of BHT allowed are 200 ppm in shortenings, 50 ppm in breakfast cereals and potato flakes.

BROMELAIN

Is an extract of pineapple and used in meat tenderizers. It will breakdown proteins and liquefy them if allowed to work long enough.

CAFFEINE

This is the number one psychoactive drug in the United States. It is used as a flavor in some root beers and found naturally in coffee, tea, and chocolate. It affects the central nervous system, heart, and is a respiratory stimulant. It is capable of altering the blood sugar release system in the body and easily crosses the placental barrier. Other side affects are extreme nervousness, insomnia, irregular heart rhythm, ringing in the ears, and even convulsions in high doses. Soft drinks that

are labeled ''cola'' or ''pepper'' that are not artificially sweetened must contain caffeine. The soft drink industry is trying to have this changed.

CALCIUM CARBONATE

The main chemical compound constituent in common chalk, limestone, marble, and coral. Commonly used as an alkali to reduce acidity in foods. Also, used as a neutralizer in ice cream and cream syrups. Commercially, used as a carrier for a variety of bleaches. It's used as a white dye in foods and was withdrawn by the FDA in 1988. Medically, is used to reduce stomach acid and as an antidiarrheal medicine. Animal studies show that overconsumption may affect mineral absorption, especially iron.

CALCIUM HYPOCHLORITE

Used as a germicide and sterilizing agent, used in washing the curd on cottage cheese, kills algae, is a potent bactericide, and fungicide. When used in a 50% solution is valuable in sterilizing fruits and vegetables. Dilute hypochlorite is commonly found in household laundry bleach. Can cause serious damage to all mucosal membranes if ingested. Should never be mixed with other household chemicals as it may produce deadly chlorine gas.

CALCIUM LACTATE

A white, odorless powder which is commonly used as a bread dough conditioner and oxidizing agent. Nutritionally, it is used as a source of calcium for calcium deficient patients, however, it may cause intestinal and heart disturbances.

CALCIUM PROPIONATE

A preservative that is used to reduce the prevalence of certain bacteria and molds. May also be used as sodium propionate depending on the food.

CALCIUM SULFATE

Also known as "Plaster of Paris." A powder that is used as a firming agent and a yeast dough conditioner. Commonly used in the brewing industry as well as other alcoholic products that need fermentation. Commercially, it is used in jellies, cereal flours, breads, rolls, bleu cheese, and canned potatoes and tomatoes. Reduces the acidity in cottage cheese and tooth pastes. Industrially, it is used in cement, wall plaster, and insecticides. Because it tends to absorb moisture and harden quickly some known problems have been related to intestinal obstruction. When it is mixed with flour it is an excellent rodent killer.

CARRAGEENAN

Also known as Irish Moss. A common stabilizer used in oils, cosmetics, and foods. Used as an emulsifier in chocolate products, chocolate milk, cheese spreads, ice cream, sherbets, French dressing, and gassed cream products. It is completely soluble in hot water and is not coagulated by acids. It is under further study by the FDA since it has caused cancerous tumors in laboratory animals, however, in the present levels used in food it should be harmless.

CHLORINE GAS

A common flour-bleaching agent and oxidizing agent. May be found naturally in the earth's crust and is a greenish-yellow gas that is a powerful lung irritant. It can be dangerous to inhale with only 30 ppm causing coughing. The chlorine in drinking water may contain carcinogenic carbon tetrachloride which is formed during the production process. Chlorination of drinking water may not be the safest chemical to use in water.

CHLOROPHYLL
This is the green color found in plants that plays the essential role in photosynthesis. It is used in deodorants, antiperspirants, dentifrices, and mouthwashes. Also, used to give a green color to soybean and olive oil.

CITRATE SALTS
Mainly used in pasteurized process cheeses and spreads. May tend to mask the results of laboratory tests for pancreatic and liver function and blood acid-base balances. If you are going for extensive blood work, try not to consume these cheeses for at least one week prior to the test.

COLORINGS
Most of the colorings presently in use are derived from coal tars (carcinogens). As the years go by, more and more of these colorings are phased out and banned for use in food.

DIACETYL
A naturally occurring substance found in cheese, cocoa, pears, berries, cooked chicken, and coffee beans. It appears as a yellowish-green liquid and tends to assist in retaining the aroma of butter, vinegar, and coffee. Also used in chocolate, ginger ale, baked goods, and flavoring in ice creams, candy, and chewing gum. Certain diacetyl compounds have been found to cause cancer in laboratory studies.

DISODIUM PHOSPHATE
Used to trap mineral ions in foods that would cause the food to spoil and affect the color of foods. Mainly used in the processing of evaporated milk, pork products, in sauces, and commonly used as an emulsifying agent in cheese spreads.

ETHYL ACETATE
This is a colorless liquid that has a pleasant fruity odor and occurs naturally in a number of fruits and berries. It is extracted and made into a synthetic flavoring agent and used in berry products, butter, a number of fruit products, rum, mint products, ice creams, baked goods, chewing gum, puddings, and certain liquors. Also used in nail enamels and nail polish remover. The vapors are an irritant to the central nervous system with prolonged inhalation leading to possible liver damage.

ETHYL VANILLIN

Has a stronger flavor than natural vanilla and is used as a synthetic flavoring agent in berries, butter, caramel, coconut, macaroon, cola, rum, sodas, chocolate, honey, butterscotch, imitation vanilla extract, and baked goods. Has caused mild skin irritations in humans and injuries to a number of organs in animals.

EUCALYPTUS OIL

Has a camphorlike odor and is used in mint, root beer, ginger ale flavoring, ice creams, candy, baked goods, chewing gum, and some liquors. Medically, it has been used as a local antiseptic, expectorant, and vermifuge. Deaths have occurred from people consuming as little as one teaspoon and reports of coma from consuming one milliliter.

GLUTEN

A combination of the two proteins gliadin and glutelin. It is obtained from wheat flour, is extremely sticky, and is produced by washing out the starch in the flour. Responsible for the porous and spongy structure of breads.

GUAR GUM

Derived from the seeds of a plant found in India. It has 5-8 times the thickening power of starch and is used as a stabilizer in fruit drinks, icings and glazes. Frequently is used as a binder in cream cheese, ice creams, baked goods, French dressing, etc. Has been very useful in keeping vitamin tablets from disintegrating. Also, used as an appetite suppressant and to treat peptic ulcers.

GUM ARABIC

This is also called acacia and is the odorless, colorless, and tasteless sap from the stem of the acacia tree which grows in Africa and areas of the Southern United States. It is considered a natural gum and has the ability to dissolve very quickly in water. It is mainly used to stop sugar crystallization, as a thickening agent in the candy-making industry, and to make chewing gum. Gum acacia is used in the soft drink and beer industry to retard foam.

HYDROGENATED OIL

An oil that has been partially converted from a liquid polyunsaturated oil into a more solid saturated fat. This process is done by adding hydrogen molecules from water to increase the solidity of the fat. Basically, it turns a relatively good fat into a bad fat which has more "mouth feel."

INVERT SUGAR

Composed of a mixture of 50% glucose and 50% fructose. It is much sweeter than sucrose (ordinary table sugar). Honey is mostly invert sugar. Invert sugar is mainly used in candies and the brewing industry. It tends to hold moisture well and prevents products from drying out. Medically, it is used in some intravenous solutions.

LECITHIN

It is a natural antioxidant and emollient composed of choline, phosphoric acid, fatty acids, and glycerin. It is normally produced from soybeans and egg yolk. Used in breakfast cereals, candies, chocolate, baked goods, and margarine.

MALIC ACID

Has a strong acid taste and occurs naturally in many fruits, including apples and cherries. Used to age wines, and in frozen dairy products, candies, preserves, and baked goods. Commercially, used in cosmetics and hair lacquers and is a skin irritant.

MANNITOL

Usually produced from seaweed and is sweet tasting. Used as a texturizer in chewing gum and candies. Commonly used as a sweetener in "sugar-free" products, however, it still contains calories and carbohydrates. Studies are underway and may show that mannitol is a significant factor leading to cancer in rats. It may also worsen kidney disorders and cause gastrointestinal upsets.

METHYLENE CHLORIDE

A gas used in the decaffeination of coffee. Residues may remain and coffee companies do not have to disclose their methods on the label. Best to drink decaf if the label states that it was decaffeinated with water.

MODIFIED STARCH

Modified starch is ordinary starch that has been altered chemically and used in jellies as a thickening agent. Since babies have difficulty digesting regular starch, modified starch is easier to digest since it is partially broken down. Chemicals that are used to modify the starch include propylese oxide, succinic anhydride, aluminum sulfate, and sodium hydroxide.

MONOSODIUM GLUTAMATE (MSG)

This is actually the salt of glutamic acid (one of the amino acids). It occurs naturally in seaweed, soybeans, and sugar beets. It has no taste of its own, however, its main purpose in foods is to intensify existing flavors especially in soups, condiments, candies, meats, and baked goods. A number of symptoms have been reported after ingesting MSG which include headaches, facial tingling, depression, mood changes, light flashes, and rapid pulse rate. A study released by the Federation of American Societies for Experimental Biology in 1995 stated that MSG was declared safe for most people, however, other reports indicate that people with asthma may be affected by as little as 0.5 grams which is the minimum amount that would be absorbed through most foods. Should be consumed in moderation if at all.

NITRATE

Potassium and sodium nitrate are also known as "saltpeter." It is mainly used as a color fixative for processed meat products. They tend to combine with saliva and food substances (amines) to form nitrosamine a known carcinogen (cancer-causing agent). Animal studies have proven that mice developed cancer after being given nitrosamines.

NITRITE

Potassium and sodium nitrite are used as color preservatives in meats as well as providing a chemical that will assist the meat product in resisting certain bacteria. Sodium nitrite will actually react with the myoglobin in meat and protect the red color for a long period of time. It is used in all processed meat products which include: Vienna sausage, smoke-cured fish products, hot dogs, bacon, lunch  meats, and canned meats. Vitamin E as well as vitamin C will block the formation of nitrites after ingestion.

When nitrites are fed to lab animals, studies have shown that malignant tumors developed in over 90% within 6 months, and death soon afterwards. A number of incidents have been reported that linked high levels of nitrites in food to "cardiovascular collapse" in humans and even death from consuming hot dogs and blood sausage that were produced by local processors in different areas of the country.

An Israeli study discovered problems related to brain damage in lab animals when they were fed an equivalent amount of nitrites that would be consumed by a person eating a large amount of processed meat products.

When nitrites in food are ingested by humans there are two possible pathways that the nitrites may take that could be harmful:

(1) the nitrites react with a person's hemoglobin to produce a pigment called meth-hemoglobin, which may seriously lower the oxygen-carrying capacity of the red blood cell,

(2) there is a possible cancer connection when the nitrites are biochemically altered into a "nitrosamine" which usually occurs in the stomach if certain proteins are present when the nitrites arrive.

If you drink some orange juice or chew a 500 mg. vitamin C tablet just before consuming foods that contain nitrites the adverse reaction by the nitrites may be reversed. Vitamin C can neutralize the reaction that takes place in the stomach by interfering with the protein combining with the nitrite. Due to recent studies relating to this neutralizing effect, some manufacturers of hot dogs are now adding ascorbic acid to their product.

PAPAIN

An enzyme that will break down meats. It is prepared from papaya and is an ingredient in a number of meat tenderizers or marinades. It is also used for clearing beverages and added to farina to reduce the cooking time. Medically, it is used to prevent adhesions. It is, however, deactivated by cooking temperatures.

PECTIN

An integral part of many plants, it is found in their roots, stems, and fruits. The best sources are derived from lemon or orange rind which contains 30% of the complex carbohydrate. It is used as a stabilizer, thickener, and bodyfier for beverages, syrups, ice creams, candies, French dressing, fruit jellies, and frozen puddings. Mainly used in foods as a "cementing or binding agent."

PEROXIDE

Three forms of peroxide are used commercially: Benzoyl, Calcium, and Hydrogen. Benzoyl peroxide is mainly used as a bleaching agent for flours, oils, and cheeses as well as medically made into a paste and used

on poison ivy and burns. It should not be heated as it may explode.
Calcium peroxide is used as a dough conditioner and oxidizing agent for
baked goods. Has also been used as an antiseptic. Hydrogen peroxide is
used as a bleaching agent, a modifier for food starch, a preservative, and
to reduce the bacterial count in milk products. It is a strong oxidant that
is capable of injuring skin and eyes. Commercially, it is used in hair
bleaches and rubber gloves should always be worn at all times when
using this product.

POTASSIUM CHLORIDE

A crystalline, odorless powder that has a somewhat salty taste. It is used
in the brewing industry to improve fermentation and to assist in the
jelling process with jellies and jams. It is also used with sodium chloride
as a salt substitute. Should be used in moderation as testing is being
done relating to gastrointestinal irritation and ulcers.

SODIUM BENZOATE

Used in acidic foods to reduce the microorganism count. Has been used
to retard bacterial growth and act as a preservative in carbonated
beverages, jams and jellies, margarine, and salad dressings. Sodium
benzoate may be found naturally in cranberries and prunes.

SODIUM BISULFATE

Used as an antibrowning agent and a preservative in beverages, corn
syrup, dehydrated potatoes, dried fruits, sauces, soups, and some wines.
Tends to destroy vitamin B_1 (thiamin) when added to foods.

SODIUM CARBONATE

An odorless crystal or powder that is found in certain ores, in lake brine,
and seaweed. Has the tendency to absorb water from the air and is used
as a neutralizer for butter, milk products, and in the processing of olives.
Commercially, it is used in antacids, soaps, mouthwashes, shampoos,
and foot preparations. If ingested may cause gastrointestinal problems,
nausea, and diarrhea.

SODIUM CASEINATE

A protein used as a thickener and to alter the color of foods. Usually
found in coffee creamers, frozen custards, and ice cream products.

SODIUM CHLORIDE

This is the chemical name for common table salt. It is used in numerous food products both as a preservative and taste enhancer. Readily absorbs water. Many breakfast cereals are high in salt, such as Wheaties with 370 mg. of sodium per ounce. Most potato chips have 190 mg. per ounce. Your daily intake should not exceed 1200 mg.

SODIUM CITRATE

Used as an emulsifier in ice cream, processed cheeses, and evaporated milk. Also, used as a buffer to control acidity and to retain carbonation in soft drinks. Has the ability to attach itself to trace metals that are present in water and prevent them from entering live cells.

TANNIC ACID

May be found in the bark of oak and sumac trees and the fruit of plants as well as in coffee, cherries, and tea. It is used as a flavoring agent and to clarify beer and wine. It has been used medically as a mild astringent. Commercially, it is also used in antiperspirants, eye lotions, and sunscreens.

SORBITOL

A sweetener that is extracted from berries and some fruits. Basically, it is an alcohol that produces a sweet taste and is used in dietetic products as a replacement for sugar. It is also used as a food binder, thickener, texturing agent, humectant, and food stabilizer.

SULFITES

There are three types of sulfites that may be used as anti-browning agents: sodium, potassium, and ammonium. They may all be used on most foods except meats or a high vitamin B content food. Physiologic reactions to sulfites are numerous with the more common being an acute asthmatic attack.

Sulfites have been used for years to retard browning of fruits and vegetables, providing a level of preservation. The most common use was on salad bars. The outside leaves of lettuce should be discarded since they have been found to contain sulfites in some instances. The United States has limited the use of sulfites, however, imported produce may still be hazardous.

SULFUR DIOXIDE

Produced from the chemical reaction of heating sulfur. Used as a food bleach, preservative, antioxidant, and anti-browning agent. Found on a number of dried fruits such as yellow raisins and apricots. It has a tendency to destroy vitamin A and should not be used on meats or high vitamin A content fruits or vegetables.

CHAPTER 16

Going with the Grain, and Some Nuts

GRAINS

Grains are one of the most important components in our diet and one that is not eaten in anywhere near the levels recommended by nutritionists. They supply complex carbohydrates and are one of the major food sources worldwide. To obtain optimum health a person should consume 5-6 servings of products that contain grains daily, which include: whole grain cereals, pasta, rice, breads, baked chips, bran muffins, corn, etc.

Only 25% of the American diet contains these complex carbohydrates, compared to countries such as Japan at 65%. As we learn more about nutrition we are beginning to realize that a diet high in meat and meat products is not the healthiest way to go. In recent years the trend is improving as more and more information reaches the public regarding nutrition and health. Americans are taking more interest than ever before in their health, unfortunately it took an increase in cancer and cardiovascular diseases to bring this change about.

One example is the level of pasta consumed per person in the United States which has risen from 11 pounds per person in 1975 to 23 pounds in 1997. The nutrient content of whole grain products, if left in their natural form is excellent.

Grain Cooking Chart				
Grain	Quantity Uncooked	Amount of Water	Cooking Time	Quantity of Cooked Grain
Amaranth	1 cup	3 cups	25 min.	2 cups
Barley	1 cup	4 cups	45 min.	4 cups
Brown Rice	1 cup	2.5 cups	45 min.	3 cups
Buckwheat	1 cup	4 cups	20 min.	3 cups
Bulgur	1 cup	2 cups	15 min.	2.5 cups
Cornmeal	1 cup	4 cups	40 min.	4 cups
Millet	1 cup	3 cups	40 min.	3 cups
Oat Bran	1 cup	3 cups	2 min.	3 cups
Oat Groats	1 cup	2 cups	30 min.	2.5 cups
Rolled Oats	1 cup	2 cups	5 min.	4 cup
Quinona	1 cup	2 cups	15 min.	2 cups
Rye	1 cup	4 cups	1 Hour	2.5 cups
Wheat Berries	1 cup	3 cups	1 Hour	2.5 cups
Wild Rice	1 cup	4 cups	40 min.	3.5 cups

Grains are composed of three parts; the bran, the endosperm, and the germ. The outer covering, or bran, contains the majority of the grain's nutrients and almost all of the dietary fiber. This nutrient-rich portion of the kernel is removed during processing to make our refined foods that need to be enriched. The endosperm accounts for the majority of the grain's weight and contains most of the protein and carbohydrates. It is this portion that is used to make white flour. The germ portion of the grain contains polyunsaturated fat and is rich in vitamin E and B complex. It is usually removed to avoid rancidity.

GRAIN VARIETIES

AMARANTH, A SUPER GRAIN
Amaranth, unlike other grains is not deficient in the amino acid listen. This grain should be consumed with either rice, wheat, or barley. It will provide a biologically complete protein containing all the essential amino acids. Amaranth was first grown by the Aztecs. The seeds are minute and there are about 70,000 in one pound.

BARLEY
It is an excellent source of B vitamins and soluble fiber. One of the favorite forms of barley consumed in this country is as grits. Malted barley can be purchased in health food stores.

BUCKWHEAT
Buckwheat is actually the fruit of a leafy plant related to rhubarb. Has a strong nutlike flavor and is especially high in the amino acid listen. Considered a minor crop in the United States, it is only found in health food stores and prepared as "kasha." Kasha (buckwheat groats) is from the buckwheat plant and can be cooked and prepared the same as rice. It has a high nutritional value.

MILLET
The only grain which is higher in B vitamins than whole wheat or brown rice. It is also an excellent source of copper and iron. People with wheat allergies can usually tolerate millet without a problem. Millet is more popular in North Africa, China, India and Ethiopia where it is used to make flatbread. One of the best nutritionally rich grains.

OATS
Oats were first produced in the United States in the 1600's. By 1852 they were being packaged and sold with oatmeal becoming the most popular breakfast food of that day. In 1997 the annual consumption of oats per person was approximately 15 pounds. Oat bran is being studied in relation to its cholesterol lowering qualities. It is high in a number of vitamins and minerals. Besides oatmeal, oats are used extensively in granola and muesli cereals.

TYPES OF OAT PRODUCTS
» Instant Oats
Oats that have been sliced into very small pieces, then pre-cooked and dried. They require very little, if any, cooking. These type of oats cannot be used in recipes that call for rolled oats or quick-cooking oats. If you do try and use them your product will probably be a gooey mess.

» Oat Bran
This is the ground outer casing of the grain. It is very high in soluble fiber, and may help to lower cholesterol levels.

» Oat Flour
The oat grain is very finely ground, it must be mixed with gluten flour due to the lack of gluten or it will not be able to rise.

» Quick-Cooking Oats
These are oats that are sliced into many pieces, then steamed and flattened. These oats take only 5 minutes to cook.

» Rolled Oats
These are just steamed, flattened and made into flakes. These oats take about 15 minutes to cook. Both the quick-cooking oats and the rolled oats can be exchanged in recipes with no problem.

» Steel-Cut Oats
These are oats that are cut instead of rolled and take a longer amount of time to cook, usually 20-30 minutes. They have a chewy texture.

QUINONA

Related to Swiss chard and spinach, its leaves can be cooked in similar fashion for a nutritious green. It has a delicate flavor and can be a substitute for almost any grain. Quinona is high in iron, potassium, and riboflavin and has good levels of zinc, copper, and manganese. Tends to increase 3-4 times in volume when cooked and is usually found only in health food stores. More expensive than most other grains.

RICE

Rice is the most common grain consumed in the United States at about 17 pounds per person, annually. This is very low compared to the 300 pounds consumed per capita in Japan and China. History records the first cultivation of rice to be in Thailand in 3500 B.C., however, China produces more rice than any other country, almost 90 percent of all the rice grown worldwide. It is an excellent source of the B complex vitamins as well as a number of minerals. Brown rice is more nutritious and higher in the B vitamins and fiber than white rice. Vitamin E is only found in brown rice. Instant brown rice is now becoming available. it is really hard to tell the difference between white rice and brown rice after it is cooked. The brown rice, however, will have a much higher nutritional content.

The only difference between brown and white rice is the removal of the husk. It is only sold in small boxes because the bran portion is higher in fat which may cause the rice to go rancid if not used up in a short period of time. If you allow brown rice to soak for about 1 hour before cooking it will be more tender.

There are more varieties of rice grown than any other food. Worldwide there are over 7,000 varieties of long, short, or medium grain rice.

» WHITE IS OUT, BROWN IS IN
Rice, unlike other processed products does not have the number of nutrients replaced that are lost. Even though rice may be sold as "enriched" the number of nutrients replaced is minimal. When the rice is then cooked in boiling water additional nutrients are lost. Brown rice is always best. The rice with the lowest nutritional content is Minute Rice and any instant rice. The burnt taste may be removed from rice by changing the rice into a clean pot and placing a piece of white bread on top for 5 minutes, then remove and discard. The white bread will absorb the odor.

» TOUGH STUFF
Salt should never be added to any food while it is cooking in water, it tends to toughen the food. Rice is very susceptible to toughening from salted water. Rice will retain its white color if you add a few drops of lemon juice to the water.

» CLEAN 'EM OUT
Always store rice at cool room temperature and make sure that you wash the rice before using it to clean out the hulls.

» COOKING RICE
The easiest method determining the amount of water to cook rice in is to place the rice in a pot, shake it to settle the rice, then pour enough water in up to your fist knuckle of your index finger that has been placed gently on top of the rice. The rice should be covered with about 1 inch of water. Then cook the rice by bringing the water to a boil, cover and simmer on low heat for 35 minutes. The heat should then be turned off and the rice allowed to stand for 8-10 minutes. If you want your rice to always be dry and fluffy, try placing a few folded paper towels under the lid to absorb the steam and excess moisture for the last 2-3 minutes of cooking time.

HOW DO THEY MAKE PUFFED CEREALS?

Puffed cereals were invented in the early 1900's by Alexander P. Anderson. He was interested in the nature of starch granules and while experimenting some of his experiments exploded into large puffy masses of starch. Making puffed cereals was somewhat like making popcorn. The starch or dough is compressed and cooked to gelatinize the starch then placed under high pressure until the water vapor expands puffing out each small morsel. The final product is produced from "oven puffing." Quaker Oats was first to produce puffed cereal and it was introduced to the public in 1904 at the St. Louis World's Fair and sold as a popcornlike snack. In 1905 it was sold as a breakfast cereal.

FAUX CORN

When prepared the same as rice, Jasmine rice smells and tastes just like popcorn. For a different treat try it as a side dish.

Long grain rice contains more protein and fewer minerals than most standard rice.

FLUFFIER BEATS MUSHIER

Converted rice is actually parboiled rice, rice which has been soaked, steamed, and dried in such a way as to make it fluffier instead of mushier.

It is not necessary to rinse packaged rice before preparing it. You may wash more nutrients down the drain. You will lose enough from the cooking.

RICE, WILD

This is not a grain, but actually a grass seed of a shallow water grass and not part of the grain family. It is more expensive than rice with the majority grown in wild rice paddies in Minnesota. It has twice the protein content of standard rice and was a staple food of the Chippewa and Dakota Native American tribes. It is high in the B vitamins, has a more chewy texture, and takes longer to cook. Wild rice will only remain fresh for one week if refrigerated.

RYE

Rye is higher in protein (86% higher than brown rice), iron and the B vitamins than whole wheat. Most breads and rye products are usually made from a combination of rye and whole wheat. It is unusual to find a rye product with rye as the single grain source. Only 25% of the rye crop goes into human food production, the balance being used for alcoholic beverage production and animal food.

TRITICALE

One of the better grains with a high protein content. It is grown by crossing wheat with rye. May be used as a bread flour due to its excellent gluten content. It has a high level of B vitamins and will most likely be found in a health food store.

WHEAT

Wheat is the number one grain crop in the world and used mainly in breads and pastas. Unfortunately the majority of wheat is processed into white flour, reducing its nutrient content. Whole wheat is very high in the B vitamins and numerous minerals including iron. Wheat bran is presently being studied in relation to colon cancer. The hardest wheat is Durham, which is made into seminola and mainly used for pastas.

» TOP OF THE LINE
The finest pasta wheat grown in the United States is grown in North Dakota, in an area known as the "Durham triangle." Over 90% of this first quality wheat is grown here. When making pasta with Durham wheat it is not necessary to wash the pasta after it is cooked. This wheat always cooks up tender and never becomes mushy.

» WHAT IS THE ANCESTOR OF WHEAT?
There are over thirty thousand varieties of wheat. They have all developed from just one common ancestor, known as "wild einkorn." Genetically, all the wheats grown today are from a different strain, however, two of the ancient strains are occasionally available in health food stores. The two that you may find are called "kamut" and "spelt" which are produced as flour and pasta. These wild wheats can be traced back thousands of years.

» FINALLY, A GOOD GERM
Wheat germ is an excellent food, high in nutrients and fiber. However, it is almost impossible to buy fresh wheat germ. Rancidity starts as soon as it is processed (exposed to air) and it should be eaten within 3-6 days of the original processing. If it leaves a bitter taste in your mouth it is not fresh and rancidity and oxidation has taken over. When fresh, wheat germ should have a sweet taste.

» A LITTLE OF THIS AND A LITTLE OF THAT = CEREAL
Be aware that your favorite brand of cereal may contain so many additives that it may not be as healthy a product as you are made to believe.

» HEALTHY CHOICE
Cracked wheat AKA wheat berries can be prepared by toasting wheat and keeping the more nutritional parts of the wheat intact (bran and germ). The cracked wheat is then ground into a variety of granulations making it easier to cook and digest. If a recipe calls for rice, cracked wheat can be a more nutritious substitute.

» NO GERMS HERE
When you purchase hot cereal products such as Cream of Wheat, grits, or Farina be aware that most of these products are

"degerminated" which reduces the available nutrients to increase their palatability.

» THE DARKER THE BETTER
Bulgur wheat is not as nutritious as 100% whole wheat products unless it has a dark brown covering. Bulgur wheat is best steamed, dried, and then pulverized into three separate sizes of granulations. The finest wheat is used to prepare "tabbouleh." The coarsest for bulgur pilaf and the medium granulation for cereals.

» TASTY DISH
A favorite Middle Eastern dish is "tabbouleh" which is prepared from bulgur wheat. It includes lemon juice, olive oil, parsley, dill or mint, plum tomatoes, onions, garlic, and an herbal blend. Vegetables are added when available.

» FOR HEALTH'S SAKE, READ THE LABEL
If the list of ingredients reads "wheat flour" it is the closest thing to white flour and has about the same nutritional quality as white flour. If you are buying bread or rolls and you want the healthier ones make sure the label reads "100% whole wheat flour" or "whole grain." 100% whole wheat flour will only store for about 2 months without the risk of rancidity. Refrigeration will allow you to store it for up to 4-5 months. The healthiest portion of the wheat is the bran. It contains between 75-85% of the niacin and pyridoxine, 40-50% of the pantothenic acid and riboflavin, almost 35% of the thiamin, and about 20% of the protein. When we process wheat to make white flour this is all discarded. Very little is added back.

SHAKE IT UP
Whole grain flours should always be sifted through a coarse sifter. This can mean a measurement difference of up to two tablespoons per cup.

OLYMPICS BOUND?
A recent product produced from wheat germ or whole wheat is "octacosanol." The product is normally somewhat expensive since it takes 10 pounds of wheat to obtain 1,000 micrograms of octacosanol. Has been used by athletes to improve endurance and slow the buildup of lactic acid. It may also improve the glycogen storage capacity of muscles. Since wheat germ is a source, it would be wise to include fresh wheat germ in an athlete's diet.

COMPETITORS

The pretzel and the bagel are neck and neck competing for the hottest selling snack foods in America. Both products are relatively fat-free which is a plus.

HIDE AND SEEK

Companies are now playing "let's hide the sugar" game with the consumer. The products are the same but the names have changed to remove any hint of sugar. Super Sugar Crisp has been changed to Super Golden Crisp and Sugar Frosted Flakes is now just Frosted Flakes.

Foods Containing Wheat			
Beverages			
Beer	Malt Liqueur	Malted Milk	Gin
Postum	Sanka	Whiskies	Home Brew
Breads			
Crackers	Cookies	Biscuits	Rolls
Pretzels	Breads	Macaroni	Spaghetti
Noodles	Dumplings	Muffins	Vermicelli
Pie Crust	Cereals	Graham	Popovers
Pastries and Desserts			
Pie	Cake	Doughnuts	Puddings
Candy Bars	Ice Cream	Cones	Waffles
Cereals			
Corn Flakes	Crackles	Grapenuts	Wheatena
Most cereals contain wheat.			
Flours			
Buckwheat Flour	Corn Flour	Graham Flour	
Rye Flour	White Flour	Gluten Flour	
Whole Wheat Flour	Patent Flour	Lima Bean Flour	
Miscellaneous			
Bouillon Cubes	Gravies	Griddle Cakes	
Matzos	Sauces	Mayonnaise	

NUTS AND SEEDS

The cultivation of nuts can be traced back to 10,000 B.C. They are nutritious, are a good source of protein, potassium, vitamin E, B vitamins and iron. The only drawback to nuts is their fat content. Nuts are approximately 70-95% fat. Macadamia nuts contain the highest level of fat and join coconut, cashews and Brazil nuts as having their fat high in saturated fats. Peanuts contain the highest level of protein of any nut.

Nuts are protected from oxidation of their oils by their shells, damaged nuts should never be purchased.

Seeds of many plants are edible and contain an excellent level of nutrients, especially trace minerals that may be deficient in many of our foods due to poor soil conditions. The most popular eating seeds are: pumpkin, sesame, and sunflower. Eating poppy seeds may cause you to have a positive urine test for drugs. Poppy seeds are a relative of morphine and codeine.

Sunflower seeds produce a similar reaction on the body as smoking a cigarette. It causes the body to produce adrenaline, which will go to the brain, resulting in a pleasant feeling. The seeds, however, must be raw, not roasted.

UP, UP, AND AWAY

When you consume a large quantity of sunflower seeds you may get somewhat high due to the body producing excess adrenaline which may result in a feeling of exhilaration. For this reaction to occur, however, you will need to eat raw seeds, not roasted ones.

ALMOND PASTE AND MARZIPAN, IS THERE A DIFFERENCE?

There is a difference, however, both are initially made from blanched almonds. Marzipan contains more sugar and is stiffer and lighter in color. Almond paste contains more blanched almonds, therefore it costs more. In California almond orchards are second only to grapes in orchard space. Almonds are California's major food export.

WHAT IS MASA HARINA?

Masa harina is a special corn flour that is made by boiling the corn in a 5 percent lime solution for one hour to increase the amount of available calcium. The corn is then washed, drained, and ground into corn flour that is mainly used to make tortillas and other Mexican dishes.

WHAT ARE GINKGO NUTS?

A ginkgo nut is actually the pit of the ginkgo fruit and has a sweet flavor. It can be found in most oriental markets, however, if you do find it with the skin still on, be cautious since the skin contains a skin irritant and you will need to wear gloves to handle the fruit until the skin is removed.

WHAT IS THE OLDEST TREE FOOD IN THE WORLD?

The oldest tree food that is known to man is the walnut, which dates back to 7000 B.C., in Persia. The first walnuts were planted in the United States in 1867 by Franciscan missionaries. The Central Valley of California produces 98% of the total U.S. crop and 33% of the world's commercial crop.

IS BEANUT BUTTER BETTER THAN PEANUT BUTTER?

A new substitute for peanut butter called Beanut Butter is now being marketed in the United States by Dixie USA. It provides a high quality protein and is made from soy. The product contains sufficient quantities of an estrogen-like substance called isoflavones which may be effective in reducing the symptoms of menopause, lowering the risk of heart disease, and osteoporosis, and is being studied in relation to reducing the risk of certain cancers. The fat content is 11 grams per 2 tablespoons compared to 16 grams in regular peanut butter and has half the saturated fat. The fat tends to separate similar to natural peanut butter and can be poured off to reduce the fat content even farther. For additional information if the product is not available call (800)347-3494.

TYPES OF NUTS

» ROASTED NUTS
Even though they are called roasted they are usually fried in oil. If they are cooked in a tropical oil which most are, they will contain a good percentage of the fat as saturated.

» DRY-ROASTED
These are never cooked in an oil. All nuts, however, are naturally high in fat content. Most of this type sold are high in preservatives and salt.

» RAW NUTS
Commonly packaged in cans which will keep them fresh for longer periods since they tend to go rancid very easily. Raw nuts should be stored in the refrigerator or freezer to slow down rancidity.

» DEFATTED (LITE) PEANUTS
Through processing, a percentage of the fat is reduced, however, they are still not a low-fat treat.

GENERAL FACTS

HEALTHIER WAY TO GO

In the early 20th century our grandparents were getting twice as much protein from grains and cereals than we are getting in 1998. We would be healthier if this was still the case.

CALCIUM FROM NUTS?

Almonds are an excellent source of calcium. A small handful equals the calcium in 4 ounces of milk. You will still have the fat content of the almonds which will be higher than non-fat milk.

CRUMMY SOLUTION

Bread crumbs are getting more and more expensive! You will never have to buy them again if you have a special jar set aside and place the crumbs from the bottom of cracker boxes or low-sugar cereal boxes in the jar.

AH HA, A NUT, THAT'S REALLY NOT A NUT

Peanuts are really not in the nut family but are actually a relative of the legume family of beans. The two varieties are the Spanish and the Virginia. If you need to store peanuts, try wrapping them in a plastic bag and keeping them refrigerated. They should last for 6 months and be fresh.

DOES PEANUT BUTTER CONTAIN A CARCINOGEN?

Yes. Aflatoxin has been found in almost all peanut butters on the market. A study that was performed by Consumers Union showed that the major brands such as Jiff, Peter Pan, and Skippy had less of the aflatoxin that most store brands. The biggest offender turned out to be the freshly ground peanut butter in health food stores which had ten times the levels of the major brands. The U.S. Government allows no more than 20 parts per billion (ppb) of aflatoxin which members of the health field feel is too high. According to Consumers Union eating levels that contain an average of 2 ppb of aflatoxin every 10 days will result in a cancer risk of seven in one million. This is a higher risk than exists from most pesticides in foods. Best to purchase a major brand or one that states on the label "aflatoxin-free."

CHEF'S SECRET
This trick is used all the time by chefs. Next time you chop nuts in a blender, try adding a small amount of sugar and the nut meat will never stick together.

GREAT TASTE TREAT
Almond paste is used to make marzipan. It is made from almonds, glycerin, sugar (or a substitute), and a liquid, usually almond extract.

THE OLD SWITCHEROO
When your recipe calls for a coarse bran and you don't have any, try substituting your favorite finely chopped unsalted nut. If you have a problem shelling the nuts, just store them in the freezer for an hour.

SLOWS THE RANCIDITY
If you want your natural peanut butter to stay fresh longer, try storing it in the refrigerator upside down. If unopened it will stay fresh for 1 year. If refrigerated after opening it will last about 3-4 months providing you don't take a taste from the jar after the spoon was in your mouth. The oil in natural peanut butter does not stay in suspension due to the lack of a stabilizer chemical.

TAKE ME TO ST. LOUIS, LOUIS
Peanut butter was first introduced at the St. Louis World's Fair in 1904. It was labeled as a health food.

GETTING ALL YOUR AMINO ACIDS
A Mexican meal of 1¼ cup of beans plus 4 cups of rice will provide you with a better source of protein than a 1 pound steak. Beans and rice are the most common meal in Mexico and extremely healthy.

EAT IN MODERATION
Macadamia nuts have more fat (96%) and calories than any other nut.

A GRAIN-RAISING EXPERIENCE
Grains should always be tested to see if they are fresh. Just pour a small amount of water into a pan and add a small amount of grain. Fresh grain sinks to the bottom and older grain floats to the top. Nuts, beans, whole

grains, corn, and peanut butter should be discarded if there is even the slightest sign of mold or unusual odor. They may contain the dangerous "aflatoxin."

CHUCK FULL OF PROTEIN

Lentils are tiny seeds that need no soaking before cooking. They are a good source of protein and will cook slower if added to highly acidic foods such as tomatoes.

HEAVVVVY

One ounce of sunflower seeds contains 160 calories and is not a "diet" food as some would have you believe.

SUPERMAN TO THE RESCUE

One of the most difficult nuts to crack open is the black walnut. My recommendation is that if you have a trash compactor, place a piece of wood on the bottom high enough so that when the compactor lowers it will crush the nut. Be sure and have a clean bag in it.

WHY IS BARLEY A COMMON THICKENER FOR SOUPS AND STEWS?

Barley contains the starch molecules (complex carbohydrates) amylase and amylopectin packed into the granule. When barley is cooked, the starch granules absorb the water molecules, swell and become soft. At 140°F. (60°C.), the amylase and the amylopectin relax and some of their internal bonds come apart and form new bonds. This new network is capable of trapping and holding water molecules. As the starch granules swell, the barley becomes soft and provides bulk. If the barley is cooked farther, the granules will rupture releasing some of the amylase and amylopectin which are able to absorb more water making the soup or stew thicker. To retain a large percentage of the B vitamins in barley, you will need to consume the liquid as well as the barley.

COMPETING WITH THE SQUIRRELS?

According to Greek legend, acorns were a popular food during the Golden Age. The high carbohydrate content made them an excellent cereal food for the North American Indians. The nuts do contain a high level of tannin which can be removed by soaking them in hot water and changing the water several times. The acorn pulp is then mashed and flat cakes made similar to tortillas.

IS THERE A FUNGUS AMONG US?

Rye is one grain that needs to be carefully inspected before processing. It is very susceptible to the fungus "ergot." In Europe 300 years ago ergot was responsible for spreading disease over a widespread area. It is even believed that ergot was responsible for causing the disease among peasants that led to the French Revolution. Ergot looks like purplish-black masses in the rye and should be removed or the entire batch discarded. Rye grain that contains more than .03 percent ergot is presently discarded and present day rye products should be perfectly safe.

THE BRAZIL NUT

The Brazil nut can only be grown in the Amazon and attempts to grow the tree in different parts of the world have all failed. The majority of the producing trees are still in the wild since commercial plantations have difficulty raising the trees. The tree grows to about 150 feet with a diameter of about 6 feet. The Brazil nut is actually the seed of a pod that resembles a coconut and is about 6 inches across with 12-20 seeds per pod. The pod weighs about 5 pounds and harvesters must wear hard hats or risk being killed. They have a high oil content and two nuts have the same number of calories as one egg.

PEANUT BUTTER, BY PRESCRIPTION?

In 1890 Dr. Ambrose Straub of St. Louis, Missouri made a batch of peanut butter for his elderly patients who needed a source of protein and were not able to chew well. Dr. Straub also patented a machine on February 14, 1903 for a peanut grinding mill. In 1904 at the St. Louis World's Fair peanut butter was first introduced to the public in the United States. The
first recorded history of "peanut paste" being consumed was by the Peruvian Indians and African tribes hundreds of years ago. The fat separation was a problem with the early peanut butters that were produced, but when hydrogenation came along keeping the oil in suspension it became one of the most popular foods in America. Peanut butter must be at least 90% peanuts to use the term "peanut butter." Almost 50% of the peanut crop in the United States goes for peanut butter production.

CASHEWS RELATED TO POISON IVY?

Cashews and almonds are the two most popular nuts that are traded worldwide. The cashew is a relative of the poison ivy family which is a good reason for never seeing the cashew in its shell. The shell contains an oil which is irritating and must be driven off by heat processing before the cashew nut can be extracted without the nut becoming contaminated. The extraction process is a delicate operation, since no residue can be associated with the nut. The oil that is liberated is then used in paints and as a rocket lubricant base. The cashew is the seed of a fruit that resembles an apple with the cashew seed sitting on top. In some countries the cashew is discarded because of the extreme difficulty of obtaining the seed in favor of consuming the apple or better yet fermenting it and using it to produce an alcoholic beverage.

FLAXSEED, A REAL DISEASE-FIGHTER?

Flaxseed is now being processed so that it no longer has any toxicity and will store longer. It is being studied by the National Cancer Institute because it is an important source of "lignans," which are plant compounds that provide a specific fiber that may contain anticancer properties. It is being studied in relation to breast, colon, and prostate cancer. Flaxseed is also rich in omega-3 fatty acids and is the richest plant source of alpha-linolenic acid, an essential fatty-acid. In a recent study, men who ate six slices of bread containing 30% flaxseed reduced their cholesterol levels by 7% and LDL's (bad cholesterol) by 19% without lowering the good cholesterol.

Over twice as much of our protein was coming from grains and cereals in the early 1900's compared to 1997.

If you need to store peanuts, try wrapping them in a plastic bag and keeping them refrigerated. They should last for 6 months and be fresh.

POP TOP

Popcorn on top of soup makes it more appealing for children.

SIMPLE MATH

The ratio of cooked pasta to uncooked pasta is 2:1. For every cup of uncooked pasta you will end up with two cups of cooked pasta. Uncooked pasta contains 3.4 grams of protein per ¾ cup.

A LITTLE OF THIS AND A LITTLE OF THAT

When eating pasta which is a high carbohydrate food, it would be wise to have some protein with the meal to balance off all that carbohydrate. This will allow the blood sugar levels to be normalized in susceptible individuals.

PASTA

In 1997 pasta consumption in the United States averaged 24 pounds per person, which is low compared to the Italians at 64 pounds per person in 1997.

» IS THE GREEN REALLY SPINACH IN SPINACH PASTA?
Actually spinach pasta contains hardly any real spinach. In a cup of cooked spinach pasta there is less than one tablespoon of spinach. The nutritional value is almost identical to regular pasta and that is true with the other vegetable-colored pastas.

» PASTA TRICKS
Cook pasta only until it becomes slightly chewy (al dente). The more you cook it, the less nutrients it will retain. When preparing pasta, always cover the pot as soon as you place the pasta into the rapidly boiling water. Keep the water boiling and do NOT allowed it to cool down to obtain the best results. When draining pasta make sure you warm the colander, a cold colander will cause the pasta to stick together. Adding a small amount of vegetable oil to the water as it is cooking will also help.

» SPEEDY PASTA
If you see the chemical "disodium phosphate" on a package of pasta it is only used to help the pasta cook faster by softening it up.

» YOU'LL TASTE THE DIFFERENCE
The finest pasta in the world is produced in Russia and is called "amber Durham."

» BAKE IN GOOD WEATHER
If you are making pasta dough, don't make it on rainy or high humidity days, it will be very difficult to knead.

» YOU'RE GETTING SLEEPY
A large pasta meal may help you relax by increasing a chemical called Serotonin. However, if you eat pasta without a protein dish, you may feel somewhat sluggish 1-2 hours later. This is related to a blood sugar level change in some individuals.

» GOOD FOR YOUNG AND OLD
Most pasta is easily digested and has a low fiber content making this

a good food for children and the elderly. Also, pasta is normally made with hardly any salt and is excellent for a low sodium diet.

» NO PEEK-A-BOO

If you are purchasing pasta with a clear plastic window or in a see through package you will have a nutrient loss due to the lights in the supermarket. Purchase pasta in boxes without a window.

» SPEEDY PASTA DISH

Capellini pasta cooks up in about 3-4 minutes and is handy if you need a pasta dish in a hurry. It is sometimes called angel hair pasta.

» RAVIOLI FIT FOR A KING For the finest handmade ravioli, call Raviolismo in Dallas, Texas at (800)80-PASTA for a free catalog. The pasta can be stored in the freezer until needed.

Pasta Shapes	
Anellini	Shaped like small rings.
Bavettine	A narrow linguine
Bucantini	Hollow thin strands
Cannaroni	Very wide tubes
Cannelloni	Hollow tubes up to 2 inches long.
Capellini	Angel hair, very thin strands
Capelveneri	Thin medium width noodles
Cappelletti	Shaped like small hats
Cavatappi	Short spiral macaroni shaped
Cavatelli	Short, shells with a rippled edge
Conchiglie	Shaped like a conch shell
Coralli	Tiny soup tubes
Cresti-di-gali	Looks like a roosters comb.
Ditali	Shaped like small thimbles
Ditalini	Small thimble shapes.
Farfalle	Shaped like a bowtie. The word means butterfly in Italian. Sold in two sizes
Fedelini	Very fine spaghetti
Fettucce	Flat egg noodles
Fideo	Very thin, coiled strands
Funghini	These pasta are related to the mushroom family and are used in soups and stews.
Fusilli bucati	Corkscrew-shaped pasta.
Gemelli	Two strands of spaghetti twisted together.
Gnocchi	Very small rippled-edge stuffed shells.
Lasagna	Very long, flat egg noodles
Linguine	Very narrow pasta ribbons.
Lumache	Pasta shaped like a snail's shell.
Macaroni	Curved pasta
Maccheroni	Italian for all types of macaroni.

Pasta Shapes	
Mafalde	Ripple-edged flat
Magliette	Short, curved pasta tubes.
Manicotti	Very large stuffed tubes.
Margherite	Narrow, flat one-sided ripple edged noodles.
Maruzze	Pasta shaped like sea shells.
Mezzani	Short, curved tubes.
Mostaccioli	Tubes
Occhi-di-lupo	Very large tubes of pasta, sometimes referred to as "wolf's eyes."
Orcchiette	Pasta shaped like ears.
Orzo	Pasta, the size and shape of rice.
Pappardelle	Wide noodles with rippled sides.
Pastina	A variety of pasta shapes, usually used in soups.
Penne	Tubes that are diagonally cut with ridged sides.
Perciatelli	Thin, hollow tubes
Pezzoccheri	Very thick buckwheat noodles.
Pulcini	Used mainly in soups and called "little chickens."
Quadrettini	Very small pasta squares.
Radiatore	Resemble small radiators.
Ravioli	Small squares of pasta stuffed with different ingredients.
Riccini	Pasta shaped like ringlet curls.
Rigatoni	Very large, grooved shaped pasta
Riso	Another rice-shaped pasta
Rotelli	Small "wagon wheel" shaped pasta.
Rotini	Very small spiral-shaped pasta.
Ruoti	Round pasta with spokes, looks like a wagon wheel.
Semi de Melone	Small, melon seed-shaped pasta.
Spaghetti	Very long, thin strands of pasta.
Spaghettini	Very thin, spaghetti.
Tagliarini	Pasta shaped like ribbons, usually paper thin.
Tagliatelle	Very long
Tortellini	Pasta that is supposed to resemble the Roman Goddess Venus' navel. "Little Twists."
Tripolini	Very small bow ties that have rounded edges.
Tubetti	Very tiny hollow tubes.
Vermicelli	Italian word for worms, which they resemble. Also known as spaghetti.
Ziti	A very short tubular-shaped pasta.

Pasta Sauces	
Genovese	A hearty meat sauce that may be spiced with garlic, tomatoes.

Pasta Sauces	
Marinara	A somewhat spicy sauce and flavored with garlic, and an herbal blend. Usually not made with meat.
Neopolitan	Made with different flavored tomato sauces, herbal blend, garlic, mushrooms, and green bell peppers.
Alfredo	A high calorie sauce made from cream, a light cheese (either Parmesan or Romano), and garlic.
Alla panna	Made with fresh cream, Marsala wine, Parmesan or Romano cheese, garlic, mushrooms, and occasionally smoked ham.
Formaggi	A blend of cream, garlic, Parmesan, Romano, and Swiss cheeses.
Pesto	Must be made from the finest grade of extra virgin olive oil, fresh basil, garlic, a few pine nuts, and cream.

CHAPTER 17

Eggciting Facts

The egg is still one of the best and most complete sources of protein, regardless of all the negative publicity it has received. Most of this publicity revolves around cholesterol and the high levels found in the egg yolk (approximately 200 mg.).

New major studies have recently shown that consuming egg yolks does not appreciably elevate blood cholesterol levels. One of these studies related the substance lecithin found naturally in eggs as a factor which may help the body clear the cholesterol. Recommendations are still to limit egg consumption to no more than 4-5 eggs per week.

WEIGHT OF ONE DOZEN EGGS

Jumbo	30 ounces
Extra Large	27 ounces
Large	24 ounces
Medium	21 ounces
Small	18 ounces
Pee Wee (bakery eggs)	15 ounces

CALORIES MEASURING EGGS

1 Large egg	80 calories
1 Large egg (2 oz)	1/4 cup
1 Egg white	20 calories
1 Med. egg(1¾oz)	⅙ cup
1 Egg yolk	60 calories
1 Small egg(1 ½oz)	⅙ cup

POURING SALT ON AN OPEN CRACK

If an egg cracks when being boiled, just remove it from the water and while it is still wet, pour a generous amount of salt over it, let it stand for 20 seconds, wrap it in tin foil, twirl the ends and replace it in the boiling water.

IT'S HARD TO GET AN "AA"

There are three grades of eggs: U.S. Grade AA, U.S. Grade A, and U.S. Grade B. The Grade B are usually used by bakeries and commercial food processors. All egg cartons that are marked "A" or "AA" are not officially graded. Egg cartons must have the USDA shield as well as the letter grade.

A FLATTENED BOTTOM

If you want your deviled eggs to have greater stability, cut a slice off the end and they will stand up for easy filling.

TRY IT WITH A SMALL ROUNDED BOTTOM

If you want to increase the volume of beaten eggs, try using a bowl with a small rounded bottom. This reduces the work area and creates the larger volume.

THE UPSIDE DOWN EGG

Eggs should be stored with the tapered end down. The larger end should be upright to reduce spoilage since it maximizes the distance between the yolk and the air pocket which may contain bacteria. The yolk is more perishable than the albumin. Even though the yolk is somewhat centered it does have some movement and will move away from any possible contamination.

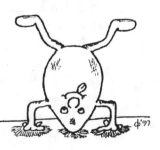

DROWN THEM

If you have used the egg whites for a recipe and want to save the yolks for a day or two, try storing them in a bowl of water in the refrigerator.

FALLING APART AT THE SEAMS
If you have problems with poached eggs breaking up, you may have salted the water. Salt tends to cause the protein to break apart.

TOUGHENING 'EM UP
Hard boiled eggs should never be frozen since egg white changes texture and becomes tough. When freezing fresh eggs always break the yolk, The whites can be frozen alone and the yolks can be frozen alone unless you plan on using them at the same time.

HEART-SHAPED EGGS?
To serve the family something different, try cooking fried eggs in cookie cutters in different shapes. Just place them in the pan and break the egg into the cookie cutter. Spray the cutter after it is placed into the pan so that the eggs will be easy to remove.

HARD BOILED FACTS

- » You can prevent boiled eggs from cracking by rubbing a cut lemon on the shell before cooking.

- » Boiled eggs should be cooled at room temperature before refrigerating them in an open bowl.

- » To make the eggs easier to peel, just add a small amount of salt to the water to toughen the shell.

- » Another trick is to add a teaspoon of white vinegar to the water eggs are being boiled in, this may also help prevent cracking. The vinegar tends to soften the shell allowing more expansion. However, they may not be as easy to peel.

- » To remove the shell from a hard boiled egg, roll it around on the counter with gentle pressure then insert a teaspoon between the shell and the egg white and rotate it.

- » Always cool a hard boiled egg before you try and slice it, it will slice easier and not fall apart.

- » After you make hard-boiled eggs, never place them in cool water after they are peeled. Eggs have a thin protective membrane that if removed or damaged and placed in water or a sealed container may allow bacteria to grow.

MIXING IT UP

When preparing scrambled eggs, allow 3 eggs per person. Most people eat more eggs when they are scrambled. If other ingredients are added, such as cheese or vegetables then 2 eggs per person is sufficient.

GENTLY DOES IT

You should never pour raw eggs or yolks into any hot mixture. If you need to add them, add them gradually for the best results. Adding the eggs too quickly may cause the dish to curdle.

PICTURE PERFECT

To guarantee a white film over the eggs when cooking, place a few drops of water in the pan just before the eggs are done and cover the pan.

GETTING DIZZY YET?

To tell if an egg is hard-boiled or raw, just spin it, if it wobbles it's raw. If it spins evenly then it's hard boiled.

MISCELLANEOUS EGG FACTS

» Egg whites contain more than ½ the protein of the egg and only 25% of the calories.

» When frying an egg, try adding a small amount of flour to the pan to prevent splattering.

» If you store your hard boiled eggs with your fresh eggs, try adding a small amount of vegetable coloring to the boiling water and it will be easier to tell them apart.

» White or brown eggs are identical in nutritional quality and taste.

» Egg whites become firm at 145°F. (62.8°C.), yolks at 155°F.(68.3°C.). Eggs should be cooked at a low temperature to guarantee a tender white and smooth yolk.

» When preparing any dish that calls for egg whites only such as a meringue, remove all traces of egg yolk with a Q-tip or edge of a paper towel, before trying to beat. The slightest trace of yolk will effect the results. Vegetable oil on your beater blades will also effect the results.

» When preparing a number of omelets or batches of scrambled eggs, always wipe the pan with a piece of paper towel dipped in table salt after every 2-3 batches. This eliminates the problem of the eggs sticking to the pan.

» The fresher the egg the better it will be for poaching. The white will be more firm and prevent the yolk from breaking. Make sure you bring the water to a boil and then to a simmer before adding the egg. If you stir the water rapidly before placing an egg in for poaching the egg won't spread as much and will stay centered.

» For the best scrambled eggs, you need to cook them slowly over a medium-low heat starting them in a cool pan.

» The total digestive time for a whole egg is about four hours due to its high fat content.

» Egg will clean off utensils easier if you use cold water instead of hot water. Hot water tends to cause the protein to bind up and harden.

» To remove an unbroken egg that has stuck to the carton, just wet the carton. If the egg is broken throw it out.

EGGNOG FACTS
If you want to reduce the calories in homemade eggnog, try separating the eggs, beat the whites until stiff, then gently fold them into the balance of the mixture just before serving. Eggnog can be substituted in many recipes that call for whole milk for a great taste. However, it may add lots of cholesterol and calories. Commercial eggnog has a very short shelf life, it will only stay fresh for about 5-6 days.

BAD SEPARATION
If you freeze eggnog and find that it separates, place it in a blender before using it.

WILL NEVER SLIP AWAY
You will never have an egg slip from your grip if you just dampen your fingers a little. The eggs will adhere to your fingers and won't slip away.

SAFETY FIRST
FDA regulations state that eggs should be refrigerated at all times during shipping and in supermarkets, however, in many instances they will be left on pallets in supermarkets without refrigeration. Best not to purchase eggs left out since the internal temperature of an egg should never fall below 45°F. (7.2°C.) and no more than 75% humidity.

EGGS VS. BACTERIA

A soft-boiled egg should be cooked at least 3 ½ minutes to kill bacteria if it is present. Fried eggs should have the white hard and the yolk may be soft. The internal temperature will be approximately 140°F. (60°C.) Some egg shells have been found to contain "micro-cracks" which allow harmful bacteria to enter. If you find a cracked egg in the carton when you get home throw it out, it is probably contaminated. Egg shells should be dull not shiny if the egg is really fresh. In very fresh eggs the yolk will hardly be visible through the white.

ALWAYS IN THE MIDDLE

To keep yolks centered when boiling eggs for deviled eggs, just stir the water while they are cooking. When storing deviled eggs, place the halves with the filling together and wrap tightly with tin foil, twirl the ends and refrigerate. Hard boiled eggs will slice easier if you use unwaxed dental floss.

SEPARATION

An easy method of separating egg yolks from the whites is to poke a small hole in the pointed end and drain the white out. If you want the yolk then just break it open. An even easier method is to use a small funnel placed over a measuring cup. This works very well, just don't break the yolk. Never separate eggs by passing the yolk back and forth from one half of the shell to the other. Bacterial contamination may be present on the shell.

BLACK EGGS?

Aluminum bowls and cookware tend to darken an egg due to the aluminum reacting with the egg protein.

SUBSTITUTIONS

You can substitute 2 egg yolks for 1 whole egg when making custards, cream pie filling, and salad dressings. You can also substitute 2 egg yolks plus 1 teaspoon of water for 1 whole egg in yeast dough or cookie batter. If you come up one egg short when baking a cake, substitute 2 tablespoons of mayonnaise. This will only work for one egg.

YOLK SUPPORTERS?

The twisted strands of egg white are called "chalazae cords." These hold the yolk in place and are more prominent in very fresh eggs.

BAD EGG?

Beware of duck eggs since they tend to develop harmful bacteria as they age. They should only be eaten within 3-5 days of laying. Once the bacteria gets a foothold it can only be destroyed by boiling the eggs for 10-12 minutes.

PLANT ME, PLANT ME

An excellent mineral plant fertilizer may be made by drying eggshells and pulverizing them in a blender.

TELLING THE AGE OF AN EGG

Using a large bowl, fill the bowl¾quarters with cold water. Drop an egg in, not from too high up or it won't matter. If the egg goes to the bottom and lies on its side it's fresh. If it stays on the bottom at a 45 degree angle it is about 3-5 days old. If it stays on the bottom and stands up at a 90 degree angle (straight up) it is about 10-12 days old. If

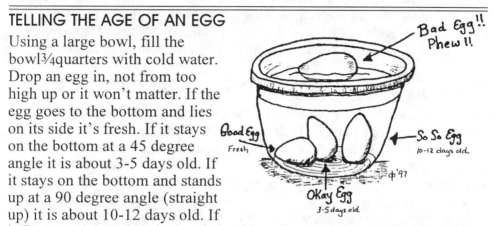

it floats to the top it is bad and should not be opened in the house. When an egg ages it develops a degree of buoyancy as the yolk and the white lose moisture and the air pocket gets larger. Egg shells are porous and moisture will go through the shell.

SPREAD 'EM!

The quality of eggs can easily be determined by the amount of spread when they are broken. U.S. Grade AA eggs will have the smallest spread, will be somewhat thick, very white and have a firm high yolk. U.S. Grade A eggs will have more spread and a less thick white. U.S. Grade B eggs will have a wider spread, a small amount of thick white, and probably a flat enlarged yolk.

BEING FRESH

The egg is really fresh when the shell is dull, not shiny. In very fresh eggs the yolk will hardly be visible through the white.

DECIPHERING THE SECRET CODE ON EGG CARTONS

Before eggs are graded they are "candled." This means that the egg is viewed by passing the egg in front of an intense light that allows a person to see the inside contents. If the yolk is obscured by a cloud of white, the egg is very fresh. If the air pocket at the base of the egg is about the size of a dime this is also an indication of a fresh egg. Grade AA eggs are the freshest, Grade A are just a bit older, Grade B goes to restaurants and bakeries. If your state requires a sell date that will also help determine the freshness. If not, there may be a 3 digit code that was placed there the day the egg was packaged. The code pertains to the day of the year that the egg was packaged. January 1st would have a code of 001 meaning that it is the first day of the year. February 1st would be coded 032 since there are 31 days in January.

WHAT IS THE CHINESE 1,000 YEAR-OLD EGG?

This a Chinese delicacy which is really not a 1,000 year old egg. It is actually a duck egg that has been coated with a mixture of ashes, salt, and lime, then buried in the ground for 3 months. The insides of the egg turn into a dark jelly-like solution that can actually be eaten without fear of food poisoning. These eggs can even be stored at room temperature for up to 2 weeks and still be edible. The combination of the ashes, salt, and lime tend to have a drawing effect on the fluids in the egg causing the proteins in both the white and the yolk to gel and to be colored by the minerals which decompose to some degree and stain the proteins.

THE LIFETIME OF AN EGG

The refrigerator shelf life of an egg is approximately 14-21 days. Always store eggs in a closed container or the original carton for longer life and to avoid the egg absorbing refrigerator odors. If they are stored with the large end up they will last longer and the yolk will stay centered. Also, try rubbing a small amount of vegetable oil on the shell to seal it.

WHAT IS EGG WASH?

Egg wash is a mixture composed of a whole egg or egg white that is combined with milk, cream, or water and beaten well. The "egg wash" is then brushed on the top of baked goods before they are baked to help the tops brown more evenly and give the top a shiny, crisp surface. It also is used to hold poppy seed or similar toppings on rolls as a sort of glue.

THE GREEN EGG

When eggs are overheated or cooked for a prolonged period of time there is a chemical change that will take place. This change tends to combine the sulfur in the egg with the iron in the yolk which form the harmless chemical ferrous sulfide. This reaction is more prevalent in older eggs since the elements are more easily released. Eggs should never be cooked for any reason more than 12-15 minutes to avoid this problem.

THE BREATHING EGG

When eggs are laid they begin to change in a number of ways. The most significant to the cook is that the ph (acid/base balance) of both the yolk and the white changes. Eggs "breathe" and release low levels of carbon dioxide even after they are laid. The carbon dioxide is dissolved in the internal liquids and causes changes in the ph of the egg. The older the egg, the more changes that occur. The yolk and the white tend to increase in alkalinity with time, the yolk going from a slightly acidic 6.0 to an almost neutral 6.6, and the white going from 7.7 to about 9.2. Because of the changes in the alkaline nature of the white, the white tends to change from a strong white color to a very weak almost clear color. Coating the shell of a fresh egg with a vegetable oil will slow this process down. The older egg tends to be more runnier which may make it more difficult for the chef to work with. The yolk is more easily broken as well.

HOT FAT

When microwaving eggs, remember that the yolk will cook first. Microwaves are attracted to the fat in the yolk.

WHAT HAPPENS TO EGG PROTEIN WHEN IT IS COOKED?

When egg white protein is cooked the bonds that hold the proteins together unravel and create a new protein network. The molecules of water that is in the egg is trapped in this new network and as the protein continues to cook the network squeezes the water out. The longer and the more heat that is used, the more water is released and the more opaque the white becomes. If you overcook the egg it will release all its moisture and will have a rubbery texture. The nutritional value of dried out eggs is the same as fresh eggs.

UP, UP, AND AWAY, SUPER EGG

A new egg is appearing in supermarkets, called EggsPlus. The hens are being fed a diet rich in flaxseed. These "super eggs" will be higher in vitamin E and omega 3 and omega 6 fatty acids. These fatty acids have been shown in studies to lower triglyceride (blood fat) levels about 6% as well as increasing the HDL (good cholesterol) levels by 20%. However, the cholesterol content is about the same as a regular egg at about 200 milligrams. A dozen eggs will sell for approximately $2.89.

THE SECRET TO A FLUFFY OMELET

To make the greatest omelet in the world just make sure that the eggs are at room temperature by leaving them out of the refrigerator for 30 minutes before using them. Cold eggs are too stiff for an omelet. Also, if you always add a little milk to your omelet, try adding a small amount of water instead. The water will increase the volume at least 3 times more than the milk. The water molecules surround the egg's protein forcing you to use more heat to cook the protein and make it coagulate. Another great addition is to add ½ teaspoon of baking soda for every 3 eggs. If you try all these tips you will have the greatest looking omelet and your guests will be impressed.

WHERE DID THE FIRST CHICKEN COME FROM?

We are still not sure whether the egg or the chicken came first, however, we do know that eggs are millions of years old. The chicken that we are familiar with today is only 5,000 years old and not one of the first domesticated animals. The ancestors of the chicken were jungle fowl that were native to Southeast Asia or India. Chickens were probably domesticated for their eggs since it is a breed that will continue to lay eggs in a nest until a specific number is reached. By removing the eggs at regular intervals the chicken feels that it must lay more eggs, which it keeps doing. Some fowls will only lay one or two eggs and no matter what you do will not lay anymore.

HOW THE CHICKEN MAKES AN EGG

The making of a chicken egg is really a remarkable feat. The trouble a chicken goes through to make sure we have our eggs for breakfast is the result of her daily reproductive efforts. A chicken is born with thousands of egg cells (ova) and only one ovary. As soon as the hen is old enough to lay eggs, the ova will start to mature usually only one at a time. If more than one matures then the egg will be a double-yolker. Since chickens will not produce any more ova, when their ova supply is depleted, they stop laying eggs and end up in the pot. The liver continually synthesizes fats and proteins to be used in the egg and provides enough nutrients for the embryo to survive the incubation period of 21 days. The egg shell is 4% protein and 95% calcium carbonate. The shell is porous and will allow oxygen in and expels carbon dioxide.

JUST PLACE THEM OVER A CONVEYER BELT

The average hen produces about 2,000-4,000 eggs in a lifetime, the laying begins 5 months after they are hatched. Most hens tend to average about 225 eggs per year.

IT'S A YOLK

The chicken egg yolk consists of 50% water, 34% fat, and 16% protein as well as traces of glucose and a number of minerals, of which sulfur is one. The yellow color is produced from pigments known as "xanthophylls" which is a distant relative of the carotene family.

WHO INVENTED MAYONNAISE?

Mayonnaise was invented by a German immigrant named Nina Hellman in New York City in 1910. Her husband Richard Hellman operated a deli in the city where he sold sandwiches and salads. He soon realized that the secret to his success was based on Nina's recipe for her dressing she put on the sandwiches and salads. He started selling the spread he called "Blue Ribbon" for ten cents a dollop and did so well that he started a distribution business, purchased a fleet of trucks, and in 1912 built a manufacturing plant. The rest is mayo history with Hellman's Mayonnaise becoming one of the best selling spreads in history. At present, we consume 3 pounds of mayonnaise per person annually. To date Hellman's has sold 3.5 billion pounds of mayonnaise without changing the original recipe.

COUNTING CHICKENS AND EGGS

In 1997 the chicken population in the United States totaled about 269 million which means that there are more chickens than people. In 1800 chickens were only laying 15-20 eggs each year while they strolled around the barnyard pecking and scratching here and there and living a pretty normal chicken lifestyle. Presently, the poor fowl are cooped up in a controlled-temperature warehouse, fed a special diet, not allowed to move about and forced to lay egg after egg to about 200-300 per year. Each "breeder house" holds 9,000 chickens and 900 roosters to keep them happy. The record for a cooped up chicken is 371 eggs in one year at the University of Missouri College of Agriculture. The larger chicken farms produce 250,000 eggs per day. Americans are consuming about 250 eggs per person down from 332 eggs per person in 1944 due to all the cholesterol scares by the medical community.

WHIPPING EGG WHITES? USE A COPPER BOWL

A copper bowl should be used when beating egg whites. Copper tends to absorb the heat friction caused by the beating which tends to stop the formation of the air pockets needed to form bubbles of air. The copper will also release ions during the beating process that causes the protein in the mixture to become stiffer. If the copper bowl is used, you will not need to use cream of tartar. Next best is stainless steel, however, a pinch of cream of tartar needs to be added to accomplish the stabilization. Make sure either bowl has a rounded bottom to allow the mixture to fall easily to the bottom and come into equal contact with the mixing blades. Also, be sure that there is not even a trace of egg yolk in your mixture. The slightest hint of fat has a negative effect on the final product. Remove any yolk with a piece of the egg shell.

THE RUBBERY EGG

Freeze raw eggs whole or separated. However, foods with cooked egg whites do not freeze well and their consistency changes.

WHY PLACE A DROP OF VINEGAR IN POACHED EGGS?

Add vinegar to the water that you are poaching your eggs in and it will create a slightly acidic medium allowing the eggs to set and retain a more desirable shape as well as helping the whites retain their bright white color. The proper amount of vinegar is 1 teaspoon to 1 quart of water. If you prefer lemon juice will also work at ½ teaspoon to 1 quart of water. To repair a cracked-egg, remove it from the boiling water and pour a generous amount of salt on the crack while it is still wet. Allow it to stand for 20 seconds then wrap it in aluminum foil and continue cooking it. When poaching eggs, add a small amount of butter to the tin or plastic cup before placing the eggs in to prevent them from sticking and the yolks from breaking.

WHY EGGS CRACK WHEN BOILED

When an egg is laid it is very warm and tends to cool down and as it does the yolk and white cools and shrinks. This cooling and shrinkage results in an air space at the egg's large (non-tapered) end. This air pocket, or trapped gas tends to expand as the egg is heated in the boiling water and the gas has no place to go except out of the shell resulting in a crack. When this occurs the albumen escapes and solidifies in the boiling water almost immediately. To relieve the problem all you have to do is make a small hole in the large end with a pushpin, one with a small plastic end and a small short pin point. It is easy to handle and will not damage the egg nor release the white.

SEND IN THE SUB

When purchasing an egg substitute, make sure you read the label. Some contain MSG.

NO MORE GRAY

If you want to cool an egg and not have a grayish coating on the yolk, try placing the egg in ice cold water after cooking.

CALL IN THE EASTER BUNNY

If you are using eggs for an Easter egg hunt, write down the location of every egg. Many children have become ill from finding eggs after they have been removed from refrigeration for more than 3 hours.

BLOOD SPOTS, ARE THEY HARMFUL?

When the yolk membrane travels down the reproductive tract before it is surrounded by the albumen it is possible for a small drop of blood to attach itself to the yolk. The blood may be the result of a small arterial rupture or from some other source of bleeding. It does not indicate that fertilization has taken place and if the egg is properly cooked is not harmful. If you feel uncomfortable with the blood spot you can remove it with a piece of the shell.

FLYING FAT

If you have a problem with fried eggs splattering, try adding a small powdering of cornstarch to the pan before adding the eggs. The butter should be very hot before adding the eggs. Reduce the heat once the eggs are in the frying pan.

CHAPTER 18

Dairyland

Milk was first consumed about 4,000 years ago from dairy animals. Animal milk is not as easily digested as human milk due to the lower amount of protein in human milk, thus resulting in less curdling when the milk hits the stomach acid. When milk is heated, however, animal milk tends to form a looser curd making it easier to digest. The percentage of protein by weight of human milk is about 1% compared to cow milk protein at 3.5%.

The fat in milk contains carotene which give the milk its yellowish color. The non-fat milks are whiter since they do not have the fat content of whole milk. Two proteins are found in milk called "curds" and "whey." Both react differently when they come into contact with acid and rennin. The casein (curds) forms a solid, while whey remains a liquid in suspension.

"A" BIG LOSS

Milk should never be purchased in see-through plastic containers. When light hits the milk it can lose up to 44% of its vitamin A content in low-fat or skim milk. Markets are now placing these type of containers under light shields. Many manufacturers are now tinting the containers which does help.

CAN FOODS CAUSE ARTHRITIS?

Recent studies are providing some alarming information regarding Salmonella, Campylobacter, and other bacteria relating these bacteria to arthritis. Recently, 198,000 people became ill from drinking milk contaminated with Salmonella. Approximately 2% of the people became arthritis sufferers after only 1-4 weeks after consuming the tainted product. The new type of arthritis is called "reactive arthritis." Symptoms include painful inflammation of joints in the knees and ankles and lower back pain.

DO COWS HAVE TO GIVE BIRTH BEFORE GIVING MILK?

Unless we have been raised on a farm few people realize that a cow must give birth before being able to give milk. The mammary glands which give milk become active by special hormones that are produced at the termination of the pregnancy. If the mammary glands are milked regularly they will produce milk for about 10 months. The gestation period for a cow is 282 days which means that the farmer has a long wait before the cow will produce milk and after the 10 months the cow must become pregnant again for the cow to produce more milk. Milk cows are usually bred again about 90 days after calving to get the cycle working again.

LOW-FAT IS GOING UP

Americans drank 26 gallons of whole milk per person in 1970. In 1997 the consumption was down to 7.7 gallons.

WE'RE JUST A FEW YEARS BEHIND

In Europe milk is processed at ultra-high-temperatures (UHT) to preserve its nutritional qualities as well as turning it into a product that does not need refrigeration and can survive on a shelf for 6 months. This milk has been sold in Europe for 30 years and accounts for 85% of all milk sold.

ADVERTISING WINS

Consumption of milk is down due to the increase in soft drink advertising. Soda is the drink of choice in the United States.

HOPE THE GRASS IS GREENER

Remember the quality of milk depends on the feeding habits of the cows. Poor quality grass produces a lower nutritional quality milk.

WHIP ME, WHIP ME

Light cream can be whipped if you add 1 tablespoon of unflavored gelatin that has been dissolved in 1 tablespoon of hot water to 2 cups of cream. After you whip it refrigerate it for 2 hours. Heavy cream will set up faster if you add 7 drops of lemon juice to each pint of cream.

GIVE ME AIR

Have you ever wondered why cream will whip and milk won't. The reason is that cream has a higher fat content than milk. Heavy cream may be as high as 38% fat while even whole milk is only 3.3% fat. When the cream is whipped the fat globules break apart and the fat molecules stick together in clumps. This also causes the air that is being forced into the mixture to be trapped between the globules.

SAVES A MESS

If you are going to freeze milk be sure and pour a small amount off allowing for some expansion.

ADDING LIFE

If you would like the milk to last an extra few days, just add a teaspoon of baking soda to the milk carton or a pinch of salt. If you allow milk to sit at room temperature for more than 30-40 minutes it will reduce its fresh lifespan

SUBSTITUTION

If a recipe calls for buttermilk and you don't have any, try using slightly soured milk. Soured milk may be used in many baking recipes. Buttermilk may be substituted for whole milk in most recipes, but you will need to add ½ teaspoon of baking soda to the dry ingredients for each cup of buttermilk you use.

DAIRY 101

Sour cream is easily made by adding 4 drops of pure lemon juice to¾cup of heavy cream. Allow the mixture to stand at room temperature for about 40 minutes.

POWDERED MILK

Dry milk comes in three forms; whole milk, non-fat, and buttermilk. Buttermilk powder is presently becoming available in most markets. The powdered whole milk requires refrigeration because of its high fat content of 49-50%. Other powdered milks can last for about 6 months without refrigeration. Once powdered milk is reconstituted it will last for about 3 days under refrigeration.

HOW FRESH I AM
Milk can retain its freshness if it is not contaminated by drinking from the carton for up to one week after the expiration date.

I'M STERILE?
Evaporated milk is now available in whole, low-fat, and nonfat, and is only sold in cans. It is heat-sterilized and will store at room temperature for 5-6 months. Partially frozen evaporated low-fat milk can be whipped and will make a low-fat whipped topping. If you need higher peaks, try adding a small amount of gelatin.

VIVA LE DIFFERENCE
Sweetened condensed milk is not the same as evaporated milk. The sugar content is about 40%.

GOAT'S BUTTER IS GREAT TOO
Goat's milk is actually healthier than cow's milk for humans and especially infants. The protein and mineral ratio is closer to mother's milk and the milk contains a higher level of niacin and thiamin (B vitamins). The protein is even of a better quality and is less apt to cause an allergic reaction.

ALLERGIES?
If you have an allergy to milk or milk products, health food stores have a number of non-dairy products that can achieve the same results.

TIMING IS EVERYTHING
Sour cream should only be added to recipes just before serving, if added hot. If it is necessary to reheat a dish containing sour cream, reheat it slowly or the sour cream will separate.

AERATION
When preparing a sauce that contains a milk product that has curdled, try placing the sauce in a blender for a few seconds.

ICE CREAM FACTS
» WHY DO ICE CRYSTALS FORM IN ICE CREAM ?
The problem is that ice cream is removed from the freezer so often

that it tends to freeze and thaw too many times. Water is released from the fat in the ice cream and the result is the formation of ice crystals. Home freezers rarely freeze ice cream solid, since most will not go down to 0°F. (-17.8°C.) and hold that temperature for any length of time.

» WHO INVENTED THE ICE CREAM CONE?
The "waffle cone" was invented at the 1904 St. Louis World's Fair. One of the concession vendors by the name of Ernest Hamwi was selling waffle pastries called "Zalibia." His neighboring booth was selling ice cream in cups and ran out of cups and was panicking. The waffle vendor came to his rescue by making a cone-shaped waffle that would hold the ice cream. The cone was called the "World's Fair Cornucopia" and was the food sensation of the fair.

» HERE YE, HERE YE, FLYING FORTRESS MAKES ICE CREAM
In 1943 an article in the New York Times titled "Flying Fortress Doubles as Ice-Cream Freezers" stated that airmen were placing special canisters with an ice cream mixture and attaching it to the tail gunners compartment of Flying Fortresses. The vibration of the plane and the cold temperature of the high altitude made ice cream as they were flying over enemy territory on their missions.

» THE SECRETS OF MAKING ICE CREAM
The following tips should be adhered to if you wish the best results when using an ice cream maker:

Before you start the freezing process, chill the mixture in the refrigerator for 4-5 hours. This will reduce the freezing time and the ice cream will be smoother and have more volume.

The canister should only be⅔full. By underfilling it will allow more room for the ice cream to expand as the air is beaten into it. The result will be ice cream that is creamier and fluffier.

» ARTIFICIAL GUNK
Ethyl vanillin, a flavoring agent, should be avoided if listed on the list of ingredients. It has caused multiple organ damage in laboratory animals. Butyraldehyde provides ice cream with a nutlike flavor and is also used as an ingredient in rubber cement and should be avoided as well.

» REDUCED-FAT ICE CREAM AKA ICE MILK
Reduced-fat ice cream used to be called ice milk. All products now have new names relating to lower fat providing they contain at least 25% less fat than the same brand of the regular ice cream product. However, you will need to read the label since the 25% refers to the corresponding brand, the amount of fat will vary from brand to

brand. So don't be fooled into thinking that all "reduced-fat ice cream" has the same level of fat per serving.

» AERATED ICE CREAM, A MUST
Air must be whipped into all commercial ice cream, it is a step in the manufacture called "overrun." If the air was not added the ice cream would be as solid as a brick and you would be unable to scoop it out. The air improves the texture and is not listed on the list of ingredients. However, ice cream must weigh at least 2¼ounces per ½ cup serving

TAPIOCA

Tapioca is usually sold as a pudding mix and is actually a starch that has been extracted from the cassava root. It is found in three forms:

» PEARL TAPIOCA
This is the type that the puddings are made from and usually has to be soaked for a number of hours before it is soft enough to be prepared.

» QUICK-COOKING TAPIOCA
This is normally sold in granular form, needs no presoaking, and is popular for use as a thickening agent.

» TAPIOCA FLOUR
Normally only found in health food stores and is also very popular as a thickening agent for soups and stews.

Tapioca should be mixed with water until it is a thin paste and then added to the food that needs to be thickened. Never add tapioca directly to the food, it tends to become lumpy. Try not to overstir tapioca when it is cooking or it may become a thick paste and not be very palatable.

IS LOW-FAT MILK REALLY LOW-FAT?

Some is and some isn't, if that sounds confusing it is meant to be by the milk producers. A good example of this is 2% low-fat milk which most people think is really low-fat, however, when the water weight is removed from the milk it is approximately 34% fat (not a low-fat product). Whole milk is actually 3.3% fat or about 50% fat, while 1% low-fat milk is about 18% fat. There is a new milk ready to hit the supermarkets which is .5% milk and that will contain about 9% fat. Best to use skim, non-fat, or buttermilk which is now made from a culture of skim milk.

NON-STICK SURFACE

When heating milk, try spreading a small layer of unsalted butter on the bottom of the pot to keep the milk from sticking. Salted butter may cause the food to stick

HOW PERISHABLE IS MILK?

Every ½ gallon of Grade A pasteurized milk contains over 50 million bacteria and if not refrigerated will sour in a matter of hours. Milk should really be stored at 34°F.(1.1°C.) instead of the average refrigerator temperature of 40°F. (4.4°C.). Milk should never be stored in light as the flavor and vitamin A are affected in 4 hours by a process known as "auotoxidation." The light actually energizes an oxygen atom that invades the carbon and hydrogen atoms in the fat.

HOW DRY I AM

Buttermilk can be used to soften dry cheese. Place the cheese in a shallow covered dish with a one inch layer of buttermilk and refrigerate overnight.

WHY IS MILK HOMOGENIZED?

Homogenization is the process where fresh milk is forced through a very small nozzle at a high pressure onto a hard surface. This is done to break up the fat globules into more uniform very tiny particles. The process is done so that the cream which is high in fat will not rise to the top and form a layer. The fat particles become so small that they are mixed in the milk and are evenly dispersed. Fresh milk cannot be homogenized until it is pasteurized because it will go rancid in a matter of minutes. If the fat is broken down before pasteurization, the protective coating on the fat is exposed to enzymes that will cause the milk to become rancid.

LOW-FAT WORKS BEST

If you are low on sour cream and need to make a dip, try placing cottage cheese in a blender and cream it.

WHAT IS CONDENSED MILK & EVAPORATED MILK?

Condensed milk is milk that is not sterilized due to its high sugar content, which is usually 40-45%. The sugar acts as a preservative retarding bacterial growth, however, the milk is not a very appetizing food. Evaporated milk is milk that is heated in the can to over 200°F. (93.3°C.) sterilizing the milk. The milk tends to end up with a burnt flavor as well as picking up additional flavor from the metal if stored for a long period.

WHY DOES A SKIN FORM ON THE TOP OF MILK?

The skin that forms on the top of milk is composed of the milk protein "casein" which is the result of the protein coagulating and calcium which is released from the evaporation of the water. The skin contains a number of valuable nutrients and should be minimized by covering the pan or rapidly stirring the mixture for a few seconds to cause a small amount of foam to form. Both of these actions will slow the evaporation and reduce the amount of skin formation.

IS IT TRUE THAT DAIRY PRODUCTS MAY CAUSE MUCUS?

As far back as I can remember I was told that I should never drink milk when I am sick because it will increase mucus production. In the last several years the "mucus-milk" connection has been studied and some interesting results have surfaced. In Australia 125 people were given chocolate-peppermint-flavored cow's milk or an identically flavored non-dairy soy milk so that they could not tell the difference by taste. The people who believed in the theory that milk produced mucus reported that both milks, even though one was a non-dairy product did produce a coating on their tongue and in their mouth. They also reported that they had trouble swallowing because of a thickened, harder to swallow saliva.

In another study the same researchers infected a group of healthy people with a cold virus and tracked their dietary habits and cold symptoms and found that there was no difference in the amount of mucus secreted. It was concluded that milk did not produce any excess mucus, and the feeling of mucus production was due to the consistency and texture of the milk.

WHAT IS ACIDOPHILUS MILK?

It is milk that is produced from low-fat or skim milk with a bacterial culture added to it. As the milk is digested the bacteria are released and become active at body temperature helping to maintain the balance of beneficial microorganisms in the intestinal tract. It is especially useful when taking antibiotics to replenish the bacteria that are destroyed, especially the ones that produce the B vitamins. Other products that can produce the similar bacteria building effect are yogurt, buttermilk, and kefir. To obtain the best result, acidophilus should be consumed one hour before breakfast.

SPINNING OFF THE CREAM

Cream is produced by spinning milk in a centrifuge which causes the fat globules to release from the watery substance and become more concentrated when removed. Supermarkets carry three grades of cream: Light cream which is between 20-30% butterfat, light whipping cream which is between 30-36% butterfat, and heavy whipping cream which is between 36-40% butterfat as compared to whole milk which is only 3.3-4% butterfat.

STICK BUTTER VS. WHIPPED BUTTER

All recipes that call for butter always calculate the measurements for standard butter. Whipped butter has a higher air content due to the whipping. If you do wish to use it, you need to increase the volume of butter used by about 33%. Whipped butter is 25% air and better to use on toast than in recipes, since it will spread more easily.

» BUTTER-B-WARE
When storing butter it will be more important where you store it than how long it will last. Butter tends to absorb odors more efficiently than any other food. If you store it near onions it will have an onion smell. If it's around fish, it will smell fishy, etc. If butter is refrigerated it will retain its flavor for about 3 weeks, then it starts losing it rather fast. If you desire a rich butter flavor it would be wise to date your butter package. Butter will freeze if you double-wrap it in plastic then foil to keep it from absorbing freezer odors. It will last for 9 months if fresh when frozen and must be kept at 0°F. (-17.8°C.).

» WHAT'S IN THE NEW IMITATION BUTTER SPRAY?
The product "I Can't Believe It's Not Butter" spray is made from water, a small amount of soybean oil, salt, sweet cream buttermilk, gums, and flavorings. The average 4 spray serving only contains 15 mg. of salt. If you spray your popcorn it will not make it soggy and 20 squirts will only give you just over 2 grams of polyunsaturated fat.

» BEST TO USE UNSALTED BUTTER IN RECIPES
Depending on the area you live in and the particular supermarket's butter product, the salt content of salted butter will vary from 1.5% to 3%. This can play havoc with certain recipes unless you are aware of the actual salt content of a particular butter and how the level of salt in that butter will react with your recipe. It is best in almost all instances to use unsalted butter and just add the salt.

» BUTTER EASILY SCORCHED, USE CLARIFIED BUTTER
When butter is heated the protein goes through as change and causes the butter to burn and scorch easily. A small amount of Canola oil

added to the butter will slow this process down, however, if you use clarified butter, butter in which the protein has been removed you can fry with it for a longer period and it will also store longer than standard butter. Clarified butter, however, will not give your foods the rich real butter flavor you may desire.

SALMONELLA IN YOUR HOLLANDAISE?

Recently some eggs have been found to contain the salmonella bacteria even if they are in perfect condition. Because of this when making sauces that call for raw eggs and the sauce is not cooked thoroughly it may give you cause for concern. When preparing a hollandaise or bernaise sauce it might be best to microwave the eggs before using them in your sauce. This can be accomplished without damaging the eggs too badly and still allowing them to react properly in your sauce. This should only be done with no more than 2 large Grade A egg yolks at a time and in a 600-watt microwave oven.

First you need to separate the egg yolks completely from the white and the complete cord. Second place the yolks in a small glass bowl and beat them until they are well mixed. Third add 2 teaspoons of lemon juice and mix thoroughly again. Fourth cover the bowl and place into the microwave on high and observe the mixture until the surface begins to move, allow it to cook for 10 seconds past this point, remove the bowl and beat the mixture with a clean whisk until they appear smooth. Return the bowl to the microwave and allow to cook again until the surface starts to move, allow it to remain another 10 seconds, remove and whisk again until it is smooth. Finally, allow the bowl to stand for about 1 minute and the yolks should be free of any salmonella and still usable in your sauce.

HOW ABOUT SOME DONKEY BUTTER, YAK, YAK

While almost all butter sold in the United States is produced from cow's milk, butter may be produced from the milk of many other animals. When cow's milk is not available butter can be made from the milk of donkeys, horses, goats, sheep, buffalo, camels, and even yaks.

WHY DOES WHIPPED CREAM WHIP?

The number of fat globules in cream is why cream whips. The cream as it is whipped causes the fat globules to be encompassed by air bubbles which causes the foam and produces a solid reinforcement to the mixture. The fat globules actually cluster together in the bubble walls. The higher the temperature of the ingredients and the utensils used the more difficult it will be to whip the cream. Fat globules are more active and tend to cluster more rapidly at low temperatures. The cream should actually be placed in the freezer for 10-15 minutes before whipping. If a small amount of gelatin is added to the mixture it will help stabilize the bubble walls and the mixture will hold up better. Sugar should never be added in the beginning as it will decrease the total volume by interfering with the proteins that will also clump on the bubble. Always stop beating whipped cream at the point when it becomes the stiffest so that it won't turn soft and have a glossy appearance. If small lumps appear in your whipping cream, this is a sign of butter formation and there is nothing that can be done to alter the situation. You will never obtain a good volume once this occurs.

IS A LOW-CHOLESTEROL MILK ON THE HORIZON?

Whole milk contains about 530 milligrams of cholesterol per gallon. A new process being developed by researchers at Cornell University may reduce the cholesterol level to just 40 milligrams per gallon. The process involves injecting carbon dioxide into butterfat at high pressures. The butterfat is then removed from the milk, the cholesterol is then extracted and the butterfat returned to the milk. The result is a milk with only 2% butterfat, low cholesterol, and taste close to 2% milk.

WHY DOES A RECIPE CALL FOR SCALDED MILK?

When a recipe calls for scalded milk it is intended to destroy certain enzymes that might keep emulsifying agents from performing their thickening task and to kill certain bacteria that might be present. However, any recipe that still calls for scalding the milk has been reproduced in its original form. Scalding is unnecessary today since all milk is pasteurized which accomplishes the same thing.

IS BUTTERMILK MADE FROM BUTTER?

While it is still possible to find the "old fashioned" buttermilk that was drawn off butter, the majority of buttermilk is produced from skim milk cultures. The milk is incubated for 12-14 hours which is longer than yogurt and kept at least 40° cooler while it is fermenting. The buttery flavor is the result of a by-product of the fermentation process and is derived from the bacterium "diacetyl."

WHY IS THERE WATER IN MY YOGURT?

To begin with it really isn't water that collects on the top of the yogurt but a substance called whey. Whey is a protein that tends to liquefy easily and may either be discarded or stirred back in. If you place a piece of cheesecloth directly on top of the yogurt it will absorb the whey, then discard the cheesecloth. If you do this for 2-3 days in a row it will stop weeping the protein and the yogurt will become much thicker, more like sour cream which will also leak whey.

CAN BUTTER GO RANCID?

Oxidation will take its toll on butter just like any other fat. It tends to react with the unsaturated fats and causes rancidity. This reaction can be slowed down to a crawl if the butter is either under refrigeration or placed into the freezer. Butter should always be kept tightly wrapped.

CAN FORMULA BE REHEATED AFTER THE BABY DRANK FROM IT?

It is best to dispose of the unused portion since bacteria from the baby's mouth will enter the formula through the nipple. Once the bacteria enter, they will multiply to high levels. Even if the formula is refrigerated and reheated there may still be enough bacteria left to cause illness. Formula bottles should be filled with enough formula for a single feeding and the leftover should be discarded.

BREAST MILK AND EXERCISE DON'T MIX

Studies show that if you are nursing your baby you should breast feed the baby before you exercise. Lactic acid tends to build up during exercise and will give the breast milk a sour taste. The lactic acid levels in breast milk will remain elevated for about 90 minutes after exercise before it can be cleared by the blood. If you need to feed during the recovery period, it would be best to collect milk for that feeding.

MICROWAVING BUTTER

We all have the experience of microwaving butter too long and ending up with a runny mess. Butter is somewhat softer on the inside than the outside. When butter is microwaved the inside melts first and causes a rupture in the outer surface and leaks out. It's best to microwave for a few seconds then allow the butter to stand for 2-3 minutes before using it, allowing the inner heat to warm and soften the outside.

WHAT IS MARGARINE MADE FROM?

Regular margarine must contain no less than 80% fat along with water, milk solids, salt, preservatives, emulsifiers, artificial colors, and flavorings. The fat may be tropical oils which are high in saturated fat or any of the polyunsaturated oils. The higher quality margarines will use corn or safflower oils. Soft margarines are produced from vegetable oils and do not have the milk solids added. They still contain salt, and the artificial flavorings and preservatives. Liquid margarines are all polyunsaturated fat and will not harden in the refrigerator. Light/diet margarines vary from 40-60% fat content and have more air and water added along with the preservatives, salt, and flavorings

SAVING THE CREAM FROM SOURING

When cream is having a somewhat off-odor and you need to use it, try mixing in⅛teaspoon of baking soda. The baking soda will neutralize the lactic acid in the cream that is causing the souring. Before you use the cream, however, make sure the flavor is within normal boundaries.

CAN COWS BE MILKED TOO SOON AFTER EATING?

If you have ever purchased a quart of milk that had a cooked flavor, the milk was poorly pasteurized, which does happen occasionally. If the milk has a grassy or garliclike flavor, it was because the cows were milked too close to their last meal.

CHAPTER 19

Cheese It!

Cheeses come in a wide variety of colors and flavors, few of which are natural. Most cheeses are naturally white, not yellow, pink, green or burgundy.

The cheese industry has perfected methods of changing a good quality nutritious product into a chemical smorgasbord. The following is just a partial list of chemicals used by the cheese industry: Malic acid, tartaric acid, phosphoric acid, alginic acid, aluminum potassium phosphate, diacetyl sodium, carboxymethyl cellulose, benzyl peroxide and an unbelievable number of dyes and coloring agents.

These chemical are used to give cheeses their sharp taste, color them, make them smell more appealing or just to change their texture. All of the chemicals have been approved by the FDA and are supposed to be harmless, however, a number of the dyes and coloring agents are being studied and are related to cancer in laboratory animals.

Many of these same chemicals are also being used in other industries for making cement, bleaching clothes, producing cosmetics, printing, and even rust-proofing metals.

Be more aware of the type of cheese you buy and try to buy cheeses without the added chemicals, especially cheeses that are low-fat or even non-fat. If the label says "all-natural" you still need to see the wording "no preservatives or coloring agents." Consumers need to read the labels more than ever these days.

WHY CHEESE MAY REFUSE TO MELT

One of the more frequent problems with melting cheeses is that the cheese is heated at too high a temperature for too long a period of time. When this occurs the protein is separated from the fat and the cheese becomes tough and rubbery. Once this occurs it cannot be reversed and the cheese is ruined. Remember to keep the heat on low and best to use a double boiler. If you are going to melt cheese don't try and melt large pieces. Cut the large piece into a number of small chunks before you attempt to melt it. Cheese should be added last to most recipes. Grating the cheese will also make it easier to melt and this method is best for sauces. Certain exceptions are ricotta, Camembert and Brie which have a higher water content and lower fat content. These are not as good for certain dishes.

MAYTAG IS A CHEESE NOT A WASHING MACHINE

The Maytag blue cheese is one of the finest in the world and is produced from the freshest unpasteurized milk obtainable from only two Holstein herds located near Newton, Iowa. The moisture content is higher than that of most other blue cheeses making it very spreadable and creamy and the cheese is aged in a special manmade cave that was dug into the side of a hill. The cheese is a somewhat sharp, yet mellow to the taste. It can be ordered by calling (515)792-1133.

HOW MANY ORGANISMS CAN A CHEESE CULTURE, CULTURE?

One teaspoon of a cheese-starter culture can contain 5 trillion living organisms. In the past cheese producers were never sure of the activity of their culture which came from milk-souring lactic acid bacteria. Today there are companies that specialize in producing cultures of bacteria in whey (a protein) which actually separates the curd in the cheese-making process. These companies use lactobacillus and lactococcus to ferment milk sugar (lactose) into lactic acid. The acid is necessary in preventing unwanted microbes from growing in the cheese.

CHEE-TOS, MADE MOSTLY OF CORNMEAL?

Cheese is not the main ingredient in Chee-Tos. It is actually fourth on the list of ingredients, after cornmeal, vegetable oil, and whey. It was invented in 1948 by Frito-Lay who uses stone-ground cornmeal, then adding moisture to turn it into a doughy mass. The dough is forced through small holes of an extruder (round wheel with holes). As the hot dough moves out of the extruder it comes into contact with the cooler air and literally "explodes" similar to popcorn. A knife then slices the long pieces into the bite-sized pieces we are used to seeing.

HOW TO BUY SOFT CHEESES

Two very popular soft cheeses are Brie and Camembert and both are sprayed with special mold to form a very thin, white, flexible rind. These cheeses ripen from the outside in and turn creamier with a more intense flavor as time passes. These cheeses are normally found in boxes which when opened may smell a little musty but should never have an ammonia smell. Ideally, the cheese should be somewhat springy when prodded and never have a hard core. These cheeses will continue to ripen when refrigerated for 1-2 days and should be consumed in 3-5 days after purchase for the best taste. If the cheese appears "runny" then it has been over-aged and may be bitter. Other cheeses in this category include Limburger, Coulommiers, and Liederkranz.

A LITTLE SQUIRT OR TWO

When grating cheese, try spraying a liquid vegetable oil on the grater before grating and cleanup will be much easier.

CHEESE TIP

Cheese making is fast becoming a popular pastime. For information call the hot line at 1(800)542-7290.

MAY AFFECT THE RECIPE

Many low-fat cheeses substitute water for the fat, reducing their shelf life.

VELVEETA, A CHEESE WITH A COLLEGE DEGREE?

A bacteriologist working at Cornell University was hired by the Phenix (yes, it's spelled correctly) Cheese Company and developed the product in 1915. The emphasis was to try to duplicate the consistency of Gerber's Swiss Gruyere cheese, which was a processed Swiss cheese. Eldridge separated the whey (the liquid protein) from the cheese and after removing the protein, used the protein mixed with real cheese and a small amount of sodium citrate as an emulsifier to help the product stay in solution and stabilize. The original name was Phen-ett Cheese named after the Phenix Company. Eldridge also developed another product at the same time for Kraft called NuKraft which eventually became Velveeta. Velveeta is presently called "cheese spread" and contains about 60% water and not less than 20% butterfat, plus a few gums to hold it together and of course sweeteners. Velveeta was marketed to stores in 1921 when Kraft patented a new method of packaging the cheese spread in a tinfoil-lined wooden box. The trick was to make the foil stick to the cheese and not the box, this created a hermetic seal and kept the cheese fresh for longer periods.

CHOOSING A GOOD CHEDDAR

One of the first things to look for when purchasing cheddar cheese is uniform color. If the cheese has white spots or streaks it has not ripened evenly or is starting to develop mold. The texture should always be relatively smooth, however, it is not uncommon to purchase cheddars that are grainy and crumbly. If the cheddar has a rind, be sure that the rind is not cracked or bulging, which may mean that the cheese will be bitter due to poor manufacturing practices. Cheddar will continue to age in the refrigerator for months and should be stored in a container with vinegar dampened paper towel underneath.

CHEESE RIPENING CLASSIFICATIONS

Unripened - Are normally consumed shortly after manufacture and are the more common cheeses such as cottage cheese which is a high-moisture soft cheese. Examples of unripened low- moisture cheeses include gjetost and mysost.

» Soft — The cheeses are cured from the outside or rind of the cheese toward the center. The process entails using specific molds or cultures of bacteria which are allowed to grow on the surface of the cheese creating the specific characteristic flavors, body and texture of that cheese. These cheeses usually contain more moisture than the semi-soft ripened cheeses.

» Semi-soft — When cheese ripens from the inside as well as the exterior curing continues as long as the temperature is warm. These cheeses have a higher moisture content than firm-ripened cheeses.

» Firm — These cheeses are ripened by utilizing a bacterial culture and the ripening continues as long as the temperature is favorable. It will have a lower moisture content than the softer cheese varieties and usually requires a longer curing period.

» Very hard — These cheeses are cured utilizing a bacterial culture and specific enzymes. They are slow-cured, have a higher salt content and are very low in moisture.

» Blue-vein— These are cured with the aid of a mold bacteria and specific mold cultures that grow throughout the inside of the cheese. This produces the familiar appearance and unique flavor.

COMMON CHEESES OF THE WORLD

» BEER

This is a smooth, soft cheese that has been compared to limburger but is somewhat milder.

» BEL PAESE

Originated in Italy. It is a semi-soft cheese with a mild flavor. Usually eaten for dessert with fruit.

» BLUE (BLEU)

Is easily identified by its white and blue streaks. Blue cheese crumbles easily and has a somewhat soft texture. It is sold in various shapes, the most common of which is a block.

» BRICK

A somewhat soft, yellow cheese with a medium-soft texture, commonly available in brick form.

» BRIE

The cheese is produced with an edible white outer coating. It has a mild flavor with a creamy white texture. Originated in the south of France, Brie is only available in wedges and occasionally in round forms.

Why is it impossible to buy a good brie cheese in the U.S.?

The finest Brie cheeses that reach their perfection in taste are made in France and are always made from unpasteurized milk. The United States will not allow this "surface-ripened" cheese to be imported unless it is made from pasteurized milk, aged for 60 days, or stored in such a manner that the flavor would be adversely affected during shipping. Natural Brie if aged for 60 days would lose its flavor and become overripe. The Brie that we do buy does not have the flavor or quality of the French Brie and has a lower fat content by about 10%.

» BOURSAULT

A French cheese that is soft and has a creamy texture. It is a delicate, mild cheese usually served at desert with wine.

» CAMEMBERT

Has a soft somewhat yellow inside, with a thin dull white coating which is edible. It ripens in about 4-8 weeks, and is reputed to be Napoleon's favorite cheese.

» CHEDDAR
The natural color of cheddar is white not yellow. The yellow color is produced by dyes since yellow cheese is more salable. It has a mild to very sharp taste, and has a fairly firm texture. It is sold in numerous shapes and is sliced. It originated in England and was imported to the United States in the 19th century.

» CHESHIRE
Mainy produced in England. It is a hard cheese with a mellow and rich flavor similar to cheddar.

» COLBY
Usually sold as a light yellow cheese and has a somewhat mild flavor. The texture is similar to that of cheddar. It is normally sold in wedges cut from a large round and it originated in Wisconsin.

» COLDPACK
Sold as both fresh and aged. It contains whey solids and usually has a somewhat mild flavor. A soft, spreadable cheese, it is sold in a variety of colors using artificial colorings and flavorings.

» CREAM CHEESE
Usually made with light cream or whole milk before the cream has been skimmed off and is 90% fat. Some cream cheeses are made with propylene glycol alginate. This chemical is not one of the more healthy chemicals and should be avoided. Sold in a semi-soft form and usually white, however, colorings may be added.

» EDAM
It is commonly sold from a large ball-shape with a red wax coating. The interior is a creamy-yellow orange color and the cheese has a light nut-like flavor. The consistency is semi-soft and has a lower milk-fat content than a Gouda cheese. Should be an additive-free cheese.

» FETA
A small curd cheese usually produced from goat's milk. The taste is somewhat salty and sharp.

» FARMER'S CHEESE (POT CHEESE)
A close relative to cottage cheese and is usually pressed into a block shape. Sold mostly in a delicatessen.

» FONTINA
One of the finest semi-soft cheeses from Italy. It has a mild, somewhat nutty flavor with a light brown rind. It is usually a fondue cheese.

» GJETOST

A relatively mellow cheese that is sold in cubes or rectangles. Usually found in a pleasant golden color and made from whey or fresh goat's milk. The consistency is semi-soft.

» GORGONZOLA

Mold plays a big role in the coloring of this cheese. It is always found with blue-green stripes and has a soft texture with an off-white exterior. The flavor is tangy and somewhat peppery and the cheese tends to crumble easily. It is usually made with whey or goat's milk.

» GOUDA

Usually sold in a bell shape with a red wax coating. The insides are a semi-soft, creamy yellow, with a nut-like flavor. The cheese contains irregular or round-shaped holes.

» GRUYERE

Similar to Swiss cheese but with a higher nutrient content. Usually sold with mold inhibitors added, check the label.

» THE LIMBURGER STORY

Once one of the most popular cheeses in America, however, few people now eat Limburger cheese. The cheese is a smooth, creamy, semi-soft aged cheese. It is a stronger smelling cheese than we have become used to and has been relegated to being produced by only one plant in the United States in Monroe, Wisconsin, the Chalet Cheese Company. This company produces about a million pounds per year using 32 cows. Limburger is "real" cheese, while most of the processed cheeses in the market are only 45 percent real cheese then fortified with whey powder and lactose. Limburger will continue to age after it is purchased and will actually develop more flavor. It will last for 5-6 months and should be stored in a well-sealed glass container.

» MOZZARELLA

Produced from part-skim or whole milk and has a firm texture. Sold in rounds, shredded, or slices. Preservatives are sometimes added to keep the moisture content low.

» MUENSTER

Usually sold in wedges or blocks and has more moisture than brick cheese. The insides are a creamy-white with a yellowish exterior and possibly small holes. The flavor is mild and the texture is semi-soft.

» MYOST

Sold in pie-shaped wedges or cubes and has a buttery consistency. The color is usually a light brown and has a sweet caramel flavor.

» NEUFCHATEL

Has a soft texture and a mild acidic flavor. The fat content is lower than cream cheese due to a lower milk-fat content.

» PARMESAN

Usually sold grated, however, will have a better flavor if it is purchased in bulk and then grated as needed. In bulk it is a creamy-white cheese with a hard granular texture. The moisture content is lower than Romano and is usually produced from partially skimmed-milk.

» PASTEURIZED PROCESSED CHEESE

Usually a blend of various cheeses with varying degrees of consistency. The flavor is relatively mild and is frequently used for cheeseburgers since it has a low melting point.

» PASTEURIZED PROCESS CHEESE FOOD

Similar to the standard processed cheeses except that milk or whey are usually added. They have a lower fat content and have a milder flavor and are softer. Moisture is added to lower the fat content per ounce.

» PORT Du SALUT

A mellow, robust creamy yellow cheese with a buttery texture and has small holes. Usually sold in wheels.

» PROVOLONE

Produced from a bleached milk, it has an off-white interior with a somewhat yellowish exterior. The texture is relatively smooth and the cheese is unsalted with a mild flavor.

» QUARK

This is a soft unripened cheese which has the texture of sour cream. The flavor is richer than yogurt.

» RICOTTA

Usually produced from whole or skim-milk with a somewhat nut-like flavor. Looks like cottage cheese.

» ROMANO

Has a sharp flavor with a dark green exterior. Sold mostly in wedges or grated and is made with whole cow's or goat's milk. A yellow-white cheese with a greenish-black exterior.

» ROQUEFORT

Mold is introduced to create a marbling and blue veins throughout the cheese. It has a white interior and is usually produced from sheep's milk. The flavor is somewhat peppery and the texture is always crumbly. Sold mostly in wedges or packaged already crumbled.

» STILTON
Similar to Roquefort, it has a white interior with blue mold streaks. However, it is normally produced from cow's milk and has a crumbly texture. It is usually sold in logs or wedges.

» SWISS
The interior is a light yellow and the cheese has a somewhat sweet nutty flavor. The texture is firm and the holes may vary in size. It is usually sold in rectangular form or sliced. Produced using bleached milk which gives it its yellow color. One ounce = 105 calories, somewhat high due to the fat content of the bleached whole milk.

HOW DID SWISS CHEESE GET ITS HOLES?
When Swiss cheese is curing, special microorganisms produce a gas that causes pockets of air to form and remain after the cheese ripens. The holes should, however, be relatively the same in size and not oversized or irregular sized holes, especially large ones. The border of the holes should also have a moist, shiny look about them. If the rind is grayish-looking it should not be purchased. The flavor of Swiss cheese will become stronger when wrapped in plastic wrap and refrigerated. Cut wedges should last for about 1-2 months.

» TILSIT
The insides are usually a light yellow color and the cheese is semi-soft. It is produced from raw milk and takes about 5 months to ripen. The fat content runs about 40%.

COTTAGE CHEESE

Cottage cheese is a United States original and is made from skimmed milk either plain-cured, or plain-cured with cream. It is always sold in a soft texture with different size curds. If the label says "curd by acidification" it will be a synthetic product. Cottage cheese only retains 25-50% of the calcium from the milk it is made from due to the processing. The higher the water content of cheeses, such as cottage cheese, the sooner they will go bad. Cottage cheese will only last until the expiration date unless it is stored as mentioned above. Cheddar cheese, however, is so low in moisture that it will last for years with the taste becoming stronger with aging.

» TOPSY TURVEY
Cottage cheese will last 7-10 days longer if you store it upside down. When you open cottage cheese spores enter from the

air and live on the oxygen layer. When you turn it upside down and allow it to fall to the top, you eliminate a percentage of the oxygen layer, many of the spores will suffocate and the rest can't grow as fast so the cottage cheese will last about 7-10 days longer.

TYPES OF COTTAGE CHEESE

» CREAMED
Creamed cottage cheese contains 4.2% fat or 9.5 grams per cup. It is not a low-fat product.

» LOW-FAT
This is produced using either 1% or 2% milk. Low-fat cottage cheese may soon be produced using the new .5% milk which will lower the fat content a little more. The 2% is really not low-fat at all.

» UNCREAMED
Can be used in recipes calling for cottage cheese. Usually sold as low-fat and possibly even salt-free.

CHEESE FACTS

» An ounce of cream cheese may contain as much as 110 calories. As advertised, it does have fewer calories than butter for a comparable weight, but we tend to use more and also use it more frequently.

» It would be best if you choose cheeses that are low-sodium, low-fat, or reduced-fat. There are new varieties appearing almost weekly in supermarkets and health food stores.

» Be sure and read the label. If a cheese is labeled "natural" the name of the cheese must be preceded by the word "natural." If not it is a chemical concoction.

» Most cheese substitutes are produced from soybean vegetable fats. Many low-fat cheeses substitute water for the fat reducing their shelf life.

» It requires 8 pounds of milk to produce 1 pound of cheese. One average slice of standard American cheese = 8oz. of milk. Best to at least purchase the 2% cheeses or the non-fat varieties.

» The wax coating on cheeses will protect it. If there is an exposed edge try covering it with butter to keep the area moist and fresh.

» To keep cheese longer without mold forming, place a piece of paper towel that has been dampened with white vinegar in the bottom of a plastic container that has a good seal before adding the cheese. Also, try adding 5-6 small sugar cubes for any mold that does get in. It'll go for the sugar, not the cheese.

» Soft cheeses can be grated using a metal colander and a potato masher. Cheeses that have dried out may still be used for dishes that require grated cheese.

» White or yellow cheddar cheeses contain about 70% fat, of which 40% is saturated.

CHEESEHEAD COUNTRY

The leading producer of cheese in the world is the United States with Wisconsin producing over 2.2 billion pounds annually. Worldwide there are over 800 varieties of cheese with only about 200 being produced in the United States.

EATING YOUR CURDS AND WHEY

Curds and whey are two proteins found in milk and milk products. The curd is actually "casein" and tends to form into a solid. The whey may be composed of several proteins, the most predominant of which being "lactoglobulin" and all are suspended in liquid. The liquid that you see on the top of yogurt or sour cream and other natural dairy products is the protein whey, not water, and should be stirred back into the product.

STORING DAIRY PRODUCTS

All dairy products are very perishable and contain tens of millions of bacteria. The optimal refrigeration is actually just over 32°F.(0°C.), however, few refrigerators are ever set that low or will hold that low a temperature. Most home refrigerators remain around 40°F. (4.4°C.) which goes higher everytime the door is opened.

BUTTER, GETTING A GOOD GRADE

To be called butter, butter must have a butterfat percentage of 80%. A natural coloring agent called annatto is added to some butters to give it a deeper yellow color. The USFDA grades butter by taste, color, aroma, texture and body. Grading is done on a point system with 100 being the best. Grade AA must have at least a 93 points, Grade A at least 92, and Grade B a minimum of 90 points. Salt is added to butter to increase its shelf life.

HOW TO GUARANTEE A CREAMY CUSTARD

The recipe for a basic custard formula calls for 1 egg, 1 cup of milk, and 2 tablespoons of granulated sugar. If you wish to increase the richness you will need to add 2-3 egg yolks, which increases the fat and cholesterol significantly. To avoid a solid custard it will be necessary to continually stir the mixture using a low heat setting to avoid setting the protein too soon.

Milk in a custard is really not the main protein source but contributes salts to assist in producing a gel. Never try and replace the milk with water. The milk and sugar will thin out the proteins and increase the volume. Abide by the recipe and never try and speed up the cooking process by increasing the heat, it will end up ruining the custard. To make the perfect custard takes time and patience.

CAN BUTTER BE EASILY MADE AT HOME?

It's really not as hard as you might think. Using a food processor, place the bowl and metal blade unit in the freezer for 20 minutes. Measure 2 cups of cold heavy whipping cream (never use ultra-pasteurized) into the ice cold bowl and metal blades. Process for 3-5 minutes, scraping down the sides to make sure that it all gets processed. Be sure to continue processing until all the solids are separated from the liquid. Then pour off the liquid which is a protein substance called "whey." The solids (butter) need to be refrigerated and used within 3-4 days. This will make about 6-7 ounces of butter.

CHAPTER 20

A Cup of Joe, A Spot of Tea, and Water Facts

WATER

Almost every day it seems as if we hear about another incident involving contaminated water supplies. Our concern about our drinking water is definitely warranted with over 50,000 chemical dumpsites identified in the United States. These dumpsites are capable of leaching over 45,000 different contaminants into the water supplies, of which only about 100 are regulated. These thousands of contaminants may include: heavy metal salts, inorganic compounds, and suspended solid particulate matter.

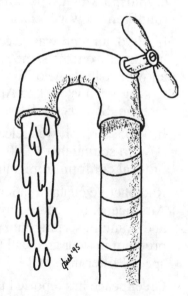

Disease outbreaks in the United States are in the news continually and easily traced to chemical or bacterial contamination of local water supplies. Remember, almost all of our drinking water originates in streams, rivers, and lakes. Even if the water source is a mountain stream it may have contact with impurities in suspension as it flows down the mountain.

Surface water frequently contains fertilizers and insecticide residues as well as pollutants from manufacturing plants and motor vehicles. Also there is the problem of chemicals that are added to our water supplies such as chlorine, fluorine, phosphates, and sodium aluminate for purification.

We should be able to rely on a safe water supply and not worry about its safety every time we take a drink. Water may contain a number of inorganic minerals which cannot be utilized by the body and are instead being deposited in bones, joints, and organs. Conditions such as arthritis, hardening of the arteries, and a variety of bone diseases, may be related to this unsafe matter in our water.

WATER FACTS

» According to the National Cancer Institute, nine recent studies correlated water quality and cancer with drinking waters in Pittsburgh, New Orleans, a number of cities in Ohio, New York, and New Jersey. Almost 66% of all households in the United States are using water that is in violation of EPA standards.

» In 1993, 110 people died and 400,000 became ill from drinking tap water in Milwaukee, Wisconsin. The water contained the parasite cryptosporidium. The problem is usually caused by agricultural runoff and sewage leaks.

» In 1996, a report was released that listed 28 cities that may be at high-risk from the same parasite. Numerous other cities were listed at a lower risk. Some of the high-risk cities were Baltimore, Boston, Chicago, Houston, Los Angeles, Denver, New York, Portland, Oregon, San Diego, West Palm Beach, Florida, and San Francisco.

» In 1995, a report was released by the Environmental Working Group (EWG) stating that 1,200 water supplies in the U.S. had a high level of fecal coliform from animal wastes affecting 12 million people.

» Radioactive contamination of water is a problem for 1.7 million Americans. It is caused by natural radioactive elements such as radon and uranium seeping into groundwater. If you feel that this may be a problem in your area call (708)505-0160 for information regarding special filter units.

» Greenpeace has reported that 1 million Americans are affected by chemicals and pesticides, some of which are now under investigation and may be phased out of use. The more serious problems are from atrazine and trichloroethylene.

» Chlorine has become a problem. It does protect us from a number of waterborne diseases, however the latest findings are that it reacts with organic matter to produce a carcinogen called trihalomethanes (THM's). This problem may affect about 650,000 Americans.

RELEASE ME

Water must be filtered if you want clear ice cubes. However, if you boil the water before placing it into the trays this will allow a number of minerals that cause the cloudiness to dissipate into the air.

SO WHAT'S NEW

A new bacterium water contaminant, Helicobacter pylori is now being studied as a possible link to stomach cancers. Studies are ongoing in attempts to control it.

GETTING HIGH ON WATER

If water is overly oxygenated (adding more oxygen) drinking it may give you a slight feeling of euphoria. The latest entry into the beverage field may be "Life 02" which will contain seven times more oxygen than regular water.

GLUB, GLUB

The average person consumes over 15,000 gallons of water if they live to age 68.

POOR CENTS

Americans in 1997 spent more than three times the dollars on soft drinks than they did on milk, and six times more on alcoholic beverages.

FLUID BALANCE

The human body is dependent on an adequate and especially healthy water supply. Air and water are two essentials without which we cease to live. Every bodily function and organ system relies on water. Water assists our bodies in dissolving foods, transports nutrients to the organ systems, then cools the body through perspiration, while assisting in regulating overall body temperature. Water washes out contaminants through the kidneys in the form of urine.

Because of all the uses for water in the body and the fact that we eliminate a good percentage of our supply every day we require an intake of about 6-7 pints of water to replace these losses. If you are thirsty, remember the body prefers a cool supply of water which it can absorb easily. Hot water in the form of tea or coffee is not absorbed as well and may act as a diuretic and actually cause the body to excrete more water.

About 70% of the human body is water. If you weigh 150 pounds, your body contains about 90 pounds of water. The following shows the percentage of water making up the tissues, organs, fluids, and bone:

Brain	76%
Kidneys	83%
Heart	74%
Bone	22%
Muscle	75%
Blood	82%
Lungs	86%
Saliva	94%
Liver	86%
Perspiration	95%

WATER TREATMENT METHODS

Since it cannot be taken for granted that the water we drink is beneficial to our health, a home filtration device or purchasing bottled water is a must. The following information will shed some light on a number of common systems:

» CHARCOAL FILTRATION
Most filtration units filter the water through activated charcoal. This method is good for filtering out odors, pesticides, chlorine, and assorted organic matter. However, it is not that effective in removing bacteria and heavy metals. The filter system will continue working until it reaches a saturation level, then it needs a replacement filter.

» CHLORINATION
Very effective in killing bacteria but tends to leave an unusual taste and odor to the water. Has the possibility of forming a dangerous element if not functioning 100%.

» MICROSTRAINERS
Will remove most chemical contaminants and bacteria. However, it is unable to remove nitrates.

» REVERSE OSMOSIS
Has a dual filtration system utilizing a sediment filter and an activated filter system. The drawback is that it does not allow the production of large quantities of water. However, it is effective in

removing up to 90% of the majority of minerals and inorganic materials.

» DISTILLATION
A very effective method of filtration. Steam is produced by boiling the water then the vapor is trapped and cooled to produce water. Gasses, however, do not seem to be eliminated completely through this method.

» AERATION
If you live in the Midwest and have a radon gas problem in your water, the best method to remove it is aeration filtration. Recent EPA estimates are that over 8 million people may be at risk.

» ULTRAVIOLET RADIATION PURIFIERS
Effective for the removal of bacteria. Usually installed on wells with other types of filters.

» OZONATORS
Found on the later model of swimming pools. Employs activated oxygen to purify and kill bacteria. Replaces chlorinators on pools. Every pool should have one.

» WATER SOFTENERS
Employs a method of ion-exchange to remove the harder minerals such as calcium and magnesium and replaces them with sodium. Sodium has a softening effect on the water and creates more suds making it more effective for washing clothes, bathing, and dishes. Best not to drink soft water due to higher sodium content.

> NOTE: Water filters are only good if they remove the particular problem in your area and are serviced properly, this includes changing the filter at regular intervals.

TYPES OF WATER

» SPARKLING WATER
There are two types of carbonated water. Naturally carbonated water is found in deep natural springs in many areas of the world. Artificially carbonated water is produced by using an acid such as phosphoric or citric mixed with water. Natural carbonation tends to last longer.

» MINERAL WATER
Is exactly what it names implies, water with minerals. The different brands will all have a different levels of minerals. Some companies use tap water and add minerals while others sell natural mineral water from springs. If you are importing water from a famous spa, the

water will have no real extra health benefit over any other mineral water in most instances.

» CLUB SODA
Most of the club soda sold in the U.S. is just tap water that has been carbonated. Some brands have added minerals and flavors. Seltzer and club soda are basically the same product.

» SOFT WATER/HARD WATER
Sofr water is water with a low mineral content. The mineral sodium is usually the primary mineral. If you have lead pipes soft water may leach out the lead into the water. Hard water is just the opposite. It contains a high percentage of minerals and will leave concentrations of calcium magnesium on plumbing fixtures

» SPRING WATER
Pure water without carbonation. Most of the bottled water falls into this category. When buying bottled water be sure it is a good quality and not just filtered tap water.

» ARTESIAN WELL WATER
Water from a well that taps into a water bearing layer of rock and sand which lies above the normal water table.

MORE WATER FACTS

GIVE IT TO THE PLANTS
Tap water should always be allowed to run for 2-3 minutes first thing in the morning in case contaminants have seeped in during the night.

DRINK A CUP OF WATER WITH EVERY SOFT DRINK

When you drink a non-diet soft drink the sugar must be broken down by the body. This process is normally conducted in the small intestine which requires water to break down the sugar. This may cause you to be thirstier than before you tried to quench your thirst with the soft drink. If you are really thirsty, the best drink is water. Alcoholic drinks also require one cup of water per drink to metabolize the alcohol.

THIRSTY, GET OUT THE BLOWTORCH
The oceans contain 97% of the earth's water as salt water. Desalinization is becoming more important as new methods are being

discovered. We are presently living on only about 3% fresh water, and 75% of that is frozen up in glaciers.

DON'T CHILL OUT

If you suffer from any form of cardiovascular disease it would be best not to drink ice cold water. The cold may cause a sudden drop in tissue temperature and may cause an unnecessary shock to the system. Also, the digestive system will function more efficiently if you drink tepid water. However, it is best if we do not drink any water with our meals since water will dilute stomach acids and digestive enzymes.

RELEASE ME

There is a higher level of contaminants in hot tap water than cold tap water. The heat tends to hold the contaminants better. Boiling hot tap water, however, tends to release contaminants.

WHY DO WE NEED TO DRINK MORE WATER AT HIGHER ELEVATIONS?

Where we live will actually have an effect on the amount of water we need to drink to hydrate the body adequately. At higher elevations water tends to evaporate faster through your skin due to the lower atmospheric pressure making the air drier. Since the air is thinner we also tend to increase our rate of breathing and lose additional moisture through exhalation. You will need to consume approximately 3-4 extra glasses of water per day if you live in the mile-high city of Denver than if you lived in New York.

WHAT TYPE OF WATER SHOULD THIRST BE QUENCHED WITH?

There has been a debate going on for years as to whether it is best to drink ice water or room-temperature water when you are thirsty. The answer is to drink ice water which will quench your thirst faster because it will cause the stomach to constrict, thereby forcing the water into the small intestine where it will be absorbed into the bloodstream faster.

DOESN'T SAY MUCH FOR THE GOVERNMENT

The bottled water industry is a $3.2 billion dollar industry. Over $2 billion dollars were spent in 1997 on home filtration systems. Home filter systems are only capable of removing larger particulate matter which leaves a good percentage of the small ones, such as some bacteria and viruses. One out of twelve households in the United States use bottled water as their main source of drinking water.

RAINDROPS

Rainwater is still considered to be mineral water and may have a number of impurities. We have all heard of "acid rain." The purest water is distilled water.

ADD A GOOD ORGANIC CLEANER

Rinsing vegetables in a sink filled with water (instead of under running water) will save about 200 gallons of water per month for the average family. You will waste another 200 gallons waiting for the tap water to warm up. Best to save the cold water for the plants.

DOES DEHYDRATION AFFECT US MORE IN THE SUMMER OR WINTER?

It is a known fact that the human body will lose more water during the summer months but you are more likely to become dehydrated in the winter. In the winter you lose the conscious need to drink more fluids and water is still lost through sweat. Sweat will not linger and is absorbed more quickly by the dryness of the atmosphere in a heated room and the rate of absorption of heavier clothing.

WASTE NOT

If you leave the water running, you will waste about 1 gallon of water every time you brush your teeth. The average family normally uses over 300,000 gallons of water annually for all personal hygiene, lawn watering, laundry, and cooking.

DRINK A VEGGIE

Some fruits and vegetables have a high water content. Carrots are 90% water and iceberg lettuce is 96% water.

WHY ICE FLOATS

When water freezes, its molecules of hydrogen and oxygen combine in a loose fashion, thus creating air pockets in the structure of the ice cube. When water is in its liquid form these pockets do not exist making water denser than ice.

SOME WET FATS

The production of food in the United States uses up 47% of our fresh water supply. Feeding one person for one year uses about 1,500,000 gallons of fresh water.

1 Large baked potato requires 18 gallons of water to grow. 1 Pat of margarine requires 85 gallons. 1 Loaf of bread requires 56 gallons. 1 Pint of alcohol requires 110 gallons. 1 Pound of flour requires 350 gallons 1 Pound of meat requires 4,850 gallons.

THINK AGAIN!

Well water should be tested every 6 months, without fail! Many farmers never have their water tested and assume that well water is always clean and healthy.

YOU NEED TO GET THE LEAD OUT

Over 5 million private wells in the United States may be exposing millions of people to high levels of lead. A warning has been issued by the Environmental Protection Agency that certain types of submersible pumps may leach lead into the water. The problem pumps have fittings made from brass that contains copper and zinc and 2-7% lead. It is possible to drink water with 51 times the allowable limits of lead in water prescribed by the EPA. Pumps should be made from stainless steel or plastic to eliminate the risk. For more information call the EPA's Safe Drinking Water Hotline at (800)426-4791.

SCRUB THOSE ICE CUBES

When ice cubes are allowed to remain in the freezer tray more than a few days they tend to pick up freezer odor from other foods, or even a degree of contamination from the air when the freezer is frequently opened. It would be wise to wash the ice cubes before using them to avoid any contamination or alteration of the flavor of the beverage.

BREAK TIME

When water is called for in a recipe, it should be between 60-80 degrees for the results. Allow water you are going to useto stand at room temperature for about 30 minutes before using.

NATURE'S CARBONATED WATER

A number of "natural" beverages advertise that their drink contains naturally carbonated water. This water is created underground by the action of a somewhat acidic water, comes into contact with limestone resulting in the production of the gas carbon dioxide. The gas is trapped by the water under the high pressure underground. Artificially, trapped by the water under the high pressure underground. Artificially, carbonation is helped along with either phosphoric acid or citric acid in most soft drinks.

HEAVY WATER, NOT REALLY

Occasionally a recipe will require a weight of water be used.
1 tablespoon = ½ ounce and 2 cups = 1 pound of water.

HAVE A SHOT OF WATER

When you're drinking an alcoholic beverage it would be wise to drink a cup of water for every alcoholic drink you consume. For every ounce of alcohol it takes 8 ounces of water to metabolize it. If you have ever had a hangover a few of the common symptoms are the result of dehydration. Symptoms, such as dry mouth, headaches, and of course an upset stomach.

Call the EPA SAFE DRINKING WATER HOTLINE
1-(800)426-4791 for a free booklet.
Additional water information and literature may be obtained by calling the following number:
Environmental Working Group — (202)667-6982
Greenpeace Internationa — (202)462-1177
Natural Defense Council — (212)727-2700

TEA

The history books tell us that tea was first grown and served in China and was originally used to flavor water that tasted flat after boiling for purification. It was introduced to Japan from China, however, the Island of Ceylon is presently the world's leading producer of tea. Tea is still picked by hand and a tea picker can pick about 35-40 pounds of tea leaves a daily. In 1904 iced tea was first sold at the Louisiana Purchase Exposition held in St. Louis, Missouri.

The most popular tea in the United States is black tea. In 1996 U.S. tea imports were approximately 140 million pounds, with our annual consumption topping 44 billion servings. Most of our tea is presently imported from India.

The average pound of tea will brew 200-250 cups. Brewed tea contains approximately half the quantity of caffeine as instant coffee. Tea has diuretic effects and should not be relied upon for providing your daily intake of water.

AT WHAT TEMPERATURE SHOULD TEA BE BREWED?

Tea experts agree that green teas should be brewed between 180°-200°F. (82.2° - 93.3°C.), oolong teas between 185°-205°F (85° - 96.1°C.), and black teas between 190°-210°F. (87.8° - 98.9°C.). The better quality teas should be brewed at lower temperatures since they tend to release their flavor more readily than the lower quality teas. The higher temperature used in the lower quality teas seems to stimulate the tea to release flavor.

CLASSIFICATION OF TEAS

» Black Teas

When tea is processed and the insides of the leaves exposed to oxygen, oxidation takes place and the tea turns black. They are then dried on long tables and allowed to ferment for 2-3 hours. The majority of supermarket teas sold are black teas. A new study from the Netherlands found no evidence linking black tea drinking and cancer prevention or cure. The study was performed on 120,000 men and women ages 55-69 who had cancer. In a Dutch study, however, drinking black tea did show that drinking 4.7 cups of black tea per day reduced the risk of stroke compared to men who only drank 2.6 cups per day.

» Green Teas

Green is the natural color of this variety of tea. Oxidation does not play a role in changing the color imparted by the presence of chlorophyll. The more common varieties found mostly in health food stores are Basket Fired and Gunpowder. Green tea comes from an evergreen related to the camellia family. The leaves are steamed, then rolled and dried.

Studies in Shanghai and Japan showed that drinking green tea was effective in protecting against stomach cancer and lowering cholesterol and triglyceride levels. However, the effective amount of tea may be 10 cups per day, which is unrealistic for most Americans. In the future the active ingredient may be isolated which will provide a more realistic preventive product.

» Oolong Teas

This tea is partially processed and somewhat oxidized. It is a greenish-brown color and is usually sold as Formosa tea or Oolong Jasmine.

TEA FACTS

THE PERFECT CUBE
Ice cubes used for iced tea or coffee should be made from the tea or coffee. Iced tea is diluted to a great degree and loses up to 40% of its flavor from the ice cubes.

CLEARING UP A PROBLEM
Cloudiness is common in iced tea but can be eliminated if you just allow the tea to cool to room temperature before placing it into the refrigerator. If the tea is still cloudy, try adding a small amount of boiling water to it until it clears up. A number of minerals are released when the tea is brewed which results in the cloudiness.

DOES TEA REALLY HAVE LESS CAFFEINE THAN COFFEE?
Actually a pound of tea has almost twice the amount of caffeine as a pound of roasted coffee. However, one pound of tea will make 160 cups, while one pound of coffee will brew only 40 cups. This is the reason that tea has only about 25% of the caffeine as coffee. One of the absurdities which we all come into contact with on a daily basis is that children are usually not allowed to drink coffee, yet some soft drinks contain up to 25% of the same caffeine found in one cup of coffee.

GETTING YOUR JOLT FROM TEA
If you want a high caffeine tea just have a cup of English Breakfast or Bigelow English Teatime. This tea has about 60 mg. of caffeine per cup.

UP TO DATE
While the latest studies still show that there are no risk factors related to tea drinking the tannins found in tea and red wine can interfere with the assimilation of iron, thiamin, and vitamin B_2 in the body.

BETTER CLEAN UP YOUR MESSY DESK
If you have ever had a puddle on your desk while drinking tea and couldn't figure it out the answer may surprise you. If you placed HOT tea and LEMON in a polystyrene cup a chemical reaction took place eating a hole in

the cup, allowing the tea to spill out. To top it off it also added a few carcinogens to the tea from the breakdown of the polystyrene.

CAN CORN SILK BE USED TO MAKE TEA?

On almost every continent corn silk has been used to prepare tea that has a diuretic effect. In fact, it is one of the best diuretics you can prepare from any herb. In some studies it was also shown that corn silk tea even lowered blood pressure, probably by controlling fluid retention. If your doctor ever recommends that you take a diuretic it would be best to ask him if you could try a natural one before a prescribed medication.

SOME TEAS CAN BE TOXIC

A number of teas may have risk factors attached and should not be used if you have any medical condition or just want to stay healthy. These include; comfrey, jimsonweed, burdock root, kava-kava, mandrake, sassafras, nutmeg, oleander, pokeweed, lobelia, hops, senna, and woodruff.

> SPECIAL NOTE: In recent literature tea has been discussed as a possible protective beverage for cancer. Research is presently being performed but there have not been any definitive, double-blind studies released that can provide information as to whether tea will act as a cancer preventive or cure.
>
> The substance in iced or hot tea that is suspected of having possible benefits is called polyphenol. Canned iced teas would be the worst source of polyphenols due to the high sugar content which reduces the potency of the chemical.

HERBAL TEA WARNING

Historically, the blossoms of the germander plant (Teucrrium chamaedrys) were used for weight-loss. However, according to researchers in France they have been found to cause liver damage.

A number of cases were reported of hepatitis (liver inflammation) in people taking Germander for 3-18 weeks. Dosages taken ranged from 600 to 1,620 mg. a day in capsule form. Teas were also used and may be just as harmful. Most manufacturers have stopped producing the product for weight control, however, it is still available through herb shoppes without a prescription.

COFFEE

Coffee is made from coffee cherries. Coffee trees originated in Africa and records of the first use of the actual beverage "coffee" have been found in the Middle East. The coffee bean was so highly prized that the Arabs would not allow the exportation of the bean. It was finally smuggled to Holland in 1660 and then to Brazil in 1727. Coffee trees need an annual rainfall of over 70 inches. Every tree only produces about 2,000 "coffee cherries" to make one pound of coffee.

The United States consumes about 50% of all coffee worldwide, approximately 400 million cups per day. Eight out of 10 adults drink at least one cup of coffee daily. On the average a person drinks 3 cups per day.

Coffee prices have risen dramatically since 1994 due to major frosts in Brazil which destroyed 1 billion pounds of coffee, about 10% of the world's coffee supply.

FRESH GROUND COFFEE BEANS, BREW IT FAST

When coffee beans are ground, a large percentage of their surface is exposed to air allowing oxidation to take place at a rapid rate as well as causing some of the natural aromatics to be lost. Another problem is that the longer the fresh ground beans sit, the more carbon dioxide is lost which contributes to the coffee's body and aroma. Coffee beans should be stored in the refrigerator and only the quantity that is needed removed and ground. The vacuum packed cans should be stored upside down to preserve the taste and flavor longer. By placing the can upside down you reduce the amount of oxygen that had contact with the surface of the coffee slowing down oxidation.

WORLD CLASS COFFEE

The Big Island (Hawaii) is the only location in the United States where coffee is grown. The mineral rich volcanic soil produces Kona coffee, one of the finest and most flavorful coffees in the world.

SURVIVAL & REVIVAL

When you keep coffee warm in a coffee pot on a warming unit, it will only stay fresh for about 30 minutes after it is brewed. If your coffee needs to be freshened up, try adding a dash of salt to your cup and then reheat it.

SO WHAT'RE A FEW WRINKLES

New studies report that caffeine and nicotine may cause your skin to age prematurely. These chemicals tend to cause the skin to dehydrate at a faster than normal rate.

MEDICAL FACTS

The effects of caffeine on your brain to keep you awake may last for about 4 hours. If you suffer from stomach ulcers you should consider giving up coffee since it will reduce the healing time. Caffeine also effects zinc absorption and reduces a man's sex drive as well as adversely affecting the prostate gland. People who consume more than 3-4 cups of coffee a day may be unable to handle stress well.

Opened coffee cans should be stored in the refrigerator upside down, The coffee will retain its freshness and flavor for a longer period of time.

Ground coffee oxidizes and loses flavor, it needs to be used within 2-3 days for the best results. Best to buy coffee vacuum packed. Fresh-roasted beans are usually packed in non-airtight bags to allow the carbon monoxide formed during the roasting process to escape. If the carbon monoxide doesn't escape, the coffee will have a poor taste.

If you run out of coffee filters, try using a piece of white paper towel with no colored design. Clean your coffee pot regularly. The slightest hint of soap or scum will alter the taste. Baking soda and hot water work well.

HOW COFFEE BECAME DECAFFEINATED

» 1973
The first chemical used to decaffeinate coffee was trichloroethylene. However, 2 years later it was found that it caused cancer of the liver in mice and use was discontinued.

» 1975
Processors switched to methylene chloride in 1981, however, this was also found to cause cancer in mice. The FDA said that the residues that did reach your coffee cup were found to be minimal and concern was low that it posed a human health risk.

» 1981
In 1981 coffee companies decided to use ethyl acetate, a chemical that is also found in pineapples and bananas. However, studies showed that when used in concentrated form the vapors alone were causing liver and heart damage in laboratory animals. This chemical

is also used as a cleaning solvent for leathers and production of plastics. This chemical is still in use today.

» 1984

Two companies have developed methods of decaffeinating coffee using water. Swiss and Belgium companies use water to harmlessly remove the caffeines, however, there is a small amount of flavor loss. A number of U. S. companies are working with the method but production is still low and more expensive than using a solvent. When purchasing coffee, try choosing a coffee that states it has been decaffeinated using a "water process."

WHAT IS THERE IN COFFEE AND TEA THAT ACTS AS A DIURETIC?

Many people switched to decaffeinated beverages so that they would stop running to the bathroom as often and were surprised that the problem was still with them. Unfortunately, many people over a period of years get used to going to the bathroom after drinking coffee and tea and their body just tells them they need to continue doing that even though it isn't necessary. Caffeine does have a diuretic effect on many people, but unfortunately even when it is removed from tea there is still another diuretic agent that remains called theophylline that may stimulate the bladder.

DOES A HOT CUP OF ANY BEVERAGE REALLY WARM YOU UP?

Other than a psychological effect hot drinks will not raise your body temperature. Research conducted by the U.S. Army Research Institute of Environmental Medicine showed that you would have to drink 1 quart of a liquid at 130°F to generate any raise in body temperature. They also stated that it would be difficult to keep that much liquid down. Hot liquids do cause a dilation of the surface blood vessels which may make you feel a slight bit warmer, but actually may lead to a loss of heat.

ARE THERE ANY SAFE METHODS OF DECAFFEINATING COFFEE?

The only safe methods are the Swiss water method and the carbon dioxide method. In the Swiss Water Process method the green coffee beans are soaked in water for several hours which will remove about 97% of the caffeine as well as a few of the flavor components. The water is then passed through a carbon filter which removes the caffeine and leaves the flavors. The same water is then added back to the beans before they are dried.

In the carbon dioxide method, the green beans are dampened with water, then placed into a pot that is then filled with pressurized carbon dioxide.

The carbon dioxide has the ability to draw the caffeine out of the bean and can remove almost 100% of the caffeine. The coffee beans are then dried to remove the excess moisture. Both methods employ only natural elements to decaffeinate the coffee beans.

DOES THE GRIND-SIZE OF COFFEE BEANS MAKE A DIFFERENCE?

The size of the grind does make a difference in the taste and level of caffeine in a cup of coffee. Espresso should be made with a fine ground, and Turkish coffee needs to have an even finer ground. Most American coffee is ground into a "drip grind." This provides the maximum surface area and will brew a rich cup of coffee that is not bitter. However, if the grinds are ultra-fine the water will take longer to filter through and this will result in an increase in polyphenols (tannins) and bitter tasting coffee.

ARE THEY REALLY MAKING CAFFEINATED WATER?

Yes, it's true and it's being sold under the names of "Water Joe" and "Java Johnny." It is being advertised as the latest cure for sleepiness when you are driving. When you go to a restaurant they will soon be asking you whether you want your water "caffeinated" or "plain."

REDUCING ACIDITY IN BEVERAGES

Acid levels can easily be reduced in a number of common beverages since certain people are overly sensitive to these beverages. To reduce the acidity just add a pinch of baking soda to the drink, especially coffee. Other high acid foods as well can have their acidity levels reduced with baking soda.

HOW YOU ABLE TO DRINK BURNING HOT COFFEE?

Drinking coffee that is hot enough to burn you skin and not your mouth is easily explained. When you sip a very hot cup of coffee, you will suck in more cool air than you ordinarily would. This air lowers the temperature through both convection (air current) and evaporation. The other factor involved is that the saliva released partially coats the inside of the mouth insulating it from being easily burned.

CAFFEINE VS. CALCIUM

Recent studies released from the University of Washington states that drinking regular coffee will cause calcium to be excreted in the urine. The loss of calcium amounts to approximately seven milligrams of calcium for every cup of coffee or two cans of caffeinated soda pop according to a researcher at the Creighton University's Osteoporosis Unit in Omaha, Nebraska. To replace the calcium losses it would be wise to add or consume 2 tablespoons of milk for each cup of coffee you drink.

DOES COFFEE KEEP YOU UP AT NIGHT?

Coffee will only keep you up if you are not used drinking a large amount. The more coffee you drink, the higher your tolerance will be to caffeine and the more it will take to keep you awake. Some individuals are actually born with a high tolerance and are never kept awake. Studies have also found that the thought that coffee is supposed to keep you awake at night is enough to make peoplestay awake.

SHOULD YOUR COFFEE-MAKER HAVE A THERMOMETER?

When brewing coffee it is necessary to have the proper temperature to allow the extraction of the maximum amount of caffeol compounds (taste and aroma enhancer) and the lowest level of polyphenol compounds (tannins which tend to give coffee an off-taste). A professional coffee brewer will keep the temperature of coffee that is brewing between 185°-205°F. (85° - 96.1°C.). If the temperature is too low the coffee grounds will not release adequate caffeol compounds and if gets too high the tannins are released. Caffeine in coffee has very little to do with the taste.

THE LATEST COFFEE CRAZE, THE CAFETIERE

The cafetiere or French coffee press or plunger pot is the latest craze in the United States. A number of coffee product retailers are touting the cafetiere as the "preferred method of brewing." The unit does not use a filter; it just presses the coffee and water which is then poured into a cup. Studies, however, indicate that this is not a preferred method if people drink 5-6 cups of pressed coffee a day since it may increase cholesterol levels by about 10% and the "bad" cholesterol (LDL) by 14% in some cases. The standard American method of brewing coffee by pouring water through a filter removes two of the risk ingredients that are implicated in raising cholesterol: cafestol and kahweol. These compounds are also found in other non-filtered coffee products such as espresso, which is produced by forcing steam or water through finely ground coffee.

COFFEE BITTER?

The best flavor will be from freshly ground coffee and always use filtered water. Coffee should never be boiled, the longer it is boiled the more tannins are released.

TYPES OF ESPRESSO BEVERAGES

» Espresso
Prepared by "rapid infusion" by forcing almost boiling water through a high quality dark coffee ground. The darker the coffee, how dense it is packed, and the quantity of water forced through determines the strength.

» Cappuccino
This is prepared by combining one shot of strong espresso with very hot steamed milk and a topping of frothy milk.

» Caffe Mocha
Prepared using one shot of espresso and topped off with the froth from hot chocolate. A somewhat sweet coffee drink.

» Caffe Latte
Prepared using one shot of espresso with about 4 ounces of steamed milk. Usually has more milk added than cappuccino. Topped with a large amount of foam.

» Macchiato
Prepared using one shot of espresso with a very small amount of foam on top.

» Latte
Prepared with a small amount of espresso on top of a glass of steamed milk.

» Cafe Au Lait
Espresso is not used, however, it is prepared with a very strong coffee blend and steamed milk. Will occasionally be served in a bowl.

CAFFEINE CONTENT IN COMMON FOODS AND DRUGS

BEVERAGE	PER 8 OZ. SERVING
Drip Coffee	178-200 mg.
Instant Coffee	90-112 mg.
Black Tea 5 Minute Brew	32-78 mg.
Iced Tea	34-65 mg.
Instant Tea	20-34 mg.
Cocoa	6-8 mg.

Jolt Cola . . . . 58 mg.
Diet Dr. Pepper . . . . 55 mg.
Mountain Dew . . . . 42 mg.
Coca Cola . . . . 38 mg.
Diet Coke . . . . 38 mg.
Dr. Pepper . . . . 37 mg.
Pepsi Cola . . . . 29 mg.
Diet Pepsi . . . . 28 mg.

DRUGS	PER TABLET
Weight Control Aids	250 mg.
Vivarin	200 mg.
NoDoz	100 mg.
Excedrin	65 mg.
Vanquish	38 mg.
Anacin	35 mg.
Midol	32 mg.
Soma	31 mg.

CHOCOLATE
Milk Chocolate (1 oz.) . . . . 5-6 mg.
Semi-Sweet Chocolate (1 oz.) . . . 20-35 mg.

Caffeine is the most popular drug in the United States and can be derived from 60 different plants. It is found naturally in cocoa beans, cola nuts, tea leaves and coffee beans.

Caffeine is a stimulant to the central nervous system and is capable of warding off drowsiness and increasing alertness. It does, however, reduce reaction time to both visual and auditory stimuli.

Studies have shown that caffeine does not cause frequent urination, but does cause an acid increase in the stomach after just two cups. Chronic heartburn sufferers should avoid coffee completely. Caffeine intake should be restricted to 300 mg. per day.

The latest information on pregnancy and caffeine consumption is relating to studies performed at U.C. Berkeley recommending that pregnant women should try and limit their caffeine consumption to a maximum of 300 mg. per day.

CHAPTER 21

The Real Facts About Booze

While alcohol is the most familiar of the multitude of available drugs, it has the distinction of being one of the least potent, ounce for ounce, of any of them. However, it is the most widely abused of all the drugs.

Since it is the least potent, large quantities are consumed which ultimately leads to the many alcohol related problems in today's society. Alcohol is one of the leading health problems in the United States today, surpassed only by heart disease and cancer.

The following is a brief description of the effects alcohol has on the various body systems after only 3 drinks of an 80 proof beverage:

» MOUTH
The taste of most alcoholic beverages is not a pleasant experience for the taste buds, unless the drink is "doctored up" (mixers, etc.). There is no permanent damage to the mouth, but the risk of oral cancer is increased four times.

» STOMACH
As the alcohol comes in contact with the stomach lining, the lining may become inflamed and irritation occurs. A number of problems can result, such as small ulcers appearing, tiny blood vessels bursting, and the normally acid resistant coating losing a high degree of protection. Approximately 20% of the alcohol is absorbed directly into the bloodstream from the stomach.

» INTESTINE
Soon the beer, whiskey, vodka or scotch finds its way into your small intestine and the remaining 80% is now absorbed into the bloodstream within 1 hour of consumption.

» BLOODSTREAM
The bloodstream transports the alcohol to the processing site, the liver.

» LIVER
The liver is assigned the task of breaking down the alcohol. This unique burden reduces the liver's efficiency and over a prolonged period of reduced efficiency may cause permanent liver damage. The liver may develop scar tissue and an increase of cellular fats, leading to the disease cirrhosis. Cirrhosis may cause the liver to stop functioning completely and thus become life threatening.

» BRAIN
If you drink more alcohol than the liver can handle it spills over, returning to the bloodstream and a percentage goes to the brain. When alcohol reaches the brain it affects the frontal lobes first, affecting our reasoning powers and judgment.

Next the alcohol affects our speech and vision centers. Following that the effects tend to affect our large muscles causing us to stagger and we lose our ability to walk a straight line. Eventually if you drink enough you will pass out due to an anesthetic effect on the brain. If you don't pass out, you would eventually kill yourself with a lethal dose.

VITAMIN/MINERAL RELATIONSHIP

 Vitamins and minerals are required in order for alcohol to be metabolized (broken down) in the liver. If these nutrients are not available in the amounts needed, the liver will have difficulty breaking the alcohol down. The following list are the nutrients needed to break down alcohol:

B Vitamins	**Minerals**
Thiamin	Iron
Riboflavin	Zinc
Niacin	Manganese
Pantothenic Acid	Phosphorus
Biotin	Copper
Magnesium	

It would probably be best to take a vitamin/mineral supplement if you plan on drinking more than 2 drinks of any kind.

ALCOHOL FACTS

WILL COFFEE SOBER YOU UP?

Alcohol in many people will first provide a feeling of euphoria then have an opposite effect of making you drowsy and incoherent. Coffee, because of the caffeine, will make you more awake; however, it will have little to do with sobering you up. The quickest way to sober up is to consume a glass of water for each drink you had and to take a multi-vitamin, multi-mineral supplement while you are drinking. This will assist the liver in metabolizing the alcohol more efficiently. The hangover effects will be reduced or eliminated. These are usually the result of a poor quality alcohol that contains too many cogeners, or by-products of the processing. High quality alcoholic beverages rarely, if ever cause a hangover.

THE PROBLEM WITH ALCOHOL

Alcohol is the major cause of accidents of all types. Examples of this are as follows:

> 69 percent of drownings
> 47 percent of industrial injuries
> 83 percent of fatal fire and burn injuries
> 50 percent of motor vehicle fatalities
> 50 percent of all divorces

SPEED IT UP OR SLOW IT DOWN

The rate that alcohol is absorbed can be slowed down if you eat while drinking. If you are in a hurry just drink without eating. Fatty foods will slow down the rate of absorption even more.

MODERATION IS THE KEY

Recently Scotch whiskey has been associated with a risk factor related to a carcinogen called a "nitrosamine." The problem has been traced to the method of drying barley used in the processing. Nitrosamines can also be formed from nitrites found in processed meats.

SURPRISED?

Only 5% of all alcoholics are on skid row, 20% are blue collar workers, 25% are white collar workers, and 50% work as managers or professionals.

WORD TO THE WISE

Alcohol may suppress the immune system increasing the risk of colds and infections. It can also cause adverse reactions with over 100 medications and reduce the potency of most vitamins you are taking. Moderation is the key.

WATCH WHAT YOU EAT

If you have a problem with food allergies, drinking alcohol may intensify any adverse effects that occur from eating the risk foods and drinking at the same time.

ALCOHOL CONTENT

Most alcoholic beverages sold in the United States contain 40% alcohol content or 80 proof. The "proof" figure will always be double the alcohol content.

HOW ALCOHOL IS DISTILLED

Alcohol is so toxic to all living organisms, even the yeasts that produce fermentation are unable to survive in a solution of more than 15% alcohol which is most of the beer and wine. Beer and wine were the only alcoholic products for hundreds of years until the process of distillation was invented. This process is only made possible because alcohol boils at 173°F. (78.3°C.) which is 39° (3.9°C.) lower than water. When alcohol and water are mixed and brought to a boil, the alcohol will predominate in the vapor. The vapor is then cooled through long curled tubes of cold metal and allowed to drip into a container.

HEAR YE, HEAR YE, ALCOHOL KILLS ANTIOXIDANT?

According to information released from the American Cancer Society, alcohol has the ability to neutralize the beneficial effects of beta carotene.

TOO MUCH PUNCH IN YOUR PUNCH?

If you have added too much alcohol to your punch (by accident, of course), try floating some cucumber slices on the top to absorb the taste of the alcohol.

MEN BEWARE

The mineral zinc is very important to prostate health. Alcohol has the tendency to increase the excretion of the mineral zinc. Magnesium, another important mineral may also be abnormally excreted which may lead to lowering your resistance to stress.

JUST ONE MORE RISK FACTOR

When alcohol is processed cogeners (toxic contaminants) are produced. The safest beverages with the lowest levels are gin and vodka (especially Russian vodka). The beverages with the highest levels are whiskeys and brandy.

CALIFORNIA WON'T AGREE

The expensive champagne Dom Perignon was invented by a seventeenth-century French monk. This discovery was instrumental in today's champagne production methods. The French feel that true champagne only comes from the Champagne region of France. Champagne should be served at 40° to 50°F. (4.4° to 10°C.) for most of the standard champagnes, especially the less expensive ones. Never refrigerate champagne for more than 1-2 hours before serving. If left in the refrigerator for long periods the flavor will be poor.

DID THE ENGLISH OR FRENCH INVENT CHAMPAGNE?

The English actually invented champagne almost 40 years before the French. The English invented the cork stopper which was made from the inner bark of an oak tree that was native to Spain. The English had been using the cork material to stopper their wine and beer bottles for hundreds of years while the French used plugs of hemp soaked in oil that would seep. When carbon dioxide would build up in the French bottles it would seep out through the hemp while the English cork held back the carbon dioxide, hence the carbonation was retained. The English imported still champagne, bottled it and the yeasts that were left in the wine produced the carbon dioxide in the closed environment. Wine needs to be stored on its side to keep the cork damp and not allow any air into the bottle which would increase the deterioration of the wine. Portugal supplies about 80% of the corks sold worldwide.

WHY DO WINE CONNOISSEURS SWIRL THE WINE?

People who enjoy wine also enjoy the aroma of the various wines. By swirling the wine around in the glass you release the full aroma of the wine. Wine may contain 400 hundred different organic molecules, 200 of which have an aroma.

WHAT ARE THE CLASSIFICATIONS OF CHAMPAGNE?

Brut is the driest and the best grade; Vintage is normally very dry; Sec or just plain Dry is slightly sweet; Extra Sec or Extra Dry is a moderate sweet champagne; Demi-sec falls into the sweet category; Doux is very sweet; and Blanc de blanc means that the only white grape used was a Chardonnay.

WHY IS CHAMPAGNE ALWAYS SERVED IN NARROW GLASSES?

Champagne is always served in "flutes" or tall narrow glasses because these glasses provide less surface from which the carbon dioxide bubbles can escape. Also, it allows a better bouquet to be released more slowly. The older type glasses that were shallow and had a wide brim allowed the bubbles and bouquet to escape at least twice as fast.

CHEERS

The quality of champagne will be altered if it is chilled for too long a period of time. It should also only be chilled up to the neck of the bottle, any higher and the cork may be more difficult to remove.

YOU GET HIGHER, QUICKER ON CHAMPAGNE THAN OTHER WINES

Yes! Champagne contains carbonation which will speed the absorption of the alcohol into the bloodstream. If you have a wine cooler using a carbonated beverage it will give you the same effect.

POP GOES THE CHAMPAGNE

Champagne is produced with a high level of trapped carbon dioxide dissolved in the liquid. The pressure in the bottle is sufficient to keep the carbon dioxide in suspension until the bottle is opened. At that point the pressure immediately drops to room-temperature pressure which draws the cork out of the bottle at a high speed. This causes the carbon dioxide to be released in the form of bubbles which will continue until all the carbon dioxide is depleted and the champagne goes flat. This does not take very long. The carbon dioxide gas also tends to increase the absorption of alcohol into the bloodstream allowing you to feel the effects sooner than you would if you were drinking any other type of wine.

DE-BUBBLER
Soap film on a champagne glass or "flute" will ruin the effervescence.

A REAL SWEETIE
Most recipes that allow you to use a small amount of an alcoholic beverage will never mention bourbon since it is too sweet for most recipes.

MEASURING UP
When figuring the total liquid in a recipe any wine that is added should be part of the total liquid figure. As a rule of thumb for almost all sauce and soup recipes, use 1 tablespoon of wine per cup of sauce or soup. When cooking with wine, it will reduce from 1 cup to ¼cup in about 8-10 minutes. Keep wine stored for cooking in small bottles. The less space between the wine and the top, the longer the wine will retain its flavor.

TYPES OF WINES

» BLUSH WINES
These are produced from the juice of red grapes which has had almost no contact with the grape skins. The color will vary depending on the type of grape and whether a small amount of white grape juice has been added. These wines are usually best if served chilled and not icy cold.

» FORTIFIED WINES
This is a wine to which brandy or another alcoholic beverage has been added to increase the alcohol content. The most common wines to which this is done are port, sherry, and Marsala.

» VINTAGE WINES
These are wines that are produced from grapes grown in a specific year. This information as to the year and even the particular vineyard are usually found on the label. A non-vintage wine may be made from grapes that were harvested in different years and never has a date on the label.

WINE CHEMISTRY 101
Wine is composed of water, alcohol, various pigments, esters, some vitamins and minerals, acids, and tannins. It does not remain in a constant state, but is continually changing.

COOKING WITH WINES

» SHERRY
Recommended for stews, soups, and sauces. Tastes best with poultry and seafood recipes.

» ZINFANDEL/CHABLIS
Chefs recommend that these wines go best with seafood and poultry meals.

» RED WINE
The richer body and stronger flavor make this the best wine to savor with meat dishes. When using it for cooking, it will taste best when used in marinades, meat sauces, stews, and hearty gravies.

» DESSERT WINES/LIQUORS
Sweeter wines normally used in dessert dishes such as compotes, fancy fruit desserts, and sweet sauces.

» BRANDY
Mostly used in poultry and meat recipes. Also frequently found in compotes and puddings.

» THERE GO THE EYEBROWS
If you are having a problem igniting brandy, it is probably not hot enough. Some chefs warm the brandy before adding it to the food to assure that it will light. If you heat it too much, however, it may ignite.

» RUM
Commonly used for rum cake, pineapple upside down cake, and sweet sauces.

CURDLING UP WITH WINE

Wine tends to cause curdling in recipes that contain dairy products. If you add the wine before you put the dairy product in the dish it should not cause curdling. Also, be sure and keep the dish warm until you serve it. If it cools too much curdling will take place.

A GENTLE TOUCH

When cooking with wine try not to use too much or the taste will overpower the recipe. Wine should only be used to improve the flavor. If you wish to make sure that you taste the wine in a recipe, just add it to the recipe about 5-7 minutes before completion.

CRYSTAL-LIKE PARTICLES ON YOUR WINE CORK?

This phenomenon only occurs when the wine is poorly processed. It is not harmful and is caused by malic acid crystals that have turned into a solid from incomplete processing during the wine-making procedure. This does not make the wine unsafe to drink but I would not purchase that brand again.

WHAT DOES WINE HAVE TO DO WITH MAKING A TOAST?

We have all been to a party when the host pops up and says "let's make a toast." This saying originated in the 17th century in England when a piece of spiced toast was placed in a carafe of wine or individual glass to improve the taste. When the "toast" was made it was polite to eat the toast so as not to offend the host. The toast has since been omitted and just the wine consumed.

The best temperature for wine storage is 55° F. (12.8°C.). White wine should be served at 50-55° F. (10 - 12.8°C.) for the best flavor. Red wine should be served at 65° F. (18.3°C.). Wine glasses should never be filled, there needs to be room to swirl the wine releasing its full flavor.

If bits of cork break off and fall into the wine, the wine must be strained into a decanter before pouring it.

Red wines that are over 8 years old tend to develop a sediment that accumulates on the bottom. This is harmless and the wine can be strained into a decanter.

NOT ALL FOODS GET ALONG WITH WINE

There are a number of foods that do not have an affinity with wine. Foods that have a high acid content such as vinegar and citrus fruits will give wine a bad flavor. Egg yolks contain sulfur which tends to have a negative effect on wine's flavor. There are also an assortment of aroma and flavor problems that can be traced to certain ingredients such as asparagus, chocolate, onions, tomatoes, pineapples, and artichokes.

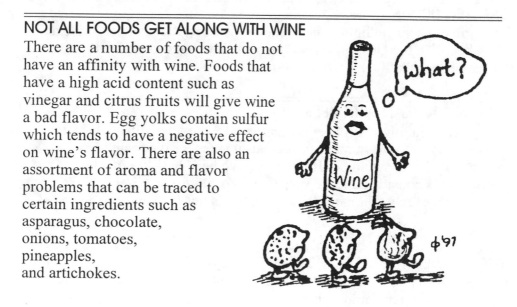

SLOW DOWN
The higher the temperature of wine the more rapidly it will age. White wines are more susceptible to aging from the heat than red wines.

TASTE BUDS KNOW THE DIFFERENCE
Always serve a dry wine before a sweet wine and a white wine before a red wine.

BEER FACTS

BEER BELLY?
The latest findings are that it is not the consumption of beer that causes the "beer belly." It is the fact that beer tends to slow down the rate at which the body burns fat, which is the real problem. It would be necessary to reduce your fat intake to reduce the problem bulge.

'TIS A SAD FACT
We are the only country in the world that consumes more beer than milk. In 1997 Americans averaged 38 gallons of beer per person opposed to 25 gallons of milk. We also spend an average of $325 per person on beer, wine, and hard liquor annually.

LIGHTEN UP!
In Europe the term "light beer" denotes the difference between pale and dark beers. In the United States "lite beer" can refer to either the color of the beer or that it is lower in calories.

GETTING A HEAD WITH BEER
The "head retention" on beer is measured by the "half-life" of the foam which equates to the number of seconds it takes for the foam to be reduced by half its volume. If the beer has a head half-life of 110 seconds it is considered to be very good. Foam will last longer if the beer is served in a tall, narrow glass that does not contain even a spec of soap scum.

THE COLDER THE BEER, THE LESS THE FLAVOR
The colder the beer, the less flavorful it will be, which is why beer is served at room temperature in many countries. If beer is allowed to sit in the sun, however, a chemical change will occur from the intensity of the

illumination. Some of the sun's wavelengths tend to react with the hop resin "humulone" which in turn reacts with the sulfur-containing molecules in the beer producing isopentenyl mercaptan which is one of the odor ingredients in "skunk spray" resulting in "skunky beer."

DRAFT BEER VS. BOTTLED OR CANNED

A real beer drinker, one that is knowledgeable in respect to how beer is brewed and stored will always order a draft beer over a bottle or can. Since all beer is subject to some degree of spoilage by microorganisms all bottled and canned beer must be pasteurized (sterilized). This high-temperature processing causes a loss of natural flavor which the discernible beer drinker will notice. Draft beer in dispensed from kegs that do not go through the pasteurization process since they are kept cold and are never stored for a period of time that would allow the microorganisms to alter the flavor or spoil the beer.

A BEER A DAY KEEPS THE DOCTOR AWAY

New studies are showing that by having 1-2 alcoholic beverages a day, either beer, wine, or hard liquor may reduce the risk of cardiovascular disease. Alcohol seems to boost the body's natural levels of a clot-dissolving enzyme called TPA. Physicians are using this enzyme to stop heart attacks in progress according to the Journal of the American Medical Association. Other studies are now showing that moderate alcohol consumption also raises the supply of the good cholesterol HDL in the bloodstream.

REMAINING REAL COOOOOL

There are any number of ways to serve beer. If you enjoy a cold beer then it would be best to keep a glass in the freezer, since an ice cold glass will keep the beer cold for about 10-15 minutes longer than a warm glass. A hard styrafoam or soft foam holder will keep the beer close to the original cold temperature for at least 25-35 minutes.

WHAT HAPPENS WHEN YOU COOK WITH BEER?

When you cook with beer the heat will cause the alcohol to evaporate leaving the flavoring agents intact. The acid, however, will react with certain metals, especially aluminum and iron to form a dark compound that will cause a discolorization of the pot. When cooking with beer always use a glass or enameled pot.

THE MAKING OF THE BREW

Beer making is a series of steps that eventually lead up to the final product. The first step is to allow dry barley kernels to soak, germinate, and accumulate specific starch-digesting enzymes such as amylase. The second step is to take the partially germinated kernels (or malt) and dry them to stop the enzyme activity, then heat them in a kiln until they are the desired color and flavor. The third step is when the malt is mashed in a warm water bath, thus reviving the enzymes resulting in a somewhat sweet, brown liquid called the "wort." The fourth step involves adding the hops into the wort and boiling the two to extract the hop resins which are responsible for flavoring the beer. This also inactivates the enzymes, enhances the color, and kills any microbes that may have been present. The fifth step ferments the wort with yeast producing the desired level of sugar and alcohol. The sixth step is to filter the beer and remove the majority of the yeast then age the beer as desired. Finally, the beer is filtered, clarified, possibly pasteurized, packaged, and sold.

THE PERCENTAGE OF ALCOHOL IN BEERS

British		American	
Brown Ale	3.0%	Low-Cal	3.75%
Light Ale	3.5	Lager	4.5
Lager	3.5	Malt Liquor	5.6
Stout	4.8		
Strong Ale	7.0		

STRAIGHTEN UP AND SETTLE DOWN

Beer should always be stored in the upright position whether it is a can or a bottle. When beer is allowed to lie on its side for any length of time more of the beer is exposed to any oxygen in the container. The more oxygen it is exposed to the more oxidation will take place and the sooner the beer will lose its flavor. Also, beer should not be moved from one location in the refrigerator to another since the slightest temperature change will affect the flavor.

FROTH AWAY

The amount of foam a beer produces is controlled by the temperature of the beer. A cold beer produces less froth than a room temperature beer. Make sure your beer mugs are soap-free. The slightest hint of soap may cause the beer foam to collapse as well as affect the color.

SPEEDY ICED BEER

Quick-chilling beer has always been a problem. Placing the beer into the freezer usually doesn't work well since it either explodes or turns into a beer slushy when you forget it is in there. The best way to fast-chill beer is to have a cooler chest filled with water and ice and plunge the beer into the chest. In about 20 minutes the beer will be ice cold. The ice water is about 32°F. (0°C.) and of course is warmer than a zero degrees freezer. The ice water, however, absorbs the warmth from the bottle faster and more efficiently than the cold air does.

BEER WILL STAY COLDER IN A BOTTLE THAN A CAN

Aluminum cans are very thin and therefore when you hold the can it is easy for the heat to transfer and lower the temperature of the beer. A glass bottle, however, is much thicker and the heat from your hands can't penetrate as easily and the beer will stay colder for a considerable amount of time.

THE YOUNGER, THE BETTER

Beer is not like wine and is best when consumed as soon as possible. Aging beer reduces the flavor and overall quality.

SOONER THAN LATER

If your beer is not pasteurized, it would be best to drink it within 1-2 weeks after it is produced. The ideal temperatures for "lite" and lager beer is 45°-50° F. (7.2-10°C.), ales and porter beers should be at 50°-60°F. (10-15.6°C.).

BEER COOKING TIP

If you like cooking with beer, try using a bock or ale for the best flavor. Light beers do not contribute much flavor to a dish.

TYPES OF BEER

» ALE
This may range in color from light to very dark amber with a slightly bitter flavor and is usually stronger than lager beer.

» BOCK
A German beer that is usually dark and full-bodied with a slightly sweet flavor and twice as strong as the lager beers.

» FRUIT BEER
These are the milder ales and usually flavored with a variety of fruit concentrates.

» LAGER
This is a pale colored beer, light-bodied, and has a somewhat mellow flavor.

» MALT LIQUOR
A hearty, dark beer that has a somewhat bitter flavor and a high alcohol content.

» PORTER BEER
A relatively strong full-bodied beer that has a slightly bittersweet flavor and is usually found as a dark beer.

» STOUT
A dark beer that is produced from a dark-roasted barley. It has a bitter flavor and is very hearty.

» WHEAT BEER
Produced from a malted wheat. Has a pale color and a somewhat lager flavor.

MISCELLANEOUS BEVERAGE FACTS

DO YOU HAVE THE MOXIE TO ORDER MOXIE?
The oldest carbonated soft drink is called "Moxie." It was introduced in the United States in 1884 by Dr. Augustus Thompson in Union, Maine. This drink was originally sold as a nerve tonic and is still available today on the east coast. The soda is formulated using the root of the yellow gentian plant which was thought to calm frazzled nerves. Moxie is still sold in orange cans with labels that resemble the original bottle. A Miss Moxie Pageant is held annually in Lisbon Falls, Maine. Presently, the Moxie headquarters is in Atlanta, Georgia within the Monarch Bottling Company. To order your Moxie call (207)353-8173.

CARBONATION LASTS LONGER IN COLD SOFT DRINKS
Two popular acids are used to make carbon dioxide which is the gas that produces the "bubbles" in a soft drink. Phosphoric acid and citric acid react with water and form carbon dioxide gas. When carbon dioxide is in warm drinks or at a warm temperature the gas expands and more of it escapes in the form of bubbles. If you add ice cubes to warm soda you will allow the gas to escape from the beverage at a faster rate since the ice cubes contain more surface (nucleation sites) for the gas bubbles to

collect on, thus releasing more of the carbon dioxide. This is the reason that the beverage goes flat in a very short period of time. To slow down the process rinse the ice cubes in cold water for about 10 seconds before adding the soft drink. This will almost eliminate the "fizzing up" or loss of carbon dioxide in too short a period of time.

HOW ABOUT A SCUPPERNONG, MUSCADINE COCKTAIL?

When the Pilgrims landed, one of their favorite foods was the muscadine berry which were growing wild. It has a great-tasting tangy berry flavor and is made into juice, jams, syrup, and jellies in the Southern United States. The berries come in two varieties, the white or "scuppernong" and the red muscadines. Muscadine juice is the first new juice introduced to supermarkets since the 1930's. No sugar, coloring agents, or water is added to the juice and it is not bottled as a concentrate. It has a little punch to it and frequently replaces apple cider. To order the juice if it not available in your area just call (800)233-1736.

DURING WORLD WAR II COKE ALMOST WENT BATTY

In 1942 caffeine was becoming scarce due to the war and reduction of imports from foreign countries. The Coca Cola Company was considering the idea of extracting caffeine from bat guano (bat feces), however, they decided against it since they were afraid that if the public ever found out that Coke had bat excrements in it, Pepsi would have won the cola wars, hands down!

IS YOUR CALCIUM GOING DOWN THE TOILET?

Physicians are getting more and more concerned about the number of soft drinks women consume. Their concern stems from the fact that most of the more popular soft drinks contain "phosphoric acid" as the carbonating agent. Excessive amounts of phosphorus can upset the calcium/phosphorus ratio in the body and may allow excess calcium to be excreted in the urine. Women who are near or who are going through menopause are especially at risk since osteoporosis is a major concern to this group.

Normally, we consume about 1500 mg. of phosphorus daily from the foods we eat. The normal daily recommended allowance is 800 mg. The following soft drinks may contribute large amounts of phosphorus per ounce of the beverage: Coke 70 mg., Pepsi 57 mg., Dr. Pepper 45 mg., Hires Root Beer 32 mg. One 12 ounce Coke can provide 840 mg. of phosphorus.

A FEW HARD, SOFT DRINK FACTS

In a 24 hour period Coke is consumed 192 million times in 35 countries. Soft drinks now account for 25% of all sugar consumed in the United States. If children drink 4 colas per day they are taking in the equivalent caffeine of 2 cups of regular coffee. Soft drinks, according to statistics, are now the beverage of choice over milk, with 3 times the dollars spent on soft drinks. This amounts to 50 gallons of soft drinks per person consumed in 1997.

DOES BLOWING ON HOT SOUP REALLY COOL IT?

Laboratory testing has shown that if a spoonful of very hot soup is held at room temperature for 45 seconds before it is consumed it will cool down to an acceptable temperature, one that will not burn the mouth. If the same spoonful is blown on to speed-up the cooling it will cool to the same acceptable temperature in 20 seconds. The fast moving air when blowing on the hot soup will carry heat away from the soup more efficiently by forcing evaporation from the surface.

WHO PUT THE POP IN SODA POP?

In 1822 a man by the name of Townsend Speakman living in Philadelphia developed the method of adding carbonation artificially to a beverage. He was asked to invent the process by none other than the father of surgery, Dr. Philip Syng Physick, who wanted to give such a beverage to his patients. The doctor charged his patients $1.50 per month for one drink a day. In 1878, the plain beverage was flavored and sold as soda water with a Hutchinson Bottle Stopper made from wire and rubber that would seal the carbonation into the bottle. When the stopper was moved to one side in order to drink the beverage, the gas escaped and caused the "pop" sound, hence the nickname "soda pop" was born.

DOES COUNTRY TIME LEMONADE MIX CONTAIN LEMON?

In all actuality Lemon Pledge furniture polish contains more actual lemon than Country Time Lemonade Mix.

FORMULA FOR LIMEADE

Squeeze out ⅓ cup of fresh lime juice into 1 cup of water and add 5 teaspoons of sugar or equivalent of artificial sweetener.

HOW LONG WILL ORANGE JUICE CONCENTRATE LAST?

Orange juice has a higher acid content and therefore will last about a week after it is reconstituted. The nutritional value, especially of the vitamin C, however, will decrease rapidly and it would be wise to consume the juice in the first 3-4 days. Water contains oxygen which is the enemy of vitamin C, that along with the airation of the mixing process adds a large amount of oxygen to the juice.

RAINBOW-COLORED BEVERAGES?

In case you haven't noticed children's foods are changing colors. Beverages are now all different colors with the most popular being blue. Kids will purchase blue drinks over any color and manufacturers are now going to make blue candy, cookies, ice cream, and even some foods. Studies performed at the University of Massachusetts showed that children "are open to the novelty of unnaturally tinted products." It was also discovered that color has an impact on how a food tastes to people. Kool-Aid now markets a green powder called Great Bluedini Punch that changes to blue when you add water.

HOW DID GATORADE ORIGINATE?

Gatorade originated in 1967 when researchers at the University of Florida decided that their football team, the Gators, needed to replace the minerals and fluids lost through strenuous exercise. In 1983 Quaker Oats purchased the brand name and sold the drink in different flavors. The drink was developed to provide water, sugar (energy), salt (fluid balance), and potassium (nerve transmission). At present Gatorade has about 85% of the sports drink market of over $800 million dollars a year.

AVOID THE NEW BEVERAGE MUGS WITH A FREEZABLE LINING

A number of companies are producing a beverage mug with a walled separation that contains a liquid that will freeze. The mugs are to be kept in the freezer and used for any type of beverage. They are safe to use, however, when a beverage is placed in them, ice crystals are formed in the beverage reducing the palatability of the beverage. Even alcoholic beverages such as beer will develop ice crystals and reduce the flavor and aroma significantly. Soda will become crunchy and not very pleasant to drink. The mugs are fine if you are going to allow a beverage to sit for some time before you drink it. Standard mugs kept in the freezer do not produce the same problem.

THE FORMULA FOR COCOA

Just mix 2 ½ tablespoons of unsweetened cocoa with 3 tablespoons of sugar and a dash of salt with ½ cup of water, heat the mixture slowly until it is thick and starts to bubble then add 2 cups of low-fat milk and stir for a few minutes.

CHAPTER 22

Substitutions That Work

If you're using a cookbook and it was published in England, the following information will be very useful since many of the common cooking ingredients are called by different names.

BRITISH FOOD	AMERICAN FOOD
Plain Flour	All-Purpose Flour
Strong Flour	Bread Flour
Single Cream	Light Cream
Double Cream	Whipping Cream
Castor Sugar	Granulated Sugar (10X)
Demerara Sugar	Brown Sugar
Treacle Sugar	Molasses
Dark Chocolate	Semi-Sweet Chocolate
Sultanas	White Raisins
Courgettes	Zucchini
Swedes	Turnips
Gammon	Ham

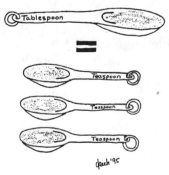

Substitutions	
Active Dry Yeast (one package)	1 cake compressed yeast
Agar-Agar	Use gelatin
Allspice	¼ teaspoon cinnamon & ½ teaspoon ground cloves or ¼ teaspoon nutmeg for baking only or black pepper other than baking
Anise	(use equivalent amount) Fennel or dill or cumin
Apples 3 medium	One cup of firm chopped pears and one tablespoon of lemon juice. 1 pound of apples = 4 small
Arrowroot	Flour, just enough to thicken
Baking Powder (one teaspoon double-acting)	½ teaspoon cream of tartar plus ¼ teaspoon of baking soda or ¼ teaspoon baking soda plus ½ cup of sour milk
Baking Powder (one teaspoon single-acting)	¾ teaspoon double-acting baking powder
Basil (dried)	Tarragon or summer savory of equal amounts or thyme or oregano
Bay Leaf	Thyme of equal amounts
Black Pepper	Allspice in cooking providing salt is also used in the dish
Borage	Cucumber
Brandy	Cognac or rum
Bread Crumbs (1/4 cup dry)	¼ cup cracker crumbs or ½ slice of bread
Bulgur Use equal amounts of:	Cracked wheat, kasha, brown rice, couscous, millet, quinona
Butter (in baking) Hard margarine or shortening *Do Not Use Oil In Baked Products*	1 pound = 2 cups 1 cup = 2 sticks 2 tbl = ¼ stick or 1 ounce 4 tbl = ½ stick or 2 ounces 8 tbl = 1 stick or 4 ounces,
Buttermilk	One cup of milk plus 1¾ tablespoons of cream of tartar or equivalent of sour cream

Substitutions	
Cake Flour	Use 1 cup of all-purpose flour minus 2 tablespoons
Capers	Chopped green olives
Caraway Seed	Fennel seed or cumin seed
Cardamom	Cinnamon or mace
Cayenne Pepper	Ground hot red ppper or chili powder
Chervil	Parsley or tarragon (use less) or anise (use less)
Chives	Onion powder (small amount) or leeks or shallots (small amount)
Chocolate, Baking, Unsweetened	(one ounce or square) 3 tablespoons of unsweetened cocoa plus 1 tablespoon of butter or 3 tablespoons of carob powder plus 2 tablespoons of water
Chocolate, Semi-Sweet	(6 ounces of chips or squares) 9 tablespoons of cocoa plus 7 tablespoons of sugar plus 3 tablespoons of butter
Cilantro	Parsley and lemon juice or orange peel and a small amount of sage or lemon grass with a small amount of mint
Cinnamon	Allspice (use a small amount) or cardamom
Cloves (ground)	Allspice or nutmeg or mace
Club Soda	Mineral water or seltzer
Cornmeal	Grits (corn) or polenta
Cornstarch	Flour a few tablespoons for thickening
Corn Syrup (one cup light)	1¼ cups granulated sugar or 1 cup granulated sugar plus¼ cup of liquid
Cream Cheese	Cottage cheese mixed with cream or cream with a small amount of butter or milk

Substitutions	
Creme Fraiche	Sour cream in a recipe or ½ sour cream and ½ heavy cream in sauces
Cumin	⅓ anise plus⅔ caraway or fennel
Dill Seed	Caraway or celery seed
Edible Flowers (garnish)	Bachelor buttons, blue borage, calendula petals, chive blossoms, mini carnations, nasturtiums,
Eggs Whole	2 tablespoons water plus 2 tablespoons of flour plus ½ tablespoons of Crisco plus ½ teaspoon of baking powder or 2 yolks plus 1 tablespoon of water or 2 tablespoons of corn oil plus 1 tablespoon of water or 1 teaspoon of cornstarch plus 3 tablespoons of water if part of a recipe
Evaporated Milk	Light cream or half and half or heavy cream
Flour	(thickeners use up to 2-3 tablespoons only) Bisquick
Garlic (equivalent of 1 clove)	¼ teaspoon of minced dried garlic or ⅛ teaspoon of garlic powder or ¼ teaspoon of garlic juice or ½ teaspoon of garlic salt (omit ½ tsp salt from recipe)
Ghee	Clarified butter
Honey (one cup in baked goods)	1¼ cups granulated sugar plus¼ cup water
Juniper Berries	A small amount of gin
Lemongrass	Lemon or lemon rind or verbena or lime rind
Lovage	Celery leaves
Marjoram	Oregano (use small amount) or thyme or savory
Masa Harina	Corn flour

Substitutions	
Mascarpone	Cream cheese whipped with a small amount of butter
Milk Evaporated	Light cream or half and half or heavy cream
Milk (in baked goods)	Fruit juice plus ½ teaspoon of baking soda mixed in with the flour
Milk (one cup)	½ cup evaporated milk plus ½ cup of water or 3 tablespoons of powdered milk plus 1 cup of water. If whole milk is called for add 2 tablespoons of butter
Molasses (one cup)	1 cup of honey
Nutmeg	Allspice or cloves or mace
Nuts (in baked goods only)	Bran
Oregano	Marjoram or rosemary or thyme (fresh only)
Pancetta	Lean bacon (cooked) or very thin sliced ham
Parsley	Chervil or cilantro
Polenta	Cornmeal or grits (corn)
Poultry Seasoning	Sage plus a blend of any of these: thyme, marjoram, savory, black pepper, and rosemary
Rosemary	Thyme or tarragon or savory
Saffron (⅛ teaspoon)	1 teaspoon dried yellow marigold petals or 1 teaspoon azafran or 1 teaspoon safflower or ½ to 1 teaspoon turmeric (adds color)
Sage	Poultry seasoning or savory or marjoram or rosemary
Self-Rising Flour (one cup)	1 cup all-purpose flour plus 1 teaspoon of baking powder, ½ teaspoon of salt
Shallots	Small green onions or leeks or standard onions (use small amount) or scallions (use more than is called for)

Substitutions	
Shortening (one cup in baked goods only)	1 cup butter or 1 cup hard margarine
Sour Cream (one cup)	1 tablespoon of white vinegar plus sufficient milk to make 1 cup. Allow the mixture to stand for 5 minutes before using or 1 tablespoon of lemon juice plus enough evaporated milk to make 1 cup or 1 cup of plain yogurt if it is being used in a dip or cold soup or 6 ounces of cream cheese plus 3 tablespoons of milk or ⅓ cup of melted butter plus ¾ cup of sour milk for baked goods
Tahini	Finely ground sesame seeds
Tarragon	Anise (use small amount) or Chervil (use larger amount) or parsley (use larger amount) or a dash of fennel seed
Tomato Paste (one tablespoon)	1 tablespoon of ketchup or ½ cup of tomato sauce providing you reduce some of the other liquid
Turmeric	Mustard powder
Vanilla Extract (in baked goods only)	Almond extract or other extracts that will alter the flavor
Vinegar	Lemon juice in cooking and salads only or grapefruit juice, in salads or wine, in marinades
Yogurt	Sour cream or creme fraiche or buttermilk or heavy cream or mayonnaise (use in small amounts)

CHAPTER 23

Insects and Other Pesky Pests

VITAMIN C FOR PREGNANT DOGS

If you find your pregnant dog searching the garden for
rose petals or citrus fruit peelings, don't get upset, they
know what they are doing. Giving your pet a vitamin C
supplement 3-4 weeks before they whelp makes the
process easier for your pet. Even though animals are able
to produce vitamin C and humans can't, they tend to burn up more than
they can produce during this period.

GETTING RID OF THE CRAWLEEES

A number of herbs will ward off crawling insects. The most potent are
cloves, bay leaves, and sage. Placing any of these herbs in locations
where a problem may exist will stop the critters cold and cause them to
do an about face and leave the premises. Ants, roaches, and spiders are
especially hard to get rid of, however, a few old remedies seem to really
work well. If the above herbs don't work, try mixing 2 cups of 20 Mule
Team Boraxo with any powdered sweetener in a large container and
sprinkle areas that you know they frequent. Crawling insects will also
not cross a fine powder such as baby powder.

WHITE OUT

If you have a problem with any type of flying insect, try keeping a basil
plant or two around the house. Keep the plant well-watered from the
bottom, this will cause the plant to release additional aroma. Hanging
small muslin bags with fresh dried basil will also repel flying insects.
Works against anything with wings.

YOU WON'T NEED THE ROD AND REEL
To get rid of silverfish, try mixing 1 part of molasses in 2 parts of white vinegar. Apply the mixture to cracks and holes where they reside. Treat the baseboards and table legs as well.

OOOOPS
If your dog or cat has an accident use a small amount of white vinegar in a spray bottle to remove the odor. However, try a small area that is out of sight to make sure the carpet is colorfast. Use paper towel first to remove as much of the liquid as possible. A mild solution of hot soapy water should do the trick as well.

ROTTEN EGGS TO THE RESCUE
Keeping deer, antelope, and reindeer away from your garden and trees is a breeze with eggs that have gone bad and float in water. Just break them open (outside of the house) around the area that you want to keep the critters away from. The smell of hydrogen sulfide from rotten eggs is not one of their favorite aromas. Another method is to grate deodorant soap (not the sweet-smelling stuff), place the gratings in small cloth sacs and hang a few sacs on each tree.

FASTER THAN RABBITS
Garbage cans and trash compactors can produce 1,000 or more flies a week unless they are sealed tight. Flies, however, are repelled by oil of lavender. Soak a sponge with the oil and leave it in a saucer, or place the oil on a cotton ball and add it to your garbage the beginning of each week. Other natural fly repellents are oil of cloves and mint sprigs.

NATURAL INSECTICIDE
If you are going to plant in window boxes, try whitewashing them first. This will deter insects and reduce the risk of dry rot.

BUG KILLER
If you place a few drops of liquid detergent in your water that is being used to clean the plant's leaves, it will keep the bugs off and if they go into the soil at night they will die.

FLEA SUCTION

Fleas can be eliminated by vacuuming with a high powered vacuum cleaner (Preferably Electrolux) with a good sealing bag. Remove the bag and dispose of it immediately after vacuuming.

THE CABBAGE PATCH SLUG

If you are having problems with slugs eating your flowers, there is a simple solution. Just plant a few cabbage plants in your garden. Slugs go crazy for cabbage plants, try it, it works great.

ONE FOR THE SQUIRREL

One of the deadliest mushrooms is the Amanita. Gray squirrels have developed a method of detoxifying the mushroom so that they can eat it without being harmed.

ODOR CONTROLLER

Citronella oil candles will rid your home of mosquitoes. The smell is pleasant and not at all offensive. Placing tall gas lights around the backyard when you are having an outdoor event with a few drops of citronella oil added to it will keep the backyard clear of moths and mosquitoes.

MOTH TRAPPER

Moths can be trapped by mixing 1 part of molasses with 2 parts of white vinegar and placing the mixture in a bright yellow container.

KEEPING YOUR DOG HOT

If you want to keep a hot dog hot until lunchtime, try placing it into a thermos filled with a hot beverage wrapped in plastic wrap or in a baggie.

WHEWWWWW

Next time you change the litter box, try adding a small layer of baking soda on the bottom to absorb odors. A small amount of baking soda applied to your armpits can replace your deodorant.

NUTRAPET

Vitamins and minerals are very important to your pet's health. Save the water from boiled vegetables or liquid from a crock pot and mix it with your animal's food for additional nutrients.

TRAPPER TOAD

Finding a toad in your garden is really good luck. One lonely toad will feast on over 100 slugs, cutworms, grubs, caterpillars, and assorted beetle larvae. If the toad is in top form, it can consume over 10,000 invaders in one season.

SNAIL ZAPPER

Place stale cheap beer in a shallow container just below ground level. Snails are attracted to beer (I don't know why). The beer tends to have a diuretic effect, causing the snail to lose excess liquids in a short period of time and die.

RODENT REPELLER

Moles, squirrels, gophers, rats, and mice hate the aroma of peppermint. If you plant mint around your home chances are you will never see one for any length of time. If you place a small amount of oil of peppermint on a cotton ball and drop it down a gopher hole you will never see the varmint again.

HERE, KITTY, KITTY

To remove a grease stain from your concrete driveway, try rubbing kitty litter into the stain and allow to stand for 1-2 hours before sweeping it up. Don't let the cat out.

WHERE DID FIDO GO?

To ward off fleas from a pet's sleeping area, try sprinkling a few drops of oil of lavender in the area. Fleas hate oil of lavender, hopefully your dog won't.

POOR BAMBI

Hanging small pieces of a deodorant bar soap on trees will keep the deer away. Works excellent on fruit trees. Also, try a piece of your clothing, they don't like the smell of humans.

TAKE TWO AND SEE ME IN THE MORNING

Chigger bites respond to a thick paste of a few aspirin tablets with water. Should ease the pain and itching.

CARPENTER ANTS A PROBLEM, FEED THEM CAT FOOD

It's not necessary to poison your pets and drive the family out of the house for a week to get rid of carpenter ants. Just mix up a batch of 4 ounces of cherry or grape jelly in 3 tablespoons of canned cat food and 1 tablespoon of boric acid. Place small amounts in locations that they are frequenting. The ants who find the food will take it to their leader (queen) and the colony will be eliminated.

SLIPPING AND SLIDING

If you place a border of petroleum jelly (Vaseline) around a plant it should keep the ants away. Also, placing it on the stem of plants will stop most insects including ants from crawling up the plant.

WORRIED ABOUT MOTH EGGS IN YOUR WOOLENS?

All you have to do is place your woolens in a plastic bag and leave it in the freezer for at least 24 hours to kill the eggs. When you do store the garments, try and place them in as airtight a bag as possible.

WEEVIL ELIMINATOR

Weevils tend to take up residency in dried and most grains. If you place a dried chili pepper in with your grains you will never find another weevil and it will not affect the grain or beans.

A SPOT OF TEA, WITH A DASH OF AMMONIA

If you want to keep bugs off your indoor plants, try spraying the plants with a solution of 10 parts weak tea and 1 part ammonia. Keep out of reach of children.

GONE WITH THE FLEAS

To rid your pet of fleas, cut a strip of cloth about an inch larger than the size of your pet's neck, fold it over so that there is an opening in the center and sew one end shut as well as placing a seam down the strip, use a funnel and fill the opening with a combination of 50/50 rosemary and oregano, then sew or tape a piece of Velcro to close the open end and attach to pet using the Velcro closure.

ROACHES LOVE ALCOHOLIC BEVERAGES

A good way to rid your home of roaches is to give them one of their favorite drinks, alcohol. A shallow dish placed wherever a problem exists filled with any type of cheap alcoholic beverage, especially wine, should eliminate the roaches.

AH CHOO

One of the more effective methods of animal control is to place small amounts of red pepper around your garden, trees, etc. Plants that are toxic to animals such as oleander need to be sprinkled with pepper.

DON'T MAKE YOURSELF ATTRACTIVE TO BUGS

A variety of different bugs are attracted to different colored clothing. If you wear blue, thrips will follow you around. Whiteflies love the color yellow. A basic brown or khaki color doesn't seem to draw flies or bugs.

SHINE ON, SHINE ON

Most animals are usually afraid of anything bright and shiny. Try hanging strips of foil on trees or shrubs.

MOSQUITOES SMARTER THAN ZAPPERS

Studies have proven that electric bug zappers have no effect on mosquitoes. They seem to have a special sense that keeps then away from electronic magnetic fields. Citronella lamps will do the trick.

USING WRIGLEY'S FOR WRIGGLERS

Mealworms will avoid your grain products (macaroni, spaghetti, etc.) if you keep a wrapped slice of spearmint gum near the products. They don't like spearmint but are attracted to Juicy Fruit.

TRAPPING MICE WITH PEANUT BUTTER

Mice love the flavor of peanut butter even more than cheese. If you are having problems trapping them with cheese, try some peanut butter.

CHAPTER 24

Assorted Hints and Tips

SOMETHING TO CUDDLE UP WITH

A large one liter plastic soda bottle can make an excellent hot water bottle in an emergency. Make sure you wrap it in a hand towel before you apply it to your skin.

A FOREIGN PROBLEM

Dinnerware being imported from foreign countries may still contain traces of lead and other heavy metals. Salad dressings that contain a mild acid such as vinegar and even tomatoes may be strong enough to release these metals.

SHAKE IT BABY, SHAKE IT

To remove an unsightly residue buildup from inside a flower vase or wine bottle, try using a solution of 2 tablespoons of salt, some raw rice, and 1 cup of white vinegar and shake vigorously.

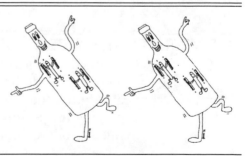

DECAL BEGONE

Transparent decals may be easily removed using a solution of luke warm water and ¼ cup of white vinegar. Place the solution on a sponge and dampen the area thoroughly for a few minutes. If this doesn't work saturate the decal and allow to stand for 15 minutes then try again with very hot water.

COVER UP

To cover a scratch on your refrigerator or freezer, try using the same color enamel paint. This really works great and will last a long time.

GREASE REMOVER

To clean your can opener, try running a piece of paper towel through it. This will pick up the grease and some of the gunk.

STREAKER

If the sun is shining on your windows, try not to wash them until they are in the shade. When they dry too fast they tend to show streaks.

PUT A LID ON IT

A fire in a pan can easily be put out by just placing a lid over the fire, thus cutting off the oxygen supply.

ALCOHOL TO THE RESCUE

Black soot marks on candles are unsightly and can be removed with rubbing alcohol.

BE GENTLE

A nick on the rim of a glass can be easily removed with an emery board. Don't use a nail file or sandpaper. They are too coarse and will scratch the glass and ruin it.

PASS ME THE PEANUT BUTTER, HOLD THE HAIR

 One of the best methods of removing chewing gum from a child's hair is to use a small amount of non-chunky peanut butter (not the natural kind). Other methods such as placing the person's head in the freezer for 45 minutes is not recommended.

LEATHER REVIVAL

If you want to revive the beauty of leather, try beating two egg whites lightly, then applying the mixture to the leather with a soft sponge. Allow it to remain on for 3-5 minutes before cleaning off with a soft cloth, just dampened with clear warm water. Dry immediately and buff off any residues.

ODOR EATERS

A number of foods are capable of removing odors. Vanilla extract placed in a bottle top in the refrigerator will remove odors, while dry mustard is commonly used to eliminate onion odors from hands and cutting boards.

ON A CLEAR DAY

To prevent windows from steaming up, rub them with equal amounts of glycerin and methyl alcohol. This combination will neutralize the buildup of minor condensation.

I WONDER WHERE THE YELLOW WENT

Stale milk will do a great job of cleaning plant leaves. The protein "casein" has a mild cleansing effect on the plant cell walls.

A SALAD SOLUTION

If you run out of wood oil, try using mayonnaise. A very light coating rubbed into the wood will help protect the finish. It should be rubbed in well and be sure not to leave a residue. Leftover tea is a beverage that can be used on wood furniture and also to clean varnished furniture.

POURING SALT ON AN OPEN SPILL

If you ever spill red wine on your carpet, try pouring salt on the area as soon as possible and watch the wine being absorbed almost instantly, then wait until it dries, and vacuum it up. Salt tends to provide a special capillary action that will attract most liquids.

SHAKE IT BABY, SHAKE IT

If you wish to make a unique salad dressing just place a small amount of olive oil and wine vinegar inside an almost empty ketchup bottle and shake.

MONEY SAVER

Don't bother buying fancy dustcloths that are treated to attract dust when all you have to do is to dip a piece of cheesecloth in a mixture of 2 cups of water and ¼ cup of lemon oil. Allow the cheesecloth to air dry and it will do just as good as the expensive cloth.

BEATS IRONING

If you want your sheer curtains to come out of the washing machine "wrinkle-free," just dissolve a package of unflavored gelatin in a cup of boiling water and add it to the final rinse. The protein has a relaxing, or softening effect on the fabric.

LEMON TREE, VERY USEFUL

For a brighter shoe shine, place a few drops of lemon juice on your shoes when you are polishing them. Also, a small amount of lemon juice mixed with salt will remove mold and mildew from most surfaces. The juice is just acidic enough to do the job.

TRY IT, YOU WILL BECOME A BELIEVER

If you want to remove glue residue on almost any surface, try using vegetable oil on a rag. Residue from sticky labels are also a breeze to remove. The vegetable oil tends to neutralize the glue's bonds.

A GIRL'S BEST FRIEND

All diamonds and gold jewelry can easily be cleaned by mixing a solution of 50/50 white vinegar and warm water. Dip a soft toothbrush into the solution and brush gently. Opals, emeralds, and pearls are too delicate for this type of treatment. Costume jewelry should only be cleaned with a weak solution of baking soda and water to avoid damaging the glue bonds.

EXTINGUISHING THE OLD FLAME

One of the best fire extinguishers is baking soda. The oxygen supply is cut off and the flame goes right out. Always keep an open box in the cupboard next to the range.

A POPPER OUTER

Tough nuts and bolts are easy to remove after you pour some cola or other carbonated water on them and allow them to sit for about 20 minutes. The mild acidic action of either citric or phosphoric acid will usually do the job.

NEUTRALIZE ME

The acid around a battery post can easily be cleaned with a thick solution of baking soda and water. Allow it to soak for 10-15 minutes before washing it off. Baking soda is a mild base and will neutralize the weak acid.

SMILE!

A method of cleaning dentures that works as well as the expensive spreads is to just soak them overnight in white vinegar.

RING AROUND THE TABLE

When you place a glass with a wet bottom on wood furniture the water may react with the stain in the wood or whatever wax was used leaving a white ring. These rings may be removed by mixing a small amount of salt with 2 tablespoons of vegetable oil. Apply the solution and allow it to stand for at least 1 hour before rubbing the area gently. baking soda may be substituted for salt if a less abrasive mixture is desired for more delicate surfaces.

A NUTTY SOLUTION

The broken edges of nuts can be rubbed gently on wood furniture to mask scratches. Just find a nut that matches the color and the results will surprise you. The most common ones are pecans, walnuts, and hazelnuts.

IT REALLY HITS THE SPOT

If you are going to wash a load of greasy clothes, try adding a bottle of cola to the load. It will really improve the cleaning action of most detergents. Colas contain a weak acid that will help to dissolve the grease. Cola can also be used to clean the rings off toilets.

FILL 'ER UP

A trick used by antique dealers to remove hairline cracks on china plates or cups is to simmer the cup in milk for 45 minutes. Depending on the size of the crack the protein (casein) in the milk will fill in the crack.

BUG SLIDE

Oven Guard or spraying vegetable oil on a clean car bumper before a trip will make it easy to remove the bugs when you return.

GREAT GRATER TIP

Cleaning the grater will never be a problem if you use a small piece of raw potato before trying to wash it out. Sometimes a toothbrush comes in handy too.

GREASE CUTTER

If you are expecting to have a problem with a real greasy pan, try placing a few drops of ammonia in the pan with your soap suds.

SLOWING DOWN TARNISH

If you place a small piece of chalk in a silver chest it will absorb moisture and slow tarnishing. Calcium carbonate (chalk) absorbs moisture very slowly from the air. If you break the chalk up and expose the rough surface it will be more efficient.

BAG 'EM, DANO

A great idea used by professional cooks worldwide is to keep a small plastic baggie handy in case you have both hands in a food dish or dough and need to answer the telephone.

LUCKY FOR YOU

If you have ever wondered why you can place your hand into a hot oven and not be burned, the answer is simple, air does not conduct heat well. However, if you leave it in there long enough it will come out medium-well. Water conducts heat more efficiently and will easily burn you.

MESSY!

The glue on any type of contact paper will easily melt by running a warm iron over it or using a hair dryer on high heat.

SPRINKLE, SPRINKLE

If you want to sharpen up your carpet colors, try sprinkling a small amount of salt around. The salt provides a mild abrasive cleaning action that won't hurt the fibers.

ROUND AND ROUND WE GO

Have you ever wondered how to efficiently get the last drop of ketchup out of the bottle? All you have to is to hold the neck of the bottle and swing the bottle in a circular motion from your side. Hold on tight!

REMOVING ODORS

To remove refrigerator odors, try leaving a small cup of used coffee grounds on 2 shelves. An excellent method of removing odors from the kitchen is to keep a few washed charcoal briquettes in a shallow dish on top of the refrigerator. Frying a small amount of cinnamon will chase all odors from the home.

VERY UPLIFTING

An easy method of raising the nap of a carpet after a piece of furniture has matted it down is to place an ice cube on the matted down area overnight.

MEASURING UP

If you want to use the fewest utensils possible, first measure out all the dry ingredients then the wet ingredients. By doing this you can use the measuring spoons or cups for double-duty.

SMART MOVE

Used microwave food containers should be saved and used for leftovers: just fill, freeze, and re-heat.

MICROWAVE SMARTS

It is always wise to check and see if a dish is microwave safe and will not melt. Just place the container next to a ½ full cup of water and turn the microwave on high for about 1 ½ minutes or until the water is boiling. If the dish is hot when you touch it, you will be able to cook with it.

SLIPPERY SUBJECT

When preparing a pan that needs to be greased, try saving your salt-free butter wrappers or use a fresh piece of bread. Remember salt butter wrappers may cause foods to stick.

DON'T BURST YOUR BUBBLE

An easy solution for children to use when blowing bubbles is to mix 1 tablespoon of glycerin with 2 tablespoons of a powdered laundry detergent in 1 cup of warm water. Any unpainted piece of metal can easily be shaped with a circle on one end to use with the solution. Blowing into the mixture with a straw will also cause smaller bubbles to float up. If you want colored bubbles add food coloring.

ONE FOR THE GRIPPER

If your glasses are slick, try placing a wide rubber band on them so that the children will get a better grip.

SAVES ON THE WASHING

Ice cream cones are notorious for leaking ice cream. To solve this problem just place a standard size or miniature marshmallow on the bottom of the inside of the cone to act as a plug.

REAL MILK SHAKE

Since fresh milk is difficult to transport on a road trip and young children require their milk, bring along some powdered dry milk and just add water and shake, a treat fit for a child.

COMING UNGLUED

Plastic wrap loves to hug itself. If you hate this problem just keep the package in the refrigerator. The cold keeps it from sticking together.

SALVAGE JOB

If you accidentally burn or scorch a food, place the pot or dish immediately into cold water. This will stop the cooking action so that the balance of the food will not be affected. The damaged food must then be discarded and a fresh piece of white bread placed on top of the rest of the food for a short period while the food is reheated to remove the burnt odor.

CRUMMY SOLUTION

Too much mayonnaise or salad dressing can ruin a dish. To fix the problem, try adding bread crumbs to absorb the excess.

REVIVAL

Almost any soft rubber ball including tennis balls can be brought back to life and the bounce returned by leaving the balls in an oven with only the pilot light overnight. This will cause expansion of the air inside the ball.

COOL IDEA

If you wish to cool a hot dish more rapidly, try placing the dish or pot into a pan of cold salted water. The salt will lower the temperature of the water even more.

SUMMERTIME

To keep salt free-flowing in a humid climate, just add some raw rice to the shaker to absorb the moisture. Rice absorbs moisture very slowly under these conditions and lasts for a long time.

ALTERNATIVE USE

Large sugar and flour bags can be used to store ice cubes. They are much thicker than plastic bags. Rubbing a clean, lightly dampened, dishrag on the inside of the bag will remove any sugar granules that might still be lurking about.

EDIBLE CANDLE HOLDER

Natural candle holders can be made from small marshmallows. If they are kept refrigerated they will work better.

CLEAN LIVING

If you have a problem with mildew forming in your refrigerator, just spray the inside with vegetable oil. Spray the freezer after it has been defrosted and next time it will be easier to defrost.

PUT ON A THIN COAT

To keep your blender and mixer working great, be sure and lubricate all moving parts with a very light coating of mineral oil (not vegetable oil). This should be done every 3 months. Before you use a measuring cup to measure a sticky liquid, try spraying the inside with vegetable oil and the liquid will flow more freely.

SLICK IDEA

If you have a problem with ice cube trays sticking to the bottom of the shelf, try placing a piece of waxed paper under the tray. Freezing temperatures do not affect waxed paper.

FREEZER MELT

A common icemaker problem is freeze-ups. Next time this happens just use the hair dryer to defrost the problem. This problem won't occur if you release a few ice cubes every few days.

WORKS LIKE MAGIC

Have you ever stuck two glasses together and couldn't get them apart? Next time it happens just fill the top glass with ice water and then place the bottom one in a few inches of hot tap water in the sink. Should only take a few seconds.

GETTING IN SHAPE

Butcher blocks will not only harbor bacteria deep down in the cracks but are also difficult to clean. They need to be washed with a mild detergent, then dried thoroughly and covered with a light layer of salt to draw any moisture that may have gotten into the crevices. The wood can then be treated with a very light coating of mineral oil. Make sure it is only a light coating since mineral oil may affect the potency of a number of vitamins in fruits and vegetables.

TIME SAVER

Keeping a grater clean so that you can continue to work and still grate a number of different foods is an old chef's secret. A chef will always grate the softest items first, then grate the firmer ones.

COMING UNGLUED

At one time or another we have all experienced the problem of postage stamps that have stuck together. Next time this happens just place the stamps in the freezer for about 10 minutes.

THRIFTY IDEA

Dishwasher soap can be expensive. If you want to save money just purchase the least expensive one and add 2 teaspoons of white vinegar to the dishwasher. You dishes will come out spot-free.

HUNDREDS OF YEARS OLD

Headaches may be relieved by taking the herb "Feverfew."

CAN PROTECTION

The lids from 1 pound coffee cans will fit a can of opened motor oil and stop the dust or debris from contaminating it.

LOCKS, NOT LOX

A hairdryer will defrost your automobile locks in the winter.

GETTING BACK ON SOLID GROUND

If you get stuck in snow or mud, try using your car floor mat or a blanket kept in the trunk for traction.

A BIT CHILLY

If you run your air conditioner for 4-6 minutes during the winter it will keep the seals in good shape for the summer.

NO NIPPING, IT'S POISON

If your windshield wipers are smearing the windows, try wiping them with rubbing alcohol.

LET THERE BE LIGHT

Used milk containers can be filled with old candle wax and kept in the car for emergencies. Place a long candle in the center for the wick. It will burn for hours.

TRY, SODIUM PHOSPHATE

TSP will remove grease stains from concrete after you scrape off the excess.

RUB-A-DUB-DUB

To prevent the rubber around your car doors from freezing, try rubbing the rubber moldings with vegetable oil.

BE GENTLE

Steel wool pads make an excellent white wall cleaner. Best to use as fine a steel wool pad as you can find.

THE ½ GALLON SIZE

Old milk cartons make excellent sand containers if you're stuck on ice.

TO THE SEAT OF THE PROBLEM

If you place a sheet of fabric softener under your car seat it will keep your car smelling fresh. Cleaning it out regularly will help too.

CHURCH KEY TO THE RESCUE

When you can't open a jar, try placing it in a sink with a few inches of hot tap water for about 10 minutes, then try again. If this doesn't work use an old type bottle opener and place the pointed tip under the lid and gently pry the cap away. Do this gently all around the top and it should release enough pressure to allow you to open it.

CHAPTER 25

Personal Grooming Facts

SLIPPERY WHEN WET?

For an inexpensive bath oil, try using sunflower oil and either lavender or rose petal herb.

A REVIVAL

Hair brushes and combs may be revived by soaking them in a pot of warm water and 1 tablespoon of baking soda or ammonia.

REFLECTING

If you lose a contact lens, turn the lights off and use a flashlight, the lens will reflect the light.

SQUEAKY CLEAN

If you want your hair to really sparkle, try adding a teaspoon of white vinegar to your final rinse.

RING AROUND THE FINGER

If you are unable to remove a ring, try placing your hand in a bowl of very cold water for a few seconds.

OR JUST WEAR GLOVES

If you would like to keep dirt from getting under your nails when you are working in the garden, just rub your nails over a bar of soap before starting work.

A CLEANER-UPPER
Laundry detergent makes an excellent hand cleaner for very hard to clean hands.

A CUP OF JOE
If you have red hair or are a brunette, try rinsing your hair with black coffee, then clear water to add luster.

FEET ADE
If you want to freshen your feet, try using a few fresh lemon slices. Just rub them in.

THIS WILL SNAP YOU AWAKE INSTANTLY
The life of pantyhose can be extended if they are placed in the freezer for the first night only. It will strengthen the fibers, but make sure you thaw them out before wearing them, unless you are having trouble waking up in the morning.

TASTES GOOD TOO
An inexpensive facial treatment is as follows: for normal to somewhat oily skin, use 1 cup of yogurt, 1 teaspoon of fresh lemon juice, 1 teaspoon of fresh orange juice, and 1 teaspoon of carrot juice. Blend all ingredients well and apply to your face for 10-15 minutes then rinse with warm water.

NEW USE FOR BREAKFAST FOOD
For a great facial scrub, try using a paste of oatmeal and water. Apply the paste then allow to dry until your skin feels tight. Then remove it with your fingers with a back and forth motion to remove the dead skin.

EAU DE REFRIGERATOR
Perfume should be stored in the refrigerator if you are not going to use it up over a reasonable period of time, approximately 30 days.

GREAT FOR HALLOWEEN
A great facial can be had by mashing ½ avocado and spreading it thickly on your face. Wait 20 minutes, then wash off with warm water. Don't let your husband see you.

WHY DIDN'T I THINK OF THAT
Place a small amount of vegetable oil on the threads of nail polish bottles and the lid won't stick.

YUK!
To make your own deodorant, mix 2 teaspoons of baking soda, 2 teaspoons of petroleum jelly, and 2 teaspoons of talcum powder.

FRUITPASTE
To remove the yellow from your teeth, try using mashed fresh strawberries to brush with.

A LITTLE DAB WILL DO YA
Many toothpastes are now adding baking soda to their formula. However, you could just use a small amount of baking soda to brush your teeth. Just dampen your brush and sprinkle it on.

A PASTY?
For a bad sunburn, try making a paste of baking soda and water, works almost as well as white vinegar.

HOW DRY I AM
If you want to make a bar of soap last longer, try unwrapping it before you use it and allow it to dry out.

SHAMPOO AWAY
To add shine to your hair and to remove shampoo buildup, try adding 2 tablespoons of apple cider vinegar to the rinse water.

A LITTLE ACID GOES A LONG WAY
Before polishing your nails, try applying a small amount of white vinegar to your nails. They will stay shiny longer and it will clean them. Bleaching your fingernails is easy. All you have to do is soak them in lemon or lime juice. The mild citric acid will do the job.

BABY YOURSELF
Baby oil will do the same job as a fancy cleansing cream at about a third of the price.

THE EYES HAVE IT

For puffy eyes, place slices of cucumber on your eyes. There is a chemical in cucumber that acts as an anti-inflammatory.

PERFUME HOLDER

If you want your perfume to last longer, try applying a small amount of petroleum jelly first on the area.

SKINADE

Skin blemishes can be cleared up quickly by dabbing them with lemon juice 4-6 times per day.

BALANCING ACT

If you want to restore the natural acid balance to your skin, try using ½ cup of apple cider vinegar in a basin of water. Splash it on your face and allow it to dry before removing with a towel.

BEING THRIFTY

To make an inexpensive shampoo mix ½ cup white vinegar, ½ cup dish detergent, ¼ cup water with 2 teaspoons of mayonnaise (not low-cal).

SWEET GRIT

To remove garden stains from your hands, try placing about ½ teaspoon of sugar with the soap lather when you wash your hands. You will be amazed how easily the stains are removed.

THE MAD SCIENTIST

The formula for a good liquid hand soap is: one 4oz. bar of soap, preferably one that has a moisturizing cream, and 3 cups of water. Grate the soap as fine as possible then add the water. Microwave on high till dissolved stirring every few minutes, then allow to cool before using.

A LITTLE SQUIRT

If you want your makeup to last longer, try spraying your face first with mineral water and allowing it to dry.

HOT AND COLD

If you break your lipstick, try heating the broken ends over a matchstick until they are soft, place them together and place in the freezer.

NO HANGING AROUND ANYMORE

If hangnails are bothersome, try rubbing vitamin E oil around the cuticles.

SHADES OF LAWRENCE WELK

To make your own bubble bath liquid, try placing soap slivers in a porous drawstring bag. Attach the bag to the tap while the water is filling the tub and instant bubble bath. Place herbs in the bag for a pleasant fragrance.

CHAPTER 26

Everyday Household Products

HOW CAN I MAKE AN EFFECTIVE GROUT CLEANER?

Cleaning grout around tiles is one of the worst cleaning jobs in the home. Most common products contain sodium hypochlorite (similar to diluted laundry bleach) and/or calcium hypochlorite and some detergent. An inexpensive grout cleaner may be made by mixing together 2 parts of liquid laundry bleach with ½ part of a phosphate-based liquid floor cleaner (or 2 tbl of Spic & Span), 3 parts of isopropyl alcohol, and 4 ½ parts of water. The solution can be placed in a clean plastic pump bottle and used the same as the store cleaners. When mixing chemicals be sure to not place any near an open flame or heating element. The isopropyl alcohol is flammable.

SHOULD WE USE A PHOSPHATE DETERGENT?

Phosphates increase the alkalinity of wash water and are more effective than the older products that used washing soda. Phosphates tend to bind certain metal salts that are found in hard water and change them into soft water which makes the fabric more accessible to the detergent. Sometimes phosphates are called sodium triployphosphate (STPP), which is an inexpensive form and harmless to humans.

WHAT CHEMICALS BESIDE SOAP ARE IN LAUNDRY DETERGENT?

There are a number of other chemicals in most laundry detergents, these include; bleaches, perfumes, enzymes, redeposition agents, surfacants, and even chemicals to prevent your washer from being damaged. Some products even use optical brighteners, which are dyes that are deposited on your garments that will transmit light to the human eye that would ordinarily be invisible, and ultraviolet light rays. When you see an advertising that claims its products will make your clothes "whiter than white" it is really not possible they only appear to be. One of the more interesting agents is the antiredeposition agents that coat the clothes with a type of cottonlike substance (carboxymetacellulose) that can prevent the dirt and grime that has been washed from the garments to be redeposited back on the clothes during the wash cycle. The agent is easily removed during the rinse cycle. The most difficult stains for a detergent to remove are the protein stains from dairy products, eggs, and blood.

WHAT DO FABRIC SOFTENERS ACTUALLY DO?

Fabric softeners are made from chemicals called "cationic surfacants" or resins. The cationic surfacants possess a positive charge and have an affinity for wet, negatively charged garments. They form an even layer on the surface of the garment removing the negative charge which is responsible for a scratchy feeling and roughness of the fabric. The softener will also remove the static electricity from the fabric and generally makes the fabric softer to the touch.

WHAT CAUSES THE RINGS ON TOILET BOWLS?

 The ring around the bowl is caused by the accumulation of dirt embedding in minerals from the hard water. Minerals that are usually found in these residues are either calcium or magnesium carbonate. A mild acid will easily remove the stains, the most common and least expensive is oxalic acid which is available in a powder or flake form. A cola drink that contains phosphoric acid and has gone flat will also do the job in some instances.

WHAT IS SOAP MADE OUT OF?

Whether you use soft soap or hard soap they are all made from sodium or ammonium hydroxide and one of the following: An animal fat product, usually tallow, coconut oil (lauric acid), oleic acid (olive oil), cottonseed oil (linoleic acid), or isethionic acid. Soaps may contain perfumes, skin conditioners, or antibacterial agents. Most are non-irritating to the skin and lather well and have good cleansing ability.

HOW IS TALLOW PRODUCED?

Tallow is a substance that is derived by passing steam through animal fat. The lighter fat is stearic acid and the sodium salt of stearic acid is called sodium sterate which is found in bar soap as sodium tallowate.

Coconut oil because of its liquid form is more unsaturated than tallow and makes it a better choice for a soap product.

WHY DOES IVORY SOAP FLOAT?

Excess air is mixed in with the ingredients which allows it to float. The floating soap was produced by accident when in 1930 an employee who was supposed to be watching the soap mixture fell asleep and the mixture accidentally filled with air. The company didn't want to discard the batch and found that the public liked the floating soap.

IS COLD CREAM THE SAME AS CLEANSING CREAM?

Cleansing creams or cold creams are basically the same product. They are composed of camphor, clove oil, menthol, phenol, linseed oil, water, stearic acid, soybean oil, eucalyptus oil, calcium hydroxide, and aluminum hydroxide. The camphor, clove oil, and the eucalyptus oil are aromatics, the menthol has some antibacterial properties as well as being an astringent, soybean oil adds a smooth texture, stearic acid prepares the skin so that the cream will penetrate, linseed oil is a softening agent, phenol is a relatively strong antibacterial agent, and a hydroxide will increase the ph.

ARE SHAMPOOS SIMILAR TO LIQUID DISH SOAP?

There are really no similarities between liquid dish soap and shampoo. Shampoos are produced from ammonium lauryl sulfonate and are much safer for your hair. Shampoos contain lauramide for producing a lather, lecithin to give your hair a shine, hydrolyzed animal protein to repair those split ends, glycol stearate to untangle your hair and give it luster, methylparaben to preserve the mixture, methylisothiozoline as an antibacterial agent, Canadian balsam as a lacquer, and some citric acid to make the mixture a bit more acidic with a lower ph. When shampoos are produced they end up too basic (alkaline) to be used on hair and must have the ph lowered.

HOW DOES HAIR SPRAY WORK?

When you spray hair spray you are depositing a thin layer of resin which is dissolved in a volatile solvent or alcohol which easily evaporates in the air. Once the solvent evaporates it leaves behind a layer of "plastic." Hair sprays in standard pump applicators (non-aerosal type) are really "plasticizers." If you don't believe that there is a thin layer of plastic on your hair, just take a flat glass surface and spray a thick layer on the glass. Allow it to dry for a minute or so then just peel off the layer in one thin sheet. Mousses, gels, and creams for the hair are also a type of plasticizer.

HOW DOES A LIQUID HAIR REMOVER WORK?

A hair remover is called a "depilatory." These products remove body hair using a concentrated chemical solution to break the sulfide bonds in hair. The main chemical used is calcium thioglycolate and in high concentrations is capable of breaking down almost 100% of the disulfide bonds in hair, thus causing the hair to literally fall apart and disintegrate. The minute fragments of hair are then removed with washing.

WHAT IS TOOTHPASTE COMPOSED OF?

There are a number of chemicals that all work together to grind off stains, help prevent cavities, wash away the debris, and a flavoring. The abrasives to remove stains may include any of the following: hydrated silica, calcium carbonate, baking soda, calcium pyrophosphate, hydrated aluminum oxide, magnesium carbonate, or tricalcium phosphate. The moisturizing agent is usually sorbitol; the chemical that prevents the conversion of plaque to tartar is tetrapotassium pyrophosphate; the sweetener may be sodium saccharin; one of the more popular whiteners is titanium dioxide; a thickening agent is needed which is carbomer; and of course a number of artificial dyes F, D, and C blue #1. Using baking soda after each meal may be just as effective as this chemical smorgasbord.

HOW DO ANTIPERSPIRANTS AND DEODORANTS DIFFER?

The first antiperspirant was produced about 1905 and was called "Odo-Ro-No." Early deodorants were actually just underarm perfumes. Antiperspirants are formulated to cause the sweat glands to constrict and actually prevent normal perspiration. Since bacteria need a certain amount of moisture to reproduce, the sweat provides a perfect medium for them to live and produce offensive odors. Antiperspirants contain chemicals that prevent the problem from occurring, these include: aluminum chlorohydrate, aluminum chloride, or zirconium chloride. Sticks are more effective due to their solid composition. Creams and sprays tend to lose effectiveness too soon.

Deodorants do not act to constrict the sweat glands but they do contain antibacterial agents, the most effective being triclosan. The antibacterial effects are only effective for about 2-3 hours and most deodorants contain a perfume to hide the offensive odors. Deodorants are used by people who would prefer a more natural approach and they would prefer not to have normal bodily process altered.

WHY ARE AFTERSHAVE LOTIONS USED?

Aftershave lotions tend to cool the skin, tighten the pores, and promote healing from the irritation of shaving. The most common ingredients used to accomplish these tasks are propylene glycol, menthol, and benzoic acid. Pre-shave lotions are only used with electric shavers and are skin lubricants that help the shaver glide more easily across the skin. Some have ingredients that may also make the facial hair stand up to be cut.

WHAT IS VASELINE MADE OUT OF?

Vaseline is produced from a mixture of hydrocarbons that are derived from purified crude oil. Petroleum jelly is excellent for sealing off the skin and protecting it from surface damage, especially from irritations and a mild abrasion.

WHAT IS THE DIFFERENCE IN OVER-THE-COUNTER PAIN RELIEVERS?

The most common analgesics (pain relievers) are aspirin, acetaminophen, ibuprofen, and naproxen. Aspirin has the capability of reducing inflammation in joints and act as an antipyretic (fever reducer). Ibuprofen is supposed to be more effective for deep muscle pain, however, it has yet to be clinically proven to the satisfaction of the medical community. Naproxen is similar in action to ibuprofen but tends to remain in the bloodstream for about 2-3 hours longer which may provide a plus. Acetaminophen (AKA Paracetamol) in England does not seem to offer any relief for inflammation and is not as good a pain reliever as aspirin but does not irritate the stomach which aspirin may do. A relative newcomer is naproxen sodium sold under the brand name of Aleve. Naproxen sodium may irritate the stomach just as much as aspirin and is sold to relieve pain, backache, muscle pain, discomfort of arthritis, and menstrual cramping.

Aspirin works by slowing the transmission of nerve impulses to the brain reducing the sensation of pain. It also interferes with prostaglandins, which when in excess, tend to dilate the small vessels in the brain causing headaches by localized inflammation.
Stomach irritation by aspirin is usually the result of not drinking a full glass of water when taking the product.

WHY ARE SO MANY HOSPITALS USING TYLENOL?

Tylenol is selling the hospitals their product at below cost to promote their product as one of the more popular analgesics used by the medical community. Bayer is also trying this method and is making some inroads. Once the patient leaves the hospital most physicians advise their patients to purchase any over-the-counter pain reliever.

WHY DO LINIMENTS REDUCE PAIN?

Liniments have been used for hundreds of years on both animals and humans to relieve pain, especially pain related to muscle overuse. They are mainly in cream form, however, there are still a few that are in liquid form. The creams tend to stay on better and allow the chemicals to do their job more efficiently. Liniments work by a process called "counter-irritation". They actually irritate the skin to such a degree that they cause a mild pain which causes the pain receptors in the area to be "switched off." A common liniment for horses, DMSO is not recommended for humans. DMSO tends to dilate surface blood vessels and will allow almost any medication or chemical to enter circulation.

WHY CAN'T I KEEP THAT NEW CAR SMELL LONGER?

A number of products have that same "new car" smell for a short period of time, especially new carpets. During the manufacture of plastics, oils are added to the plastic to keep it from drying out. These special oils are absorbed into the plastic and over a short period of time their vapors come into the air. The oils that are left on the surface are the ones you smell when you purchase a new item. Over a period of time, the deeper internal oils come to the surface but are not strong enough to create a noticeable odor.

ARE OVEN CLEANERS DANGEROUS?

The majority of aerosol oven cleaners contain sodium hydroxide (lye) which is also found in drain cleaners. When lye is sprayed on burnt fats and carbohydrates it converts them into a soap that is easily wiped off with a damp cloth. It would be best to use a number of the newer products that use organic salts and are less dangerous, however, with any type of oven cleaner make sure that there is good ventilation or they may burn the lining of your mouth and throat.

HOW DOES ANTIFREEZE WORK?

Antifreeze is composed mainly of propylene alcohol which when added to water lowers the freezing point and also increases the boiling point. Therefore water can't freeze at 32°F.(0°C.) and it will not boil at 212°F. (100°C.). The coolant is circulated through the engine by the water pump and the engine heat is transferred to the coolant which returns to the radiator. The radiator is cooled by the outside air which cools the antifreeze preventing boilovers.

CAN COLA REALLY CLEAN MY CAR BATTERY?

Carbonated beverages especially those that are carbonated using phosphoric acid will dissolve metal oxides that cake on battery terminals. However, the best way to clean the terminals is with a metal brush and some baking soda sprinkled on first to neutralize the acid. Never clean the battery terminals with water, the battery may short out and explode.

WHY DON'T CARS WANT TO START ON COLD DAYS?

The problem usually has nothing to do with the battery but with the oil. Freezing temperatures tend to turn your oil into a thick syrup making your battery work harder to turn the engine over. Manufacturers make higher amp batteries that may help alleviate this problem or you may want to consider a heated blanket to keep the motor oil from becoming a semi-solid.

WHAT IS THE DIFFERENCE BETWEEN A CAR POLISH AND A WAX?

A car polish is only meant to enhance and restore the luster to a wax coating. They remove dirt and debris trapped in the wax and restore a smooth finish to the surface. The polish will not provide any protection, it will just keep the wax clean.

WHAT IS THE DIFFERENCE BETWEEN CEMENT AND CONCRETE?

Cement is mainly composed of limestone (calcium carbonate), calcium oxide, clay, and usually shale. The ingredients absorb water which turns it into a paste. Concrete is cement with the addition of sand, gravel, and crushed rock. The addition of these ingredients lowers the cost since pure cement is very expensive. The hardening process of cement is somewhat complicated, however, the moistened mixture containing calcium, aluminum, and silicon salts tend to interact and produce a new substance called tricalcium aluminates. These are inorganic compounds that after a few days form interlocking crystals that produce the concrete's strength.

WHAT IS STAINLESS STEEL MADE OF?

When stainless steel is produced, iron and chromium are mixed together with the percentage of chromium at about 12%. As long as the alloy contains the 12% a percentage of the chromium will rise to the surface of the metal and will form a thin coating of chromium oxide which protects the iron from rusting and gives it a shiny surface. Other metals are sometimes added such as nickel to increase the strength of the stainless steel.

WHAT MAKES A DISINFECTANT DIFFERENT FROM AN ANTISEPTIC?

Antiseptics are chemical agents that kill a percentage of bacteria, however, they don't kill all bacteria but they are effective in preventing the growth of most bacteria. Antiseptics are mainly used on a cut or abrasion. Disinfectants are formulated to kill all bacteria and viruses but are too harsh to be applied to your skin.

KEEP YOUR FIZZLE IN

The refrigerator is a good place to store many chemicals such as hydrogen peroxide. It will stay active for a longer period of time. Nail polish is another chemical that likes the cold and will go on smoother.

HOW DO THE INSTANT HOT SHAVING CREAMS WORK?

A number of shaving creams advertise that they heat up on your face to provide a more comfortable shaving experience. These products use compounds such as methyl salicitate or salicylic acid to actually irritate the skin causing a sensation of heat by increasing the circulation of blood in that area where it is applied. The same ingredients can be found in a number of liniments.

WHAT HAPPENS WHEN YOU HAVE YOUR HAIR STRAIGHTENED?

Hairs are linked together by a chemical bond called a "disulfide bond." These sulfur atoms are attracted to each other and form a bond which can be broken using a chemical called thioglycolic acid. When this is applied the bonds release and become free allowing the hair to relax.

DO I NEED A SPECIAL DETERGENT FOR COLD WATER WASHING?

It is not necessary to purchase a special cold water detergent. The differences in hot and cold water detergents are so insignificant that it is a waste of money if there is a difference in cost. There is only one compound that is capable of changing the effectiveness of any detergent when it is used in cold water and that is the amount of surfacant they use and almost all are at the same level. A surfacant will actually make the water "wetter" by changing the surface tension allowing the water and detergent to more freely enter the garment.

DO DRY BLEACHES WORK BETTER THAN LIQUID BLEACHES?

There is a misconception that bleaches remove stains. Bleaches do not remove stains, they only mask the stain so that you will not see it. This process is known as oxidation and utilizes one of two types of bleach. The dry bleach is composed of sodium perborate which is converted to hydrogen peroxide, which continues to break down liberating oxygen gas which then oxidizes the clothing. Liquid bleach contains the chemical sodium hypochlorite which causes the release of chlorine gas that oxidizes the clothing, thus bleaching the stain out. The more powerful of the two bleaching agents is the liquid bleach.

THE SECRET FORMULA OF THOSE MAGICAL SPOT REMOVERS

The TV commercials and newspaper ads announcing that there is a cleaner that will take any spot or stain out of any fabric is just a combination of a detergent and bleach combined. Most of these are sold through good advertising and sales techniques. Most do work well, however, you could probably make them with two or three ingredients you already have at home.

THE DIFFERENCE BETWEEN SYNTHETIC AND NATURAL FIBERS

Synthetic or permanent press fabrics are produced from either 100% synthetic or natural fibers that contain sufficient quantities of plastic added to give the desired qualities the manufacturer requires. Permanent press fabrics will retain their shape up to the point that they will start to melt which is a very high temperature and never achieved when they are washed or dry cleaned. Because of the plastic used in the synthetics, the fabrics are very dense and will not lose their shape. Natural fiber garments are not very dense therefore they are unable to retain their shape very well, especially creases.

ARE THE EXPENSIVE BATHTUB CLEANERS REALLY NECESSARY?

Most bathtub cleaners advertise that they contain powerful disinfectants that will kill bacteria as well as cleaning off the soap scum and dirt residues. While they do contain disinfectants, the bacteria killing action only lasts for about 3-4 hours and then the bacteria come right back. The best cleaner for tubs is diluted laundry bleach. If you can't handle the smell, purchase one that is scented. Be sure and wear gloves and ventilate the room well when using bleach of any type.

WHAT DO THOSE LARGE TOILET CLEANING TABLETS REALLY DO?

The bowl-cleaning tablets that are placed into the toilet tank are not going to clean your toilet, they are only designed to slow down the process of hard-water buildup which contains imbedded dirt and debris. They contain a strong chlorine bleach compound or quaternary ammonium chloride. Both are strong disinfectants and have good cleaning properties. Some products, however, may be so strong that they will cause scaling of any metal surface in the tank and may cause the toilet to clog up.

DO THE COLORED RIBBONS OF TOOTHPASTE CONTAIN DIFFERENT INGREDIENTS?

Toothpastes that come out of the tube in different colors are all the same product, just dyed red and green. Recently, a new product did come on the market with a plunger and two compartments in the container that provides you with two different ingredients to care for your teeth and gums. Check with your dentist before using the product since it contains hydrogen peroxide.

WHAT'S IN A BREATH MINT AND HOW DOES IT WORK?

Breath mints contain sweeteners, moisturizers, and may contain a germ killer. Most brands contain sorbitol as the sweetener which may cause diarrhea if too much is consumed in susceptible individuals. The odor eaters are probably chlorophyll and "Retsyn" which is another name for cuprous (copper) gluconate.

WHAT IS THE DIFFERENCE IN PERFUME, COLOGNE, & TOILET WATER?

The main difference is the concentration of the compounds used that are responsible for the aroma of each product. Perfumes are produced with the highest concentrations and therefore last longer. If you place a small amount of Vaseline on the areas you are applying the perfume to it will last twice as long. Colognes contain less of the same compound and more fillers, while toilet water is just diluted cologne. The cost of most perfumes is determined by the amount of money that is spent in advertising and in-store marketing of the product.

WHAT MAKES TOILET TISSUES DIFFERENT?

The better brands and of course, the more expensive ones are made from purified wood pulp and skin softeners. The other products are only made from purified wood pulp and they do not go through any softening process and you should have no problem telling the difference. Colored toilet paper contains traces of metals that produce the different colors. Occasionally people with very sensitive skin may experience a reaction from the colored papers.

DO ACNE MEDICATIONS WORK?

Acne medications do not cure acne, they only provide a measure of control. Studies show that diet doesn't have much of an effect either. Keeping the face clean with soap and water seems to work almost as well as some of the medications. The preparations contain a chemical sponge which may contain sulfur and salicylic creams as the absorbent to possibly soak up the excess skin oils. The oils are actually more related to pimples than acne. One of the more common methods is to soak a cotton ball in alcohol and use that to cleanse the area.

HOW DO STOMACH COATING PREPARATIONS ACTUALLY WORK?

These preparations absorb large quantities of water and waste food materials in the stomach and upper small intestine. By doing this it allows the areas to "dry out" and protects the delicate stomach lining against any additional infection. These coating products contain purified clay, aluminum magnesium silicate, bismuth salts, and usually activated charcoal.

DOES COLA REALLY CONTROL NAUSEA AND VOMITING?

Nausea and vomiting can be controlled by medications called "antiemetics." These antiemetics, of which Emetrol is one of the most popular ones, control the "gag reflex" and are very effective. However, Coca-Cola syrup or almost any other cola syrup which contain sugar and phosphates are every bit as effective in most instances. Your pharmacist may be able to assist you in obtaining a cola syrup. Diet colas will not work since they do not contain sugar.

HOW DOES BAKING SODA REMOVE ODORS?

Sodium bicarbonate (baking soda) is an inorganic powder, which simply means that it is not produced from living matter and is sold in very fine particles with a high surface area. House odors are composed of organic oils that become stuck in the powder and neutralized as if taken into a sponge. When the oils remain in the soda they eventually become inactivated permanently.

HOW DO ELECTRIC AIR CLEANERS WORK?

The newer electric air cleaners draw the air over a series of electrically charged metal plates that attract dust and pollutants. The plates must be removed periodically and cleaned. Another type is the porous silicon plate which traps the particles like a magnet. This type of unit utilizes a blower motor to pass the air over the filters which need to be washed.

DO WINDSHIELD DEICERS REALLY WORK?

Most windshield deicers are made from alcohol and are overpriced products. They do, however, work fairly well depending on the thickness of the ice. If the ice is very thick it will take quite a while for the ice to melt. Never place hot water on your windshield, it may cause the glass to expand from the heat and then contract when it cools, cracking the windshield. Most deicers are similar to antifreeze. You can place a solution of homemade deicer in your window washer unit, just mix 1 part of any commercial antifreeze with 9 parts of 50/50 mixture of alcohol and water.

WHAT IS A PAINT PRIMER?

These are usually colorless and will cause paint to adhere to surfaces better. Colored primers hide a color that may bleed through. Primers may also be used to protect a metal surface from corrosion as an undercoat. Since many paints do not adhere well to a number of surfaces, primers are a necessity in many instances.

WHAT CAN I USE TO CLEAN SILVERSTONE AND TEFLON POTS?

For the most part these plastic coated pots are easy to keep clean, however, they do stain and may over time develop a buildup of grease and oil. If this occurs it will adversely affect the efficiency of the non-stick surface. To clean the surface, just mix 2 tablespoons of baking soda with ½cup of white vinegar in 1 cup of water and clean the pot by placing the ingredients into the pot, place the pot on the range and boil it for about 10 minutes. Wash the pot, then rub vegetable oil on the surface of the plastic coating to re-season it.

CAN I UNCLOG A DRAIN USING INGREDIENTS AROUND THE KITCHEN?

After trying a plumber's helper with no success, try the following method:

Remove all standing water so that you are able to pour the ingredients into the drain. First pour 1 cup of baking soda, 1 cup of table salt, and ½ cup of white vinegar into the clogged drain. These will start dissolving any organic matter and grease away immediately. Allow to stand for 5 minutes then flush 1-2 quarts of boiling water down the drain.

HOW DO YOU CLEAN A THERMOS BOTTLE?

The easiest way to eliminate the odors and stains is to fill the container with hot water and drop in a denture cleaning tablet, then allow it to stand overnight. Baking soda will also work, but not as well.

HOW DO YOU MAKE A CANDLE ALMOST DRIPLESS?

Prepare a solution of 2 tablespoons of salt per candle in just enough water to cover the candles. Allow the candles to soak in the saltwater solution for about 2-3 hours, then rinse them, let them dry, and wait at least 24 hours before you use them. The saltwater hardens the wax and allows the wax more time to burn cleaner reducing the chance of dripping on the tablecloth.

ALL CHOPSTICKS ARE NOT THE SAME

If you have ever eaten in a Japanese restaurant you will notice that the chopsticks are pointed. In a Chinese restaurant the chopsticks are blunt. Many restaurants will Americanize the chopsticks by placing a rubberband around them about ¼ of the way down from the top. This will hold them together and make them easier to handle.

WHAT IS AN EASY METHOD OF OVEN CLEANING

If you have an oven that is not equipped with a self-cleaning feature then just preheat the oven to 200°F.(93.3°C.) and turn it off. Place a small bowl with ½ cup of ammonia on the center shelf then close the oven and allow it to stand overnight. The next day open the oven and allow it to air for 30 minutes in a well ventilated kitchen then wipe up the mess with a warm, damp paper towel.

CHAPTER 27

Home and Garden Tips

MODERATION, A MUST

If you are going to paint cabinet doors, try rubbing a small amount of Vaseline on the hinges, it will make removing the paint easier.

THE DISAPPEARING ACT

If you are sure you will use up all the paint in a can, try punching a few holes near the rim you are removing the paint from. The paint that is wiped off the brush will go back into the can.

PAINT DROPS KEEP FALLING ON YOUR HEAD

If you are going to paint a ceiling, try cutting a tennis ball in half and placing a half on the brush to catch the drips.

NOT A SHOCKING EXPERIENCE

To remove a broken light bulb, turn off the electricity, then try placing ½ a raw potato or ½ a small apple into the broken base and screwing it out.

CALL SMOKY

If you have a charcoal filter in your rangehood it can be recharged by placing it in a 450°F. (232.2°C.) oven for 30 minutes after completely cleaning the frame. If there is any grease left on the frame it may catch on fire or smoke up the house.

DUNK IT, DIP IT

When painting anything, make sure you dip a 3 X 5 index card into the paint to make it easier to match it at a later date if needed.

GOING DOWN

Old nuts and bolts make excellent sinkers when you are going fishing.

STATIC ELECTRICITY

If a pin or needle will not penetrate an article, try rubbing it in your hair before trying it again.

I CAN SEE A RAINBOW

If you want to add color to a campfire, try soaking pinecones in a solution of ½ gallon of water and ½ pound of Borax.

REAL SHARPIE

An easy way to sharpen scissors is to fold a piece of aluminum foil 3-4 times, then cut through it several times.

RETURNING TO LIFE

Those dented up ping pong balls can be revived by placing them into very hot water for about 20 minutes. The air in the ball will expand enough to pop out the dents.

DON'T GET ZAPPED

Microwave doors may become misaligned, especially if you tend to lean on them occasionally. They will leak radiation and should be checked periodically with a small inexpensive detector that can be purchased in any hardware store.

FILLER UP

If you need to repair a hole in a piece of wood, try adding a small amount of instant coffee to the spackling or a thick paste made from a laundry starch and warm water.

BUY A NEW LID

If you lose a top knob to a saucepan lid, try placing a screw with the thread side up into the hole and then attach a cork on it.

SNOW SLIDE

If you want the snow to slide off your snow shovel with ease, all you have to do is save your empty butter wrappers and wipe the shovel off with them before using it.

SEEING THE LIGHT

Mirrors can be brightened by rubbing them with a cloth dampened with alcohol. Alcohol will remove a thin film of oil that is left from cleaning agents.

GETTING A NEW LEASE ON LIFE

If your flashlight batteries are becoming weak while on a camping trip, try placing them in the sunlight for 6-8 hours. This should give them some additional life.

DOING THE TWIST

Hair dryer cords can be kept neat using ponytail holders.

SPRINKLE, SPRINKLE, LITTLE SALT

Place salt on fireplace logs to reduce the soot in the house.

A SWEETER YULE

To preserve your Christmas tree for a few extra days, try adding a small amount of sugar or Pinesol to the water.

NATURAL FERTILIZERS

A number of foods make excellent fertilizers. Banana skins and egg shells are on top of the list. The minerals provided are for the most part not found in many fertilizers. Flat club soda also makes an excellent fertilizer. A sip or two occasionally will perk up their colors.

SMOOTHIE

When applying wallpaper, try using a paint roller instead of a sponge to smooth the paper out.

HOP SCOTCH

If you need to paint steps, try painting every other step, when those are dry go back and paint the rest. This will allow you continued access to the upstairs.

COLA WORKS GREAT TOO

If you are having a problem with a rusty nut or bolt, try placing a few drops of ammonia or hydrogen peroxide on it for 30 minutes.

MAY HAVE A NEGATIVE EFFECT

If you run out of salt or sand to deice your walkway, try using kitty litter. Keep the cat in the house!

FOR SAFETY'S SAKE

If you want to fireproof your Christmas tree, try spraying a mixture of 8 ounces boric acid in one gallon of water on the tree then allow to dry.

BE FIRM WITH YOUR GUTTERS

If you need to clean your gutters, try using an old fan belt. It has excellent flexibility, and is firm enough to do the job without scraping the paint off.

DON'T TREAD ON THEM

Linoleum or floor tiles are excellent for covering the tops of picnic tables. A piece of linoleum can also be used instead of contact paper on kitchen shelves. It will last longer and is easier to keep clean.

ELECTRICIAN'S TRICK

Electrical cords should be stored in cardboard tubes from rolls of paper towels. Then label them as to which appliance they go to.

GETTING ON THE RIGHT TRACK

Windows will slide more easily if you rub a bar of soap across the track occasionally.

RUST PREVENTION

If you place a few mothballs, a piece of chalk, or a piece of charcoal in your toolbox you will never have any rust on the tools.

STOP SMOKING
To reduce fireplace smoking, try placing a brick under each leg of the grate.

OUCH
Use a split piece of old garden hose to cover the blades of a saw when storing it, to be safe.

GOING DOWN?
If you need to use a ladder on soft earth, try placing a coffee can under each leg.

BIG BAGGIE
If you need to store furniture or chairs outdoors, place a large plastic bag over them.

GLUB, GLUB
When cutting flowers from your garden, be sure and cut them only in the late evening or early morning. Have a bucket of water with you and use very sharp shears. After you cut the flowers, place the stem under water and cut the stem again on the diagonal, the stem will then take in water and not air.

WEED-A-WAY
To remove unwanted grass from between sidewalk and driveway cracks, try using vinegar and salt. Place the solution in a spray bottle and squirt.

HOW DRY I AM
When transplanting, always use pre-moistened soil and peat moss to help retain the moisture.

A CLEAN LEAF IS A HAPPY LEAF
If you want your plant's leaves to shine, try placing a small amount of glycerin and water on them. Mix 1 tablespoon of glycerin to 1 quart of water. Another method is to just dip a cotton ball in milk or mineral oil and clean the leaves.

CLAY IS POROUS
Never place a clay pot on wooden furniture, water seeps through and can damage the wood.

HAPPY SEEDS
½gallon milk carton cut in half makes an excellent seed starter flat.

PLANT SAVER
If you are going on a long vacation and are unable to find someone to care for your plants, try placing a large container of water near your plants. Place pieces of yarn in the water and then lay the ends across the stalks of the plants. Capillary action will keep the plants in good shape until you return.

GETTING POTTED
If you are going to re-pot a plant, try placing a small coffee filter on the bottom of the pot to eliminate the soil from leaking out.

ROCKY ½
Be sure and place a ½ inch layer of gravel on the top of the soil in window boxes to prevent splattering when they are watered.

ESPECIALLY HARD ROCK ONES
Broken cassette tapes make excellent ties for plants.

HEAD FOR THE SWAP MEET
Old ice cube trays make excellent herb starters.

GETTING A LEG UP
Nylon stockings or pantyhose make excellent storage holders for storing bulbs during the winter. Air is able to circulate avoiding a problem with mold. Store in a cool dry location.

THE LIVING CUP
Styrofoam cups make excellent plant starters and are easy to break apart when you decide to plant the plant in the garden.

IT WON'T MAKE THE ICE GROW
A lawn seeder or fertilizer spreader make an ideal unit for scattering sand or salt on ice.

FILLER UP
If you have a small hole in a window screen, try using a number of layers of clear nail polish.

MR. CLEAN
If you place masking tape on the rim of a paint can before pouring the paint out, you can remove the tape later and the rim will be clean.

LUMPLESS PAINT
If you have lumps in your paint can, try cutting a piece of screen the size of the can and allowing it to settle to the bottom, it will carry the lumps to the bottom.

FOUR EYES
When painting ceilings, try wearing a pair of old plastic goggles.

PAM TO THE RESCUE
Squeaky door and cabinet hinges as well as sticky locks can be sprayed with a non-stick vegetable spray.

SAFETY FIRST
If you need to get a closer look at your roof or second story, try using a pair of binoculars instead of a ladder.

FINDING A REAL STUD
If you don't have a stud finder, try using a compass, holding it level with the floor and at a right angle to the wall. Then slowly move the compass along the surface of the wall, when the needle moves that's where you will find a stud.

HOW TO GET A RUN IN YOUR PANTYHOSE
Whenever you are using sandpaper to finish a wood surface, try placing an old nylon stocking over your hand and running it over the surface, the slightest rough spot will be found.

PEEK-A-BOO

To avoid getting locked out of your house, try placing an extra key in a plastic baggie and placing it under a rock in the garden or bury it behind a plant or tree.

DRIP, DRIP, DRIP

If you are worried about your water lines freezing just leave one of the taps running very slightly to avoid the problem. If you have a two story house, open one on the first floor.

DON'T PAINT YOUR PORES

Using a hand moisturizer when painting or doing other dirty chores, will prevent dirt and paint from seeping into your skin's pores making personal cleanup easier.

HANDY RULER

Remember a dollar bill is 6 inches long and almost 3 inches wide.

BUBBLE, BUBBLE, TOIL AND TROUBLE

Varnish never needs stirring. Stirring only creates air bubbles which may ruin a smooth finish.

ODE DE CEDAR CHEST

If you would like the original cedar odor from an old cedar chest, try rubbing the inner surface lightly with a fine sandpaper.

ALL-PURPOSE, OF COURSE

If you are painting old woodwork that has small holes that need patching, try filling the holes with flour and some of the paint, it will harden and will not be noticeable.

ARE YOUR DRAWERS A PROBLEM

If you are having problems with sticky drawers, try rubbing a candle along the tops of the runners.

A CHILLING SOLUTION

If you don't feel like cleaning a roller. place it in a plastic bag and place in the freezer. This will keep it moist and usable for a few days.

AND A LONNNNG EXTENSION CORD

If your pipes freeze and do not burst, try using a hair dryer to defrost them.

TRY TO KEEP IT TOGETHER

Lightweight materials that need to be glued together are easily held in place with spring clothespins.

SOFTENING THEM UP

When your paint brushes harden, try softening them by soaking them in full strength white vinegar, then cleaning them with a comb.

PAINT HOLDERS

Empty nail polish bottles make excellent holders for touch-up paints.

KEEPING GREASE IN ITS PLACE

If you have grease spots after removing old wallpaper, try applying a coat of clear varnish to the spots. The grease won't soak through to the new paper.

BALLOONING

If you are going to store a partially used can of paint, try placing a blown-up balloon the size of the space in the can. It will reduce the air in the can and keep the paint fresher longer.

SUN-DRYING YOUR BOTTOM

If you have a cane-bottomed chair that has loosened, try applying very hot water to the underside and allowing the chair to stand in direct sunlight until it dries.

A WASTE OF A COOL ONE

If you wish to "frost" a bathroom window, use a solution of 1 cup of "Lite" beer mixed in 4 tablespoons of Epsom salts. Paint the mixture on the window, it will wash off easily.

HOW DRY I AM

Bathroom fixtures should be painted with a special epoxy paint because of exposure to moisture.

A SHINING EXAMPLE

Enamel or oil paint can easily be removed from your hands with paste floor wax then washing with soap and water.

SKIN TIP

To prevent a skin forming on top of the paint, try placing a piece of waxed paper the size of the opening on top of the paint.

OIL YOUR BRISTLES

After you clean out a paint brush rub a few drops of vegetable oil into the bristles to keep them soft.

I WONDER WHERE THE YELLOW WENT

If you add 7-10 drops of black paint to each quart of white paint it will not yellow.

TILL YOU'RE OLD AND GRAY

If you "weather" wood before applying stain, the stain will last years longer.

DON'T CRACK-UP

To prevent plaster walls from cracking when driving a nail in for a picture hanger, try placing a small piece of tape over the spot before hammering in the nail.

CHAPTER 28

Stains Begone

GENERAL RULES TO REMOVE STAINS

Never wash any fabric before attempting to remove the stain. Washing in a detergent may actually set the stain and make it impossible to remove later.

Stains on washable fabrics should be treated as soon as possible. Remember, fresh stains will come out more easily than old ones. Non-washable items that normally go to the cleaners should be taken to the cleaners as soon as possible. Identify the stain for the dry cleaner. If you know what the stain is be sure and tell them.

LIGHTS ON

When trying to remove stains at home, make sure you do it on a clean, well-lighted work surface. Always use fresh clean rags or a towel.

RUST REMOVAL

Rust stains can be removed by wetting the areas with lemon juice, then sprinkle with a small amount of salt and allow to sit in direct sunlight for 30-45 minutes.

THAT BURNING SENSATION

A scorch can be removed by rubbing a raw onion on the scorched area and allowing the onion juice to soak in thoroughly for at least 2-3 hours before washing.

MAKE SURE IT'S CHILLED
Blood stains may be cleaned with club soda.

A SHINING EXAMPLE
To shine chrome fixtures, try rubbing them with newspaper while they are still damp. Baby oil and a soft cloth works well. Aluminum foil will also do the job.

A WORD TO THE WISE
If you are going to use a commercial stain removal substance, be sure and follow directions carefully.

TESTING, ONE, TWO
Always test a stain remover on an area of the fabric that will not show to be sure of the colorfastness of the fabric. Allow the product to stand on the area for at least 3-5 minutes before rinsing off. If there are any changes in the fabric's color, do not use.

HIDE THAT SPOT
When treating a spot, it should be placed face down on paper towel, then apply the stain remover to the underside of the garment, allowing the stain to be forced to the surface and not back through the fabric. The paper towel should be replaced a number of times if it is a tough stain to remove.

WHERE ART THOU COLOR
If you are going to use a bleach product, never use it on a colored garment. It is necessary to bleach the whole garment to avoid uneven color removal. If there is a change in color it will at least be uniform.

STAIN BEGONE
As soon as the stain is removed, launder immediately with your favorite laundry detergent. This will also remove the residues from the stain remover.

STAIN REMOVAL PRODUCTS
Prompt treatment is the key to stain removal, and it would be wise to have the supplies on hand at all times. The following list are some of the

more common ingredients needed for most stain removal, however, more natural stain and general cleaning preparations are recommended.

Bleaches	Miscellaneous Removers
Chlorine bleach	Ammonia
Fabric color remover	Rust stain remover
Non-chlorine, all fabric Bleach	White vinegar
Detergents	**Solvents**
Enzyme detergent	Dry cleaner spot remover
Enzyme presoaker	Nail polish remover
Liquid detergent	Rubbing alcohol
	Turpentine
Soaps	**Supplies**
Laundry detergent	Clean white cloths
White bar soap	Paper towels

Any of the above products that cannot be found at the supermarket will be found at any drug store.

> CAUTION
> Some stain removal materials are inflammable, while others are poison or toxic. Store them safely and use with care.

CHEMICAL ALERT
Keep stain removal supplies out of reach of children. They should be stored in closed containers with childproof lids and in a cool, dry location away from any food products.

SMELLS NICE TOO
Lemon extract will remove black scuff marks from shoes and luggage.

HARD ONE TO GET OUT
Stains from ball point pens can be removed with hair spray or milk.

READING THE WRITING
Read the labels on cleaning products and follow directions. Heed all label warnings and always try to store them in their original containers.

CONTAINER SMARTS

Empty and wash all containers immediately after using them. It is best to store stain removal supplies in glass or unchipped porcelain containers. Solvents will ruin plastic containers. Rusty containers should never be used.

Be careful, never allow chemicals near your face and especially your eyes. Wash any spilled chemicals off your hands as soon as possible.

WEAR A GAS MASK

Use chemicals that give off vapors in a well ventilated location, preferably outside. Try not to breathe the vapors.

POOOOF

Never use a solvent near an open fire or an electrical outlet.

YUM, YUM, FABRIC

Never add solvents directly into the washing machine. Always allow a solvent-treated fabric to dry before washing or placing it into the dryer.

A WITCH'S BREW

Never mix stain removal materials with each other, especially ammonia and chlorine bleach. If it is necessary to use both, make sure one is thoroughly rinsed out before adding the other.

RECIPES FOR SAFE CLEANING PRODUCTS

The following recipes are safe when mixed in the quantities indicated below. The mixing of other household chemicals may be dangerous.

» All-Purpose Household Cleaner
  Add 1 teaspoon of any liquid soap and 1 teaspoon of trisodium phosphate (TSP) to 1 quart of warm water.

  This is a very effective cleaner for many cleaning jobs including countertops and walls. However, try an area of the wall that will not show before using in case your walls are painted with a poor quality water-based flat paint.

» Chlorine Bleach
  Best to use a hydrogen peroxide-based bleach.

» Degreaser (engines, etc.)
  Best to use a water-based cleaner that is well diluted instead of

kerosene, turpentine, or a commercial engine degreaser. These are available in parts stores and the label should read "nonflammable," "non-toxic," or "store at temperatures above freezing." These will be water-based products and will do the job.

» Degreaser (kitchen, grill)
Add 2 tablespoons of TSP to 1 gallon of hot water or use a non-chlorinated scouring cleanser with a scouring or steel wool pad.

» Fabric Softener
Fabrics produced from natural fibers do not need fabric softeners only synthetics.

» Floor Cleaner
Vinyl Floors - Use ½ cup of white vinegar to 1 gallon of warm water.

» Wood Floors - May be damp mopped with a mild liquid soap.

» Furniture Polish
Mineral oil may be used, however, most wood surfaces may be cleaned with a damp cloth.

» Oven Cleaner
Mix 2 tablespoons of baking soda or TSP in 1 gallon of warm water and scrub with a very fine steel wool pad (0000). Rubber gloves should be worn and the area rinsed well. For difficult baked-on areas, try scrubbing with a pumice stone.

If all of the above fails, try using an oven cleaner that states "no caustic fumes" on the label.

» Glass Cleaner
Use a 2-3 cup spray bottle with ½ teaspoon of liquid soap, 3 tablespoons of white vinegar and 2 cups of water.

If the windows are very dirty, try using more liquid soap.

» Laundry Detergent
Use laundry soap in place of the detergents. Washing soda may be used in place of a softener. An alternate would be to use detergents with no added bleaches or softeners. Bleach should be used in moderation when needed.

» Mildew Remover
Scrub the area with baking soda or if very stubborn with TSP.

» Scouring Powder
Baking soda will work well in most instances.

» Toilet Bowl Cleaner
Use a non-chlorinated scouring powder and a stiff brush. To remove hard water deposits, pour white vinegar or a commercial citric

acid-based toilet bowl cleaner into the toilet and allow to sit for several hours or overnight before scrubbing.

> NOTE: Washing soda and TSP are caustic and should be kept out of the reach of children.

FABRIC ADVICE

It is best to know the fiber content in clothing items. If sewn in labels are to be removed a note should be made as to which item it was removed from.

» Any durable press or polyester fabric such as a Dacron, holds soil very well and especially stains. A dry cleaning solvent will work the best. If the stain remains after the first treatment, try once more. If the fabric has been washed or has been placed in a dryer, the stain may never come out.

» Never use chlorine bleach on silk, wool, or Spandex.

» Never try to remove a stain from leather, take it to a dry cleaners to send to an expert.

STAIN REMOVAL FROM WASHABLE FABRICS

A number of stains can be removed right in your washing machine. Laundry detergents that state that they contain enzymes will provide the best cleaning and stain removal. Enzyme presoak products provide extra cleaning and stain removal for fabrics that may have a more difficult stain.

An enzyme detergent or enzyme presoak product should be able to remove the following common stains:

Blood	Gravy	Body soils	Egg
Fruits	Milk	Chocolate	Grass
Cream soups	Baby formula	Puddings	Vegetables
Baby foods	Ice cream	Most food soils	

I WONDER WHERE THE YELLOW WENT

Yellowed fabrics can be restored and even old unknown stains may be removed by first soaking in an enzyme presoak product (Proctor & Gamble has excellent ones) such as Biz and then laundering.

CAN'T PERFORM MAGIC

Remember, even the best enzyme detergent or enzyme presoak product is not capable of removing all types of stains. A number of grease soils and highly colored stains may require special pretreatment before laundering. Since many stains require a variety of different soil removal treatments and techniques, it is important to identify a stain before trying to remove it. A number of stains may actually be set if the wrong method is used.

The following stains will usually be removed with the following recommended methods:

Stain	Method Of Removal
Beverage	Sponge the area with cold water or soak then sponge again. Launder with oxygen bleach and the hottest water that is safe for the fabric.
Blood	Soak the fabric in cold water as soon as possible. If the stain persists, soak in warm water with a presoak product before laundering. Try club soda.
Candle Wax	The surface wax should be removed with a dull knife. The item should then be placed stain face down on paper towels and then sponge the remaining stain with dry cleaning solvent. Allow to dry and then launder. If traces of color from the wax remains, try soaking it in Biz or an oxygen bleach before laundering again. If the color is still present, try laundering again using chlorine bleach, if the fabric is chlorine bleach safe.
Catsup Tomato Products	Remove excess with a dull knife, then soak in cold water then launder using the hottest water the fabric will stand.
Chewing Gum Rubber cement Adhesive tape	First apply ice to the stain to harden it. Remove excess stain material with a dull knife. Place the item face down on paper towels and sponge with a dry cleaning solvent.
Chocolate, Cocoa	Soak in cold water then launder with oxygen bleach using the hottest water the fabric will stand.

Stain	Method Of Removal
Coffee Tea	Best to soak in Biz or an oxygen bleach using the hottest water that is safe for the stained fabric then launder. If the stain persists, try laundering again using chlorine bleach if it is safe to do so.
Cosmetics	Dampen stain and rub gently with a white bar soap, then rinse well and launder.
Crayon	If there are only a few spots they can be treated the same as candle wax. If there are many items that are stained, first wash the items with hot water and laundry soap (e.g. Ivory Snow) and 1 cup of baking soda. If the spots remain, have the clothes dry cleaned.
Deodorants And Antiperspirants	Apply white vinegar, then rub and rinse. If the stain remains, try saturating the area with rubbing alcohol, rinse then soak in Biz or an oxygen bleach and launder. If the stain remains wash in chlorine bleach if safe for fabric.
Dye Transfer	If you have white fabrics that have picked up dye from a colored garment that "bled" try restoring the white by using a fabric color remover. Launder if any of the dye remains using chlorine bleach, if it is safe for the fabric.
Egg and Meat Juice	Remove excess with a dull knife then soak in cold water. Launder in oxygen bleach in very hot water.
Fabric Softeners	These stains usually result from accidental spills and can be removed by rubbing the area with a piece of cloth moistened with bar soap then launder.
Formula	Soak in warm water then launder with oxygen bleach and the hottest water that is safe for the fabric.
Fruit and Fruit Juices	Soak in cold water before laundering.
Grass	The green area should be sponged with denatured alcohol before washing in very hot water and oxygen bleach.

Stain	Method Of Removal
Grease Stains	The stained area should be placed face down on paper towels. Dry cleaning solvent should be placed on the back side of the stain and then brushed from the center of the stain to the outer edges using a clean white cloth. Moisten the stain with warm water and rub with a bar soap or a mild liquid detergent, then rinse and launder.
Gum	Rub with ice and carefully remove the gum with a dull knife before laundering.
Ink Stains	For removal of ball point stains, place the stain face down on paper towels and sponge the back of the stain with dry cleaning solvent. If there is some ink left, try rubbing the area with moistened bar soap, rinse and then launder. For any other type of ink stains, just try and remove the stain with a dampened cloth and bar soap, rinse and soak in Biz or an oxygen bleach using very hot water. If the stain won't come out, try using chlorine bleach, if the fabric is safe. Some permanent inks may never be removed.
Ink, Felt Tip	Rub the area with Fantastic or Mr. Clean, rinse and repeat if necessary. May be impossible to remove.
Iodine	Rinse the fabric from the underside with cool water, then soak in a solution of fabric color remover, rinse and then launder.
Lipstick	The stain should be placed face down on paper towels and then sponged with dry cleaning solvent replacing the paper towels frequently while the color is being removed. Moisten the stain with cool water and then rub with bar soap, rinse and launder.
Mildew	The fabric should be laundered using chlorine bleach if it is safe for the fabric. If not try soaking it in oxygen bleach and then laundering.
Milk	The fabric should be rinsed in cold water as soon as possible, then washed in cold water using a liquid detergent.

Stain	Method Of Removal
Mustard	Moisten stain with cool water, then rub with bar soap, rinse and launder using a chlorine bleach, if it is safe for the fabric. If not, soak in Biz or an oxygen detergent using very hot water, then launder. It may take several treatments to remove all of the stain.
Nail Polish	The fabric stain should be placed face down on paper towels then sponge the back of the stain frequently and repeat until the stain disappears then launder. Never use nail polish remover on fabric, best to have them dry cleaned.
Paint	Try to treat the stain while it is still wet. Latex, acrylic, and water based paints cannot be removed once they have dried. While they are wet, rinse in warm water to flush the paint out then launder. Oil-based paints can be removed with a solvent that is recommended on the paint can. If it does not give this information, try using turpentine, rinse and rub with bar soap, then launder.
Perspiration	Moisten the stain and rub with bar soap. Be gentle as perspiration may weaken some fibers, especially silk. Most fabrics should be presoaked in Biz or an enzyme detergent and then laundered in hot water and chlorine bleach, if the fabric is safe.
Perfume	Same as beverages.
Rust	Never use chlorine bleach on rust, apply a rust stain remover, rinse then launder. You can also use a fabric color remover and then launder or if the stain is really stubborn, try using 1 ounce of oxalic acid crystals (or straight warm rhubarb juice) dissolved in 1 gallon of water, mixed in a plastic container, then rinse and launder.
Scorch	Soak the fabric in a strong solution of Biz and an oxygen bleach using very hot water if safe for the fabric, then launder. If the scorch remains, it will be necessary to repeat the procedure using chlorine bleach, if the fabric will take it.

Stain	Method Of Removal
Shoe Polish	Try applying a mixture of 1 part rubbing alcohol and 2 parts of water for colored fabrics and only the straight alcohol for whites.
Suede	Rain spots can be removed by lightly rubbing the area with an emery board. If there are grease spots, try using white vinegar or club soda then blot out the stain. Afterwards brush with a suede brush.
Tar	The area should be rubbed with kerosene until all the tar is dissolved, then wash as usual. Test a small area first to be sure it is color fast.
Tobacco	Moisten the stain and rub with bar soap, rinse and then launder. If the stain persists, try soaking it in Biz or an oxygen detergent, then launder. As a last resort use chlorine bleach, if the fabric is safe.
Urine, Vomit Mucus	Soak the fabric in Biz or an enzyme detergent, launder using chlorine bleach, if safe for the fabric. If not use an oxygen bleach with a detergent.
Wine Soft Drinks	Soak the fabric with Biz or an oxygen bleach using very hot water then launder. Use chlorine bleach if need and the fabric is safe.

SOME NATURAL METHODS TO TRY FIRST

TOTALLY THRIFTY

If you wish to use less detergent and save money, try using slivers of old soaps placed in a sock with the neck tied. Place the sock into the washer and you will use less detergent.

SETTING IT PERMANENTLY

To colorfast a possible problem garment, try soaking the colored garment in cold, salty water for 30 minutes before laundering.

DON'T GET STUNG

After washing a piece of clothing with a zipper that has given you problems, try rubbing beeswax on the zipper to resolve the problem and remove any grime that has accumulated.

THE OLD BUBBLE MACHINE
Placing too much soap in the washing machine can cause problems. If this happens, just pour 2 tablespoons of white vinegar or a capful of fabric softener into the machine to neutralize some of the soap.

BEGONE OLD SOAP
When washing clothes, to be sure that all the soap has been removed, try adding 1 cup of white vinegar to the rinse cycle. The vinegar will dissolve the alkalinity in detergents as well as giving the clothes a pleasant fragrance.

THE GREEN, GREEN, GRASS OF HOME
Grass stains will be easily removed with toothpaste, scrub in with a toothbrush before washing. Another method is to rub the stain with molasses and allow to stand overnight, then wash with regular dish soap by itself. If all else fails, try methyl alcohol, but be sure the color is set, best to try an area that won't show first.

GREASELESS
Spic and Span placed in the washer is a great grease remover, ¼ cup is all that is needed.

WRINKLE REMOVER
To avoid ironing many different types of clothes, just remove them from the dryer the second it stops and fold or hang up immediately.

CATCH THAT COLOR
Washing colored material for the first time may be risky unless you wash it in Epsom salts. One gallon of water to 1 teaspoon is all that is needed. The material will not run.

THE DISAPPEARING ACT
An excellent spot remover can be made using 2 parts of water to 1 part rubbing alcohol.

A DIRTY JOB

To remove difficult dirt, such as collars, mix⅓cup of water with⅓cup of liquid detergent and⅓cup of ammonia. Place the ingredients in a spray bottle. Rubbing shampoo into the area may also work.

LINT MAGNET

To keep corduroy garments from retaining lint, turn them inside out when washing.

HAIRBALLS?

To avoid hairballs on acrylic sweaters, turn them inside out when washing them.

ONE OF THE TOUGHEST

Iodine stains can be removed using a mixture of baking soda and water. Allow to remain on for about 30 minutes rub with mild action.

USE ONLY THE UNSALTED

Butter or margarine will remove tar from clothing, just rub until it's gone. The butter is easily removed with any type of spray and wash product.

INKA-KA-DINKA-DOO

Rubbing alcohol or hair spray may remove a number of ink pen stains.

BEWARE OF A TIGHT FIT

If you wash slipcovers, be sure and replace them when they are still damp. They will fit better and will not need to be ironed.

BLOW DRYING

If sweater cuffs are stretched, dip them in hot water and dry with a hairdryer.

A SPOT OF TEA, PERHAPS

Tea stains on tablecloths can be removed with glycerin, try leaving it sit overnight in the solution before washing.

INTO THE FREEZER
Candle wax on tablecloths can be removed by freezing with ice cubes.

YUK
Lace doilies should be hand washed in sour milk for the best results.

HOLD THE SHAVING CREAM
If you have a problem with small burrs on sweaters, try using a disposable razor to remove them.

EASY DOES IT
If you are washing a woolen garment, be careful not to pull on it. Wool is very weak when wet. Lay the garment on a towel and roll it up and squeeze the excess water out.

NEUTRALIZER
If you have a difficult blood stain, try making a paste of meat tenderizer and cold water. Sponge on the area and allow to stand for 20-30 minutes. Rinse in cold water, then wash. Hydrogen peroxide may also work.

BATHING STUFFED ANIMALS
To clean stuffed animals that cannot be placed in the washer, just place them in a cloth bag and add baking soda, then shake.

POWDER ME
White flour will clean white gloves, just rub.

A SLIPPERY SUBJECT
Lipstick stains will clean out of clothes by using Vaseline.

A REVIVAL
If you shrink a woolen garment, try soaking it in a hair cream rinse. This will usually make it easy to stretch back into the original size. Another method is to dissolve 1 ounce of Borax in 1 teaspoon of hot water then add it to 1 gallon of warm water. Place the garment in, stretch back to shape then rinse it in 1 gallon of warm water with 2 tablespoons of white vinegar added.

BE STINGY, BE SMART
When you are doing a small wash load tear the fabric-softening sheet in half for the same results.

A SOLID FACT
To make your own spray starch, purchase 1 bottle of liquid starch concentrate and mix one part of liquid starch to 1 part of water, use a spray bottle.

BUTTON, BUTTON, WHO'S GOT THE BUTTON
If you lose buttons regularly from children's clothing, try sewing them on with dental floss.

TRUE GRIT
If your iron is sticking, try running it over a piece of paper with sprinkled salt on it.

WELL SEASONED CURTAINS
Water stained fabrics should be placed in salt water and soaked until the stain is gone.

BRING IN THE SUB
If you prefer not to use bleach, try substituting 3 tablespoons of hydrogen peroxide to the washload.

SAVE THE BUTTONS
Always remove buttons before discarding a garment. They may come in handy at a later date.

ATTRACTIVE SALT
Cleaning silk flowers is easy if you place them in a plastic bag with 2 tablespoons of salt and shake vigorously while holding on to the stems. Salt tends to attract the dust.

IRONING SMARTS
When ironing, always iron the fabrics that require a cool temperature first as the iron heats up.

DEW TELL

Mildew on shower curtains can be removed with a mixture of ½cup bleach, ½cup powdered detergent, and 1 gallon of water. To prolong the life of shower curtains add 1 cup of white vinegar to the final rinse.

MAKING COLORS FAST

To prevent jeans from fading (if you want to) soak the jeans in ½cup of white vinegar and 2 quarts of water for 1 hour before you wash them for the first time.

JEAN SMARTS

Blue jeans should only be washed in cold water then placed in a moderate heat dryer for only 10 minutes. Then they should be placed on a wooden hanger to continue drying.

DOLLAR SAVER

If you would like to save dollars on dry cleaning of woolen blankets, try washing them in a mild dishwasher soap on a very gently cycle then air fluff to dry.

NO ONE WILL EVER KNOW

If you scorch a garment, try removing the scorch with a cloth that has been dampened with vinegar. Only use a warm iron, not too hot. Cotton scorch marks tend to respond better to peroxide.

INSULATION

A sheet of aluminum foil placed underneath the ironing board cover will allow the heat to be retained for a longer period of time.

BUTTON, BUTTON

Always remember to place a small amount of clear nail polish in the center of every button on a new garment. This seals the threads and they will last longer.

A SHOCKING SITUATION

A pipecleaner dipped in white vinegar should be used to clean the holes in the iron after it is completely cool. Make sure it is unplugged.

IF YOU'RE IN A SPOT

Glass cleaner sometimes makes an excellent spot remover if you need something in a hurry. Make sure the fabric is colorfast.

BRIGHTEN-UP

If you want to whiten your whites, try adding a cup of dishwasher detergent to the washer. Even whitens sweat socks.

ANY PENCIL WILL DO

A sticky zipper will respond to a rubbing with a lead pencil. Does an excellent job of lubricating it.

A TEMPORARY SOLUTION

If a button comes off, try reattaching it with the wire from a twist tie.

DON'T SUCK YOUR THUMB

If you use a thimble to sew or sort papers, try wetting your finger before you place the thimble on. This creates a suction and holds the thimble on.

A SEALER

When you wash you sneakers, spray them with a spray starch to help them resist becoming soiled.

DIRTY BOTTOM

If the bottom of the iron gets dirty, just clean it with a steel wool soap pad. If you want to make it shiny again, just run a piece of waxed paper over it.

RUSTADE

Rust marks on clothing can be removed with lemon juice and a small amount of salt easily rubbed in and then allowed to sit in the sun for 2 hours.

A LITTLE BUBBLY

Red wine can be removed from a tablecloth by wetting the area with club soda and allowing it to stand for 20 minutes before washing.

AND AWAY WE GO
To dry the insides of shoes or sneakers, try placing the blower end of the vacuum hose inside.

A TRIPPER-UPPER
If you have problems with your shoelaces becoming undone, just dampen them before tying them.

A WORD OF CAUTION
Silk clothing should be hand washed using cool water with Ivory liquid soap. When you rinse, try adding a small amount of lanolin to help preserve the material. Always drip dry, never place the garment in the dryer, then iron using a soft piece of cloth over the garment.

SHAPE-UP, AND DON'T LOSE YOUR COLOR
Cold water should always be used in the rinse cycle to help the clothes retain their shape and color.

CHAPTER 29

Getting Fit and Staying Fit

METABOLISM, WHAT IS IT?

Metabolism is the process by which the body releases energy derived from nutrients. It is the sum of all chemical reactions of the body's cells. The cells produce the energy in the form of heat, or in muscle cells in the form of mechanical work.

The basic fuels are proteins, carbohydrates, and fats which are converted into glucose by the liver, then travel to the cells for chemical processing by way of the Krebs cycle (complex biochemical pathway) and turned into usable energy.

Metabolic rates vary from individual to individual dependent on a person's age, sex, body size, activity level or thyroid activity. Metabolism is first in line when the body distributes the energy it produces, the body must have energy to run the heart and vital organs before anything else. Physical activity energy is only available after the more important needs are met.

A common question asked physicians is how to increase the metabolic rate as we age. There is still no magic pill that has been invented that will raise the metabolic rate naturally. Recently, a number of supplement companies claim to have invented a number of different herbal combinations and special nutrients, but none have ever proved true in double-blind studies performed by a major university or testing laboratory.

Unfortunately for women, men tend to have a higher metabolic rate throughout their lives. This may be due to the male's greater percentage of lean tissue. The more muscle tissue a person has will also increase their metabolic rate.

The thyroid gland's level of activity has a direct influence on the basal metabolic rate. The thyroid secretes a hormone, thyroxin and the less it secretes, the lower the energy requirement for the running of the body.

The following is an example of the total energy output by a moderately active homemaker:

Energy for basal metabolism . . . . . 1,400 calories

Energy for moderate physical activity . 500 calories

Energy to burn 2,000 calories . . . . . 200 calories
2,100 calories total

When more calories are burned than are ingested weight loss will occur.

THE ENERGY BALANCE

Approximately 70% of all food consumed is utilized in keeping the essential life processes going, such as the heart pumping and the liver functioning. The other 30% is turned into "external energy" and used in conscious activities, such as walking, playing sports or working.

The actual energy value of foods are determined by their caloric content. A Kilocalorie is a measure of heat needed to raise the temperature of a liter of water one degree centigrade (a single calorie is a thousandth of a Kcal).

When we discuss energy balance the input/output theory of weight control usually comes up. This simply means if you burn more calories than you take in you will lose weight. This is a true statement, however, it is still the type of calories you consume that will ultimately determine your actual level of health.

EXERCISE

Exercise is a must for everyone, regardless of your age. The type of exercise you do should be one you enjoy doing and one you will continue for an extended period of time. Many people have the initial motivation and good intentions in starting a program but end

up doing exercise they don't enjoy and would never stick with.

It is not the intention of the following information to suggest one form of exercise over another, you need to choose the one that fits your lifestyle. The easiest for most people is walking and this chapter will provide you with guidelines for a walking program.

Before starting any exercise program it would be best to have a complete physical from your physician, not just a series of tests by a local athletic club. If you will be walking, swimming, jogging or any very active exercise, a treadmill stress test is a must. A resting cardiogram is a poor test in detecting early heart disease or how your heart will respond to the exertion of exercise.

BENEFITS OF EXERCISE

Cardiovascular System Exercise increases the efficiency of the cardiovascular system in several ways:

» The heart grows stronger and pumps more blood with each stroke, reducing the number of strokes necessary.

» It increases the number and size of your blood vessels as well as your total blood volume. Enhances oxygenation of your cells.

» It increases your body's maximal oxygen consumption by increasing the efficiency of the red blood cells. By doing this, it improves the overall condition of the body, especially the heart, lungs, and blood vessels.

» It improves the muscle tone of your blood vessels, changing them to strong and firm tissue, possibly reducing blood pressure.

» Lungs – Improves the efficiency of the lungs, making them capable of processing more air with less effort.

» Aging – Slows the aging process and physical deterioration that accompanies it.

» Stress – Helps you relax more easily and develop a better self-image. Relieves the tension and stress of daily living.

» Job – Allows you to get more work done at a lower fatigue level.

HEART RATE RESPONSE TO EXERCISE

Resting Heart Rate

The rate will vary widely from individual to individual and also within the individual from one observation to another. It is therefore meaningless to speak of a "normal heart rate." We may say that the average heart rate is 72 beats per minute, but cannot imply that a variation from this figure in either direction is borderline or abnormal.

To determine your own resting heart rate; first take your pulse, 3 times, either radial (side of wrist), or carotid (side of neck), and count for a total of 60 seconds, average the three figures to give you your resting pulse rate.

After 10 days of exercising, repeat the procedure to determine your new resting heart rate. If your new rate is lower than the first one, you are experiencing a positive training effect and are starting to get in condition.

FACTORS AFFECTING HEART RATE

» AGE
Resting heart rate at birth is approximately 130 beats per minute. It gradually decreases until the teens where it averages out to about 72 beats per minute.

» SEX
Resting heart rate in adult females is 5-10 beats faster than the average male.

» SIZE
Resting heart rate in animals vary inversely with the size of the species. A canary may have a heart rate of 1,000 beats per minute, while an elephant is only 25 beats per minute.

» POSTURE
A change from a sitting to a standing position may increase the heart rate 10-12 beats per minute.

» FOOD
The ingestion of food affects the resting heart rate as well as the exercising heart rate. Both rates are higher during digestion than in the pre- consumption period.

» EMOTIONS
Increases resting heart rate as well as exercising heart rate. It also tends to slow the recovery rate.

» ENVIRONMENT
An increase in ambient temperature causes an increase in the exercising heart rate.

» SMOKING
Even one cigarette will cause an increase in the resting heart rate.

AEROBICS AND FITNESS

The term "aerobics" refers to the type of metabolism utilizing oxygen in the production of energy. It relates to modes of training that are designed to improve the efficiency of the body's oxygen exchange system. Thus, delivering more oxygen to the cells while improving the efficiency of the cardiovascular system (heart, lungs, and blood vessels).

The degree to which the cardiovascular system becomes more efficient (and healthier) is dependent upon the total work performed by a particular exercise and its effect on the system.

By gradually increasing the amount and intensity of an exercise program, your fitness level will increase accordingly.

The following is a listing of the most realistic aerobic activities for the average person in their order of aerobic value. Remember, however, these are not recommended prior to a physical evaluation.

Exercise	Duration (Min.)	Times Per Week
Jogging 6 MPH	20	4
Bicycling 12 MPH	30	5
Swimming 25-50 YD/Min.	20	4
Walking 4 MPH (O Elev.)	30	5
Rowing Machine	20	5
Tennis (Singles)	45	4
Handball (Singles)	30	4
Skating (Ice Or Roller)	45	5
Racquetball (Singles)	25	4

FAST AND SLOW TWITCH MUSCLE FIBERS

Slow-Twitch Muscle Fibers

These muscle fibers are usually utilized first during a sport or exercise until the body determines the need for the "fast twitch muscles."

The following are facts that apply to the slow twitch muscle fibers:

» Aerobic type muscles, which must burn glucose in the presence of oxygen to produce needed energy.

» Used for long distance endurance, exercises, or sports.

» The number of slow-twitch muscles and the intensity of their movement is usually determined by heredity.

» The size and strength of the fibers can be improved with exercise.

» They are also capable of burning fatty acids which reduces the body's fat stores. The leg muscles of a long distance runner may contain up to 90% of the slow-twitch fibers.

Fast-Twitch Muscle Fibers

Activated when sudden bursts of energy are needed, such as in a "dash" or other fast movement.

The following are facts related to fast-twitch muscle fibers:

» These muscles are for the most part anaerobic and burn fuel without the presence of oxygen.

» The leg muscles in world-class tennis players may contain up to 70% fast-twitch muscle fibers.

» As with slow-twitch muscle fibers, the number of fast- twitch muscle fibers is controlled by heredity.

» With training the size of the fibers can be increased and provide faster response.

JUST FOR THE FUN OF IT:

SPECIAL EXERCISE CALORIE CHART	
Jumping on the bandwagon	200
Beating around the bush	75
Jogging your memory	125
Jumping to conclusions	100
Climbing the walls	150
Swallowing your pride	50
Passing the buck	25
Grasping at straws	75
Beating your own drum	100
Throwing your weight around	50-300
Dragging your heels	100
Pushing your luck	250
Making mountains out of molehills	500
Spinning your wheels	175
Flying off the handle	225
Hitting the nail on the head	50
Turning the other cheek	75
Wading through paperwork	300
Bending over backwards	75
Balancing the books	23
Beating your head against the wall	150
Running around in circles	350

SPECIAL EXERCISE CALORIE CHART	
Chewing nails	200
Eating crow	225
Fishing for compliments	50
Tooting your own horn	25
Climbing the ladder of success	75
Pulling out the stoppers	75
Adding fuel to the fire	150
Pouring salt on the wound	50

HOME FITNESS EQUIPMENT

» Rowing Machines

These are an all-around exerciser, involving the activity of numerous muscle groups. They are excellent for the legs, upper body, and arms. However, they are not recommended for persons who are not in condition. They also do not provide the best aerobic workout.

» Treadmills

An inexpensive method of exercising by either walking or jogging. Employs a moving belt which may be motorized. Most motorized models will allow you to adjust both the speed and elevation. The most frequent complaint is that they tend to become boring after a short period of time. Earphones with music or a TV to watch seems to solve the problem. Computerized models are best.

» Mini-Trampolines

A fun way to exercise indoors or out. They provide an inexpensive aerobic alternative to jogging. Can be used by almost any age group and can provide a fairly good workout if sufficient time is spent.

» Stationary Bike

(Ergometer) This by far the most popular piece of exercise equipment. It provides good aerobic training without the problems that may be caused by the continual pounding of jogging, especially for the unfit. Combining workouts on the rowing machine and the bicycle will provide a well-rounded exercise program.

The cost of the bicycle in most cases will determine the overall quality, ease of making adjustments, and the degree of comfort. Many of the less expensive models do not have adjustable handlebars which is a comfort feature. Computerized models tend to hold your interest better and give you feedback.

» Multi-Gyms

Usually expensive but competition has brought the prices down in recent years. Incorporates a multitude of different exercises into one unit which makes it handy for home use. Best to try out a unit before buying one, either in a store or a gym. Many of the more unusual units will not hold your interest too long. Be wary of some of the new ones advertised on TV unless you can send it back if you don't like it. Watching a person on TV using the unit is different from you using it in many instances.

FITNESS FACTS

INJURIES AND PREVENTION

» Blisters
Blisters are a common problem, particularly when breaking in a new pair of shoes. Prevention begins with properly fitting shoes and socks that stay in place and do not creep or bunch up. When blisters occur, puncture the edge of the blister with a sterile needle, drain the fluid and apply a topical antiseptic solution, then cover with a bandaid.

» Arch Conditions
Painful arches are usually the result of improperly fitting shoes, overweight, excessive activity on a hard surface, faulty posture, or fatigue. The symptoms are divided into three stages:

1. Slight soreness in the arch area.

2. A chronic inflammatory condition that includes soreness, redness, swelling, and a slightly visible drop in the arch. See your physician.

3. A completely fallen arch, accompanied by extreme pain, immobility, and deformity. See your physician.

Caring for arch disorders should include the following suggestions: Shoes should be properly fitted. Whirlpool hydrotherapy. Ultrasound deep therapy. Arch orthotics. Exercise program, if detected early.

» Sprained Ankle
Generally caused by a lateral or medial twist that results in external and internal joint derangement. Sprains may be classified as first, second or third degree. The majority of ankle sprains are the inversion type, resulting in the stretching or tearing of the lateral ligaments. In handling a sprained ankle, these first aid measures should be followed:

1. The ankle should be compressed with an ice pack and then elevated for 24 hours.

2. If swelling is more than minor or if a fracture is suspected, a physician should be contacted for x- rays.

3. With severe ankle sprains, continue cold applications through the second or even the third day.

4. Apply heat therapy if swelling has subsided by the third day.

» Knee Problem

Although the knee is the largest joint in the body, it is extremely vulnerable to traumatic injuries because of poor bony arrangement. Knee injuries fall mainly into four categories: compression injuries, lateral and medial sprains, torsion injuries, and hyperextending injuries. See your physician.

» Lower Back Pain

Lower back pain is usually the result of poor flexibility, weak abdominal and back muscles, and poor posture. Stretching and strengthening exercises, with a conscious effort to improve posture, improves the problem in the majority of cases.

» Muscle Soreness

Engagement in activities different from those to which one is normally accustomed often produces muscular soreness. In some cases pain has been reported to occur during the latter stages of high-intensity exercise. More often, it occurs as many as 24-48 hours after the activity. This type of pain is less understood than immediate pain, but it most commonly occurs after an endurance workout. Reports show that the delayed pain to be caused by alterations in the muscle connective tissue (stretching of the elastic components). Recovery from this type of soreness can be enhanced by warm compresses or warm baths, accompanied by light exercise to help prevent adhesions during the healing process.

» Side Stitch

A side stitch usually develops in untrained individuals during aerobic activities. Manifested in mild to agonizing pain in the area of the lower rib cage and may be on either side of the body, but usually the right side. There are several explanations for this occurrence, none of which is completely satisfactory. It is probable that all of the following factors contribute to the discomfort:

1. Accumulation of metabolic wastes (lactic acid) in the diaphragm.

2. Severe shaking of the abdominal contents, which causes pain in the supporting structures.

3. Formation of gas in the ascending colon.

4. Reduced blood flow to the affected area due to the rerouting of blood to other areas.

Relief is usually accelerated by the application of pressure on the affected side while the exercise is continued. If the pain becomes too severe, the alternative is to terminate the workout and rest.

» Achilles Tendon Rupture
This usually follows a history of chronic inflammation and gradual degeneration caused by microtears. When the rupture occurs, the individual complains of a sudden snap or that something has hit them in the lower leg. Severe pain, point tenderness, swelling, and discoloration are usually associated with the trauma. Signs of a rupture are obvious indentations at the tendon site or a positive Thompson Test.

» Achilles Tendon Bursitis and Tendinitis
Bursitis and tendinitis usually occur from the overstretching of the Achilles tendon, resulting in a constant inflammatory condition of the Achilles bursar. The condition is chronic, developing gradually over a period of time, and takes many days to heal. An excellent therapeutic approach is ultrasound (electrical heat transfer). Activity should be held to a minimum, and heel lifts should be placed in the shoe to relieve the Achilles tendon of as much tension as possible. After a workout, the tendon should be cooled with ice packs or ice massage. Gradual heel cord stretching is recommended.

» Shin Splints
These are characterized by pain and irritation in the shin region of the leg, and are usually attributed to an inflammation localized mostly in the tendon of the tibialis posterior and the flexor digitorum longus. Inflammation in this area is often a mystery. Speculation of cause include: faulty posture alignment, falling arches, muscle fatigue, overuse stress, body chemical imbalance or a lack of reciprocal muscle coordination between the anterior and posterior aspects of the leg. All these factors singly or in combination, may contribute to shin splints.

While rest is the only sure cure, limited exercise is possible with an ice massage and a leg wrap. Prevention of shin splints can be accomplished by using proper footwear, running on soft surfaces, stretching, and strengthening the surrounding musculature.

WALKING NECESSARY TO WALK OFF COMMON SNACK FOODS
The following will provide the walking distance required to work off the calories of a number of common snacks and foods.

Snack	Serving	Calories	Miles
That Little Sandwich			
Ham	½ oz. w/butter	335	5.8
Cheese	½ oz. w/mayo	400	6.7

Snack	Serving	Calories	Miles
Peanut butter and jelly	2 tablespoon peanut butter	425	7.4
Hamburger on bun	3" patty	445	8.0
Tortilla w/cheese	1 piece cheese	190	3.2
Beverages			
Carbonated soft drink	12 oz. can	160	2.7
Chocolate malt	12 oz. glass	485	8.2
Ice cream soda	12 oz. glass	290	4.7
Milk/whole	8 oz.	8 oz. glass	160
Tea or Coffee (w/ 2 tablespoon cream and 2 teaspoon sugar)	8 oz. cup	90	1.6
Beer	12 oz. can	165	2.8
Highball (w/ginger ale)	8 oz. glass	140	2.8
Martini	average	160	2.7
Manhattan	average	175	3.0
Sherry	4 oz. glass	120	2.1
Scotch, Bourbon	1 shot glass	80	1.3
Fruits			
Apple	1 medium	90	1.5
Orange	1 medium	85	1.4
Pear	1 medium	100	1.7
Grapes	25 medium	70	1.2
Banana	1-6" long	100	1.7
Date	1 medium	27	0.4
Salted Nuts			
Almonds	10	130	2.2
Pecans	10	150	2.5
Cashews	10	60	1.0
Walnuts	1 oz. shelled	175	2.9
Peanuts	1 medium	6	0.1
Candies			
Chocolate bar	1¼ oz.	185	3.1
Bonbon	1 piece	90	1.5

Snack	Serving	Calories	Miles
Caramel	1 piece3/4"	40	0.7
Jelly Bean	1 average	6	0.1
Desserts			
Doughnut	1 medium	140	2.3
Ice Cream Cone	1 scoop	190	3.2
Ice Cream Sundae	2 scoops with toppings	400	6.7
Cake (layer)	1 average piece	290	4.8
Pie (fruit),⅙pie	340	5.7	
Cream puff	4" diameter	365	6.1
Brownie	1 medium	300	5.0
Graham cracker	1	42	0.7
Miscellaneous			
Potato Chips	10 medium	115	11.8
Popcorn (w/o butter) modest amount for popcorn	1 cup	60	1.0
1 tablespoon butter	1 tablespoon	85	1.4
Saltine Crackers	4	50	0.8
Midnight Ice Box Raid			
Piece of Chicken	1 oz.	105	1.8
Chicken Leg	1 average	85	1.5
Hard Boiled Egg	1 medium	80	1.3
Jello	½ cup	70	1.2

Exercise and Calories

The purpose of the following information is to create an awareness of which foods are higher in calories and the number of minutes needed to work off the foods. The information is based on a 150-pound adult.

	Calories	Walking 3 mph	Bicycling 15 mph	Jogging 5 mph
Bread and Cereals				
Raisin Bran (½ cup)	73	15	7	10
Special K (½ cup)	30	6	3	4
Cornbread (2" square)	107	21	10	13
White bread (1 slice)	62	12	6	8

	Calories	Walking 3 mph	Bicycling 15 mph	Jogging 5 mph
Whole wheat bread (1 slice)	56	11	5	7
Donut	1 medium	150	30	14
Blueberry muffin	110	22	10	14
Cinnamon bun	158	32	14	20
Pancake (medium)	110	22	10	14
Waffle (medium)	165	34	15	20
White Rice (¾ cup)	103	21	9	13
Egg noodles (¼ cup)	70	14	6	9
Air popcorn (1 cup)	54	11	5	7
Popcorn oil (1 cup)	82	16	7	10
Graham cracker (1)	30	6	3	4
Macaroni/cheese (1 cup)	530	110	57	70
Spaghetti/meat balls (1 cup)	310	68	35	46
Taco (beef, 3 oz.)	195	45	22	30
Saltine cracker (1)	14	3	1	2
Meats				
Bacon/cooked (2 slices)	100	20	8	12
Beef hash (½ cup)	230	46	21	29
Regular hamburger	225	45	20	28
Lean hamburger	140	28	13	18
Beef pot pie (medium)	445	90	40	55
Chili//meat (5 oz.)	185	39	17	25
Hot dog (plain)	125	25	12	16
Ham slice (2 oz.)	185	35	18	22
Lamb (3 oz.)	300	60	25	35
Meat loaf (3 oz.)	285	61	30	40
Chicken TV dinner	542	108	49	68
Bologna (1 slice)	66	13	6	8
Sausage (1 regular link)	95	19	9	12
T-bone steak (4 oz.)	175	35	22	22
Fish/Shellfish				
Deviled crab (1)	188	38	17	24
Baked flounder (3 oz.)	200	41	19	28
Broiled lobster (1 medium)	310	62	28	39
Fried oysters (7)	235	48	22	30
Broiled salmon (4 oz.)	200	45	23	29
Fried shrimp (3 oz.)	205	40	16	22

	Calories	Walking 3 mph	Bicycling 15 mph	Jogging 5 mph
Tuna/water (4 oz.)	127	26	11	16
Tuna/oil (4 oz.)	205	49	19	29
Anchovies (3)	21	4	2	3
Poultry				
Fried chicken (½)	460	100	45	58
Fried chicken leg	150	30	13	19
Roast turkey (1 slice)	80	16	8	10
Nuts				
Almonds (14)	90	18	8	11
Cashews (7)	84	17	8	11
Peanuts (1 tablespoon)	86	18	8	11
Peanut butter (1 tablespoon)	88	19	9	12
Pecans (6)	100	21	9	13
Sunflower seeds (3 oz.)	502	110	50	65
Prepared Salads				
Coleslaw (1 cup)	79	21	10	15
Carrot/raisin (3 oz.)	150	31	14	19
Macaroni salad (1 cup)	335	67	30	41
Potato salad (1 cup)	200	40	19	24
Salad dressing (1 tablespoon)	71	14	6	9
Dairy Products				
Milk/whole (1 cup)	160	32	14	20
Milk/non-fat (1 cup)	105	21	10	13
Buttermilk (1 cup)	88	18	8	11
American cheese (1 oz.)	110	21	10	14
Cottage cheese (½ cup)	120	29	14	18
Ice cream (½ cup)	225	41	20	27
Yogurt/non-fat (1 cup)	122	24	11	15
Soups				
Cream of mushroom (1 cup)	150	30	14	19
Chicken noodle (1 cup)	60	12	7	8
Split pea (1 cup)	120	24	11	15
Tomato (1 cup)	73	15	7	9
Sweet Treats				
Chocolate bar	215	44	20	27
Milky Way (regular)	285	57	26	35
Chocolate chip cookies (3)	150	30	14	19

	Calories	Walking 3 mph	Bicycling 15 mph	Jogging 5 mph
Banana Split (2 scoop)	600	120	54	74
Éclair	300	60	27	37
Apple pie (1 slice)	390	79	35	48
Brownie (1 square)	150	30	14	19
Beverages				
Beer (12 oz.)	230	42	20	53
Lite beer (12 oz.)	100	20	9	13
Brandy (3 ½ oz.)	75	15	7	9
Martini (3 ½ oz.)	140	28	13	18
Wine (4 oz.)	110	22	10	14
Champagne (4 oz.)	85	17	8	10
Milkshake (8 oz.)	420	85	38	55
Eggnog (8 oz.)	235	48	22	29
Cola soda (12 oz.)	155	31	14	21
Restaurant Sandwiches				
Club (3 slices of bread)	600	120	59	78
Egg salad	280	56	25	35
Tuna salad	280	56	25	35
Bacon/Lettuce/Tomato	285	58	27	39
Vegetables				
Asparagus (½ cup)	17	3	2	3
Broccoli (½ cup)	26	5	3	3
Cabbage (½ cup)	20	4	2	3
Sweet corn (1 ear)	96	20	9	12
Sweet pickle (1 large)	140	30	14	18
Baked potato (1 medium)	100	20	10	14
French fries (10 average)	140	30	12	17
Mashed potatoes (½ cup)	90	16	7	10
Potato chips (small bag)	115	22	10	14
Fruits				
Apple (medium)	50	10	4	6
Banana (1 small)	88	17	8	12
Cantaloupe (¼ melon)	45	9	4	6
Grapefruit (½ small)	40	8	4	5
Orange (1 small)	50	10	5	7
Watermelon (1 cup)	45.	9	4	6

CHAPTER 30

Vitamins, Antioxidants, & More

WHY WE NEED SUPPLEMENTS

How often have we heard that if we eat a balanced diet with all the food groups in the right proportions, we will be able to obtain all the necessary nutrients our bodies need. We are all tired of listening to this statement from professionals who have a limited education in the field of nutrition or have been brainwashed to really believe this is possible.

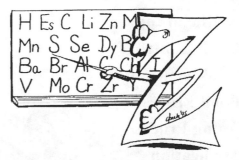

The above statement was, however, true 70 years ago before we were bombarded with more environmental insults than our bodies know how to cope with. The following information will alert you to all the reasons why we cannot possibly remain in optimum health without taking supplements.

Every week on television there seems to be another show telling of another problem with our food supply. We are not inspecting our foods properly due to the lack of inspectors. Our fruits and vegetables are grown in soils that are nutrient-deficient due to the depletion of trace minerals from over-farming.

Our products are stored too long before they are sold and many of the natural nutrients are processed out before they reach us. No one will ever convince me that they are enriching our foods sufficiently to provide us with anywhere near the original levels.

We use preservatives and coloring agents that are borderline chemical agents and many have been proven to cause cancer in laboratory animals. We don't have time to eat a balanced diet and we kill off all the enzymes with heat before we eat the food.

Then we take a supplement that has probably lost a percentage of its potency and has a low level of "biologic activity" to save a few dollars. Many supplement products are just not active enough and cannot provide you with the level of nutrients you buy them for.

The following information will give you some insight into the "real" world of nutrition and the many factors that relate to your obtaining the level of nutrients from the foods you purchase. It will also provide some additional information regarding the need for supplementation in relation to a variety of lifestyle factors.

Loss Of Nutrient Availability In Foods

Depleted Soil Minerals

Artificial Ingredients

Birth Control Pills

Cooking Methods

Food Processing

Aging Process

Medication

Smoking

Sickness

Dieting

Some Reasons For Nutrient Losses

Unbalanced Diets

Lack of Enzymes

Bioavailability

Sugar Intake

Restaurants

Fertilizers

Alcohol

Storage

Smog

Stress

Temperature changes take their toll on nutrients. The following is an example of why these losses occur:

» FRIED FOODS
The higher the temperature and the longer the food is fried, the higher the nutrient loss. Most frying temperatures reach 375°F. (190.6°C.) making an oil such as Canola oil best for frying because of its high smoke point of over 400°F. (204.4°C.) This allows Canola oil to be used for a longer period of time before breaking down and smoking.

» CANNED FOODS
Vitamin and mineral potency losses occur mainly from cooking and the sterilization process, which can involve temperatures of 240°F. (115.6°C.) or higher for up to 30 minutes.

» FROZEN FOODS
It will depend on whether these foods were cooked before being frozen. This determines the level of nutrient loss from processing. In many instances the higher quality foods and better appearing foods are sold fresh, while lower quality ones are usually processed for frozen foods.

» DEHYDRATED FOODS
If these are processed using a high quality product, the nutritional content for the most part will be retained. However, many companies choose to use lower quality goods since they cannot be distinguished from the quality ones. The most commonly used method of dehydrating foods uses temperatures of 300°F. (148.9°C.) or higher. Air dehydrating takes too long.

» DAIRY PRODUCTS
The pasteurization process takes its toll on nutrients. Many vitamins either lose their potency or are totally destroyed. When dairy products are homogenized, the process is designed to break down the normal-sized fat particles and may allow the formation of an enzyme called "xanthane oxidase." Studies performed in Canada stated that this enzyme may enter the bloodstream and destroy specific chemicals that would ordinarily provide protection for the smaller coronary arteries.

» REFINING OUT AND REPLACING NUTRIENTS
Bread is a good example, many nutrients are processed out and only a few replaced. Vitamin D is added to milk and almost all breakfast cereals are fortified unless they contain the whole grain. Vitamin C and calcium are added to numerous products.

> NOTE: White and wheat flours (not the 100% or whole grain type) may lose up to 90% of their vitamin E potency during processing. Cereal products, especially rice, may lose up to 70% of their vitamin E.

» CANNED AND PACKAGED PRODUCTS

The length of time on the shelf of a supermarket as well as possible warehousing time may result in reduced potencies of many vitamins and minerals.

» FRUITS AND VEGETABLES

Frequently these are picked before they are fully ripened, then allowed to ripen while being transported to the supermarket. Produce departments tend to cut a number of fruits into smaller, more salable pieces. This causes more of their surface to be exposed to the effects of air and light. Oxidation takes place more rapidly, thus reducing their nutrient content.

» ROTATION OF FOODS

When bringing home any food it should be dated and rotated. This is one of the more frequent mistakes most people make. Nutrients are only potent for a period of time which varies with every product.

» WAREHOUSING

Most supermarket foods are warehoused before being shipped to the market. The time they are delayed will have a lot to do with the ultimate level of nutrients.

» RESTAURANTS

To save money restaurants purchase in large quantities, possibly resulting in long storage times before the food is served. Most fast food restaurants avoid this problem since they serve a great number of people.

» MEAL PLANNING

Too few people plan their meals in advance. This results in poor combinations of foods, leading to inadequate vitamin and mineral intake.

> NOTE: In a recent study it was found that some oranges from supermarkets were found to contain no vitamin C content, while a fresh picked one contains approximately 80 mg. This due to a number of factors previously mentioned.

Tests have shown that a potato which has been in storage for up to 4-6 months will lose at least 50% of its vitamin C content. The nutritional information panels on foods now deduct 25% of the nutrient value of that food to allow for storage, effects of light, type of packaging material, transportation times, processing, preservation chemicals, and cooking.

» SOIL PROBLEM

Only the minerals that are crucial to crop growth are replaced back into the soil, these usually only include: phosphorus, potassium, and nitrates. Selenium, a trace mineral may vary by a factor of 200 in soils in the continental United States. You never know how much selenium you are really getting from the foods that should contain an adequate amount. Wheat is a good example and may contain from 50 mcg. to 800 mcg. depending on where it is grown.

Two other important minerals, chromium and zinc, are also critically deficient in the soil. The problem is significant and is presently under study by the USDA.

» SMOKING AND VITAMIN C

Recent studies have shown that smokers require approximately 40% more vitamin C than non-smokers to achieve adequate blood levels. Every cigarette may reduce bodily stores by about 30 mg., which means that a pack of cigarettes requires at least a 600 mg. increase in vitamin C intake.

» SMOG

All major cities in the United States have some form of chemical air pollution. This pollution will effect your lungs' capacity to deliver oxygen efficiently to the cells of the body. The antioxidant vitamins A, C, E, selenium, the mineral OptiZinc, and proanthocyanidin have proved to be effective in combating some of the effects of chemical pollution.

» SMOKE

The smoke from cigarettes, cigars, and pipes all effect the oxygen-carrying efficiency of your red blood cells. Smoke contains carbon monoxide which may compete for the site on the red blood cell that should be always carrying oxygen. This is one reason why smokers are short-winded, a percentage of their red blood cells are carrying carbon monoxide instead of the needed oxygen.

» DAIRY PRODUCT INTOLERANCE

The mechanism to produce the enzyme to break-down lactase loses it efficiency over time in many people. This may lead to a reduction of available calcium by not eating dairy products. Dark green leafy vegetables will help supply calcium and a new product "Lactaid" will assist the body in breaking down lactase.

» HORMONAL CHANGES
Aging and hormonal changes may lead to an increase in the loss of calcium and supplementation, especially of calcium, should be considered.

» Vitamin B_6 absorption is effected by the hydrazines in mushrooms. If you are taking birth control pills, it may be best to only consume mushrooms occasionally.

» Boiling any food for more than 5-10 minutes will destroy 100% of the vitamin B and C content.

» Make sure you cook all fish, shellfish, Brussels sprouts, and red cabbage. They contain thiaminase, a chemical which may destroy the B vitamins in these foods. Cooking inactivates the thiaminase, however, that will also kill the B vitamins.

» The tannins in teas and red wines may interfere with the utilization of iron, thiamin and B_{12}. Moderation is the key word. Iron absorption can be also be affected by coffee consumption and may leach magnesium out of the body. Vitamin C is required to assist in the metabolism of iron. If it is not present in adequate amounts, less than 30% of the ingested iron will be utilized by the body.

» Studies have shown that PABA may retard or even aid in returning original hair color.

» The American Medical Society cited studies that revealed eating excessive amounts of foods that are high in vitamin A, such as: liver, carrots, and cantaloupe, may result in headaches and nausea.

GETTING THE MOST

» Calcium supplements are best absorbed when taken with meals, since the calcium likes the acid medium. Calcium is also best utilized by the bones when boron is present. The better sources of boron may be found in prunes, raisins, almonds, peanuts, dates, and honey. Studies have also shown that if you consume a small amount of sugar the absorption rate will improve.

» A good laxative would be to take one teaspoon of crystalline vitamin C when you first awake with 8oz. of water. This will usually result in a bowel movement within 30 minutes.

» Studies show that Caucasian men and African-American women lose calcium stores at a faster pace than the rest of the population after age 30. For Caucasian women it begins at age 18. African-American men do not seem to have the problem.

» Vitamins A, D, E and K are best absorbed in the intestines when a small amount of fat is present. If you are taking a vitamin E supplement as a single supplement it would be best to take it with a small amount of 2% milk.

» When taking a vitamin C supplement, remember that if it isn't time-released, your body is only capable of metabolizing about 250 mg. per hour. A 500 mg. supplement in a non-time release is all that should be taken.

» Vitamin supplements will maintain their freshness longer if stored in the refrigerator. Most will maintain a good level of potency for about 2 years.

» Aspirin tends to reduce the effectiveness of vitamin C.

» Vitamin A is important for a healthy immune system as well as assisting the body in the retention of vitamin C and zinc metabolism.

» Americans spent $4.2 billion on nutritional supplements in 1997.

HIGH PROTEIN INTAKE = DANGER

Can shorten life expectancy, increase the risk of cancer, deplete calcium from bones, can cause fluid imbalances, may stress and damage the liver and kidneys, cause a hazard to premature infants, one cause of obesity, and will increase the need for vitamin B_6.

Studies are being done relating low vitamin D levels to breast cancer. Areas of the country with low sunlight levels seem to have a higher incidence of breast cancer.

Beta-carotene which assists the body to produce vitamin A is only available from plants while the actual vitamin A is only available from animal sources.

VITAMIN ROBBERS

The following information will provide information regarding some of the environmental factors, drugs, and everyday product use that can significantly affect the potency and availability of many nutrients. The awareness of these factors should assist you in making choices regarding your supplement program.

Vitamin/Mineral	Robber
Vitamin A	Mineral oil, air pollution/smog, fertilizer nitrates, antacids, corticosteroids.
Vitamin D	Anti-convulsive drugs (dilantin), consumption, alcohol, stressful situations, oral contraceptives, mineral oil, antacids, oral contraceptives, alcohol.
Thiamin B₁	Antibiotics, excess heat/cooking, sugar
Riboflavin B₂	Antibiotics, exposure to light, diuretics, reserpine.
Niacin	Excessive heat, alcohol, most illnesses reduce intestinal absorption, nitrites and nitrates, penicillin.
PABA	Sulfa drugs.
Pantothenic Acid	Methyl bromide insecticide (fumigant for foods).
Pyradoxine B₆	Aging causes levels to decline after 50, steroids, hormones, hydralazine (hypertension drug), excessive heat, food processing, corticosteroids, hydralazine.
Folic Acid	Oral contraceptives, stress situations, vitamin C deficiency.
Vitamin B₁₂	Prolonged iron deficiency, stress, oral contraceptives.
Biotin	Excess heat, antibiotics, sulfa drugs, avid in raw egg white, oral contraceptives.
Calcium	Antacids, aspirin, corticosteroids, diuretics, lidocaine.
Choline	Sugar consumption, alcohol.
Inositol	Antibiotics.
Magnesium	Thiazides, alcohol, diuretics.
Vitamin C	Overexertion, fatigue, stress, aspirin, smoking, alcohol, corticosteroids, antihistamines, fluoride, oral contraceptives, barbiturates.
Vitamin E	Oral contraceptives, food processing, rancid fats, mineral oil.
Vitamin K	Antibiotics, mineral oil, radiation, anticoagulants, phenobarbital, alcohol.

NEW SUPPLEMENTS OF THE 90'S

PHYTOCHEMICALS

These chemical extracts from fruits and vegetables are becoming the latest fad in prevention. Basically, they are the biologically active, non-nutritive substances, found in plants that give them their color, flavor, odor, and provide them with their natural defense system against diseases. Simply put, these are not nutrients, nor vitamins or minerals, just chemical compounds that exist in fruits and vegetables. Their new name in many publications is "Nutraceuticals." They have been known to exist for years, but never received much press or attention until recent studies started linking them to cancer prevention in laboratory animals.

Studies on phytochemicals are presently being conducted by numerous agencies and universities including The National Cancer Society and The National Academy of Science. Phytochemicals are presently showing results in animals, arresting cancer in all stages of cellular development. Exactly which phytochemicals will be beneficial to humans and in what types of cancer are questions that will take years to answer.

We have always known that whole grains, fruits and vegetables should be consumed in adequate amounts on a daily basis for optimum health, and that cancer was not as prevalent in the early part of the century as it is today. The possible explanation is that our grandparents ate a healthier diet with more unprocessed foods and more fruits and vegetables. The naturally occurring compounds in these foods provided a degree of "natural" protection.

Cancer has only become more prevalent since the 1940's when we learned how to process foods, can them, use chemicals more efficiently in our foods and heat them until almost all the nutrients were either lost or biochemically altered. Phytochemicals may, however, be one answer to reducing the incidence of cancer.

One very important factor is that phytochemicals are not destroyed by cooking or processing to any great degree. The problem is that we just don't eat enough of them. If that is the case then we should consider taking a "Nutraceutical" supplement or any supplement that contains these phytochemicals or phytoextracts.

There are over 100,000 phytochemicals and the more sophisticated our analysis equipment becomes over time, we will probably identify even more. The following list provides the most current 1998 information obtainable on the more potent and important of these extractions. All information has been taken from laboratory animal testing only.

Phytochemicals In Fruits, Vegetables, and Herbs	
Food	**Phytochemical**
Broccoli, Cauliflower, Brussels sprouts, Kale, Turnips	*Sulforaphane* Activates enzyme that aids in turnips removing carcinogens from the body. *Dithiolthiones* Triggers production of enzymes that may block carcinogens from damaging DNA. The phytochemicals have shown special cancer fighting benefits by inhibiting cancer of the breast tumors in laboratory animals. Cooking methods such as microwaving and steaming increase the availability of the phytochemical. Broccoli has 40 phytochemicals.
Sweet potatoes, Yams, Artichokes, Red Grapes, Red Wine, Strawberries	*Flavinoids/Polyphenols* Attaches to cancer cells and stops hormones from attaching. May reduce the risk of cancer by attaching to free radicals and flushing them out of the body. This may also reduce the risk of cardiovascular diseases. This phytochemical is a part of the red wine/lower heart disease factor in France. However, it would be wise to avoid the red wine and consume the foods until additional studies are more conclusive. Recommendations are 1/3 cup per day.
Cabbage, Turnips, Dark green leafy vegetables	*Indoles* Studies show that they reduce risk of breast cancer. Tends to improve immune system function and may protect against cancer by allowing the body to eliminate toxins more easily. Stimulates the production of an enzyme that may make estrogen less effective
Soy, Dried beans, Mung bean sprouts	*Genistein* Cuts off the blood supply to tumor cells by retarding their capillary growth. This phytochemical is called a "phytoestrogen" and may offer protection against breast cancer, osteoporosis, heart disease, and most female hormone associated problems. Additional phytochemicals found in soybeans may help reduce blood cholesterol levels and slow replication of cancer cells. Three 4-oz servings of tofu or three cups of soy milk daily is recommended.

| Phytochemicals In Fruits, Vegetables, and Herbs ||
Food	Phytochemical
Chili peppers	*Capsaicin* Stops toxic molecules from attaching to DNA. An anti-inflammatory substance that prevents carcinogens from attaching to DNA and discourages the growth and replication of cancer cells. Other potential uses are in killing bacteria that may cause stomach ulcers and as a treatment for bronchitis and colds. Eat in moderation as red chili peppers tend to stimulate gastric acid
Citrus fruit	*Limonene* Activates enzyme that disposes of carcinogens. The active substance d-limonene has been shown to offer protection against breast cancer in laboratory animals. It also increases the production of additional enzymes that may assist the immune system in disposing of carcinogens. Future studies may also show that this phytochemical will actually reduce plaque in arteries. The pulpier the product, the better. Recommendations are 16-24 ounces of pulpy orange juice daily or 3-4 pieces of citrus fruit. Orange juice has 59 known phytochemicals.
Apples Fruits	*Caffeic Acid* Increases the solubility of toxins so they can be flushed from the body. *Ferulic Acid* Binds to nitrates in stomach.
Grapes, Strawberries, Rasperries	*Ellagic Acid* May prevent carcinogens from entering DNA.
Garlic, Onions, Leeks	*Allylic Sulfide* Detoxifies carcinogens.
Chives	*Allium Compounds* Slows reproduction of carcinogens
Grains, especially Rye, Wheat, Rice, Sesame Seeds, and Peanuts	*Phytic Acid* Binds to iron

| Phytochemicals In Fruits, Vegetables, and Herbs ||
Food	Phytochemical
Tomatoes, Green Peppers	*P-Coumaric and Chlorgenic Acids* Kills cancer-forming substances in their formation stages. This group contains over 10,000 phytochemicals.
Carrots, Seaweed, Squash, Peaches, Red, yellow, dark-green vegetables.	*Alpha-Carotene/Beta-Carotene* Fights free radicals which may invade the DNA causing an abnormal cell to be produced. Tends to improve vitamin A effectiveness and improves immune system responses as well as decreasing the risk of lung cancer in laboratory mice. Carrots should be cleaned thoroughly and left unpeeled to preserve the phytochemicals. Recommendation is 1-2 carrots or one cup of seaweed daily.
Licorice root	*Glycyrrhizin and Triterpenoids* Has disease-fighting properties. Still under investigation. Increases the effectiveness of the immune system and tends to slow the rate at which cancer cells replicate. Also useful in treating gastrointestinal problems and ulcers. Contains antibacterial properties and helps fight tooth decay and gingivitis. Prevents breast cancer in laboratory animals by activating the production of liver enzymes, reducing the level of tumor-promoting estrogens. Persons with high blood pressure should not eat licorice. Anise, a licorice flavoring, does not contain the phytochemical; only licorice root does.
Green tea Black tea (not herbal teas)	*Polyphenol Catechins and Theaflavin* Studies are ongoing regarding cancer-fighting abilities. May have a tendency to increase fat metabolism as well as increasing the effectiveness of the immune system and lowering cholesterol. The phenols have been found in recent studies to protect tissues from oxidation. Tea must be brewed for at least 5-10 minutes to get maximum catechin content. Excessive consumption may cause stomach upsets and provide a large dose of caffeine. Moderation is the key.
Rosemary	*Carnasol* An antioxidant that tends to reduce the development of certain types of tumors and may protect fats in the body from oxidizing. May be used freely on salads or other foods.

| Phytochemicals In Fruits, Vegetables, and Herbs ||
Food	Phytochemical
Flaxseed	*Ligans* Antioxidant of which flaxseed is the precursor. Flaxseed contains elements that are capable of producing ligans, a potent antioxidant. It also contains Omega-3 fatty acids which may have anti-cancer properties. Recommendations are to use ground, fortified flaxseed with B_6 and zinc added. Daily dose is 1 tablespoon of grain or 1 teaspoon of oil.
Red Grapefruit, Tomatoes, Watermelon, Apricots	*Lycopene* An antioxidant May decrease the risk of colon and bladder cancer in laboratory mice as well as reducing the risk of heart disease. Protects DNA and cells against damage from free radicals. Fruits should be eaten uncooked and as fresh as possible. One cup daily is recommended.
Yellow Squash, Spinach, Collard, Mustard, Turnip greens	*Lutein/Zeaxanthin* Slows growth of cancer cells. Reduces the risk of lung cancer
Cranberry Juice	*Anthocyanins* May prevent and cure urinary tract problems. It is best to use unsweetened cranberry juice in water or tea. Two 8-oz glasses per day is the recommendation.
Ginger root	*Gingerol* Relieves motion sickness. Has anti-inflammatory properties and may relieve symptoms of headaches. One-half teaspoon of powdered root or 1 teaspoon of fresh ginger daily. Tea can be made by simmering several slices in 2-3 cups of water for 8-10 minutes then strain.
Horseradish, Cabbage, Turnips	*Phenethyl Isothiocyanates* Tends to reduce tumor growth.
Kidney , Chickpeas, Soybeans, Lentils	*Saponins* Slows the growth of cancer cells and may even prevent them from replicating.

| Phytochemicals In Fruits, Vegetables, and Herbs ||
Food	Phytochemical
Basil, Carrots, Parsley, Mint, Carraway Seeds, Citrus Fruits, Cabbage	*Monoterpenes* May interfere with the replication of cancer cells.

Nutraceuticals, at present, are regulated by the FDA as dietary supplements only and are not classified as drugs. They are extractions from natural foods, to date have had no definitive extensive studies completed, and all claims made for them as mentioned above are still speculative. Studies that have been reported have all been on laboratory animals. Hopefully, more human studies will be forthcoming in the very near future.

Claims made for products that offer cancer protection and cure should be viewed with caution. Products that contain herbal or botanical ingredients should indicate the part of the plant the product was produced from. Be sure labels list all the ingredients that are present in significant amounts.

A future statement that may appear on these products may read; "This food product is not intended to diagnose, treat, cure or prevent any disease." Phytochemicals in the future will be transferred to different foods and produce foods that will be called "functional foods." The Functional Foods For Health project is presently underway at the University of Illinois.

Phyto-Fortified Foods (FFH) will be the new wave of the future.

PROANTHOCYANIDIN (PAC)

A relatively new antioxidant that may be purchased under a brand name (Pycnogenol) or by its generic name (proanthocyanidin) has only recently appeared in many products. It is a natural plant product, originally extracted from the bark of pine trees. However, it is now being extracted from grape seeds as well as pine bark. The substance is found in many natural foods, however, it is relatively expensive to extract from most of them.

Proanthocyanidin is stated to be 20 times more powerful than vitamin C and 50 times more powerful than vitamin E. It also, may have the ability to protect a number of antioxidants from being destroyed before they are able to perform their functions or be utilized by the cell.

PAC is water soluble and has the ability to be absorbed and utilized by the cell very shortly after ingestion. PAC remains in the body for three days circulating in body fluids and is gradually eliminated. If taken regularly, cells will acquire a saturation level which provides a continuum of beneficial antioxidant activity.

PAC is one of the most efficient free radical scavengers known. It has the unique ability to actually adhere to collagen (connective tissue) fibers and ward off the potential damage that might be done by circulating free radicals. This function may be the emphasis of future studies that relate to aging of the skin and joint diseases, such as arthritis.

DHEA (dehydroepiandrosterone)

This a naturally occurring hormone which may enhance the efficiency of the immune system. It is normally produced by the adrenal gland and is a component of a number of hormones, such as; testosterone, progesterone, estrogen, and corticosterone.

As we age the blood levels of DHEA decline and studies are being done to determine if this decline may speed up the aging process. It has been used successfully to increase libido in persons that have experienced a lowering of their sex drive as related to aging. Many of the degenerative effects of aging may be slowed with the supplementation of this as we age.

Studies, however, are not conclusive at this time to actually prescribe a dosage that would be beneficial for a specific problem. DHEA has been banned by the government until more studies are done. However, herbal products are being sold that companies claim to be the precursor of DHEA. These herbal products are for the most part derived from the Mexican Yam (Dioscorea villosa) roots. Also called diosgenin and can be converted to DHEA in the body.

High dosages when given to rats have caused liver damage.

SHARK CARTILAGE

Studies are continuing in all major countries regarding the use of shark cartilage and the prevention or treatment of cancer. Most studies are finding that there is an ingredient that seems to reduce the growth of tumors. The following results have been taken from a small study of only 21 patients and should be viewed in that context: 61% had a reduction in tumor size. 87% stated that they had improved their quality of life and 100% of prostate cancer patients had a lower PSA level

When claims are made it is best to obtain a copy of the study and review it before taking this or any new product for an extended period of time.

CAROTENOIDS

Fruits and vegetables contain over 500 carotenoids. Carotenoids are a pigment that give these foods their colors. About 10% of the carotenoids will convert to vitamin A and provide 25% of the bodies usable vitamin A. Studies are continuing and the future may show that carotenoids are more effective when taken together as a potent antioxidant.

Beta-carotene may not be the "magic bullet" to slow down or stop a cancer cell from replicating, however, a combination of carotenoids may provide the protection we are hoping for. One of the more interesting findings is that carotenoids improve communications between pre-malignant cells and normal cells. Tumor growth is slowed when they receive regulating signals from the normal cells.

Animal studies have shown that when a combination of carotenoids were given there was a decrease in the number of cancer cells.

MAJOR CAROTENOIDS

Major Carotenoids		
Carotenoid	**Food Source**	**Possible Benefit**
Alpha Carotene	Carrots	Activity of vitamin A decreased the risk of lung cancer and slowed the growth of cancerous cells in mice as well as increasing immune system response.
Beta-Carotene	Broccoli, Cantaloupe, Carrots	Same response as alpha-otene, with the additional decrease of colon, bladder, and skin cancers in mice.
Beta- cryptoxanthin	Mangos, Oranges, Papayas, Tangerines	Vitamin A activity.

Major Carotenoids		
Carotenoid	**Food Source**	**Possible Benefit**
Canthaxanthin	Natural food color added to jellies, Jams, Soft drinks, and Tomato sauce	Found to slow skin cancer in mice as well as slowing the growth of cancer cells and improving immune response in mice.
Lutein	Broccoli, Dark green leafy vegetables	Decreased the risk of lung cancer in mice.
Lycopene	Tomatoes, Tomato products	Decreased the risk of colon and bladder cancer and slowed the replication of cancer cells in mice.
Zeaxanthin	Cress leaf, Swiss chard, Okra, Beet greens.	May prevent macular degeneration. Blocks peroxide free radicals.

CO-ENZYME Q_{10} (ubiquinone)

Ubiquinone$_{10}$ is not a vitamin and can be produced by the body from two proteins tyrosine and mevalonate. Ubiquinone$_{10}$ is necessary for the cell to produce energy and has proved to be an active antioxidant in reducing free radical production. A number of factors may reduce the available Ubiquinone$_{10}$ in the body causing lower energy levels. Dietary sources of the nutrients needed to produce Ubiquinone$_{10}$ are lean meats, nuts, vegetables, and grains.

Studies have shown that if levels of Ubiquinone$_{10}$ are low (below 25% of normal levels) cells cannot produce enough energy to live and cells will start to die until the level increases. The elderly, malnourished, and chronically ill have lower levels of Ubiquinone$_{10}$ and may need to be supplemented. However, if a sufficient supply is always available energy levels are maintained.

Ubiquinone$_{10}$ may also be active in keeping the immune system healthy and at optimum efficiency.

ANTIOXIDANT ENZYMES

» Superoxide Dismutase (SOD)
One of the first lines of defense the body has from free radicals is from a substance called SOD. SOD is a natural antioxidant that keeps the free radicals under control and eliminates them. SOD always has

a partner called "catalase" which helps ry away some of the debris when SOD reacts with a free radical. The most dangerous element of the debris is hydrogen peroxide which if left alone will create additional more destructive free radicals.

This partnership is one of the most effective free radical eliminators in our bodies. A deficiency of SOD can reduce the body's effectiveness in fighting free radicals and increases the risk and severity of a number of diseases such as arthritis, bursitis, and gout.

» Glutathione Peroxidase (GP)
The main constituents of this antioxidant enzyme is the amino acid glutathione and the mineral selenium. One of selenium's main functions in the body is to become a component of the glutathione peroxidase enzyme.

The key role of GP in the body is to protect the lipids in the cells, walls from being destroyed by a group of free radicals known as lipid peroxides. Studies are being done to determine the significance of the cell damage by peroxides (when adequate GP is not present) in relation to diseases such as: heart disease, premature aging, cancer, liver and pancreas damage, and skin disorders.

» Methionine Reductase (MR)
This antioxidant enzyme has been effective in neutralizing another free radical called a hydroxyl radical. These are formed by the reactions involving heavy metals and other free radicals. Hydroxy radicals are also formed by the exposure of the body to x-rays and radiation. MR plays a significant role in the destruction and neutralization of these free radicals, especially the ones formed by athletes or during strenuous exercise periods.

Hydroxy radicals are a by product of fat metabolism which occurs after the depletion of our bohydrate stores. An athlete who can keep a high level of MR during a strenuous exercise period or sport may be able to improve their performance.

CHLORELLA

Chlorella is derived from freshwater algae and is one of the newest green algae products. It has 50 times the chlorophyll content of alfalfa and scientists estimate it has survived for approximately 2.5 billion years. Studies have concluded that the longevity of chlorella is due to the strength of its hard cell wall and unique DNA repair mechanism.

Only recently has science discovered a method of breaking down the hard cell wall and be able to produce it as a health food. At present, chlorella is the fastest-selling health food product in Japan and is used as both a dietary supplement and for medicinal purposes. Chlorella has a high protein content, approximately 60% compared to soybeans' 30% making it an excellent non-meat protein source.

Chlorella contains over 20 vitamins and minerals and is an excellent source of vitamin B_{12}, especially for vegetarians. Chlorella is far superior to spirulina in all categories. Studies are surfacing showing that chlorophyll has been related to improved metabolism, tissue growth (wound healing), and lowering cholesterol levels. Additional studies are ongoing relating to cancer prevention since chlorella may stimulate the immune system to produce macrophages which kill abnormal cells. At present, all studies regarding cancer and chlorella are being conducted in Japan.

CHAPTER 31

The Quick Cuisine Dilemma

FAST FOODS, THE GOOD AND THE BAD

Fast food restaurants over the past 5 years have had to make a number of changes and are now offering a number of low-fat alternatives to their usual fare of high-calorie, high-fat foods. The level of education and media information that has been released has had an impact and raised the public's level of health consciousness.

IT'S THE REAL THING, OR IS IT?

If you are going to Arby's to get a "real" roast beef sandwich you are in for a surprise. According to Arby's, the roast beef is just processed ground beef, water, salt, and sodium phosphate. It is lower in cholesterol and fat than "real" roast beef or the average hamburger making it still a good choice for fast food fare. Arby's also has an excellent roasted chicken sandwich.

SALT SHAKE?

Most thick shakes contain so many additives that are derived from sodium that they contain more sodium than an order of french fries.

SLOP ON THE CHOCOLATE FAT

When they dip a soft-serve ice cream product into a vat of chocolate coating, it is actually a high-fat product made from oils that have a very low melting point.

YUM, YUM, FRIED CHICKEN FAT

When the skin and special coatings are consumed on your fried chicken, the product ends up providing you with more fat and calories than a regular hamburger.

GEE, WE GOT FOOLED AGAIN, SO WHAT'S NEW

The fast food restaurants are now advertising that they do not use any animal product to fry in. However, what they neglect to mention is that some are using tropical oils such as coconut and palm oils which are both high in saturated fat. Also, some chains are pre-frying their fries to reduce cooking time. The pre-frying may be done in high saturated fat oils.

NUMERO UNO FRENCH FRIES

The number one fast food restaurant french fry is made by the In-N-Out Burger restaurant chain. They are never fried twice and always cut up fresh and fried immediately.

THE GOOD IS OUT, THE BAD IS BACK

McDonald's removed the Mclean hamburger which had only 350 calories and 12 grams of fat and replaced it with the Arch Deluxe hamburger which contains 570 calories and 31 grams of fat. Taco Bell removed the Border Light Taco from its menu which had only 140 calories and 5 grams of fat and replaced it with the Big Border Taco which has 290 calories and 17 grams of fat.

WELL SHIVER MY TIMBERS

If you are ordering a fried fish sandwich, be aware that the coating and frying oil make the sandwich a 50% fat meal. Might as well eat a burger.

HAR, HAR, HAR
Baked fish is available at Long John Silvers, a reduction of over 200 calories over fried fish. Even the sodium content is in an acceptable range of 361 mg. instead of the usual 1200 mg.

THIS WILL MAKE YOU POP-UP
Make sure you use a "lite" dressing and the shrimp salad at Jack-In-The-Box will only have 115 calories and 8% fat.

ONE FATTY CHICKEN
If you think you are getting a low-fat meal by ordering the Burger King chicken sandwich, think again. It contains 42 grams of fat and can be compared to eating a pint of regular ice cream in one sitting.

THE ROASTED CHICKEN INVASION
» Boston Chicken
½ chicken with skin contains 650 calories and 9.2 teaspoons of fat.

» Kenny Rogers Roasters
½ chicken with skin contains 750 calories and 8.7 teaspoons of fat.

» Kentucky Fried Chicken
½ chicken with skin contains 670 calories and 9.0 teaspoons of fat.

There isn't enough difference to really make an intelligent choice. Kenny Rogers Roasters in my opinion has the best flavored product and the best side dishes as long as they are kept fresh.

GREAT BUNS
Fast food restaurants are finally getting more health conscious and offering multi-grain buns which are an excellent source of fiber.

ALL OF ME, WHY NOT TAKE ALL OF ME
When you see an advertisement that reads "100% pure beef" and your biting down on unusually chewy material it might be almost any part of the beef. Legally, bone, gristle, fat, and almost any other part of the animal can be ground up and used in a number of processed meat products. It is sometimes referred to as "edible offal."

GOOD GOING JR.

If you go to Carl's Jr. you may see a number of small red hearts next to an item. They have a few sandwiches that are actually approved by the American Heart Association.

A small order of McDonald's Chicken McNuggets (6) have 21.3 grams of fat, 36.5% of which is saturated.

Common Fast Food Meal				
Food	Cal.	Chol.	Sodium	Fat
Hamburger on a bun	550	80mg.	800mg.	57%
Regular Fries	250	10mg.	115mg.	52%
Thick Shake	350	31mg.	210mg.	8%
Apple Pie	260	13mg.	427mg.	21%
Total	1,410	134mg.	1,552mg.	no % given

HOLD THE BAD STUFF

When ordering in a fast food restaurant always order your food "special order" so that you can tell them that you do not want the special sauce (fat), ketchup (sugar), mayonnaise (fat), and pickles (salt).

EASILY BEATS THE BURGERS

Pizza is the most popular fast food in America (44,000 units) and pepperoni is the number one topping. In Japan the favorite pizza topping is tuna and scallops.

STUFF IT?

The new "stuffed pizza crusts" add 13-23 grams of fat to the pizza and an additional 400-500 calories.

FAT CITY

If you really want a high-fat meal, try l's Jr.s Double Western Cheeseburger. This one is on top of all charts with over 1,000 calories and 63 grams of fat, half of which is saturated. If you want to double the fat just add a thickshake and a large order of fries.

SALAD FAT?

If you think that a salad is a better meal try adding one packet of ranch dressing to a McDonald's Chef's Salad, it will have more fat than a Big Mac.

HEALTHY CRUST OR UNHEALTHY CRUST?
Nutritionally, pizza may or may not be reasonably healthy. Some restaurants use flour that is not "enriched" since it is the cheaper product.

IT'S A HOLY CATASTROPHE
In 1997 we ate over 11 billion doughnuts. 90% of Americans eat doughnuts on a regular weekly basis.

KEEPING YOUR DIOLOGIST BUSY
Between McDonald's, Burger King, and Wendy's, they sell almost 4 million pounds of french fries daily that contain a total of 1 million pounds of saturated fat.

HIGH-FAT SALAD?
One of the worst salads found at a fast food restaurant was the Taco Bell Taco Salad containing 838 calories and 55 grams of fat, 16 grams of which is saturated.

THE UNINFORMED LEADING THE ADULT
In over 83% of American families, kids make the decision as to which fast food restaurant to go to. The deciding factor is the toy promotion.

WHO'S RUNNING THE SHOW?
Over 2 million children every day eat in a fast food restaurant. In most cases they are given the right to choose what food they will order and usually order whatever has a prize in it, which are all high fat meals. The sad part is that the adults will allow a six year old to determine what is healthy and not healthy for them. In 85% of families the children even choose the restaurant.

THE ADULT'S FAVORITE
The most popular fast food chain with the adults is Burger King. Burger King's Weight Watcher's Fettucini Broiled Chicken, however, is 33% fat by calories.

ADDING THEIR OWN TOUCH

If you are curious about additives in fast foods you might send away for the list of ingredients in the fast foods. You may be surprised at the number of additives such as MSG in chicken and roast beef seasonings, yellow dyes in shakes, soft ice cream, chicken nuggets, hot cakes, and sundae toppings, etc., etc.

Rating The Fast Foods	
Food	**Best Restaurant**
1. Pizza	Fasolini's, Las Vegas, NV
2. Rotisserie Chicken Kenny	Rogers Roasters
3. Roast Beef Sandwich	Roy Rogers
4. Hamburger (single)	In-N-Out Burgers
5. French fries	In-N-Out Burgers
6. Baked Fish Sandwich	Long John Silver's
7. Chicken Sandwich (grilled)	McDonald's

GREATEST PIZZA IN AMERICA

Having traveled extensively and tasted thousands of pizza's, the finest pizza has got to be a Fasolini's pizza. The pizza is completely hand made with an array of seasonings that are a secret, producing a pizza sauce that is second to none. This is a true gourmet pizza. To order call (702)877-0071 and ask for Josie or Jim Fasolini.

REASONABLE FAST FOOD CHOICES

Food	Calories	Teaspoons of Fat
Burger King		
Plain Bagel	270	1.0
Chef's Salad	178	1.9
Garden Salad	95	1.3
Side Salad	25	0.0
Tater Tenders	213	2.6
l's Jr.		
Chicken Salad	200	1.8
Hamburger, Plain	320	3.2

Food	Calories	Teaspoons of Fat
Domino's Pizza		
Cheese Pizza (2 lg. slices)	375	2.3
Ham Pizza (2 lg. slices)	417	2.5
Hardee's		
Chicken Fiesta Salad	280	3.4
Chicken Stix	210	2.0
Fried Chicken Leg (no skin)	120	1.1
Garden Salad	210	3.2
Grilled Chicken Sandwich	310	2.0
Roast Beef Sandwich (reg.)	310	2.7
Jack In The Box		
Chicken Fajita Pita	292	1.8
Hamburger, Plain	265	2.5
Hash Browns	115	1.6
Taco	190	2.5
Kentucky Fried Chicken		
Baked	133	0.4
Chicken Little Sandwich	169	2.3
Cole Slaw	119	1.5
Corn on the Cob	175	0.7
Long John Silver's		
Catfish Fillet (1 pc.)	180	2.5
Chicken Plank	110	1.4
Chicken, Baked	140	0.9
Clam Chowder Soup (w/cod)	140	1.4
Cod, Baked	130	0.0
Hushpuppies	70	0.5
Rice Pilaf	250	0.7
Seafood Salad	270	1.6
Vegetables	120	1.4
McDonald's		
Apple Bran Muffin	190	0.0
Chunky Chicken Salad	140	0.8

Food	Calories	Teaspoons of Fat
Garden Salad	110	1.5
Hamburger, Plain	260	2.2
Hashbrown Potatoes	130	1.7
Subway		
Ham Sandwich	360	2.5
Roast Beef Sandwich	375	2.5
Turkey Sandwich	357	2.3
Taco Bell		
Pintos and Cheese	190	2.0
Chicken Taco, Soft	210	2.3
Steak Taco, Soft	218	2.5
Taco	183	2.5
Tostada	243	2.5
Wendy's		
Chili	220	1.6
Garden Salad	102	1.1
Grilled Chicken Sandwich	340	3.0
Jr. Cheeseburger	310	3.0
Jr. Hamburger	260	2.1

Almost everyday fast food restaurants are changing their menus, many of these changes are low-calorie and low-fat. Send for their up-to-date nutritional information brochure or ask for one at any restaurant.

If you would like a copy of the list of ingredients in your favorite fast food, just write to the restaurant chain listed below:

Arby's
Ten Piedmont Ctr.
3495 Piedmont Rd. NE
Atlanta, GA 30305

Burger Chef
College Park Pyramids
P.O. Box 927
Indianapolis, IN 46206

Hardee's
1233 N. Church St
Rocky Mount, NC 27801

Burger King
P.O. Box 520783
General Mail Facility
Miami, FL 33152

Church's Fried Chicken
P.O. Box BH001
San Antonio, TX 78284

Jack In The Box
Foodmaker Inc
9330 Balboa Ave.
San Diego, CA 92123

Kentucky Fried Chicken
P.O. Box 32070
Louisville, KY 40232

Long John Silver's
P.O. Box 11988
Lexington, KY 40579

McDonald's
McDonald Plaza
Oak Brook, IL 60521

Pizza Hut
P.O. Box 428
Wichita, KS 67201

Roy Rogers
Marriot Corp.
Marriot Dr.
Washington, D.C. 20058

Wendy's
4288 W. Dublin Granville
Dublin, OH 43017

Kenny Rogers Roasters
899 West Cypress Creek Road, Ste #500
Fort Lauderdale, FL 33309
(305)938-0330

CHAPTER 32

Consumers Beware

CONSUMER AWARENESS

The safety of our foods is becoming more of a public concern than it has ever been. Our methods of inspection are lacking, the foods are not as nutritious, meats are suspect of disease, some chicken ovaries are contaminated with salmonella, our water supplies are going bad, we allow a degree of contaminants in our foods, and we use hundreds of chemicals in our foods.

Most of these statements were topics of TV expose shows during the 1995-96 season or could be found in newspapers nationwide. The public is becoming more aware that the food we eat may not be as good as we think it is or as nutritious as it should be.

Awareness is the key to eating healthy and knowledge is the key to awareness.

THE BOARD OF CONTROVERSY

Studies keep going on and on regarding the safety of cutting boards. Plastic cutting boards were then thought to be the best since they were less porous than wood, However, in a 1996 study the Wisconsin's Food Research Institute reported that
wooden cutting boards may be best and bacterial levels were low after only a few minutes. The studies are continuing and all we can suggest is that if you cut up any meat product, clean the board thoroughly with very hot soapy water immediately afterwards. A new study in 1995 completed by the federal government Center for Food Safety and Applied Nutrition showed that only one out of four people wash their

cutting boards after cutting or preparing raw meats and poultry.
However, any cutting surface has the potential of harboring dangerous
bacteria. Cutting boards and especially butcher block surfaces are often
used to place hot pots down. When this occurs some of the heat is
transferred to the surface and into the wood where bacteria may be
lurking. The bacteria like the heat and it may activate them for a longer
period of time or provide an area for them to survive as you are
preparing foods.

GERM SPREADERS

Dish rags and sponges should be placed in the wash or dishwasher every
day. Paper towels are safer to use in most instances. The can opener is
still the number one germ spreader.

IS YOUR FAVORITE RESTAURANT CLEAN?

Salmonella food poisoning is on the rise and in 1996 almost 44,000
cases of salmonella poisonings were reported (how many were not?).
Most of these cases were caused by human error and many have been
associated with restaurant and employee cleanliness. There are 1800
strains of salmonella, most of which will cause food poisoning.

SHOULD BE CALLED "POT RISKY"

A large majority of food poisonings are related to the "pot luck" type of
event. These are usually a result of poor temperature controls of the
foods containing egg, dairy, or meat products.

BEST TO USE THEM FOR A VASE

Imported lead crystal decanters may cause an excessive amount of lead
to be consumed if you store wine or vinegar in them for any length of
time. A number of fluids can leach the lead out of crystal and into the
product.

BACTERIAL SAUNA

A number of cooks insist on cooking their turkey on low heat overnight.
When this is done it gives the bacteria plenty of time to multiply and if
the bird is not heated to 185°F. (85°C.) in the center a problem may
exist and food poisoning is a possibilty.

SNIFF, SNIFF

Never purchase a can or jar if there is any sign of damage or a bulge. When you open a can or jar always smell the contents to see if there is any off-odor and check the top for mold. Foods can also be contaminated rather easily by tasting the foods from a container with a utensil that has been in your mouth.

UPSIDE DOWNER

Never drink from a glass that has been stored upside down over a bar. Smoke and other contaminants are able to get into the glass and remain there.

MED FACT

Just in case you were not advised by your doctor or pharmacist, antibiotics should never be taken with food. Food tends to slow down the absorption of the medication and may reduce its potency.

DOES FOOD NEED TO BE CHEWED & CHEWED & CHEWED?

Over the centuries a number of medical professionals have investigated digestion and how food can be utilized more efficiently. Chewing your food seems to top most lists as one of the most effective methods of gaining more nutrition out of less food. In the early 1900's Horace Fletcher was one of the most outspoken advocates of chewing your food and called the mouth "Nature's Food Filter." He felt that the sense of taste and the desire to swallow was a poor guide to proper nutrition practices. He felt that food should be chewed until there is no taste left, which he calculated at about 50 chews per mouthful. He once said that he had to chew 722 times to eliminate the taste of onions before swallowing. In fact, "Fletcherism" was very popular at Dr. Kellogg's Battle Creek sanitarium. In England they actually held "munching parties" to honor him. All this hard work he explained would also make people eat less and thus reduce their overall caloric intake.

WHAT ARE THE INSPECTORS, INSPECTING?

Food-borne illnesses will make over 6,000,000 Americans ill in 1998 according to the Center for Disease Control. However, a more accurate total is probably closer to 85,000,000. Approximately 10,000 people will die from food-borne illnesses in 1998. The majority of the cases are relatively mild and most people get over the illness in about 2-3 days.

However, almost 10,000 of these cases are fatal with most of the fatalities caused by meat and poultry.

RUN, DON'T WALK TO THE NEAREST EXIT
If you can see the cooks in a restaurant and any of them are smoking it would be wise to leave as soon as possible. Saliva contamination from smokers touching the cigarette then the food is relatively common.

HEAT THEM FOR SAFETY
If you have leftovers in the refrigerator for more than 36 hours they should be recooked. Refrigerator temperatures are usually not cold enough to slow down bacterial growth for any longer period of time, especially on meat products.

A DEFINITE NO, NO
When working with raw meat or poultry for barbecueing never use the same plate or utensil that touched the raw food. Placing the cooked food back on the same plate that held the raw food has caused many people to get food poisoning.

DON'T EAT CHILLY, CHILI
If you make chili with beef, be sure and reheat it to a temperature of 160°F. (71.1°C.) before serving it.

NO PICNIC
Recently, a supermarket placed barbecued birds from the oven onto a pan that had held fresh chickens without washing the pan. Every barbecued chicken was contaminated with Salmonella typhimurium and caused food poisoning at a picnic.

A SULFITE BY ANY OTHER NAME
Sulfites in foods for the most part are becoming a chemical of the past, especially after salad bars that were using the chemicals to retard the browning killed a number of people and brought on an untold number of asthmatic attacks. Occasionally, however, they seem to still appear in a few processed food products. The ones to watch out for are the following:

Sodium metabisulfite   Sodium sulfite
Sodium bisulfite   Potassium metabisulfite
Potassium bisulfite   Sulfur dioxide

FOOD CANNING FACTS

STERILIZATION A MUST

When canning anything the jars should always be sterilized regardless of the method used. The only exception is when you cook the foods in the jars, then the jars do not need sterilization, but should be thoroughly washed.

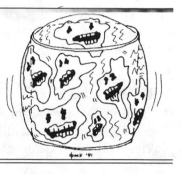

PLAYING IT SAFE

No preservatives, additives, or artificial colorings should ever be added to a home canned product. Always wipe the outside of all jars with white vinegar before storing to reduce the risk of mold forming on any food that wasn't cleaned off well.

SEAL SAFETY

As long as the seal is intact frozen home-canned goods are still safe to eat. However, as with all fresh frozen foods the taste and texture may change.

DON'T BE AFRAID OF THE DARK

If you see a black deposit on the lid after you open a canned food it is usually nothing to worry about (as long as the jar seal is intact). The mold-looking deposits are actually caused by tannins in the food or by hydrogen sulfide released by the foods when processed.

HELP! I'M EXPANDING

Foods high in starch such as corn, Lima, and peas need to be packed loosely since they tend to expand during and after being processed. Fruits and berries should be packed solidly due to shrinkage and the fact that their texture does not stop the heat penetration.

KEEP IT IN THE CLEAR
If you see a jar that has a cloudy liquid the food is probably spoiled. Be very cautious, these jars should be disposed of without being opened. Spores can be released that may be harmful.

BEST VINEGAR FOR CANNING
Pure apple cider vinegar is the best to use when pickling. It has a 4-5% acidity level.

SOLVING A SOFT PICKLE PROBLEM
If you don't want your pickles to become soft, make sure that the vinegar has adequate acidity and that enough is used. Also, keeping the pickles in the refrigerator will help them remain hard.

INFINITY?
As long as the seal is intact, canned foods can last for many years. Nutrient content will be diminished, however, to a great degree.

ONE RINGY, DINGY
After canning the food, tap the top, you should hear a clear "ringing note." If the food is touching the top, this may not occur, but as long as the top does not move up and down, the food does not have to be reprocessed.

THE DUNGEON?
Canned foods need to be stored in a cool, dark location. Summer heat may cause a location to develop enough heat to damage the canned foods. Heat causes dormant bacteria to become active and multiply.

SWEETNESS
Always slowly thaw frozen fruits in the refrigerator. The fruit will have time to absorb the sugar as it thaws.

WHERE DID THAT STRING GO?
A small piece of string placed on top of the warm wax before sealing a jar of preserves will make it easier to remove the wax.

DINING OUT

» If you order a dish made from custard, whipped cream, or has a cream-filling, be sure they are served cool to the touch. These are all supposed to be refrigerated desserts.

» If the server touches the top of your water glass, either ask for a new glass or ask for a straw with your water when you first order.

» Check the cream for your coffee. If it has small white objects floating around it has been left out too long and is starting to go sour. If it is not cool don't use it.

» If the menu, server's uniforms, or bathrooms are dirty get out while the going's good.

RADIATION EXPOSED FOODS

It is still the feeling by many scientists and doctors that radiation exposed foods are not as safe to eat as foods that have not been irradiated. This view, of course, is not shared by the companies that plan to irradiate the foods. It is felt that exposure will destroy the nutritional quality of foods, especially vitamins A, C, E, K and some B's. Certain amino acids and enzymes will also be destroyed.

Studies have shown that radiation exposed foods can cause the following problems in lab animals:

Chromosomal damage   Testicular tumors
Reduced rate of offspring   High infancy mortality
Sperm-count reduction   Mutagenicity

The following symbol denotes radiated foods.
CONSUMER NUTRITION SAFETY HOTLINE
1-(800)366-1655

GOVERNMENT FILTH IN FOOD FACTS

The "Filth in Food" guidelines are controlled by the FDA. The following levels of contamination (insects, etc) if found in food would be the cause for the FDA to take legal action to remove the food from the supermarket. However, the following is just a small sample of foods and contaminants, there is a complete manual listing all foods available from the U.S. Government Consumer Affairs office in Washington.

The following is just a sample taken from the Consumers Affairs Booklet:

» Apricots
Canned, average of 2% insect infested or damaged.

» Coffee Beans
If 10% by count are infested or insect damaged or show evidence of mold.

» Citrus Juice
Canned, microscopic mold count average of 10%. Drosophila and other fly eggs: 5 per 250 ml. Drosophila larva: 1 per 250 ml. If average of 5% by count contain larvae.

» Peaches
Canned, average of 5% wormy or moldy fruit or 4% if a whole larva or equivalent is found in 20% of the cans.

» Popcorn
One rodent pellet in one or more sub-samples or six 10 ounce consumer-size packages, and 1 rodent hair in other sub-samples; or 2 rodent hairs per pound and any rodent hairs in 50% of the sub-samples. 20 gnawed grains per pound and rodent hairs in 50% of the sub- samples.

» Asparagus
Canned. 15% of the spears by count infested with 6 attached asparagus beetle eggs or egg sacs.

» Broccoli
Frozen, average of 80 aphids or thrips per 100 grams.

» Tomato Juice
10 fly eggs per 3 ½ oz. or 5 fly eggs and 1 larva per 3½oz. or 2 larva per 3½oz.

» Raisins
Average of 40mm. of sand and grit per 3 ½ oz. or 10 insects and 35 fly eggs per 8 oz. of golden bleached raisins.

» Wheat
One rodent pellet per pint. 1% by weight of insect-damaged kernels.

» Brussels Sprouts
Average of 40 aphids per 3 ½ oz.

» Flour
The FDA allows wheat flour to contain approximately 50 insect parts per 2 ounces of flour. These are harmless and won't affect your health.

The government allows 350 pesticide ingredients to be used on crops. Approximately 70 of these have been classified as possible cinogens.

RING AROUND THE BOTTOM
Check the bottoms of lettuce, to be sure that the ring is white, not brown.

Common Food Poisoning Bacteria/virus			
Organism	**Sources Appear**	**Symptoms Appear**	**Typical Duration**
Salmonella	Undercooked, raw poultry, eggs, beef, port, raw milk	12-48 hours	1-4 days
Campylobacter Jejuni	Raw poultry & milk	2-7 days	1-2 weeks
Staphlococcus Aureus	Improperly handled cooked food	1-6 hours	12-24 hours
Clostridium Perfringens	Improperly handled meats & foods only kept warm.	8-15 hours	6-24 hours
Clostridium Botulinum	Improperly canned foods, raw honey	18-48 hours	1-7 months
Bacillus cereus	Cooked grains and vegetables left at room temperature	1-15 hours	6-24 hours
Campylobacter	Undercooked chicken	1-5 hours	12-24 hours
Shigella	Contaminated food with feces from very young children.	36-72 hours	4-8 days
Escherichia	Ground meat, raw milk, organic vegetables.	5-48 hours	3 days-2 wks
Norwalk Virus	Fecal contaminated food or hands.	35-40 hours	2 days
Vibrio	Raw shellfish	12 hours	2-4 days
Listeria	Processed meat, deli-type salads, un-aged cheese.	3-12 hours	2-7 days

CAUTION
Symptoms of food poisoning will vary depending on the level of the germ or viruses ingested. Symptoms usually include chills, stomach ache, nausea, muscle aches, and diarrhea. If diarrhea occurs shortly after a meal it is usually a sign of food poisoning. If you experience any abnormal symptom or even feel that you have eaten a contaminated food, contact your doctor immediately.

Every day 20,000 people get sick from eating foods that are contaminated in the United States.

NUTRIENT PROTECTION
The latest fad is buying vegetables in bags that are ready to open and eat. Studies were conducted as soon as these appeared on the market, and to everyone's surprise the nutrient content was excellent, even to the point of surpassing fresh in most cases.

UP, UP, AND AWAY
Melons that have been sliced in half and fresh fruits that are sliced and packaged usually have a high nutrient loss, especially in vitamin C. This is caused by the effects of light and air (oxidation).

JUST THE OIL FACTS, MA'M
When an oil is processed the breakdown process is started and rancidity occurs at a slow pace, however, it can increase at a faster pace if the oil is left under the light in a market in a clear container. It is best to purchase oil in dark containers or tins and store in the refrigerator if the oil will not be used up within 30 days.

Healthy Restaurant Eating	
Chinese	
Soup choices	Wonton or hot and sour soup.
Main courses	Vegetable dishes cooked in a wok (stir fried), white rice, chow mein dishes and most vegetable-based dishes.
Stay clear of	Anything fried, especially egg rolls and breaded fried anything. Sweet and sour dishes are high in calories and any dish sauteed in large amounts of oil such as Szechwan style foods.
Italian	
Soup choices	Minestrone.
Main courses	Any grilled lean meats or seafoods, not creamed, vegetable dishes without creams, pasta with marinara sauce.
Stay clear of	Antipasto, garlic bread, dishes topped with cheese, breaded and fried foods.
French	
Soup choices	Broth or vegetable soups.
Main courses	Any grilled lean meats or seafoods, stews with a tomato base, vegetable dishes without cream sauces.

Healthy Restaurant Eating	
Stay clear of	French onion soup unless they leave the cheese topping off, pate, anything in butter sauce, croissants, au fromage or au gratin dishes.
Mexican	
Soup choices	Corn tortilla soup
Main courses	Bean and rice dishes without cheese, chicken fajitas without cheese, corn tortilla or taco.
Stay clear of	Flour tortilla and chips, cheese sauces, guacamole, beef dishes, fried tortilla dishes, enchiladas, burritos.
Fast Food Chains	
Breakfast	Recommended are scrambled eggs, English muffin with no butter, orange juice.
Lunch	Smallest single burger with no cheese or sauce, Carl's Jr. or Roy Rogers roast beef sandwich, baked fish, rotisserie chicken with a salad at Kenny Rogers Roasters, salads with low-cal dressing, small single layer cheese pizza with vegetable toppings, Wendy's chili, Jack-In-The-Box Club Pita
Stay clear of	Anything else.

CHAPTER 33

Grocery Stores Smarts

BRIMMING OVER WITH POSSIBLE CONTAMINATION

One of the major problems in supermarkets are foods that are placed in a chest freezer in the center of an isle around the holidays and filled up over the freezer line. Chickens and turkeys that are over the line have probably thawed and defrosted a number of times. When you are ready to use them they may be bad.

CLEAN IS IN

The cleanliness of a market is important. This includes the floors, counters and even the employees. Check the bathrooms.

THE TEMPERATURE MAKES A DIFFERENCE

The meat freezer cases should have a thermometer in plain view and should read between 28° and 38°F. (2.2 and 3.3°C.). The dairy products should be stored between 35° and 45°F The ice cream should be at -12° F. (-24.4°C.). If you see ice crystals, don't buy the product, moisture has crept in.

WHAT'S IN A NAME

Many supermarkets have their own brand names to make you think that the product is of a higher grade than it really is. These names are usually similar to ones used by the USDA. They include "Premium," "Quality," "Select Cut," "Market Choice," "Prime Cut," etc.

MORE SUPERMARKET SMARTS

» Shop in a store when it is not crowded so that you can see the specials.

» Processed hams should be under refrigeration, because of the large volumes sold, they may not be around Easter time.

» Never buy a jar if it is sticky or a can if it's damaged.

» Remember, most weekend specials start mid-week.

» Foods placed on the lower shelves are usually the least expensive.

» The most commonly purchased items are always found in the center of the shelf.

» Tumble displays are more common than the old pyramid displays, since shoppers did not want to disturb a neat display.

» Buy by the case whenever possible, if the market has a sale.

» Don't be afraid to return poor quality goods.

KOSHER FOODS, BETTER OR WORSE?

While kosher foods do not contain any animal-based additives such as lard, or edible offal they still may contain tropical oils (palm and coconut) which are high in saturated fats. Kosher meats usually have a higher sodium content than any other type of meat or meat product due to the heavy salting in their special type of processing. Kosher products for the most part are no more healthful than any other product and the additional cost is just not worth it unless you adhere to the religious restrictions.

NUTRIENTS IN SUPERMARKET FOODS

The variation in the level of nutrients in supermarket products varies to such a degree that trying to calculate whether you really are ingesting the level you think you are is almost impossible. The following are results from one study, the variance in nutritional content was caused by many factors such as; storage times, transportation times, original quality of the food, washings in the markets, effects of direct light, packaging, canning procedures, freezing techniques, preservatives used, processing, variations in the nutrient content of the soil or feed, etc.

The following is the vitamin A content in 3 ½ oz. servings in a few common foods:	The following is the vitamin C content in 3 ½ oz. servings in a few common foods:
Calf Liver 470-41,200IU	Oranges (no skin) Trace-116mg.
rots (with skin) 70-18,500IU	Tomatoes (with skin) 9-38mg.
Tomatoes 640-3,020IU	Calf Liver 15-36mg
White Cheddar Cheese 735-1,590IU	rots (with skin) 1-8mg.
Eggs (without shell) 905-1,220IU	

SHOPPING CARTS, A LOSING PROPOSITION

Shopping carts are a necessity, however, they are an expensive necessity. Supermarkets lose about 12% of their carts every year, with another 17% wearing out. The cost of the average cart is $100 which is an average cost to the market of $5,000 annually. The number of carts a store has is also an indication of its total dollar business. Most markets average $1,000 for every cart they have in service every week. If the market has 200 carts then it probably does $200,000 per week in business which equals $10.4 million dollars a year.

IN 1997 THE AVERAGE AMERICAN CONSUMED THE FOLLOWING

132 pounds of refined sugar
 61 pounds of fats and oils
339 cans of soft drinks
195 sticks of chewing gum
 21 pounds of candy
 15 pounds of potato chips, corn chips, popcorn, & pretzels
 66 dozen doughnuts
 52 pounds of cakes and cookies
 22 gallons of ice cream
105 tablespoons of peanut butter
  7 pounds of carrots
  5 pounds of bell peppers
  4 pounds of broccoli

SALES PRODUCED FROM PRODUCE

The produce department in a supermarket is one of the more successful departments. In 1997 produce sales totaled about $35 billion dollars. Apples are the most popular item with oranges second, then lettuce, potatoes, and tomatoes following close behind. Some of the least popular are broccoli, squash, asparagus, and cauliflower. Fruits account for 44% of the sales with vegetables accounting for 56%. According to law tomatoes which are botanically a fruit are counted as a vegetable and watermelons which are actually a vegetable are counted as a fruit.

THE MOST COMMON ITEMS STOLEN FROM SUPERMARKETS

Shoplifting is a real problem in supermarkets with security cameras popping up everywhere. The losses are estimated to be $5 billion per year. The most common items stolen are cigarettes, health and beauty aids, meats, fish, and batteries. Two of the most common problems are stock boys that steal and cashiers not ringing up items for friends.

WHEN WERE AMERICA'S MOST POPULAR FOODS INTRODUCED?

Year	Food	Year	Food
1691	First Patent For A Food Additive	1927	Kool-Aid
1853	Potato Chips	1928	Rice Krispies
1875	Heinz Ketchup	1930	Snickers
1880	Hot Dog	1930	Twinkies
1894	Chocolate Bar	1932	3 Musketeers
1896	Tootsie Roll	1934	Ritz Crackers
1897	Grape Nuts Cereal	1937	Spam
1897	Jell-O	1941	Cheerios
1906	Instant Coffee	1941	M & M's
1906	Planter's Peanuts	1944	Hawaiian Punch
1907	Hershey's Kisses	1946	Frozen French Fries
1911	Crisco	1946	Minute Rice
1912	Oreos	1947	Almond Joy
1912	Life Savers	1948	Chee-Tos
1912	Goo Goo Clusters	1950	Sugar Corn Pops
1914	Mary Jane	1952	Sugar Flakes
1914	Clark Bar	1953	Sugar Smacks
1915	Velveeta	1956	Brownie Mix
1916	All Bran	1956	Jif Peanut Butter
1917	Moon Pie	1958	Tang Orange Drink
1920	Baby Ruth	1965	Shake 'n Bake
1921	Mounds Candy Bar	1966	Cool Whip
1923	Milky Way	1968	Pringles Chips
1923	Peanut Butter Cup	1976	Country Time Lemonade
		1978	Weight Watcher's Food

SHOPPING FOR A PARTY?

The following chart is based on 20 guests, adjust accordingly.

Type Of Food	Serving Size	Amount Needed
Coffee	1 Cup	¾ - 1 Lb.
Soft Drinks	12 Oz.	(4) 2 Liter Btls
Tea, Iced	1 Cup	1 ½ Gallons, 30 Bags
Cake	1/12 Cake	(2) 13 X 9 Inch Cakes
Ice Cream	1 Cup	5 Quarts
Pie	⅙ Pie	(4) 9 Inch Pies
Butter/margarine	2 Pats	One Pound
Pizza	⅓ Of 12" Pie	(7) 12 Inch Pizzas
Potato/corn Chips	1 Ounce	1 ½ Pounds
Olives	4	1 ½ Quarts
Pickles	½ Pickle	10 Medium Pickles
Pasta	1 Cup Cooked	Two Pounds
Uncooked Spaghetti	1 ½ Cups	3 ½ Pounds
Uncooked Mashed Potatoes	½ Cup	6 ½ Pounds
Potato Salad/slaw	½ Cup	2 ½-3 Quarts
Soup	1 ½ Cups	(3) 50 Oz. Cans
Canned Vegetables	½ Cup	Six Pounds

SUPERMARKET STATISTICS

For every $100 spent on food, almost $18.00 is spent on meat, seafood, or poultry. Produce takes almost $10.00, snack foods take just over $5.00, and beans, rice, and dried vegetables take $1.00. Potato chips are purchased every two weeks by over 80% of all households. In 1997 $55 million dollars worth of Twinkies were sold.

SUPERMARKET PROFITS ARE ON THE EDGE?

Almost 50% of the profits a supermarket makes is from the edges of the store. Most of the money you spend is spent on foods that are placed at the edges, such as produce, meats, dairy, and the salad bar. Breakfast cereals make more money for the store than any interior store product and are given a large amount of space. Shoppers are still beeped out of about $1 billion dollars a year by scanner errors. This problem is being worked on and is improving. The meats are always at the end of the aisles so that you will notice them every time you reach the end of an aisle. Milk is always as far from the entrance as possible since it is such a popular item the market wants you to pass other foods. Anchor displays are placed at the end of each aisle. These are products the market needs to sell out of or are a higher profit item. The produce department is the showcase of most stores and you will have to go past the great-looking fruits and vegetables first.

The produce area usually has the most influence on where the shopper shops. Produce is the second highest profit for the market while meat is always first. In supermarket terms, the aisles are called the "prison" since once you enter you cannot get out until you reach the other end. The "prison," however, is where the least profitable foods are found in most instances.

SNIFF, SNIFF, THAT'S AN ORANGE

The checkout counter scanners will soon have aroma detectors that will identify every kind of produce to save the checker time. It may be available by 2001.

GETTING CANNED

The United States cans over 1,500 different kinds of foods with billions of cans being sold annually. There are over 40 varieties of beans alone, 75 varieties of juices, and over 100 different types of soups. If stored in a cool, dry location a can of food will last for about 2 years and still retain a reasonable level of nutrients.

SUPERMARKETS LOVE PETS

Americans spend an unbelievable amount of money on pet foods. In 1997 over $6 million dollars was spent a day on cat food and over $8.6 million dollars on dog food. Pet foods are an $8 billion dollar a year industry. The higher quality pet foods contain more protein and less sugar as well as fewer artificial dyes and additives. National estimates by veterinarians place household pets to be about 50% overweight and a study showed that overweight pets had overweight owners. Feeding cats that saucer of milk may not be a real treat since cats have a difficult time digesting lactose and would prefer a lower lactose treat like cottage cheese or yogurt. Too much chocolate can actually kill a dog, cats won't even touch it since they don't possess a sweet taste bud.

LABEL TERMINOLOGY

» Low Calorie
The food is allowed to contain 40 calories per serving.

» Reduced Calorie
Must have at least 33% fewer calories
than the original product and must show a comparison of both
products.

» Diet or Dietetic
The product may be lower in calories, sodium or sugar than a
comparable product.

» Lite or Light
This is one of the more confusing terms. It can have any meaning the
manufacturer wants it to have, such as a relation to taste, texture,
color, or may have a lowered calorie, fat or sodium content.

» No Cholesterol
Means that the item has no cholesterol, but still may be high in
saturated fat.

» Low Cholesterol
If the label states "low cholesterol" the food cannot contain more
than 20mg. of cholesterol per serving and 2 grams of fat.

» Low Fat
Usually related to dairy products, they must only contain between
0.45-2% fat by weight. Per serving the food must not contain more
than 3% fat per serving size.

» Lean
Meat and poultry must have no more than 10% fat by weight.

» Leaner
Meat and poultry must have at least 25% less fat than the standard
lean.

» Extra Lean
Meat and poultry must have no more than 5% fat by weight.

» Sugar-Free
Product should contain no table sugar, but still may contain some of
the following: Sugarless honey, corn syrup, sorbital, or fructose.
Most of which are just other forms of sugar and still high in calories.

» Sodium-Free
Product should contain less than 5mg. per serving.

» Very Low-Sodium
Contains 35mg. or less per serving.

» Low-Sodium
Contains 140mg. or less per serving.

» Reduced Sodium
The normal level of sodium in the product has been reduced by at least 75%.

» No Salt Added
Salt cannot be added during the unsalted processing. The food may still have other ingredients that contain sodium.

» Imitation
A food which is a substitute for another food and is usually nutritionally inferior, it may still contain the same number of calories and fat. Imitation crab meat is a good example.

» Organic
This term may pertain to almost anything. This usually,incicates a food that is grown without the use of artificial fertilizers. This term needs further clarification by the FDA.

» Natural
This term may mean anything, no regulations apply and may be seen on foods that have no additives and preservatives.

» Enriched
A degraded, processed product that is sometimes fortified with a percentage of the nutrients that were originally there.

SCRATCHING YOUR HEAD?

If this seems confusing, it is! This is just another way to fool the consumer into thinking they are getting a much better product, when there is only a minor difference. The reason for this is that a manufacturer can list the percent of nutrients by weight (which includes water weight), not percent of fat by calories. The "light" hot dogs are 80% fat free by weight, which is determined by the total weight including the water content, not by the actual food value.

SUPERMARKET SAVVY

» The loss of nutrients before you get products home is a real problem. Most of us believe that when we purchase a product from the market it will be fresh and have its full compliment of nutrients, not so!

A survey was done in 1988 to see if the public reads labels on products before purchasing them. The study reported that 97% of people who purchased processed foods never read the label. In 1994 the survey was repeated and showed that 84% still didn't read the labels. Progress has been made since the labels have become easier to understand.

repeated and showed that 84% still didn't read the labels. Progress has been made since the labels have become easier to understand.

FOOD LABEL DECODING AND TERMINOLOGY

Food labels contain a large amount of important information. To make the information useful, you must first understand the labels. The following facts may make it somewhat easier:

Proteins contain . . . . 4 calories per gram
bohydrates contain . . . 4 calories per gram
Fats contain . . . . . 9 calories per gram
Alcohol contains . . . . 7 calories per gram

If a label says that it is 80% fat free, it will be necessary to understand what that really means. As an example let's look at two hot dogs.

Hot Dog

Nutritional information per serving   8 links per package

Portion Size—1 link (56g.) . . . Calories 180
Protein . . . . 6g.
bohydrate . . . . 2g.
Fat . . . . 17g.
Cholesterol . . . . 35mg.
Sodium . . . . 600mg.

17 grams of fat X 9 calories per gram equals 153 calories from fat

153 divided by 180 X 100 = 85% of calories from fat.

Light Hot Dog (80% fat free)

Nutritional information per serving   8 links per package

Portion size . . . . 1 link (56g.)
Calories 130
Protein . . . . 7g.
bohydrate . . . . 1g.
Fat . . . . 11g.
Cholesterol . . . . 25mg.
Sodium . . . . 600mg.

11 grams of fat X 9 calories per gram equals 99 calories from fat

99 divided by 130 X 100 = 76% of calories from fat.

NEEDS SUN GLASSES

When milk is purchased in clear plastic containers and allowed to sit under the light for 4 hours you will have a 44% loss of vitamin A in low-fat and non-fat milks. The reduction in fat content, which protects the vitamin A is for the most part, absent. Supermarkets in some areas of them. Juices have a similar problem to milk in that the light may affect their nutrients, especially vitamin C. The juice containers should not be clear.

Food Terminology

A ACID
A sour tasting substance that is soluble in water.

ACIDULATED WATER
A number of fruits and vegetables turn brown easily and need to be sprayed with a solution of a mild acid found in fruits called ascorbic acid (vitamin C). To prepare acidulated water, just mix 1 part of lemon or lime juice to 5 parts of water and place the mixture in a bowl or spray bottle.

AL DENTE
This is an Italian term meaning "to the tooth." It is used to describe the cooked stage of pasta when the pasta has been cooked to the stage that is has a slight resistance when you bite down on it.

ALKALI
A substance that is capable of neutralizing an acid. Sodium bibonate is a good example.

ALLEMANDE
A thick sauce made from meat stock with egg yolks and lemon juice.

AMEL RULERS
Also, called chocolate rulers. They are used to contain the hot chocolate or amel as they cool. They are usually 20-30 inches in length with½ inch stainless steel or chrome bars. The bars are lightly oiled or dusted with corn starch to keep the product from sticking and are placed on a marble working counter. The hot mixture is then poured into the center of the mold.

ANGELICA
A sweet aromatic herb whose candied stems are used in cake decorating and to flavor alcoholic beverages.

ANGLAISE
A typical English dish that is boiled or roasted.

ANTIPASTO
An Italian word for an assortment of appetizers, such as, cold cuts, olives, pickles, peppers, and vegetables.

ARROWROOT
A fine powder that is produced from dried rootstalks of a subtropical tuber. It is used to thicken soups, sauces, and pastes. Has 1½ times the thickening power of flour.

ASPIC
Gelatin made from concentrated vegetables and meat stocks. Usually contains tomato juice.

A BUERRE
Means either "with" or "cooked in butter."

AU GRATIN
Usually refers to a dish that has a browned covering of bread crumbs, usually mixed with cheese and butter.

ANTIOXIDANT
A substance that has the capability of protecting another substance from being destroyed or damaged by oxygen.

APERITIF
An alcoholic beverage such as sweet vermouth, dry sherry, or champagne served before a meal to stimulate the appetite.

ASTRINGENT
These are compounds that are capable of drawing skin or other soft tissue together. They are used to close the pores of the skin and block toxins from entering surface cells.

AVIDIN
A protein that is found in egg white that will inactivate biotin.

AVERAGE FLOUR VALUE
This is derived from four factors: the color of the flour, loaves per barrel, the size of the loaf, and the quality of the bread as compared to any given flour shipment.

B BAKING CHOCOLATE

This is also called bitter or unsweetened chocolate and is pure chocolate liquor that has been extracted from the cocoa bean. Usually has lecithin and vanilla added for flavor and to keep it in a usable suspension.

BASTING

This is the process of covering meats or fowl with added fat to keep the flesh moist. It is usually done to meats that only have a small fat covering and is accomplished by basting the meat with any fat source.

BEAN THREADS

Translucent threads that are produced from the starch of mung beans. These are also known as Chinese vermicelli or glass noodles. They may be found in oriental markets.

BENZYL PEROXIDE

A fine powder that is mixed into the flour in very small amounts to bleach the flour.

BIGARADE

Food that has been cooked in orange juice.

BISQUE

A rich, creamy soup made from fish or game. May also refer to a frozen dessert.

BLANCH

The process of plunging food into boiling water, usually to remove the skin from fruits and vegetables or to kill bacteria prior to freezing.

BOILED ICING

Made by beating cooked sugar syrup into egg whites that have been firmly whipped. The mixture is then beaten until it is smooth and glossy. Also, known as Italian meringue.

BOLTING

Removing the bran from ground grain by sifting.

BRIX SCALE

This is a measurement of the density of sugar that has been dissolved in water to prepare a syrup. The scale is designed to provide a measurement of the amount of water, which will determine whether the syrup is at a low or high density level. The instrument used to accomplish this is called a saccharometer.

BRUNOISE
A generic term referring to a food that contains finely diced vegetables.

C CAKE BREAKER
A comb with 3-4 inch long metal teeth that is used to slice angel food and chiffon cakes. Cuts the cakes cleanly instead of tearing them which a knife will do.

CAKE LEVELER
A U-shaped metal frame that is used to cut cakes into even horizontal layers. It stands on plastic feet and has a thin, very sharp, serrated cutting blade. Adjusts to any size slice. The cake is pushed against the blade and will cut cakes up to 16 inches in diameter.

CARBON DIOXIDE
A colorless, odorless gas that is noncombustible. Used commonly as a pressure-dispensing agent in gassed whipped creams and carbonated beverages. It is also, used as dry ice in the frozen food industry and has been used in stage productions to produce harmless smoke or fumes. However, it may cause shortness of breath, nausea, elevated blood pressure, and disorientation if inhaled in larger quantities.

CARCINOGEN
A substance that may contribute to producing a cancer cell in the body.

CASEIN
The main protein in cow's milk is used as a a water absorbing powder with no odor. It is used as a texturizer for a number of dairy products including ice cream and frozen custards. Casein is also used in hair preparations to thicken thin hair and as an emulsifier in cosmetics.

CHEESECLOTH
A natural white cotton cloth which is available in either fine or coarse weaves. It is lint-free and maintains its shape when wet. Primarily used for straining jellies or encompassing stuffing in turkeys.

CHELATING AGENT
A compound that has the capability of binding with and precipitating trace metals from the body. The most common agent is EDTA (ethylenediamine tetraacetic acid).

CHEVRE CHEESE
Any cheese made from goat's milk, usually found coated with an herb or ash.

CHOCOLATE BLOOM
This has also been called "fat bloom." The bloom is actually accomplished when the cocoa butter and the chocolate separate during cooking and the cocoa butter floats to the top and crystallizes. The streaks of fat look like the bloom of a plant, hence the name. As soon as the chocolate melts, the cocoa butter goes back into the mixture.

CHOU PASTE
The French name for a special pastry dough used in cream puffs and chocolate eclairs.

CLARIFICATION
The process of removing small particles of suspended material from a liquid. Butyl alcohol is used to remove particles from shampoos. Traces of copper and iron are removed from certain beverages and vinegar.

CLOTTED CREAM
May also be known as Devonshire cream in recipes. It is a thick, rich, scalded cream that is made by slowly cooking and skimming cream or unpasteurized milk. The thickened cream floats to the surface and is removed after the cream cools. it is traditionally served with scones in England.

COCKLE
A very small mollusk that resembles a clam. May be sold either shucked or canned.

CRACKLING
The crisp, browned pieces that remain in the bottom of the pan after fresh pork fat is rendered into lard. May be added to a number of dishes, especially beans, corn bread, or vegetables.

CUTIN
The process of adding fat into a flour mixture with a pastry blender or other mixing utensil.

D DEMULCENT
A thick or creamy substance, usually oily that is used to relieve pain and inflammation in mucosal membranes. One of the common demulcents is gum acacia.

DOCKER

This is a tool made for making holes in pastry dough, especially puff pastries so that steam can escape as the dough is baking. It looks like a paint roller with protruding metal or plastic spikes.

E ## EMULSIFIER

A commonly used substance used to stabilize a mixture and to ensure the proper consistency. One of the most common emulsifiers is lecithin which will keep oil and vinegar in suspension. Cosmetics use stearic acid soaps which include potassium and sodium stearates.

F ## FERMENTATION

The breakdown of starch (grains) using certain enzymes that speed up the reaction. The end product may depend on the particular enzyme that is used. If the enzyme diastase is used, the end product will be maltose.

FILE POWDER

A spice used by Cajun chefs made from ground sassafras leaves to thicken as well as adding a thymelike flavor to gumbos. Tends to become stringy when boiled and needs to be added just before serving.

FLOATING ISLAND

A dessert made from chilled custard and topped with a special "poached" meringue. The custard usually contains fruit and the meringue is occasionally drizzled combined with a thin stream of caramel syrup.

FLUMMERY

A soft custard like dessert that is served over berries or other types of fruit. Resembles a thickened fruit sauce.

FOCACCIA

An Italian yeast bread that resembles a deep-dish pizza crust with a breadlike texture and is usually topped with a variety of toppings.

FRAPPE

A beverage or slushy dessert that is made with crushed ice and usually with liquor poured over it.

G ## GLYCOGEN

The body's main storage carbohydrate. Is easily converted into energy.

GNOCCHI
A small Italian dumpling made from potatoes and 100% seminola flour. They may be found in many shapes from squares to balls and usually served as an appetizer in better Italian restaurants.

H HARICOT
A term used to describe a thick meat stew.

HYDROLYZED
To be put into a water form.

I ISOPROPYL ALCOHOL
This is not an alcohol that can be drank. It is not for human consumption and only used for massages, as a disinfectant, and to remove moisture from gasoline tanks. If you are trying to remove moisture from a gas tank, be sure the isopropyl alcohol is 100% not 70% or you will have more problems.

J JAGGERY
This is also known as palm sugar and is semi-refined sugar which is produced from the sap of the Palmyra palm tree. It may also be made from Hawaiian sugar cane. It looks like a coarse, crumbly, brown sugar with a strong flavor, and is sold in cakes. It is mostly used in Asian and Indonesian dishes.

L LEAVENING
A chemical placed in baked goods to make them lighter and more porous by causing the release of bon dioxide gas during cooking.

M MARYANN PAN
Also, known as the "shortcake pan." It is a shallow, round, aluminum pan that looks like a tart pan. It has fluted sides and is made with a deep hollow area around the edges making the center look like it is raised. Used mainly for sponge cakes and pastry shells.

METABOLIZE
A substance that undergoes physical and chemical changes and placed into a usable form.

P PARCH
Browning with a dry heat.

ph
This refers to the scale to measure acidity and alkalinity. The ph is actually the hydrogen (H) ion concentration of a solution. The small p is for the power of the hydrogen ion. The scale used

to determine the level of acidity or alkalinity of a product or solution is measured with the number 14 as the highest level and 7 as a neutral point where the acidity and alkalinity are balanced. Water is 7, and if the number goes above 7 the solution is considered to be alkaline. If the number falls below 7 then the solution is considered to be acidic. Human blood has a ph of 7.3, vinegar and lemon juice are 2.3, and common lye is 13.

PHYLLO DOUGH
A very thin pastry dough, usually sold in one pound tons. Sold fresh in the Middle East and sold frozen in the United States. Must be kept wrapped, otherwise the dough will dry out rapidly.

PIQUANT
Refers to any food that has a sharp flavor, usually used to describe cheeses.

Q QUENELLE
A small delicate, round dumpling made from finely chopped fish or meat in a flour and egg mixture. They are poached and served as an appetizer with a rich sauce over them.

R RACLETTE
A Swiss cheese snack prepared by placing a piece of cheese near a flame so that it will remain soft enough to scrape a small amount of the cheese off and use it as a spread on bread or boiled potatoes as the meal progresses.

RICE STICK
This is an almost transparent Oriental noodle that is flavorless. It is made from rice flour and may be sold as rice noodles or rice vermicelli. They will expand to 8-10 times their original volume and are usually cooked in liquid or deep fried.

ROUX
A special cooked mixture of flour and butter, usually used to thicken sauces and stews.

RUSK
A slice of bread that is crisp and used as a cracker. The bread is baked then sliced very thin and allowed to dry out and is browned.

S SEQUESTRANT
A substance that will absorb iron and prevents chemical changes that would affect the flavor, texture, and the color of foods. Sodium is an example that is used for water softening.

SHELF STABLE

This is a term that is used to describe foods that have been sterilized, then sealed in airtight plastic bags, containers, or special paper foil. This is a type of preservation of food that does not require refrigeration or freezing and sometimes referred to as aseptic packaging. The most popular products to be sold in this manner are dairy products, puddings, and sauces.

SUET

This is a semi-hard fat found in the loin and kidney areas of beef and pork. Occasionally beef suet will be used to make mincemeat.

T TOXIN

An organic poison that is produced in or on living or dead organisms.

Z ZEST

The oil found in the outer yellow or orange rind of citrus fruits.

Index

Dr. Myles H. Bader's Formulas to the Rescue!

Certain chemicals, vitamins, and minerals act as antioxidants to help the body's own scavengers destroy free radicals. The role of antioxidants is still being studied. However, in all reasearch to date,they are "highly recommended in over 60 diseases as a preventative measure or to reduce the severity of a disease in patients who already show symptoms."

Dr. Myles H. Bader's Formulas declare war on free radicals. A 100% natural product, it may help:

* **shield your cells against free radicals,**
* **dislodge existing free radicals from cellular tissue,**
* **flush free radicals from your body, and**
* **stimulate the natural biochemicals in your body to maximize their potential to fight free radicals and rebuild damaged cells.**

Dr. Myles H. Bader's Formulas combine, in one potent compound, the most effective antioxidants now known through research: proanthocyanidin, phytochemicals (powdered vegetables), selenium, and vitamins A (Beta Carotene), C and E.

TWO FORMULAS TO MEET YOUR NEEDS:

**For Further Information Call:**

1-800-717-6001